AF696592

EU Management of Global Emergencies

Studies in EU External Relations

Edited by

Marc Maresceau (*Ghent University*)

Editorial Board

Marise Cremona (*European University Institute*)
Günter Burghardt (*former EU ambassador Washington*)
Alan Dashwood (*University of Cambridge*)
Frank Hoffmeister (*European Commission*)
Pieter Jan Kuijper (*University of Amsterdam*)

VOLUME 8

The titles published in this series are listed at *brill.com/seur*

EU Management of Global Emergencies

Legal Framework for Combating Threats and Crises

Edited by

Inge Govaere and Sara Poli

Lifelong Learning

BRILL
NIJHOFF

LEIDEN | BOSTON

Aerial photo of Norway. © Przemyslaw Wasilewski, available at http://www.iStock.com.

Library of Congress Cataloging-in-Publication Data

EU management of global emergencies : legal framework for combating threats and crises / edited by Inge Govaere and Sara Poli.
pages cm. — (Studies in EU external relations ; v. 8)
Includes bibliographical references and index.
ISBN 978-90-04-26832-6 (hardback : alk. paper) — ISBN 978-90-04-26833-3 (e-book) 1. Emergency management—Law and legislation--European Union countries. 2. War and emergency legislation—European Union countries. 3. Emergencies—Law and legislation—European Union countries. 4. Crisis management in government—European Union countries. 5. Terrorism—Law and legislation—European Union countries. I. Govaere, Inge, editor of compilation. II. Poli, Sara, editor of compilation. III. Title: European Union management of global emergencies.

KJE7520.E97 2014
344.2405'34—dc23

2014014580

This publication has been typeset in the multilingual 'Brill' typeface. With over 5,100 characters covering Latin, IPA, Greek, and Cyrillic, this typeface is especially suitable for use in the humanities. For more information, please see brill.com/brill-typeface.

ISSN 4875-0451
ISBN 978 90 04 26832 6 (hardback)
ISBN 978 90 04 26833 3 (e-book)

Copyright 2014 by Koninklijke Brill NV, Leiden, The Netherlands.
Koninklijke Brill NV incorporates the imprints Brill, Brill Nijhoff, Global Oriental and Hotei Publishing.
All rights reserved. No part of this publication may be reproduced, translated, stored in a retrieval system, or transmitted in any form or by any means, electronic, mechanical, photocopying, recording or otherwise, without prior written permission from the publisher.
Authorization to photocopy items for internal or personal use is granted by Koninklijke Brill NV provided that the appropriate fees are paid directly to The Copyright Clearance Center, 222 Rosewood Drive, Suite 910, Danvers, MA 01923, USA. Fees are subject to change.

This book is printed on acid-free paper.

MIX
Paper from responsible sources
FSC® C109576
FSC www.fsc.org

Printed by Printforce, the Netherlands

Contents

Preface

Nothing comes out of nowhere.

The broader context to this book on "Management of Global Emergencies, Threats and Crises by the European Union" is to be situated in a joint Pisa-Ghent project on "EU Governance of Global Emergencies". The working basis was first provided by a duo-VLAC Fellowship sponsored by the Royal Flemish Academy of Sciences and Arts. It was in this framework that Sara was invited to develop the project further and for us to collaborate in performing research at the beautiful location of the Palace of the Academies in Brussels.

As the ambitions of the project grew both in terms of objectives and scope, financial input for the substantive research, the organisation of a high level conference and platform for discussion as well as the current book project was sought and graciously provided by the European Commission in the framework of Jean Monnet funding. Without the financial support in the form of a Jean Monnet life-long learning project hosted at Ghent University these activities would simply not have been possible.

The book in itself has led to a very fruitful collaboration with many people, first of all of course the contributors who accepted to share their knowledge and insights in this book. We are also much obliged for the enthusiastic support and help from the following persons who may be less visible throughout the book yet proved to be crucial to its production. Without the dedicated IT, linguistic and editorial help from Barbara Van Laere, Magali Carel, Grant Stirling and in the crucial last phase especially also Maaike Cornelli and Anne-Lise Van der Meulen the book would surely look very different in appearance. Our special thanks goes also to our publishers Lisa Hanson and Marie Sheldon from Brill Academic Publishers for their patience as well as the always very helpful advice and tips. We are confident the final production and distribution of the book is safe in their professional hands.

Inge Govaere and Sara Poli

Foreword

Humanitarian Aid and Crisis Response

We live in a fragile world. Through force of nature, conflict or economic meltdown—emergencies are becoming more frequent and more severe. In more cases than ever before, they affect people regardless of national borders and go beyond the capacity of any one country to respond effectively on its own. The global financial crisis has demonstrated the speed with which contagion can tear through the markets in an interconnected world economy. The collective effort to deal with its consequences—be it at the G20 summit in London in 2009, or the massive mobilization of the EU and Eurozone since then—has underscored that only a concerted response can be effective.

Natural disasters, too, are striking with greater frequency and severity. Parts of the world that have traditionally been prone to recurrent emergencies—such as the Sahel, or the Horn of Africa—are being hit harder and with increasing frequency. It is the most vulnerable people who are most exposed but the developed world is not immune. Events such as Hurricane Sandy have underscored that we are all vulnerable. Climate change is an important driver of this, but it is by no means the only factor. Population growth and urbanization are compounding existing fragilities. All too often, conflict overlaps with and aggravates natural disasters—such as in the Horn, or in parts of the Sahel.

The only way to deal effectively with the impact of such emergencies is to strengthen our capacity to anticipate them, to mobilize our collective assets and respond swiftly—in short, to improve the governance of emergencies. It is heartening in this context that the economic and financial crisis has not diminished the willingness of European citizens to help respond to emergencies outside Europe's borders. Collectively, together with its Member States, the EU has done a great deal to step up its capacity not only to respond, but also to help prepare for the worst. To mobilize assets when emergencies strike but also to help the most vulnerable become more resilient to crises which we know will not go away and which in many cases are likely, if anything, to hit with ever greater frequency and severity.

This book is timely in that it allows us to take stock of how far Europe has come in dealing with global emergencies, including emergencies originating outside Europe but which affect the EU as well as emergencies outside Europe in which Europe plays a major role as a responder. It will also no doubt show how much more remains to be done. This book is timely also because it comes just as the dust from the first few years of implementation of the Lisbon Treaty is starting to settle and we are getting a clearer idea of how a new institutional architecture, new legal bases and new instruments may contribute further to responding to and preventing emergencies. It promises to be an invaluable compass to a complex issue that will not go away.

Kristalina Georgieva
European Commissioner for International Cooperation

List of Abbreviations and Acronyms

AASM	Association of the Associated African States and Madagascar
ACP	African, Caribbean and Pacific countries
AGIR	Alliance Globale pour l'Initiative Résilience Sahel
AJIL	American Journal of International law
AMISOM	African Union Mission in Somalia
ASEM	Asia-Europe Meeting
ATAA	Air Transport Association of America
Aust. YBIL	Australian Yearbook of International Law
BIMCO	Baltic and International Maritime Council
BMP	Best Management Practices
CBD	Convention on Biological Diversity
CBRN	Chemical, biological, radiological and nuclear defence
CCA	Crisis Coordination Arrangements
CCP	Common Commercial Policy
CCS	Carbon Capture and Storage
CDM	Clean Development Mechanism
CECIS	Common Emergency Communication and Information System
CFSP	Common Foreign and Security Policy
CGPCS	Contact Group on Piracy off the Coast of Somalia
CISAR	Chinese International Search and Rescue Team
CJEU	Court of Justice of the European Union
CMCO	Civil-Military Coordination
CMF	Combined Maritime Forces
CMPD	Crisis Management Planning Department
CO_2	Carbon dioxide
COP	Conference of the Parties
COSI	Committee on Internal Security
CPCC	Civilian Planning and Conduct Capability
CPM	Civil Protection Mechanism
CPR	European Civil Protection Mechanism
CRED	Centre for Research on the Epidemiology of Disasters
CSDP	Common Security and Defence Policy
DG ECHO	Directorate-General for Humanitarian Aid and Civil Protection
DG HOME	Directorate-General for Home Affairs
DG SANCO	Directorate-General for Health and Consumers
EBA	Everything But Arms initiative
EC	European Community

ECB	European Central Bank
ECHO	European Community Humanitarian Office
EDA	European Defence Agency
EEA	European Economic Area
EEAS	European External Action Service
EEC	European Economic Community
EFSF	European Financial Stabilisation Facility
EFTA	European Free Trade Association
EGS	European Global Strategy
EJIL	European Journal of International Law
EMO	Chinese State Council Emergency Management Office
EMU	European Monetary Union
EPA	Economic Partnership Agreement
ERC	European Emergency Response Centre
ERCC	Emergency Response Coordination Centre
ESA	European Space Agency
ESCAP	United Nations Economic and Social Commission for Asia and the Pacific
ESM	European Stability Mechanism
ESS	European Security Strategy
ETS	Emissions Trading Scheme
EU	European Union
EUCAP	EU Capacity building mission
EUMC	European Union Military Committee
EUMS	European Union Military Staff
EUSF	European Union Solidarity Fund
EUTM	EU Trainings Mission
FAO	Food and Agriculture Organization
FLEGT	Forest Law Enforcement, Governance and Trade
FTA	Free trade agreement
GATT	General Agreement on Tariffs and Trade
GDP	Gross Domestic Product
GEO. L.J.	Georgetown Law Journal
GHGs	Green House Gases
GSP	Generalised System of Preferences
HFA	Hyogo Framework for Action
HFC-23	Trifluoromethane
IAEA	International Atomic Energy Agency
ICAO	International Civil Aviation Organization
IFRC	International Federation of the Red Cross and the Red Crescent Societies
IfS	Instrument for Stability

ILC	International Law Commission
ILO	International Labour Organisation
IMB	International Maritime Bureau
IMF	International Monetary Fund
IMO	International Maritime Organization
INSARAG	International Search and Rescue Advisory Group
INTCEN	EU Intelligence Analysis Centre
IRTC	Internationally Recommended Transit Corridor
ITTO	International Tropical Timber Organisation
LDC	Least developed country
LRRD	Linking relief, rehabilitation and development
MCDA	Military and Civil Defence Assets
MEAs	Multilateral Environmental Agreements
MFN	Most Favoured Nation
MIC	Monitoring and Information Centre
MoU	Memorandum of Understanding
MSCHOA	Maritime Security Centre Horn of Africa
N_2O	Nitrous Oxide
NATO	North Atlantic Treaty Organization
NAVFOR	Naval Force
NIEM	Chinese Institute for Emergency Management
nyr	not yet reported
OCHA	UN Office for the Coordination of Humanitarian Affairs
OECD-DAC	Development Assistance Committee of the Organization for Economic Cooperation and Development
OJEU	Official Journal of the European Union
OPCW	Organisation for the Prohibition of Chemical Weapons
OpsCenter	Ad-hoc military Operations Center
PCIJ	Permanent Court of International Justice
PS	Participating States
PSC	Political Security Committee
QMV	Qualified Majority Voting
RCSC	Red Cross Society of China
ReCAAP	Regional Cooperation Agreement on Combating Piracy and Armed Robbery against Ships in Asia
REDD+	Reducing Emissions from Deforestation and forest Degradation in developing countries; and the role of conservation, sustainable management of forests and enhancement of forest carbon stock in developing countries

SARS	Severe Acute Respiratory Syndrome
SCO	Shanghai Cooperation Organisation
SHADE	Shared Awareness and Deconfliction
SHARE	Supporting Horn of Africa Resilience
SLOCs	Sea Lines of Communications
TEU	Treaty on European Union
TFEU	Treaty on the Functioning of the European Union
TFG	Transitional Federal Government
TSCG	Treaty on Stability, Coordination and Governance in the Economic and Monetary Union
UAE	United Arab Emirates
UK	United Kingdom
UKMTO	United Kingdom Maritime Trade Operations
UN	United Nations
UNCTAD	United Nations Conference on Trade and Development
UNDP	United Nations Development Programme
UNFCCC	United Nations Framework Convention on Climate Change
UNISDR	United Nations Office for Disaster Risk Reduction
UNOCHA	United Nations Office for the Coordination of Humanitarian Affairs
UNODC	United Nations Office on Drugs and Crime
UNPOS	United Nations Political Office for Somalia
UNSC	United Nations Security Council
USA	United States of America
USAR	Urban search and rescue
VPAs	Voluntary Partnership Agreements
WASH	Water, Sanitation and Hygiene
WEU	Western European Union
WFP	World Food Programme
WG	Working Group
WTO	World Trade Organisation

List of Contributors

Alberto Alemanno

is Jean Monnet Professor in EU Law and Risk Regulation at HEC Paris. He is also Global Clinical Professor at NYU Law School where he directs the HEC-NYU EU Regulatory Policy Clinic and Adjunct Professor at Georgetown University Law Center where he teaches Global Risk Regulation. Prior to joining the HEC faculty, he clerked at the Court of Justice of the European Union, worked as a Teaching Assistant at the College of Europe in Bruges and qualified as an attorney at law in New York. Originally from Italy, Alemanno earned a *Laurea in Giurisprudenza* cum laude from the Università degli Studi di Torino, LLM degrees from Harvard Law School and the College of Europe, and a PhD in International Law and Economics from Bocconi University. He has published extensively in the areas of EU law, international economic law and risk regulation, including the books *Trade in Food—Regulatory and Judicial Approaches in the EU and the WTO* (Cameron May, 2007), *Governing Disasters—The Challenges of Emergency Risk Regulation* (Edward Elgar, 2011) and *Better Business Regulation in a Risk Society* (Springer, 2013). His latest edited volume is *Foundations of European Food Law & Policy—The First Ten Years of the European Food Safety Authority* (Ashgate, 2013). He is currently co-editing a volume provisionally titled *Regulating Lifestyle Risks—Europe, Alcohol, Tobacco and Unhealthy Diets* (Cambridge University Press, 2014—with Amandine Garde). He is the founder and editor of the *European Journal of Risk Regulation* he serves in the editorial boards of the *Revue du Droit de l'Union européenne* and the *European Food and Feed Law Review*.

Giacomo Biagioni

is Assistant Professor of International Law at University of Cagliari, where he teaches International Law and Global Governance Law. He holds a degree in Law (magna cum laude) from University of Florence and a Ph.D. in European Union Law from University of Trieste. He taught at several institutions in Europe. He is regular speaker at various meetings and author of a monograph and about forty articles, especially on European Union law and private international law, as well as the co-editor of two books.

Michal Bobek

is Professor of European Law at the College of Europe, Bruges. He is also research fellow at the Oxford University Institute of European and Comparative Law. He has qualified as a judge in the Czech Republic and previously worked as legal secretary to the Chief Justice and the head of the Research and Documentation Department at the Supreme Administrative Court of the Czech Republic. His areas of research interest include various aspects of EU law, European human rights law, comparative (public) law, and legal theory. He (co)authored ten books, two academic commentaries and dozens of articles and case notes, published in Czech, English, French and German, with works translated also into Romanian, Polish, Russian and Chinese. His latest book entitled "Comparative Reasoning in European Supreme Courts" appeared with the Oxford University Press.

Steven Blockmans
is Senior Research Fellow and Head of the EU Foreign Policy Programme of the Brussels/based think tank Centre for European Policy Studies (CEPS), Professor of EU External Relations Law and Governance at the University of Amsterdam (part-time), and one of the founding members of the Centre for the Law of EU External Relations (CLEER).

Jenő Czuczai
is Legal Adviser in the Legal Service of the Council of the EU (since April 2006–). Visiting Professor at the College of Europe in Brugge-Warsaw (since 1997–). Graduated from ELTE Law Faculty with summa cum laude (1991). He was Head of Unit (Prime Minister Office, Budapest, 1991–1992), Director of the different Hungarian Privatization Institutions (1992–1995). He was Legal Adviser to the EC Delegation in Budapest (1995–2001) and Vice-President of the European Law Academy in Hungary (1999–2006). He is Member of the Hungarian Bar Association (since 2001–). He was founding President of the Hungarian European Law Association (2003–2006) and Member of the Board of Directors of the World Federation for European Law (since 2003). He was Chief Legal Adviser to the Hungarian Presidency of the EU Council (seconded from the GSC to Budapest). He is the author, editor, co-editor of 13 books, and author of about 100 articles.

Sanderijn Duquet
is a research fellow at the research Foundation—Flanders (FWO), the Leuven Centre for Global Governance Studies and the Institute for International Law, University of Leuven, Belgium, where she is preparing a Ph.D. on the contribution of the European Union to international diplomatic and consular law. She holds a Master of Laws, Ghent U. and an LL.M. in International Legal Studies, American U. Washington College of Law.

Florika Fink-Hooijer

has spent most of her career in the Commission on foreign external policy matters and in particular on crisis management and conflict prevention. She is currently the Director for Strategy, Policy and International Cooperation at the Directorate General for Humanitarian Aid and Civil Protection. Previously she was Head of Cabinet of Commissioner Kristalina Georgieva, who is responsible for humanitarian aid, international cooperation and crisis response. Inside the Commission Florika had set up the managerial and financial structures for CFSP and crisis management and has been directly involved in initiating numerous EU police, rule of law or protection missions in third countries. Her professional experience includes the design and management of various conflict prevention schemes such as instruments to counter the financing of terrorism as well as the EU's sanctions management in general. Florika has also been negotiating for the EU the Kimberley Process Certification Scheme to curb the trade in blood diamonds and has been responsible for EU relations with Japan, Korea, Australia and New Zealand. Inside the Secretariat General of the Commission she has been responsible for the Commission's external policy coordination after having advised various Commissioners as member of their cabinet on EU external policies at large as well as on justice and home affairs and internal market matters.

Kristalina Georgieva

is currently the European Commissioner for International Cooperation, Humanitarian Aid and Crisis Response. Before taking her position in the Commission she has been Vice President and Corporate Secretary of the World Bank Group, directly reporting to the President, from 2008 to 2010. She was the interlocutor between the World Bank Group senior management, its Board of Directors, and the 186 country shareholders of the World Bank Group. Previously, she was the institutions' Director and Resident Representative in the Russian Federation based in Moscow. She has also been the Director, Strategy and Operations, Sustainable Development in charge of overall directions and delivery of World Bank policy and lending operations in infrastructure, urban development agriculture, environment, and social development, including coordination of World Bank support to fragile and conflict-affected countries. Kristalina Georgieva received her graduate and postgraduate education from the University of National and World Economy, Sofia.

Inge Govaere

holds the Jean Monnet Chair in EU Legal Studies at Ghent University where she is Director of the Ghent European Law Institute (G.E.L.I.) and is Director of the European Legal Studies Department at the College of Europe, Bruges. She studied law at Ghent University and obtained her Ph.D at the European University Institute (E.U.I.) in Florence (Italy). She was a Fulbright Scholar-in-Residence at Cornell University, N.Y. (USA) and was invited as a Visiting Professor and to give guest-lectures and conferences in the EU and abroad, a.o. European University Institute (E.U.I., Firenze), Cambridge University (UK), Yale University (USA), Columbia University (N.Y., USA), Pittsburgh University (USA), Bond University (Queensland, Australia), Sao Paolo (Brazil), Lima (Peru), La Paz (Bolivia), Sofia (Bulgaria), Budapest (Hungary), Warsaw (Poland), Tunis (Tunesia), Ankara (Turkey). Her publications include, inter alia, The 1992 Challenge at National Level (Nomos Verlagsgesellschaft, 1990), The Use and Abuse of Intellectual Property Rights in EC Law (Sweet & Maxwell, 1996), The Oxford Encyclopaedia of EC Law (Oxford University Press, 2005), European Legal Dynamics/Dynamiques Juridiques Europeennes (PIE, 2007), Intellectual Property, Public Policy and International Trade (PIE, 2007), Intellectual Property, Market Power and the Public Interest (PIE, 2008), La Fonction Publique Communautaire (Bruylant, 2008), Trade and Competition Law in the EU and Beyond (Edward Elgar, 2011), as well as many articles in law journals and contributions to edited books.

Sieglinde Gstöhl

is Director of the Department of EU International Relations and Diplomacy Studies at the College of Europe in Bruges, Belgium. She has been fulltime professor at the College since 2005. From 1999–2005 she was Assistant Professor of International Relations at the Institute of Social Sciences at Humboldt University Berlin, Germany. She holds a PhD and an MA in International Relations from the Graduate Institute of International and Development Studies in Geneva as well as an MA in Public Affairs from the University of St. Gallen, Switzerland. She was, inter alia, a research fellow at the Liechtenstein-Institut, Liechtenstein, and at the Center for International Affairs at Harvard University, United States.

Christophe Hillion

is professor of European Law at the Universities of Leiden and Stockholm, and Senior Researcher in Law at the Swedish Institute for European Studies (SIEPS, Stockholm). He has published on EU external relations, enlargement and constitutional law. He is a member of the editorial boards of the Common Market Law Review, the European Foreign Affairs Review and the Ukrainian Journal of European Legal Studies. He is also member of the governing board of the Centre for the Law of EU external Relations (CLEER, The Hague), academic fellow at the European Policy Centre (EPC, Brussels), and member of the Jean Monnet Wider Europe Network (Sussex European Institute).

Christine Kaddous

is professor at the University of Geneva and head of the Centre for European Legal Studies. She holds a Jean Monnet Chair *ad personam*. After studying in Switzerland (University of Neuchatel), England (Cambridge University) and Belgium (Free University of Brussels), she was a professor at the University of Fribourg until 2002 and taught at the Europa Institute in Basel and the University of Bern before joining the University of Geneva. His academic interests and activities cover various areas of law of the European Union, including external relations, internal market, litigation of the European Union, role of the EU in international organizations as well as protection of human rights. She publishes also in the field of international economic law, particularly the law of the WTO. She co-directs the Collection "Dossiers de droit européen". She is author and editor of several books on the law of the European Union, the most recent ones cover the "Free movement of persons and services" (2012), "European Energy Law" (2011) and "From Amsterdam to Lisbon: ten years an area of freedom, security and justice" (2010).

Kati Kulovesi

is Senior Researcher and Adjunct Professor (docent) in climate law at the Department of Law, University of Eastern Finland. She holds PhD and LL.M degrees from the London School of Economics and Political Science, and an LL.M from the University of Helsinki. She has published widely on climate law and WTO law, and worked on climate change issues as a practising lawyer and consultant for various organizations and governmnents.

Jing Men

has been the InBev-Baillet Latour Chair of European Union-China Relations since 2008 in the Department of EU International Relations and Diplomacy Studies, College of Europe. She obtained a PhD in Political Science (2004) at the Vrije Universiteit Brussel. She published widely on Chinese foreign policy and EU-China relations. She is the founder of the electronic journal EU-China Observer, launched at the beginning of 2009, where she edits and publishes articles on EU-China relations.

Elisa Morgera

is Lecturer in European Environmental Law at the University of Edinburgh School of Law, where she directs the LLM Programme in Global Environment and Climate Change Law. Her recent publications include: as editor, The External Environmental Policy of the European Union: EU and International Law Perspectives (CUP, 2012); and as a co-author, Environmental Integration in the EU's External Relations: Beyond Multilateral Dimensions (Hart, 2012).

Madalina Moraru
is currently a PhD candidate in law at the European University Institute (EUI) in Florence, working on the subject of 'Protecting EU citizens in the world—What role for the European Union?'. She has a magna cum laude LLM in EU Law from Durham University (2008), as well as from the EUI (2010), and a bachelor degree in law from the Faculty of Law, Bucharest (2007). Ms Moraru participated as Country Correspondent for Romania, legal expert and project leader in several European Projects financed by the European Commission, European Parliament and the European University Institute on a different range of topics: protection of EU citizens abroad, fundamental rights of EU citizens and third country nationals, and training of national judges from EU Member States on the due process rights. In 2009, Ms Moraru has worked as legal expert on fundamental rights issues for a Member of the European Parliament. She has organized several conferences on the law of EU external relations and published articles in Romanian, Italian and European journals on: protection abroad of EU citizens, the EU fundamental right of due process and judicial dialogue between domestic courts and the CJEU. Her research interests include the law and policies of EU external relations, fundamental rights, judicial cooperation and treatment of asylum seekers and refugees.

Veronika Orbetsova
has, since August 2012, been Research Assistant for the Inbev-Baillet Latour Chair of European Union-China Relations in the Department of EU International Relations and Diplomacy Studies at the College of Europe in Bruges. She graduated from Paris 1—Pantheon-Sorbonne University in Paris with a double degree Master's in "International Relations and Activities Abroad" (MRIAE) and "European Affairs". At the College of Europe, she assists with the organisation of seminars, workshops and conferences related to EU-China relations and is part of the editorial board of the *EU-China Observer*. Before joining the College of Europe, Ms. Orbetsova was a Blue Book trainee at the China and Mongolia Unit of the EEAS.

Jan Orbie
is a Professor at the Department of Political Science of Ghent University. He is also the co-director of the Centre for EU Studies which forms the political

science pillar of the Jean Monnet Centre of Excellence at Ghent University, and a member of the university's Research Council. Jan Orbie teaches and researches on the 'soft' (trade, development, social) dimensions of EU external relations and on the EU's role as a civilian/normative power. He has published various journal articles and book chapters on these topics. He has also coordinated two Jean Monnet Information and Research Activities on 'The EU and the social dimension of Globalization' and 'The substance of EU international democracy promotion'. Jan Orbie has edited two books on EU trade and development politics (with Gerrit Faber, Routledge, 2007 and 2009), one book on European external policies (Ashgate, 2008), and one book on Europe's global social policies (with Lisa Tortell, Routledge, 2008), and he has been the co-editor of special issues of the European Foreign Affairs Review (2009 and 2011), of Res Publica (2008), and the Journal of Contemporary European Research (forthcoming).

Sara Poli

is Professor of European law at the University of Pisa as of 2012. She has worked as researcher at the European University Institute (Fiesole) in 2002 and 2009, as lecturer of European Law at the University of Southampton (2001) and teaching assistant of the College of Europe (law department) in Bruges (1999–2001). She obtained her Master of legal studies degree at the College of Europe, and her PhD from the Scuola Superiore S. Anna (Pisa) where she also did her undergraduate studies. She graduated from the University of political science in (Pisa). Sara has received a number of research grants such as the Vlac fellowship of the Royal academy of Belgium for science and the arts, the Marie Curie intra-european, the Jean Monnet and the Fulbright-Schuman fellowships. She has published in several areas of EU law, including the external dimension of the area of freedom security and justice, EU counter terrorist measures, EU judicial remedies and institutional law, EU food safety and environmental law.

Lorenzo Schiano di Pepe

is currently a professor (professore associato) of international law at the University of Genoa, after having studied and researched at the University of Genoa, the University of Milan, Georgetown University Law Centre and the University of London. His teaching is in particular focused on EU law (institutional and substantive aspects) whilst his fields of expertise include international and European transport law, international and European environmental law, institutional law of the EU and international law of the sea.

Peter Van Elsuwege
is professor of European Union law at Ghent University. His research activities essentially focus on the law of EU external relations. Specific attention is devoted to the legal framework of the relations between the EU and its East European neighbours. He is also the academic coordinator of a Jean Monnet Module on "The Legal Dimension of EU External Relations" and an affiliated member of the Centre for the Law of EU External Relations (CLEER) and the Centre for Russian International, Socio-Political and Economic Studies (CERISE). His recent publications include, amongst others: *From Soviet Republics to EU Member States. A Legal and Political Assessment of the Baltic States' Accession to the European Union* (Martinus Nijhoff, 2008); "The Four Common Spaces: New Impetus to the EU-Russia Strategic Partnership", in: A. Dashwood and M. Maresceau (eds.), *Law and Practice of EU External Relations. Salient Features of a Changing Landscape* (CUP, 2008) "EU External Action after the Collapse of the Pillar Structure. In Search of a new Balance between Delimitation and Consistency", *Common Market Law Review* (2010) 987–1019; (with R. Petrov), "Article 8 TEU: Towards a New Generation of Agreements with the Neighbouring Countries of the EU?", *European Law Review* (2011) 688–703 and (with G. Vanderloo), "Competing Paths of Regional Economic Integration in the Post-Soviet Space: Legal and Political Dilemmas for Ukraine", *Review of Central and East European Law* (2012), pp. 421–447.

Bibi van Ginkel
is a senior research fellow of the Netherlands Institute of International Relations Clingendael, as well as a research fellow of the International Centre for Counter-Terrorism (ICCT)—The Hague. She is a member of the Committee on Peace and Security of the Dutch Advisory Council for International Affairs. Her areas of expertise are related to the nexus between law and security, in particular issues of (counter-) terrorism and (counter-) piracy, public international law, human rights and international relations in general.

Jan Wouters
is full Professor of International Law and International Organizations, Jean Monnet Chair ad personam EU and Global Governance and Director of the Leuven Centre for Global Governance Studies and Institute for International Law at the University of Leuven (KU Leuven). In Leuven, he teaches public international law, international organizations, the law of the World Trade Organization and humanitarian and security law. As Visiting Professor at Sciences Po (Paris) and the College of Europe (Bruges) he teaches EU external relations law. As a Visiting Professor, he also teaches international law in the

Master of Laws in International Economic Law (IELPO) at the University of Barcelona and international criminal law in the European Master's in Human Rights and Democratisation (EMA, Venice). He is President of the Flemish Foreign Affairs Council, which advises the Flemish Government, and practises law as Of Counsel at Linklaters, Brussels. He is Member of the Royal Flemish Academy of Belgium for Sciences and Arts. He studied law and philosophy in Antwerp and Yale University (LLM 1990), was a Visiting Researcher at Harvard Law School and obtained his PhD at KU Leuven (1996). He taught at the Universities of Antwerp and Maastricht, was Visiting Professor at Liège and Kyushu University and Référendaire at the European Court of Justice (1991–1994). He is Editor of the International Encyclopedia of Intergovernmental Organizations, Vice-Director of the Revue belge de droit international and editorial board member in ten international journals. He has published widely (around 480 publications including 44 books and 85 international journal articles). Recently he published inter alia a treatise on international law (Grondlijnen van Internationaal Recht, 2005) and on The World Trade Organization (2007) and co-edited The European Union and Conflict Prevention (2004), Legal Instruments in the Fight Against International Terrorism (2004), The United Nations and the European Union (2006), Multilevel Regulation and the EU (2008), The Europeanisation of International Law (2008), European Constitutionalism Beyond Lisbon (2009), Belgium in the Security Council (2009) Accountability for Human Rights Violations by International Organizations (2010), Upgrading the EU's Role as Global Actor (2011), The European Union and Multilateral Governance (2012), International Prosecutors (2012), Informal International Lawmaking (2012), Private Standards and Global Governance (2012) and China, the European Union and Global Governance (2012). Apart from his participation in many international research networks and networks, he advises various international organizations, often trains international officials and frequently comments international events in the media.

Introduction to EU Governance of (Global) Emergencies, Threats and Crises

Inge Govaere and Sara Poli

In recent years, the EU has dealt with situations of emergency affecting third countries, threats of a global nature as well as EU-generated crises. The expression "emergency" is an umbrella term which is used to refer to sudden events causing the death of a large number of people, their internal displacement and even exodus. Extreme climate events (such as flooding or drought), and regional or internal conflicts often create situations of humanitarian emergency. The distinguishing features of the latter are that their *actual* impact in terms of human lives is very high and the catastrophic effects may become apparent either immediately or over the course of a long period of time.

The word 'threat' does not refer to sudden and unpredictable events such as the ones mentioned above. It refers to phenomena that may affect regional or global security for a protracted period of time. For instance, piracy is an example of a persistent menace to the security of the Gulf of Aden which has also affected EU economic interests. By contrast, terrorism and climate change are of world-wide concern. These three different categories feature highly on the EU agenda.

Emergencies and threats may be distinguished from situations of "crisis". The fiscal and economic turbulence of the eurozone countries, which started with the Greek case in May 2010, can be considered the most notable example of "EU generated crises." The eruption of an Icelandic volcano, leading to the protracted closure of European airspace, is another example of a "local emergency" affecting the EU. It goes without saying that these two crises are very different from each other not least because of their effects, which are durable in the former case and temporary in the latter. Yet, they are both exceptional events that had a direct impact upon the rights and the lives of many EU citizens.

In the situations mentioned above the EU has joined its Member States or other international organizations in the effort to manage emergencies and crises, or to counter threats. The aim of this book is to examine the contribution that this special kind of organization, the EU, has made to the management of selected emergencies, threats and crises with respect to its constituent Member States or other international organizations. The objective is two-fold.

© KONINKLIJKE BRILL NV, LEIDEN, 2014 | DOI 10.1163/9789004268333_002

Firstly, the book seeks to identify the strengths and weaknesses of the EU in countering emergencies, threats and crises on the basis of the toolbox that the Lisbon Treaty has made available to the EU institutions. In doing so, the institutional practice, including the contribution of the CJEU in shaping the legal toolkit, is also taken into account. Secondly, the book seeks to highlight how the EU legal order has itself been changed by these exceptional events.

To achieve this double objective the various contributions assess the role of the EU in managing global emergencies in particular in the domains of the environment, humanitarian aid, terrorism, as well as the economic and financial crisis. The reasons for focusing on these selected areas are manifold. Firstly, it is apparent that some emergencies directly threaten the EU integration process as a whole, such as the economic and financial crisis. Secondly, the question arises as to how the EU manages global emergencies in areas where the nature of EU competences differ widely. This explains the attention given to the financial crisis as it affects areas of exclusive competence (such as monetary policy) as well as the lighter form of EU competence, such as in the field of economic policy (Article 5(1) TFEU). The domain of humanitarian aid is singled out because it falls within a 'sui generis' category of shared competence, characterised by the 'non-affectation' clause. Environmental policy is a classic area of shared competence. Whereas the fight against terrorism is an objective which can be ascribed to the area of freedom, security and justice and is therefore included within the EU shared competence, although it can be singled out by classic areas of shared competence since it belonged to the third pillar in the pre-Lisbon era. It goes without saying that situations of emergency may also occur in other policy fields. For example, the influx of illegal immigrants to the borders of the EU is a very real and recurrent concern for the EU but is not focused upon in this book as other studies have already addressed this particular emergency.

The book is structured in two complementary parts, one more EU 'inward' looking in focus, reflecting upon the implications for the EU and its Member States, and the other more 'outward' looking, assessing the impact on relations with third countries and other international organisations.

Part 1 examines the new legal instruments that the EU has at its disposal to tackle situations of humanitarian emergency and to fight terrorism outside the EU, following the Treaty of Lisbon. In addition, it examines the obligations of solidarity stemming from Article 222 TFEU for the EU and its Member States in the event that the territory of a component of the EU family is the subject of a terrorist attack or a natural/man-made disaster. It further explores what the effects are of the economic and fiscal crises of the eurozone countries as well as the volcanic ash crisis on the European integration process and considers judicial review of EU measures addressing emergencies, crises or threats.

The opening contribution sets out the scrutiny of the EU policy approach from the perspective of the EU policy makers. Commissioner Kristalina Georgieva explains and comments upon how the EU currently responds to disasters taking place both inside and outside the EU's borders. European cooperation on civil protection has been developed from 2001 onwards, thus enabling the Union to respond to disasters caused by conflicts or by natural phenomena. It is illustrated how crises such as food emergencies are caused by other crises and need to be addressed within the framework of the humanitarian aid and development cooperation policies. The emphasis is put upon the need for the EU to focus on the prevention of disasters and on building resilience among the most vulnerable populations.

This is followed by an academic, both legal and political, analysis of the humanitarian aid policy, as explicitly set out by the Lisbon Treaty in Article 214 TFEU. In their joint contribution, Peter Van Elsuwege and Jan Orbie discuss the second pillar of the EU's disaster response mechanism. They explore the historical development of the humanitarian aid policy, the legal nature of the EU's competence in this field and the link between the EU's humanitarian aid policy and the principles of international humanitarian law. Finally, specific attention is devoted to the interaction between this policy and other components of the EU external action such as the Common Security and Defence Policy, development cooperation and trade policy. The more theoretical analysis is complemented by a case study by Sieglinde Gstöhl on how the EU has supported the economy of a country hit by a natural catastrophe through trade instruments. The Treaties do not explicitly envisage that the common commercial policy may be used to pursue humanitarian objectives. On the contrary it appears that the principles underpinning the two policies are at odds with one another. Indeed, conditionality is attached only to the former policy but not the latter. Yet, in the practice of the EU institutions there is a case in which trade preferences were granted to Pakistan on account of the situation of emergency caused by the 2010 floods. The contribution examines the first case in which the EU granted trade preferences to a country severely affected by a natural catastrophe related emergency. The political background motivating the adoption of such a unique concession is explained. Attention is also paid to the considerable opposition that the grant of preferential access to the EU market for Pakistan's goods met with from the WTO, the EU institutions and amongst a few Member States. Eventually, numerous conditions were attached to the aforementioned trade concessions, despite the humanitarian purpose of the measure. This case well-illustrates the shortcomings of using trade measures for humanitarian objectives.

The legal toolkit that the Treaty of Lisbon offers to fight the threat of terrorism is the focus of the next two contributions. First of all an analysis of Articles 43 TEU and 215 TFEU is carried out by Christophe Hillion. The former provision establishes an express competence to combat terrorism through the Common Security and Defence Policy (CSDP). It is argued that the CSDP contribution to counterterrorism has now become more tangible than in the past. Two CSDP missions were set up with the specific aim of fighting terrorism. Yet, the ambitions of these missions are limited since they are aimed merely at supporting third countries in their efforts to counter terrorism. The latter provision has been interpreted by the CJEU as conferring a competence upon the Union to adopt sanctions against non-state organisations and individuals, on the ground of their association with terrorism. As a result of the CJEU judgment in Case C-130/10, *European Parliament v. Council,* the CJEU waters down the external dimension of the AFSJ to the benefit of the CFSP. In sum, the inclusion within EU primary law of the above mentioned legal bases contributes to enhance the CFSP dimension of EU counterterrorism. This analysis is complemented by Jeno Czuzai in the subsequent contribution. Here the focus is put on the practical consequences of the Court's judgment in Case C-130/10, *European Parliament v. Council* in terms of the powers of the Council in relation to the threat of international terrorism. The major importance of this judgment is spelled out in terms of "providing stability and continuity in the EU legal order and efficiency in the given EU external action policy areas".

The newly introduced solidarity clause under Article 222 TFEU, and its implementing arrangements, is tackled by Steven Blockmans. He examines this provision which enshrines an explicit obligation upon the Union and its Member States to act jointly, 'in a spirit of solidarity', if a Member State is subject to a terrorist attack or the victim of a natural or man-made disaster. This clause offers a breadth of solidarity that other international organisations do not provide and have no intent of acquiring. The analysis is mainly theoretical as at the moment the provision has not been used by the EU institutions.

Article 196 TFEU is another new legal basis introduced by the Lisbon Treaty. This provision relates to the area of civil cooperation in respect of which the EU is conferred a supporting competence. Florika Fink Hooijer's practical analysis of the EU Civil Protection Mechanism shows that the EU facilitates and coordinates national action in responding to natural and man-made disasters occurring both inside and outside the EU. It is demonstrated that European integration does not need to be based upon a formal operational competence at EU level to work effectively. Reference is *inter alia* made to a Commission proposal to widen the cooperation between the Member States to new situations of emergency which cannot adequately be addressed by action at national level.

The following contribution by Madalina Moraru takes the perspective of an EU citizen in the case of a natural or man-made disaster occurring in a third country. It focuses upon the EU's role in affording consular and diplomatic protection to its citizens. These tasks fall within the primary responsibility of the Member States of origin. Yet, if European citizens cannot benefit from the consular protection of their Member State of nationality, they can find themselves in a vulnerable position. The absence of an external representation of a Member State in a third country may endanger EU citizens' fundamental rights and in certain urgent circumstances it can actually imperil their lives. In such a situation, the responsibility falls upon the other Member States that are represented in the specific third countries, and, lastly, responsibility falls upon the EU delegations, if requested by one of the Member States. Since the Treaty of Lisbon, the Union delegations have taken over the coordination of Member States' embassies from the embassies of the Member States holding the Rotating Presidency. It is argued that the EEAS and the EU delegations could prove useful for ensuring more efficient consular assistance for unrepresented Union citizens in third countries. In particular, the fact that the EEAS is given more powers and instruments in the field of consular protection of EU citizens may lead to a more efficient horizontal co-operation among the external representations of the Member States.

The crucial issue of judicial control at EU level is central to the next contribution. Sara Poli assesses the role that the CJEU sets for itself in cases such as *McDonagh, Kadi* and *Pringle*, which respectively concern the situation of emergency following a natural phenomenon such as the eruption of a volcano, the threat of terrorism and the financial crisis within the eurozone. This piece highlights the Court's broad interpretation of EU-derived rights available to victims of an emergency such as the passengers of airline flights during the volcanic ash crisis in *McDonagh*. Furthermore, it is demonstrated how unusually intense judicial review is when the threat of terrorism affects fundamental human rights. Hence, the *Kadi II* judgment may be contrasted with the case-law in which the fight against terrorism has heavily impinged upon individual freedom, as emphasised by Michal Bobek. In these two cases the judicature prescribes the conduct that the EU institutions and private parties have to take in the management of the threat of terrorism or the emergency caused by the ash cloud of the volcano Eyjafjallajökull. By contrast, in the *Pringle* case, by deciding to uphold the Member States' decision to use an international agreement rather than the Treaty provisions, the CJEU has pragmatically opted for judicial containment.

Biagioni's chapter focuses on one of the weaknesses of the EU in countering the sovereign debt crisis at the current stage of EU integration process. The EU should respect its values and good governance principles, including the democratic principle, even in the administration of crises. The author argues that the management of the sovereign debt crisis by the Member States and the Union institutions fails to comply with the democratic principle for various reasons. First of all, the control of economic policy is diverted from national Parliaments, usually involved in the budgetary procedures, to institutions not directly accountable to the citizens. The intervention of technical bodies such as the Commission and the European Central Bank somehow neutralises democratically elected Governments and/or Parliaments insofar as they prove unable to provide economic and financial stability to their countries, causing adverse effects for the European Union as a whole or for the Eurozone. This is, of course, especially true for the countries that have received financial assistance. In addition, even where the national Parliaments do vote on the international agreements concluded by Member States, they do not exercise any meaningful power of control over these acts. Indeed, voting against a political commitment already assumed by the Government is not legally and politically possible. Thirdly, the loss of political weight in economic matters by national Parliaments is not compensated by a comparable enhancement of the role of the European Parliament. The prevalence of the intergovernmental method is also a cause for democratic concern since the discussion leading to crucial political decisions is not disclosed to the general public. Finally, the author assesses the contribution of judicial review to the implementation of the democratic principle and finds that in economic and monetary matters this is not significant.

The last two contributions, to conclude the more inward looking first part of the book, offer more practical case studies. The first examines how the substantive aspects of risk management decisions were taken to avoid a disaster, following the eruption of an Icelandic volcano in 2010. Alberto Alemanno points to the co-ordinated European approach in response to the volcanic ash crisis and the measures taken to restore the situation to one of normality. One of the legal issues explored is whether the crisis contributed to the establishment of a more integrated EU-wide airspace. The second contribution offers an assessment of the impact which the declared aim of the 'fight against terror' and the EU legislative measures adopted on its basis has had on the state and the 'quality' of the EU legal order. Michal Bobek takes two significant examples of legislative measures, which have been adopted in recent years in two different sectors with the aim of contributing to the 'fight against terror': regulation(s) on airport and aviation security and the Data Retention Directive. In both cases the legality of these measures has been unsuccessfully challenged before the CJEU. The legality of the former measure was questioned on the basis that it was not published in the Official Journal. By contrast, the legal basis of the latter act was contested. It is argued that the regulation on aviation security should have been annulled because it disregarded the rule of law and it impinged upon the right to privacy in a disproportionate manner. A more active role for the Court of Justice in acting as the guardian of EU political institutions is advocated.

Part 2 of the book broadly considers the EU as an international actor in managing emergencies, threats and crises. Three problematic aspects were selected with regard to the manner in which the EU interacts with other international actors or contributes to tackling problems within the framework of multilateral/regional Treaties. The first issue concerns the EU external representation in international organisations and the question of whether this representation is adequate for the EU to contribute to tackling problems related to the economic and financial crisis. The second question is whether the EU has an added value with respect to other international organisations in tackling marine disasters and threats such as climate change, terrorism and piracy. Finally, attention is paid to how the EU interacts with a third country, namely China which has experienced the highest number of disasters per year since 2000, in the field of humanitarian aid and disaster management.

The first 'outward' looking contribution by Christine Kaddous analyses the legal basis enabling the Council to adopt a decision establishing common positions on matters of particular interest for economic and monetary union within the competent international financial institutions and conferences. An assessment is made of the EU's role in international financial and monetary *fora* such as the IMF, the World Bank and the G20. Particular attention is given to the question of whether and how the EU's performance may be strengthened within international financial institutions.

Lorenzo Schiano di Pepe examines the issue of the EU's participation in international instruments dealing with marine pollution. He enquires on whether the EU's activity in this area provides an added value with respect to that of the Member States and of international organisations. Although there are a number of international Treaties that are applicable to this area, the EU is not always a party to them. The author illustrates with a specific example that when the EU participates to international conventions it may play a positive role. It is argued that by adopting a Directive in the area of oil spills and by acceding to the Offshore Protocol within the framework of a regional agreement (the Barcelona Convention), the EU has promoted the adoption of high standards in order to both prevent the likelihood of marine pollution and counter the effects of possible accidents such as that of the *Deepwater Horizon* oil platform. In addition, the EU has filled an important gap within the UNCLOS.

In a joint contribution, Elisa Morgera and Kati Kulovesi assess whether and to what extent the EU can be considered a world leader in stimulating the development of international climate change standards. It is stated that climate change is considered to be the most severe contemporary environmental challenge as well as a key threat to global security. The Lisbon Treaty now expressly lists combatting climate change among the objectives of EU environmental policy in Article 191(1) TFEU. Special attention is given to the legitimacy issue arising from the clearly identified and exposed multi-faceted strategy pursued by the EU in promoting international climate change standards.

Bibi Van Ginkel poses the question of whether one can truly speak of a comprehensive approach to combating piracy. A critical analysis is provided as to whether the EU action shows a genuine added value in this respect as compared to that of the international community at large and the individual Member States. The case study at hand is piracy off the coast of Somalia and the multi-layered response to it by the international community, the Member States and the EU. It is argued that the effectiveness of the EU's action is altogether questionable.

Counter-terrorism cooperation between the EU and UN is the focus of attention of the joint contribution by Jan Wouters and Sanderijn Duquet. The added value of the EU in tackling emergencies with respect to that of other international organisations is clearly illustrated here. It is argued that multilateral approaches have been successfully applied, although different actors and issues are involved. It is maintained that the UN and the EU have developed a partnership in fighting terrorism whereby the cooperation has largely been instigated by the EU, whereas on the part of the UN there has been a responsiveness to interacting with the EU.

The concluding contribution considers the interaction between the EU and China in managing emergencies. Veronika Orbetsova and Jing Men join efforts in analysing the China-EU experience and cooperation in emergency management. An assessment is first made of China's enhanced efforts in emergency management and its growing global experience in disaster relief, before turning to a review of the EU's experience in this field. The main focus is on examining the recently developed EU-China cooperation in managing emergencies, such as the EU-China Disaster Risk Management Project and the setting up of the EU-China Institute for Emergency Management, and its potential for future cooperation. The concluding sentence is very promising in this respect, pointing out that 'the rapid development of cooperative projects between China and the EU is not only mutually beneficial, but also supportive to international emergency management'.

Many of the ideas, insights and arguments presented in this book were first introduced and discussed at a High-level Conference on 'EU Governance of Global Emergencies' which took place in Brussels on 22–23 October 2012. The conference brought together academics, policy makers, practitioners and civil society from several countries with the financial support of the Lifelong Learning Programme Jean Monnet action (information and research activities) and the Royal Flemish Academy for Belgium for Science and the Arts which provided the distinguished location of the Palace of Academia. This proved to be an excellent setting for stimulating thought-provoking cross-disciplinary debate which was further deepened and strengthened in the process leading up to the production of this book.

PART 1

Global Emergencies, Threats and Crises: Impact on the EU and Its Member States

CHAPTER 1

Stakes and Challenges of EU Response to Global Emergencies: An EU Policy Perspective

Kristalina Georgieva

1 What is at Stake Globally: The Rising Fall-Out from Disasters

Let me start with a simple observation: the world is becoming more vulnerable to shocks. For example, there has been a five-fold increase in the number of natural disasters since 1975. The ensuing human suffering and economic costs are huge. With more people (and higher population density) as well as greater wealth, more people are affected and more livelihoods and assets lost when a disaster strikes. 2011 was the costliest year on record where natural disasters are concerned, with almost €285 billion in economic damage, in addition to 30,000 people killed.[1] There is an increasing body of evidence to suggest that climate change is an important driver of this trend and around 80 per cent of disasters are climate-related. Urbanisation and population growth are compounding the picture both by placing more people in situations of vulnerability and by heightening the potential for conflict, which in many cases, such as the Sahel or the Horn of Africa, is linked to environmental degradation and climate change.

Conflict and fragility are not declining. While there may be fewer all-out international conflicts, we are seeing more endemic internal conflicts of which Syria and Mali are the most obvious examples. Moreover, conflicts and natural disasters are overlapping more and more often. The Sahel is a case in point. The situation in Mali is a crisis in a crisis in a crisis, namely a conflict superimposed (and triggered by) a political crisis, superimposed on a massive food and nutrition crisis (the droughts which hit the entire Sahel region in 2005, 2010 and 2012).

We are also seeing more shocks of a cross-border nature than ever before. Some disasters are local but trigger a global response, such as the Haiti earthquake. Others have a direct impact way beyond the borders of the country directly hit, such as the triple disaster in Japan (Fukushima) which prompted nuclear stress-tests in the EU but also affected long-term policy choices in a

1 UNISDR, at <http://www.unisdr.org/archive/24588>.

© KONINKLIJKE BRILL NV, LEIDEN, 2014 | DOI 10.1163/9789004268333_003

number of countries. And pandemic health emergencies, almost by definition, tend not to stop at national borders.

It goes without saying that the EU is itself subject to shocks. There have been 100,000 excess deaths in Europe caused by natural disasters or extreme climate events in the last 10 years alone. In recent years, in addition to forest fires and floods, we have also seen the 2010 red sludge disaster in Hungary and the munitions explosion and power plant disaster in Cyprus in 2011.

2 How Does the EU Respond to Conflict and Disasters—and What are the Challenges?

2.1 *Disaster Response: How Europe Has Been Stepping Up to the Plate*

Europe's capacity to respond to disasters both inside and outside its borders has, as often in the development of the EU, been built up incrementally and in response to very concrete challenges. The EU's humanitarian aid policy started in earnest in 1992, prompted by a small number of major crises notably in former Yugoslavia, in the Great Lakes and in Iraqi Kurdistan. Structured cooperation within the EU on civil protection began only in 2001 with the creation of the Community (now EU) Civil Protection Mechanism, as a very practical way of helping EU Member States draw on each other's disaster response assets when dealing with major disasters. Over the years Europe has become a major player in responding to disasters, both natural and man-made. Some 150 million people worldwide are assisted every year thanks to humanitarian aid funded by the European Union (totalling some €1.3 billion in 2012). The humanitarian aid and civil protection department of the European Commission now has a network of teams around the world (140 senior experts and nearly 300 junior and support staff in 44 offices), assessing humanitarian needs and coordinating closely with the United Nations, the Red Cross, NGOs and other donors. European cooperation on civil protection, too, has developed substantially from just 3 requests for assistance in 2002 to 28 in 2010 and a total of some 170 EU-coordinated civil protection operations since 2002. In 2010, the EU for the first time designated a dedicated Commissioner for crisis response and humanitarian aid, with new provisions in the Lisbon Treaty on humanitarian aid and civil protection. Again, this has underscored the extent to which the issue has moved up the policy agenda in Europe.

The 2010 Haiti earthquake tragically confirmed the need for strong European and international disaster response capacities. Since then we have been confronted with a string of conflicts and disasters requiring substantial international (including European) assistance, such as the Pakistan floods in 2010, the Horn of Africa drought in 2011, the Libyan crisis in 2011, the Fukushima disaster in 2011; successive food and nutrition crises in the Sahel, the gruesome conflict in Syria or the Mali crisis. In all of these, Europe has stepped up to the plate in terms of funding but also by mobilizing in-kind assistance through the EU civil protection mechanism both in terms of advocacy for humanitarian access and in terms of raising the alarm on impending crises (collectively, the international community managed to avoid a massive catastrophe in 2012 in the Sahel by responding early, and the EU did its bit in this effort).

Faced with the challenge of more frequent and more severe disasters, the EU has not only stepped up the resources it devotes to humanitarian aid and disaster response. It has also modernized important aspects of the way it does emergency response. The Commission set out its vision for a more effective EU disaster response in a major policy paper in 2010, adopted soon after the Haiti earthquake.[2] The central aim is to make EU assistance, both inside and outside Europe, more predictable. At present, the EU civil protection mechanism relies largely on ad-hoc offers of assistance from Member States which are frequently, and very generously, provided but lack the certainty that the types of assistance actually required will be forthcoming. The central plank of the system proposed by the Commission will be a stand-by pool of Member States' civil protection assets so that Europe can draw on the assets it needs to respond to a given crisis and does not have to improvise its response every time. In addition, in line with the proposals put forward in 2010, a European Emergency Response Centre has been set up building on the Monitoring and Information Centre, the hub of the EU Civil Protection Mechanism. The Emergency Response Centre is designed as a one-stop shop for requesting and organizing European emergency assistance.

Moreover, the EU's emergency food assistance, by far the biggest component of its humanitarian aid by volume of funding, has been transformed. The 'traditional' way of providing food assistance consisted in many cases of dumping agricultural surpluses on markets of developing countries. The EU has moved away from this entirely and we have been in the vanguard of using cash and vouchers instead promoting local farmers and local food markets, funding the delivery of food from outside only when it cannot be sourced adequately in the region and aiming to direct assistance towards the most vulnerable people. The EU led the way in negotiating a new international Food Assistance

2 Communication from the Commission to the European Parliament and the Council 'Towards a stronger European disaster response: the role of humanitarian aid and civil protection' of 26 October 2010, COM(2010)600 final.

Convention, which entered into force on 1 January 2013, and which reflects this new approach.

We have also put resilience at the heart of what we do, focussing not only on the response to disasters but also on helping communities and countries prepare better for coping with disasters when they happen.[3] Implementing this approach will require close cooperation between the humanitarian and development sides of the EU, something that is now happening in the Horn of Africa and in the Sahel region where building resilience to food and nutrition crises is a key objective for the EU.[4]

2.2 *Working with Other Actors, Inside and Outside the EU*

Of course the EU's emergency relief assistance is only one part of the picture in many natural and man-made disasters. It is certainly an important one, because it addresses the immediate human cost of crisis and it is in many cases the first, and often the only, part of the EU response present on the ground from the first few days or even hours after a disaster. Other parts of the EU come into play to address other aspects of a crisis such as the European External Action Service for the political and security dimension in conflicts outside the EU, the EU's Maritime Safety Agency for maritime incidents, the Home Affairs Directorate-General of the Commission for terrorist incidents in Europe, the European Centre for Disease Control (ECDC) and the Health and Consumer Protection Directorate-General of the Commission for communicable diseases. Whereas of course the EU's own humanitarian aid is complementary with that provided by EU Member States. Cooperation and exchange of information among EU Member States, and between the Member States and the Commission, has made significant progress since the adoption in 2007 of the European Consensus on Humanitarian Aid, as a shared statement of basic principles, and the consequent creation of a specific working group on humanitarian and food aid in the EU Council, bringing together Member States and the Commission.

---

3 Cf. the Communication from the Commission to the European Parliament and the Council 'The EU approach to resilience: learning from food security crises' of 3 October 2012, 2012(586) final.

4 For the Sahel region, the EU was instrumental in initiating the "AGIR Sahel" alliance, which was formally launched in Ouagadougou on 6 December 2012, and which seeks to mobilize governments of the region, regional organization, donors and agencies behind key actions to build resilience across the Sahel. For the Horn of Africa, the EU is actively working with other donors, agencies and governments in the "Global Alliance" led by the United States.

Good cooperation among these different actors, based on a clear understanding of who does what, is of the essence in ensuring a solid European approach to crisis response. We have made great strides in recent years in ensuring consistency between different strands of European crisis response. At the operational level, the single most significant step has been to bring together under a single Commissioner, in 2010, humanitarian aid and civil protection, as the EU's primary instruments for responding to disasters. But we have also worked to ensure stronger cooperation between all the EU actors who may intervene in a crisis situation, namely through the creation of the Emergency Response Centre as a one-stop shop for EU relief assistance, through the EEAS crisis platform for conflicts outside the EU such as those in Syria or Mali, through a much more consistent effort to ensure smooth linkages between humanitarian relief and development (with a huge improvement, for example, in the way the EU has ensured transition from humanitarian aid to longer term assistance in Haiti; or successful EU-sponsored initiatives such as the Partnership for Transition in Cote d'Ivoire), through close cooperation between EU Delegations and the ECHO experts in crisis countries, or through successful practical cooperation between the Commission's humanitarian aid and civil protection service on the one hand, and Member States' militaries and the EU Military Staff, on the other (which made possible, for example, military airlift support to humanitarian operations in the 2011 Pakistan floods).

Finally, in this context, it is worth mentioning the increasing importance we have been attaching to cooperation and dialogue with new and emerging actors in humanitarian and disaster relief, such as the Gulf states, or the Organization of Islamic Cooperation (which has played a central role in coordinating relief assistance in Somalia, for example), or the BRICs. The humanitarian world is infinitely more diverse now than it was even ten years ago. This is very much to be welcomed but it will also require a real commitment from the EU to maintain a permanent and open conversation with key players significantly beyond the 'traditional' humanitarian community of UN agencies, the Red Cross and international NGOs.

3 What Next for EU Emergency Response?

There is no doubt that the EU's response to emergencies has in recent years become faster, better coordinated and more effective. But we also need to gear up to prevent and anticipate disasters, both natural and man-made. We need to get better at identifying and mapping vulnerabilities and risks. Within the EU, a substantial effort to improve risk mapping is under way building on the experience already developed in a number of Member States.[5] Outside Europe, we need to improve our capacities for early warning of conflicts. At the end of 2012, for example, the world was taken largely by surprise by the sudden flaring-up of two separate conflicts in central Africa, namely the intensification of the conflict involving a myriad of armed groups, not least the M23 movement, in the Eastern DRC in November 2012 as well as the events in the Central African Republic in December, when the long-running low-intensity clashes between the government and armed groups suddenly turned into an acute and fast-moving conflict that required substantial mobilization by humanitarian actors and triggered intense political mediation efforts in the region. Collectively, the international community needs to do better in being ahead of the curve on such developments and enable political and diplomatic actors to be more effective in preventing conflict; and for humanitarians to be better equipped to prepare and pre-position when conflicts threaten to bring about serious humanitarian consequences.

Prevention and preparedness are all the more important at a time where the resources available for humanitarian action and disaster response have come under huge pressure. This has certainly been the case in many EU Member States, some of whom have reduced their overseas aid budgets in a context of budgetary austerity. It has also been the case at EU level and it has affected other big traditional donors outside Europe. As we saw earlier, the trend for humanitarian case-loads and damage from disasters is going up, driven by factors such as climate change. In addition, the cost of delivering humanitarian aid in some crucial contexts is also going up (it costs significantly more, for example, to provide for refugees in an urban setting than in a traditional refugee camp—just as urban displacement is on the increase). The upshot is that the international community (the EU included) will need to do better on preventing conflict before it triggers serious humanitarian consequences. We will need to focus in a sustained way on building resilience of the most vulnerable populations, not least in countries that will be more, rather than less, subject to climate-related disasters in the future.

Finally, while much has changed in the EU's response to crisis, one thing has not, namely our commitment to the humanitarian principles of humanity, impartiality, independence and neutrality as the cornerstone of EU humanitar-

5 Communication from the Commission to the European Parliament and the Council 'A Community approach on the prevention of natural and man-made disasters' of 23 February 2009, COM(2009)82 final, and Council Conclusions on a Community framework on disaster prevention within the EU, 2979th Justice and Home Affairs Council meeting, Brussels, 30 November 2009.

ian aid, as enshrined in the European Consensus on Humanitarian Aid. There are voices that argue that the humanitarian principles are being rendered obsolete by the increasing diversity of humanitarian actors. Or by the increasing engagement of humanitarian actors in resilience-building and transition to development which, by definition, require cooperation and coordination with the governments of states affected by disaster. Or else by the changing nature of modern warfare. In fact, I would argue that the opposite is true. The rise in protracted asymmetrical warfare as seen in Syria or the Sahel makes it all the more important that humanitarians are clearly identified and perceived as not taking sides. When leaning forward to build resilience or help rebuild communities after disasters, humanitarian actors of course need to engage with government authorities who have the primary responsibility, after all, for the wellbeing of their population. This should not interfere with the imperative to remain impartial when saving lives in a crisis. For the EU, these principles will continue to remain 'hardwired' into its approach to emergency relief.

4 Conclusion

'Global' emergencies have in recent years moved dramatically up the EU's agenda. Particularly since the Haiti earthquake, humanitarian aid and disaster response are no longer marginal 'niche' areas of EU activity. Collectively, we have stepped up to the plate in the EU. On the whole, EU citizens have recognized this and, surprisingly in a period of financial austerity, appear if anything to be more rather than less supportive of the EU's action in this area.[6] But much remains to be done, particularly as regards resilience, prevention and preparedness as well as regards more effective upstream engagement with the root causes of conflict. I am hopeful that in the next few years we will make further headway on all of these issues.

6 European citizens' support to the EU's humanitarian action increased from 79% in 2010 to 88% in 2012. Cf. the Special Eurobarometers 343 and 384 on Humanitarian Aid, at <http://ec.europa.eu/public_opinion/archives/ebs/ebs_343_en.pdf> and <http://ec.europa.eu/public_opinion/archives/ebs/ebs_384_en.pdf,> respectively.

CHAPTER 2

The EU's Humanitarian Aid Policy after Lisbon: Implications of a New Treaty Basis

*Peter Van Elsuwege and Jan Orbie**

1 Introduction

Despite the long-term involvement of the European Union (EU) in humanitarian actions, it is only with the Treaty of Lisbon that a specific provision devoted to humanitarian aid has been introduced into the primary legal framework of the EU. Accordingly, the granting of "*ad hoc* assistance and relief and protection for people in third countries who are victims of natural and man-made disasters, in order to meet the humanitarian needs resulting from these different situations" is an EU external policy in its own right.[1] With this explicit recognition, the Treaty of Lisbon underlines the separate nature of humanitarian aid in comparison to other external policies such as development co-operation or Common Foreign and Security Policy (CFSP). It also clearly distinguishes humanitarian aid and civil protection as two different yet complementary pillars of the EU's disaster response mechanism.[2]

Notwithstanding the absence of an explicit legal basis in the pre-Lisbon period, the EU has a long-standing tradition of providing humanitarian assistance to third countries. Already in 1969, a humanitarian aid programme was initiated in the context of the Yaoundé II Convention with the countries of Africa, the Caribbean and the Pacific (ACP). In 1992, the European Community Humanitarian Office (ECHO) was set up for the purpose of "managing humanitarian actions for the benefit of the populations *of all third countries* suffering from natural disasters or exceptional events requiring swift response or

* The authors thank Mrs. Kathrin Schick, Director of "Voluntary Organisations in Cooperation in Emergencies" (VOICE) and Mr. Hervé Delphin, Head of Cabinet of Commissioner Kristalina Georgieva, for their comments on a draft version of this text.

1 Article 214 TFEU.

2 With regard to civil protection, the Lisbon Treaty introduced new Article 196 TFEU. On the link between humanitarian aid and civil protection as the two main tools of the EU's disaster response policy, see COM (2010) 600 final.

© KONINKLIJKE BRILL NV, LEIDEN, 2014 | DOI 10.1163/9789004268333_004

the implementation of accelerated procedures".[3] The adoption of Council Regulation 1257/96 provided the basic legal framework for the further elaboration of a specific humanitarian aid policy on behalf of the European Community.[4]

Since the early 2000s, the EU's humanitarian aid policy has gradually become more independent from the development realm on the one hand, and from the foreign and security policy sphere on the other. This became clear for the first time during the drafting of the Constitutional Treaty by the European Convention in 2002–2003. The European Consensus on Humanitarian Aid, adopted in December 2007 and signed on behalf of the Council, the European Commission, the European Parliament and the Member States, also stresses the independent nature of the EU's policy in this field. The principles that apply to humanitarian aid (neutrality, impartiality, humanity and independence) are specific and distinct from other forms of aid.[5] They differ from development cooperation, the practices and principles of which are outlined in a separate European Consensus,[6] and from the EU's involvement in crisis management, civil protection and consular assistance. Of course, given the close connection between the origins of a humanitarian crisis (a civil war, natural disaster, extreme poverty etc.) and its consequences (large numbers of displaced people, social and economic difficulties), humanitarian aid is almost always closely related to other policy areas. One of the key challenges for the EU is therefore to ensure coherence and complementarity in its response to crisis situations while respecting the constitutional division of competences and the specific characteristics of its different policies.

In this contribution it will be argued that the attribution of an explicit legal basis for the elaboration of an EU humanitarian aid policy is the logical next step in a gradual process to achieve this objective. After analysing the historical development of the EU's humanitarian aid policy (2), the legal nature of the EU's competence in this field is discussed (3). Subsequently, the link between the EU's humanitarian aid policy and the principles of international humanitarian law is scrutinised (4). Finally, specific attention is devoted to the

3 <http://ec.europa.eu/europeaid/how/evaluation/evaluation_reports/reports/acp/951474_2_en.pdf> (emphasis added) (accessed 1 May 2013).

4 Council Regulation (EC) No 1257/96 of 20 June 1996 concerning humanitarian aid, *OJ*, 2006, L 163/1.

5 European Consensus on Humanitarian Aid, *OJ*, 2008, C 25/1, para. 22. For an analysis of the humanitarian principles, see *infra* part 4.

6 European Consensus on Development, *OJ*, 2006, C 46/1.

challenge of coherence in the EU's response to global emergencies and the place of humanitarian aid in this respect (5).

2 The Evolution of an EU Humanitarian Aid Policy: From Yaoundé to Lisbon

The introduction of Article 214 TFEU consolidates a long process of gradual European integration in the area of humanitarian assistance. This integration encompasses three distinct but related processes: (i) the legal framework to pursue an EU humanitarian aid policy has been strengthened over the years (ii) the EU's humanitarian aid policy has become more and more professionalised through subsequent institutional reforms within ECHO, and (iii) EU humanitarian aid policy has increasingly become an independent policy area that is separate from e.g. crisis management and development policy, in line with international humanitarian principles.

Whereas the Treaty of Rome contained a separate Part IV on development policy entitled 'Association of the Overseas Countries and Territories', humanitarian aid was not mentioned. It was only in 1969 that the European Economic Community (EEC) for the first time engaged in this domain through the Yaoundé II Convention with the AASM (Association of the Associated African States and Madagascar). Article 20 of the Yaoundé II Convention refers to 'exceptional aid', understood as the aid given to address exceptional economic difficulties or natural disasters. The receiving country's national government was in charge of the emergency aid granted by the EEC. The scope of humanitarian aid was extended with the Lomé II Agreement between the EEC and the ACP, which replaced the notion of 'exceptional aid' with that of 'emergency aid' (Article 254). From then on, man-made disasters could also be covered, in which case support could go directly to the victims of the emergency situation rather than to the national government.[7] This mirrors a broader evolution at the end of the 1970s when the EEC started to take a more critical stance towards violation of democratic and human rights principles by ACP governments.[8] Meanwhile, the geographical scope of EEC humanitarian aid had also been extended to include all the developing countries and not just the ACP group by means of a separate budget line created by the European Parliament in 1971.

7 H. Versluys, European humanitarian aid policy from a political science perspective: an analysis of delegation and coherence (Unpublished PhD, Ghent University, 2008b), p. 9.

8 K. Smith, European Union foreign policy in a changing world, Cambridge: Polity Press, 2003, pp. 97–101.

In 1992, the EU humanitarian aid policy was further institutionalised with the creation of ECHO[9] as a separate service within the European Commission. This decision can be put down to a combination of different factors.[10] Firstly, there were efficiency concerns. Since the 1970s the EEC had spent an increasing amount of its budget on humanitarian aid, while responsibilities remained scattered among different Directorate-Generals (e.g. DG Agriculture, External Relations, Development). An administrative structure exclusively dedicated to humanitarian assistance would make the EU a more efficient actor in this area. Secondly, as principal-agent models have shown at length, the delegation of a specific task to an agency makes it easier to pursue policy goals that should not be distorted by political considerations. In this sense, the creation of a separate office in the form of ECHO should allow for the straightforward application of humanitarian principles without undue interference from the sphere foreign and security policy. Thirdly, the early 1990s witnessed severe challenges in terms of humanitarian crises, for instance in Iraq after the first Gulf War and in the former Yugoslavia. Fourthly, the post-Cold War context provided the EU with a window of opportunity to play a more prominent international role. In this respect, the creation of ECHO also served to enhance the EU's visibility and legitimacy as an actor on the world scene. Indeed, the Commission regarded the lack of visibility to the general public within and outside Europe as one of the shortcomings that the creation of ECHO should address.[11] EU humanitarian aid could also be seen as a foreign policy 'by default': when a unified position proves difficult to achieve the EU can often fall back on its significant budget for humanitarian assistance.

However, this institutionalisation process was not reflected in the Treaties. The decision to create ECHO was made during the same period as the

---

9 Originally ECHO stood for 'European Office for Emergency Humanitarian Aid', then it became 'European Community Humanitarian Office', and later 'European Commission's Humanitarian Aid Office'. Since 2010, ECHO has been the European Commission's office for Humanitarian Aid and Civil Protection.

10 See also H. Versluys, "European Humanitarian Aid: Lifesaver or Political Tool?", in: J. Orbie (ed.), Europe's Global Role. External Policies of the European Union, Aldershot: Ashgate, 2008a, pp. 91–116; Versluys 2008b *op. cit.*, n. 7; C. Bretherton and J. Vogler, The European Union as a Global Actor, London: Routledge, 2006, p. 131; M. Holland and M. Doidge, The European Union and the Third World, Basingstoke: Palgrave, 2012, pp. 109–110; T. Mowjee, "The European Community Humanitarian Office (ECHO): 1992–1999 and Beyond", Disasters 22 (3), 1998, pp. 250–267.

11 European Commission Decision to set up a European Office for Humanitarian Aid, P/91/69, 06/11/1991.

intergovernmental conference leading to the Treaty of Maastricht,[12] but the latter did not include a single reference to humanitarian aid. In 1996, the basic legal framework for EU humanitarian aid was provided through secondary law, namely Council Regulation 1257/96.[13] This Regulation was adopted on the legal basis of ex Article 130w of the EC Treaty (later Article 179 EC; now Article 209 TFEU) relating to development cooperation. This choice of legal basis, which may be explained by the historical links with humanitarian assistance to the ACP countries and the absence of a more specific Treaty basis at the time, is at least somewhat controversial.[14] Firstly, the scope of application of Regulation 1257/96 is not restricted to developing countries, and, following the logic of the *Community Guarantee to EIB* case, it may well be argued that such a legal act cannot be adopted on the grounds of development competences alone.[15] Secondly, the adoption of a humanitarian aid instrument in the framework of development cooperation risks undermining the specificity of humanitarian assistance.

Despite the Community's expanding activities in the field of humanitarian aid in the 1990s, supported by ECHO and based on Regulation 1257/96, several problems emerged. ECHO's increased financial responsibilities combined with understaffing of the agency contributed to malfunctions, ranging from long delays and cumbersome procedures to financial scandals. In 1997, the Court of Auditors issued a critical report about ECHO and the internal evaluation following ECHO's seven-year trial period also voiced strong criticisms.[16] Fraudulent

12 Emergency humanitarian aid from the Community: Commission guidelines (Memo P 91/56, 24/07/1991) European Commission Decision to set up a European Office for Humanitarian Aid, P/91/69, 06/11/1991.

13 Council Regulation (EC) No 1257/96 of 20 June 1996 concerning humanitarian aid, *OJ*, 2006, L 163/1.

14 M. Broberg; "Undue Assistance? An Analysis of the Legal Basis of Regulation 1257/96 concerning Humanitarian Aid", *EL Rev.*34 (5), 2009, pp. 769–778.

15 In this case, the CJEU found that a decision granting a Community guarantee to the European Investment Bank (EIB) against losses under loans and loan guarantees for projects outside of the Community had to be adopted under the dual legal basis of ex Article 179 EC (now Article 209 TFEU) and ex Article 181a EC (now Article 212 TFEU) reflecting the adoption of such measures with respect to developing countries, on the one hand, and non-developing countries, on the other hand. See CJEU, Case C-155/07, *European Parliament* v. *Council* [2008] ECR I-8103, paras. 67–72.

16 Court of Auditors Special Report No 2/97 Concerning humanitarian aid from the European Union between 1992 and 1995 together with the Commission's replies, *OJ*, 1997, C 143/1–65.

contracts in the context of Bosnia and the African Great Lakes region were part of the scandals that led to the demise of the Santer Commission in 1999. Apart from these management-related challenges, ECHO's compliance with the humanitarian principles was also questioned at times. Under Commissioner Emma Bonino (1995–1999) ECHO became a visible part of the EU's international policies, but according to Versluys it "sometimes engaged in activities which, strictly speaking, went beyond humanitarian assistance and were more oriented towards conflict resolution or development."[17]

The next decade saw an improvement in both respects. Firstly, internal reforms following the 1999 evaluation led to a more professional management of ECHO with several changes such as the fast-track procedure for decision-making in Brussels and the elaboration of clear performance indicators for partners on the ground. Under Commissioner Poul Nielson (1999–2004), ECHO "lost some of its idealism and romance, but gained in efficiency and speed" and became "more middle aged and mature, less high spirited perhaps, but a leaner, meaner, more professional aid machine".[18] Secondly, a number of legal and political initiatives were undertaken to guarantee the observance of the humanitarian imperative *vis-a-vis* developmental and security related objectives, while also safeguarding the coherence of the EU's humanitarian aid policies. The work of the European Convention has been important in this respect. The initial mandate and discussion papers informing the Convention's Working Group on External Relations did not contain any suggestion to incorporate humanitarian aid into the new constitutional document.[19]A number of Member States even wanted to reinforce the operational links between humanitarian aid and CFSP because of their disappointment with the slow progress in military cooperation.[20] It was only after Commissioner Nielson's appeal to the Convention that "humanitarian assistance should be covered by a distinct chapter of external policy, subject to specific Community decision-making mechanisms and not fall under crisis management procedures"[21] that subsequent draft documents incorporated a

17 Versluys 2008b, *op. cit.*, n. 7 p. 93.

18 ICG 2001, quoted in Versluys 2008a, *op. cit.*, n. 10 p. 93.

19 CONV 161/02, 3 July 2002; CONV 200/02, 16 July 2002; CONV 252/02, 10 September 2002.

20 P. Nielson "EU Aid: What Works and Why", ReCom/UNU-WIDER Working Paper No. 2012/76, p. 15.

21 CONV WG VII—WD 48, 21 November 2002.

separate article on humanitarian aid.[22] When analysing the subsequent discussions and amendments within the European Convention, it is remarkable that this upgraded status of humanitarian aid into primary EU law has barely been contested.[23] The new Treaty provision on humanitarian aid was modelled upon that on development cooperation, with an emphasis on the specific nature of humanitarian operations following the definitions included in Regulation 1257/96.

The Convention work revealed the emergence of a political consensus on the need for a more professional and independent humanitarian aid policy at EU level. This trend would be further strengthened through the transformation of ECHO from a specialised service into a full-fledged Directorate-General (2004), the drafting of a European Consensus on Humanitarian Aid (2007), and finally the Treaty of Lisbon, which literally recycled the Constitutional Treaty's humanitarian aid provision. With the European Consensus and Article 214 TFEU, "the EU has put in place a solid humanitarian policy, anchored in relevant legislation and applicable across the Commission and Member States", and the appointment of a separate Commissioner for humanitarian aid (Kristalina Georgieva, 2009–2014) has "helped solidify this move".[24]

In sum, a remarkable evolution has been observed beginning with limited competences ensuing from a bilateral agreement (Yaoundé 1969 and subsequent Lomé Agreements) and a budget line of the European Parliament (1971), developing with an internal decision of the European Commission (creation of ECHO in 1991 and upgrade to a Directorate General in 2004) and a Council Regulation (1996, based on the Maastricht Treaty's article on development cooperation), culminating in primary law in the ill-fated Constitutional Treaty and, finally, the Treaty of Lisbon (2009). In addition to these legal and institutional evolutions, the EU has also developed a number of substantial policy initiatives in the area of humanitarian aid, as witnessed by e.g. the European Consensus on Humanitarian Aid (2007),[25] the Commission Communications

22 WG VII—WD 21 REV 1, 22 November 2002; WG VII—WD 21 REV 2, 29 November 2002; CONV 685/03, 23 April 2012.

23 The only two elements that provoked some debate in the Convention were the questions of whether 'neutrality' should be added to the principles in paragraph 2 and whether a reference to the European Voluntary Humanitarian Aid Corps in the Treaty would be desirable (see *infra* part III). For a summary of the amendments, see CONV 685/03, 23 April 2012.

24 OESO-DAC report 2012, p. 88, available at: <http://www.oecd.org/dac/peer-reviews/50155818.pdf> (accessed 1 May 2013).

25 European Consensus on Humanitarian Aid, *OJ*, 2008, C 25/1.

on Linking Relief Rehabilitation and Development (1996 and 2001)[26] and the Commission Communication on Disaster Risk Reduction (2012).[27]

Several reasons behind this evolution have already been mentioned: increasing efficiency and economies of scale, insulating the humanitarian principles from political pressures, and enhancing the legitimacy and visibility of the EU as an international actor. In addition, some have argued that, somewhat paradoxically, the expansion of a Common Foreign and Security Policy at the EU level may also have contributed to the growing independence of the EU humanitarian aid sphere: since the EU now has several foreign policy related instruments in its armoury, there is no need to rely on humanitarian resources for these purposes.[28] Nevertheless, privileged observers such as former Commissioner Nielson[29] and the VOICE network of humanitarian aid NGOs[30] warn that the humanitarian principles are often poorly understood and constantly under pressure from actors involved in development as well as foreign and security policies. The next sections will take a closer look at the possible implications of the Lisbon Treaty in terms of guaranteeing the specific position of humanitarian aid within the broader context of the EU's external action.

3 The Nature of the EU's Competence in the Field of Humanitarian Aid

Already in the *Bangladesh* case of 1993, the European Court of Justice observed that "the Community does not have exclusive competence in the field of humanitarian aid, and that consequently the Member States are not precluded from exercising their competence in that regard collectively in the Council or outside it".[31] The Treaty of Lisbon codified the shared nature of the EU's

26 European Commission Communication on Linking Relief, Rehabilitation and Development (LRRD), Brussels, 30.04.1996, COM (96) 153 final; European Commission communication on Linking Relief, Rehabilitation and Development—An Assessment. Brussels, 23.04.2001, COM (2001) 153 final.

27 European Commission communication on 'The EU Approach to Resilience: Learning from Food Security Crises', Brussels, 3.10.2012, COM (2012) 586 final.

28 H. Versluys 2008b, *op. cit.*, n. 7.

29 P. Nielson, "EU Aid: What Works and Why", ReCom/UNU-WIDER Working Paper No. 2012/76.

30 Interview with Kathrin Schick, Director of VOICE, 4 February 2013.

31 Joint cases C-181/91 and C-248/91, *European Parliament* v. *Council* [1993] ECR I-3685, para. 16.

humanitarian aid competences. Pursuant to Article 214(1) TFEU, humanitarian assistance provided by the EU and the Member States "shall complement and reinforce each other". Just as in the area of development cooperation, EU initiatives to develop a common humanitarian aid policy do not have a pre-emptive effect on the Member States.[32] Both the EU and its Member States can conclude international agreements with third countries and international organisations on matters related to humanitarian assistance.[33]

The existence of parallel EU and Member State competences regarding development cooperation and humanitarian aid can be linked to the particular characteristics of both policies. Taking into account the important budgetary implications as well as the visibility of development and humanitarian aid, Member States appear reluctant to accept a far-reaching competence transfer to the EU level. Moreover, parallel action by the Union and the Member States, either individually or collectively, can contribute to a better burden-sharing of the technical and financial efforts related to development and humanitarian aid. This may result in more intensive assistance than would be the case if Union action excluded further Member State activities in support of developing countries and/or in the wake of an emergency. To paraphrase Advocate General Kokott: the more development and humanitarian assistance, the better.[34] Of course, the duties of consistency and loyal cooperation, which have been given an even more prominent place by the Treaty of Lisbon,[35] fully apply to the implementation of the EU and Member State development and humanitarian aid initiatives.

Despite the similarities between the EU's development and humanitarian aid competences, subtle differences do exist. Whereas Article 209(1) TFEU allows for the adoption of "measures necessary for the *implementation* of development cooperation", Article 214(3) TFEU only refers to "measures defining the *framework* within which the Union's humanitarian aid operations shall

32 Article 4(4) TFEU.

33 Article 214(4) TFEU.

34 See Opinion of Advocate General Kokott in Case C-13/07, *Commission* v. *Council*, not published in the ECR, para. 70. The Opinion of the Advocate General only concerned the parallel nature of the Community's development cooperation competences at the time but the same reasoning applies *mutatis mutandis* with regard to humanitarian aid.

35 See, in particular, Articles 4(3) TEU, 13 TEU and 7 TFEU. For comments, see E. Neframi, "The duty of loyalty: rethinking its scope through its application in the field of EU external relations", *CML Rev.* 47, 2010, pp. 329–359 and C. Hillion, "Cohérence et action extérieure de l'Union européenne", in: E. Neframi (ed.), *Objectifs et compétences de l'Union européenne*, Paris: Bruylant, 2012, pp. 229–241.

be implemented".[36] This may be linked to the specific features of EU humanitarian assistance, which is essentially implemented by NGOs and specialist international organisations or bodies.[37] A key objective of the EU's humanitarian aid policy is to operate as a facilitator for providing first aid and relief in emergency situations. In this context, Article 214(6) TFEU gives a mandate to the European Commission to "take any useful initiative to promote *coordination* between actions of the Union and those of the Member States, in order to enhance the efficiency and complementarity of Union and national humanitarian aid measures". Arguably, this general focus on coordination reveals that the division between 'shared' and 'coordinating' competences in Articles 4 and 6 TFEU is not straightforward.[38] As far as humanitarian aid (and development cooperation) is concerned, the EU is both a significant actor/donor and coordinator of Member State actions.

The Commission's competence to promote coordination between humanitarian actions of the Union and the Member States is nothing new since it is already explicitly included in Article 10(1) of Regulation 1257/96. Article 10(2) of the same Regulation deals with the Commission's coordinating role in relation to international organisations and agencies, in particular those which form part of the United Nations system, and Article 10(3) provides that the Commission "shall endeavour to develop collaboration and cooperation between the Community and third-country donors in the field of humanitarian aid". It is worth noting that Article 214(7) TFEU gives the task of coordination with international organisations and bodies to the Union, rather than specifically to the Commission, whereas Article 214 TFEU remains silent on the task of coordination with other third country donors. This is a direct consequence of the Lisbon Treaty innovations, which grant the responsibility for cooperating with international organisations to the High Representative and the Commission[39] and resulted in the establishment of Union—rather than Commission—Delegations. In practice, the Commission actively pursues a coordinating role with regard to the activities of both the Member States and other international actors, be it international organisations, agencies or third country donors. The initiative of Commissioner Georgieva to convene a major donor conference in response to the unfolding humanitarian crisis in Syria

36 Emphasis added.

37 Articles 7 and 8 of Regulation 1257/96. Article 9 of the same Regulation provides that "where necessary, the Community may also finance humanitarian operations by the Commission or the Member States' specialized agencies".

38 P. Craig, *The Lisbon Treaty. Law, Politics and Treaty Reform*, Oxford: OUP, 2010, p. 395.

39 Article 220(2) TFEU.

provides a good illustration of the Commission's coordinating activities in the field of humanitarian aid.[40]

4 Humanitarian Aid as a Separate EU External Policy Based on Principles of International Humanitarian Law

Article 214 TFEU endows the EU with an explicit competence to tackle the humanitarian consequences of natural or man-made disasters such as, for instance, floods, droughts, earthquakes, volcano eruptions, tsunamis, civil wars, state failures or ethnic cleansings. Whereas the wording of Article 214 TFEU may be considered to be very broad,[41] it also contains important limitations upon the scope of application of the EU's humanitarian actions. Firstly, humanitarian aid is limited to emergencies in third countries. Disaster relief within the EU is subject to the solidarity clause in Article 222 TFEU.[42] Secondly, measures adopted under Article 214 TFEU are designed to provide *ad hoc* support in the event of emergencies whereas long-term and structural assistance fall under either Article 208 TFEU (development cooperation) or Article 212 TFEU (economic, financial and technical cooperation). Thirdly, EU humanitarian aid is confined to addressing 'humanitarian needs'. In this respect, it differs from civil protection cooperation, which is another tool at the disposal of the EU to provide relief assistance to people faced with the immediate consequences of natural or man-made disasters. The latter is based on Article 196 TFEU and can be mobilised both internally within the EU and in third countries. It typically focuses on search and rescue operations and often includes technical types of assistance such as fire fighting (in case of forest fires), pumping capacity (floods), ships to combat pollution (oil spills) and detection and decontamination facilities (chemical, biological or nuclear incidents).[43] Last but not least, EU humanitarian aid operations "shall be conducted in compliance with the principles of international law and with the

40 "Humanitarian response to the Syrian crisis: EU Commissioner convenes donors, Syria's neighbours and aid agencies", available at: <http://europa.eu/rapid/press-release_IP-12-1032_en.htm> (accessed 1 May 2013).

41 A. Dashwood, "Conflicts of Competence in Responding to Global Emergencies", in: A. Antoniadis, R. Schütze and E. Spaventa (eds.), *The European Union and Global Emergencies. A Law and Policy Analysis*, Oxford: Hart, 2011, p. 38.

42 On the 'solidarity clause', see also the contribution of S. Blockmans to this volume.

43 On 'civil protection', see also the contribution of F. Fink Hooijer to this volume.

principles of impartiality, neutrality and non-discrimination".[44] It follows that, in contrast to civil protection, EU humanitarian aid cannot be used as a tool for facilitating and supporting CFSP crisis management operations.[45]

It is noteworthy that Article 214(2) TFEU refers to "impartiality, neutrality and non-discrimination" as fundamental principles guiding the EU's humanitarian aid whereas the European Consensus refers to "humanity, neutrality, impartiality and independence". The latter also provides a definition of those terms. Humanity implies that "human suffering must be addressed, wherever it is found, with particular attention to the most vulnerable in the population". Neutrality means that humanitarian aid "must not favour any side in an armed conflict or other dispute". Impartiality requires that "humanitarian aid must be provided solely on the basis of need, without discrimination between or within affected populations". Respect for independence entails "the autonomy of humanitarian objectives from political, economic, military or other objectives". So the sole purpose of humanitarian aid is "to relieve and prevent the suffering of victims of humanitarian crises".[46]

The four humanitarian principles as defined in the European Consensus correspond to the practice of the United Nations Office for the Coordination of Humanitarian Affairs (UNOCHA)[47] and are based on a number of UN General Assembly and Security Council Resolutions.[48] Despite the absence of an explicit reference to humanity and independence in Article 214(2) TFEU, it is difficult to maintain that those principles would not bind the institutions

44 Article 214(2) TFEU.

45 The European Consensus explicitly states that "EU humanitarian aid is not a crisis management tool", para. 15.

46 *Ibid.*, para. 14.

47 See <http://ochanet.unocha.org/p/Documents/OOM_HumPrinciple_English.pdf> (accessed 1 May 2013).

48 General Assembly Resolution 46/182 of 19 December 1991 on "Strengthening of the coordination of humanitarian emergency assistance of the United Nations" laid down that "humanitarian assistance must be provided in accordance with the principles of humanity, neutrality and impartiality", A/RES/46/182. General Assembly Resolution 58/114 of 17 December 2003 reaffirmed those principles and recognised that "independence, meaning the autonomy of humanitarian objectives from the political, economic, military and other objectives that any actor may hold with regard to areas where humanitarian action is being implemented, is also an important guiding principle for the provision of humanitarian assistance, A/RES/58/114. Security Council Resolution S/RES/1674 of 28 April 2006 on the protection of civilians in armed conflicts also "stresses the importance for all, within the framework of humanitarian assistance, of upholding and respecting the humanitarian principles of humanity, neutrality, impartiality and independence".

and the Member States in pursuing the EU's humanitarian aid policy.[49] After all, Article 214(2) also contains a reference to "the principles of international law" and pursuant to Article 21 TEU the Union's external action shall by guided by, amongst other things, "respect for human dignity, the principles of equality and solidarity and respect for the principles of the United Nations Charter and international law". Respect for the key rules of international humanitarian law falls within the scope of those provisions.[50] Moreover, Article 1 of the Charter of Fundamental Rights unequivocally states that "[h]uman dignity is inviolable. It must be respected and promoted". This reflection of the humanity principle binds the institutions, bodies, offices and agencies of the Union and the Member States when they are acting under Article 214 TFEU.

The principles of humanity, neutrality and impartiality are generally recognised as the common denominator of international legal instruments related to humanitarian aid in disaster situations.[51] The notion of independence, which is also often mentioned, may be considered as a 'derived principle' insofar as its substance, i.e. the autonomy of humanitarian objectives from political, military or economic influences, follows from the other principles.[52] The same reasoning applies with regard to the principle of non-discrimination. Nevertheless, just as in the case of independence, non-discrimination is sometimes explicitly included as a separate concept alongside the notions of humanity, neutrality and impartiality. This is, for instance, the case in Article 9 of Additional Protocol I to the Geneva Conventions relating to the protection of victims of international armed conflicts,[53] in the International Code of Conduct for the Red Cross and Red Crescent Movement,[54] and in Article 6

49 See also F. Casolari, "The External Dimension of the EU Disaster Response", in: A. De Guttry, M. Gestri and G. Venturi, (eds.), *International Disaster Response Law*, New York: Springer, 2012, p. 152.

50 Significantly, the EU's Strategic Framework on Human Rights and Democracy specifies that the Union will, amongst other things, promote the observance of international humanitarian law in the context of its external action. Council of the EU, doc. 11855/12, 25 June 2012.

51 Memorandum by the Secretariat of the International Law Commission, "Protection of Persons in the Event of Disasters", A/CN.4/590, para. 11. See also G. Venturi, "International Disaster Response Law in Relation to Other Branches of International Law", in: A. De Guttry, M. Gestri and G. Venturi, (eds.), *International Disaster Response Law*, New York: Springer, 2012, p. 52.

52 Casolari, *op. cit.*, n. 49 p. 134.

53 Available at: <http://www.icrc.org/eng/> (accessed 1 May 2013).

54 Available at: <http://www.ifrc.org/Docs/idrl/I259EN.pdf> (accessed 1 May 2013).

of the draft Convention on Protection of Persons in the Event of Disasters currently prepared by the International Law Commission.[55]

Despite the reference to humanitarian principles in Article 214(2) TFEU, NGOs appear to be not entirely satisfied with the drafting of the new provision.[56] For instance, Article 214(5) TFEU explicitly provides for the establishment of a European Voluntary Humanitarian Aid Corps (EVHC). The NGO community fears that this may undermine the increasing professionalism in the humanitarian aid sector potentially leading to dangerous situations in conflict areas. In general, there is a feeling that this initiative may be used as a promotional tool to increase the visibility of the EU's humanitarian actions. The Commission's proposal on establishing an EVHC does not conceal the fact that raising "the levels of awareness about the Union's humanitarian aid and its visibility" is an underlying objective of this initiative.[57] Such visibility requirements may conflict with the humanitarian imperative to provide aid on a needs-based approach. Moreover, it may affect the independence from political, economic, military or other objectives.[58]

There is also a more general concern that the integration of humanitarian assistance within the framework of the EU's external action may negatively affect the independence of the EU's humanitarian action. According to Article 214(1) TFEU, EU humanitarian aid shall not only be implemented in compliance with the general principles of international (humanitarian) law, it shall also be conducted "within the framework of the principles and objectives of the external action of the Union". This reference is included as a standard clause in all Treaty provisions dealing with EU external policies[59] and reflects a general preoccupation of the Lisbon Treaty with ensuring the coherence of

---

55 Draft Article 6 of this Convention provides that "Response of disasters shall take place in accordance with the principles of humanity, neutrality and impartiality, and on the basis of non-discrimination, while taking into account the needs of the particularly vulnerable". See International Law Commission, A/CN.4/L776.

56 Available at: <http://www.ngovoice.org/documents/HA-Dev_NGO_response18Jun03.pdf> (accessed 1 May 2013).

57 Proposal for a Regulation of the European Parliament and of the Council, Establishing the European Voluntary Humanitarian Aid Corps, COM (2012) 514, Brussels, 19.9.2012, p. 2.

58 This problem of visibility is explicitly addressed in the most recent OECD-DAC Report, which recommends the EU to consider a different logo for its humanitarian aid operations than for other, less neutral, activities such as election monitoring or CSDP operations. See OECD-DAC Report, 2012, p. 98.

59 Article 207 TFEU (Common Commercial Policy); Article 208 TFEU (development cooperation); Article 212 TFEU (economic, technical and financial cooperation with third countries); Article 24 TEU (Common Foreign and Security Policy).

the Union's action on the international scene.[60] The key reference point listing the EU's general principles and objectives is Article 21 TEU.

A strict reading of Article 214(1) TFEU might suggest that humanitarian aid can be used as an instrument to achieve the entire list of objectives mentioned in Article 21 TEU including, for instance, the ambition to preserve peace, prevent conflicts and strengthen international security.[61] Obviously, such an interpretation potentially affects the independence of humanitarian operations. However, the inclusion of a horizontal list of external action objectives in Article 21 TEU does not absolve the institutions from respecting the principle of conferral as expressed in the specific legal bases mentioned in the Treaties.[62] Pursuant to Article 214(2) TFEU, the Union is only competent to pursue a humanitarian aid policy in respect of international (humanitarian) law and the principles of impartiality, neutrality and non-discrimination (cf. *supra*). The latter principles preclude that humanitarian operations are used to pursue the political, military or economic objectives of the EU's external action listed in Article 21 TEU. The first sentence of Article 214(1) TFEU cannot affect this legal obligation. Moreover, Article 40 TEU forms an additional guarantee for the independence of EU humanitarian aid in relation to potential foreign policy and military influences. According to this provision, the implementation of CFSP measures cannot affect the application of the procedures and the extent of the powers of the institutions under the EU's non-CFSP action and *vice versa*.[63] The incorporation of a specific Treaty provision on humanitarian aid therefore helps to consolidate the specific features of EU action in this field without, however, solving the often blurred boundaries with other policy areas in practice.

---

60 See Articles 23 TEU and 205 TFEU.

61 Article 21(2)(c) TEU.

62 This can be derived from Article 3(6) TEU, which states that "The Union shall pursue its objectives by appropriate means commensurate with the competences which are conferred upon it in the Treaties". See also A. Dashwood, "Conflicts of Competence in Responding to Global Emergencies", in: A. Antoniadis, R. Schütze and E. Spaventa (eds.), *The European Union and Global Emergencies. A Law and Policy Analysis*, Oxford: Hart, 2011, p. 35.

63 For comments on Article 40 TEU, see P. Van Elsuwege, "EU External Action after the Collapse of the Pillar Structure: In Search of a new Balance between Delimitation and Consistency", *CML Rev.* 47, 2010, pp. 987–1019 and I. Govaere, "Multi-faceted Single Legal Personality and a Hidden Horizontal Pillar: EU External Relations Post-Lisbon", *Cambridge Yearbook of European Legal Studies* 13, 2010–2011, pp. 87–112.

5 Humanitarian Aid as an Integral Part of the EU's External Action: The Challenge of Coherence

Rather than regarding the reference to the principles and objectives of EU external action in Article 214(1) TFEU as a potential threat to the independence of humanitarian operations, it may be considered as a general call for coherence in the EU's response to global emergencies. Even though humanitarian aid is subject to specific conditions and principles, which implies that it is distinct from other forms of aid, humanitarian assistance can only be effective when it is linked to other policies. Such an interpretation is fully in line with the European Consensus, which explicitly states that:

> EU humanitarian aid, including early recovery, should take long-term development objectives into account where possible, and is closely linked to development cooperation [...] EU humanitarian aid is delivered in situations where other instruments related to crisis management, civil protection and consular assistance may also come into play. Hence, the EU is committed to ensure coherence and complementarity in its response to crises, making the most effective use of the various instruments.[64]

With the Treaty of Lisbon, several innovations have been introduced to increase the coherence of the EU's external action. Apart from the creation of new institutional functions and structures, the inclusion of a general list of EU external action objectives in Article 21(1) TEU is of particular significance. Following the horizontal application of Article 21 TEU, the objective "to assist populations, countries and regions confronting natural or man-made disasters"—laid down in Article 21(1)(g)—does not exclusively relate to the EU's humanitarian aid policy but can, in principle, also be pursued on the basis of other EU policies.[65] In this respect, the links between humanitarian aid and crisis management (5.1.), development (5.2.) and trade (5.3.) deserve particular attention.

64 European Consensus on Humanitarian Aid, *OJ*, 2008, C 25/1, para. 22.

65 According to Article 21(3) TEU, the principles and objectives of the EU's external action, set out in paragraphs 1 and 2 of this provision, are respected and pursued in the development and implementation of the different EU external policies and the external aspects of its other policies.

5.1 *The Nexus between Humanitarian Aid and Crisis Management Operations*

The European Consensus explicitly states that "EU humanitarian aid is not a crisis management tool".[66] This also follows from the EU's humanitarian principles mentioned in Article 214(2) TFEU and the division between CFSP and non-CFSP measures under Article 40 TEU (cf. *supra*). Nevertheless, Article 43 TEU provides that the Union may use civilian and military means to pursue, amongst other things, humanitarian tasks. In other words, whereas Article 214 TFEU and the European Consensus prohibit that humanitarian operations are used for political or military objectives, the opposite is possible. Under certain circumstances, measures adopted within the context of the EU's Common Security and Defence Policy (CSDP) may be used to support humanitarian operations. This is in line with the horizontal application of Article 21(2)(g) (cf. *supra*). Nevertheless, the use of CSDP instruments in the context of humanitarian operations remains controversial. This is particularly the case for man-made disasters.

In terms of responding to natural disasters, civil protection resources can provide an essential contribution to humanitarian assistance without posing any risk to the neutrality and impartiality of the latter. With regard to man-made disasters, on the other hand, the situation is completely different. For this reason, the European Consensus provides that "in complex emergencies, recourse to civil protection assets should rather be the exception".[67] A similar reasoning applies with regard to the use of military assets in support of humanitarian actions:

> In order to avoid a blurring of lines between military operations and humanitarian aid, it is essential that military assets and capabilities are used only in very limited circumstances in support of humanitarian relief operations as a 'last resort', i.e. where there is no comparable civilian alternative and only the use of military assets that are unique in capability and availability can meet a critical humanitarian need.[68]

Respect for international humanitarian law also requires that EU military operations supporting humanitarian assistance are subject to strict conditions.[69]

66 European Consensus on Humanitarian Aid, *OJ*, 2008, C 25/1, para. 15.

67 *Ibid.*, para. 60.

68 *Ibid.*, para. 61.

69 Those conditions are laid down in the "Guidelines on the use of military and civil defense assets in disaster relief" (Oslo guidelines) and the "Guidelines on the use of military and

For instance, such operations can only be deployed upon the request of UNOCHA and if all civilian alternatives have been explored and exhausted. Crucially, any military assets used in this scenario must remain under civilian coordination and must respect the need-based and neutral nature of humanitarian aid. In other words, the humanitarian imperative has to be respected under all circumstances.

A concrete example of the interplay between CSDP activities and humanitarian assistance is the adoption by the Council, on 1 April 2011, of Decision 2011/210/CFSP on a European Union military operation in support of humanitarian assistance operations in response to the crisis situation in Libya (EUFOR Libya).[70] This decision did not imply the immediate deployment of an EU mission on the ground but only allowed for further and more detailed contingency planning by appointing an EU operation commander (Rear Admiral Claudio Gaudiosi) and EU operational headquarters located in Rome. High Representative Catherine Ashton was given the responsibility of ensuring consistency with the EU's external action as a whole, 'including the Union's humanitarian aid activities'.[71] Significantly, the actual implementation of the EUFOR mission required a prior request from UNOCHA and an additional decision of the Council. Since the approval from UNOCHA never came, EUFOR has never been operational in Libya.

The preparation of the EUFOR mission with full respect for the European Consensus and international humanitarian guidelines has been regarded as a 'good practice example that could be used to guide future European civil military co-operation'.[72] Nevertheless, the Union's response to the Libyan crisis also revealed a number of institutional tensions between the European External Action Service (EEAS) and the European Commission. Within the EEAS, the 'Crisis Response and Operational Coordination Department' was mandated to coordinate the EU's reaction to the unfolding crisis. This created certain frictions with DG ECHO of the European Commission, particularly after the Managing Director of the EEAS crisis response unit depicted a visit

---

civil defense assets to support United Nations humanitarian activities in complex emergencies" (MCDA guidelines). See European Consensus on Humanitarian Aid, *OJ*, 2008, C 25/1, para. 57.

70 Council Decision 2011/2010/CFSP of 1 April 2011 on a European Union military operation in support of humanitarian operations in response to the crisis situation in Libya, *OJ*, 2011, L 89/17.

71 Article 4 of Decision 2011/210/CFSP.

72 OECD-DAC Report 2012, p. 96.

to Benghazi and meetings with the Libyan National Transitional Council as a 'humanitarian mission'.[73]

These types of actions explain why the humanitarian community is concerned that the further development of EU crisis management capabilities may lead to the erosion of humanitarian principles.[74] In particular, there is a fear that an expanded interpretation of the coordinating role of the EEAS and the evolution towards a more comprehensive approach to crisis management[75] may lead to a politicisation of humanitarian aid delivery.[76] Concrete examples of the trend towards a more comprehensive approach are the adoption of strategic frameworks for the Horn of Africa and the Sahel region. Both strategies aim to bring together all relevant actors and instruments in order to ensure a more coherent EU external action *vis-à-vis* the respective regions. Whereas such an approach certainly has its merits, adherence to the humanitarian principles of humanity, neutrality, impartiality and independence implies that the humanitarian sector cannot have the same role as other EU capabilities.

5.2 *The Nexus between Humanitarian Aid and Development*

Humanitarian aid and development cooperation are closely intertwined. On the one hand, humanitarian interventions often address emergency situations in developing countries. On the other hand, complex emergencies have an impact upon the development process and the development policy's central objective of poverty eradication. Funds allocated to mitigating or preventing disasters relate to both humanitarian and development cooperation. In other words, there is sometimes an overlap between both policies and it is often difficult to draw an exact boundary between the *ad hoc* assistance under Article 214 TFEU and the structural assistance under Article 208 TFEU. In order to address

73 N. Helwig, P. Ivan and H. Kostanyan, "The European External Action Service in the New EU Foreign Policy Architecture: Reviewing Two Years of Practice", Brussels: Centre for European Policy Studies, 2013, p. 41, available at: <http://www.ceps.eu/ceps/dld/7711/pdf> (accessed 1 May 2013).

74 VOICE briefing paper, "EU crisis management—A Humanitarian Perspective", Brussels, January 2004.

75 The European Commission and High Representative prepared a joint communication on "The EU's comprehensive approach to external conflicts and crises", JOIN (2013) 30 final, Brussels, 11 December 2013.

76 Conference report "From comprehensive approach to comprehensive action: enhancing the effectiveness of the EU's contribution to peace and security", Wilton Park, 17–18 December 2012, available at: <https://www.wiltonpark.org.uk/wp-content/uploads/WP1202-final-report.pdf> (accessed 1 May 2013).

this reality, the European Commission has taken the lead in linking relief, rehabilitation and development (LRRD).[77]

However, the implementation of the LRRD concept has not always been easy, and synergies between DG ECHO and DG Development in the 'grey zone' of rehabilitation have sometimes been difficult to achieve.[78] This is related to different views between the development and humanitarian actors within the EU, but also to institutional and operational obstacles.[79] In 2003, an Inter-Service group on Transition, co-chaired by DG ECHO and EuropeAid, was created to ensure a more coherent approach but in practice the inter-service group has not been very functional.[80] Experience from field missions reveals that LRRD remains a challenge for the Union. An evaluation of the EU's response to the humanitarian crisis in Chad conducted by the Development Assistance Committee of the Organisation for Economic Cooperation and Development (OECD-DAC) showed that the coordination between the different instruments for funding recovery and transition faced significant bureaucratic hurdles.[81] The case also revealed the lack of flexibility of the EU's funding instruments in dealing with post-emergency situations.[82]

In its reaction to the 2010 earthquake in Haiti, the EU proved to be a quick and generous provider of emergency aid. However, it has experienced more problems in dealing with the transition towards long-term development.[83] Several studies show that there was a considerable funding gap between short-term relief and long-term development. The Haiti Task Force set up after

---

77 European Commission communication on Linking Relief, Rehabilitation and Development (LRRD), Brussels, 30.04.1996, COM (96) 153 final; European Commission communication on Linking Relief, Rehabilitation and Development—An assessment. Brussels, 23.04.2001, COM (2001) 153 final.

78 Versluys 2008b, p. 105; K. Koddenbrock and M. Büttner, "The Will to Bridge? European Commission and U.S. Approaches to Linking Relief, Rehabilitation and Development", in: *Humanitarian Assistance. Improving U.S. European Cooperation*, 2009, pp. 127–129, available at: <http://www.gppi.net/fileadmin/gppi/RTB_book_chp8.pdf>; Bretherton and Vogler, 2006, *op. cit.*, n. 10 pp. 131–132.

79 Koddenbrock and Büttner, *op. cit.*, n. 78 pp. 127–129; P. Morazán, F. Grünewald, I. Knoke and T. Schäfer, Strengthening the link between Relief, Rehabilitation and Development (LRRD) in the EU's Financing Instruments for Development and Humanitarian Aid under the MFF 2014–220, study requested by the European Parliament's Subcommittee on Security and Defence Committee on Development, August 2012, 18.

80 *Ibid.*, p. 5.

81 OECD-DAC Report 2012, p. 90.

82 Morazán *et al.*, *op. cit.*, n. 79 p. 20.

83 G. Werleigh and E. J. Brouwer, "How to help Haiti help itself", European Voice, 13 January 2011.

the earthquake to deal with ad hoc crisis management, has "created more competition and power struggles between the Commission and the European External Action Service (EEAS) and more delays than concrete results".[84]

Even the more critical voices in the European Parliament and the humanitarian aid community acknowledge that the EU has recently taken some promising initiatives in the area of LRRD, such as the piloting programmes in the Horn of Africa ('SHARE', Supporting Horn of Africa Resilience) and in the Sahel ('AGIR', Alliance Globale pour l'Initiative Résilience Sahel) and the 'Partnership for Transition' launched by the government of Côte d'Ivoire, DG ECHO and DG DEVO.[85] Nevertheless, almost 20 years after the first Commission Communication on LRRD it can only be concluded that the concept has never been put into practice beyond some pilot projects.[86] Humanitarian NGOs call for an increased political commitment to LRRD, an Action Plan with clear definitions and concrete measures for progress, and adequate funding mechanisms.[87] Both Development Commissioner Piebalgs and Humanitarian Aid Commissioner Georgieva admit that the EU's approach to LRRD could be improved in terms of concrete output on the ground, for example by making the EU's funding tools more flexible.[88]

A recent EU initiative regarding the development-humanitarian aid nexus is the Commission Communication on resilience. Resilience is defined as "the ability of an individual, a household, a community, a country or a region to withstand, to adapt, and to quickly recover from stresses and shocks".[89] As such, it requires a comprehensive approach that includes adequate risk assessment tools, a focus on prevention and preparedness, and an enhanced

84 Morazán *et al.*, 2012, *op. cit.*, n. 79 p. 18.

85 See VOICE-CONCORD position paper "Linking Relief Rehabilitation and Development: Towards a more joined up approach enhancing resilience and impact", July 2012; Morazán *et al.*, *op. cit.*, n. 79 p. 23.

86 V. Hauck, "What can bridge the divide between humanitarian aid and development?", ECDPM Talking Point, 19 September 2012, available at: <http://www.ecdpm-talkingpoints.org/what-can-bridge-the-divide-between-humanitarian-aid-and-development> (accessed 1 May 2013).

87 *Ibid.*

88 A. Piebalgs, "Haiti, one year after: Keeping our promises and accelerating our efforts", speech at the conference "Haiti, One Year after the Earthquake", Brussels, Egmont Palace, 23 February 2011; K. Georgieva, "Policy Priorities—achievements and mapping the ways ahead", speech at the Development Committee of the European Parliament, 25 May 2011.

89 Communication from the Commission to the European Parliament and the Council, "The EU Approach to Resilience: Learning from Food Security Crises", Brussels, 3.10.2012, COM (2012) 586, p. 5.

response to crises. A policy based on enhancing resilience implies that donors do not just intervene to address the consequences of emergency crises, but that they also tackle the root causes of recurrent crises.[90] Since this requires a coherent approach between humanitarian aid and development assistance, the concept of resilience has been central to debates about improving the EU's LRRD policy. Different from previous LRRD initiatives, it puts more emphasis on the role of the recipient side in EU interventions.[91] The above-mentioned SHARE and AGIR Sahel piloting programmes are considered to be best practices in the new EU approach to resilience in the area of food security.[92]

5.3 *The Nexus between Humanitarian Aid and Trade*

Already before the entry into force of the Lisbon Treaty, the EU had attempted to use trade measures in response to a humanitarian crisis.[93] In the aftermath of the 2004 Indian Ocean Tsunami, the Commission suggested bringing forward the entry into force of the new Generalised System of Preferences (GSP) to 1 April 2005 from 1 July 2005.[94] As a result of this initiative, countries that suffered from the Tsunami such as Sri Lanka, Thailand and Indonesia would benefit more quickly from more favourable import tariffs for products such as shrimps, textiles and clothing. Although all Member States appeared to be in favour of the Commission's Tsunami proposal, the Council's approval of the new GSP was eventually delayed because of disagreements about the graduation threshold for textiles from India,[95] thereby jeopardizing this potentially coherent link between humanitarian aid and trade policy.

In response to devastating floods in Pakistan, and shortly after the entry into force of the Lisbon Treaty, the September 2010 European Council called not only for the provision of traditional humanitarian aid but also for the adoption of additional measures essential for the country's recovery and growth. In this context, it was agreed "to grant exclusively to Pakistan increased market access to the EU through the immediate and time limited reduction of key imports

90 *Ibid.*, p. 2.

91 See e.g. Public Hearing in the European Parliament about LRRD, 3 September 2012.

92 COM (2012) 586, p. 7.

93 On the use of trade preferences as a humanitarian aid instrument, see also the contribution of S. Gstöhl to this volume.

94 Commission communication concerning amendment of the Commission's proposal for a Council Regulation applying a scheme of generalised tariff preferences for the period 1 July 2005 to 31 December 2008, Brussels, 10.02.2005, COM (2005) 43 final.

95 *Agence Europe* 22 January 2005, 18 March 2005, 25 March 2005, 8 April 2005.

from Pakistan".[96] As argued by Gstöhl elsewhere in this volume, the proposed emergency trade preferences for Pakistan were to a large extent motivated by the country's geostrategic importance and its unsatisfactory access to the EU market under the Generalised System of Preferences (GSP).[97] Whereas the approach of the European Council to use a trade policy instrument for the achievement of a humanitarian objective is fully in line with the rationale of Article 21 TEU and the Lisbon Treaty to increase the coherence of the EU's external action, this initiative faced significant legal and political obstacles.

After the adoption of a European Commission proposal for a regulation introducing emergency autonomous trade preferences for Pakistan,[98] several members of the European Parliament as well as import-sensitive industries from France, Italy, Portugal and Spain challenged the appropriateness of such a measure. In particular, they raised concerns about the economic implications for the EU's textiles and ethanol industries and the absence of any political conditionality in the Commission's proposal.[99] The latter point is of particular interest, taking into account the humanitarian rationale for the trade initiative. According to the humanitarian principle of independence, aid to people in need cannot be subject to any political, economic or military conditions (cf. *supra*). Adding such conditions to the granting of temporary autonomous trade preferences adopted to address an emergency situation would thus, arguably, contradict the spirit, the nature and the purpose of the proposed measure.[100]

On the other hand, the measure is adopted in the context of the EU's Common Commercial Policy (CCP) under the legal basis of Article 207(2) TFEU and not as part of the EU's humanitarian assistance under Article 214 TFEU. That being the case, the humanitarian principles laid down in Article 214(2) TFEU and reflected in the European Consensus do not automatically apply to this type of measure. Within the context of the CCP, the granting of trade preferences can be made conditional upon respect for fundamental rights.[101]

---

96 European Council Conclusions, 16 September 2010, Annex II, Declaration on Pakistan, EUCO/21/1/10 REV 1, p. 10.

97 See further, in this volume, S. Gstöhl, "No Strings Attached? The Emergency Trade Preferences for Pakistan".

98 COM (2010) 552 final, 7 October 2010.

99 Debate in the European Parliament on emergency autonomous trade preferences for Pakistan, 9 May 2011.

100 See, in this respect, the intervention of Commissioner Neelie Kroes during the Parliamentary debates, 9 May 2011.

101 However, granting trade preferences for reasons related to foreign policy may not always be compatible with international trade law, as became clear in the EC-Tariff Preferences case (WTO Appellate Body Report, WT/DS246/AB/R, 20 April 2004). See e.g. L. Bartels,

It is, therefore, not surprising that the European Parliament only accepted the proposed regulation after the inclusion of explicit conditionality provisions. For instance, Pakistan is only entitled to benefit from the preferential arrangements if it does not engage in "serious and systematic violations of human rights, including core labour rights, fundamental principles of democracy and the rule of law."[102] Other crucial European Parliament amendments concern the introduction of an economic safeguard clause[103] and the more limited duration of the preferential trade measures.[104]

Problems with the EU's initiative to support Pakistan also emerged at the level of the World Trade Organisation (WTO). Given that the unilateral introduction of trade preferences would be in breach of the Most Favoured Nation (MFN) principle (Article I(1) GATT) and of the principle of non-discriminatory administration of quantitative restrictions (Article XIII GATT), the EU had to request a waiver from the application of those provisions in accordance with Article IX of the Agreement establishing the WTO. A first attempt to obtain such a waiver, which requires consensus within the WTO Council for Trade in Goods, failed due to resistance from Pakistan's neighbours. Only the introduction of further amendments, including the increased use of tariff rate quotas instead of full liberalisation, secured the acceptance of the EU's waiver.[105]

The Pakistan case illustrates how the EU's trade policy may be used as an instrument to promote humanitarian objectives in the wake of a global emergency. It also reveals the limits and challenges of such an approach. The final EU Regulation was adopted in October 2012, i.e. more than two years after the catastrophic events, and is a watered down version of the original Commission proposal.[106] The addition of conditionality and safeguard clauses, the more

---

"The WTO Legality of the EU's GSP+ Arrangement", *Journal of International Economic Law* 10 (4), 2007, pp. 869–886; I. Govaere and A. Van Bossuyt, "Le commerce à visage de plus en plus humain? Les droits de l'homme dans la politique commerciale commune, in: M. Candela Soriano (ed.), *Les droits de l'homme dans les politiques de l'Union européenne*, Brussels: De Boeck/Larcier, 2006, pp. 225–254.

102 Article 2 of Regulation No 1029/2012 introducing emergency trade preferences for Pakistan, *OJ*, 2012, L 316/43.

103 *Ibid.*, Article 4.

104 *Ibid.* Article 11.

105 <http://www.wto.org/english/news_e/news12_e/good_02feb12_e.htm> (accessed 1 May 2013).

106 In a statement added to the adoption of the EU Regulation introducing emergency autonomous trade preferences for Pakistan, Sweden expressed its regret "that the adoption of the regulation comes late, is limited in scope, and will endure, de facto, only a short period of time". Council document 13867/12, 21 September 2012.

limited scope as well as the shorter duration of the trade preferences raise questions about the effective added value of such a measure.[107] The conclusion may thus well be that the implementation of "an package of short, medium and longer term measures" including humanitarian aid, development and trade instruments as an EU response to global emergencies remains a challenging task also after the entry into force of the Lisbon Treaty and its innovations aimed at increasing the coherence of the EU's external action. More generally, this case shows that for various reasons it is difficult for the EU to employ its trade instrument for objectives related to other external policies.[108]

6 Conclusion

What initially entered the European Community's armoury as an instrument of development co-operation with the countries of Africa, the Caribbean and the Pacific (ACP) under the 1969 Yaoundé II Convention, gradually developed into an independent external policy. The Treaty of Lisbon may be regarded as a further and logical step in this long-term process. Humanitarian aid is now formally recognised as a specific form of engagement with third countries, apart from development cooperation and economic, financial and technical cooperation.[109] With the introduction of Article 214 TFEU and the adoption of the European Consensus, the EU has put in place a solid legal and political framework for the implementation of a strong humanitarian aid policy.

The Lisbon Treaty not only raises the profile of humanitarian aid as a separate external policy of the Union, it also aims to increase the coherence of the EU's external action. The implications of the new institutional and legal provisions to combine humanitarian aid activities with other external action instruments and institutions have raised concerns within the humanitarian aid community. In principle, there are sufficient safeguards to protect the independence of the EU's humanitarian operations. Decision-making in the field of humanitarian aid is still essentially steered by DG ECHO of the Commission.

107 See also S. Khorana, M. T. Yeung, W. A. Kerr and N. Perdikis, "The Battle over the EU's Proposed Humanitarian Trade Preferences for Pakistan: A Case Study in Multifaceted Protectionism", *Journal of World Trade*, 46, 2012, pp. 33–60.

108 See F. Bossuyt, J. Orbie and L. Drieghe, "Living Apart Together: EU Comprehensive Security from a Trade Perspective", *European Foreign Affairs Review*, 2013, 18, pp. 63–82.

109 Title III of Part V of the TFEU devoted to "Cooperation with third countries and humanitarian aid".

The integration of civil protection functions into the activities of DG ECHO has improved the coherence of the EU's strategy for crisis response and relations with the EEAS do not appear to have undermined the fundamental role of humanitarian principles.[110]

Nevertheless, several challenges continue to exist. Firstly, the trend towards a more comprehensive approach to crisis management, including a more active coordinating role for the EEAS, may lead to further institutional tensions with DG ECHO of the European Commission. A clear-cut division of responsibilities as well as a sufficient awareness of the humanitarian aid specificities among all actors are crucial to ensuring effective cooperation on the ground. Secondly, there has still been little practical progress on linking emergency aid, rehabilitation and development. A recent assessment conducted by the services of the OECD revealed that "opportunities for greater programme coherency between ECHO, EuropeAid and EEAS are sometimes being missed".[111] Thirdly, the ambition of the Lisbon Treaty to facilitate the combination of different policy instruments in response to global emergencies faces political and legal obstacles. This has been clearly illustrated with the Pakistan case, where the temporary introduction of autonomous trade preferences faced strong opposition both from within the EU and at the level of the WTO. So, it appears that the EU is a key player when it comes to providing and coordinating humanitarian assistance but difficulties remain regarding the integration of humanitarian aid programmes into more comprehensive strategies of disaster response.

110 OECD-DAC Report 2012, pp. 90–95.

111 *Ibid.*, p. 95.

CHAPTER 3

No Strings Attached? The EU's Emergency Trade Preferences for Pakistan

Sieglinde Gstöhl

1 Introduction: Trade Preferences and Humanitarian Aid

The European Union (EU) has several instruments at its disposal to react to global emergency situations, ranging from the humanitarian aid regulation and the Stability Instrument to the civil protection mechanism and crisis management missions within the framework of the Common Security and Defence Policy (CSDP).[1] Trade policy is normally not among these instruments, except for food safety emergencies which might require export or import restrictions. Such trade restrictions *directly* address the causes of food safety crises, originating within or outside the EU, whereas the use of *indirect* trade measures to alleviate the consequences of a natural disaster is less straightforward, depending on the particular situation of the country affected.

On 26 December 2004 an earthquake that occurred off the northwest coast of Sumatra triggered the single worst tsunami in recorded history in the Indian Ocean. It killed over 220,000 people in fourteen countries, including around 1,400 tourists from the European Union enjoying their Christmas holidays in Southeast Asia.[2] The EU responded to this disaster with unprecedented humanitarian and reconstruction efforts. The European Community Humanitarian Office (ECHO) was the first donor to respond to the tsunami. The European Commission and the 25 Member States pledged €560 million for humanitarian assistance and €1.5 billion for longer-term reconstruction. The Commission alone committed €123 million in humanitarian aid and €350 million towards rehabilitation and reconstruction.[3] Moreover, the EU

1 See M. Cremona, "The EU and Global Emergencies: Competence and Instruments", in A. Antoniadis, R. Schütze and E. Spaventa (eds.), *The European Union and Global Emergencies: A Law and Policy Analysis*, Oxford: Hart, 2011, pp. 11–31.

2 Eurostat, "Causes of deaths in the EU", *Statistics in Focus: Population and Social Conditions*, 10/2006, pp. 7–8.

3 European Commission, "Post-Tsunami reconstruction: 2 years on", MEMO/06/507, Brussels, 20 December 2006.

© KONINKLIJKE BRILL NV, LEIDEN, 2014 | DOI 10.1163/9789004268333_005

Trade Commissioner sought to fast-track the adoption and implementation of the revised Generalised System of Preferences (GSP) since Sri Lanka, Indonesia, Thailand and India were expected to be among the greatest beneficiaries.[4] In addition, a suspension of anti-dumping duties and the reorientation of trade-related technical assistance in areas such as sanitation and food safety standards were considered. However, more extensive tariff concessions for individual countries were not suggested because they would have contravened the rules of the World Trade Organisation (WTO), in particular the principle of non-discrimination.[5]

When cyclone Nargis hit Myanmar in May 2008, killing an estimated 140,000 people, the EU also provided substantial humanitarian assistance.[6] It did not, however, reinstate the country's suspended trade preferences. While trade between the EU and Myanmar has never been fully banned, it was the first country that faced a withdrawal from the list of GSP countries in 1997, as a reaction to the practice of forced labour, as confirmed by the International Labour Organisation (ILO).[7] The sanctions that the EU had gradually imposed on Myanmar since 1991 ranged from a visa ban and asset freeze for the leadership to an arms embargo, the partial suspension of non-humanitarian aid as well as a ban on investment and on the export of equipment for the timber and gems industries. It was only in the light of the domestic political reforms that the Burmese government began in 2011 that the EU suspended its sanctions under the Common Foreign and Security Policy (CFSP) in April 2012.[8] The resumption of trade privileges, however, is less straightforward as the GSP is, following the entry into force of the Lisbon Treaty, subject to the ordinary legislative procedure. The European Commission proposed in September 2012 to bring Myanmar, which is classified as a least developed country (LDC), into the 'Everything But Arms' (EBA) preferential trade regime. The European Parliament endorsed this proposal in May 2013, after which formal approval by the Council is required.

---

4 European Commission, "EU Trade Commissioner seeks trade measures to relieve tsunami victims", press release, IP/05/25, Brussels, 11 January 2005.

5 *Ibid.*

6 European Commission, "Commission welcomes launch of Post-cyclone Nargis recovery and preparedness plan for Myanmar/Burma", press release, IP/09/231, Brussels, 9 February 2009.

7 See "Council Regulation (EC) No 552/97 of 24 March 1997 temporarily withdrawing access to generalized tariff preferences from the Union of Myanmar", *OJ*, 1997, L85, pp. 8–9.

8 M. Bünte and C. Portela, "Myanmar: The Beginning of Reforms and the End of Sanctions", *GIGA Focus International Edition* 3, Hamburg: GIGA, 2012.

After a devastating earthquake struck Haiti in January 2010, taking more than 220,000 lives, the European Commission did not consider special trade measures.[9] Unlike Myanmar, this LDC benefitted from the EBA and thus from duty-free and quota-free access to the EU market.

When heavy monsoon rains led to severe floods that massively devastated Pakistan in July and August 2010, causing almost 2,000 deaths and requiring urgent humanitarian assistance for more than 12 million people,[10] the EU adopted emergency trade preferences as an additional measure to help the country. This was the first time that the EU granted a country autonomous trade preferences with a humanitarian justification. The question then arises as to why the EU granted Pakistan emergency trade preferences, whereas it did not offer comparable trade measures to countries in similar situations? What lessons can be drawn?

It has to be kept in mind that the Common Commercial Policy and humanitarian aid are of a different nature, with distinct goals and instruments. Trade is an exclusive EU competence, whereas humanitarian assistance is a shared parallel competence. Humanitarian aid provided by the EU and the Member States is to be complementary. According to the first European Consensus on Humanitarian Aid of December 2007, "[t]he objective of EU humanitarian aid is to provide a needs-based emergency response aimed at preserving life, preventing and alleviating human suffering and maintaining human dignity wherever the need arises if governments and local actors are overwhelmed, unable or unwilling to act".[11] The non-political character of humanitarian assistance stands in contrast to EU development policy, trade policy or foreign policy in general, which have since the end of the Cold War increasingly become linked to political conditionality, in particular concerning the recipient country's

9 European Commission, "Factsheet Haiti earthquake", MEMO/10/81, Brussels, 15 March 2010, available at: <http://europa.eu/rapid/press-release_MEMO-10-94_en.htm> (accessed April 2013). Haiti had signed the EU-CARIFORUM Economic Partnership Agreement in December 2009 which aims to establish a comprehensive, and eventually fully reciprocal, free trade agreement between the EU and the Caribbean ACP countries as well as supporting development assistance programmes. Ratification is still pending.

10 European Commission, "Humanitarian Aid: remembering the 2010 floods in Pakistan, helping recovery", press release, IP/11/941, 1 August 2011.

11 "European Consensus on Humanitarian Aid", Joint Statement by the Council and the Representatives of the Governments of the Member States meeting within the Council, the European Parliament and the European Commission, *OJ*, 2008, C25, para. 8.

respect for human rights, labour rights and democratic principles.[12] The lack of conditionality should facilitate access to crisis victims and enhance the security of humanitarian aid workers, "based on the understanding that assistance comes with no strings attached".[13] Versluys finds that although in the 1990s the EU sometimes used humanitarian aid "as a substitute for political engagement or a gap-filler for development cooperation", such instances of 'securitisation' and 'developmentalisation' have in the past decade been replaced by a more consistent commitment to provide non-political, needs-based assistance.[14]

In terms of Article 214 TFEU, the Treaty of Lisbon introduces an explicit legal basis for humanitarian aid, which had previously been operated under development cooperation powers.[15] Although this assistance is to be conducted within the framework of the objectives of EU external action, listed in particular in Article 21 TEU, it is to be guided by the principles of impartiality, neutrality and non-discrimination. Humanitarian operations should therefore not be subject to political conditionality but should be pursued independently of political, military or economic objectives.[16] Additionally, the European Consensus on Humanitarian Aid emphasises "that the provision of aid should not be influenced by specific interests be they economic, political, cultural or religious".[17] On the other hand, however, the EU may, under the CSDP, use civilian and military means to pursue humanitarian tasks (Article 43 TEU).

The Common Commercial Policy is generally aimed at a liberalisation of international trade and investment. Article 206 TFEU stipulates that "the Union shall contribute, in the common interest, to the harmonious development of world trade, the progressive abolition of restrictions on international trade and on foreign direct investment, and the lowering of customs and other barriers". The Treaty of Lisbon also places the Common Commercial Policy (Article 207(1) TFEU) under that part of the Union's external action to which the general provisions of Article 21(2) TEU apply. Therefore, EU trade

12 See, for instance, S. Gstöhl, "The Common Commercial Policy and Political Conditionality: 'Normative Power Europe' through Trade?", *Studia Diplomatica* LXIII (3–4), 2010, pp. 23–41.

13 H. Versluys, "European Union Humanitarian Aid: Lifesaver or Political Tool?", in J. Orbie (ed.), *Europe's Global Role: External Policies of the European Union*, Aldershot: Ashgate, 2008, p. 100.

14 *Ibid.*, p. 112.

15 See chapter by P. Van Elsuwege and J. Orbie in this volume.

16 *Ibid.*

17 "European Consensus on Humanitarian Aid", *op. cit.*, n. 11 p. 12 (Annex "Principles, standards and evaluation criteria for humanitarian aid").

policy is also to be guided by much broader goals. This 'quasi-constitutional' framework for EU external action creates the legal foundation for coordinating trade policy with other external policies and for pursuing non-trade objectives through trade.[18] Although trade policy was never really 'apolitical', this arrangement bestows greater weight on the non-trade objectives. The Treaty of Lisbon acknowledges that the pursuit of diverse goals may lead to tensions by explicitly enshrining the aim of ensuring consistency between all areas of EU external policies and between these and its other policies in several articles, including in Article 21(3) TEU itself.

It is argued in this contribution that the EU granted Pakistan emergency trade preferences because of the country's geostrategic importance and because of the setback that Pakistan faced in accessing the EU market. In 2005 Pakistan had lost its additional preferences under the GSP 'drugs arrangement' as a result of a WTO ruling and it did not qualify for the 'GSP+' scheme that replaced the former. The emergency trade preferences also pre-empted the revised 'GSP+' entering into force in 2014 for which Pakistan is again eligible. Regarding the effectiveness of these emergency trade preferences, the economic impact still has to be assessed once the analyses become available.[19] However, in view of the Commission's initial intentions, it can be argued that they provided too little too late. Vested domestic interests in some EU Member States and WTO countries significantly reduced and delayed the potential value of the trade preferences. Moreover, in terms of trade policy, the Lisbon Treaty empowered the European Parliament, a traditional advocate of political values, which, with its new responsibility, also became a more prominent lobbying target for organised economic interests. As a result, although there should *a priori* be 'no strings attached' to humanitarian trade preferences, the case of Pakistan shows that aiming at consistency in this regard comes close to squaring the circle. While emergency aid should be unconditional, trade preferences are fraught with political and economic interests.

This contribution first introduces the GSP as the EU's standard tool for granting autonomous trade preferences, which serves as a background for the

---

18 A. Dimopoulos, "The Effects of the Lisbon Treaty on the Principles and Objectives of the Common Commercial Policy", *European Foreign Affairs Review* 15 (2), 2010, p. 161.

19 The Commission shall be submitting a report to the European Parliament and to the Council on the effects of the emergency trade preferences no later than December 2015. See Regulation (EU) No 1029/2012 of the European Parliament and of the Council of 25 October 2012 introducing emergency autonomous trade preferences for Pakistan, *OJ*, 2012, L 316, Article 10.

case study. In the second part, it turns to the case of Pakistan's emergency trade preferences, and finally, the chapter draws some conclusions.

2 The EU's Generalised System of Preferences (GSP)

As a customs union, the EU applies its Common Customs Tariff to products imported from third countries, irrespective of the Member State of destination. There are, however, many derogations from the common external tariff rates negotiated in the WTO and from its principle of most-favoured-nation (MFN) treatment, either through preferential trade agreements or through autonomous non-reciprocal trade preferences for certain countries.[20] The primary objective of the GSP is to contribute to the reduction of poverty and the promotion of sustainable development in the beneficiary countries.

2.1 *The Creation of the GSP*

The GSP goes back to a recommendation by the second United Nations Conference on Trade and Development (UNCTAD) in 1968, calling on the industrialised countries to grant non-reciprocal trade preferences to all developing countries, including special measures for the least developed countries.[21] The underlying expectation was that a generalised non-reciprocal, non-discriminatory system of preferences in favour of developing countries would increase their export earnings and promote their industrialisation.[22] This also explains the focus on preferences for manufactures and semi-manufactures instead of primary products. In 1971 the Contracting Parties to the General Agreement on Tariffs and Trade (GATT) agreed a general waiver of the MFN principle to allow for discriminatory treatment between developed and

20 The MFN principle (Article I(1) GATT) states that any favourable treatment (e.g. a tariff concession) granted by a Contracting Party to any product originating in or destined for any other country shall be extended immediately and unconditionally to the like product originating in or destined for the territories of all other contracting parties.

21 UNCTAD, Resolution 21(II) "Preferential or free entry of exports of manufactures and semi-manufactures of developing countries to the developed countries, 77th plenary meeting, 26 March 1968", in UN, *Proceedings of the United Nations Conference on Trade and Development, Second Session, New Delhi, 1 February–29 March 1968, Volume I: Report and Annexes*, TD/97, New York, p. 38.

22 On the development of the GSP see N. Breda dos Santos, R. Farias and R. Cunha, "Generalized System of Preferences in General Agreement on Tariffs and Trade/World Trade Organization: History and Current Issues", *Journal of World Trade*, 39 (4), 2005, pp. 639–656.

developing countries for ten years.[23] While countries could designate themselves as 'developing countries' and thus potential beneficiaries, the developed countries had reserved the right to exclude countries from their tariff concessions. Besides the principle of self-election, membership of the UN 'Group of 77', which today has more than 130 members,[24] has been a main criterion for the EU to classify developing countries. The UN only provides a definition of least developed countries based on per capita gross national income, human assets and economic vulnerability to external shocks.[25]

Against the background of the oil crises, the breakdown of the fixed exchange-rate regime and the rise of non-tariff barriers to trade, the GATT waiver was, in 1979, perpetuated by the so-called 'Enabling Clause' negotiated in the Tokyo Round.[26] The Enabling Clause allows derogations from MFN treatment in favour of developing countries, both for preferential tariff treatment accorded by developed Contracting Parties to products originating in developing countries, including special treatment for LDCs, and for preferential arrangements among developing countries themselves. It also permits graduation mechanisms which phase out non-reciprocal preferential market access to developing countries which have attained a sufficient degree of progress.

The European Community (EC) was the first actor to create a GSP of non-reciprocal discriminatory treatment in 1971.[27] Several phases can be distinguished in the development of the EU's GSP (see Table 1 in the annex). The *first phase* of the Community's GSP ran from 1971 to 1980 and was then renewed for another ten years until 1990. Within the framework of the ten-year cycles, the GSP was implemented through different regulations and decisions (for example for industrialised products, textiles, agricultural products and those covered by the European Coal and Steel Community), adopted on a yearly basis. It distinguished several degrees of product sensitivity, depending on the extent

---

23 GATT, "Waiver Decision on the Generalized System of Preferences", GATT doc. L/3545, 25 June 1971, BISD 18S/24.

24 See <http://www.g77.org> (accessed April 2013).

25 See <http://www.unohrlls.org> (accessed April 2013).

26 GATT, "Decision on Differential and More Favourable Treatment, Reciprocity, and Fuller Participation of Developing Countries", GATT doc. L/4903, 28 November 1979, BISD 26S/203.

27 On the origins of the EU's GSP see P. Tullock, *The Politics of Preferences: EEC Policy Making and the Generalised System of Preferences*, London: Overseas Development Institute, 1975, pp. 37–64. However, the Community continued to require reciprocal preferences from the African countries associated with it under the Yaoundé Convention. Only the Lomé Convention of 1975 with the ACP countries introduced non-reciprocity into the relationship.

to which imported goods competed with domestic goods. The Commission's initial list of products to be covered was heavily cut back by the Council, virtually eliminating any processed agricultural goods about which any Member State (and particularly France and Italy) felt sensitive.[28] The Community imposed tariff quotas and ceilings, and within these maximum limits there were restrictions at national level on either the importing Member State or the exporting developing country in order to 'spread' the burden or benefit, respectively. Generally, 'non-sensitive' goods were afforded duty-free access within the fixed quantities, while 'sensitive' goods were only granted a reduction on the MFN tariff. During this phase, the EC GSP was reviewed each year, leading to changes in product coverage, quotas, ceilings and beneficiaries as well as the depth of tariff cuts for agricultural products.

Although the GSP was initially thought to be only a temporary measure, the EC has since then regularly renewed the system, thereby broadening its product and country coverage and increasing the level of differentiation as well as the degree of political conditionality. Besides the EU, a dozen of countries presently have GSP schemes in place.[29] The reform due for 1991 was postponed in order to await the results of the Uruguay Round which ended in 1994 and led to the creation of the WTO. Yet, as a first differentiation, a special arrangement was established in 1991 for the Andean countries (Bolivia, Colombia, Ecuador and Peru), which received exemptions from quotas and ceilings as well as duty-free access for certain industrial and agricultural products in order to combat the production and trafficking of cocaine.[30] It was subsequently extended to some other Latin American countries.

2.2 *The Increasing Differentiation of the EU's GSP*

The *second phase* began with a new system that entered into force in 1995 for the next decade. Two regulations—one for industrial goods and one for agricultural goods—set out the new GSP with a review period of up to four years.[31]

28 *Ibid.*, p. 61.

29 Australia, Belarus, Bulgaria, Canada, Estonia, Japan, New Zealand, Norway, the Russian Federation, Switzerland, Turkey and the USA. See <http://unctad.org/en/Pages/DITC/GSP/About-GSP.aspx> (accessed April 2013).

30 Council Regulation (EEC) No 3835/90 of 20 December 1990 amending Regulations (EEC) No 3831/90, (EEC) No 3832/90 and (EEC) No 3833/90 in respect of the system of generalized tariff preferences applied to certain products originating in Bolivia, Colombia, Ecuador and Peru, *OJ*, 1990, L 370/126–132.

31 Council Regulation (EC) No 3281/94 of 19 December 1994 applying a four-year scheme of generalized tariff preferences (1995–1998) in respect of certain industrial products originating in developing countries, *OJ*, 1994, L 348/1–56; Council Regulation (EC)

The main innovations were the replacement of tariff quotas and ceilings with a tariff modulation, the introduction of a system of graduation and the creation of 'special incentive arrangements' alongside the general arrangement. The system of graduation by country and sector combined criteria of a development and a specialisation index and aimed "to transfer preferential margins gradually from advanced to less-developed countries".[32] Preferential tariffs were either suspended or re-established when a country's performance on the EU market exceeded or fell below a set threshold. This graduation system did not apply to the LDCs.

The special incentive arrangements were an attempt to induce developing countries to pursue particular political goals in order to obtain additional trade preferences as a reward. The policy thus entailed positive conditionality. The GSP also made use of negative conditionality by allowing the temporary withdrawal of trade preferences in certain cases such as any form of forced labour (in 2002 extended to the core labour standards),[33] export of goods made by way of prison labour, or insufficient controls on the drugs trade or money laundering (since 1999 also in manifest cases of infringement of the objectives of international conventions concerning the conservation and management of fishery resources).[34] In addition, countries could, in case of non-compliance, lose the additional preferences provided by the special incentive arrangements. Following a Commission investigation into forced labour in Myanmar, the Council suspended the country's GSP benefits in 1997; Belarus had its trade

No 3282/94 of 19 December 1994 extending into 1995 the application of Regulations (EEC) No 3833/90, (EEC) No 3835/90 and (EEC) No 3900/91 applying generalized tariff preferences in respect of certain agricultural products originating in developing countries, *OJ*, 1994, L 348/57–68; and Council Regulation (EC) No 1256/96 of 20 June 1996 applying multiannual schemes of generalized tariff preferences from 1 July 1996 to 30 June 1999 in respect of certain agricultural products originating in developing countries, *OJ*, 1996, L 160/1–64.

32 Council Regulation (EC) No 3281/94, *op. cit.*, n. 31 p. 2.

33 Following the 1995 World Summit for Social Development in Copenhagen and the commitment by the 1996 Singapore WTO Ministerial Conference to the "observance of internationally recognized core labour standards", the ILO Declaration on Fundamental Principles and Rights at Work was adopted in 1998. WTO, Singapore Ministerial Declaration, adopted on 13 December 1996, T/MIN(96)/DEC, 18 December 1996, para. 4.

34 See Council Regulation (EC) No 2820/98 of 21 December 1998 applying a multiannual scheme of generalized tariff preferences for the period 1 July 1999 to 31 December 2001, *OJ*, 1998, L 357, Articles 20 and 22; and Council Regulation (EC) No 2501/2001 of 10 December 2001 applying a scheme of generalised tariff preferences for the period from 1 January 2002 to 31 December 2004, *OJ*, 2001, L 346, Articles 14 and 26.

preferences withdrawn in 2007 due to a failure to respect its ILO obligations relating to freedom of association for workers.[35]

Five arrangements were therefore available for beneficiary countries under the GSP in the second phase: the general arrangement, the special incentive arrangement for the protection of labour rights, the special incentive arrangement for the protection of the environment, the special arrangement for the least developed countries, and the special arrangement for combating drug production and trafficking. These special schemes were the predecessors of what in 2006 became the 'GSP+' (see below). The 'labour arrangement' encouraged beneficiary countries to introduce effective policies for the protection of workers' rights, more precisely according to the ILO Conventions concerning the freedom of association, the right to bargain collectively, and the minimum age for employment. The 'environmental arrangement' rewarded the sustainable management of tropical forests in conformity with the International Tropical Timber Organisation (ITTO), at the time the only internationally recognised set of environmental standards. More favourable treatment also continued to be granted to countries undertaking effective programmes to combat drug production and trafficking. Whereas the EU decided whom to grant additional preferences to under the 'drugs regime', interested countries had to apply for the two special incentive arrangements related to the protection of labour rights (from which only Moldova and Sri Lanka benefited) and of the environment (which no country requested).[36]

The special arrangement for LDCs ensured that for them, tariffs were suspended on all products covered by the GSP. Unlike the other arrangements, the EBA is not subject to periodic renewal, and the graduation mechanism does not apply. A country is withdrawn from the list of beneficiaries if the UN removes it from its list of LDCs. WTO members, including the EU, pledged at the Singapore Ministerial Conference in 1996 to improve access to their markets for LDCs.[37] In 1998, the EU granted the LDCs not party to the Lomé

35 Council Regulation (EC) No 552/97, *op. cit.*, n. 7; and Council Regulation (EC) No 1933/2006 of 21 December 2006 temporarily withdrawing access to the generalized tariff preferences from the Republic of Belarus, *OJ*, 2006, L 405/35–40.

36 See J. Orbie and L. Tortell, "The New GSP Beneficiaries: Ticking the Box or Truly Consistent with ILO Findings", *European Foreign Affairs Review* 14 (5), 2009, pp. 669–670. In addition, Ukraine, Uzbekistan, Georgia, Mongolia and Russia (which withdrew later on) had applied for the EU's special labour arrangement, but pending the GSP reform no decision was taken.

37 WTO, Singapore Ministerial Declaration, *op. cit.*, n. 33 para. 14.

Convention, preferences equivalent to those enjoyed by the ACP countries.[38] In 2001, in view of the launch of the Doha Round negotiations, the EU adopted the 'Everything-but Arms' initiative for least developed countries. This grants the least developed countries duty-free and quota-free market access for all products, except for arms and ammunitions (and with transitional periods for sugar, rice and bananas).[39] Orbie argues that the WTO agenda was complementary to the EU's efforts to reform its relationship with the ACP countries: on the one hand, the EBA initiative helped gain the developing countries' support for a new trade round, while on the other hand, it helped differentiate the ACP group and discourage more interventionist trade regimes.[40] The Cotonou Agreement was negotiated between 1998 and 2000. Its section on trade foresees a gradual shift from non-reciprocal trade to asymmetrical, reciprocal free trade agreements (FTAs) between the EU and regional groups of ACP countries. These Economic Partnership Agreements (EPAs) are thus WTO compatible and cover trade in goods, services, investment and trade-related areas such as intellectual property rights, public procurement, competition law, trade facilitation or sustainable development.

Besides the increasing differentiation of the EU's GSP according to non-trade concerns, this phase was also impacted upon by a WTO dispute settlement. The terrorist attacks of September 2001 in the United States and the subsequent US-led invasion of Afghanistan—an important opium producer—to overthrow the Taliban, an Islamic fundamentalist regime which hosted the Al-Qaeda leadership, turned the neighbouring country of Pakistan into a frontline state in the war against drug trafficking and production as well as counter-terrorism. In this post-9/11 context, the European Commission proposed in November 2001 to add Pakistan to the list of beneficiaries of the 'drugs arrangement'. The rationale was to support Pakistan's campaign against illicit drugs and to help stabilise the country's economic and social structures.[41]

38 Council Regulation (EC) No 602/98 of 9 March 1998 extending the coverage of Regulations (EC) No 3281/94 and No 1256/96 concerning Community schemes of generalised tariff preferences for the benefit of the least-developed countries, *OJ*, 1998, L 80/1–2.

39 Council Regulation (EC) No 416/2001 of 28 February 2001 amending Regulation (EC) No 2820/98 applying a multiannual scheme of generalised tariff preferences for the period 1 July 1999 to 31 December 2001 so as to extend duty-free access without any quantitative restrictions to products originating in the least developed countries, *OJ*, 2001, L 60/43–50.

40 J. Orbie, "The Development of EBA", in G. Faber and J. Orbie (eds.), *European Union Trade Politics and Development: 'Everything but Arms' Unravelled*, London: Routledge, 2007, pp. 20–42.

41 European Commission, "Explanatory Memorandum concerning amendment of the Commission's proposal for a Council Regulation applying a scheme of generalised tariff

As a result of Pakistan's participation in the 'GSP drugs', its exports of textiles and clothing to the EU increased by 23% in 2003 and 18% in 2004.[42]

The addition of Pakistan to the EU's GSP 'drugs regime' prompted the Indian government to contest its WTO compatibility. India considered that the tariff preferences under the EU's special arrangements would have to be granted on a generalised, non-reciprocal and non-discriminatory basis in order not to treat developing countries differently. In December 2003, the Panel found that the 'GSP drugs' was indeed inconsistent with Article I(1) GATT (MFN principle) and not justified under the Enabling Clause.[43] The EC appealed and in April 2004 the Appellate Body partly modified the Panel's findings, yet with the same outcome. It found that preference-granting countries are required, by virtue of the term 'non-discriminatory', to ensure that identical treatment is available to all similarly-situated GSP beneficiaries, that is, to all GSP beneficiaries that have the same "development, financial and trade needs" to which the treatment in question is intended to respond.[44] This need must meet an objective standard, for instance broad-based recognition as set out in the WTO Agreement or in multilateral instruments adopted by international organisations. The identified need should be such that it can be effectively addressed through tariff preferences. Finally, a sufficient nexus should exist between the preferential treatment provided and the likelihood of alleviating the relevant 'development, financial or trade need'. The 'GSP drugs' was discriminatory because it operated through a 'closed list' that precluded an assessment of potential beneficiaries and the same treatment of countries in the same situation.[45]

Due to this dispute, the enduring Doha Round negotiations and the EU's 2004 enlargement, the new ten-year cycle was postponed for one year.

---

preferences for the period 1 January 2002 to 31 December 2004, in order to include Pakistan in the list of beneficiary countries of the special arrangements to combat drug production and trafficking", COM(2001) 688 final, 2001/0131(ACC), Brussels, 14.11.2001, p. 2.

42 M. Gulati, "Unblocking of NATO Supply Routes by Pakistan: Logistics or Plain Politics?", *Occasional Paper*, New Delhi, Vivekananda International Foundation, December 2012, p. 17.

43 WTO, *European Communities—Conditions for the Granting of Tariff Preferences to Developing Countries, Report of the Panel*, WT/DS246/R, Geneva, 1 December 2003.

44 WTO, *European Communities—Conditions for the Granting of Tariff Preferences to Developing Countries, AB-2004-1, Report of the Appellate Body Report*, WT/DS246/AB/R, Geneva, 7 April 2004, para. 165.

45 See L. Bartels, "The Appellate Body Report in *European Communities-Conditions for the Granting of Tariff Preferences to Developing Countries* and its Implications for Conditionality in GSP Programmes", in T. Cottier, J. Pauwelyn and E. Bürgi Bonanomi (eds.), *Human Rights and International Trade*, Oxford: Oxford University Press, 2005, pp. 463–487.

2.3 *The Growing Political Conditionality of the EU's GSP*

The *third phase* began with a new GSP in 2006 and lasted until 2013.[46] In response to the WTO ruling, the EU replaced the labour, environmental and drugs arrangements with an integrated special incentive arrangement for sustainable development and good governance ('GSP+').[47] The new system was thus composed of just three arrangements. Firstly, the general arrangement granted duty-free access for non-sensitive products or tariff reductions for sensitive products (mainly agriculture and textiles) to all 176 beneficiary countries and territories (Myanmar and Belarus being suspended). Secondly, the 'GSP+' provided duty-free access to all the products covered by the GSP's general arrangement (plus a few more), without differentiation in terms of their sensitivity. Thirdly, the EBA continued offering duty-free and quota-free access to the products from LDCs.

Another new feature was that beneficiaries were expected to abide by 16 UN/ILO conventions. In case of serious and systematic violations of the principles laid down in these international conventions, any arrangement could temporarily be withdrawn. In addition to this 'negative conditionality', allowing for preferences to be suspended if a beneficiary country no longer adheres to certain values, the GSP+ also relies on 'positive conditionality', offering better market access if certain values are accepted. Countries wishing to benefit from the extended preferences of 'GSP+' had to apply, qualify as 'vulnerable' economies and commit to ratifying and implementing a list of 11 additional international conventions in the fields of human rights, labour standards, sustainable development and good governance. A 'vulnerable' country was defined in terms of three cumulative conditions: it is not classified by the World Bank as a high-income country, its exports are poorly diversified (i.e. its five largest sections represent more than 75% of its GSP-covered exports to the EU), and its EU share of GSP-covered imports is lower than 1%.[48] So the 'GSP+' beneficiaries faced more political conditionality and risked losing the additional preferences if their national legislation no longer incorporated or effectively implemented the international conventions. The 15 beneficiary countries that had qualified for the first round of 'GSP+' in 2005 were Bolivia, Colombia, Costa Rica, Ecuador, El Salvador, Georgia, Guatemala, Honduras, Moldova, Mongolia, Nicaragua, Panama, Peru, Sri Lanka and Venezuela. So all

---

46 The 'GSP+' already entered into force in July 2005 to conform with the WTO ruling.

47 Council Regulation (EC) No 980/2005 of 27 June 2005 applying a scheme of generalised tariff preferences, *OJ*, 2005, L 169/1–43.

48 *Ibid.*, Article 9.

countries that had already participated in the earlier 'GSP drugs' and the special labour arrangement were admitted to the 'GSP+'[49]—except for Pakistan.

In sum, countries could cease to benefit partially or totally from the EU's GSP for various reasons: because they were classified as diversified high-income countries, because they graduated, because of the application of political conditionality (withdrawal clause) or of a safeguard clause, or because they obtained at least equivalent treatment under a preferential trade agreement concluded with the EU.

The role of political conditionality in the GSP has, since the mid-1990s, developed from a few labour standards to the core human and labour rights as well as good governance and environmental issues in the 'GSP+'. The EU's application, however, has not been very consistent. "The fact that an important number of countries with similar workers' rights records as Belarus, such as Uzbekistan or Turkmenistan, continue to have access to the EU's GSP indicates some arbitrariness in its implementation."[50] The same can be said with regard to the 'GSP+' because candidates such as Colombia or Guatemala have been granted such preferences despite being seriously criticised by the ILO.[51] The European Commission conducted investigations into El Salvador's effective implementation of labour standards in 2009 and for Bolivia in 2012 and found no justification for a temporary withdrawal from the 'GSP+'. Only Sri Lanka was suspended in 2010 due to significant shortcomings in respect of its human rights record. It thus fell back on regular GSP treatment.

In view of the failings of the WTO Doha Round, the EU partly reconsidered its approach to concluding trade agreements, which in the past had often followed political rather than commercial purposes. With its 2006 'Global Europe' trade strategy, embedded in the Lisbon Strategy for Growth and Jobs, the Commission aimed at reinforcing the EU's competitiveness by opening up more, and in particular emerging markets, by means of FTAs: the key economic criteria for new partners were now market potential, the level of protection against EU export interests and the partner's negotiations with EU competitors.[52] The EU's active pursuit of new bilateral trade agreements,

---

49 Moldova was removed in 2008 because the EU granted it more far-reaching autonomous preferences under a separate legal instrument in the context of the European Neighbourhood Policy. Armenia, Azerbaijan and Paraguay were added in 2009 and Cape Verde in 2011 (after it had lost its UN LDC status). Sri Lanka was suspended in 2010 due to significant shortcomings in respect of its implementation of UN human rights conventions.

50 J. Vandenberghe, "On Carrots and Sticks: The Social Dimension of EU Trade Policy", *European Foreign Affairs Review*, 13 (4), 2008, p. 572.

51 Orbie and Tortell, *op. cit.*, n. 36 pp. 663–681.

52 See European Commission, Communication from the Commission to the Council, the European Parliament, the European Social and Economic Committee and the Committee

together with the expansion of the unilateral GSP over time and multilateral tariff reductions in the GATT/WTO rounds, reinforced the preference erosion, especially for least developed countries.

In late 2009, the Lisbon Treaty entered into force and introduced the ordinary legislative procedure for the Common Commercial Policy. Although the ten-year cycle 2006–2015 was not yet over, the need for reform in terms of both contents and institutional procedure accelerated the entry into force of a new system.

2.4 *The Refocused GSP as of 2014*

The revised GSP will enter its *fourth phase* in 2014, starting another ten-year cycle. For the first time the European Parliament participated in the drafting of the regulation within the framework of the ordinary legislative procedure as a result of the Lisbon Treaty. Moreover, the Treaty enables the Commission to adopt delegated acts, a new category of legal act by which the legislator delegates the power to amend non-essential elements of a legislative act, while it retains a veto (Article 290 TFEU). The main changes in the GSP regulation concern the coverage of countries, the criteria for graduation and vulnerability and political conditionality.[53]

First of all, the new GSP focuses on the countries 'most in need', although the product coverage remains the same. The three arrangements (GSP, 'GSP+' and EBA) continue to exist, but the general GSP will have fewer beneficiaries and the 'GSP+' more than in the past. Countries which the World Bank classifies as either high-income or—new—upper-middle income countries are no longer eligible. The graduation mechanism has been relaxed by increasing the threshold, redefining the product sections and by abolishing the graduation mechanism for the 'GSP+'. The regulation lists 89 countries to benefit from the general GSP as of 2014.[54]

---

of the Regions, *Global Europe: Competing in the World: A Contribution to the EU's Growth and Jobs Strategy*, COM(2006) 567 final, Brussels, 4 October 2006, p. 9. This trade strategy was in the context of the 'Europe 2020 strategy' updated: European Commission, Communication from the Commission to the Council, the European Parliament, the European Social and Economic Committee and the Committee of the Regions, *Trade, Growth and World Affairs: Trade Policy as a Core Component of the EU's 2020 Strategy*, COM(2010) 612 final, Brussels, 9.11.2010.

53 Regulation (EU) No 978/2012 of the European Parliament and of the Council of 25 October 2012 applying a scheme of generalised tariff preferences and repealing Council Regulation (EC) No 732/2008, *OJ*, 2012, L 303/1–82.

54 *Ibid.*, Annex II, but Azerbaijan and Iran have in the meantime been removed. See Commission Delegated Regulation (EU) No 154/2013 of 18 December 2012 amending Annex II to Regulation (EU) No 978/2012 of the European Parliament and of the Council of 25 October 2012 applying a scheme of generalised tariff preferences, *OJ*, 2013, L 48/1–4.

In order to further strengthen the conditionality within the 'GSP+', the 'burden of proof' for compliance is on the beneficiary and no longer on the EU side. The vulnerability criteria have been loosened by increasing the maximum threshold of GSP-covered imports into the EU in terms of value of the total imports to 2% (instead of 1%) and by increasing the number of a country's largest sections of its imports into the Union to seven (instead of five). Instead of fixed deadlines, applications for the 'GSP+' can be launched at any point in time. There are now 15 international conventions relevant to all GSP schemes and 12 additional international conventions for the 'GSP+'.[55] Effective implementation of the ratified conventions requires that the relevant monitoring bodies do not identify a serious failure. Finally, the review of the GSP every three years has been dropped, but the Commission shall report to the European Parliament and to the Council on the need to review the scheme five years after its entry into force.

Pakistan will continue to be included in the general GSP, and thanks to the vulnerability criteria it is also eligible to apply for the new 'GSP+'. In fact, its share of total GSP imports into the EU, which is now required to be lower than 2%, is, at 1.6%, the highest of all eligible 'GSP+' beneficiaries.[56] The Commission identified 35 countries to be considered for the new 'GSP+'.

Table 1 summarizes the development of the EU's Generalised System of Preferences in the four phases and locates Pakistan's place in it (see annex to this contribution).

3 The EU's Emergency Trade Preferences for Pakistan

The EU's emergency trade preferences for Pakistan were to a large extent motivated by the country's geostrategic importance and its unsatisfactory access to the EU market resulting from the GSP's development outlined above.

---

55 The UN Framework Convention on Climate Change has been added (the Kyoto Protocol was already included), while the International Convention on the Suppression and Punishment of the Crime of Apartheid has been removed.

56 European Commission, "Information Notice for countries which may request to be granted the special incentive arrangement for sustainable development and good governance under Regulation (EU) No 978/2012 of 31 October 2012", available at: <http://trade.ec.europa.eu/doclib/docs/2012/november/tradoc_150043.pdf> (accessed April 2013).

3.1 *Pakistan's Economic and Geostrategic Importance to the EU*

The relationship between the EU and Pakistan builds upon the bilateral cooperation agreement which entered into force in 2004. One of its main objectives is to secure the conditions for and to promote the increase and development of two-way trade between the parties.[57] Moreover, Pakistan has been benefitting from preferential access to the EU market under the GSP scheme. Almost 20% of Pakistan's exports have entered the EU with no tariff and more than 70% at a preferential rate.[58] In 2011 Pakistan accounted for only 0.3% of the EU's trade, while the EU was—with a share of 14.5%—Pakistan's second largest trade partner after China (14.8%).[59] In terms of exports only, the EU was, in fact, the most important market for Pakistan (22.6%), and textiles and clothing accounted for 74.5% of Pakistani exports to the EU.[60] In addition, leather and ethanol were also important export products.

Pakistan's requests to adhere to the 'special incentive arrangement for sustainable development and good governance' were rejected because EU imports from Pakistan were just over the eligible threshold for a 'vulnerable' country (see above). In addition, Pakistan's record of human rights and governance might have posed problems in terms of its qualification for the 'GSP+'. In 1995, the International Confederation of Free Trade Unions lodged complaints about labour conditions in both Myanmar and Pakistan, but only the former case was followed up.[61] While Myanmar's suspension was a fairly uncontentious decision, "when a more problematic situation arose in the case of forced labour in Pakistan, a country with economic ties and geopolitical significance for the EU, the system came to a halt".[62]

While Pakistan is not an important trade partner for the EU, it has acquired great geostrategic importance. The country plays a crucial role in the Afghanistan conflict and in the fight against terrorism. In October 2009, the Council of the EU adopted the 'EU Action for Afghanistan and Pakistan' which

57 Cooperation Agreement between the European Community and the Islamic Republic of Pakistan, *OJ*, 2004, L 378/23–36.

58 EEAS, Delegation of the European Union to Pakistan, available at: <http://eeas.europa.eu/delegations/pakistan/eu_pakistan/trade_relation/index_en.htm> (accessed April 2013).

59 European Commission, DG Trade, "Pakistan: EU bilateral trade and trade with the world", 29 November 2012 and 23 May 2013, available at: <http://trade.ec.europa.eu/doclib/docs/2006/september/tradoc_113431.pdf> (accessed March 2013 and May 2013).

60 *Ibid.*

61 "EU's trade muscles need exercising to wield political clout", *European Voice*, 14.11.1996.

62 G. Tsogas, "Labour Standards in the Generalized Systems of Preferences of the European Union and the United States", *European Journal of Industrial Relations* 6 (3), 2000, p. 365.

underlined the EU's security interests and its intention to enhance the bilateral trade relationship as well:[63]

> The EU and Pakistan have agreed to step up a dedicated dialogue in order to enhance the bilateral trade relationship, including the possibility of a free trade agreement. [...] The EU will explore how aspects of the EU's preferential tariff regime (GSP+) might be looked at in the context of the preparation of the next GSP Regulation, thereby allowing new beneficiaries, including possibly Pakistan, to take advantage of this scheme.[64]

Since India had in 2004 won a WTO ruling against the EU's GSP 'drugs arrangement' (see above), Pakistan had lobbied the EU for more trade preferences. Given the structure of Pakistan's semi-industrialised economy, with its strong reliance on textiles and agriculture, a new-generation free trade agreement with the EU does not seem the most likely option, even though India has already been negotiating a FTA with the EU since 2007.[65] Nevertheless, the Pakistani government did in 2008 ask the EU to initiate the process for an EU-Pakistan FTA, a request of which the Council 'took note'.[66]

Part of the explanation for the emergency trade preferences might be sought in the fact that "[a] stable, democratic and prosperous Pakistan is key to addressing global issues such as counter-terrorism, non-proliferation or counter-narcotics".[67] So the difference with other cases was Pakistan's geostrategic importance. Additionally, the legacy of the country's GSP participation seemed to reinforce the case for autonomous trade preferences.

---

63 Council of the EU, Council Conclusions "Strengthening EU Action in Afghanistan and Pakistan", 2971st External Relations Council meeting, Luxembourg, 27 October 2009, available at: <http://www.consilium.europa.eu/uedocs/cms_data/docs/pressdata/en/gena/110789.pdf> (accessed April 2013).

64 *Ibid.*, para. 16.

65 Moreover, a study commissioned by the European Commission in 2008 to consider the impact of the EU's (third party) trade policies in South Asia on Pakistan's preferential access to the EU market found that the "impact on Pakistan from any of the EU agreements with countries in Asia is negligible although the effects in various sectors (e.g., textiles and apparel) are potentially more significant". See Centre for the Analysis of Regional Integration at Sussex (CARIS), *The impact of trade policies on Pakistan's preferential access to the European Union*, TRADE08/C3/C18, Brighton, University of Sussex, December 2008, p. 100.

66 Council of the EU, "Council Conclusions on Pakistan", 2914th General Affairs Council meeting, Brussels, 8 December 2008, para. 8.

67 *Ibid.*

3.2 *The Road to the EU's First Emergency Trade Preferences*

Against this background, a number of EU Member States were favourably inclined to support Pakistan's quest for better market access. The main driving force behind the emergency trade preferences was the UK government, backed by other Member States and High Representative Ashton. In May 2009 the UK and Pakistan had launched their high-level Strategic Dialogue.[68] Media reports suggested that the proposal was supported by the High Representative in a bid "to demonstrate the effectiveness of the EU's new External Action Service" after she had faced criticism regarding the response to Haiti's earthquake in January 2010.[69]

The Commission's DG Trade would have preferred to offer unilateral liberalisation on a non-discriminatory basis for products in which Pakistan was competitive.[70] Such an initiative would have been easier and faster as no WTO waiver would have been required. The suggested temporary suspension of MFN duties for a number of products from the textiles and clothing sector would have had a minor impact on EU production and created trade in particular for Pakistan, to a lesser extent also for India and China, while diverting trade mainly from Turkey, Nepal, Tunisia and Morocco.[71] However, this idea did not gain the necessary support.

On 16 September 2010, the European Council, following discussions a week earlier in the Foreign Affairs Council, adopted a Declaration on Pakistan underlining

> its firm commitment to grant exclusively to Pakistan increased market access to the EU through the immediate and time limited reduction of duties on key imports from Pakistan *in conformity with WTO rules*, to be implemented as soon as possible, and to [...] Pakistan's eligibility for GSP+ for 2014, provided it meets the necessary criteria. The Commission is invited to explore options with WTO partners and to present its

---

68 "Brown vows to stand by Pakistan", *BBC News*, 13 May 2009, available at: <http://news.bbc.co.uk/2/hi/uk_news/politics/8047142.stm> (accessed April 2013).

69 J. Chaffin and F. Bokhari, "EU considers tariff cuts for Pakistan", *Financial Times*, 29 August 2010.

70 European Commission, "Pakistan—Info Note for College", Possibilités d'aide au Pakistan dans le domaine commercial, Note d'information de M. De Gucht, *OJ* 1928, SEC(2010) 1046, Brussels, 7 September 2010.

71 *Ibid.*

> finalised proposal in October *taking account of industrial sensitivities in the EU*.[72]

The European Council invited the Commission "to present its finalised proposal in October taking account of industrial sensitivities in the EU" and mandated the Ministers to urgently agree a comprehensive package, including ambitious trade measures.[73] While the call for emergency trade preferences responded to Article 21(2)(g) TEU, according to which the EU's external action should "assist populations, countries and regions confronting natural or man-made disaster", this was the first time that trade preferences were used for humanitarian purposes.

In October 2010 the Commission proposed liberalising a list of 75 dutiable product lines, accounting for approximately 27% of EU imports from Pakistan, which would result in an estimated increase in imports of around €100 million per year.[74] Despite its humanitarian objective, the Commission's proposal was challenged in the Council of the EU and in the European Parliament. Opposition came in a *volte face* especially from France, Italy, Portugal and Spain which have significant textiles sectors.[75] As a result, the Council adopted a weaker package on 11 November 2010, with tariff suspensions for only two years (with a possible third year after an assessment) and limiting the duty-free access by annual quotas for the most sensitive products, while no tariffs were cut on bed linen, one of Pakistan's main exports.[76]

In order to grant tariff concessions to one developing country while denying them to others, the EU needed a WTO waiver to deviate from its commitments such as the MFN principle. This required the consent of Pakistan's commercial and geopolitical rivals.[77] On 30 November 2010, at a meeting of the WTO Council for Trade in Goods, the EU requested a waiver on trade preferences

---

72 European Council, "Declaration on Pakistan", Annex to the Conclusions of the European Council, EUCO 21/10, Brussels, 16 September 2010 (emphasis added).

73 *Ibid.*

74 European Commission, "Proposal for a Regulation of the European Parliament and of the Council introducing autonomous trade preferences for Pakistan", COM (2010) 552 final, Brussels, 7 October 2010, p. 2.

75 International Centre for Trade and Sustainable Development, "EU Trade Concessions to Pakistan Fail to Obtain WTO Waiver", *Bridges*, 14(4), December 2010, Geneva, ICTSD, available at: <http://ictsd.org/i/news/bridges/98780> (accessed April 2013).

76 *Ibid.*

77 Pakistan's export competition in the EU market is strongest from China, Turkey, India and Bangladesh and is mainly concentrated in the textiles and clothing sectors. CARIS, *op. cit.*, n. 65 p. 21.

for Pakistan for two years. India, Vietnam, Bangladesh and Peru, supported by some other countries, asked for consultations.[78] Bangladesh has been a major beneficiary of the EBA initiative, enjoying quota- and duty-free access for its exports to the EU, of which in 2011 92.1% were in textiles and clothing.[79] By comparison, India's share of exports in textiles and clothing to the EU was 19.4%.[80]

In the European Parliament concerns were voiced in May 2011 that the EU textiles, clothing and ethanol industries would suffer, which would lead to an unequal sharing of the 'burden' within the EU. The proposal came from Northern Member States such as the UK, while the brunt of the economic impact would be felt in the Southern Member States. In addition, the absence of any political conditionality was criticised.[81] The Commission contended that making the granting of autonomous trade preferences conditional upon Pakistan respecting certain fundamental principles would be contrary to the regulation's spirit and purpose.[82] Nevertheless, the European Parliament made Pakistan's entitlement to benefit from the preferential arrangement subject to its respect for human rights, including core labour rights, democracy and the rule of law. It introduced a safeguard clause and shortened the duration of the trade preferences to one year. The vote was postponed to a later plenary session.

India's opposition in the WTO seemed to block any progress. Yet, after India and Pakistan had both qualified to face each other in the semi-finals of the 2011 Cricket World Cup, a fresh round of 'cricket diplomacy' was launched by the Indian Prime Minister who used this opportunity to invite the Pakistani Prime Minister to India to watch the match at the end of March 2011. In September 2011, the first visit of a Pakistani Trade Minister to India for 35 years took place. Pakistan still had to grant MFN status to India. Both countries agreed

---

78 WTO, "EU requests waiver on trade preferences to Pakistan", 30 November 2010, available at: <http://www.wto.org/english/news_e/news10_e/good_30nov10_e.htm> (accessed April 2013).

79 European Commission, DG Trade, "Bangladesh: EU bilateral trade and trade with the world", 29 November 2012, available at: <http://trade.ec.europa.eu/doclib/docs/2006/september/tradoc_113349.pdf> (accessed April 2013).

80 European Commission, DG Trade, "India: EU bilateral trade and trade with the world", 29 November 2012, available at: <http://trade.ec.europa.eu/doclib/docs/2006/september/tradoc_113390.pdf> (accessed April 2013).

81 European Parliament, "Debate on emergency autonomous trade preferences for Pakistan, CRE 09/05/2011–19", Strasbourg, 9 May 2011. Just one week earlier, al-Qaida leader Osama bin Laden was killed by US forces in Abbottabad, Pakistan.

82 *Ibid.*

to increase bilateral trade and loosen visa restrictions for businessmen, and India withdrew its objection to the WTO waiver.[83] February 2012 saw the first-ever visit by an Indian Trade Minister to Pakistan. The Indian opposition might indeed have been less motivated by economic than political factors. Due to their highly differentiated and concentrated export baskets, Indian and Pakistani exports do not necessarily compete directly with each other.[84]

The EU submitted a revised request for a waiver, taking into account the concerns expressed by several WTO members during the consultations. In February 2012 the world trade body finally approved the EU's demand to temporarily waive tariffs on imports from Pakistan. The waiver still applied to a list of 75 products, yet it now included 20 on which tariff rate quotas applied instead of full liberalisation. It was stressed that the waiver constituted an exceptional measure and should not be treated as a precedent.[85]

The amendments adopted by the European Parliament in September 2012 were the result of a trialogue compromise negotiated between the Parliament and the Council.[86] The Council agreed in October 2012, and the EU regulation introducing emergency autonomous trade preferences for Pakistan was finally adopted.[87] The measures entered into force in mid-November 2012 and will be in place until the end of December 2013. Whereas the Commission proposal had originally foreseen a duration of three years and only one product (ethanol) with an annual tariff rate quota, the final regulation will last approximately one year with about one third of the 75 product lines subject to duty-free tariff quotas.

---

83 Z. Mahmood, Pakistani Commerce Secretary, "Moving toward Pakistan-India Trade Normalization: An Overview", in M. Kugelman and R. Hathaway (eds.), *Pakistan-India Trade: What Needs To Be Done? What Does It Matter?*, Washington, D.C.: The Wilson Center, 2013, pp. 23–24.

84 S. Khorana, M. Yeung, W. A. Kerr and N. Perdikis, "The Battle over the EU's Proposed Humanitarian Trade Preferences for Pakistan: A Case Study in Multifaceted Protectionism", *Journal of World Trade* 46 (1), 2012, p. 2.

85 WTO, "Members approve EU waiver request for trade aid to Pakistan", 1 February 2012, available at: <http://www.wto.org/english/news_e/news12_e/good_02feb12_e.htm> (accessed April 2013).

86 European Parliament, "Position of the European Parliament adopted at first reading on 13 September 2012 with a view to the adoption of Regulation (EU) No.../2012 of the European Parliament and of the Council introducing emergency autonomous trade preferences for Pakistan (EP-PE_TC1-COD(2010)0289)", PE 493.534, 13.9.2012.

87 Regulation (EU) No 1029/2012 of the European Parliament and of the Council of 25 October 2012 introducing emergency autonomous trade preferences for Pakistan, *OJ*, 2012, L 316/43–53.

The humanitarian purpose of the emergency trade preferences was thwarted by a combination of domestic interests in Member States which were afraid of increased competition for sensitive products and Pakistan's competitors among developing countries fearing a potential loss of their preferential access to the EU market.[88] The potential impact of 'veto players' in both fora is considerable given that the practice in the Council of the EU and the WTO Councils is that decisions are taken by consensus.[89] Moreover, the Treaty of Lisbon had added the European Parliament as a 'veto player' by extending the scope of the ordinary legislative procedure to trade measures.

This case effectively illustrates the shortcomings of using trade measures as an additional instrument to promote humanitarian objectives. The adoption of the regulation took more than three years after the emergency, and the negotiations within the EU and with the WTO members watered down the original proposal. The addition of economic safeguards and of political conditionality sits squarely with the provision of impartial, neutral and independent help. Humanitarian aid should be provided with no political and economic strings attached, whereas trade policy is often conditional.

4 Conclusion: No Strings Attached?

This chapter investigated why the EU granted Pakistan emergency trade preferences in 2010, whereas in comparable situations it had not responded in the same manner. It has been argued that the humanitarian trade preferences can be explained by Pakistan's geostrategic importance and the problems that Pakistan faced in its access to the EU market in the context of various GSP initiatives.

It seems safe to conclude that the emergency trade preferences offered too little too late. Vested interests in some EU Member States and WTO countries reduced the potential value of the trade preferences and delayed their entry into force. As a result, "trade policy might not be an effective means to

88 Khorana, Yeung, Kerr and Perdikis, *op. cit.*, n. 84 p. 54.

89 Voting only takes place when consensus cannot be achieved and requires a high threshold in both institutions. The Council of the EU decides by qualified majority, which consists until the end of 2013 of a majority of Member States (at least 14 out of 27), a majority of votes (at least 255 out of 345 or 73.91%) and—if requested by a Member State—a majority of the population (at least 62%). In the WTO three fourths (75%) of the members' votes are needed for granting a waiver (Article IX(2) WTO Agreement).

provide humanitarian assistance".[90] Moreover, the Lisbon Treaty empowered the European Parliament, a traditional advocate of political values, but with its new responsibility it also became a more prominent lobbying target for organised economic interests.

The Pakistani trade preferences might well remain a one-off experiment. As the regulation itself emphasises: the emergency measures are "part of an exceptional package, in response to the specific situation in Pakistan" and should "[u]nder no circumstances [...] constitute a precedent for the Union's trade policy with other countries".[91] Although there should be 'no strings attached' to humanitarian measures, the EU's policy was not consistent in this regard. This case shows that the use of trade preferences in response to an emergency is likely to face a dilemma. The good intention to provide more (unconditional) humanitarian aid by commercial means is challenged by (conditional) trade preferences resulting from a lengthy co-decision procedure, reflecting the EU's political values and economic interests, and the uncertainty of obtaining a WTO waiver.

Article 214 TFEU does not foresee that the objectives of humanitarian aid take priority over those of trade, nor does it list specific instruments. Poli therefore argues that the Treaty on the Functioning of the EU should include a clause integrating humanitarian aid into all other relevant EU policies, similar to environmental policy (Article 11 TFEU) or the objectives of development policy (Article 208(1) TFEU).[92] However, such a clause would not necessarily eliminate the risk of conditions being attached to trade measures with a humanitarian purpose. Although the Lisbon Treaty aims at increased consistency in EU external action, emergency trade preferences suffer from the fundamental tension between values and interests that can sometimes also be observed in other areas (such as trade and human rights or security and development). Article 21(2) TEU specifies no prioritisation of goals, and the adoption of trade measures is subject to the institutional procedures at EU and WTO levels—with all the 'strings attached'.

---

90 Khorana, Yeung, Kerr and Perdikis, *op. cit.*, n. 84 p. 33.

91 Regulation (EU) No 1029/2012, *op. cit.*, n. 87 p. 44.

92 S. Poli, "Commento all'art. 214 TFUE", in Antonio Tizzano (ed.), *Commentario al Trattato di Lisbona*, Milan: Giuffrè, 2013, forthcoming.

ANNEX: TABLE 1 *Development of EU's GSP*

	Phase 1: 1971–1994	Phase 2: 1995–2005	Phase 3: 2006–2013	Phase 4: 2014–2023
Background factors	UNCTAD support for GSP 1968 2 ten-year cycles (1971–80, 1981–90), extended to 1994 due to pending GATT Uruguay Round End of Cold War	WTO support for LDCs at Singapore 1996; ILO Declaration on Fundamental Principles and Rights at Work 1998 EU-India 'GSP Drugs' Dispute 2002–04 Ten-Year Cycle (1995–2004), extended to 2005 due to EU enlargement, on-going Doha Round and WTO dispute	'Global Europe' trade strategy 2006 & 'Trade, Growth and World Affairs' 2010 with focus on competitiveness Ten-Year Cycle (2006–15), shortened due to Lisbon Treaty and other need for reform	Application of ordinary legislative procedure due to Lisbon Treaty Preference erosion Ten-year cycle (2014–23)
Type of preferences	*Tariff quotas & tariff ceilings:* fixed duty-free amounts for (sensitive, semi-sensitive & non-sensitive) industrial goods, fixed reduced-duty amounts mainly for agricultural goods	*Tariff modulation:* duty-free access for non-sensitive products, reduced tariff rates for 3 degrees of sensitivity (as of 2002 only sensitive & non-sensitive products)	*Tariff modulation:* duty-free access for non-sensitive products, reduced tariff rates for sensitive products	*Tariff modulation:* duty-free access for non-sensitive products, reduced tariff rates for sensitive products

ANNEX: TABLE 1 (*Cont.*)

	Phase 1: 1971–1994	Phase 2: 1995–2005	Phase 3: 2006–2013	Phase 4: 2014–2023
Different arrangements	*1 arrangement:* – general arrangement (plus as of 1991 special arrangement for certain Latin American countries to combat drugs)	*5 arrangements:* – general arrangement – special incentive for protection of labour rights as of 1998 (first 3, later 8 ILO conventions) – special incentive for protection of environment (ITTO) as of 1998 – special arrangement to combat drugs – special arrangement for LDCs (extended into EBA in 2001)	*3 arrangements:* – general arrangement – special incentive for sustainable development and good governance ('GSP+' as of 1 July 2005) – EBA	*3 arrangements:* – general arrangement – special incentive for sustainable development and good governance ('GSP+') – EBA
Product coverage	Industrial goods & selected processed agricultural goods Annual review (with declining number of sensitive goods over time)	Industrial & agricultural goods 3 to 4-year review (except for EBA)	Industrial & agricultural goods 3-year review (except for EBA)	Industrial & agricultural goods None (report assessing the need for review after 5 years)

	Phase 1: 1971–1994	Phase 2: 1995–2005	Phase 3: 2006–2013	Phase 4: 2014–2023
Country coverage	In 1971 132 eligible countries & territories (in 1981 147) No graduation mechanism **Pakistan included in general GSP**	In 1995 170 eligible countries & territories (of which 49 LDCs; 5 in 'GSP drugs'), later 2 in 'GSP labour', none in 'GSP environment', 12 in 'GSP drugs' Country-sector graduation (except for LDCs) **Pakistan included in general GSP & in 'GSP drugs' (2002–05)**	In 2006 178 eligible countries & territories (of which 50 in EBA, 15 in 'GSP+') Simplified country-sector graduation (except for EBA) **Pakistan included in general GSP & emergency trade preferences for 2013**	In 2014 89 eligible countries & territories (of which 49 in EBA, South Sudan to be added, and 35 countries eligible to apply for GSP+) Relaxed country-sector graduation for GSP, no graduation for 'GSP+' and EBA **Pakistan included in general GSP & eligible for 'GSP+' as of 2014**
Political conditionality	None	Forced labour, extended to core labour standards as of 2002 Suspension from the special labour or environmental arrangements as of 1998 Infringement of intl fisheries conventions as of 1999	Core human & labour rights for all arrangements (16 intl conventions), intl fisheries conventions, plus for 'GSP+' environmental & good governance standards (11 intl conventions)	Core human & labour rights for all arrangements (15 intl conventions), intl fisheries conventions, plus for 'GSP+' environmental & good governance standards (12 intl conventions) Reverse burden of proof

Source: own compilation based on GSP regulations.

CHAPTER 4

Fighting Terrorism Through the Common Foreign and Security Policy

*Christophe Hillion**

1 Introduction

This paper discusses the contribution of Articles 43 TEU and 215 TFEU to the European Union's fight against terrorism. Three propositions are put forward about these two provisions: First, they formally confer new CFSP competences on the EU to combat terrorism (1). Secondly they contribute to the increasingly hybrid character of EU counterterrorism (2). Thirdly, they establish competences that are potentially more constraining on EU institutions and Member States and more constrained in their exercise than pre-Lisbon CFSP competences, given the increased integration of the old 'second pillar' with the EU constitutional order (3).

2 Post-Lisbon CFSP Competences to Combat Terrorism

Articles 43 TEU and 215 TFEU confer additional competences on the Union to fight terrorism within the specific context of the CFSP. Introduced into EU primary law by the Treaty of Lisbon, Article 43 TEU establishes an express competence to combat terrorism through the Common Security and Defence Policy (CSDP) (A), whereas Article 215 TFEU confers a competence on the Union to adopt sanctions against non-state organisations and individuals, implicitly on the grounds of their association with terrorism (B).

2.1 *Article 43 TEU: A Potential CSDP Contribution to EU Counterterrorism*

Article 43 TEU makes it clear that the EU is empowered to combat terrorism through the CFSP, and more specifically by using CSDP means. According to this provision:

---

* Many thanks to Anne Myrjord for her helpful comments. The usual disclaimer applies.

© KONINKLIJKE BRILL NV, LEIDEN, 2014 | DOI 10.1163/9789004268333_006

1. The tasks referred to in Article 42(1),[1] in the course of which the Union may use civilian and military means, shall include joint disarmament operations, humanitarian and rescue tasks, military advice and assistance tasks, conflict prevention and peace-keeping tasks, tasks of combat forces in crisis management, including peace-making and post-conflict stabilisation. All these tasks may contribute to the fight against terrorism, including by supporting third countries in combating terrorism in their territories.
2. The Council shall adopt decisions relating to the tasks referred to in paragraph 1, defining their objectives and scope and the general conditions for their implementation. The High Representative of the Union for Foreign Affairs and Security Policy, acting under the authority of the Council and in close and constant contact with the Political and Security Committee, shall ensure coordination of the civilian and military aspects of such tasks.

This is the first time that EU primary law makes such an express connection between counter-terrorism and the CSDP.[2] The linkage is nevertheless not new, but rather a codification of an approach previously forged by the European Council in the aftermath of the terrorist attacks on the United States, and elaborated following the Madrid and London bombings.[3] Thus, the Seville *Declaration by the European Council on the contribution of the CFSP, including the ESDP, to the fight against terrorism* underlined that the CFSP, including the ESDP "can play an important role in countering this threat to our security and in promoting peace and stability", and called for enhanced coordination among the EU Council bodies to "increase the effectiveness of the contribution

1 According to Article 42(1) TEU: "The common security and defence policy shall be an integral part of the common foreign and security policy. It shall provide the Union with an operational capacity drawing on civilian and military assets. The Union may use them on missions outside the Union for peace-keeping, conflict prevention and strengthening international security in accordance with the principles of the United Nations Charter. The performance of these tasks shall be undertaken using capabilities provided by the Member States".

2 The final sentence of paragraph 1 was added by the Convention on the Future of Europe, and was included in then Article III-309 of the Treaty establishing a Constitution for Europe. Updating the list of ESDP tasks was recommended by the Convention's Working Group VIII on Defence to take account of new threats, such as terrorism; see Final Report, CONV 461/02, para. 56.

3 Declaration on the contribution of the ESDP in the fight against terrorism presented at European Council meeting in Seville (2002).

of the CFSP, including the ESDP, to the fight against terrorism".[4] The putative ESDP 'contribution' was reiterated notably in the *Declaration on combating terrorism* adopted at the European Council in March 2004.[5] In many respects therefore, Article 43 TEU codifies an earlier conception of the role that the EU security and defence policy could play in combating terrorism.

This earlier practice lessens the innovative character of Article 43 TEU, and suggests that the empowerment it encapsulates is rather modest, as similarly to ESDP documents referred to earlier, Article 43(1) TEU uses the phrase '*may contribute*' when conceiving of the role of CSDP missions in the fight against terrorism. The optional contribution that the TEU provision thus envisaged denotes that CSDP tasks are not specifically, let alone primarily, devoted to combating terrorism. The formulation of Article 43(1) TEU cannot be understood as *mainstreaming* the fight against terrorism into CSDP tasks, in the sense of obliging the EU institutions systematically to consider this aspect in setting up CSDP missions. Instead the formulation of Article 43 TEU makes it plain that this is a *possibility* which EU decision-makers may decide to take up, or not.

Indeed, past ESDP 'contributions' to combating terrorism have been rather unimpressive. Despite the ostentatious pledges of the European Council to use the ESDP to combat terrorism, none of the pre-Lisbon EU security and defence missions was crafted with counterterrorism as its primary objective. Moreover in line with the pre-Lisbon record, most CSDP missions adopted on the basis of Article 43 TEU have been silent on the fight against terrorism, despite the

---

4 The Declaration also pointed out that "priority action for the European Union, in the fields of the CFSP and the ESDP in particular, in the fight against terrorism should focus on: devoting greater efforts to conflict prevention; deepening political dialogue with third countries to promote the fight against terrorism, including the promotion of human rights and democracy as well as non-proliferation and arms control, and providing them with appropriate international assistance strengthening arrangements for sharing intelligence and developing the production of situation assessments and early warning reports, drawing on the widest range of sources; developing our common evaluation of the terrorist threat against the Member States or the forces deployed under the ESDP outside the Union in crisis management operations, including the threat posed by terrorist use of weapons of mass destruction; determining military capabilities required to protect forces deployed in European Union-led crisis management operations against terrorist attacks; exploring further how military or civilian capabilities could be used to help protect civilian populations against the effects of terrorist attacks".

5 European Council, "Declaration on Combating Terrorism" (25 March 2004); see also European Council, "European Security Strategy. A Secure Europe in a Better World" (12 December 2003).

recurring topicality of the matter,[6] and the formal EU empowerment contained in the TEU.[7]

This modest CSDP contribution to fighting terrorism, be that pre- or post-Lisbon, may partly be explained by the taxing procedural arrangements of the CFSP in general, and the CSDP in particular. Like any other CSDP mission, the EU fight against terrorism based on Article 43 TEU remains in principle dependent upon the unanimous support of the Member States, as required by Article 42 TEU. Indeed, as frequently recalled in EU counterterrorism documents, the prime responsibility for fighting terrorism lies with the Member States, and the CSFP dimension, particularly under Article 43 TEU, remains *complementary*. In the same vein, the EU financial support of CSDP operations is limited to civilian missions, leaving CSDP operations that have a military or defence aspect, to be financed by the Member States themselves, possibly another deterrent to their extensive use for combating terrorism.[8]

In sum, the Lisbon Treaty's empowerment of the EU to fight terrorism using the means of the CSDP is seemingly limited, particularly in the light of previous practice. However, the growing perception in some Member States that the terrorist threat is getting closer to EU shores[9] contributes to changing the approach, as evidenced in two CSDP missions which have recently been set up with the specific aim of combatting terrorism. Thus, an EU CSDP Mission in Sahel ('EUCAP Sahel Niger') was established in July 2012[10] the aim being "to support the capacity building of the Nigerien security actors to fight terrorism

---

6 See e.g. Draft Council Conclusions calling for an update of the EU Strategy for Combating Radicalisation and Recruitment to Terrorism; 9447/13, Brussels, 15 May 2013; European Council, *The Stockholm Programme—An Open and Secure Europe Serving and Protecting Citizens, OJ*, 2010, C 115/1, p. 24.

7 Further see J. Argomaniz, "A Rhetorical Spillover? Exploring the Link between the European Union Common Security and Defence Policy (CSDP) and the External Dimension of Counter-Terrorism", in: H. Carrapico and F. Trauner (eds.), "Special Issue—The External Dimension of EU Justice and Home Affairs: Post-Lisbon Governance Dynamics", European Foreign Affairs Review 17, 2012, pp. 35–52; G. de Vries, "The nexus between EU crisis management and counter", in: S. Blockmans (ed.), *The European Union and Crisis Management—Policy and Legal Aspects*, The Hague: T.M.C. Asser Press, 2008, pp. 355–372, S. Duke, "CESDP and the EU response to 11 September", *European Foreign Affairs Review* 7, 2002, pp. 153–169.

8 Articles 41(2) and (3) TEU.

9 See speech by French President Hollande at the 67th UN General Assembly, 25 September 2012, available at: <http://www.franceonu.org/france-at-the-united-nations/press-room/statements-at-open-meetings/general-assembly/article/25-september-2012-67th-united> (accessed 1 June 2013).

10 Council Decision 2012/392/CFSP of 16 July 2012; *OJ*, 2012, L 187/48.

and organised crime".[11] Additionally in Mali, a military operation has been set up to contribute to the training of the Malian Armed Forces ('EUTM Mali').[12] In particular, the operation purports to:

> provide, in the South of Mali, military and training advice to the Malian Armed Forces ... in order to contribute to the restoration of their military capacity with a view to enabling them to conduct military operations aiming at restoring Malian territorial integrity and reducing the threat posed by terrorist groups.[13]

Both missions correspond to the only *specific* facet of counterterrorism through the CSDP envisaged in Article 43(1) TEU, in addition to the standard CSDP tasks, namely "supporting third countries in combating terrorism in their territories". In other words, the CSDP competence to fight terrorism has thus far not materialised in terms of direct handling of terrorism by the EU through the CSDP actions enounced in the first part of Article 43(1) TEU, but has taken the more modest form of support for third parties. So while the CSDP contribution to counterterrorism has now become more tangible, it nevertheless remains limited, thus confirming the feeling of a 'proclamation-implementation' gap as regards the CSDP and counterterrorism.[14]

2.2 *Article 215: EU Restrictive Measures against Terrorists*

Alongside the CSDP dimension of counter-terrorism, Article 215 TFEU provides a legal basis for the EU to adopt 'restrictive measures' against individuals, groups or states, following a preliminary CFSP decision:

> 1. Where a decision, adopted in accordance with Chapter 2 of Title V of the Treaty on European Union, provides for the interruption or reduction, in part or completely, of economic and financial

---

11 Article 1, Council Decision 2012/392/CFSP.

12 Council Decision 2013/34/CFSP of 17 January 2013; *OJ*, 2013, L 14/19. See also the conclusions of the Foreign Affairs Council on Mali, Brussels, 18 February 2013.

13 Article 1, Council Decision 2013/34/CFSP.

14 See further J. Argomaniz, "A Rhetorical Spillover? Exploring the Link between the European Union Common Security and Defence Policy (CSDP) and the External Dimension of Counter-Terrorism", in: H. Carrapico and F. Trauner (eds.), "Special Issues—The External Dimension of EU Justice and Home Affairs: Post-Lisbon Governance Dynamics", *European Foreign Affairs Review* 17 (35), 2012, pp. 36–52; R. Coolsaet, "EU Counter-Terrorism Strategy: Value Added or Chimera?", *International Affairs* 86 (4), 2010, pp. 857–873.

relations with one or more third countries, the Council, acting by a qualified majority on a joint proposal from the High Representative of the Union for Foreign Affairs and Security Policy and the Commission, shall adopt the necessary measures. It shall inform the European Parliament thereof.

2. Where a decision adopted in accordance with Chapter 2 of Title V of the Treaty on European Union so provides, the Council may adopt restrictive measures under the procedure referred to in paragraph 1 against natural or legal persons and groups or non-State entities.
3. The acts referred to in this Article shall include necessary provisions on legal safeguards.

More than replacing the old Article 301 EC, Article 215 TFEU encapsulates in its second paragraph the combination of pre-Lisbon Articles 301-60-308 EC which had previously been used by the Community institutions as a legal basis for adopting restrictive measures against individuals and groups associated with terrorism, pursuant to CFSP decisions. That practice was endorsed by the European Court of Justice in its famous *Kadi I* judgment,[15] and is now constitutionalised.

That Article 215 TFEU replaces the pre-Lisbon composite legal basis was confirmed by the European Court of Justice in a judgment of 19 July 2012 in case C-130/10 *European Parliament v Council*. The case will be examined in further detail later; at this point it will suffice to highlight the Court's view on Article 215 TFEU:

> 51 (...), as a result of the amendments made to primary law after the Treaty of Lisbon entered into force, the content of Articles 60 EC, relating to restrictive measures with regard to capital movements and payments, and 301 EC on the interruption or reduction, in part or completely, of economic relations with one or more third countries, is mirrored in Article 215 TFEU.
>
> (...)

15 Joined Cases C-402/05 P and C-415/05 P, *Kadi and Al Barakaat International Foundation v Council and Commission* [2008] ECR I-6351.

> 53 Furthermore, Article 215(2) TFEU allows the Council to adopt restrictive measures against natural or legal persons and groups or non-State entities, namely, measures that, before the Treaty of Lisbon entered into force, required Article 308 EC too to be included in their legal basis if their addressees were not linked to the governing regime of a third country (see, to that effect, *Kadi and Al Barakaat International Foundation* v *Council and Commission*, paragraph 216).

It is indeed in the light of that pre-Lisbon arrangement that the Court interprets the provisions of Article 215 TFEU. In particular, while the provision does not specifically refer to the fight against terrorism, the Court nevertheless deduces that:

> As regards combating terrorism and its funding, it is to be noted that there is nothing in Article 215 TFEU to indicate that measures designed to combat them, taken against natural or legal persons, groups or non-State entities, could not constitute restrictive measures provided for in subparagraph 2 of that article. It is to be observed here that, although neither Article 60 EC nor Article 301 EC referred expressly to combating terrorism, those two provisions did, none the less, constitute the legal basis for the adoption, before the Treaty of Lisbon entered into force, of restrictive measures designed to combat that phenomenon (see, inter alia, in this respect, the measures at issue in *Kadi and Al Barakaat International Foundation* v *Council and Commission*).

Like Article 43 TEU, Article 215 TFEU thus appears to codify past practice. It confirms that the Union is empowered to adopt sanctions against individuals and organisations, and endorses the counter-terrorism objective that such restrictive measures may pursue. In turn, the judgment makes it plain that the CFSP may aim at combatting terrorism, confirming that Article 215 TFEU indirectly preserves the CFSP dimension of counterterrorism.

Also akin to Article 43 TEU, but in contrast to Article 215 (1), the competence conferred on the Union by Article 215(2) is, somewhat surprisingly, couched in *optional* rather than mandatory terms. It foresees that the Council "*may* adopt restrictive measures ... against natural or legal persons and groups or non-State entities", following a CFSP decision. The Council is thus not bound to act, and may leave it to the Member States to implement the CFSP decision, at least in areas where they have competence, while they also remain at liberty not to follow the CFSP route in the first place, and to opt for the national level. Another EU route could also be explored, as discussed below.

In sum, Articles 43 TEU and 215 TFEU expressly confer EU competences to combat terrorism through CFSP means. These provisions appear to codify pre-Lisbon practice, a fact that relativises their innovative character, which in turn might limit their added value in terms of enhancing the EU capacity to fight terrorism. Indeed, both of them depend in principle upon the unanimous support of the Member States in view of the recurrent unanimity requirements of the former second pillar.[16]

Arguably, however, the inclusion of these competences within Treaty provisions amounts to more than a mere codification of the status quo. The 'constitutionalisation' of such competences might create a new momentum for EU counterterrorism measures, as suggested by recent practice.

3 A Rampant "*PESCalisation*" of EU Counterterrorism?

The inclusion within EU primary law of the above mentioned competences increases the CFSP *component* of the EU fight against terrorism. The question could therefore be raised as to whether this development has taken place at the expense of more communitarian (i.e. TFEU) instruments (A), or whether the two dimensions ought to be seen as complementary. Conversely, rather than being merely 'PESCalised',[17] has counterterrorism become a hybrid policy framework combining CFSP and non-CFSP instruments (B)?

3.1 *CFSP v. TFEU Counterterrorism*

A closer look at Articles 43 TEU and 215 TFEU, and their context, increases the impression of an enhanced CFSP dimension to EU counterterrorism, possibly at the expense of the other EU instruments in the field, based on the TFEU.

The apparent 'PESCalisation' of counterterrorism is, for instance, illustrated by the subtle modification of the *procedural* arrangements for the adoption of restrictive measures, which affects the nature of the competence involved. Whereas ex Article 301 EC envisaged that the adoption of the regulation to implement the preliminary CFSP Common Position was to be proposed by the

---

16 Article 24 TEU. See further P. Eeckhout, "The EU's Common Foreign and Security Policy after Lisbon: From Pillar Talk to Constitutionalism", in: A. Biondi, P. Eeckout and S. Ripley (eds.), *EU Law after Lisbon*, Oxford: Oxford University Press, 2012, pp. 265–291.

17 The term can be found in Y. Buchet de Neuilly, "La politique étrangère et de sécurité commune. Dynamique d'un système d'action", *Politix* 46, 1999, pp. 127–146; and R. A. Wessel, "Fragmentation in the governance of EU external relations: legal institutional dilemmas and the new Constitution for Europe", in: J. W. de Zwaan (ed.), *The European Union: An ongoing Process of Integration—Liber Amicorum Alfred E. Kellermann*, The Hague: TMC Asser Press, 2004, pp. 123–140.

Commission following a classic Community procedure, Article 215 TFEU requires a joint initiative of the Commission and the High Representative for Foreign and Security Policy. As such, the provision does not only confirm the CFSP dimension of counterterrorism, it also encapsulates a stronger CFSP *presence* in the implementation of sanctions in the context of the TFEU.[18]

The impression of EU counterterrorism being PESCalised is also borne out by the CJEU's 2012 judgment in case C-130/10 *European Parliament v Council*, briefly referred to above. Here, the Court of Justice found that Article 215 TFEU was the appropriate legal basis for adopting the Regulation amending the 2002 "Regulation imposing certain specific restrictive measures directed against certain persons and entities associated with Usama bin Laden, the Al-Qaeda network and the Taliban". It thus rejected the claim made by the European Parliament that the Regulation ought to have been adopted on the basis of Article 75 TFEU,[19] relating to the area of freedom, security and justice.[20] As mentioned earlier, the Court first established that Article 215 TFEU replaces the combination of Articles 60, 301 and 308 EC that serves as legal basis for the pre-Lisbon regulation which the impugned act was deemed to replace, distinguishing it from the more restricted function of Article 75 TFEU:

> 54. (…) its context and tenor differ from those of Articles 60 EC and 301 EC. Article 75 TFEU does not, in fact, refer to the interruption or reduction,

18 In Case C-130/10, *Parliament v Council* [2012] ECR n.y.r: the Court appears to accept that the endorsement by the HR of a Commission's proposal is sufficient, for the proposal to be considered as a joint proposal for the purposes of Article 215 TFEU. The Court specifies that Article 215 "does not make it necessary for the High Representative to present a separate statement of reasons or to supplement that in the Commission's proposal" (para. 105).

19 According to Article 75 TFEU: "Where necessary to achieve the objectives set out in Article 67, as regards preventing and combating terrorism and related activities, the European Parliament and the Council, acting by means of regulations in accordance with the ordinary legislative procedure, shall define a framework for administrative measures with regard to capital movements and payments, such as the freezing of funds, financial assets or economic gains belonging to, or owned or held by, natural or legal persons, groups or non-State entities.

The Council, on a proposal from the Commission, shall adopt measures to implement the framework referred to in the first paragraph.

The acts referred to in this Article shall include necessary provisions on legal safeguards".

20 Council Regulation (EU) No 1286/2009 of 22 December 2009 amending Regulation (EC) No 881/2002 imposing certain specific restrictive measures directed against certain persons and entities associated with Usama bin Laden, the Al-Qaeda network and the Taliban, *OJ*, 2010, L 346/42.

> in part or completely, of economic relations with one or more third countries. Incorporated in Part Three of the FEU Treaty on Union policies and internal actions, and more specifically in Title V thereof, entitled 'Area of freedom, security and justice', that article simply refers to the definition, for the purpose of preventing terrorism and related activities and combating the same, of a framework for administrative measures with regard to capital movements and payments, when this is necessary to achieve the objectives set out in Article 67 TFEU.

While admitting that "the combating of terrorism and its financing may well be among the objectives of the area of freedom, security and justice, as they appear in Article 3(2) TEU", the Court opined that:

> the objective of *combating international terrorism and its financing in order to preserve international peace and security* corresponds, nevertheless, to the objectives of the Treaty provisions on external action by the Union (emphasis added).[21]

It then concluded:

> 63. Given that terrorism constitutes a threat to peace and international security, the object of actions undertaken by the Union in the sphere of the CFSP, and the measures taken in order to give effect to that policy in the Union's external actions, in particular, restrictive measures for the purpose of Article 215(2) TFEU, can be to combat terrorism.

Since the provision of Article 75 TFEU is "incorporated in Part Three of the FEU Treaty on Union policies and internal actions",[22] whereas Article 215 TFEU is included in the external action part of the Treaty, and linked to the CFSP, the Court held that:

> 78. (…) Article 215(2) TFEU constitutes the appropriate legal basis for measures… directed to addressees implicated in acts of terrorism who, having regard to their activities globally and to the international dimension of the threat they pose, affect fundamentally the Union's external activity.

21 Para. 61.

22 Para. 54.

The Court of Justice thus confirms the significant CFSP dimension of the EU external fight against terrorism envisaged by the Treaty of Lisbon, while seemingly circumscribing the external dimension of the AFSJ,[23] and incidentally its ability to underpin an implied external power.[24] It is indeed noticeable that, in its judgment, the Court referred to Article 43 TEU and its new express reference to the possible contribution of CSDP missions to combating terrorism, to corroborate its findings. Reference is also made to the first subparagraph of Article 24(1) TEU according to which "the Union's competence in matters of [the CFSP] shall cover all areas of foreign policy and all questions relating to the Union's security". It is the first time that the Court points out the all-encompassing character of the CFSP,[25] *in casu* to substantiate that counterterrorism cannot be excluded from its ambit. This in turn formally permits the EU to rely on Article 215 TFEU to adopt restrictive measures against terrorists/terrorist organisations, despite the provision's silence on the matter.

The Court thereby takes account of various structural innovations introduced by the Treaty of Lisbon to substantiate the significant CFSP dimension of counter-terrorism. First, it places considerable importance upon the separation now enshrined in the TFEU between internal policies and external action, for the purposes of determining the correct legal basis of an act.[26] Consequently, in case of conflict between an 'external' (i.e. Part V TFEU) and an 'internal' (Part III TFEU) legal basis, a measure having an external objective will thus more likely rely on the former than on the latter.[27] Taken further, this argument could paradoxically have the effect of watering down the implied powers doctrine, constitutionalised by Article 216 TFEU.

The other element which appears to pervade the Court of Justice's approach, though implicitly, is the rule enshrined in Article 40(2) TEU, whereby the implementation of the policies listed in Articles 3 to 6 TFEU must "not affect the application of the procedures and the extent of the powers of the institutions laid down by the Treaties for the exercise of the Union competences

---

23 See further on the external dimension of the AFSJ, e.g. M. Cremona, J. Monar and S. Poli (eds.), *The External Dimension of the Area of Freedom, Security and Justice*, Brussels: Peter Lang-P.I.E., 2011; J. Monar, *The External Dimension of the EU's Area of Freedom, Security and Justice*, SIEPS Report 2012: 1.

24 Indeed, the Court fails to expound the purpose of Article 75 TFEU in the fight against terrorism.

25 Cf. Case C-91/05, *Commission v Council* (*'ECOWAS'*) [2008] ECR I-3651.

26 Cf. Council Conclusions on enhancing the links between internal and external aspects of counter-terrorism, Justice and Home Affairs Council, Luxembourg, 9–10 June 2011.

27 See, in this respect, the judgment of the Court of Justice in Case C-414/11, *Daiichi Sankyo Co. Ltd*, of 18 July 2013 (n.y.r.), para. 50.

under the CFSP Chapter", and more generally the principle of equality of the Treaties, enshrined in Article 1 TEU. While the Court does not mention Article 40 TEU in its judgment,[28] despite the Council and the AG having raised the point,[29] its interest in various CFSP provisions, which none of the parties invoked, arguably materializes the protective and implicit interpretative jurisdiction over the CFSP which it is endowed with on the basis of Article 40(2) TEU.[30]

In this respect, it is symptomatic that the Court points out that adopting measures like the contested one only on the basis of Article 75 TFEU "would render Article 215(2) TFEU largely redundant".[31] It thereby protects the *effet utile* of Article 215 TFEU, and by doing so indirectly preserves the CFSP, at least in terms of its counterterrorism dimension. Indeed, had the Court decided otherwise, it would not only have emptied Article 215(2) of much of its relevance, it would also have reduced the size of the CFSP quite considerably given that sanctions represent in qualitative and quantitative terms the most significant instrument of CFSP.[32] While this might not be the primary ratio decidendi in this case, this judgment could nevertheless be read as a nascent intention by the Court to protect the integrity of the CFSP, in line with the requirements of Article 40(2) TEU.

3.2 *An Increasingly Hybrid Policy?*

Another reading of the above developments is nevertheless possible: it may be argued that while the CFSP dimension of the EU fight against terrorism has undoubtedly been enhanced, the legal framework of the policy appears *hybrid* rather than simply PESCalised. Not only does the non-CFSP dimension of counterterrorism remain, but various legal bases related to counterterrorism also now involve procedures and actions where CFSP and TFEU competence and instruments *interact*, if not merge.

In the judgment referred to above, the Court of Justice opines that:

---

28 I. Bosse-Platière, "L'action extérieure de l'Union européenne—3. La Cour confirme le rattachement de la lutte contre le terrorisme international et son financement à la PESC", *RTDeur* 2, 2013, pp. 118–120.

29 Para. 41 of the judgment as regards the Council's argument and para. 67 of AG Bot's Opinion.

30 See further C. Hillion, "A Powerless Court? The European Court of Justice and the Common Foreign and Security Policy", in: M. Cremona and A. Thies (eds.), *The ECJ and External Relations: Constitutional Challenges*, Oxford: Hart Publishing, 2014.

31 Para. 84.

32 See C. Eckes, "EU Counter-Terrorist Sanctions against Individuals: Problems and Perils", *European Foreign Affairs Review* 17, 2012, pp. 113–132.

> Article 215(2) TFEU *may* constitute the legal basis of restrictive measures, including those designed to combat terrorism, taken against natural or legal persons, groups or non-State entities by the Union *when the decision to adopt those measures is part of the Union's action in the sphere of the CFSP.*[33] (emphasis added)

Not only does the Court's pronouncement echo the optional nature of the competence set out in Article 215, it suggests a *contrario*, as indeed made clear in an earlier paragraph (para. 58), that in the absence of such CFSP action, Article 215 TFEU could not be used. This raises the question of whether alternative routes could be envisaged by the Union.

To be sure, the Court does not hold that the only external route to combat terrorism is the CFSP. Instead, the judges chose a careful formulation whereby:

> the objective of combating international terrorism and its financing in order to preserve international peace and security corresponds … to the *objectives of the Treaty provisions on external action by the Union.*[34] (emphasis added)

Thus, should the EU Common Position 2002/402, which the impugned regulation implements be replaced or repealed, it may be questioned whether the new legal framework would automatically be established on the basis of the CFSP chapter of the TEU. Unlike Advocate General Bot, the Court does not clearly establish that:

> action by the European Union on the international stage which pursues one or more of the objectives referred to in Article 21(2)(a) to (c) TEU, in particular the objective of preserving peace and strengthening international security, must be regarded as falling within the sphere of the CFSP.[35]

---

33 Para. 65. While in this paragraph the Court uses the phrase 'may' (translated in French as 'vocation à'), para. 78 is more affirmative in establishing that Article 215 is the appropriate legal basis: "Article 215(2) TFEU constitutes the appropriate legal basis for measures, such as those at issue in the present case, directed to addressees implicated in acts of terrorism who, having regard to their activities globally and to the international dimension of the threat they pose, affect fundamentally the Union's external activity".

34 Para. 61.

35 Para. 64, Opinion of AG Bot (31 January 2012). In this context, it may be questioned whether para. 77 of the judgment could be read as an indication that a discussion could have been held on the legal basis of the Common Position; the Court held: "although, in connection with the second plea in law, the Parliament denies that Common Position

Instead, the Court of Justice points to Article 21(2)(c) as forming "part of Chapter 1 laying down general provisions on the Union's external action in Title V of the EU Treaty".[36] It thus rightly confirms that the preservation of peace, prevention of conflicts and strengthening international security is not the exclusive domain of the CFSP. As any other external action of the Union is equally determined by the objectives enounced in Article 21 TEU, other instruments of external action could be considered to combat international terrorism as a threat to international peace and security.[37]

In this context, the question may be raised as to whether Article 75 TFEU could still be relied upon, despite the Court having significantly restricted its use for external purposes. One argument, made by AG Bot, is the difficulty in systematically distinguishing between international and internal terrorism. He thus suggests that Article 75 TFEU:

> 79. (…) constitutes the appropriate legal basis for the European Union, autonomously and independently of any initiative falling within the sphere of the CFSP, to adopt measures freezing the funds and economic resources of persons and non-State entities engaged in terrorist or related activities, there being no need to endeavour to classify the addressees of such measures as 'internal', 'external' or 'international' terrorists.
>
> 80. The nature of Articles 215(2) TFEU and 75 TFEU as mutually complementary provisions should serve to allay the concern, fundamental in the context of combating terrorism, that the system must not contain any flaw such as to jeopardise the aim pursed, which is to protect democracies against actions which in fact seek to bring an end to their existence.

One could add that in stipulating that "in its relations with the wider world, the Union shall uphold and promote its values and interests and contribute to the protection of its citizens", Article 3(5) TEU makes it clear that the EU's interactions with the rest of the world are intimately connected to the objectives of the area of freedom, security and justice, thus mitigating the over-emphasis

---

2002/402 can possibly amount to a decision under the CFSP for the purpose of Article 215(2) TFEU, it has not, however, called in question whether it was possible for that Common Position, having enabled adoption of Regulation No 881/2002 in accordance with Articles 60 EC and 301 EC, to be validly based on Title V of the EU Treaty, as it stood before the Treaty of Lisbon, that is to say, the title of that treaty concerning the CFSP".

36 Para. 62.

37 A point also made by AG Bot at para. 77 of his Opinion.

which the Court has put on the distinction between Part III TFEU (internal), and Part VI TFEU (external), to circumscribe the function of Article 75 TFEU.

As a consequence of the Lisbon Treaty, EU counterterrorism in general, and the sanction instrument in particular, is multidimensional. The two-pronged system of EU sanctions, which predates the Lisbon Treaty, persists with distinct procedural arrangements, and indeed a different geographical scope of application in view of some Member States' opt-outs in relation to the area of freedom, security and justice.[38] One may incidentally wonder whether, in this respect, Article 215 TFEU has simplified the system.[39]

The cross-pillar (or 'cross-sectoral')[40] character of EU counterterrorism has seemingly been consolidated by the post-Lisbon arrangements and other forms of 'cross-pillarisation' have become evident. As briefly mentioned earlier, the procedure to establish restrictive measures based upon Article 215 TFEU involves *a joint proposal* of the Commission and High Representative, in contrast to the previous procedural arrangements of Article 301 EC which only involved a Commission initiative. The sanction procedure has thus changed in nature, in that it is no longer an entirely 'Community-type' procedure to fulfil a CFSP objective. All the same, it has not been turned into a CFSP procedure governed by the canons of Article 24 TEU. Instead, the restrictive measures under Article 215 TFEU appear to belong to a distinct category of *hybrid* CFSP/TFEU measures altogether.[41]

In the area of counterterrorism, the solidarity clause of Article 222 TFEU is another case of such hybridity. It establishes, in its first paragraph, that the Union shall mobilise all the instruments at its disposal, including the military resources made available by the Member States, to "prevent the terrorist threat in the territory of the Member States, [and] protect democratic institutions and the civilian population from *any* terrorist attacks". Despite its apparent

38 See Protocol 21 on the position of the United Kingdom and Ireland in respect of the area of freedom, security and justice, and Protocol 22 on the position of Denmark, both annexed to the Treaties.

39 Further on this see C. Eckes, "EU Counter-Terrorist Sanctions against Individuals: Problems and Perils", *European Foreign Affairs Review* 17, 2012, pp. 113–132.

40 The expression was coined by C. Timmermans to replace the pre-Lisbon 'cross-pillar' expression. See C. Timmermans, "Evolution of Mixity since the Leiden 1982 Conference", in: C. Hillion and P. Koutrakos (eds.), *Mixed Agreements Revisited—The EU and its Member States in the World*, Oxford: Hart Publishing, 2010, pp. 1–8.

41 The European Court of Justice's jurisdiction over restrictive measures adopted in the context of the CFSP, foreseen in Article 275 TFEU, further illustrates the distinctiveness of such measures.

focus on "the territory of the Member States", these provisions may also be read as having an external dimension, in terms of involving CSDP tasks in tackling terrorist threats with external ramifications. To be sure, the location of the specific Title on Solidarity clause (Title VII) in Part V of the TFEU, on the External Action of the Union, points strongly in the direction of its possible external dimension. Article 222(1) TFEU could thus strengthen the EU's counterterrorism capacity envisaged in Article 43 TEU.[42]

The hybrid CFSP-TFEU character of the solidarity clause contained within Article 222 TFEU is further borne out by the decision-making procedure envisaged in paragraph three, defining the arrangements for the implementation of the clause. Akin to the procedure set out in Article 215 TFEU, the decision is to be adopted by the Council acting on a joint proposal by the Commission and the High Representative.[43] The same provision adds that the Council shall act in accordance with Article 31(1) of the Treaty on European Union where the decision has defence implications, the European Parliament simply being informed.[44]

In sum, while Articles 43 TEU and 215 TFEU epitomise a strengthening of the CFSP dimension of EU counterterrorism, preserved by the European Court of Justice under Article 40(2) TEU, they do not remove other EU competences in the field, which are to be equally safeguarded under Article 40(1) TEU. Indeed, the cross-sectoral nature of counterterrorism is confirmed, if not enhanced, through the amalgamation of procedural requirements typical of the CFSP and TFEU, in line with the spirit of the Lisbon Treaty, and its consolidated consistency requirement.[45]

---

42 See the contribution of S. Blockmans, "*L'union fait la force*: making the most of the solidarity clause (Art. 222 TFEU)" in this volume. See also the Opinion of AG Bot in case C-130/10, *European Parliament v Council* [2012] n.y.r., para. 65.

43 See in this respect, Joint Proposal for a Council Decision on the arrangements for the implementation by the Union of the Solidarity clause, JOIN (2012) 39, 21.12.2012.

44 It should be noted that the provisions on restrictive measures and on solidarity are both the subject of specific titles within the part of the TFEU on the EU's external action. One might wonder whether this distinctiveness in the architecture of the Treaty could be taken as an additional signal of the specificity of the two areas of the EU external action, albeit included in the TFEU.

45 See e.g. C. Hillion, "Cohérence et action extérieure de l'Union", in: E. Neframi (ed.), *Objectifs et compétences de l'Union européenne*, Bruxelles: Bruylant, 2012, pp. 229–261.

4 Integration of Counterterrorism into EU Constitutional Framework

The increased CFSP dimension of counterterrorism, and its contribution to the hybridisation of the Union's competence in the field, does not *ipso facto* mean that the latter is subject to a laxer legal framework. Not only have some facets of counterterrorism been 'communautarised', but the exercise of CFSP competence is also legally more constrained as a result of the increased 'constitutionalisation' of the CFSP, entailed by the Lisbon Treaty.[46] This could, in turn, reinforce the constraining effects of CFSP instruments of counterterrorism notably vis-à-vis the Member States.

Hence, whether pursued through CFSP or TFEU competences, EU external counterterrorism is determined, as suggested earlier, by a *common teleological framework*, namely the principles and objectives of Articles 3(5) TEU and 21 TEU. It is also governed by the *structural principles* of the EU legal order, notably the principles of conferral, subsidiarity, proportionality (Article 5 TEU) and respect for fundamental rights (Article 6 TEU), but also by the requirements of sincere cooperation (Article 4(3) TEU and 13(2) TEU), and consistency (Article 21(3) TEU), which have all been emboldened by the Treaty of Lisbon, and generalised in their application as a result of the new architecture of the Treaties. All these principles, with the exception of consistency, belong to the Common Provisions of the TEU. As such, they govern the operation of the entire EU legal order. Located within the General Provisions on the EU's External Action, the principle of consistency plays a similar structuring role for the external action of the EU, and for the functioning of the EU more generally, given its inclusion also in Part One 'Principles' of the TFEU. This final section does not discuss the application of each of such structural principles to the EU fight against terrorism. Rather, it flags up the way in which those that are particularly relevant in view of the nature of EU counterterrorism, could operate notably in relation to its CFSP dimension: respect for fundamental rights, the requirement of consistency and the principle of sincere cooperation.

As regards fundamental rights, the Court of Justice recalled in its pronouncement in case C-130/10 that:

46 See P. Eeckhout, "The EU's Common Foreign and Security Policy after Lisbon: From Pillar Talk to Constitutionalism", in: A. Biondi, P. Eeckout and S. Ripley (eds.), *EU Law after Lisbon*, Oxford: Oxford University Press, 2012, pp. 265–291.

> the duty to respect fundamental rights is imposed, in accordance with Article 51(1) of the Charter of Fundamental Rights of the European Union, on all the institutions and bodies of the Union.[47]

It also pointed out that the "respect for fundamental rights equally bears on Union measures giving effect to resolutions of the Security Council",[48] making no difference whether such implementing measures are CFSP or TFEU-based. In principle therefore, the strengthening of the CFSP dimension of counter-terrorism does not necessarily entail a diminished requirement of fundamental rights compliance in the EU fight against terrorism.[49] Indeed, the provisions of Article 275 TFEU make it clear that the Court has jurisdiction to exercise judicial control over restrictive measures adopted in the context of CFSP, in line with the *Kadi* jurisprudence, and thus to guarantee that fundamental rights are respected in relation to these measures.[50]

The principles of sincere cooperation and consistency are particularly important in view of the complementary and cross-sectoral nature of EU counterterrorism, and the multiplicity of actors involved.[51] The principle of sincere cooperation binds EU institutions in accordance with Article 13(2) TEU. As a result, EU counterterrorism institutions acting within the context of the CFSP are bound to cooperate with those acting in the framework of the TFEU, and vice-versa. In the same vein, the EU CFSP activities in the area of counterterrorism are subject to the duty of consistency, which imposes procedural obligations between the Council and the Commission, assisted by the

---

47 Para. 83.

48 Para. 84.

49 The same cannot be said about democratic control, as confirmed by the Court's judgment in Case C-130/10, *European Parliament v Council* [2012] ECR n.y.r.

50 See Joined Cases C-402/05 P and C-415/05 P *Kadi and Al Barakaat International Foundation* v *Council and Commission* [2008] ECR I-635, and the more recent judgment of 18 July 2013 in Cases C-584/10P, C-593/10 and C-595/10P, *Commission, Council, United Kingdom v Kadi* (*'Kadi II'*), and AG Bot's Opinion of 19 March 2013 (n.y.r.).

51 As mentioned earlier, the CFSP instruments of counterterrorism are primarily in the hands of the High Representative and the Council acting unanimously, whereas other non-CFSP external policies that relate to, or have a bearing on counter-terrorism, e.g. the area of freedom, security and justice, or development cooperation, have the Commission as principal initiator. Other actors include the Counter-Terrorism Coordinator, who has external functions too (he regularly meets foreign counterparts, but also meets representatives of third states, including at the highest level: see <eeas.europa.eu/delegations/niger/press_corner/all_news/news/2013/20130514_02_fr.htm> (accessed 1 June 2013)) and who is part of the Council administration, and several agencies such as Europol.

HR, to strive to achieve synergies between the different areas of its external action and between these and its other policies.[52] Importantly, both principles, and notably the procedural obligations derived from them, are in principle enforceable before the Court of Justice, irrespective of the fact that EU institutions are operating within the CFSP context.[53] As argued elsewhere,[54] the constitutional restrictions of the Court's jurisdiction in relation to the CFSP (e.g. Article 24(1) TEU, Article 40 TEU, Article 275 TFEU, Declarations 13 and 14 annexed to the Treaties) do not amount to limitations upon the Court's jurisdiction as regards the application of principles of EU law enshrined in the non-CFSP parts of the Treaties.

In the same vein, the principle of sincere cooperation compels Member States following Article 4(3) TEU. As made clear by the phrase 'tasks which flow from the *treaties*' (emphasis added) included in the first sentence of the provision, as well as its inclusion in the Common Provisions of the TEU, the rebranded principle of 'sincere cooperation' relates to all the objectives and tasks of the Union, thus including those previously related to the non-EC pillars of the EU. While this all-encompassing application is not entirely new,[55] its Lisbon formulation nevertheless makes it clearer, notably as regards objectives that hitherto related specifically to the Common Foreign and Security Policy.

---

52 Further, see e.g. C. Hillion, "Cohérence et action extérieure de l'Union", in: E. Neframi (ed.), *Objectifs et compétences de l'Union européenne*, Bruxelles: Bruylant, 2012, pp. 229–261.

53 *Ibid.*

54 C. Hillion, "*Tous pour un, Un pour tous!* Coherence in the External relations of the European Union", in: M. Cremona (ed.), *Developments in EU External Relations Law, Collected Courses of the Academy of European Law*, Oxford: Oxford University Press, 2008, pp. 10–36; M. Cremona, "Coherence in European Union Foreign Relations Law", in: P. Koutrakos (ed.), *European Foreign Policy. Legal and Political Perspectives*, Edward Elgar, 2011, pp. 55–92.

55 See Case C-105/03, *Pupino* [2005] ECR I-5285, where the Court pointed out at para. 42 that: "It would be difficult for the Union to carry out its task effectively if the principle of loyal cooperation, requiring in particular that Member States take all appropriate measures, whether general or particular, to ensure fulfilment of their obligations under European Union law, were not also binding in the area of police and judicial cooperation in criminal matters, which is moreover entirely based on cooperation between the Member States and the institutions". Further: C. Hillion and R. A. Wessel, 'Restraining External Competences of EU Member States under CFSP', in: M. Cremona and B. de Witte (eds.), *EU Foreign Relations Law—Constitutional Fundamentals*, Oxford: Hart Publishing, 2008, p. 79.

Given the generalisation of the application of the principle, the CFSP dimension of counterterrorism is not immune from its effects.[56] It could thus be argued that the counterterrorism dimension of the CFSP, which the Court of Justice acknowledged in its 2012 pronouncement, entails positive obligations of support on the part of the Member States, and obligations to refrain from taking action that could jeopardize the fulfilment of EU tasks. Failure to comply with this duty would amount to a violation of the obligation of sincere cooperation, potentially leading to a judicial sanction.[57]

In sum, the exercise of CFSP competence, notably in the area of counterterrorism, is not immune from the application of the principles underpinning the EU legal order. These principles may not only entail constrains upon EU institutions while exercising CFSP competence, they can also increase the normative effects of CFSP instruments on the Member States.

5 Concluding Remarks

This paper has discussed the contribution of Articles 43 TEU and 215 TFEU to the EU's fight against terrorism. It was argued that, while codifying past practices, the two provisions underpin the strengthening of the CFSP dimension in the area. It was then suggested that more than a mere *PESCalisation*, they also contribute to a broader phenomenon of *hybridisation* of the EU's fight against terrorism, considering the simultaneous *communautarisation* of pre-Lisbon

56 Article 24(3) TEU does not appear to restrict the general obligation under Article 4(3) TEU to the CFSP domain, contrary to what is occasionally contended in view of the Treaties' insistence on the specificity of the CFSP and the non contamination clause of Article 40(2) TEU. The latter foresees that the exercise of EU non-CFSP competences set out in Articles 3–6 TFEU cannot affect the application of CFSP procedures. As the principle of sincere cooperation does not amount to an EU competence, the provisions of Article 40 TEU are of no relevance as regards the effects of Article 4(3) TEU.

57 See in this respect: Case C-266/03, *Commission* v *Luxembourg* [2005] ECR I-4805, para. 60 and Case C-433/03, *Commission* v *Germany* [2005] ECR I-6985, para. 66, Case C-246/07, *Commission v Sweden* [2010] ECR I-03317. Further see M. Cremona, "Case C-246/07, Commission v. Sweden (PFOS), Judgment of the Court of Justice (Grand Chamber) of 20 April 2010", *Common Market Law Review* 48, 2011, pp. 1639–1666; C. Hillion, "Mixity and coherence: The significance of the duty of cooperation", CLEER Working Papers 2/2009, available at: <http://www.asser.nl/upload/documents/9212009_14629clee09-2full.pdf> (accessed 1 June 2013).

Title VI TEU.[58] In view of the recent case law of the European Court of Justice, one might nevertheless wonder whether the strengthening of the CFSP dimension is offsetting the effects of such communautarisation, with resulting inter-institutional strife, and challenges to the coherence of the EU action in the field.[59] It is to be hoped that the tighter integration of the CFSP into the EU constitutional order, safeguarded by the Court, could help contain the implications of such a paradoxical development.

58 On third pillar instruments of EU counter-terrorism, see e.g. Council Framework Decision on Combating Terrorism (2002/475/JHA), *OJ*, 2002, L 164/3. On the interface between the former second and third pillars in the area of counter-terrorism, see E. Spaventa, "Fundamental Rights and the Interface between the Second and Third Pillars", in: A. Dashwood and M. Maresceau (eds.), *Law and Practice of EU External Relations. Salient Features of a Changing Landscape*, Cambridge: Cambridge University Press, pp. 129–151; C. Eckes, *EU Counter-terrorist policies and Fundamental Rights. The case of individual sanctions*, Oxford: Oxford University Press, 2009; A. Rosas, "Terrorist listings and the Rule of Law: The Role of EU Courts", *Robert Schuman Centre for Advanced Studies*, RSCAS 2011/31.

59 See e.g. P. van Elsuwege, "The adoption of "Targeted Sanctions" and the Potential for Inter-institutional Litigation after Lisbon", *Journal of Contemporary European Research* 7, 2011, p. 488.

CHAPTER 5

The Powers of the Council Concerning the Emergency of International Terrorism after the Judgment in Case C-130/10 *Parliament v. Council*

*Jenő Czuczai**

1 Introduction

After September 11, 2001 and the terrorist attack on the US World Trade Centre it can justifiably be stated that international terrorism has become a global emergency.[1] This has required a well-coordinated and in practical terms very effective response from the international community in the last decade at two levels, namely in the context of multilateral cooperation within the framework of the United Nations (especially in close synergy with the UN Chapter VII-based Sanctions regime) and, what is particularly relevant for the purposes of this contribution, at the level of the European Union as well.

It is widely discussed within the relevant scientific literature that the EU legal and institutional framework and the available legal tool-box for combating international terrorism were perhaps not developed sufficiently to effectively manage the globally unexpected and newly emergent situations and threats, in 2001 and 2002, caused by the new forms of international terrorism.[2] In particular the EU decision-making mechanisms, based on the former EU three-pillar structure as well as the pre-Lisbon rules on delimitation of powers of the relevant EU institutions could not provide the room for manoeuvre

* The views and opinions expressed in this contribution are strictly personal and exclusively those of the author and cannot be attributed at all to the Council or to its Legal Service. This manuscript was completed in March 2013.

1 For more detail see, for example, A. Antoniadis, R. Schütze and E. Spaventa (eds.), *The European Union and Global Emergencies*, Oxford: Hart Publishing, 2011, in particular Part II, Chapter V etc.

2 For more detail, see D. Spence (ed.), *The European Union and terrorism*, London: John Harper Publishing, 2007, in particular the introductory Part and Chapter I, pp. 1–53, or L. Benoit, *La PESC au lendemain des attentats du 11 septembre 2001*, available at: <http://generisfrance.free.fr/esgeaa/benoit0802.html> (accessed on 11 March 2013), in particular pp. 4 *et seq*. It should be added that the UN Sanctions regime should have also been reformed especially after 2008, see n. 3 below.

© KONINKLIJKE BRILL NV, LEIDEN, 2014 | DOI 10.1163/9789004268333_007

required by the EU to take all the necessary and effective restrictive measures (even so-called smart sanctions e.g. freezing of financial assets etc.) against all types of actors of international terrorism (including natural or legal persons and groups or even non-state entities, associated with international terrorist activities), while at the same time fully respecting all the requirements of fundamental rights' protection.

A striking element of this incomplete and fragmented legal environment was, for example, the legal basis issue (e.g. the necessary reference to ex Article 308 TEC when restrictive measures against terrorist-individuals or entities with no sufficient connection to a given third country were taken etc.).[3]

The other debated component was about the human rights protection questions relating to the administrative management of the necessary antiterrorist measures either of reactive nature, or of temporary precautionary nature, or of preventive nature in more general terms, following the emergency of international terrorist attacks or threats world-wide, taken at EU level as a rule and typically within a relatively short period of time (e.g. listing of terrorist-suspects etc).

This is exactly why, already in 2002–2003, the Convention and the 2003–2004 IGC working on the draft Treaty establishing a Constitution for Europe—and after the failed ratification of that Treaty, in 2007 the IGC working on the Lisbon Treaty, devoted particular attention to a better integrated, more consistent and coherent, and much clearer legal drafting of all the provisions dealing with restrictive measures as an EU response in combating international terrorism in the broader context of EU external action based on lessons learned from previous years' controversies in legal practice.

The purpose of this contribution, therefore, is to give a short summary of the results of this Treaty-making process in the light of the first leading judgment of the Court of Justice of the European Union (CJEU or the Court) in December 2009 on the most important provisions of the Lisbon Treaty determining the Council's powers with regard to the emergency of international terrorism.[4]

---

3 For more detail, see, for example, G. de Búrca, *The European Court of Justice and the International Legal Order after Kadi*, Jean Monnet Working Paper 01/2009, available at: <http://www.JeanMonnetProgramme.org> or P. van Elsuwege, "EU external action after the collapse of the pillar structure. In search of a new balance between delimitation and consistency", *CML Rev* 47 (4), 2010, pp. 987–1019 etc.

4 Except for Article 222(1)–(2) TFEU, which is dealt with in another contribution to this book as well as Article 43 TEU in connection with the EU Common Security and Defence Policy, which will not be addressed in my contribution either, although it provides that: "(EU civilian and military missions) *may contribute to the fight against terrorism, including by supporting*

My intention, however, is not to provide another detailed case-note on the judgment of the CJEU, handed down on 19 July 2012 in Case C-130/10 European Parliament v. Council (hereinafter: the Judgment), since this has already been done by other authors.[5] Rather, I would like to concentrate on putting this important Judgment into the context of an organic development of EU law over recent decades. This process has led to the current clear-cut legal framework of the EU counter-terrorism sanctions' regime and a stable judicial interpretation of Article 215 TFEU, in particular when the EU implements UN Security Council Resolutions relating to the multilateral cooperation and global reactions to threats, caused by international terrorism, and concrete terrorist activities endangering international peace and security.

Andrea Ott summarised the main message of the Judgment as follows:

> Case C-130/10 decided by the CJEU on 19 July 2012 is important in regard to two aspects covering EU external relations and institutional law. This is the first case since the Lisbon Treaty which analyses the revised and amended provisions on smart sanctions found in Article 215 TFEU and Article 75 TFEU. *Article 215 TFEU can be seen as a 'dinosaur' of intergovernmentalism in the TFEU. It merely foresees that the European Parliament must be informed during the legislative process and this is the only provision of its kind in the TFEU.*[6] This decision also explains, in the Post-Lisbon setting, the criteria for the choice of the correct legal basis. In a broader context, this ruling contributes to the debate on how the relationship between the CFSP and other external actions could develop after Lisbon, in the light of depillarization.[7] (emphasis added)

In this contribution, I would like to add some further aspects to an objective assessment of Article 215 TFEU and to prove that by its Judgment, although

third countries in combating terrorism in their territories", but this CSDP aspect would also go much beyond the scope of my chosen topic.

5 See, for example, A. Ott, *Case note* on Case C-130/10, *European Parliament v. Council of the European Union,* not yet reported, *Maastricht Journal* 19 (4), 2012, pp. 589–594 etc.

6 It should be mentioned that a similar provision can also be found in Article 222(3) TFEU in relation to the so-called Solidarity clause, where it is required that the European Parliament shall be informed about the Council Decision on the arrangements for the implementation by the Union of the solidarity clause, which can also relate to actions, carried out jointly by the Union and its Member States if a Member State is the object of a terrorist attack etc. Moreover, Article 218(10) TFEU provides the right of the EP to information in relation to the EU Treaty-making process as well.

7 *Op. cit.*, n. 5 above, p. 589.

within the merits of the case in question, the Court gave clear guidance on the proper interpretation of Article 215 TFEU, provided stability and continuity in legal practice and took into account even practical aspects in the context of full respect for international law and an effective and rapid implementation of international law obligations undertaken by the EU and its Member States in fighting globally against the emergency of international terrorism.

2 A Brief Analysis of the Case and the Main Questions, Raised by It from an Institutional (Delimitation of Powers) Point of View

In general, the Lisbon Treaty[8] has substantially strengthened and increased the powers of the European Parliament in EU decision-making and introduced the ordinary legislative procedure (or co-decision procedure) even into those policy fields where only the Council had powers to decide upon without any involvement of the European Parliament prior to 1 December 2009.[9] One of the existing legal bases, which switched to the ordinary legislative procedure[10] was Article 75(1) TFEU (ex Articles 60 and 301 TEC)[11] concerning the fight against terrorism and defining a framework for administrative measures on capital movements and payments, such as the freezing of funds, financial assets or economic gains belonging to, or owned or held by, natural or legal persons, groups or non-State actors. Precisely because of this change in institutional power-distribution, at the first possible opportunity, on 9 March 2010, the European Parliament brought the Council before the Court based on the reasoning that the Council had adopted a Regulation, after the entry into force of the Lisbon Treaty, in relation to the fight against international terrorism (instead of the new Article 75(1) TFEU legal basis) based on an incorrect legal basis, namely Article 215(2) TFEU, which requires merely informing the EP of a restrictive measure adopted only by the Council.

---

8 *OJ*, 2008, C 115/1.

9 See in more detail J.-C. Piris, *The Constitution for Europe—a legal analysis*, New York: Cambridge University Press, 2006, in particular pp. 90, 181 & 198–210.

10 See in more detail J.-C. Piris, *The Lisbon Treaty- a legal and political analysis*, New York, Cambridge University Press, 2010, in particular Appendix 4 on pp. 365–368.

11 It should be noted that in the consolidated version of the Lisbon Treaty (see n. 8 above), in my view in a misleading manner, at Article 75 TFEU, "ex Article 60 TEC" is stated in brackets, while at Article 215 TFEU, also in brackets "ex Article 301 TEC" is stated, thus giving the reader the impression that the two former TEC Articles have been 'transposed' into two different new Articles of the Lisbon Treaty! In my view, this is not true—see the reasoning given in Section 4 below.

In Case C-130/10, more concretely, the European Parliament was seeking the annulment of Council Regulation (EU) 1286/2009 of 22 December 2009 amending Regulation (EC) 881/2002 imposing certain specific restrictive measures directed against certain persons and entities associated with Usama Bin Laden, the Al-Qaeda network and the Taliban (hereinafter: the contested Regulation).[12]

The contested Regulation was adopted in December 2009 in order to comply with the requirements laid down by the previous judgment of the Court in Joined Cases C-402/05 P and C-415/05 P, *Kadi and Al Barakaat v. Council*,[13] concerning the procedure to be followed by the EU when giving effect to decisions of the 'Sanctions Committee' established by UN Security Council Resolution 1267 (1999). In particular, the contested Regulation introduced new provisions into Regulation (EC) 881/2002 which require the Commission to communicate to designated persons and entities the statements of reasons concerning them, as drawn up by the UN Sanctions Committee (right to motivation) and to give those persons and entities an opportunity to present observations on such statements (right to defence and right to be heard).[14]

In my view, the Court's ruling addresses important questions in the post-Lisbon legal context about: a) the relationship between the Treaty provisions on the EU's external action and those on the EU area of freedom, security and justice, with regard to the fight against international terrorism; b) the prerogatives of the European Parliament after the entry into force of the Lisbon Treaty in relation to the choice of legal basis for adopting restrictive measures in the context of fighting against international terrorism and by implementing related UN Security Council Resolutions; and finally c) the cumulation of legal bases and incompatibility of procedures (the ordinary legislative procedure and unanimity requirement within the Council in a two-stage special decision-making process).[15]

---

12 *OJ*, 2009, L 346/42.

13 See Joined Cases C-402/05 P and C-415/05 P, [2008] ECR I-6351.

14 See paras. 1–5 of the Judgment.

15 See paras. 10–41 of the Judgment. For the sake of completeness, it should still be mentioned that the Court also examined whether the procedural requirements, stemming from Article 215 TFEU, were met when the Council adopted the contested Regulation (see paras. 88–110 of the Judgment).

3 The Post-Lisbon EU Legal and Institutional Framework for Responding to International Terrorism as a Global Emergency and to Terrorist Threats to International Peace and Security

As mentioned above, the Lisbon Treaty has established a more coherent, better structured and more focused set of legal rules on restrictive measures, which provides a much more integrated legal approach concerning the external dimension of the EU counter-terrorism policy as well as giving much more legal clarity in terms of distribution of powers among EU institutions by better defining the applicable decision-making procedures. All this intention is more followable today from a Treaty-drafting point of view as well e.g. by having clearer titles to the related Chapters and Parts of the Treaties as well as by clearer objectives-settings, by introducing bridging provisions or cross-references into the interlinked Treaty provisions, or, for example, by having an *expressis verbis* exclusion clause, in which case a Treaty legal basis can simply not apply and finally by using coherent and logical legal terminology in a consistent manner in the related Treaty provisions.

In order to show the relationship between Article 75 TFEU and Article 215 TFEU as possible legal bases for EU counter-terrorism measures, the following 7 elements of the new Post-Lisbon EU legal and institutional settings could be highlighted in brief:

Firstly, the location of the two possible legal bases within the Lisbon Treaty clearly shows their different functional determination. Article 75(1)–(2) TFEU is located in Part III, Title V of the TFEU under the title of "Union policies and *internal actions*, Area of freedom, security and justice", while Article 215 TFEU can be found in Part V, Title IV of the TFEU under the heading of "*External actions* of the Union". It can therefore be seen that the Lisbon Treaty clearly distinguishes between internal and external actions of the EU when addressing a relevant Union policy area thus determining at the same time the main focus and the priorities of the related decision-making objectives and procedures.[16]

Secondly, it is important to stress that based on previous experiences and in order to make Article 215 TFEU the only legal basis which can be chosen for restrictive measures with an EU external action orientation, the Lisbon Treaty now clearly excludes the possibility that Article 352 TFEU (ex Article 308 TEC)

16 It should be noted that when the draft Treaty establishing a Constitution for Europe was drafted there was a clear intention to merge all provisions relating to EU external action and the related competences of the newly established office of the Union Minister for Foreign Affairs into one single Title in the Treaty, for more details see J.-C. Piris, *The Constitution, op. cit.*, n. 10 above, in particular pp. 94, 108 & 145–154.

could be used in any way as a legal basis for CFSP purposes. This is clear from Article 352(4) TFEU, which provides that: "*This Article cannot serve as a basis for attaining objectives pertaining to the CFSP* and any acts adopted pursuant to this Article shall respect the limits set out in Article 40, second paragraph, of the Treaty on European Union." (emphasis added)

Thirdly, the legal drafting technique for Article 215 TFEU—as opposed to that of Article 75 TFEU—clearly links that Article to Chapter 2 of Title V of the TEU in terms of a prior decision-making obligation under the EU CFSP, for the adoption of which EU foreign policy decision unanimity is required in the Council.[17] This "two stages decision-making procedure",[18] whereby first there shall be a CFSP decision, adopted under Chapter 2 of Title V of the TEU, which defines the overall foreign policy objectives of the measure and, thereafter, the more detailed technical rules are adopted already in a Council legal act, based on Article 215 TFEU, shall apply to both types of restrictive measure, namely to those adopted against third countries, but also to those, adopted against natural or legal persons and groups or non-state entities.

Fourthly, it should be noted that while Article 75 TFEU makes its objectives[19] and thus its scope of application clear at the beginning of the Article,[20]

17 Article 215 TFEU provides that: "(1) *Where a decision,* adopted in accordance with Chapter 2 of Title V of the Treaty on European Union, *provides for an interruption or reduction,* in part or completely, *of economic and financial relations with one or more third countries,* the Council, acting by a qualified majority on a joint proposal from the High Representative of the Union for Foreign Affairs and Security Policy and the Commission, shall adopt the *necessary measures. It shall inform the European Parliament thereof.* (2) *Where a decision,* adopted in accordance with Chapter 2 of Title V of the Treaty on European Union *so provides,* the Council *may adopt restrictive measures* under the procedure referred to in paragraph 1 *against natural or legal persons and groups or non-State entities.* (3) The acts referred to in this Article shall include necessary provisions on legal safeguards". (emphasis added)

18 See in more detail G. M. Zagel, "Article 215 TFEU on Restrictive measures", in: H. Smith and P. Herzog (Eds.), *The Law of the European Union,* LexisNexis, 2010 Wien, pp. 215/1–215/25, in particular 215/3 *et seq.*

19 It is interesting perhaps to note that when Article 3(2) TEU defines the Union's aims in more general terms in relation to the area of freedom, security and justice etc, it refers only to "the prevention and combating of crime", without any specific reference to the fight against international terrorism.

20 Article 75 TFEU provides that: "(1) *Where necessary to achieve the objectives set out in Article 67, as regards preventing and combating terrorism and related activities,* the European Parliament and the Council, acting by means of regulations in accordance with the ordinary legislative procedure, *shall define a framework for administrative measures* with regard to capital movements and payments, such as the freezing of funds, financial assets or economic gains belonging to, or owned or held by, natural or legal persons,

Article 215 TFEU in this respect needs to be read together with Article 205 TFEU, which is a bridging provision in Part Five, Title I TFEU under the title of 'General provisions on the Union's external action'. It provides that: "The Union's action *on the international scene*, pursuant to this Part, shall be guided by the principles, *pursue the objectives* and be conducted in accordance with the general provisions laid down in *Chapter 1 of Title V of the Treaty on European Union*." (emphasis added)

In Chapter 1 of Title V TEU under Article 21(2) points (b)–(c) the Treaty-makers made it absolutely clear that one of the main objectives of EU external actions shall be a high degree of cooperation in all fields of international relations in order to preserve international peace and security *inter alia* in accordance with all the UN Charter requirements and with full respect for international law etc. This is a bit of a complicated legal drafting solution. It is, however, coherent and makes it incontestable that Article 215 TFEU is an inherent part of a well-integrated and consistent common set of Treaty provisions on the EU external action framework.[21]

Fifthly, in order to make the EU external action-related legal basis, namely Article 215(2) TFEU, distinct and self-standing and the only appropriate and sufficient legal basis for the adoption of restrictive measures against natural or legal persons and groups and non-State entities in this context, the Treaty-makers opted for a decision-making procedure (merely requiring the informing of the Parliament as well as a prior CFSP decision by the Council acting unanimously), which is procedurally incompatible with Article 75 TFEU, which provides for use of the ordinary legislative procedure. This means that these two Treaty legal bases cannot be used together for the adoption of any Union measure or legal act.[22]

Sixthly, another important legal drafting distinction, which should be noted, is that Article 215 TFEU uses the legal terms "necessary measures" and "restrictive measures", which are of a more operational and individual nature, as well as more reactive (or precautionary) to the emergency of a concrete terrorist threat at international level (when human lives are in danger and, therefore, quick and operative actions must be carried out). This is by contrast to the

---

groups or non-State entities. (2) The Council, *on a proposal from the Commission*, shall adopt measures to implement the framework referred to in the first paragraph. (3) The acts referred to in this Article shall include necessary provisions on legal safeguards". (emphasis added)

21 For a full explanation of this sophisticated Treaty-drafting solution see J.-C. Piris, *The Lisbon Treaty, op. cit.*, n. 10 above, in particular pp. 242–243 as well as Article 21(3) TEU.

22 This intention of the Treaty-makers was confirmed by the Court in paras. 48–49 of the Judgment as well.

more general terminology, used in Article 75 TFEU with regard to the ordinary legislative procedure, namely "definition of the framework for administrative measures". This expression is rather about a legislative framework of general application, more of a preventive nature, while when concrete "measures" shall be adopted in order to implement the established "general administrative framework", then the Council already remains the only decision-maker even under Article 75 TFEU.[23]

Seventh, a further important legal drafting specificity in the context of establishing a more coherent legal framework for the external dimension of EU counter-terrorism actions (or in more general terms concerning the integrated EU external action policy) is that the role of the High Representative of the Union for CFSP is consistently underlined in the relevant Treaty provisions when addressing the right to initiate. That is also the reason why in Article 215 TFEU the decision-making procedure shall be always based "on a joint proposal from the High Representative of the Union for Foreign Affairs and Security Policy and the Commission",[24] while in Article 75 TFEU the decision-making process is always initiated only "on a proposal from the Commission". This difference clearly shows that the later Treaty legal basis is not designed for serving EU external action purposes.

4 Commenting on the Judgment and Summarising Its Impact from an Emergency Governance Point of View

When deciding on the subject Case C-130/10 on 19 July 2012, the CJEU simply reaffirmed its long-standing case law on the choice of legal basis for the adoption of a Union measure[25] as well as its doctrine of incompatibility of

23 The Lisbon Treaty uses this legal drafting distinction between "common framework measures" versus "concrete implementing measures" when defining the powers of the EU institutions and the applicable decision-making procedures in other policy areas as well, for example: Article 43(2) versus Article 43(3) TFEU, Article 207(2) TFEU or 214(3) TFEU etc. One could even submit, although in my view it still requires further research, that typically the more operational decision-making (adoption of measures of implementing, operational or individual nature), in particular, when there is an emergency, is conferred in the Treaty on the Council in the pre-Lisbon intergovernmental pillars' fields so, for example, today in the fields of EU external actions or area of freedom, security and justice instead of having the time-consuming ordinary legislative procedure.

24 See paras. 104–105 of the Judgment in relation to the relevance of a joint proposal under Article 215 TFEU.

25 See Case C-155/07, *Parliament v. Council* [2008] ECR I-8103, paras. 34 *et seq* and paras. 42 *et seq* of the Judgment.

procedures, laid down in the 'Titanium dioxide' jurisprudence.[26] This means that the Court first of all and primarily examined the purpose and the content of the contested Regulation from the point of view of whether the measure in question serves to maintain international peace and security regardless of the precise geographical location or the scope of the terrorist threat at stake or, whether it rather serves to combat international terrorism and the financing of terrorism by cutting off the financial resources of terrorist groups and individuals by freezing the financial and economic funds etc. of persons suspected of involvement in activities linked to terrorism or associated with "external terrorism" etc.

4.1 *The Summary of the Judgment*

The Court ruled that the contested Regulation (EU) 1286/2009 was correctly based on Article 215(2) TFEU, since it is aimed at natural and legal persons etc., involved in acts of terrorism and who, "*having regard to their activities globally and to the international dimension of the threat they pose, affect fundamentally the Union's external activity*".[27]

The Court first of all recalled that Regulation (EC) 881/2002, which the contested Regulation amended, was adopted on the basis of ex-Articles 60, 301 and 308 TEC, and it noted that the content of ex-Articles 60 and 301 TEC is currently reflected in Article 215 TFEU. With regard to the scope of Article 215(2) TFEU, which refers to "*restrictive measures… against natural or legal persons and groups*", the Court observed that there is nothing in this provision to suggest that it cannot cover the combating of terrorism. The Court acknowledged that the combating of terrorism and its financing may also come within the objectives of the EU area of freedom, security and justice, but it considered that: "the objective of combating international terrorism and its financing in order to preserve international peace and security corresponds, nevertheless, to the objectives of the Treaty provisions on external action by the Union."

In this respect, it specifically referred to Article 21(2)(c) TEU, which stipulates that: "The Union… shall work for a high degree of cooperation in all fields of international relations, in order to… preserve peace, prevent conflicts and strengthen international security, in accordance with the principles and purposes of the United Nations Charter."[28]

In further detailing the UN link, the Court recalled that Regulation (EC) 881/2002, which the contested Regulation amended, was adopted by the EU in

26 See Case C-300/89, *Commission v. Council*, [1991] ECR I-2867, paras. 17–21 and paras. 45 *et seq* of the Judgment.

27 See para. 78 of the Judgment.

28 See paras. 51–52 and 60–61 of the Judgment.

order to put into effect an action decided upon by the UN Security Council under Chapter VII of the UN Charter with a view to preserving international peace and security, since terrorism involving persons and entities associated with Al Qaeda clearly being a phenomenon of the emergency of international terrorist threats. The Court still observed that the contested Regulation falls within the same line of action by supplementing Regulation (EC) 881/2002 aimed at reconciling the fight against international terrorism with respect for fundamental rights. It added, furthermore, that together with Common Position 2002/402/CFSP, Regulation (EC) 881/2002 as amended thus establishes a system of interaction between the UN Security Council and the aims of the European Union CFSP.[29]

The Court, therefore, concluded that: "Given that terrorism constitutes a threat to international peace and security, the object of actions undertaken by the Union in the sphere of the CFSP, and the measures taken in order to give effect to that policy in the Union's external actions, in particular, restrictive measures for the purpose of Article 215(2) TFEU, can be to combat terrorism."

It also added that in so far as Articles 75 and 215 TFEU relate to different EU policies that pursue objectives which, although complementary, do not have the same scope, Article 75 TFEU cannot be considered as a more specific legal basis (*lex specialis*) than Article 215(2) TFEU.[30]

The Court emphasised that although the use of Article 215(2) TFEU had significant consequences as far as the role of the Parliament is concerned, this could not affect the choice of legal basis, which must only rest on objective factors amenable to judicial review. It includes the examination of the aim and the content of the measure. In this respect, the Court stressed: "that fact (namely the fact of the institutional consequences) cannot, however, determine the choice of legal basis... it is not procedures that define the legal basis of a measure but the legal basis of a measure that determines the procedures to be followed in adopting that measure."

It still added that: "the difference between Article 75 TFEU and Article 215 TFEU, so far as the Parliament's involvement is concerned, is the result of the choice made by the framers of the Treaty of Lisbon conferring a more limited role on the Parliament with regard to the Union's action under the CFSP."

Equally, the Court did not follow the Parliament's argument that measures directly affecting the fundamental rights of individuals cannot be adopted under a procedure excluding the Parliament's participation. It observed that: "the duty to respect fundamental rights is imposed, in accordance with

29 See paras. 67 and 70–71 of the Judgment.

30 See paras. 63 & 66 of the Judgment.

Article 51(1) of the Charter of the Fundamental Rights of the European Union, on all the institutions and bodies of the Union. In addition, under both Article 75 TFEU and Article 215/3/ TFEU, the acts referred to in those articles are to include necessary provisions on legal safeguards."[31]

4.2 *Some Comments on the Judgment from an Emergency Governance Point of View*

First of all, I fully agree with the Judgment and also with its reasoning to which I would add two additional comments, which, in my view, further strengthen the Court's final conclusion in the subject case from the view-point of daily legal practice.

Firstly, I think that it is worth going back to the original wording of ex Article 228a of the Maastricht Treaty, which inserted into the Treaty the predecessor text of Article 215 TFEU. This Article number thereafter changed to ex Article 301 TEC under the Amsterdam Treaty, with no further changes under the Nice Treaty. The text of ex Article 301 TEC stipulated that: "Where it is provided, in a common position or in a joint action adopted according to the provisions of the Treaty on European Union relating to the common foreign and security policy, for an action by the Community to interrupt or to reduce, in part or completely, economic relations with one or more third countries, the Council shall take the *necessary urgent* measures. The Council shall act by a qualified majority on a proposal from the Commission".[32] (emphasis added)

Interestingly, the word "urgent" does not appear in the current wording of Article 215 TFEU despite the fact that historically and taking into account practical developments in relation to the use of economic sanctions in the last 20 years it has always been clear—as Gudrun Monika Zagel underlines—that:

> Article 301 provides *for a simplified procedure allowing a quick reaction to foreign policy events* and the imposition of sanctions by the Community.... *In order to speed up the adoption of the decision, the European Parliament has not been given a role in the decision-making process.* Furthermore, economic sanctions are always enacted through regulations, which don't require implementation by the Member States and are

31 See paras. 79–83 of the Judgment.

32 It should be noted that in ex Article 60(1) TEC there was also reference to "the necessary *urgent* measures", specifically: "If, in the cases envisaged in Article 301, action by the Community is deemed necessary, the Council may, in accordance with the procedure provided for in Article 301, take the *necessary urgent* measures on the movement of capital and on payments as regards the third countries concerned". (emphasis added).

applicable directly and *immediately* after their publication in the Official Journal."[33] (emphasis added)

I think that in the context of today's world, for the purposes of managing the global emergency of international terrorism effectively at EU level, the Court properly interpreted Article 215 TFEU in its Judgment from an 'interpretatio legis historica' point of view as well.

The second practical comment on the Judgment relates to the *traveaux préparatoires* of the ex Article III-219 (ex Article 31) of the draft Treaty establishing a Constitution for Europe (the predecessor of Article 215 TFEU) and the relevance of the 2002–2003 Convention documents in this respect.

It is clear from the Convention documents[34] that it was always the intention to merge ex Articles 60 and 301 TEC into one Article in the course of the Treaty-revision process and clearly within the context of external relations (which resulted finally in Article 215 TFEU) by including a reference to "economic and *financial* relations" in the operative part of the given Treaty provision on restrictive measures. This historical research of the former Treaty-drafting process of the 2002–2003 Convention fully confirms the same conclusion of the Judgment in this respect in paragraph 52 and further justifies the Court's correct interpretation on the well-integrated and coherent set of common rules in the Lisbon Treaty on the EU external policy approach towards fighting against international terrorism.

4.3 *The Impact of the Judgment on the Powers of the Council Concerning the Emergency of International Terrorism*

In order to properly assess the impact of the Judgment on the effective EU governance of the emergency of international terrorism, it should be noted that the number of EU restrictive measures (sanctions) either in the form of Regulations, adopted based on Article 215 TFEU or of decisions, adopted in the framework of the EU CFSP is constantly and steadily increasing.[35] The most

---

33 See G. M. Zagel, *Article 215 TFEU on Restrictive measures, op. cit.*, n. 18 above, p. 215/3 *et seq.* On the other hand, Zagel welcomes the fact that the previously existing practice whereby the European Parliament shall be informed about the economic sanctions is now codified in the Treaty, with which I fully agree, see *op. cit.*, n. 18 p. 215/17, point (iii).

34 See CONV 821/03 p. 132., CONV 729/03 p. 132 (together with footnotes 56–57), CONV 727/03 p. 54 at point VIII. and p. 73, finally CONV 685/03 p. 8 and p. 63. See also G. M. Zagel, *Article 215 TFEU on Restrictive measures, op. cit.*, n. 18 above, p. 215/6 at point 215.04(2).

35 For an updated List of Union sanctions see <http://europa.eu.int/comm./external_relations/cfsp/sanctions/measures.htm> (last update was on 21.2.2013), which also

recently updated list of the subject restrictive measures (only the references) is almost 100 pages, of which almost 30 pages cover restrictive measures against terrorist organisations, natural and legal persons, groups or non-State entities etc. (including implementation measures by the EU of UN terrorist listing decisions).[36] For this reason the Judgment should be considered, in my view, as a landmark decision of the Court providing stability and continuity in the EU legal order and efficiency in the given EU external action policy areas. In this respect, the impact of the Judgment is forward-looking and, indeed, important.

5 Conclusions

By virtue of the Judgment the CJEU has clearly clarified and strengthened the powers of the Council within the context of the EU governance of the global emergency of international terrorism in terms of the adoption of EU external action-driven effective restrictive measures against all type of actors of international terrorist activities. It gave a coherent and consistent description of the post-Lisbon legal and institutional setting in this respect.

On the other hand, one could perhaps legitimately submit that the Court might have still left some related questions open. In particular regarding the *effet utile* of Article 75 TFEU "*when necessary to achieve the objectives set out in Article 67, as regards preventing and combating terrorism and related activities*", with a view to the EU primarily ensuring its own internal security against the threats of terrorism through adopting EU rules on autonomous financial restrictive measures or by virtue of any other means than adopting restrictive measures in the context of EU external action and with the clear-cut aim of implementing UN Security Council Resolutions, based on Chapter VII of the UN Charter, because for the latter purpose the appropriate legal basis after Lisbon is undoubtedly Article 215 TFEU.[37]

---

includes the Commission implementing legal acts, adopted based on Article 7(1)a and 7a(5) of Regulation (EC) 881/2002 as amended (accessed on 11 March 2013).

36 See *op. cit.*, n. 35 above, pp. 64–91.

37 See in this respect the Opinion of *AG Bot*, delivered on 31 January 2012 in the subject case, in particular paras. 79–82. A good occasion for the Court to further develop its jurisprudence in the given field is provided in Case C-658/11 *Parliament v. Council*, which pending case is also about a choice of proper legal basis for EU external action, but concerning the conclusion of international agreements etc., see in more detail *OJ*, 2012 C 58/6.

CHAPTER 6

L'union fait la Force: Making the Most of the Solidarity Clause (Article 222 TFEU)

Steven Blockmans

1 Introduction

In recent decades natural and man-made disasters have increased in frequency and scale, and a further increase is expected with the aggravation of climate change. Pollution and contamination issues pose long-term threats to public health and the environment, including agriculture and the food supply. The EU's 2010 Internal Security Strategy points out that serious and complex security threats, from armed attacks to terrorism to natural disasters to cyber-attacks, can easily overwhelm the capacities of any single EU Member State. These threats have long called for improvements to EU crisis and disaster management practices in terms of efficiency and coherence: "They require both solidarity in immediate response and responsibility in prevention and preparedness with an emphasis on better risk assessment and risk management at EU level of all potential hazards."[1]

For the first time in its history, the EU's constituent treaties now include a so-called 'solidarity clause' to address the above-mentioned concerns. Laid down in Article 222 of the Treaty on the Functioning of the European Union (TFEU), this article imposes an explicit obligation upon the Union and its Member States to act jointly, 'in a spirit of solidarity', if a Member State is the object of a terrorist attack or the victim of a natural or man-made disaster. Although closely related, this particular strand of the 'three-musketeer' principle is not to be confused with the 'mutual defence clause', enshrined in Article 42(7) of the Treaty on European Union (TEU). Yet, like the EU constitutional paradigm of solidarity, the precise meaning of the solidarity clause has yet to be fully assessed.[2] Arguably, 'solidarity' is in the eye of the beholder:

---

1 Communication from the Commission to the European Parliament and the Council, "The EU Internal Security Strategy in Action: Five steps towards a more secure Europe", COM(2010) 673 final, 22 November 2010.

2 See S. Myrdal and M. Rhinard, "The European Union's Solidarity Clause: Empty Letter or Effective Tool? An Analysis of Article 222 of the Treaty on the Functioning of the European Union", *UI Occasional Papers* 2, 2012. See also T. Konstadinides, "Civil Protection Cooperation

© KONINKLIJKE BRILL NV, LEIDEN, 2014 | DOI 10.1163/9789004268333_008

> for some, solidarity is measured by how much support flows to a country in need. For others, solidarity means everyone doing their own 'homework' to avoid the need for assistance in the first place. Still others believe that solidarity against today's risks and threats is best pursued outside of EU frameworks.[3]

It is perhaps due to these conceptual differences that the practical implementation of the solidarity clause has lagged behind. Indeed, one can observe a certain neglect which has befallen the clause, in spite of terrorist activities (cf. the 2012 bombing of a bus with Israeli tourists in Burgas), ash clouds (cf. the fall-out from the explosion of Iceland's Eyjafjallajokull volcano in 2010 and 2012), chemical spills (cf. 2010 red sludge spill in Hungary), forest fires (e.g. in Portugal in 2012) and pandemics (cf. outbreak of swine flu at the end of 2009) which have overwhelmed national emergency capacities since the Lisbon Treaty entered into force.[4] Additionally, in the absence of any judicial interpretation derived from case law, we can only speculate about the solidarity clause's implications for both EU institutions and Member States. However, now that solidarity in cases of emergency has been established on a solid legal basis in the TFEU, differences about its interpretation should be reconciled so as to promote the implementation of the clause. This chapter offers a guide to the origins of the solidarity clause (Section 2), a legal commentary on Article 222 TFEU (Section 3), a contextual interpretation of the Article (Section 4), an anthology of challenges for its implementation and some suggestions as to how to overcome them (Section 5). Section 6 will draw some conclusions.

2 Travaux Préparatoires

The origins of Article 222 TFEU can be traced back to the European Convention on the future for Europe. Working group VIII on defence considered two types of solidarity. The first was a 'mutual defence clause',[5] which was intended to

in EU Law: Is There Room for Solidarity to Wriggle Past?", *European Law Journal* 19, 2013, pp. 267–282.

3 Myrdal and Rhinard, *op. cit.*, n. 1. For essays on the rhetoric and reality of the constitutional paradigm in EU law, see the contributions to M. Ross and Y. Borgmann-Prebil (eds.), *Promoting Solidarity in the European Union*, Oxford: OUP, 2010.

4 In other domains too, in particular that of the single currency, intra-EU 'solidarity' has been tested to its core.

5 See Section 4.1 below. Although some policy-makers and academics refer to Article 42(7) TEU as the 'mutual assistance clause', both a textual interpretation (cf. "armed aggression") and a contextual one (cf. the position of the clause among the specific provisions on CSDP in

commit EU Member States in showing solidarity in the event of 'armed aggression' against one or more of them, similar to the provision in the WEU Treaty which some hoped to incorporate into the Constitutional Treaty,[6] without prejudice to either "the specific character of the security and defence policy of certain Member States" or existing NATO relationships (cf. Article 42(7) TEU).

The second form of solidarity would bind Member States together in an obligation to respond to a range of other (non-conventional) threats. With September 11, 2001 fresh in their minds, some members of the Convention felt that a mutual defence clause could not, and would not, mobilise the full range of crisis and disaster response capacities available to the EU.[7] A broad solidarity approach, it was believed, would distinguish the EU from a military defence alliance.[8] The advocates of a stronger role for the EU in managing unintentional disasters, both man-made and natural, fought hard to see these types of threats covered by a solidarity clause. Spurred by the March 2004 terrorist attacks in Madrid, the European Council adopted a draft version of the working group's solidarity clause, albeit one very much premised on counter-terrorism, in the form of a 'Declaration on Combating Terrorism' and matching action plan.[9] The Declaration refers to the spirit enshrined in the precursor to

Section 2 of Chapter 2 of Title V TEU) leads this author to believe that the more popularly used term 'mutual defence' is in fact the most apt one to describe the character of the clause, even if the nature of the response need not be military. This reading gains extra weight in view of the announcement, on 31 March 2010, by the 10 founding members of the Western European Union that, with the adoption of the Lisbon Treaty, they had decided to terminate the modified 1954 Brussels Treaty. Additionally, the first part of Article 42(7) TEU bears remarkable resemblances to the mutual defence clause in Article V of the modified Brussels Treaty. The WEU's remaining 'sleeper' cells were incorporated into the EU's crisis management structures. See further <http://www.europarl.europa.eu/ftu/pdf/en/FTU_6.1.3.pdf> (last accessed on 19 July 2013).

6 The WEU Council facilitated this ambition of the EU by deciding "to prepare the WEU legacy and the inclusion of those functions of the WEU, which will be deemed necessary by the EU to fulfil its new responsibilities in the area of crisis-management tasks". See WEU Ministerial Council, Luxembourg Declaration, 23 November 1999.

7 Myrdal and Rhinard, *op. cit.*, n. 1, with reference to the Final report of the WG VIII—Defence, CONV 461/02, Brussels, 16 December 2002, at pp. 20–21.

8 *Ibid.* Commission representatives argued that there was no need for definitions, as this would be too constraining on the implementation of the solidarity clause, especially in view of the different levels of preparedness of Member States. Some MEPs, on the other hand, wanted clear definitions. See further below.

9 Available at: <http://www.consilium.europa.eu/uedocs/cmsUpload/DECL-25.3.pdf> (last accessed on 19 July 2013).

Article 222 TFEU[10] and sets out the commitment of the Member States, as well as the acceding countries, to act jointly in cases where one of them becomes the victim of a terrorist attack.[11] The Madrid bombings had a catalytic effect that led the working group on defence to forward its recommendations for an expanded solidarity clause (covering natural and man-made disasters) to the plenary session, which approved the new provision.

As Myrdal and Rhinard describe, the process of reflection and treaty revision which followed the rejection of the Constitutional Treaty by France and the Netherlands did not affect the wording of the solidarity clause, with one exception: "a joint declaration, originally formulated in the Solidarity Declaration, was added to the clause to give Member States more latitude in deciding how they would provide assistance."[12] The Member States' core legal obligations, i.e. to act jointly and to assist fellow Member States, remained unchanged.

3 Legal Commentary

The first paragraph of Article 222 TFEU reads as follows:

> The Union and its Member States shall act jointly in a spirit of solidarity if a Member State is the object of a terrorist attack or the victim of a natural or man-made disaster. The Union shall mobilise all the instruments at its disposal, including the military resources made available by the Member States, to:

10 Articles I-43 and III-329 of the Treaty establishing a Constitution for Europe, *OJ*, 2004, C 310. For an early critique on the legal geography of the solidarity clause in the Constitutional Treaty, see K. Lenaerts and D. Gerard, "The Structure of the Union According to the Constitution for Europe: The Emperor Is Getting Dressed", *European Law Review* 29, 2004, pp. 289–322, at p. 316.

11 There is also the following clarification: "It shall be for each Member State or acceding State to the Union to choose the most appropriate means to comply with this solidarity commitment towards the affected State".

12 Myrdal and Rhinard, *op. cit.*, n. 1, with reference to Declaration No. 37 on Article 222 of the Treaty on the Functioning of the European Union reads: "Without prejudice to the measures adopted by the Union to comply with its solidarity obligation towards a Member State which is the object of a terrorist attack or the victim of natural or man-made disaster, none of the provisions of Article 222 is intended to affect the right of another Member State to choose the most appropriate means to comply with its own solidarity obligation towards that Member State".

(a) – prevent the terrorist threat in the territory of the Member States;
– protect democratic institutions and the civilian population from any terrorist attack;
– assist a Member State in its territory, at the request of its political authorities, in the event of a terrorist attack;

(b) assist a Member State in its territory, at the request of its political authorities, in the event of a natural or man-made disaster.

The first sentence of paragraph 1 defines the types of events covered by the solidarity clause: terrorist attacks, natural and man-made disasters. This broad formulation allows for sufficient flexibility as regards the types of attacks and disasters for which the clause may be triggered and ensures that no significant calamities, such as attacks in cyberspace, pandemics or energy shortages, are overlooked.[13] In the same vein, the provision can be activated when one or more Member States are the victim of an attack or disaster, as long as the situation overwhelms the capacities of the affected Member State(s) or requires a multi-sector response involving a number of actors. Conversely, if the wording and structure of the solidarity clause are to be taken literally, then the prevention and protection provisions apply only to counter-terrorism.[14]

The first sentence also states that the Union and its Members States "shall act jointly in a spirit of solidarity" when a Member State is hit by an attack or disaster. This mandatory formulation emphasises the shared responsibility of EU institutions and Member States, and thereby gives the solidarity clause a character which supersedes the intergovernmental obligation of the 'mutual defence clause'. The remainder of paragraph 1 uses the same mandatory language to oblige 'the Union', i.e. the institutions and bodies of the EU, to

13 By using this broad remit of the solidarity clause, Article 222 TFEU could serve as an additional legal basis in developing new legislative proposals in a number of specific areas. It is not at all certain that Article 222 TFEU on its own could serve as a legal basis for the development of new legislative proposals that aim at protecting civilian populations through cooperation. See also Konstadinides, *op. cit.*, n. 1 p. 275.

14 Myrdal and Rhinard, *op. cit.*, n. 1 have pointed out that the first and second indents of Article 222(1)(a) TFEU imply actions ahead of an attack, but how far in advance is a question open to interpretation. A restrictive interpretation would suggest that these duties apply only to the immediate moments before an unfolding attack (e.g. intervention teams to stop the attack). It may be suggested that these duties apply also to increased protection of critical infrastructures, enhanced intelligence cooperation, advanced protocols for police cooperation, and capacity for quicker deployment of EU military missions.

"mobilise all the instruments at its disposal, including the military resources made available by the Member States".

The reference to 'all Union instruments' implies the EU's own institutional tools, mechanisms, and resources related to attacks and disasters. In this context, one might think of the kind of assistance provided for in Article 4 of Regulation (EU) No 230/2014 establishing an instrument contributing to stability and peace , i.e. assistance in the context of 'stable conditions for cooperation': situations of crisis not amounting to (emerging) military crisis. The focus is on different kinds of assistance, i.e. (i) assistance in the pursuit of strengthening the capacity of law enforcement and judicial and civil authorities involved in the fight against terrorism and organised crime, including illicit trafficking of people, drugs, firearms and explosive materials and in the effective control of illegal trade and transit; (ii) support for measures to address threats to international transport, energy operations and critical infrastructure, including passenger and freight traffic and energy distribution; (iii) contributing to ensuring an adequate response to sudden major threats to public health, such as epidemics with a potential trans-national impact; (iv) support for risk mitigation and preparedness relating to chemical, biological, radiological and nuclear materials or agents; and (v) support for pre- and post-crisis capacity building. Arguably, much of this represents national resources deployed through European means.[15] Thus, the phrase in the second sentence of paragraph 1 suggests that the EU institutions must be capable of drawing upon instruments in a coherent, coordinated, and effective fashion.[16]

This is certainly the case for the 'military resources made available by Member States' mentioned in Article 222(1) second sentence TFEU. There are several likely scenarios for the use of military capabilities in relation to the solidarity clause, for example for large-scale disaster clean-up or the protection of civilian populations outside the framework of the EU's Common Security and Defence Policy (CSDP).[17] In this respect, the implementation of the solidarity clause is likely to put additional pressure on the Union and its Member States to consider how to coordinate and combine the Commission's civil protection

---

15 See EP Committee on Foreign Affairs, Rapporteur Ioan Mircea Pascu, Report of 9 August 2012 on the EU's mutual defence and solidarity clauses: political and operational dimensions (2012/2223(INI)), at p. 16.

16 See Section 5.1, below.

17 One particular scenario for the use of military resources is the kind of assistance provided for in Articles 3 and 6 of Regulation (EU) No 230/2014 establishing an instrument contributing to stability and peace, i.e. assistance in the context of unstable conditions for cooperation, in response to situations of (emerging) military crisis.

coordination capacities with the use of the EEAS's civilian crisis management structures and military resources.[18]

In the elaboration of the kinds of situations in which the European Union, its institutions, bodies and agencies, are held to provide assistance, the focus is first on counter-terrorism. In ascending order, paragraph 1a specifies that the EU shall mobilise all the instruments and resources at its disposal to prevent terrorist threats in the territories of Member States, to "protect democratic institutions and the civilian population from terrorist attack", and to "assist a Member State in its territory, at the request of its political authorities" after a terrorist attack. Paragraph 1b then turns the focus to natural and man-made disasters (other than terrorist attacks), specifying that the EU is obliged to respond to a request of the political authorities of a Member State by using all the instruments and resources at its disposal to assist that stricken state in its territory. Without doubt, in all four cases identified in paragraph 1, the Union acts under the auspices of the political authorities of the Member State in question.[19]

18 The upcoming revision of the Headline Goals will also need to account for these implications of the solidarity clause. Additionally, in the field of chemical, biological, radiological, nuclear (CBRN) policy, close cooperation between Member States and coordination at EU level is a necessity. The EU Civil Protection Mechanism is currently the appropriate instrument for dealing with CBRN disasters. An EU CBRN Action Plan (COM(2009) 273 final, 24 June 2009), could offer an opportunity to enable the EU and its Member States to find the legislative means to effectively implement the solidarity clause in this specific area. As described in MEP Ana Gomes' Draft Report on strengthening chemical, biological, radiological and nuclear security in the European Union, Doc. 2010/2114(INI), such an Action Plan could also facilitate "the efficient interaction of national and EU initiatives in addressing CBRN risks and in preparing the necessary responses, enhancing both 'horizontal' coordination between the Commission and Member States and 'vertical' coordination between the EU-level instruments and Member States' instruments, in order to increase the effectiveness and speed of information sharing, the exchange of best practices, analytical reporting at all stages, joint planning, the development of operational procedures, operational exercises and the cost-effective pooling of existing resources". To this end, the EU's civil protection capacity should include infrastructures and capabilities, as well as strategic cooperation with the EDA, ESA, IAEA, OPCW and other international CBRN centres or programmes of excellence. In this context, dual-use civil-military technologies could also be exploited as a source to create synergies.

19 Formally consent is not required in all 4 situations described in para. 1, but consent to act in the territory of a Member State to prevent a terrorist attack and to protect democracy would nevertheless be required under public international law.

Whereas paragraph 1 of the solidarity clause places the onus on EU-level responses to natural, terrorist-induced or other man-made disasters, paragraph 2 addresses the Member States:

> Should a Member State be the object of a terrorist attack or the victim of a natural or man-made disaster, the other Member States shall assist it at the request of its political authorities. To that end, the Member States shall coordinate between themselves in the Council.

The provision prescribes that Member States make assistance available, in addition to acting jointly with EU institutions. However, this former obligation kicks in only upon the express invitation of the political authorities of the affected Member State. In practice, the 'duty to assist' should nevertheless be interpreted as also imposing a 'duty to be prepared to assist', as the meaning of offering immediate crisis response within the framework of Article 222 TFEU would otherwise be rendered meaningless. The solidarity clause should also raise the profile of EU coordination and cooperation in crisis and disaster response, both for national governments and in the eyes of the public. This, in turn, should force national governments to take a more principled stance on such issues. Free-riders should not be allowed.[20] This is not to say that Member States should duplicate each other's state-of-the-art response capabilities. Coordination is the name of the game.[21] The mandatory tone of the first sentence of paragraph 2 is couched in the softer language of Declaration No. 37 attached to the treaties, which allows each Member State that is requested to offer assistance to choose the most appropriate means available to it without reneging on its solidarity obligation towards the stricken Member State:

> Without prejudice to the measures adopted by the Union to comply with its solidarity obligation towards a Member State which is the object of a terrorist attack or the victim of natural or man-made disaster, none of the provisions of Article 222 is intended to affect the right of another Member

20 See EP Committee on Foreign Affairs, Rapporteur Ioan Mircea Pascu, Report of 9 August 2012 on the EU's mutual defence and solidarity clauses: political and operational dimensions (2012/2223(INI)), at p. 15: "Stresses the need to prevent any moral hazard, in that some Member States may be tempted to excessively rely on the solidarity of others while under-investing in their own security and disaster response capabilities; emphasises the primary responsibility of Member States for civil protection and security in their territory."

21 See para. 2, second sentence.

> State to choose the most appropriate means to comply with its own solidarity obligation towards that Member State.

Paragraph 3 of Article 222 TFEU states that:

> The arrangements for the implementation by the Union of the solidarity clause shall be defined by a decision adopted by the Council acting on a joint proposal by the Commission and the High Representative of the Union for Foreign Affairs and Security Policy. The Council shall act in accordance with Article 31(1) of the Treaty on European Union where this decision has defence implications. The European Parliament shall be informed.
>
> For the purposes of this paragraph and without prejudice to Article 240, the Council shall be assisted by the Political and Security Committee with the support of the structures developed in the context of the common security and defence policy and by the Committee referred to in Article 71; the two committees shall, if necessary, submit joint opinions.

The third paragraph is thus a procedural provision which is supposed to give hands and feet to the rest of Article 222 TFEU. The arrangements for the implementation of the solidarity clause 'by the Union', i.e. the institutions, bodies and agencies of the EU, shall be defined by a decision adopted by the Council acting on a joint proposal by the Commission and High Representative.[22] At the time of writing, the joint proposal had been published but had not yet led to the adoption of a Council decision.[23] As the proposed decision does not have any defence implications,[24] the Council could decide by qualified majority. The Council will be assisted by the Political and Security Committee (PSC) which, in turn, is supported by the crisis management bodies embedded within the structures of the European External Action Service (EEAS) and by the Committee on Internal Security (COSI), which must, 'if necessary', and will, in

22 See Section 5, below.

23 Joint Proposal for a Council Decision on the arrangements for the implementation by the Union of the Solidarity clause, JOIN (2012) 39 final, Brussels, 21 December 2012. Going by the time it took for the civil protection mechanism to get adopted after publication of the communication, and the process essentially being a dialogue between the Council and the Commission, the expectation is that the Council decision on the arrangements for the implementation by the Union of the Solidarity clause should be adopted within a period of 1 to 2 years.

24 *Ibid.*, recital 13.

all likelihood, both offer joint opinions on the matter. The European Parliament only needs to be informed, which exposes a lacuna in the democratic structure of the prescribed decision-making process.

Paragraph 4 wraps up the solidarity clause by imposing an obligation on the European Council, i.e. the highest political level, to "regularly assess the threats facing the Union in order to enable the Union and its Member States to take effective action".

4 Contextual Interpretation

4.1 *Umbilical Link with the TEU*

Whereas the solidarity clause is located within Title VII of the TFEU's Part Five on the Union's external action, it has a clear security and defence dimension. This is illustrated by the reference to the military resources of the Member States in Article 222(1) TFEU, as well as by the clause's procedural provisions in paragraph 3.[25] Arguably, the core of the solidarity clause could well have been placed within Title V TEU.[26] In fact, with the increasingly blurry boundaries between internal and external security,[27] it is striking that there is no reference to the solidarity clause (or terrorism for that matter) in the mutual defence clause of Article 42(7) TEU. On the other hand, the reference to military resources in Article 222 TFEU illustrates the broader understanding of security which informs the Union's activities, not just in the framework of the EU's Common Security and Defence Policy (CSDP), and stresses the need for a com-

25 See also Opinion of AG Bot delivered on 31 January 2012 in Case C-130/10, *Parliament v Council*, ECLI:EU:C:2012:50, para. 65: "[I]t is clear from the wording of the solidarity clause contained in Article 222 TFEU, which can be triggered where a Member State is the object of a terrorist attack, that that clause relates to the CFSP, particularly in so far as concerns the CSDP."

26 See P. Koutrakos, *The EU Common Security and Defence Policy*, Oxford: OUP, 2013, Chapter 3.

27 See H. Krieger, "Common European Defence: Competition or Compatibility with NATO", in M. Trybus and N. White (eds.), *European Security Law*, Oxford: OUP, 2007, pp. 174–195, at p. 195. Hence, the Lisbon Treaty may create extra 'fuzziness' of competence delimitation between the TEU and TFEU in the field of security. See already C. Hillion and R. Wessel, "Competence Distribution in EU External Relations after ECOWAS: Clarification or Continued Fuzziness?", *Common Market Law Review* 46, 2009, pp. 551–586.

bination of a broad range of instruments,[28] all in keeping with the decision that it:

> will be for Member States (...), acting in a spirit of solidarity and without prejudice to (...) traditional polic[ies] of military neutrality—to determine the nature of aid or assistance to be provided to a Member State which is the object of a terrorist attack or the victim of armed aggression on its territory.[29]

The link between the solidarity clause and the CSDP thus merits a small excursion to another major innovation in the Union's constitutional history: the introduction in the Lisbon Treaty of a 'mutual defence clause', which is laid down in Article 42(7) TEU:

> If a Member State is the victim of armed aggression on its territory, the other Member States shall have towards it an obligation of aid and assistance by all the means in their power, in accordance with Article 51 of the United Nations Charter. This shall not prejudice the specific character of the security and defence policy of certain Member States.
>
> Commitments and cooperation in this area shall be consistent with commitments under the North Atlantic Treaty Organisation, which, for those States which are members of it, remains the foundation of their collective defence and the forum for its implementation.

Contrary to the solidarity clause, the mutual defence clause is purely intergovernmental in nature: it binds Member States without transferring any competence to EU institutions; nor does it require coordination at the EU level in situations where the mutual defence obligation is invoked.[30] Article 42(7)

---

28 *A Secure Europe in a Better World—European Security Strategy*, Brussels, 12 December 2003, at p. 7. See also *Report on the Implementation of the European Security Strategy—Providing Security in a Changing World*, Brussels, 11 December 2008; and the anticipated Joint Communication on a comprehensive approach in EU external action.

29 Decision of the Heads of State or Government of the 27 Member states of the EU, meeting within the European Council on 18–19 June 2009, laid down in the Protocol on the Concerns of the Irish People on the Treaty of Lisbon, *OJ*, 2013, L 60/131.

30 Earlier versions of the Draft Treaty (Article III-214) included implementation arrangements with procedures for Member States to meet at ministerial level when the mutual defence obligation was to be called upon (assisted by the Political and Security Committee and the EU Military Committee). However, as part of the redrafting done at the Intergovernmental Conference, these arrangements were eliminated. See the report by

TEU reminds the Member States of their unequivocal obligation of aid and assistance "by all the means in their power" if a Member State is the victim of "armed aggression" on its territory.[31] In principle this formulation allows for many forms of assistance but, in practice, the explicit reference to armed aggression points most specifically to military means.[32] Whereas large-scale aggression against a Member State appears improbable in the foreseeable future, the Treaty constitutionalizes both traditional territorial defence and defence against new threats, while at the same time stipulating that, for the EU countries that are members of NATO, the Alliance remains the foundation of their collective defence and the forum for its implementation, and that commitments and cooperation in the area of mutual defence must be consistent with commitments under NATO.

Whereas the clause imposes a duty on Member States, the scope of which appears to be very broad, the caveats embedded therein are broad too, as they relate to compliance with the UN Charter,[33] the neutrality of some Member States, and the existential choices about security and defence made by others in relation to NATO. As Koutrakos explains, "[t]his formulation of the mutual defence clause is entirely consistent with the tenor of CSDP, and the balance that it seeks to strike between the security and defence choices made by the

T. Tiilikainen, "The Mutual Assistance Obligation in the European Union's Treaty of Lisbon", *Publications of the Ministry of Foreign Affairs of Finland*, 4/2008, referred to by Myrdal and Rhinard, *op. cit.*, n. 1.

31 One could take the view that even cyber-attacks, used as arms with the aim of causing severe damage and disruption to a Member State and identified as coming from an external entity, could qualify for being covered by the mutual defence clause, if the Member State's security is significantly threatened by its consequences. On the other hand, there are theoretical possibilities that both Articles 222 TFEU and 42(7) TEU could be triggered together, particularly in cases when a 'threat agent' is unclear (e.g. cyber-attacks on Estonia). See M. Schmitt, "Classification of Cyber Conflict", *Journal of Conflict and Security Law* 17, 2012, pp. 245–260.

32 It is worth mentioning that the WEU's Article V, from which the EU's mutual defence clause draws its inspiration, states that all members shall "afford the Party so attacked all the military and other aid and assistance in their power".

33 According to Article 51 UN Charter, "[n]othing in the present Charter shall impair the inherent right of individual or collective self-defence if an armed attack occurs against a Member of the United Nations, until the Security Council has taken measures necessary to maintain international peace and security. Measures taken by Members in the exercise of this right of self-defence shall be immediately reported to the Security Council and shall not in any way affect the authority and responsibility of the Security Council under the present Charter to take at any time such action as it deems necessary in order to maintain or restore international peace and security".

individual Member States and the common policy which it envisages for the Union."[34]

This nevertheless begs the question how far the Member States are required to go in order to comply with their duty under Article 42(7) TEU, and how rigorous the enforcement of this duty can be. As Koutrakos observes, its wording suggests that "military means constitute merely one option open to a Member State when it examines how best to comply with its duty." It also suggests that "compliance with the mutual defence clause cannot but depend on the subjective assessment of a Member State as to how best it may assist another Member State which is a victim of armed aggression on its territory. This assessment is subject to multifarious considerations, not least of a political and economic nature. Such inherently indeterminate criteria do not lend themselves to a rigorous mechanism of verification or control[35] and distinguish the EU's mutual defence clause from that laid down in Article 5 of NATO's Washington Treaty.

The above does not mean to suggest that the provision of Article 42(7) TEU is not significant: "On the one hand, it is a specific illustration of political solidarity, one of the main pillars of the EU's Common Foreign and Security Policy (CFSP) as laid down in Article 24(3) TEU.[36] (...) On the other hand, the interpretation of the mutual defence clause is subject to continuous redefinition: the development of the CSDP and political solidarity in general, and of common structures of military capabilities in particular, is bound to have an impact on how close to the military end of the scale Member States would be prepared to go in order to assist a Member State under attack".[37] There is another function of the mutual defence clause which is noteworthy: "against the various CSDP missions which are carried out in far-flung places and export EU values to third parties, it renders the CSDP relevant to the Union's citizens in a much more direct manner. In other words, it bolsters a sense of belonging by reaffirming the solidarity between Member States. However, its practical relevance should a crisis occur is a different matter altogether."[38]

---

34 See Koutrakos, *op. cit.*, n. 26, at 68, and Article 42(2) subparagraph 2 TEU.

35 See P. Koutrakos, 'The Role of Law in Common Security and Defence Policy: Functions, Limitations and Perceptions', in P. Koutrakos (ed.), European Foreign Policy: Legal and Political Perspectives (Cheltenham, Edward Elgar 2011), 235–258, at 238.

36 See J. Monar, "The CFSP and the Leila/Perejil Island Incident: The Nemesis of Solidarity and Leadership", *European Foreign Affairs Review* 7, 2002, pp. 251–255.

37 Similarly, international law concepts such as 'armed aggression' are not static but evolve together with a changing security landscape. This creates uncertainty in defining the applicability of the mutual defence clause. See Koutrakos, *op. cit.*, n. 25, at 70.

38 P. Koutrakos, 'The European Union's Common Foreign and Security Policy After Lisbon', in D. Ashiagbor, N. Countouris and I. Lianos (eds.), *The European Union After the Treaty of Lisbon* (Cambridge, Cambridge University Press 2012), 185–209, at 207.

4.2 *Solidarity within the TFEU*

The solidarity clause is not the only mutual assistance provision within the Lisbon Treaty, nor is it the only reference to 'solidarity'.[39] The Treaty on the Functioning of the European Union covers several aspects of health security, including EU disaster prevention and control. Other mechanisms related to EU disaster prevention, response and control are dealt with under civil protection (Article 196 TFEU),[40] EU financial assistance to Member States (Article 122 TFEU), and humanitarian aid to third countries (Article 214 TFEU). Furthermore, EU secondary legislation establishes specific rules in the field of EU disaster prevention and control (e.g. Seveso II).[41]

Under the provisions of Article 122 TFEU the Council may take a decision on measures to address a difficult economic situation in a spirit of solidarity and assist a Member State, in particular if severe difficulties arise in the supply of certain products or services, notably in the area of energy (para. 1). The Article provides for the possibility of "Union financial assistance" to an affected Member State (para. 2). The Council is given the authority to determine when to offer financial assistance during "exceptional occurrences" or "natural disasters" that may impact upon supply (para. 2). The problem of energy shortages reappears in a separate, more explicit location in the treaties. Article 194 TFEU on the EU's energy policy states that Member States should act "in a spirit of solidarity (…) to ensure the security of energy supply in the Union". This provision has prompted discussions on a "solidarity mechanism" for natural gas crises and the subsequent adoption of a gas security regulation.[42]

References to solidarity are also found in the Area of Freedom, Security and Justice. Article 67 TFEU calls for the development of a common policy on

39 See F. Hoffmeister, "Das Prinzip der Solidarität zwischen den Mitgliedstaaten im Vertrag von Lissabon", in: I. Pernice (ed.), *Der Vertrag von Lissabon: Reform der EU ohne Verfassung?*, Baden-Baden: Nomos, 2008, pp. 152–157.

40 See in this respect also the amendments to civil protection introduced by the Lisbon Treaty in Article 6(f) TFEU, endowing the EU with a supporting competence in risk prevention.

41 Directive 2003/105/EC of the European Parliament and of the Council of 16 December 2003 amending Council Directive 96/82/EC on the control of major-accident hazards involving dangerous substances, *OJ*, 2003, L 345/97.

42 Regulation (EU) No 994/2010 of the European Parliament and of the Council of 20 October 2010 concerning measures to safeguard security of gas supply and repealing Council Directive 2004/67/EC *OJ*, 2010 L 295/1.

asylum, immigration and borders "based on solidarity". This type of solidarity is made in reference to recent refugee flows across the Mediterranean, but could take on a wider scope in the future.[43]

In sum, the EU has a comprehensive EU solidarity toolbox to address some major new security challenges. What is needed above all when operationalizing *the* 'solidarity clause' is a coordinated approach to comprehensive action.

5 Implementation

5.1 *Rules and Procedures*

In line with the EU's constitutional organizing principles of consistency, effectiveness and continuity of its policies and actions (Article 13 TEU), and due to the wide scope of Article 222 TFEU, the implementation of the solidarity clause should form an integral part of a permanent EU crisis response, crisis management and crisis coordination system, building upon the existing policies, sectoral instruments and capabilities[44] to deliver a coherent response when needed.[45] Arguably, the building of such a new framework is a continuous process which demands not only the adoption of rules and procedures but also a common approach to capacity-building, prevention and preparedness by EU institutions and Member States alike. Hence the relevance of risk assessments and crisis response, coordination and control exercises, tailored for

---

43 See, e.g., the package of proposals of 15 November 2011 for Regulations of the European Parliament and of the Council establishing, as part of the Internal Security Fund, the instrument for financial support for external borders and visa (COM/2011/0750 final), establishing the Asylum and Migration Fund (COM/2011/0751 final), laying down general provisions on the Asylum and Migration Fund and on the instrument for financial support for police cooperation, preventing and combating crime, and crisis management (COM/2011/0752 final), and establishing, as part of the Internal Security Fund, the instrument for financial support for police cooperation, preventing and combating crime, and crisis management (COM/2011/0753 final).

44 These include the EU Internal Security Strategy, the Union Civil Protection Mechanism and the Civil Protection Financial Instrument, the EU Solidarity Fund; the health security initiative for serious cross-border threats to health, crisis response and analysis structures in the EEAS; the Crisis Coordination Arrangements in the Council; and the efforts geared towards the establishment of a European Area of Justice in the Union.

45 See recital 1 of the preamble and Article 1 of the Joint Proposal for a Council Decision on the arrangements for the implementation by the Union of the Solidarity clause, JOIN (2012) 39 final, Brussels, 21 December 2012.

specific contingencies covered by the clause.[46] Thus, through the implementation of the solidarity clause the EU aims to be better organised and more efficient at managing crises, in terms of both prevention and response.

As mentioned before, the arrangements for implementing the solidarity clause will be defined by a decision adopted by the Council, on a joint proposal by the Commission and the High Representative of the Union for Foreign Affairs and Security Policy. The joint proposal was published on 21 December 2012 and provides some more clarity about the definitional scope of the solidarity clause and its activation. Draft Article 2 provides that the Council Decision shall apply in case of terrorist attacks or natural or man-made disasters,

> irrespective of whether they originate inside or outside the territory of the Member States: (a) Within the territory of Member States to which the Treaty applies, including land area, territorial sea and airspace. (b) When affecting ships (when in international waters) or airplanes (when in international airspace) or critical infrastructure (such as off-shore oil and gas installations) when under the jurisdiction of a Member State.

The proposed Council decision therefore brings the territorial scope of the solidarity clause in line with the regime on territorial sovereignty and exercise of jurisdiction which is applicable under general public international law. Strictly speaking, there is thus no question of extra-territorial application of the solidarity clause, even if this might be the case in practice (see below).

Contrary to earlier resistance to a specification of the types of situations covered by Article 222 TFEU, Article 3 of the proposed Council decision does lay down the following definitions which determine the scope of crisis prevention and disaster relief:

> (a) Crisis: a serious, unexpected and often dangerous situation, requiring timely action; a situation that may affect or threaten lives, environment, critical infrastructure or core societal functions, may be caused by a natural or man-made disaster or terrorist attacks;

46 See EP Committee on Foreign Affairs, Rapporteur Ioan Mircea Pascu, Report of 9 August 2012 on the EU's mutual defence and solidarity clauses: political and operational dimensions (2012/2223(INI)).

(b) Disaster: any situation, which has or may have an adverse impact on people, the environment or property;
(c) Terrorist attack: a terrorist offence as defined in the Council Framework Decision of 13 June 2002 on Combating Terrorism, 2002/475/JHA, as amended by Council framework decision of 28 November 2008, 2008/919/JHA;
(d) Preparedness: a state of readiness and capability of human and material means enabling them to ensure an effective rapid response to an emergency, obtained as a result of action taken in advance;
(e) Response: any action taken during or after a disaster or an actual or imminent terrorist attack to address its immediate adverse consequences.

Apart from clarifying Treaty concepts such as 'terrorist attack' and 'disaster', the proposed legislation also introduces new terminology. After all, the terms 'crisis', 'preparedness' and 'response' do not appear in Article 222 TFEU.[47] Conversely, whereas the Treaty and the proposal make repeated references to the concept of 'threats', this term is not defined.

At a meeting of the Council's Article 36 Committee in October 2011,

> delegations agreed in general that the solidarity clause should only be invoked in specific exceptional and emergency circumstances (…). The

47 Some have argued that that the introduction of the term 'crisis' into the proposal would allow the solidarity clause to be used to address virtually all cases of unrest, similar to the Instrument for Stability, "in order to fund whatever cannot be funded from other EU budgets". See Statewatch, "Solidarity or militarisation? Proposed 'solidarity clause' legislation criticised for lack of clarity and 'encouraging armament' ", available at <http://www.statewatch.org/news/2013/feb/01-solidarity-clause.htm> (last accessed on 19 July 2013). In the light of Article 4 of the proposed Council decision, one should be more cautious in the interpretation of the term 'crisis' and not consider cases of, e.g., social unrest as falling under the term 'man-made disasters'. This issue became topical in the context of the Greek government's 'civil mobilisation order', through which it threatened metro workers with dismissal, arrest and even imprisonment if they did not end their strike in response to wage reductions demanded by the Troika of the European Commission, the IMF, and the ECB, as part of the conditions of Greece's financial bailout. See C. Brennan, "Greece crisis: Athens 10-day metro strike ends", *BBC News*, 25 January 2013: "It was the first time the conservative-led coalition had invoked a 2007 emergency law to deal with 'peacetime emergencies'. Such emergency legislation has only been used nine times since the collapse of Greece's military dictatorship in 1974".

> general triggering criteria to be defined would have to take account of the differences in size and capacities of Member States as well as the nature of the event.[48]

Article 4 of the proposed Council decision provides the linchpin of the solidarity clause. It provides that:

> 1. A Member State being the object of an actual or imminent terrorist attack or the victim of a natural or man-made disaster may invoke the Solidarity Clause if, after having exploited the possibilities offered by existing means and tools, at national or Union level, it considers that the situation overwhelms its response capacity.
> 2. The Member State affected shall address its request to the President of the European Commission, through the Emergency Response Centre, and notify simultaneously the Presidency of the Council.
> 3. The Emergency Response Centre shall act as the initial single 24/7 point of contact for the competent authorities of the Member State affected.

Acting at EU level in a coherent, efficient and timely fashion to prevent, respond to, or control crises requires a single set of arrangements, built on best practices of Member States in streamlining their national crisis coordination procedures and the interaction of their national crisis coordination centres with the EU. At present there is a multitude of EU-level monitoring centres,[49] specialised services and networks.[50] This raises questions of efficient coordination in the event of complex crises. The need to avoid unnecessary duplication and to ensure coherence and effective coordination in action is particularly pertinent given the current scarcity of resources. To this end, the EP has noted

---

48 Council of the European Union, doc. 15498/11 (CATS 98), 3 November 2011, at p. 3.

49 E.g., the EU Intelligence Analysis Centre (EU INTCEN) and EU Situation Room within the EEAS (see below); a number of sectoral monitoring centres within Commission departments and specialised EU bodies: the Monitoring and Information Centre (MIC) of DG ECHO, the Strategic Analysis and Response Capability of DG HOME, the Health Emergency Operations Facility of DG SANCO, the situation room of Frontex, Europol, and the European Centre for Disease Prevention and Control.

50 See also, Commission, "Inventory of Crisis Management Capacities in the European Commission and Community Agencies", Internal Document, 31 July 2009, with a Corrigendum of January 2011 to take account of the changes after the entry into force of the Lisbon Treaty.

that all specialised communication systems at EU level should be integrated within a single secured information system, so as to allow an uninterrupted, free and effective flow of information across sectoral and institutional boundaries.[51] The Commission and the High Representative should work on strengthening the internal coordination platform.[52]

Similarly, the EP has noted a necessity to develop a common situation awareness, which is essential in dealing with major multi-sector crises when rapid and comprehensive updates need to be provided to the political authorities. Article 222(4) TFEU requires the European Council to regularly assess the threats facing the Union. However, this duty casts questions over where precisely responsibility will lie within the institutions for preparing such assessments. Arguably, assessments need to be made at least at two distinct levels. Firstly, frequent comprehensive overviews analysing threats, hazards and risks in various sectors (e.g. terrorism, organised crime, civil protection, health, environment, climate change, etc.) in the light of existing vulnerabilities, thus taxing the level of preparedness and identifying the most pressing capability gaps to be addressed.[53] Here, according to the proposed Council decision, the Commission and the High Representative will, starting in 2015, regularly produce a joint integrated threat and risk assessment report at Union level.[54] These integrated threat and risk assessment reports will form the basis of a regular but more long-term assessment by the European Council, in a process which should also feed strategic thinking to be reflected in future updates of

51 See AFET Report 2012/2223(INI), *op. cit.*, n. 45. There exists a plethora of web-based platforms for communication and information sharing on emergencies, including the over-arching EU Emergency and Crisis Coordination Arrangements webpage (CCA, which brings together Member States, in capital and EU Delegations, European Commission, Council General Secretariat and EEAS in political coordination), ARGUS (the Commission's general internal rapid alert system for crisis coordination, which is open to other EU users during exercises), and two sectoral systems, namely the Common Emergency Communication and Information System (CECIS) and the Health Emergency & Diseases Information System (HEDIS).

52 At the time of writing there are ideas to link up the CCA and ARGUS so as to increase inter-operability, without merging the systems.

53 Pursuant to Article 9 of the proposed Council decision, "the Member States, the Commission and the High Representative may assess the means available throughout the Union and the Member States to meet the major threats, identifying possible gaps and the most efficient and cost effective ways to address those gaps and build the means of effective solidarity".

54 Article 8(1) of the proposed Council decision.

the European Security Strategy (ESS)[55] and the EU Internal Security Strategy,[56] perhaps every 5 years in synch with the EU political cycle.

As the EP has pointed out, "common situation awareness is hardly possible without a culture of information sharing, and the development of a culture of information sharing is hardly possible without a clear division of roles."[57] It is to this end that a European Emergency Response Centre (ERC) was created in 2013 as a one-stop-shop. The Centre is based on the existing crisis room for humanitarian crises and the Monitoring and Information Centre (MIC) for civil protection within DG ECHO. The MIC currently runs the Civil Protection Mechanism, which plays a fundamental role as a key solidarity-based instrument for European rapid response to a wide spectrum of crises, mainly in third countries but also in Member States.[58] The ERC is expected to initially act as the single 24/7 point of contact for the competent authorities of the Member State affected,[59] and the single operational hub with Member States at Union level. The Commission, in consultation with the High Representative, may subsequently designate another centre better placed to assume that function taking into account the nature of the crisis.[60] The designated operational hub shall act as the primary entry point for Member States. It will lead operational

---

55 See the think tank-led project to update and upgrade the ESS to an EGS, a 'European Global Strategy', available at: <http://www.euglobalstrategy.eu/> (last accessed on 19 July 2013).

56 COM(2010) 673 final, *op. cit.*, n. 1.

57 AFET Report 2012/2223(INI), *op. cit.* n. 45.

58 Council Decision 2007/162/EC, Euratom of 5 March 2007 establishing a Civil Protection Financial Instrument, *OJ*, 2007, L 71/9, and Council Decision 2007/779/EC, Euratom of 8 November 2007 establishing a Community Civil Protection Mechanism, *OJ*, 2007, L 314/9. The Commission has proposed strengthening the mechanism, building upon the Commission Communication "Towards a stronger European disaster response: the role of civil protection and humanitarian assistance", COM(2010) 600 final of 26 October 2010, and drawing inspiration from the May 2006 report by M. Barnier, "For a European civil protection force: Europe aid", available at: <http://ec.europa.eu/archives/commission_2004-2009/president/pdf/rapport_barnier_en.pdf> (last accessed on 19 July 2013). In line with this disaster response strategy, the EU should establish a European Emergency Response Capacity based on pre-committed Member States' assets on-call for EU operations and pre-agreed contingency plans. Efficiency and cost-effectiveness should be improved through shared logistics, and simpler and stronger arrangements for pooling and co-financing transport assets. See also ECHO Factsheet, 'Civil Protection', March 2013, available at: <http://ec.europa.eu/echo/files/aid/countries/factsheets/thematic/civil_protection_en.pdf> (last accessed on 19 July 2013).

59 Article 4(3) of the proposed Council decision.

60 Article 5(2) of the proposed Council decision.

response coordination and produce situation assessment reports, in collaboration with the EU Situation Room.[61] The preparation of such reports will draw upon contributions from the different situation awareness and crisis management centres, in Member States, in the Commission, in the EEAS[62] and in the relevant EU agencies, as well as in relevant international organisations (e.g. UN Office for the Coordination of Humanitarian Affairs (OCHA)). The Standing Committee on Operational Cooperation on Internal Security (COSI), provided for in Article 71 TFEU, will participate, if necessary, by submitting joint proposals with the PSC to the Council. This committee aims "to ensure that operational cooperation on internal security is promoted and strengthened within the Union" and "facilitate[s] coordination of the action of the Member States' competent authorities".[63] The Council is assisted by the PSC, along with the CSDP structures (such as the EU Military Committee and the EU Military Staff), if military resources are used.

---

61 Article 7 of the proposed Council decision. The EU Situation Room is part of the EEAS Crisis Response Department. It has been operational since 15 July 2011. The main tasks of the EU Situation Room are, *inter alia*, to lead, manage and develop all EEAS permanence and situational awareness capabilities; to staff and support the EEAS Crisis Platform; and to manage and develop relations with similar crisis mechanisms in certain international organisations and a number of third countries. See "High Representative Catherine Ashton visits the new EU Situation Room", Press release A 286/11, Brussels, 18 July 2011. For arrangements between the EEAS and the Commission in relation to disaster and crisis management cooperation, see European Commission, "Vademecum on Working Relations with the European External Action Service (EEAS)", 1 January 2011, section 6.2, and "Working Arrangements Between Commission Services and the European External Action Service (EEAS) in Relation to External Relations Issues", SEC(2012) 48, 13 January 2012, paras. 3.7 (IfS) and 4 (cooperation on crisis outside the EU).

62 Within the EEAS, EU INTCEN and the network of approx. 140 EU Delegations in the world are crucial in gathering intelligence and providing analysis, early warning and situational awareness on terrorist attacks on the EU plotted from the outside, in emergency situations, providing risk assessment, and coordination of crisis responses among EU institutions and Member States' embassies on the ground. Incidentally, the EEAS also offers opportunities to improve the Union's overall crisis response through actions under the IfS when they are undertaken overseas. In the current global environment where interdependencies are multiplying, major crises on a scale that would justify the triggering of the solidarity clause are likely to be multidimensional and have an international dimension, with respect to third country nationals affected by them or to international action needed to respond to them. The EEAS plays an important role in such cases.

63 See Council Decision 2010/131/EU of 25 February 2010 on setting up the Standing Committee on operational cooperation on internal security, *OJ*, 2010, L 52/50. Article 3(3): "The Standing Committee shall assist the Council in accordance with the provisions of Article 222 of the Treaty".

Overall, the proposed legislation can be criticized for its imbalance in mutual support and responsibilities. Indeed, if the Council agrees to the proposal in its current form, this would oblige EU institutions to "identify and use all relevant Union instruments that can best contribute to a response to the crisis, including sector-specific, operational, policy or financial decisions (…) as well as military resources" (Article 5), while each Member State, beyond what it would be obliged to contribute towards the response of EU institutions, would have to "choose the most appropriate means to comply with its own solidarity obligation towards another Member State" (Article 222(2) TFEU and Declaration 37 annexed to the Treaty). The outside observer cannot help but wonder how this imbalance in mutual support and responsibilities engrained into the implementing arrangements for Article 222 TFEU chimes with the very nature of the 'solidarity' clause. After all, pursuant to the principle of sincere cooperation laid down in Article 4(3) TEU, the Member States would be obliged to take "any appropriate measure, general or particular, to ensure fulfilment of the obligations arising out of [Article 222 TFEU] or resulting from the acts of the institutions of the Union", i.e. the Council decision.

5.2 *EU Solidarity Fund*

In essence, the solidarity clause demonstrates that in very special circumstances the EU is considered to be not only a community of socio-economic interests, but also a union of 'common destiny'. This was the main motivation for the creation of the European Union Solidarity Fund (EUSF) in 2002,[64] when massive flooding of rivers struck Central Europe (Germany, Austria, Czech Republic). This instrument for internal action foresees a re-financing mechanism for crisis response to major natural disasters affecting Member States or countries negotiating their accession to the EU. Man-made disasters and terrorist attacks are excluded from the scope of the Fund.[65] Implementation of the solidarity clause will encompass the EUSF, fully respecting its specific procedures and functioning under the new Multi-Annual Financial Framework.

---

64 Council Regulation (EC) No 2012/2002 establishing the European Union Solidarity Fund, *OJ*, 2002, L 311/3.

65 Emergency funding possibilities in case of a major terrorist attack or other security-related incidents will be supported under the Internal Security Fund. See the Proposal for a Regulation of the European Parliament and of the Council establishing, as part of the Internal Security Fund, the instrument for financial support for police cooperation, preventing and combating crime, and crisis management, Brussels, COM(2011) 753 final, 15 November 2011. For reasons of space, a commentary on this particular instrument is left out of this contribution.

As noted above, the EUSF works in a retro-active mode. Until the end of 2010 the Commission received 85 applications for financial assistance from 23 different countries: 27 of these applications fell within the category of "major natural disaster" which is the main field of application of the Fund.[66] The Regulation defines major disasters as disasters having caused damage exceeding a threshold specific to each country and defined as the lower of 0.6% of Gross National Income (GNI) or EUR 3,536 billion (in 2011 prices).[67] 53 applications have been presented as so-called "extraordinary regional disasters" and 4 under the criteria for disasters in a "neighbouring country". In the latter case, an eligible country affected by the same disaster as another eligible country where the occurrence of a major disaster has been accepted may also benefit from the Fund irrespective of the size of the damage. Extraordinary regional disasters are defined as having affected the major part of the population in the region concerned and having serious and lasting repercussions for the living conditions and the economic stability of the region. Overall, between the creation of the EU Solidarity Fund in 2002 and the end of 2010, 42 applications were approved with financial aid totalling more than EUR 2.4 billion.[68]

Requests for assistance have concerned a variety of different types of natural disaster including storms, floods, mudslides, earthquakes, volcanic eruption, forest fires and drought. The most serious case was the devastating 2009 earthquake that hit L'Aquila in Italy with over EUR 10 billion worth of damage and thousands of people made homeless, where the Fund intervened with over EUR 492 million, the highest grant paid out so far. The Commission claims that "[i]t has been widely recognised that the EUSF—judged against the purpose for which it was set up—has been successful. Assistance from the Fund has helped to alleviate the financial burden on disaster-stricken countries and offering help and additional resources at times of particular hardship has created a positive image of the Union in the eyes of its citizens. Nonetheless, the experience gathered shows that there are limitations and weaknesses in the operation of the Fund".[69] These relate essentially to the lack of rapidity with which aid from the EUSF is made available and the transparency of the criteria

66 The data in this section are drawn from the Communication from the Commission to the European Parliament, the Council, the European Economic and Social Committee and the Committee of the Regions, "The Future of the European Union Solidarity Fund", Brussels, COM(2011) 613 final, 6 October 2011.

67 In 2011, the EUR 3 billion threshold applies to France, Germany, Italy, Spain, and the United Kingdom, for all other countries the 0.6% of GNI threshold applies, ranging in absolute terms from EUR 32.7 million for Malta to EUR 3,339 billion for the Netherlands.

68 COM(2011) 613 final.

69 *Ibid.*

for mobilising the Fund. For example, the time-consuming bureaucracy in EUSF procedures leads to the cumulated effect that in many instances grants can only be paid out 9 to 12 months after the disaster, sometimes longer. While in need of change, a majority of Member States have serious reservations about any major amendments to the principles and functioning of the EUSF, in particular if these might lead to higher spending. With this in mind, the practical adjustments which the Commission has proposed in order to make the Fund function in a more business-like manner, are to be welcomed.[70] Yet, the current state of political debate is not likely to give much room to those who seek to enlarge the support of the EUSF to new categories of 'disasters', nor to those who wish to modify the thresholds or to soften criteria for regional disasters.

While it may be suggested that the solidarity clause should cover only major kinds of calamities requiring a combination of available EU instruments, practice under the EUSF has shown that less complex events (e.g. more frequent natural disasters) might also push Member States to trigger the clause to increase the likelihood of a coordinated and/or well-resourced response.

6 Concluding Remarks

Conceived during the Convention on the future of Europe and boosted by a Declaration set out in European Council conclusions of March 2004 following the terrorist attack in Madrid, the 'solidarity clause' has been codified by the Treaty of Lisbon in Article 222 TFEU. It thereby establishes a constitutional obligation upon the Union and its Member States to jointly act for the prevention of, and immediate response to, terrorist attacks and natural and man-made disasters in an affected Member State. Broad in scope and firm in resolve, the solidarity clause suggests with aplomb that, in special circumstances of crisis or disaster, the EU is considered to be not only a community of socio-economic interests, but also a union of common purpose, mutual respect and shared responsibilities. This finding is reinforced when reading the solidarity clause in conjunction with the mutual defence clause. Together, these clauses offer a breadth of solidarity that other international organisations do not provide and have no intent of acquiring.

Yet, in the wake of the entry into force of the Lisbon Treaty, the solidarity clause has fallen victim to a certain neglect, in spite of a host of crises and disasters which have since hit parts of the EU, some of which have exceeded

70 Opinion of the European Economic and Social Committee on COM(2011) 613 final, *OJ*, 2012 C 181/52.

the capacities of single Member States to deal with them. While efforts have been made to join up different EU centres, services and networks in the field of crisis prevention and response, the main rules and procedures for the implementation of the solidarity clause remain to be adopted. In this respect, the joint proposal by the Commission and High Representative for a Council decision that sets forth the implementing arrangements of Article 222 TFEU reveals a striking imbalance in terms of mutual support and responsibilities. Indeed, if the Council agrees to the proposal in its current form (the European Parliament only has to be informed), then this would oblige EU institutions to "identify and use all relevant Union instruments that can best contribute to a response to the crisis, including sector-specific, operational, policy or financial decisions (...) as well as military resources" (draft Article 5), while each Member State, beyond what it would be obliged to contribute towards the response of EU institutions, would only have to "choose the most appropriate means to comply with its own solidarity obligation towards another Member State" (Article 222(2) TFEU and Declaration 37 annexed to the Treaty). One cannot help but wonder how this imbalance chimes with the core characteristics of the 'solidarity' clause. The Council would be best advised to correct this weaving fault in the proposed legislation. After all, pursuant to the principle of sincere cooperation laid down in Article 4(3) TEU, the Member States are obliged to take "any appropriate measure, general or particular, to ensure fulfilment of the obligations arising out of [Article 222 TFEU] or resulting from the acts of the institutions of the Union", i.e. the Council decision. By simply agreeing to the current proposal, the Member States would sanction a certain level of free-riding in the implementation of the solidarity clause and thus do a disservice both to 'their' European Union, as indeed to one of their own affected by a terrorist attack or natural or man-made disaster. A friend in need is a friend indeed. For solidarity in the EU to endure, the ends and means should be willed not because an individual Member State desires them, but because the group does.

CHAPTER 7

The EU's Competence in the Field of Civil Protection (Article 196, Paragraph 1, a–c TFEU)

Florika Fink-Hooijer

1 Introduction

The EU has only a supporting competence in the field of civil protection. The primary responsibility lies with the Member States, in line with the principle of subsidiarity. When protecting people, property and the environment, including cultural heritage, the local, regional, and national levels are generally best placed to prepare for and respond to disasters be it earthquakes, floods, forest fires, acts of terrorism, technological accidents or other events. However, as will be argued in this contribution, civil protection cooperation among EU Member States has its particular benefits in situations where disasters may overwhelm the national capacity or where it offers important cost or network advantages, including in the fields of prevention and preparedness. This is why the EU Member States created the EU Civil Protection Mechanism back in 2001 and it has been growing ever since.[1] The Union's civil protection policy is therefore an area where even a supporting competence has stimulated and advanced EU integration.

2 The EU Civil Protection Mechanism—A Success Story

Over the past decade, the EU Civil Protection Mechanism has become an effective cooperation tool in the immediate response phase among all so-called Participating States, i.e. the 27 Member States of the EU, as well as Norway, Iceland, Liechtenstein, Croatia[2] and the Former Yugoslav Republic of Macedonia, together with the European Commission. Cooperation developed also quickly in the fields of disaster preparedness and more recently also for disaster prevention. Activations of the EU Civil Protection Mechanism have

1 2007/779/EC, Euratom: Council Decision of 8 November 2007, establishing a Community Civil Protection Mechanism (recast) (Text with EEA relevance) *OJ* L 314, 1.12.2007, pp. 9–19.

2 Croatia becoming the 28th Member State of the European Union as of 01.07.2013.

© KONINKLIJKE BRILL NV, LEIDEN, 2014 | DOI 10.1163/9789004268333_009

delivered assistance both inside Europe as well as the rest of the world. Participating States and the Commission are working together to build safer societies through a number of concrete and very effective actions.

To begin with, Participating States and the Commission are connected through a network of dedicated contact points. This network of emergency centres and authorities allows communicating in real-time through the secured Common Emergency Communication and Information System (CECIS) platform. At the push of a button, 32 emergency centres exchange information about disaster early warning alerts and forecasts, situational developments reporting, in-depth analyses of emergency situations, satellite maps, and various reporting formats. Information products are immediately available to everyone. CECIS also provides the IT platform to share requests for assistance and functions as a clearinghouse between the official requests from affected countries' governments and the voluntary offers from Participating States. The EU Monitoring and Information Centre (MIC), which as of May of this hear has been developed and upgraded into the European Emergency Response Coordination Centre (ERCC), has also served as a facilitator for regular discussions among Participating States, e.g. on coordinating their forest fire fighting efforts.

The MIC is part of the Commission. It is embedded into the Directorate-General for Humanitarian Aid and Civil Protection (DG ECHO). As will be illustrated hereafter, political will and operational needs can be powerful drivers of steady integration whereby the EU level is acting as facilitator at conceptual and operational level but not as a legislator. Yet the current state of EU integration in the field of civil protection is difficult to imagine without the support role of the Commission which makes civil protection a showcase of a specific form of cooperation between Member States and 'Brussels.'

Another element of the cooperation lies in the extensive preparedness work. Civil protection experts from Participating States participate in joint trainings and exercises, where they exchange experiences and learn to work together in an international context. The EU-financed civil protection training programme has trained and exercised more than 2500 national experts. Every year some 130 experts take part in the exchange of experts programme between the authorities. Several EU-funded exercises are carried out every year and held in high regard for their realistic testing of national capacities and the interaction between intervention forces in a simulated disaster scenario. A couple of large-scale exercises per year involve the emergency response staff of various countries, for several days in a row. A particular aspect of the exercises is the practice with civil protection 'modules', i.e. pre-defined teams and assets, such as high capacity pumping modules, advanced medical post with or without surgery, or urban search and rescue modules with or without CBRN capability. Participating States have agreed a number of criteria for these modules, such as time to deploy, days of autonomy, minimum capacities, etc. The modular approach simplifies coordination in complex emergency settings, as the module characteristics are well known, trained and tested.

When a country inside or outside the EU is overwhelmed by a disaster and makes a request for (international) assistance, Participating States in the EU Civil Protection Mechanism can deliver a more effective European response than that provided in isolation or coordinated bilaterally. They can also make use of complementarities, avoid duplication, and make sure that the European assistance is delivered as a coordinated package, which relieves the disaster-affected country of the organizational burden of receiving aid from abroad. The more concerted the European response, the better it also fits under the global UN coordination umbrella when acting outside EU borders. EU Member States are in favour of this coordinated approach, as can be illustrated by the following examples.

During the civil unrest in Libya in 2011, thousands of 'third-country nationals' (people mainly from Egypt, Bangladesh and Sub-Saharan countries) fled from Libya to neighbouring countries. In order to repatriate these people to their home countries and avoid the establishment of long-term camps at Libya's borders, the MIC worked closely with the International Organization for Migration and ten countries participating in the EU Civil Protection Mechanism. In a coordinated effort, Belgium, Bulgaria, Germany, Spain, France, Hungary, Italy, Malta, Sweden and the United Kingdom provided over 150 flights and five sea vessels to repatriate roughly 30,000 people, who were stranded in Tunisia and Egypt.

After the earthquake, tsunami and nuclear disaster in Japan on 11 March 2011, the Japanese government explicitly requested European assistance to be coordinated and the EU responded exactly according to that request by channelling almost 400 tons of in-kind assistance through the EU Civil Protection Mechanism. This coordination also resulted in considerable cost-efficiency gains on the EU side, with the MIC grouping cargo from different Participating States on the flights to Japan. This coordinated approach helped to avoid gaps and duplications.

In addition, the EU has the possibility to co-finance the transportation of assistance. Especially in the case of Japan, it was important that this funding was made available to cover a part of the (substantial) transport costs. It is routine practice to send EU civil protection teams on site in any major disaster.

In Japan, this team made sure that all cargo arriving from Europe was quickly transported onwards to the affected prefectures, in coordination with local authorities and humanitarian organizations on the ground.

Another example is Poland. In May 2010, heavy rainfall caused severe floods that triggered Poland asking for European assistance. Eight European countries (namely the Czech Republic, Estonia, France, Germany, Denmark, Latvia, Lithuania and the Netherlands) immediately responded with over 50 high capacity pumps, more than 20 expert teams, and 300 rescuers. In operations lasting two weeks, flood water that would fill close to 300 Olympic-size swimming pools was removed.

These examples of practical cooperation in the face of disasters show that European integration does not need to be based on a formal operational competence at the EU level. The success of European civil protection is based on the operational logic in emergency situations and supported by an evolving policy framework. The Commission thus acts as a facilitator, providing policy support and analysis as well as practical input to help coordinating national responses and bundling the individual strengths. This is a form of integration which Member States actively solicit and drive forward. It has become successful because institutional and legal limits are respected by all sides.

In the face of a disaster, pragmatic solutions and common will to serve and help those in distress prevails. The policy development in the field of civil protection inside the EU is setting standards globally with more and more third states wanting to connect with the EU on disaster management in legal and/or practical terms.

3 Proposals for the Further Advancement of the EU Civil Protection Mechanism

The operational success of the EU Civil Protection Mechanism is embedded in a steadily evolving policy framework. In December 2011, the Commission proposed to further enhance this framework through a revised decision on a Union Civil Protection Mechanism.[3] The legislative proposal is currently being negotiated in the Council and the European Parliament. It maintains the successful cooperation elements and includes a few innovative provisions. One such innovation is a virtual voluntary pool that will allow better planning for everybody. Another element will allow responding to new risks in Europe, for

3 COM(2011) 934 final, 2011/0461 (COD), Proposal for a Decision of the European Parliament and of the Council on a Union Civil Protection Mechanism.

which cooperation among countries is increasingly crucial, such as pandemics, nuclear disasters, volcanic eruptions (possibly with poisonous gases), solar flares or space debris. For such events with significant effects, it may be too expensive for one country alone to critically assess the risks, develop strategies for prevention, take preparedness countermeasures and respond. High impact/low probability scenarios also plead for joining forces among neighbouring states that face recurrent similar threats.

Currently, the deployment of EU civil protection assets is still based on *ad hoc* assistance offers by Participating States after an official request for assistance has been received. This way of working inevitable creates a degree of improvisation and decisions are sometimes unnecessarily delayed. However, in situations where every hour counts, the countries in Europe need a system that allows better pre-planning, which can ensure that key assets are mobilized swiftly. The key to this is pre-commitment of crucial assets.

The pool of voluntarily pre-committed civil protection response capacities will be a shared effort of all Participating States who commit assets for a period of time for common missions. In return, these assets benefit from higher co-financing rates when they are used in operations. However, ownership, command and control fully remain with the Participating States, which can also decline deployment if the capacities are needed domestically or if there are other serious reasons that make them not available. The assets in the voluntary pool would need to meet certain quality criteria.

This voluntary pool of response assets will create a system where everybody knows which assets can be counted on in case of need. This will enable every disaster management authority in Europe to improve its planning and speed of reaction, and it will thus improve the organisation of the overall civil protection system in the interest of all, both inside Europe and in the rest of the world.

4 Synergies between Humanitarian Aid and Civil Protection

As mentioned above the MIC is a part of DG ECHO, which has two major relief instruments at its disposal: humanitarian aid, which is channelled through international partners, and the mobilisation of civil protection in-kind assistance from EU Member States and other Participating States. The objective of both instruments is to relieve the suffering of populations afflicted by major disasters, to save lives, assist populations in need, and to support populations in becoming more resilient when facing these situations. Neither instrument shall follow political agendas or be used as a foreign policy tool when it intervenes outside the Union. Instead, both instruments provide assistance based exclusively on need. Furthermore, both instruments recognize the overall coordination role of the United Nations in emergencies outside the EU. Humanitarian and civil protection actors therefore liaise with UN OCHA and other relevant actors in order to seek complementarities.

In emergency situations, humanitarian and civil protection actors often work side by side. This creates plenty of opportunities to take advantage of synergies. For example, after the 2010 earthquake in Haiti the MIC encouraged Participating States to deploy Water, Sanitation and Hygiene (WASH) personnel and equipment, based on the results of a needs-assessment that had been conducted jointly by DG ECHO's humanitarian field personnel and EU civil protection experts.

Likewise, DG ECHO-funded humanitarian projects can integrate appropriate in-kind contributions from the civil protection side. In some cases the staff of DG ECHO's humanitarian partners is trained by civil protection specialized personnel on the installation, maintenance and operation of equipment, thus ensuring these installations are used in longer term, when international relief teams have already left, or to respond to the future emergencies in the affected country. In specific cases, DG ECHO's humanitarian implementing partners have been consignees for in-kind assistance coming from Participating States' civil protection authorities. For example, in the 2010 flood disaster in Pakistan, European assistance was delivered not directly to the government of the affected country but rather channelled to humanitarian implementation partners as alternative consignees.

Building further on these synergies, the Commission uses its MIC/ERCC, not only for the coordination among civil protection authorities of Participating States, but also for other purposes, including the coordination with DG ECHO field-based humanitarian experts, coordination with other Commission departments involved in disaster response, such as DG HOME, DG SANCO, and the Secretariat-General, and among the relevant EU institutions and services, including notably the Council, the European Parliament, as well as the European External Action Service. The overall capacity of the EU as a first responder in emergencies benefits from this integration, which ensures comprehensiveness and better coherence of our actions.

Further synergies between humanitarian aid and civil protection exist in the areas of disaster risk management and disaster preparedness, which are becoming increasingly important for humanitarian aid too. Focus on these elements of disaster management cycle is being systematically strengthened in civil protection authorities in Europe, which engage in an ever closer sharing of information and experience. The proposed revised EU Civil Protection

Mechanism will, for example, include obligations on Participating States to regularly update their national risk assessments and share assessments of their risk management capability. The Commission will discuss common guidelines with Participating States' authorities and thus through better prevention systems help mitigate the enormous costs of disasters[4] and the human suffering not reflected in statistic. Europe can take a leading role in this area and actively engage in knowledge transfer to countries around the world afflicted by humanitarian crises. Disaster risk management, prevention and preparedness actions have been recognised as important concepts among the new operational challenges for humanitarian action, not least because often assistance is not only about saving lives but also about preserving dignity and enabling to cope with recurrent disasters.

Finally, with the intensifying cooperation among Participating States, civil protection has constantly developed its lessons learned system, something that should become a standard for all emergency interventions around the globe.

A word of explanation on the notion of 'needs-based assistance may be called for in this respect'. Even though civil protection is mobilised on the basis of an official request, this does not mean that the response is not needs-based. After the request, the Commission/ERCC sends EU civil protection teams or joint ECHO humanitarian/civil protection teams on the ground to do a need assessment and coordinate with UN OCHA in order to have a credible and independent needs assessment. In most cases the type of assistance given by the EU civil protection community is deploying experts and specialised intervention teams on the ground. But the assistance can also include giving medicine, food and non-food items.

5 EU Civil Protection is Not a Military Force

While there is no common definition of 'civil protection' in Europe, there are a number of unifying elements. Firstly, Civil protection is essentially of a civilian nature (this is not the case everywhere in the world). Secondly, Civil protection services are responsible for preparing and coordination the national response to disasters on their territory (and for providing assistance to third countries when requested). And thirdly, Civil protection actors have no responsibilities

4 See for cost examples i.a. the 2013 UNISDR Global Assessment Report on Disaster Risk Reduction): "From Shared Risk to Shared Value: the Business Case for DRR" <http://www.preventionweb.net/gar>.

in maintaining law and order. They are never armed, neither inside Europe nor outside. Civil protection teams may carry uniforms for corporate identity and visibility reasons (most often bright orange or red). However, this should not be confused with military uniforms.

This being said, most national military will support the civil protection response to large domestic emergencies, for example with transport assets, CBRN capabilities, tents, water purification, field hospitals, etc., but they will not be in the lead.

The EU civil protection is thus a civilian actor but accepts that the military can play a useful role in emergency relief contexts, as a matter of last resort, by contributing to the provision of security and in certain well defined conditions provide relief and logistics, as governed by international norms (Oslo guidelines and MCDA guidelines) when acting outside the Union. The principle of 'last resort' is adhered by the EU and throughout all international civilian crisis response structures, especially the UN. For example, during the 2011 floods in Pakistan, and also in the year before, EU civil protection assistance was delivered to the UN and humanitarian implementing partners rather than the Pakistani government, which organised its relief efforts mainly with the help of the military.

To ensure correct civilian-military cooperation, EU civil protection has developed arrangements with military colleagues from the EU Military Staff and has many positive cooperation stories to build on (e.g. evacuation of third country nationals from the war in Libya, relief operations in Sudan and Pakistan). While fully respecting the principle, in the discussions on who responds when and how, due account must be taken also of the need to find an effective solution, without wasting taxpayer's money in duplications. In third countries, the EU Civil Protection Mechanism effectively ensures that operational co-ordination is fully integrated in the UN OCHA overall co-ordination, the cluster system, and the respect for the Oslo and MCDA Guidelines and the European Consensus on Humanitarian Aid.

Trainings for civil protection actors systematically explain the humanitarian system, so that the personnel is well aware of humanitarian principles. Although they are not 'humanitarian actors' as such, they are very aware of humanitarian constraints when acting outside of Europe.

6 Conclusion

The relationship between the European Commission's MIC/ERCC and the EU Member States/ Participating States is based on voluntary contributions. The

Member States have a habit of working with the MIC/ERCC, as well as on a bilateral basis (outside the EU framework), as appropriate in the circumstances. However, whenever the national capacities are overwhelmed, they use the facility at the EU level to coordinate their actions. This was the case in practically all major European and international disasters in the recent past. A supporting EU competence and voluntary contributions by Member States can thus be drivers for EU integration, especially when they are based on European added value, mutual trust and genuine political will, and where they effectively respond to expectations of EU citizens.

CHAPTER 8

Securing Consular Protection of the EU Citizens Abroad: What Role for the EU?

*Madalina Moraru**

One of the EEAS priorities shall be to bring the Service closer to the public.[1]

1 Introduction

There are several areas of State action where the EU's involvement has raised strong opposition from the Member States. These have usually been the areas perceived as being reserved to the nation-State, e.g. citizenship, budgetary matters, military affairs, and foreign policy affairs of high political sensitivity such as: taking a position on the recognition of states, or on civil and military intervention in the internal affairs of a third country. Of these, the CFSP and CSDP have been the EU foreign policy areas that have for a long time attracted strong opposition from the Member States to the integration of these policies into the supranational EU system.[2] It also seems that the fervent opposition

* The present paper is based on data collected for a previous paper written by the author: "Practical and Legal Consequences of Absence of EU and Member States' External Representations for the Protection of EU Citizens in Third Countries", in J. T. Arrighi, R. Bauböck, M. Collyer, D. Hutcheson, M. Moraru, L. Khadar and J. Shaw (eds.), Franchise and Electoral Participation of Third Country Citizens Residing in the European Union and of European Citizens Residing in Third Countries. Study of the European Parliament, Policy Department of Citizens' rights and Constitutional Affairs, 2013.

1 Speech of Pierre Vimont, Secretary General of the EEAS, made during the Workshop concerning the role of the EEAS in Consular Protection and Services for EU Citizens organised at the European Parliament in Brussels on 9 January 2013. See more in *The role of EEAS in consular protection and services to EU citizens*, Directorate-General for External Policies of the Union, European Parliament, available at: <http://www.europarl.europa.eu/committees/de/studiesdownload.html?languageDocument=EN&file=85428> (accessed May 2013).

2 B. van Vooren, *EU External Relations Law and the European Neighbourhood Policy: A Paradigm for Coherence*, New York: Routledge, 2012; H. Merket, "The External Action Paradox of the Lisbon Treaty: reconciling integration with delimitation", paper prepared for the

© KONINKLIJKE BRILL NV, LEIDEN, 2014 | DOI 10.1163/9789004268333_010

of certain Member States has been successful since, in spite of the fact that each Treaty amendment has toned down the distinct status of the CFSP from the other areas of EU external relations,[3] the reality is that even after the entry into force of the Lisbon Treaty, the CFSP is still distinct and primarily an area of intergovernmental cooperation.[4]

Another area that has for centuries been perceived as a discretionary State prerogative is slowly being covered by EU supranational norms, and, arguably, in a more intruding way than in the similarly politically sensitive CFSP, namely, consular and diplomatic protection of EU citizens in non-EU countries. The Lisbon Treaty expanded, arguably, even more so than in the CFSP/CSDP areas, the EU's role and competence by infusing supranational features into the area, in spite of the fervent opposition of certain Member States towards increasing the EU's involvement in this field,[5] and the critiques of international academics as to the legality of the EU mechanism.[6] The peculiarity of consular and diplomatic protection of EU citizens in the world is that even if the field is incorporated into the Founding Treaties within the part on Non-Discrimination and Citizenship of the Union as one of the four EU citizenship rights, and as a fundamental right,[7] the field does not qualify as a purely Union internal area of action. The specificity of the EU citizenship right consists in

---

Copenhagen Business School Graduate Conference "United We Stand—The EU, its current challenges and the way forward", 21–22 June 2012, available at: <https://biblio.ugent.be/publication/3064009> (accessed July 2013).

3 The distinct character of the CFSP (Article 24(1) TEU) has been slightly reduced by the Lisbon Treaty by extending the possibilities for QMV (Article 31(2) second indent and 31(3) TEU) of enhanced cooperation in the field of the CFSP as a whole (Article 20 TEU), extending the rights of the European Parliament within the CFSP (Articles 17(7)(3), 36(1) last sentence TEU, 314 and 315 TFEU) and the extent of the CJEU jurisdiction (it now has jurisdiction over the legality of restrictive measures against natural or legal persons (Article 24(1)TEU), overseeing both sides of the CFSP-TFEU boundary (Article 40 TEU) and the duty of consistency that includes CFSP as well as other EU policies (Article 21(3) TEU)). For more discussion on this see H. Merket, *op. cit.* n. 2, p. 7.

4 I. Govaere, "Multi-faceted Single Legal Personality and a Hidden Horizontal Pillar: EU External Relations Post-Lisbon?", *Cambridge Yearbook of European Legal Studies*, 13, 2010–2011, pp. 87–112.

5 See Section—*The Treaty of Lisbon—strengthening the role of the Union delegations in the field of protection of Union citizens in the world.*

6 For more details, see *ibid.*

7 Articles 20(2)(c) and 23 TFEU are located in Part Two on Non-Discrimination and Citizenship of the Union of the TFEU, while Article 46 of the EU Charter, entitled Diplomatic and consular protection, is located in Title V on Citizens' Rights.

the fact that it mixes these internal Union market objectives with a significant external dimension resulting from the fact of being exercised completely outside the Union market and pursuing strong external objectives.[8]

Since 1993[9] EU citizenship has offered concrete benefits to the citizens of EU countries not only within the borders of the EU but also outside those borders. Any EU citizen, who is not represented by her Member State of origin, who is caught in an emergency or difficult situation in a non-EU country, has the right to receive equal consular protection from the consular and diplomatic services of any of the other Member States represented in that third country.[10] Consular and diplomatic protection of individuals has long been characterized in public international law as a prerogative of the State of nationality.[11] In spite of the increased influence of contemporary international human rights law on traditional public international law norms,[12] the concept of diplomatic

8 Article 3(5) TEU provides as one of the Union's objectives: "In its relations with the wider world, the Union shall [...] contribute to the protection of its citizens". (external objective); external objectives combining with internal ones are also present in Article 35(3) TEU; on the other hand, Articles 20(2)(c) and 23 TFEU, being located in the scheme of the TFEU under the Part on Non-discrimination and citizenship, have also embedded a Union internal objective, namely making EU citizenship more effective. On the qualification of the EU citizenship right to equal protection of unrepresented Union citizens abroad as an external dimension of EU citizenship, see F. Geyer, "The External Dimension of EU Citizenship Arguing for Effective Protection of Citizens Abroad", CEPS Policy Brief, No. 136, July 2007.

9 The Treaty of Maastricht was signed on 7 February 1992 and entered into force on 1 November 1993, available at: <http://europa.eu/legislation_summaries/institutional_affairs/treaties/treaties_maastricht_en.htm> (accessed May 2013).

10 Article 8(c) of the Maastricht Treaty became Article 20 EC Treaty and now Article 23(1) TFEU.

11 See E. Vattel, *The Law of Nations*, 1758, p. 136; E. M. Borchard, *The Diplomatic Protection of Citizens Abroad or The Law of International Claims*, 1919, p. 17; the Mavrommatis Palestine Concessions Case, judgment of 30 August 1924, PCIJ Ser. A, No. 2, 6 et seq., p. 12; Report on the Work of the International Law Commission during its 50th session (1998), UN Doc. A/53/10 (General Assembly, Official Records, Supplement No. 10), Chapter V, 70–84, (§§ 56–110), p. 84 (§ 108, point c) (hereinafter ILC Report 1998); R. B. Lillich, Commentary, "The Diplomatic Protection of Nationals Abroad: An Elementary Principle of International Law Under Attack", *AJIL*. 69, 1975, p. 359. For more on the traditional theory of diplomatic protection, see generally Special Rapporteur on Diplomatic Protection, Seventh Report on Diplomatic Protection, ILC (hereinafter ILC), p. 3, U.N. Doc. A/CN.4/567 (Mar. 7, 2000).

12 In 1998, the Working Group of the ILC established the approach to the topic of diplomatic protection and declared that "[t]he work on diplomatic protection should take into

protection has remained primarily defined as a discretionary right of the State of nationality.[13] Public international law does not impose an obligation upon States to secure diplomatic or consular protection for individuals subject to injuries in foreign countries, not even in cases of gross violation of *jus cogens* rights.[14]

The situation is different within the EU. For almost 20 years, the EU countries have consented to limiting their internationally recognised discretionary powers for the purpose of advancing protection of their citizens abroad, and in this way enlarging the territorial effectiveness of EU citizenship also outside the EU. The Lisbon Treaty amendments together with the Council Decision establishing the European External Action Service[15] further challenged the

---

account the development of international law in increasing recognition and protection of the rights of individuals and in providing them with more direct and indirect access to international forums to enforce their rights", in UN Doc. A/CN.4/L.553, point (d), reprinted in: ILC Report 1998, note 7, at 84 (§ 108). The ILC has also slightly changed the definition of diplomatic protection from a purely legal fiction where only the interests of the State were recognised, to one where the interests of the individual are recognised alongside those of the State. See A. M. H. Vermeer-Künzli, "Where the Law becomes Irrelevant: Consular Assistance and the European Union", *International and Comparative Law Quarterly* 60, 2011, pp. 965–995.

13 See more in Section entitled *The Treaty of Lisbon—strengthening the role of the Union delegations in the field of protection of Union citizens in the world.*

14 In spite of existing State practice across continents recognising a right of the individual to protection abroad, the ILC did not adopt the recommendation proposed by its Rapporteur, J. Dugard, which would have required states to guarantee an individual right to diplomatic protection in the case of serious and repeated violations of fundamental human rights recognised by international law. Instead, Draft Article 19, entitled 'Recommended Practice', only proposes that states can consider exercising diplomatic protection "especially when significant injury occurred" to the national. Drafted in soft language, the Article does not purport to create any binding obligations on States. See more details in J. Dugard, "Diplomatic Protection and Human Rights: The Draft Articles of the International Law Commission", *Aust. YBIL* 24, 2005, pp. 75–92; A. M. H. Vermeer- Künzli, "As If: The Legal Fiction in Diplomatic Protection", *EJIL.* 18, 2008, p. 37. ILC Draft Articles on "Diplomatic Protection with commentaries of 2006" available at <http://untreaty.un.org/ilc/texts/instruments/english/commentaries/9_8_2006.pdf> (accessed July 2013); N. T. Hooge, *Responsibility to Protect (R2P) as Duty to Protect?—Reassessing the Traditional Doctrine of Diplomatic Protection in light of Modern Developments in International Law,* LLM Thesis, 2010, available at: <https://tspace.library.utoronto.ca/bitstream/1807/25618/1/Hooge_Nicholas_T_201011_LLM_thesis.pdf> (accessed July 2013).

15 Council Decision 2010/427/EU of 26 July 2010 Establishing the Organisation and Functioning of the European External Action Service, *OJ*, 2010, L 201/30.

traditional public international law conception of consular and diplomatic protection of citizens by conferring powers ensuring protection abroad of EU citizens directly upon the body of an international organisation, i.e. the EU's diplomatic service.

Recent events have shown that many EU citizens have been caught up in crisis situations or in difficult day-to-day situations such as, war, illness, crimes, and violations of non-derogable human rights that have endangered their lives. A high number of these EU citizens located in third countries did not, at the time that the crisis in question occurred, have an external representation of their Member State of nationality to resort to for help. In January 2013, all the then 27 Member States were represented in only four non-EU countries.[16] Due to the financial crisis affecting national budgets, most of the Member States have had to reduce their external representation in the world, while at the same time more EU citizens travel or take up residence outside the EU. It is thus expected, that in the years to come, more EU citizens will find themselves in situations where they cannot benefit from the consular services and more importantly from consular protection from their Member State of nationality.

This paper will explore whether EU citizenship confers certain concrete benefits to citizens of the Member States who find themselves in difficulty in third countries, or whether EU citizenship stops at the Union's borders and every EU citizen returns to being a citizen of their Member State of nationality when travelling or taking residence in a non-EU country.

In the following paragraphs we will first identify what are the consequences of absence of an external representation of a Member State for its citizens located in third countries (section 2). We will continue with a short overview of the methods of ensuring protection of EU citizens abroad during the pre-Lisbon Treaty period, concentrating mostly on consular protection (section 3). This section will explain why from all the different EU instruments, the chosen method was one that permitted the widest possible discretion of action for the Member States and the almost complete absence of the EU's involvement. The chapter will then briefly point out how consular protection of EU citizens, as an EU primary law obligation on the Member States, was implemented in practice, revealing the good practice examples as well as those cases where the implementation proved problematic (section 3.2). The paper allocates an

16 The People's Republic of China, the Russian Federation, the United States of America, and Canada, see <http://ec.europa.eu/consularprotection/index.action> (accessed January 2013).

important part to the analysis of the exercise of the pre-Lisbon Treaty instruments on consular protection of EU citizens since, in spite of the change of the EU legal framework brought about by the Reform Treaty, the previous regional legal instruments specifically addressing the issue of protection of EU citizens abroad is still in force and operative.[17] We will then continue by assessing the impact of the Treaty of Lisbon on the exercise of consular protection of unrepresented Union citizens and establish whether and how the Lisbon Treaty has changed the roles played by the Member States and the Union in the exercise of a State-like function: consular and diplomatic protection of EU citizens in the world (section 4). It will be pointed out that the EU mechanism for protecting citizens abroad no longer follows the equivalent traditional public international law mechanism of consular and diplomatic protection of individuals, but has established yet another area of action autonomous and exceptional from the public international law norms (section 5).[18]

In conclusion, the paper will consider several options whereby the EU can effectively use the normative and institutional settings established by the Lisbon Treaty for the purpose of helping the Member States to effectively ensure consular protection to the growing number of unrepresented Union citizens in the world. The main argument of the paper is that the Treaty of Lisbon entrusted the EEAS and the EU delegations with certain functions of coordination and support of the Member States' consular assistance responsibilities which, even if received with divided reactions by the Member States,[19] could prove useful for ensuring a more efficient consular assistance for unrepresented Union citizens in third countries.

---

17 At the time of writing (April 2014).

18 M. Ličková, "European Exceptionalism in International Law", *Eur J Int Law* 19 (3), 2008, pp. 463–490; M. Cremona, "Disconnection Clauses in EC Law and Practice", in: C. Hillion and P. Koutrakos (eds.), *Mixed Agreements Revisited—The EU and its Member States in the World*, Hart Publishing (Oxford), 2010, pp. 160–187; J. W. van Rossem, "The Autonomy of EU Law: More is Less?", in: R. A. Wessel and S. Blockmans (eds.), *Between Autonomy and Dependence*, The Hague: T.M.C. ASSER PRESS, 2013, pp. 13–46.

19 Consular and Diplomatic Protection: Legal Framework in the EU Member States, Report of the EU CARE Project, December 2010, pp. 673–674, available at: <http://www.careproject.eu/images/stories/ConsularAndDiplomatic-Protection.pdf>.

2 The Negative Consequences of Absence of Member States' External Representations in Third Countries

Recent surveys[20] have shown that the Member States have had to reduce their external representation networks for financial reasons,[21] and certain Member States plan to further reduce their external representation network.[22] As a result, there are more third countries with no Member States' external representation,[23] and others with just a few Member States being represented

---

20 See Annex on *Member States' External Representations and EU Delegations in third countries* in the European Parliament Report on *Access to Electoral Rights: Citizenship, Residence and the Franchise in Local, Regional, National and European election*, Annex drafted by the present author.

21 Several academics have pointed out that the Member States are under pressure to rationalize their external representations network, for example, D. Rijks, *EU Diplomatic Representation in Third Countries*, available at: <http://www.ies.be/files/repo/conference 2008/EUinIA_VIII_1_Rijks.pdf>. See also the written observations of K. Raik in the European Parliament Report on *The Role of the EEAS in consular services*, available at: <http://www.europarl.europa.eu/committees/de/studiesdownload.html?languageDocument=EN&file=85428> (accessed July 2013).

22 Several Ministries of Foreign Affairs (MFAs), including the Netherlands, the Czech Republic and Estonia, have significantly reduced their personnel. Other MFAs have closed several embassies and consulates due to financial constraints and/or are planning to do so in the near future. In many cases, including Bulgaria, the Czech Republic, Denmark, Finland, Greece, Latvia and Portugal, the number of national diplomatic missions has significantly decreased. See R. Balfour and K. Raik, *The European External Action Service and National Diplomacies*, EPC Issue Paper No. 73, p. 17, available at: <http://www.fiia.fi/assets/news/The%20EEAS%20and%20National%20Diplomacies.pdf> (accessed July 2013); See, M. M. Schilbach, for France, in B. Hocking and D. Spence (eds.), *Foreign Ministries in the European Union: Integrating Diplomats,* London: Palgrave Macmillan, 2005, p. 123; for Hungary, see <http://euobserver.com/economic/28315>; For Netherlands, see the Ministry of Foreign Affairs' 'Nota modernisering Nederlandse diplomatie', 8 April 2011, p. 10 and 18. Balfour and Raik also argued that "even without the crisis, and even in those countries that have not experienced major economic shocks, European public administrations are facing cuts", in: *The European External Action Service and National Diplomacies*, EPC Issue Paper No. 73, p. 19.

23 Many of the following third countries are highly sought tourist destinations. There are 26 countries outside of the EU where *no Member State is represented* (Andorra, Bahamas, Belize, Bhutan, Brunei Darussalam, Chad, Comoros, Dominica, Liechtenstein, Maldives, Marshall Islands, Nauru, Palau, Panama, Saint Kitts and Nevis, Saint Vincent and Grenadines, Samoa, San Marino, Seychelles, Somalia, Swaziland, Timor Leste, Tonga, Tuvalu, and Vanatau), *while the EU has a delegation in 8 of these third countries* (Antigua

in situ[24] as compared to several years ago.[25] In January 2013, all 27 Member States were represented in only four non-EU countries.[26] In parallel with the shrinking of the external representation network of EU countries, there is a trend towards more and more EU citizens taking up residence in third countries.[27] The result of these combined trends is that more EU citizens are not represented by their Member States of nationality and, in case of a natural or man-made disaster occurring in a third country, these EU citizens may find themselves in a vulnerable position.

The concept that States are entitled to protect the interests of their nationals in other countries is a basic principle of international consular law and practice.[28] According to Article 5 of the Vienna Convention on Consular Relations (VCCR), consular officials can provide a long list of consular services to citizens of their sending State, such as: facilitating administrative procedures

---

and Barbuda, Belize, Brunei, additional delegation in Bosnia and Herzegovina—Banya Luke, Chad, Panama, Samoa, Timor-Leste, and Vanatau);

24 There are 10 third countries where *only one Member State is represented* (Barbados, Central African Republic, Chad, Djibouti, Gambia, Guyana, Sao Tome and Principe, Sierra Leone, Syria, and Vanuatu), while *the EU has a delegation in all of these third countries, with the exception of Sao Tome and Principe*; and 13 countries where *two Member States are represented* (Fiji, Haiti, Kyrgyzstan, Laos, Liberia, Malawi, Madagascar, Mauritius, Niger, Papua New Guinea, Saint Lucia, Suriname, and Togo), while *the EU has a delegation in all of these third countries, except one—Saint Lucia.* The Member States' diplomatic and consular representations are especially limited in Central America and the Caribbean, Central Asia and Central and West Africa. Data taken from the following website: <http://ec.europa.eu/consularprotection/index.action> (accessed January 2013).

25 See for examples the numbers provided by a survey of the European Commission from 2007. At that time, there were only eighteen non-EU countries in which none of the twenty-seven Member States had either an embassy or a consulate, while currently the number has increased to twenty-six; see "Action Plan 2007–2009" and related "Impact Assessment", European Commission, Communication to the European Parliament, the EU Council, the Economic and Social Committee and the Committee of Regions, Document COM (2007) 767 final of 5 Dec. 2007 and Document SEC (2007) 1600 of 5 Dec. 2007.

26 The People's Republic of China, the Russian Federation, the United States of America, and Canada, see <http://ec.europa.eu/consularprotection/index.action> (accessed January 2013).

27 Commission Staff Working Paper, Impact Assessment, accompanying the document, *Proposal for a Directive of the Council on co-ordination and co-operation measures regarding consular protection for unrepresented EU citizens*, SEC(2011) 1556 final, Brussels, 14.12.2011.

28 L. T. Lee and J. Quigley, *Consular Law and Practice*, Third Edition, Oxford: Oxford University Press, 2008; A. James and M. Warren, *A Universal Safeguard: Providing Consular Assistance to Nationals in Custody An Introductory Guide for Consular Officers*, available at: <http://www.internationaljusticeproject.org/pdfs/GenericVCCRprint.pdf> (accessed July 2013).

concerning to repatriation in cases of death or serious illness; the exercise of notary and public register functions; the control of maritime and aerial navigation; international judicial co-operation and the extension of passports and visas; and the protection of the interests of minors and other persons lacking full capacity.[29] Securing the exercise of voting rights of citizens resident in a third country is, in certain Member States, also part of the numerous consular functions entrusted to the diplomats and consular officials.[30] Therefore, the existence of a consular or diplomatic mission of Member States can secure participation of EU citizens in national and European elections.

Some of the situations in which consular assistance is most important are those where there are indications that individuals have been subjected to torture or other prohibited ill-treatment, or face a real risk of such treatment, and, especially in cases of detention or incarceration, where such mistreatment is more likely to occur.[31] In these latter situations, the assistance that consuls may give is of utmost importance for the integrity of the judicial proceedings, preventing or stopping mistreatment or abuses from being perpetrated upon citizens. The consular and diplomatic officials can give information and advice on local legal proceedings and may also protest and seek redress when a wrong is committed against one of their co-nationals by local authorities. The overall purpose of consular assistance in situations of deprivation of liberty is to provide necessary humanitarian assistance or access to legal assistance to nationals in custody, and to ensure that the minimum standards of international human rights protection are respected by the public authorities of the receiving third country throughout the legal proceedings.[32] Timely consular

29 However, according to Article 5(m) VCCR, the list is not intended to be exhaustive and consuls can perform functions "which are not prohibited by the laws and regulations of the receiving State or to which no objection is taken by the receiving State".

30 For more details on the exercising of voting rights by third countries outside the Union, please, see the European Parliament, AFCO Committee Report on electoral rights and participation of third country nationals in EU member states, and of EU citizens in third countries (forthcoming).

31 See the REDRESS Report *Tortured Abroad: The UK's obligations to British Nationals and Residents*, September 2012, available at: <http://www.redress.org/downloads/publications/121001tortured_abroad.pdf> (accessed June 2013).

32 The Inter-American Court of Human Rights described the assistance of nationals in foreign countries, especially in situations where they are facing criminal proceedings to be one of the paramount functions of a consular officer: "It is evident that the Vienna Convention on Consular Relations recognizes assistance to a national of the sending State for the defence of his rights before the authorities of the host State to be one of the paramount functions of a consular officer… the real situation of the foreign nationals

assistance is essential for ensuring that foreign nationals facing prosecution and imprisonment receive fair and equal treatment by domestic courts and penal authorities. In third countries that still apply the death penalty, receiving prompt consular assistance ensures not only the foreigner's absolute human rights, such as the prohibition of torture and inhumane and degrading treatment, and procedural human rights, such as the right to a fair trial, but also the most fundamental of human rights, *i.e.*, the right to life. The importance of the assistance services that consular officials can secure for nationals in a foreign country, and the dramatic consequences of the absence of such timely consular assistance were clearly revealed in the *LaGrand* case.[33] In this case, the fate of two German citizens could probably have been different, and their execution could have possibly been prevented if consular assistance had been provided more promptly by the consular missions of their State of nationality.[34]

It can therefore be concluded that the absence of an external representation of a Member State in a third country not only deprives the national of mere administrative services, or endangers her fundamental rights, but in certain urgent circumstances it can actually endanger her life, or even lead to her death.

The negative consequences of absence of an external representation of the Member State of nationality in third countries for EU citizens became most evident in past situations of natural[35] or man-made[36] disasters affecting the

---

facing criminal proceedings must be considered. Their most precious juridical rights, perhaps even their lives, hang in the balance". The Right to Information on Consular Assistance in the Framework of the Guarantees of the Due Process of Law, Advisory Opinion OC-16/99, October 1, 1999, Inter-American Court of Human Rights (Ser. A) No. 16 (1999).

33 *LaGrand Case* (*Germany* v *United States of America*), International Court of Justice (ICJ), 27 June 2001.

34 See the *LaGrand* case. For more legal literature on the *LaGrand* judgment and other similar jurisprudence, see A. James, M. Cross and M. Warrant (eds.), *Equal Protection: Consular Assistance and Criminal Justice Procedures in the USA. An Introductory Guide for Consulates*, third edition, available at: <http://www.internationaljusticeproject.org/pdfs/VCCRguide.pdf> (accessed February 2013); Note, "Too Sovereign but Not Sovereign Enough: Are U. S. States beyond the Reach of the Law of Nations?", *Harvard Law Review* 116 (8), 2003, pp. 2654–2677; P. Van Alstine, "The Death of Good Faith in Treaty Jurisprudence and a Call for Resurrection", *GEO. L.J.* 93, 2005, pp. 1885–1937.

35 For example, the 2010 Icelandic volcanic ash cloud, the same year as the Haiti earthquake.

36 For example, the 2011 World Trade Centre terrorist attack, pandemics, the 2008 Georgian conflict.

whole or large geographical regions of receiving third countries,[37] when thousands of EU citizens sought to return to their Member State of origin, and realised that they did not have an external representation of their Member State to resort to for help. Not even the Member States with the widest network of consular and diplomatic representations were able—on their own—to ensure the protection of all their nationals located in all those affected areas. With the reduction of the external representation network of the Member States and the increasing number of EU citizens residing and travelling in third countries,[38] it is expected that, in the years to come, more EU citizens will find themselves in situations where they cannot benefit from the consular services and more importantly from consular protection from their Member State of nationality.

In the following section we will explore how the specific EU mechanism for securing protection of EU citizens abroad was developed, its functioning during the pre-Lisbon period, and we will identify the successful examples as well as those more problematic cases of implementation of the EU mechanism.

3 Pre-Treaty of Lisbon Forms of Consular Protection of Unrepresented Union Citizens: A Member States' Prerogative

Since 1993, EU citizens travelling to or living in a third country, who do not have an embassy or consulate of their Member State of nationality to resort

37 As happened for example, during the democratic uprising in the Southern Neighbourhood in spring 2011, the earthquake and the tsunami that hit Haiti in January 2010, the Icelandic volcanic ash cloud of 2010 (For a detailed analysis of the implications of the Icelandic volcanic ash cloud (A. Alemanno (ed.), *Governing Disasters—The Challenges of Emergency Risk Regulation*, Edward Elgar, 2011; for a more updated analysis, see, by the same author, the chapter in the present volume), the several acts of local or international terrorism (Sharm el-Sheik 2005, 11 September 2001 Attacks on World Trade Centre in New York), and military conflicts (Lebanon conflict of summer 2006, and the Georgian conflict of August 2008).

38 According to the European Commission's survey of December 2011, the number of unrepresented EU citizens travelling to third countries will increase from 5.12 million to 7.18 million in five years, and to 10 million in ten years, while the number of unrepresented EU citizens resident in third countries will increase from 1.74 million to 2.4 million in five years and to 3.3 million in ten years. Commission Staff Working Paper, Impact Assessment, accompanying the document, *Proposal for a Directive of the Council on co-ordination and co-operation measures regarding consular protection for unrepresented EU citizens*, SEC(2011) 1556 final, Brussels, 14.12.2011, p. 56.

to for help, have enjoyed increased protection abroad under the EU legal system compared to the general international law framework. Unlike the ordinary international law framework, where consular and diplomatic protection of individuals in foreign countries is a mere discretionary right of the State of nationality,[39] the Maastricht Treaty imposed on all the Member States an EU primary law obligation to ensure protection for unrepresented Union citizens abroad under the same conditions as the nationals of those Member States.

Although the EU citizenship right to equal protection abroad has been given an autonomous meaning from its equivalent traditional international law concept,[40] the EU citizenship right is not a novel legal product of the European Union integration project.

This EU citizenship right was inspired by the historical regional and bilateral consular and diplomatic cooperation agreements between the European countries which are to a large extent still in force. European countries offered their citizens a similar right before the creation of the European Community, or their accession to the Union, based on regional and bilateral consular cooperation agreements concluded between them for the purposes of sharing the responsibility of consular and diplomatic representation.[41] Thus, Article 8(c)

39 The 2006 ILC Draft Articles on diplomatic protection include, in Article 19, only a recommendation for States to give due consideration to the possibility of considering diplomatic protection as a necessary remedy in cases of significant human rights violations. As to the exercise of consular protection of individuals, Article 36 of the VCCR recognises an international individual right to consular assistance only between the foreigner and the receiving State and not between the individual and her State of nationality (*Breard, LaGrand, Avena I* and *II*, and *Diallo* judgments of the ICJ).

40 See P. Vigni, "The Protection of EU Citizens: The Perspective of International law" in: J. Larik and M. Moraru (eds.), *Ever-Closer in Brussels—Ever-Closer in the World? EU External Action after the Lisbon Treaty*, EUI Working Paper 2011/10, pp. 91–107; as well as P. Vigni, "Diplomatic and consular protection: Misleading Combination or Creative Solution?", EUI Law Working Paper 2010/11; A. Ianniello-Saliceti, "The Protection of EU Citizens Abroad: Accountability, Rule of Law, Role of Consular and Diplomatic Services", in *European Public Law* 17 (1), 2011, pp. 91–109; M. Moraru, "Protection of EU citizens abroad: A legal assessment of the EU citizen's right to consular and diplomatic protection", *Perspectives on Federalism*, 3 (2), 2011, pp. 67–105.

41 See, inter alia, the Helsinki Convention on Nordic Co-operation (hereinafter the Helsinki Treaty), concluded on 23th of March 1962 between the Scandinavian countries (Denmark, Sweden, Finland, Iceland and Norway), or the Agreement on Consular Assistance and Cooperation signed between the three Baltic States of Estonia, Latvia and Lithuania, before they acceded to the EU on 5 February 1999. For the entire list of bilateral and regional agreements between the European countries on consular cooperation, see Chapter Three, Section 2.1.2 of the Final Report of the CARE (Consular and Diplomatic

of the Treaty of Maastricht did not invent a new consular cooperation mechanism between the Member States, but it built upon numerous previous bilateral or regional consular and diplomatic co-operation agreements concluded between the European countries for the purpose of ensuring the widest possible representation of their foreign interests and protection of their citizens in the world.

European countries having long cultural and diplomatic ties, such as the Benelux countries, some of the Central and Eastern European countries, and the Baltic States,[42] have concluded agreements the substantive scope of which was very similar to that envisaged later on by Article 8(c) of the Maastricht Treaty[43] and sometimes even broader. For example, Article 3 of the Baltic Agreement signed in 1999 provides, in addition to the limited situations where EU law currently also requires Member States to ensure consular protection to unrepresented Union citizens,[44] a new consular function which, in principle, could be exercised also for the benefit of non-nationals who are citizens of one of the contracting States. Namely a type of provision of consular services that has traditionally been perceived as being reserved to the State of nationality—notary services.[45]

The added value of the Maastricht Treaty was to unite this fragmented consular and diplomatic cooperation framework under the ambit of the EU, and

---

Protection: Legal Framework in the EU Member States) Project (hereinafter CARE Report), available at: <http://www.careproject.eu> (accessed February 2013).

42 The Baltic cooperation is dedicated entirely to issues of consular assistance. For example, Article 3 of the Baltic Agreement reiterates the cases set out in Article 5(1) of Decision 95/553/EC and adds a new consular function in Article 3(g)—[the consular and diplomatic officials of the Contracting Parties] acting as notary in capacities and performing certain functions of an administrative nature, in conformity with the laws and regulations of the receiving State.

43 Article 34 of the Helsinki Treaty reads as follows: "Public Officials in the Foreign Services of any of the High Contracting Parties who are serving outside the Nordic countries shall, to the extent that it is compatible with their duties and when no objection is lodged by the country in which they are serving, also be of assistance to citizens of the other Nordic countries, should the latter not be represented in the territory concerned".

44 See Article 5(1) of Decision 95/553/EC.

45 See Article 3(g) which reads as follows: "[*the consular and diplomatic officials of the Contracting Parties*] *acting as notary in capacities and performing certain functions of an administrative nature, in conformity with the laws and regulations of the receiving State*". The entire content of the Baltic Agreement as well as other similar consular and diplomatic cooperation agreements can be accessed in the CARE database, available at: <http://www.careproject.eu/database/browse.php> (accessed June 2013).

to impose on all Member States the obligation to provide equal protection of all Union citizens who are unrepresented in third countries.

The Maastricht Treaty did not, though, define what it meant by "protection of unrepresented Union citizens abroad", and the term was not clarified by the several subsequent Treaty amendments. The term 'protection abroad' of citizens is also to be found in national Constitutions[46] and national laws[47] of some of the Member States and has usually been interpreted by academics as encompassing both consular and diplomatic protection and assistance.[48] During the preparation of the Maastricht Treaty some of the Member States proposed more concrete terms, such as: consular and/or diplomatic protection.[49] The drafters of the Maastricht Treaty opted for a general term due to two main considerations. In the light of the very different conceptual approaches of the Member States to consular and diplomatic protection of nationals, a general term was needed that would ensure the exercise of the EU right to equal protection abroad under all of these domestic legal constituencies.[50] Secondly, the drafters did not want to limit the substantive ambit of the right from the start, but to leave the door open for the future evolution of the right to equal protection of unrepresented Union citizens abroad.

In concrete terms, protection of unrepresented EU citizens abroad during the pre-Treaty of Lisbon period could have been secured by way of different EU instruments and under different pillars (Community[51] and CFSP).[52] The Member States preferred, however, to keep the exercise of protection

46 Bulgaria, Estonia, Hungary, Latvia, Lithuania, Poland, Portugal and Romania, CARE Report, Chapter three, point 4.1 at 608.

47 Denmark, Finland, Greece, Slovakia and Slovenia.

48 See S. Faro and M. Moraru, "Comparative analysis of legislation and practice on consular protection and assistance of the 27 EU countries", in: S. Faro, M. P. Chiti and E. Schweighofer (eds.), *European Citizenship and Consular Protection. New Trends in European Law and National Law*, Naples: Editoriale Scientifica Napoli, 2013, pp. 157–291.

49 See for example, Spain's proposal, Documentation de la RIE, Vol. 18, 1991, pp. 333–338 and 405–409; L. Nuergas, "De la ciudadania europea a la ciudadania de la Union", *Gaceta Juridica*, 1992, pp. 93–94.

50 The topic of the EU citizenship right to equal protection of unrepresented EU citizens abroad is not an exception within EU law formation, since in many areas, and particularly those touching upon foreign policy matters, EU law is a product of complex political bargaining: the law therefore usually contains a degree of—sometimes even intentional—politically necessary fuzziness. See, K. Koskinen, *Beyond Ambivalence. Postmodernity and the Ethics of Translation*, Tampere: *Tampereen yliopistopaino*, 2000, p. 86.

51 Possibly under ex-Articles 308 and 3(u) EC Treaty.

52 Ex. Articles 20(1) and 12 EU Treaty.

of EU citizens abroad under their exclusive control. Thus the most widely employed mechanism was *ad-hoc* horizontal cooperation among the consulates and embassies of the Member States under a limited number of EU measures: 1) Decision 95/553/EC[53] and Decision 96/409/CSFP[54] adopted for the purpose of implementing former Article 20 EC Treaty, in conjunction with 2) the Civil Protection Mechanism.[55] These rules are still in force, with the ex-Article 20 EC Treaty remaining substantially unchanged by the Treaty of Lisbon.[56] Complementary to the Civil Protection Mechanism, protection of unrepresented Union citizens in third countries could also have been secured through the military and civilian capabilities of CSDP missions, but only in cases of emergencies, and only for the purpose of evacuating European citizens.[57] However, military assets can only be used for humanitarian purposes as a last resort and where there is no other available civilian alternative.[58] In spite of the theoretical possibility of ensuring protection of Union citizens

53 Decision 95/553/EC, regarding protection for citizens of the European Union by diplomatic and consular representations, *OJ*, 1995, L 314/73.

54 Decision 96/409/CFSP, on the establishment of an emergency travel document, *OJ*, 1996, L 168/11.

55 Council Decision 2007/779/EC Euratom establishing the EU Civil Protection Mechanism (Recast), *OJ*, 2007, L 314/9. The Civil Protection Mechanism has been triggered for the purpose of consular assistance of Union citizens only in crisis situations affecting third countries.

56 Former Article 20 EC Treaty is currently Article 23 TFEU. The only important change brought about by the Treaty of Lisbon to former Article 20 EC Treaty consists in a new paragraph conferring legislative power upon the Council to adopt, by way of special procedure, Directives in the field of protection of unrepresented Union citizens abroad. Apart from this addition, paragraph one, which reproduces word for word Article 20(2) (c) TFEU, remained substantially the same.

57 Consular and diplomatic protection as an external dimension of Union citizenship is only one aspect of the protection of EU citizens abroad. Consular protection can also be conferred upon EU citizens in third countries hit by disasters by ESDP missions. Interestingly, the first Decision adopted on the basis of former Article 17 TEU concerned the evacuation of EU nationals whenever they are in danger in third countries. It was adopted as a *sui-generis* Decision that was not published in the Official Journal. See Doc. 8386/96, Decision de Conseil du 27 juin 1996, relative aux operations d'evacuations de ressortisants des Etats membres lorsque leur sécurite est en danger dans un pays tiers—see more in R. A. Wessel, *The European Union's foreign and security policy: a legal institutional perspective*, Dordrecht: Martinus Nijhoff Publishers, 1999, p. 133.

58 *European Council on the Enhancement of the European Security and Defence Policy of 2008* and Article 43(1) TEU, according to which CSDP missions have, *inter alia*, rescue and assistance tasks.

by way of military forces, in practice, the CSDP missions have, so far, never been used towards this end.[59]

3.1 *Horizontal Implementation of the Unrepresented EU Citizen's Right to Equal Protection Abroad*

Former Article 20 of the EC Treaty provided that the Member States shall establish the necessary measures amongst themselves to secure the protection required under that Article. Following this EU primary law obligation to adopt positive integration measures, the Member States have adopted two measures in a peculiar legal form, the main purpose of which was to preserve their sovereign powers in a traditional state-like field, i.e. Decisions of the Representatives of the Governments of the Member States meeting within the Council.[60] The first of these Decisions was adopted on 19 December 1995, and although generally entitled Decision 95/553/EC regarding protection for citizens of the European Union by diplomatic and consular representations, it referred only to consular assistance functions in five limited sets of circumstances. On 25 June 1996, the second implementing measure was adopted, being attributed a very narrow subject—Decision 96/409/CSFP establishing a common European Emergency Travel Document.

Decision 95/553/EC limits the Treaty based right to equal protection abroad of the unrepresented EU citizen to consular protection by any Member State's diplomatic and consular representation to the following five situations: death; serious accident or serious illness; arrest or detention; victims of violent crime; and relief and repatriation of distressed citizens. In addition, Member States agreed to offer assistance in cases of loss of travel documents by issuing a European Travel Document that would allow the EU citizen to return to his or her EU country of residence.[61] All Member States offered some kind

59 For a more detailed analysis, see J. Larik, "Operation Atalanta and the Protection of EU Citizens: Civis Europapaeus Unheeded?", in: J. Larik and M. Moraru (eds.), *Ever-Closer in Brussels—Ever-closer in the world? EU External Action after the Lisbon Treaty*, EUI Working Paper LAW 2011/10, pp. 129–144.

60 For a detailed comment on these types of Decisions see B. de Witte, "Chameleonic Member States: Differentiation by Means of Partial and Parallel International Agreements", in: B. de Witte, D. Hanf and E. Vos (eds.), *The Many Faces of Differentiation in EU law*, Antwerpen: Intersentia, 2001, pp. 261–62; and for a legal assessment of the nature of these two particular Decisions (95/553/EC and 96/409/CFSP), see M. P. Chiti and M. Moraru, "The right to consular protection before and after Lisbon", in S. Faro, M. P. Chiti and E. Schweighofer (eds.), *op. cit.*, n. 48 pp. 17–41.

61 Decision 967409/CFSP of the Representatives of the Governments of the Member States, meeting within the Council of 25 June 1996 on the establishment of an emergency travel document, *OJ* L 168, 6.7.1996, pp. 4–11.

of assistance in cases in which a national found herself in financial need, although this assistance tended to be very restrictive.[62]

Decision 95/553/EC ensures a minimum common denominator for the substantive scope of the equal consular protection right of the unrepresented Union citizen. However, it also permits the Member States to offer consular assistance in other situations, and certain, although very few, Member States have taken up this possibility and provide equal consular assistance in other situations in addition to the five mandatory ones.[63]

The other numerous consular services and functions mentioned in Article 5 of the VCCR as falling under the competence of the consular and diplomatic[64] officials were not included by the Member States within the substantive scope of the Union citizen's right to equal protection abroad, such as: passport and visas, refugees, marriage and divorce, extradition and civil procedure, child abduction, other notarial functions, international, cultural, scientific and tourist functions, shipping and aviation, promotion and protection of trade etc. However, some of these functions, in particular visas, extradition and civil procedure, are already regulated to a certain extent by other EU legal acts.[65]

The EC and CFSP Decisions were harshly criticized by legal academics[66] for being an inadequate legal measure for the implementation of a right of the EU citizen and for substantially limiting the consular assistance from which EU citizens benefit under the Treaty-based EU citizenship right. These Decisions are not unilateral EU acts, but "Decisions of the Representatives of the Member States" meaning a form of *sui-generis* international agreement concluded between the Member States in a simplified form. Usually, this format of legal

---

62 This kind of financial aid is provided mainly for the purposes of helping citizens to return to their home country (repatriation), and on condition that a reimbursement commitment is undertaken by the EU citizen; more on the comparative analysis of the Member States' practice in this area can be found in the CARE Report, Section 4.5.6.

63 See, for example, Sweden. For a detailed analysis of the exact services that consular and diplomatic officials of each of the Member States provide to their citizens, see the National Reports included in the Final CARE Report.

64 Although the exercise of consular functions is the prerogative of consular officials, under certain circumstances, diplomatic officials can exercise consular functions (Articles 3 and 70 VCCR).

65 See A. M. Fernandez, "Consular Affairs in the EU: Visa Policy as a Catalyst for Integration?", *The Hague Journal of Diplomacy* 3, 2008, pp. 21–35.

66 A. Ianniello-Saliceti, *op. cit.*, n. 40 pp. 91–109; M. Moraru, "Protection of EU citizens abroad: A legal assessment of the EU citizen's right to consular and diplomatic protection", *op. cit.*, n. 40 pp. 67–105; E. M. Poptcheva, "Judicial and non-judicial guarantees of the right to consular protection", in: S. Faro, M. P. Chiti and E. Schweighofer, (eds.), *op. cit.*, n. 48 pp. 111–123.

measure does not regulate substantive matters, nor does it have legal effects for individuals.[67] The EC and CFSP Decisions, on the other hand, establish the substantive scope of a Treaty based right of the Union citizen to equal protection abroad, and the conditions that Union citizens have to fulfil in order to exercise this right.

By restricting the substantive scope of the Treaty based right of unrepresented EU citizens to equal protection abroad (the EC Decision) and conferring a concrete consular assistance right upon unrepresented EU citizens (CFSP Decision), these two Decisions clearly create legal effects for EU citizens, even though this type of Decision is not designed to directly affect the rights of individuals. This category of act is commonly used for regulating procedural, EU institutional matters, and therefore, even if, in certain limited circumstances, such acts produced binding legal effects, these were limited to the Member States, having no direct impact on the rights and obligations of individuals.[68] Therefore, in the light of their limited legal effects, the fact that individuals enjoyed limited judicial guarantees against this hybrid type of Decision did not create problems, in practice, for the protection of the fundamental human rights of EU citizens.

On the other hand, the two Decisions adopted in the field of protection of EU citizens abroad are exceptions from this rule since they directly affect EU citizens' right to equal protection abroad by restricting the substantive scope of the EU citizen's right[69] without conferring upon the EU citizen sufficient legal remedies to claim before national and European courts.[70] Despite being part of EU law, the legal nature of international agreements under these Decisions restricts the available EU legal remedies to infringement procedures. The main effective judicial remedy which the EU legal order conferred upon individuals, namely the direct action of annulment, is not available to injured EU citizens against these Decisions, nor is it clear whether domestic courts can refer preliminary questions to the CJEU on the interpretation and application of these

67 See R. H. Lauwaars, "Institutional Structure" (Chapter IV) in P. J. G. Kapteyn, A. M. McDonnell, K. J. M Moterlmans and C. W. A. Timmermans (eds.), *The Law of the European Union and the European Communities*, fourth edition, Alphen aan den Rijn: Kluwer Law International, 2008, p. 221; B. de Witte, *op. cit.*, n. 60 pp. 261–65.

68 For a detailed analysis of this type of act, see B. de Witte, *op. cit.*, n. 60 pp. 261–62.

69 The EU primary law right guaranteeing equal protection to EU citizens abroad has been substantially limited to five mandatory cases of consular assistance by these *sui-generis* types of legal measure: death; serious accident or serious illness; arrest or detention; victims of violent crime; and relief and repatriation of distressed citizens.

70 See R. H. Lauwaars, *op. cit.*, n. 67 p. 221.

Decisions, or afford damages to individuals on the basis of claims based upon the civil liability of the State.[71]

The limited judicial guarantees enjoyed by individuals under the EU and national legal framework have prevented the citizens of the EU from lodging complaints against domestic violation of their EU citizenship right to equal protection abroad, and also contributed to the minimal exercise and knowledge of this right by EU citizens.[72]

At the time of writing, the EC and CFSP Decisions are still in force without ever having been amended, even if the Decisions provided for a mandatory amendment by the end of 2007.[73] In 2011, following the new EU legal framework introduced by the Lisbon Treaty, the Commission put forward a proposal for a Council Directive on consular protection of unrepresented Union citizens abroad.[74] However, until the Directive is adopted, the two *sui generis* EU acts of questionable legality and effectiveness continue to be in force and to regulate the field of the EU citizenship right to equal protection abroad.

In addition to day-to-day consular assistance, the Member States' external representations have closely co-operated in cases of crisis affecting third countries. In such circumstances, the assistance of unrepresented EU citizens has usually involved providing updated guidance on the latest developments, issuing emergency travel documents required to return home, and securing the evacuation of EU citizens from a third country affected by natural or man-made disasters.[75] In recent years, the EU countries have shared human and technical resources on a constant basis in cases of crisis for the purposes of ensuring the prompt evacuation of all EU citizens from the affected third countries, without differentiating based upon nationality between the EU citizens. An example of

71 On the legal status, effects and judicial remedies against Decisions of the Representatives of the Governments of the Member States concluded within the Council, in general, see R. H. Lauwaars, *op. cit.*, n. 67 p. 221; and B. de Witte, *op. cit.*, n. 60 pp. 261–62.

72 According to the information collected by the following surveys: Eurobarometer No. 188 of July 2006 and Flash Eurobarometer No. 213 of February 2008. Along the same line, see also the more recent Flash Eurobarometer No. 294 'EU citizenship' of March 2010.

73 Article 7 of Decision 95/553/EC reads as follows: *"Five years after its entry into force, this Decision shall be reviewed in the light of experience acquired and the objective of Article 8c of the Treaty establishing the European Community"*. A similar Article was incorporated into Decision 96/409/CFSP.

74 For more details see the Section of The Treaty of Lisbon entitled "strengthening the role of the Union delegations in the field of protection of Union citizens in the world".

75 See the contribution to this volume of the European Commissioner for International Cooperation, Humanitarian Aid and Crisis Response, K. Georgieva.

this good practice can be found in relation to Cyprus, where over 60,000 non-nationals were repatriated during the 2006 Lebanon conflict.[76]

In 2007, the concept of 'Lead State' was introduced by the Council of the EU,[77] whereby a Member State that is represented *in situ* accepts responsibility for the consular assistance of all unrepresented EU citizens. It was first put into practice by France in Chad, in early 2008, when it evacuated more than 1,200 citizens from 12 Member States and several third countries (60 nationalities in all). According to the Council Guidelines, the responsibility of the Lead States is limited to bringing the Union citizens to a place of safety. Once all Union citizens in need of evacuation arrive at such a place, the mission of the Lead State ends.

Independently of the Lead State role, both small and large Member States continued to assume the responsibility of evacuating EU citizens of other nationalities than their own, when they found themselves in need of urgent help. This happened, for example, during the 2008 Georgian conflict, where Estonia, a small State, secured the repatriation of non-national EU citizens.[78] More recently, when the democratic revolution shook Libya in the spring of 2011, only 8 Member States were represented, while around 6,000 EU citizens, many of whom were not represented, were evacuated.[79]

To conclude, it can be noted that although former Article 20 EC Treaty conferred a right upon "all" unrepresented EU citizens to receive help from "any" of the Member States represented in a third country, the Member States have limited the substantive and personal scope of this Treaty-based Union citizenship right by way of different international burden-sharing agreements: first by adopting the EC and CFSP Decisions; then by way of ad-hoc arrangements limiting the choice of the Union citizens to only one Member State represented *in situ*, the identity of which is made public in only a few cases, therefore delaying

---

76 See the CARE Final Report, p. 649.

77 Council Conclusions, General Affairs and External Relations, 2808th Council meeting, 10654/07, Presse No. 137.

78 As, for example, happened during the 2008 Georgian conflict, when Estonia secured the repatriation of non-national EU citizens. After the earthquake that hit Haiti in 2010, Italy arranged the evacuation of 1,300 EU citizens of which around 250 were not represented by diplomatic or consular authorities of their EU country of nationality. Numbers and facts were taken from the CARE Final Report and from European Commission Communication *Consular protection for EU citizens in third countries: State of play and way forward*, COM (2011) 149/2 of 23 March 2011.

79 European Commission—ECHO, *Libyan Crisis*, Factsheet, 21 June 2011, available at: <http://ec.europa.eu/echo/files/aid/countries/libya_factsheet.pdf> (accessed March 2013).

the provision of help that a Union citizen might urgently need. Certainly, these burden-sharing agreements pursued a legitimate aim, namely that of distributing the consular assistance responsibilities among the Member States' representations in third countries and thereby prevented concentration of requests for consular protection, thus ensuring an efficient implementation of the right. Yet, such arrangements have constantly represented a threat to the effectiveness of consular protection when leading to referrals from one Member State to another.

3.2 *Limited Vertical Consular Cooperation during the Pre-Treaty of Lisbon Period*

Even if the implementation of the unrepresented Union citizen's right to equal protection abroad was, in the pre-Lisbon period, carried out primarily by way of horizontal consular cooperation among the Member States due to the Member States' desire to preserve their full powers in the field of consular protection of citizens abroad, once the Member States started to feel overwhelmed by the magnitude and frequency of disasters affecting their citizens in third countries, forms of vertical consular cooperation started to appear. For instance, the Community Civil Protection Mechanism was amended in 2007 for the purposes of also covering consular protection of Union citizens in need of urgent help in third countries.[80]

To date, the EU's Civil Protection Mechanism has often been activated for the purposes of supporting the Member States in ensuring consular assistance to EU citizens in major emergencies in third countries. The Mechanism was activated in past crises such as: Libya (2010),[81] Mumbai (2008)[82] and Libya

80 Preamble 18 of the Civil Protection Mechanism (Council Decision 2007/779/EC Euratom establishing the EU Civil Protection Mechanism (Recast), *OJ*, 2007, L 314/9 reads as follows: "The Mechanism could also be used for supporting consular assistance to EU citizens in major emergencies in third countries, regarding civil protection activities, if requested by the consular authorities of the Member States".

81 In particular, two grants (with a value of €112,000) were awarded to two Member States which evacuated about 150 EU citizens. See Commission Staff Working Paper, Impact Assessment, accompanying the document, *Proposal for a Directive of the Council on co-ordination and co-operation measures regarding consular protection for unrepresented EU citizens*, SEC (2011) 1556 final, Brussels, 14.12.2011, p. 18.

82 In Mumbai, the Mechanism was triggered by the French Presidency and activated in order to assist severely wounded EU citizens after the Mumbai attacks; this operation complemented bilateral operations undertaken by Member States to evacuate more than 100 non-wounded EU citizens to Europe. The costs of the evacuation were 50% co-funded by the Civil Protection Financial Instrument. See Commission Staff Working Paper, Impact Assessment, *ibid.*, p. 18.

again in early 2011.[83] During the Gaza crisis in January 2009, nearly 100 people were evacuated in armoured buses thanks to the EU Delegation's support.

Co-operation among the external representations of the Member States for the purposes of securing the protection of EU citizens abroad has, for the most part, been a success story. However, several problems have been documented in practice. For example, during the 2008 terrorist attacks in Mumbai, it was reported that certain Member State representations rescued only their own citizens while refusing to rescue EU citizens of other nationalities.[84] Problems have also been encountered by EU citizens when trying to obtain European Travel Documents in situations that were not the result of disasters.[85]

Most of the problems concerning the effective exercise of the EU citizen's right to equal protection abroad,[86] registered before the entry into force of the Treaty of Lisbon, were the result of the discretionary implementation of the EU primary law obligation by the Member States, which resulted in: different legal status and effects of the right to consular and diplomatic protection of citizens (certain Member States recognise a fundamental right to their nationals, others only a right, while others have an approach whereby consular and diplomatic protection is a matter of policy under the executive's control); the right to equal protection abroad of EU citizens had a different substantive and personal scope depending on the specific domestic approach adopted by the Member States in relation to their own citizens; different forms of the transposition of the relevant EU legal regime;[87] and different legal remedies, if any, were recognised for the unrepresented EU citizen.[88]

---

83 See EU press release of 23.02.2011 available at: <http://europa.eu/rapid/pressReleasesAction.do?reference=IP/11/222&format=HTML&aged=0&language=EN&guiLanguage=en> (accessed March 2013).

84 See the Article entitled "MEP attacks EU consular reaction in Mumbai" in *EU Observer*, available at: <http://euobserver.com/justice/27253> (accessed march 2013). See also F. Forni, brief comment on the situation in: "The Consular Protection of EU Citizens during Emergencies in Third Countries", in: A. de Guttry, M. Gestri and G. Venturini (eds.), *International Disaster Response Law*, Springer T.M.C. Asser Press, 2012, pp. 155–177.

85 See CARE Report, Chapter Three, Section Five.

86 For a detailed assessment of the problems concerning the effective exercise of EU citizens' right to equal protection abroad, see S. Faro and M. Moraru, *op. cit.*, n. 48 pp. 157–291.

87 Moreover, Member States have transposed the Decision 95/553/EC into their national legislation at different times and in different ways (e.g., through laws, circulars, and constitutions) or in some cases they have failed to transpose both this Decision and Decision 96/409/CFSP entirely. For a detailed analysis, see the CARE Report, Chapter Three, Section 2.3.1.

88 In addition to the unclear *ratione personae* and *ratione materiae* scope of the right to equal protection of the EU citizen abroad, the concrete implementation of this right by the Member States and the EU was also not well established. For instance, the functioning of

The solution, so far, in cases of Member States facing difficulties in ensuring prompt consular assistance for all their nationals abroad has generally come from horizontal consular cooperation, whether initiated solely through intergovernmental cooperation mechanisms[89] or through EU instruments.[90] However with the financial crises sharply affecting all Member States budgets, horizontal cooperation had already proved to be insufficient and will become increasingly insufficient in light of the growing number of unrepresented Union citizens, especially in third countries where no Member States are represented.[91]

The solution to the on-going reduction of the external representation network of the Member States and their budget allocation for consular and diplomatic assistance services therefore also has to come from outside national capabilities. The Treaty of Lisbon has revolutionized the conduct of EU foreign affairs both substantially and institutionally.[92] Among the most relevant amendments with regard to ensuring protection of EU citizens in the world, we

---

the co-ordination and co-operation among the Member States' external representations, and the precise role of EU delegations on the ground is unclear; additionally the procedure for the reimbursement of consular assistance services was cumbersome and not uniform across domestic jurisdictions. For more on this see the *CARE Final Report*, Chapter Three (available online), and S. Faro and M. Moraru, "Comparative analysis of legislation and practice on consular protection and assistance of the 27 EU countries", in: S. Faro, M. P. Chiti and E. Schweighofer, (eds.) *op. cit.*, n. 48 pp. 157–291.

89 For example, under Decisions of the Representatives of the Governments of the Member States 95/553/EC and 96/409/CFSP, or ad-hoc arrangements concluded between the Member States' external representations existent in a third country, and by way of Lead State arrangements.

90 As for example, under the Civil Protection Mechanism, Council Decision 2007/779/EC Euratom establishing the EU Civil Protection Mechanism (Recast), *OJ*, 2007, L 314/9.

91 There are 26 countries outside the EU where no Member State is represented, while the EU has a delegation in 8 of these third countries, see *op. cit.*, n. 24.

92 Spatial constraints do not allow an in-depth analysis here of all substantive and institutional amendments brought about by the Treaty of Lisbon in the field of the EU's external relations. For a complete assessment of the Treaty of Lisbon changes in EU external relations, please, see M. Cremona, "Defining Competence In EU External Relations: Lessons from the Treaty Reform Process", in: A. Dashwood and M. Maresceau (eds.), *Law and Practice of EU External Relations—Salient Features of a Changing Landscape*, Cambridge: Cambridge University Press, 2008, and by the same author, "The Union's External Action: Constitutional Perspectives", in: G. Amato, H. Bribosia and B. de Witte (eds.), *Genèse et Destinée de la Constitution Européenne: Commentaire du traité établissant une Constitution pour l'Europe à la lumière des travaux préparatoires et perspectives d' avenir*, Bruxelles: Bruylant, 2007.

would point out the establishment of a diplomatic service for the EU[93] which includes around 140 Union delegations operating globally and making the EU better represented externally than most of the Member States. In several third countries,[94] only the EU has an 'embassy'.[95] In this context, what becomes evident is the potential added value of the EU delegations for ensuring the protection of unrepresented EU citizens *in situ* by providing certain consular services or opening their premises to EU citizens.

4 The Treaty of Lisbon—Strengthening the Role of the Union Delegations in the Field of Protection of Union Citizens in the World

The above mentioned normative deficiencies in the EU citizen's right to equal protection abroad, which diminished the effectiveness of this right, have, to a large extent, been remedied by the Treaty of Lisbon. The legal nature and scope of the EU citizen's right to equal protection abroad was clarified as being both an EU citizenship right,[96] and a fundamental right of the EU citizen (Article 46 EU Charter). The Treaty of Lisbon did not change the wording of the EU citizenship right to equal protection abroad, thus maintaining the previous convoluted text. However, the clarification of the substantive scope of this right came from the EU Charter which, by entering into force together with the Treaty of Lisbon and having the same legal force as the Founding Treaties, had the legal force to clarify the substantive content of the EU citizenship right to equal protection abroad. Article 46 of the EU Charter clarifies the substantive scope of the EU citizen's right to equal protection abroad as being

93 The European External Action Service established by Article 27(3) TEU and Council Decision 2010/427/EU of 26 July 2010 establishing the organisation and functioning of the European External Action Service, *OJ*, 2010, L 201/30.

94 See *op. cit.*, n. 24.

95 Although the founding Treaties and the Council Decision establishing the EEAS refer formally to Union delegations, academics have also used the term Union 'embassy' when referring to Union delegations, unlike the Member States, notably, the UK, which have long fought for the Treaty of Lisbon to drop any reference to the terms 'embassy' or 'Minister for Foreign Affairs' used by the Constitutional Treaty. See J. Wouters and S. Duquet, "The EU and International Diplomatic Law: New Horizons?", *Hague Journal of Diplomacy* 7, 2012, pp. 31–49.

96 The right to equal protection abroad is provided by Article 20(2)(c) TFEU which is located among the other three EU citizenship rights and under the Chapter on Non-Discrimination and Citizenship.

both consular and diplomatic protection of the unrepresented EU citizen by the Member States represented in third countries on equal terms as the citizens of such Member States receive in similar situations.[97] This maximalist interpretation of the substantive scope of the unrepresented Union citizen's right to equal protection abroad, which includes both consular and diplomatic protection, has been criticized by both Member States[98] and legal academics on grounds of violation of the general norms of international law and of the intention of the Treaty drafters.[99]

It is true that the Member States have divided opinions on whether diplomatic protection also falls within the scope of the right to equal protection of EU citizens abroad.[100] However the main opposition to the maximalist interpretation of the EU concept of "protection abroad" of unrepresented Union citizens comes from international law academics[101] who argue that such a maximalist interpretation would run contrary to public international law which still shares a traditionalist interpretation of diplomatic protection as

---

97 Article 46 is entitled "the right to consular and diplomatic protection" thus indicating that whilst outside the EU, any EU citizen can enjoy both consular and diplomatic protection from any of the Member States that is represented in the third country where the EU citizen is located under the same conditions as the nationals of those Member States.

98 See the UK's position from a recent report in relation to the Commission's proposal for a Directive on consular protection of unrepresented Union citizens: "The Government's view—endorsed by both the Committee and its predecessor—has consistently been that: *consular services are the responsibility of Member States*; are, quite rightly, at the top of Ministers' and officials' agenda, at home and abroad; a good level of cooperation between Member States already exists, and work was underway to improve it further; missions staffed by EU officials could not provide a service of the same standard, with the level of immediate accountability that ensured that it remained thus; the *Government would resist the expansionist elements in these proposals with vigour and determination*". (emphasis added). See the Thirty-third Report of Session 2012–13 of the Foreign and Commonwealth Office, available at: <http://www.publications.parliament.uk/pa/cm201213/cmselect/cmeuleg/86-xxxiii/8615.htm> (accessed June 2013).

99 A. M. H. Vermeer-Künzli, "Where the Law becomes Irrelevant: Consular Assistance and the European Union", *op. cit.*, n. 12 pp. 965–995.

100 Not all Member States agree with this maximalist interpretation of Article 46 EU Charter and Article 20(1)(c) TFEU, see, notably, the UK's position in the UK National Report from the CARE Final Report, p. 521.

101 Legal scholars, especially international law academics, have also argued in favour of a minimalist interpretation of the substantive scope of the fundamental right to equal protection abroad of unrepresented EU citizens, as encompassing only consular protection (*i.e.*, the fundamental right to consular and diplomatic protection should be understood as encompassing only consular protection and not also diplomatic protection). See A. M. H. Vermeer-Künzli, *ibid.*

a discretionary right of the State which can only be exercised for the benefit of its citizens.[102] The EU mechanism establishes certain exceptions from the traditional public international law mechanism of consular and diplomatic protection for the purpose of ensuring effective protection of EU citizens also outside the EU. These exceptions refer to the legal nature of consular and diplomatic protection as a discretionary right of States,[103] and the requirements for its legal exercise under the public international law framework, such as: nationality of claims or, in their absence, the consent of third countries for consular and diplomatic protection exercised by non-nationality States.

As to the requirement of nationality of claims, the legal basis for the exercise of consular and diplomatic protection under the general international law framework is the nationality of the State exercising protection for the injured individual, while the EU mechanism is premised on the EU citizenship, which is itself established based upon the nationality of a Member State.[104] This precise bond between an unrepresented Union citizen and a non-nationality EU country is challenged by public international law academics as not being sufficiently strong and genuine to justify the exercise of diplomatic protection.[105]

---

102 See Article 3(1) of the ILC Draft Articles on Diplomatic Protection. See J. Dugard, *Seventh Report on diplomatic protection*, United Nations General Assembly, A/CN.4/567, United Nations, New York, 7 March 2006, p. 10; A. M. Vermeer-Künzli, "Exercising Diplomatic Protection, the fine line between litigation, demarches and consular assistance", *ZaöRV* 66, 2008, pp. 339–340; T. Stein, Interim Report on "Diplomatic Protection Under the European Union Treaty", in: *ILA Committee on Diplomatic Protection of Persons and Property, Second Report*, New Delhi, 2002, pp. 36–7.

103 Unlike public international law, which describes consular and diplomatic protection of citizens as a discretionary prerogative of the State of nationality, EU law has limited to a certain extent this discretionary State prerogative in the situation of EU citizens who are not represented by their Member State of nationality in third countries. In these situations, the Member States no longer dispose of a discretionary prerogative, but have a binding legal obligation to ensure consular and, arguably, also diplomatic protection to the unrepresented non-national EU citizens.

104 The fact that EU citizenship is established on the basis of the nationality of an EU country could be interpreted as contributing to considering the EU citizenship as possibly fulfilling the requirement of nationality of claims for the purposes of the public international law concept. See F. Geyer, "The External Dimension of EU Citizenship Arguing for Effective Protection of Citizens Abroad", *CEPS Policy Brief*, No. 136, July 2007. For a different opinion, see A. M. Vermeer-Künzli, *ibid.*

105 For a detailed account of the criticism of the EU mechanism on account of absence of the 'genuine' link test, see A. V. Künzli, *When Law becomes irrelevant: Consular assistance and the European Union*, *op. cit.*, n. 12; J. Dugard, 2006, *op. cit.*, n. 102 at p. 10. A. V. Künzli, "Comments on the Green Paper on diplomatic and consular protection of Union citizens in third countries", Leiden University, the Netherlands, on the European Commission's

However, the complex issue of whether EU citizenship can make the link between the non-national Member State exercising diplomatic protection and the injured unrepresented EU citizen a genuine one, does not need to be settled as long as third countries have consented to the exceptional EU practice. The EU mechanism of consular and diplomatic protection exercised by non-nationality States is accepted by international law as long as the States involved, including third countries,[106] have consented[107] to these exceptional norms conferring more favourable treatment to individuals.[108] Article 23(1) second sentence of the TFEU stipulates that "Member States shall adopt the necessary provisions and start the international negotiations required to secure this protection." Apart from a few exceptions,[109] neither the Member

website section entitled "Contributions on Diplomatic and consular protection of Union citizens in third countries", available at: <http://ec.europa.eu/justice_home/news/events/news_events_en.htm> (accessed 18 June 2007). See also R. Wessel and B. van Vooren—"The EEAS' Diplomatic Dreams", in: P. Quinn (ed.), *Making European Diplomacy Work: Can the EEAS Deliver?*, EU Diplomacy Papers 8/2011; J. Wouters and S. Duquet, "The EU and International Diplomatic Law: New Horizons?", *The Hague Journal of Diplomacy* 7, 2012, pp. 31–49, who also spotted the possible tension between the EU legal framework and general international norms on diplomatic protection of individuals.

106 A non-EU country is not bound by EU Law, but it can be bound by international treaty provisions, if party to the Treaty, or international customary norms on the "consent" to the protection by a State other than the State of nationality of the protected person. These norms are Article 8 of the 1963 Vienna Convention on Consular Relations, and Articles 45(c) and 46 of the 1961 Vienna Convention on Diplomatic Relations.

107 In the case of the sending State and the non-nationality State the consent has to be expressed, while in the case of receiving third countries, the consent can also be only implicit, resulting from established practice, see Article 8 VCCR with regard to consular assistance, and the ICJ Judgment in "*ELSI*" for diplomatic protection. In this regard, in the *ELSI* case, the USA granting diplomatic protection to a non-US company was considered legitimate by the ICJ due to the fact that it was based on an agreement, i.e. the 1948 Treaty of Friendship between Italy and the USA. By analogy the same argument also applies to the exercise of diplomatic protection for the benefit of private individuals, and not solely to legal persons as in the ELSI case. *Elettronica Sicula S.p.A.* (ELSI) Judgment of 20 July, 1989, in ICJ Reports (1989): 15.

108 Even though public international law has gradually developed into a legal order that is more than the sum of state wills and now also other internationally recognised actors, such as international organisations' wills, it still primarily follows a voluntarist construction approach. See S. Besson, "How international is the European legal order? Retracing Tuori's steps in the exploration of European legal pluralism", No Foundations, 2008, available at: <http://www.helsinki.fi/nofo/> (accessed June 2013).

109 These Treaties are concluded by Italy: the bilateral agreements signed by Italy after the entry into force of the Maastricht Treaty are: the Conventions with Ukraine in 2003 (Article 62), Republic of Moldova in 2000 (Article 61), Georgia in 2002 (Article 60), Great

States, nor the Union[110] have concluded international agreements with all the countries around the world securing an explicit acceptance of the EU exceptional mechanism. However, in 20 years of the existence of the EU mechanism of protection of unrepresented Union citizens abroad, no third country has opposed the exercise of the mechanism by the Member States of the EU. This widely spread practice could be argued to contribute to the formation of a customary norm of international law accepting the exceptional EU practice as legitimate practice.

By virtue of its international legal personality[111] and express Treaty requirements,[112] the EU is bound by international law, both customary[113] and

People's Libyan Arab Jamahiriya Socialist in 1998 (Article 2) and Russian Federation in 2001 (Article 37); and Portugal: the Consular Convention between Portugal and the Russian Federation (2001), Article 36(5). See CARE Final Report, Chapter three, Section 2.1.2.

110 Since 2006, the European Commission has proposed, on several occasions, that Member States include a "consent clause" i.e. a clause providing for the agreement of a third State that the consular and diplomatic authorities of a represented Member State can provide protection to nationals of unrepresented Member States under the same conditions as to its own nationals, within mixed agreements that are to be concluded or amended with non-EU countries. In 2011, in a Report of the European Commission it was mentioned that "the Commission—taking due account of the specificity of each negotiation—proposed to include a consent clause in mixed agreements with certain third countries. Negotiations are ongoing". See European Commission, Green Paper on diplomatic and consular protection of EU citizens, COM(2006) 712 of 28 November 2006; Communication from the Commission to the European Parliament and the Council, Consular protection for EU citizens in third countries: State of play and way forward, Brussels, 23.3.2011 COM(2011) 149 final.

111 The Lisbon Treaty has conferred explicit legal personality upon the EU, according to Article 47 TEU.

112 According to Article 3(5) TEU. In addition to express founding Treaty requirements, there is also the established case law of the CJEU. The CJEU has stressed time and again that the EU "must respect international law in the exercise of its powers" in Case C-181/73, *R. & V. Haegeman v. Belgian State* [1974] ECR I-449, Case C-162/96 *Racke v Hauptzollamt Mainz* [1998] ECR I-3655; C-286/90 *Ankagemyndigheden v Peter Michael Poulsen and Diva Navigation Corp* [1992] ECR I-6019, para. 9 f; C-405/92 *Mondiet* [1993] ECR I-6133, paras. 13–15; Joined cases C-120/06 P and C-121/06 P *FIAMM and Fedon v Council and Commission* [2008] ECR I-6513; C-308/06 I*ntertanko et al. v Secretary of State for Transport* [2008] ECR I-4057; Joined Cases C-402&415/05 P *Yassin Abdullah Kadi and Al Barakaat International Foundation v Council and Commission of the European Union* [2008] ECR I- 6351, para. 291; C- 91/05 Commission v Council (*ECOWAS*) [2008] ECR I- 3651, para. 65.

113 Racke, para. 45 f; C- 432/92 Anastasiou [1994] ECR I-3116, para. 46 f.; *Poulsen*, paras. 9 and 10; Case C-366/10 *Air Transport Association of America and others v Secretary of State for Energy and Climate Change*, Judgment of 21 December 2011, para. 108, nyr.

treaty law; it is thus responsible for breaches of international law. In spite of the public international lawyers' view,[114] the present author argues that by establishing the right to equal protection abroad for EU citizens, the EU has not violated international law. The legitimacy of the EU mechanism rests upon the fact that international law allows more favourable norms with regard to the protection of citizens abroad, and the EU exceptional norms have been consented to, on the one hand by all EU countries and, so far, also tacitly accepted by numerous third countries.[115]

As to the issue of whether or not the drafters of the Maastricht Treaty and the subsequent Treaty amendments intended to include the public international law concept of diplomatic protection within the EU concept of "protection abroad" of unrepresented Union citizens, it seems that the Member States preferred to adopt an open-ended substantive legal concept whereby, if practice requires, services that qualify as diplomatic protection under public international law could be secured in the future under the scope of the EU concept.[116] However, for the moment, all the implementation measures refer only to consular protection of unrepresented Union citizens, excluding the mechanism of diplomatic protection.

Turning now to the precise role envisaged under the Treaty of Lisbon for the EU in relation to the protection of EU citizens abroad, it can be noted that the EU is now legally obliged to protect the interests of its citizens abroad (Article 3(5) TEU) and has a foreign service (the EEAS)[117] empowered to enforce this obligation (Article 221 TFEU), while the Member States are required, according to Article 4(3) TEU and Article 35 TEU to ensure sincere cooperation with the EEAS for the purpose of ensuring the Union objective of protecting the Union citizens in the world.

The Treaty of Lisbon has thus made the EU directly responsible for the protection of EU citizens located outside the European Union. However, the idea of ensuring external protection of Union citizens *via* the Union diplomatic delegations did not first appear during the development of the Treaty of Lisbon

114 See, *inter alia*, J. Dugard, *Seventh Report on diplomatic protection*, United Nations General Assembly, A/CN.4/567, United Nations, New York, 7 March 2006, p. 10; A. M. Vermeer-Künzli, *op. cit.*, n. 12 pp. 339–340; T. Stein, *op. cit.*, n. 102 pp. 36–7.

115 For examples of relevant practice of third countries accepting the EU mechanism of protection abroad of unrepresented EU citizens, see CARE Final Report, Section 4.6.1–4.6.4.

116 Linan Nuergas, *op. cit.*, n. 49 pp. 93–94.

117 The European External Action Service was formally launched on 1 December 2010 and became operational in January 2011. See European External Action Service established by Article 27(3) TEU and Council Decision 2010/427/EU of 26 July 2010 establishing the organisation and functioning of the European External Action Service, *OJ*, 2010, L 201/30.

or the Constitutional Treaty. The possibility was put forward for consideration, as early as 1993, at the initiative of the Commission which proposed that protection of Community citizens should be ensured directly by EC Missions.[118] Furthermore EU vessels fishing in the maritime waters of third countries with which the EU had concluded fishing agreements benefited for many years from the diplomatic protection of the Union *via* the then Commission delegations.[119] It thus seems that under areas of exclusive Union competence, the Union had been recognised as having the right to exercise diplomatic protection directly to legal persons. However, it is difficult to imagine practical situations where, private individuals of the EU countries, and not legal persons, could by way of their actions fall under the exclusive competence of the EU and thus benefit from a right to diplomatic protection from the EU even before the Lisbon Treaty.

For the purpose of ensuring effective equal protection abroad, the Treaty of Lisbon has conferred both internal and external legislative powers upon the EU Institutions. On the one hand, the Council was conferred with express legislative competence to adopt, based upon the Commission's proposals, Directives for the purpose of enhancing the effectiveness of EU citizen protection abroad (Article 23(2) TFEU).[120] After consulting the European Parliament,

---

118 Report from the Commission on the Citizenship of the Union, COM(93)702 final, Brussels, 21 December 1993, available at: <http://eur-lex.europa.eu/LexUriServ/LexUriServ.do?uri=COM:1993:0702:FIN:EN:PDF> (accessed March 2013).

119 For example fishing agreements concluded between the EU and certain third countries include two provisions of relevance for the subject: 1) Seizure of fishing vessels flying the flag of a MS shall be notified to the Delegation of the Commission of the EU and simultaneously to the consular agent of the MS of the flag; 2) Before any judicial procedure is started, an attempt shall be made to resolve the presumed infringement through an administrative procedure. This latter provision was interpreted by the then Court of First Instance in Case T-572/93, *Odigitria*, Judgment of the Court of First Instance of 6 July 1995. The then Court of First Instance interpreted this article as a form of diplomatic protection by the EU with respect to vessels that fly the flag of a Member State. The Court of Justice of the EU (at that time of the European Communities) ruled on this case by acknowledging that the EU Delegation abroad had a "duty to provide diplomatic protection" to the detained crew under the fisheries agreement that the European Commission negotiated bilaterally with the non-EU countries concerned. For a complete list of these fisheries agreements, see <http://ec.europa.eu/fisheries/cfp/international/agreements/> (accessed March 2013).

120 As a response to the differences between the 27 national legal frameworks on consular and diplomatic protection highlighted in the previous Sections, the Commission has already made a proposal for a Directive on Consular Protection for Citizens of the Union Abroad, Brussels, 14.12.2011 COM(2011) 881 final 2011/0432 (CNS) approved with

the Council acts by qualified majority (Article 16(3) TEU). The involvement of the European Parliament and the replacement of unanimous decision-making with qualified majority voting limited the long defended prerogatives of the Member States in the field of consular and diplomatic affairs. On the other hand, it should be noted that Article 23(2) TFEU maintained part of the inter-governmental language, since the directives which the Council is entitled to adopt are limited to 'cooperation and coordination' measures, recalling the pre-Lisbon framework limited to cooperation and coordination among the Member States. The 'coordination and cooperation' language of Article 23(2) TFEU gives an indication that the Directive to be adopted might not be used for harmonising the national law and practice on the legal nature, force, material and personal scope of consular and diplomatic protection of citizens. The Council might be entitled to establish only a common model for operational actions in cases of assisting EU citizens in distress. Thus, it could be argued that the ambit of the Directive mentioned in Article 23(2) TFEU is similar to the ambit of the *sui generis* measures that the Member States could have adopted under the previous pillar structure.[121]

Regardless of whether it is only a 'coordination and cooperation' or harmonising Directive, the change of the legal nature of the implementing measures brought about by the Lisbon Treaty is significant in terms of the judicial guarantees available to individuals. Unlike the *sui generis* Decisions of the Representatives which are not Union acts, Directives are subject to the full panoply of EU judicial remedies, thus increasing the effectiveness of the EU citizen's fundamental right to consular and diplomatic protection at both EU and national levels.

In December 2011, the European Commission finally[122] succeeded in making a proposal for a Directive on the Consular Protection of Unrepresented

amendments by the European Parliament, see Report on the proposal for a Council directive on consular protection for citizens of the Union abroad (COM(2011)0881-C7-0017/2012–2011/0432(CNS)), of the Committee on Civil Liberties, Justice and Home Affairs Rapporteur: Edit Bauer (PE 492.575v03-00) of 10 October 2012.

121 The so-called Decisions of the Representatives of the Governments of the Member States meeting within the Council.

122 Since 2006 the Commission has searched for legal ways to eliminate discrepancies between the Member States' exercise of consular protection of unrepresented Union citizens. The most popular method has seemed to be by way of pushing forward the Unionization of the Member States' exercise of consular protection of EU citizens. See Green Paper—Diplomatic and consular protection of Union citizens in third countries (COM/2006/712 final), 28/11/2006. However, it seems that the Commission's proposal of 2011 lost its integrationist spur in favour of the horizontal cooperation framework,

EU Citizens, which has been approved with amendments by the European Parliament,[123] and is currently under negotiation in the Council. The Commission's proposal aims at developing a common set of rules on the procedural applicability and the substantive and personal scope of the right,[124] and a more precise role for the EU with regard to the implementation of the fundamental right of unrepresented EU citizens to equal consular protection. Such a proposal was necessary especially in the light of the Member States' continuous failure to fulfil their obligation to amend the Decision 95/553/EC and Decision 96/40/CFSP for the last 4 years, and the fact that increased judicial guarantees for the protection of the EU citizen's right to equal protection abroad were necessary, but available only with regard to an EU type of legal measure, such as a Directive.

In addition to increased internal legislative competence, the Treaty of Lisbon has also clarified the external legislative competence of the Union. According to Articles 4(1) and 216(1) TFEU, the EU shares its external competence to conclude international agreements with third countries for the purpose of enhancing the protection of EU citizens abroad with the Member States.

---

most favoured by the COCON Working Group, namely, sharing of experiences between the diplomatic and consular representatives on their own unanimous accord so as to establish common practice. See Proposal for a Council Directive on consular protection for citizens of the Union abroad, Brussels, 14.12.2011 COM (2011) 881 final 2011/0432.

123 The amendments proposed by the European Parliament go beyond the intergovernmentalist type of advancement of the right to protection of EU citizens abroad, i.e. horizontal cooperation among the Member States and promoting the Lead State concept. Instead the EP sees the EU's ability to provide consular assistance as a way to enhance the meaning of EU citizenship and bring the EEAS closer to the public by taking full advantage of the consular functions which the EU primary and secondary law has conferred upon the EEAS. See European Parliament legislative resolution on the proposal for a Council Directive on consular protection for citizens of the Union abroad, Rapporteur: Edit Bauer (EPP/SK), 25 October 2012, A7-0288/2012 / P7_TA-PROV (2012) 0394.

124 One of the most important clarifications that the Commission's proposal for a Directive could bring to the scope of the fundamental right to consular and diplomatic protection is a more accurate definition of 'accessible' Member States consulate or embassy, which in turn determines the scope of unrepresented Union citizens. Article 3 of the Commission's proposal defines an accessible external representation of the Member States based on the travelling-time which must be calculated at least on the basis of the same-day return to the place of departure, while in emergency situations the time period can be even shorter. See Proposal for a Council Directive on consular protection for citizens of the Union abroad Brussels, *op. cit.*, n. 122.

The Treaty of Lisbon gave high importance to the practical application of the equal protection of unrepresented EU citizens in specific third countries since it laid down a vertical obligation of cooperation among the EU delegations and the Member States' external representations in several different provisions of both EU primary and secondary law. Firstly, Article 35(3) TEU provides for a vertical obligation of cooperation among the EU delegations in third countries and the external representations of the Member States for the purposes of contributing to the implementation of this right. Secondly, the national consulates and embassies' obligation of vertical cooperation is provided for in addition to the EU primary law and secondary law, first in Articles 5(9) and (10) of the EEAS Council Decision,[125] whereby, the EU delegations are provided with the competence to support the Member States, upon their request, in their role of providing consular protection to citizens of the Union in third countries.

In addition to the obligation of vertical cooperation, the effective implementation of the EU citizen's right to equal protection abroad is ensured by also adding an obligation of horizontal cooperation among the consulates and embassies of the Member States.[126]

It has to be pointed out that the qualification of the EU delegations' competence in the field of protection of Union citizens abroad, according to Article 5(10) of the Council Decision, as 'supplementary' does not necessarily imply a qualification of the nature of this EU competence as supportive in the sense of one of the three main EU competences from the catalogue of competences introduced by the Treaty of Lisbon (Articles 3–6 TFEU). The consular and diplomatic protection of EU citizens in the world is not among the list of supplementary competences of the EU enumerated under Article 6 TFEU, nor are they to be found under one of the other Articles stipulating the different types of EU competences.[127] Therefore, according to the fall-back Article 4(1) TFEU, the EU's competence in the field of consular and diplomatic protection of EU citizens is shared with the Member States, without thus creating a hierarchy between the competences of the Member States and those of the EU to secure protection abroad for unrepresented EU citizens. Article 5(10) of the Council Decision should be seen more as an operational principle guiding the co-operation in practice between the EU delegations and the Member States' external representations.

---

125 Council Decision 2010/427/EU of 26 July 2010 Establishing the Organisation and Functioning of the European External Action Service, *OJ*, 2010, L 201/30.

126 See Article 35 TEU.

127 Article 3 TFEU on exclusive EU competences, Articles 4(2) or 5 TFEU on shared competences.

It should be noted that, in the area of consular affairs, the extent to which specific sub-categories of consular services might be handled by the EU delegations is not regulated in detail by either the founding Treaties, or the EEAS Decision. Both primary and secondary EU law only provide guiding principles for the responsibilities of the EEAS in the area of consular affairs, without detailing the exact consular services that the EU delegations are entitled to exercise in relation to EU citizens.[128] Article 221(1) TFEU is the only provision in the founding Treaty which makes reference to the substantive scope of action of EU delegations. However, this article entrusts the EU delegations with only a general external representation for all EU external relations competences, without specifying what precise consular functions the EU delegations possess.

5 The Role of Union Delegations in Ensuring Consular Services to the EU Citizens

The above short analysis of the relevant amendments brought about by the Treaty of Lisbon has shown that the Union currently possesses explicit substantive competence and the necessary institutional setting to ensure its legally binding objective of ensuring protection of Union citizens in the world.[129]

Even though many of the EU citizens might be relieved to hear this news in times of budgetary cuts being announced by several Ministries of Foreign Affairs, the fact is that the EU still has to make sure that by developing its autonomous norms,[130] it respects ordinary international norms.[131]

---

128 The EEAS Chief Operating Officer David O'Sullivan pointed out that the gaps left by the Lisbon Treaty which only provided the legal basis for the EEAS, and the very basic provisions of the 2010 Council Decision establishing the EEAS, had to be filled in by the EEAS itself. Speech by EEAS Chief operating Officer David O'Sullivan at the Institute of International and European Affairs in Dublin, 6 October 2011, available at: <http://www.eeas.europa.eu/top_stories/2011/061011_en.htm> (accessed March 2013).

129 Article 3(5) TEU.

130 See the jurisprudence of the CJEU in the smart sanctions saga and its Opinion 1/09, *Re draft agreement on the European and Community Patents Court*, 9 March, [2011] ECR I-nyr.

131 Article 3(5) TEU states that the European Union shall contribute to "the strict observance and the development of international law", including the respect for the principles of the Charter of the United Nations (UN Charter): Article 21(1) TEU provides the "the Union's action on the international scene shall be guided by [...] the respect for the principles of the United Nations Charter and international law". The EU is also bound to respect customary rules of international law, *Racke* and *Poulsen*, *op. cit.*, n. 112.

The ability to provide consular services to citizens and secure assistance in emergency situations has traditionally been defined under the international legal framework as a symbol of statehood.[132] This explains why academics, especially international law academics, have argued that the EU, as an international organisation, cannot possess such a competence vis-a-vis its citizens. The issue of the EU's competence to directly secure consular protection to the EU citizens in third countries thus raises sensitive constitutional questions regarding the on-going debate about the legal nature of the EU: Is it *a sui generis* international organisation or a federal type of state? It also explains the position adopted by several Member States which have fervently opposed the recognition of consular powers to the EEAS.[133]

In spite of the explicit opposition of certain Member States to the allocation of more external representations tasks, especially in the field of consular affairs, the Treaty of Lisbon nonetheless found agreement among the Member States on transferring more external representation responsibilities from the national diplomacies to the EU actors. For example, the coordination of the EU positions and demarches which were, pre-Lisbon, the responsibility of the Rotating Presidency, are currently under the direct responsibility of the High Representative, the EEAS and Union delegations.[134]

The difficult task of ensuring external representation of the Union by the Member State holding the Rotating Council Presidency as well as the need to present a more coherent external image of the Union[135] might have influenced the Member States, including those vehemently opposing the idea of the Union taking over more external representations functions, to accept, during

132 See the Montevideo Convention on Rights and Duties of States, Article 1. See also K. Raik, *Serving the citizens?, op. cit.*, n. 22 *Consular role of the EEAS grows in small steps,* CEPS Policy Brief, 30 April 2013, available at: <http://www.epc.eu/documents/uploads/pub_3488_consular_role_of_the_eeas.pdf> (accessed May 2013).

133 See, *inter alia*, Foreign and Commonwealth Office, Thirty-third Report of Session 2012–13, Draft Council Directive on consular protection for citizens of the Union abroad, available at: <http://www.publications.parliament.uk/pa/cm201213/cmselect/cmeuleg/86-xxxiii/8615.htm>; and the National Report on the UK legislation and practice on consular and diplomatic protection of citizens in the CARE Final Report, available at: <http://www.careproject.eu/images/stories/ConsularAndDiplomaticProtection.pdf>

134 European External Action Service, "Report by the High Representative to the European Parliament, the Council and the Commission", 22 December 2011, p. 6.

135 See J. Larik, "The EU on the Global Stage after the Lisbon Treaty: External Action and the External Action Service", in S. Cassesse, B. Carotti, L. Cassini, E. Cavalieri and E. MacDonald (eds.), *Global Administrative Law: The Casebook*, IRPA–IILJ, 2012, pp. 16–25.

the development of the Treaty of Lisbon, to transfer more external representation tasks from the national to the EU diplomatic sphere.

The transfer of external representations tasks from the Rotating Council Presidency to the High Representative, Union delegations and the President of the European Council is a welcome step in the light of the past practice which proved that ensuring external representations functions by the Member States holding the Rotating Council Presidency in third countries was a cumbersome task not only for the small Member States, but also for those possessing one of the wider networks of external representations. It was pointed out that even during the German Presidency in the first half of 2007, the 27 local Presidencies were exercised by seven different Member States. The external representation of the EU becomes even more cumbersome for the Member States in those third countries where only few of them are represented, since such Member States would have to exercise the local Presidency almost on a continuous basis, with all the financial and non-financial burdens which that requires from an embassy. The external representation of the EU in foreign affairs that fell within the competence of the Rotating Presidency posed serious problems not only in terms of its capacity to cover as many regions as possible, but also in terms of continuity. The changing every 6 months of the Member State holding the Rotating Presidency created confusion for third countries in terms of the face, name, telephone numbers, and all the bureaucratic administrative aspects of external relations.

The Union delegations have now taken over the coordination of Member States' embassies from the embassies of the Member States holding the Rotating Presidency,[136] however the transfer of the coordination function was not smooth in all cases.[137] In spite of opposition from several Member States, it seems that there is a progressive recognition of the EU's role in exercising consular and diplomatic protection functions for the benefit of EU citizens.

---

136 Several Reports on the EEAS activities mention the gradual taking over of the external representation and internal coordination role from the rotating Council Presidency in third countries and various multilateral fora by the EU delegations. See, for example: EEAS, *EU diplomatic representation in third countries—second half of 2011*, 11808/2/11 *REV 2*, Brussels, 25 November 2011, and EEAS, "EU diplomatic representation in third countries—first half of 2012", 18975/11, Brussels, 22 December 2011; N. Helwig, *The New EU Foreign Policy Architecture: Reviewing the first two years of the EEAS*, CEPS February 2013, available at: <http://www.ceps.be/ceps/dld/7711/pdf> (accessed may 2013).

137 For example, P. M. Kaczyński pointed out that in Washington some national ambassadors did not show up for local coordination meetings for months. See, P. M. Kaczynski, "Swimming in Murky Waters: Challenges in Developing the EU's External Representation", *FII Briefing Paper* 88, September 2011, p. 9.

Comparing the catalogue of functions that Member States' embassies and consulates are empowered to exercise in third countries with the list of responsibilities of Union delegations, one arrives at the conclusion that there is not much difference between the list of consular and diplomatic functions of Member States' external representations and the list of functions that the embassies of the European Union, an international organisation, can now exercise. The consular functions which a consular mission of a Member State can exercise are specified in Article 5 of the VCCR, and they are thirteen in number. Of this list, only the visas and the notary related functions are not currently performed by the EU. As to the other consular functions, the EU has certain competence to exercise them, including: supervision of judicial proceedings in which EU citizens are involved;[138] Article 5(h) safeguarding, within the limits imposed by the laws and regulations of the receiving State, the interests of minors and other persons lacking full capacity who are nationals of the sending State, particularly where any guardianship or trusteeship is required with regard to such persons;[139] and Article 5(k) and (l) assistance to vessels and ships carrying the EU flag, but also those of the Member States, as long as they are carrying out actions which fall under the exclusive competence of the EU. For example, fishing agreements[140] concluded between the EU and certain third countries include two provisions of relevance to the subject: 1) seizure of fishing vessels flying the flag of a Member State shall be notified to the Delegation of the Commission of the EU and simultaneously to the consular agent of the Member State of the flag; and 2) before any judicial procedure

138 "The EU has informed the Ministry of External Affairs of its intention to send representatives from its Delhi-based missions of Belgium, Denmark, Germany, France, Hungary, Sweden, the United Kingdom, and the EU, to attend the court hearing in the case of Human Rights Defender and National Vice-President of the People's Union for Civil Liberties, Dr. Binayak Sen, as observers. The hearing is scheduled to take place at the Chhattisgarh High Court in Bilaspur on Monday 24 January. This is in line with the EU's agreed policy on Human Rights Defenders. The EU has also expressed to the Indian authorities its concern about the conditions pertaining to the detention of Dr. Sen". Available at: <http://eeas.europa.eu/delegations/india/press_corner/all_news/news/2011/20110121_en.htm> (accessed may 2013).

139 See the reply of the EEAS to a petition of an EU citizen whose child was abducted in Egypt, available at: <http://eeas.europa.eu/petitions/2012/20120820_rights_eucitizens_egypt_en.pdf> (accessed May 2013).

140 See *inter alia*, Article L of the Agreement between the European Economic Community and the Republic of Cote d'Ivoire on fishing off the coast of Cote d'Ivoire, *OJ*, 1990, L 379/0003-0013.

is started an attempt shall be made to resolve the presumed infringement through an administrative procedure.[141]

There is growing cooperation between the EU delegations and the Member States whereby the Union delegations have provided the Member States with significant logistic assistance on numerous occasions for the purpose of ensuring consular assistance for both represented and unrepresented EU citizens in third countries affected by disasters.[142] The delegations have helped with the logistics, including: opening their premises to the EU citizens and the Member States' consular and diplomatic officials and helping with transportation and with communications.[143] Furthermore, according to a Commission study, unrepresented EU citizens perceive Union delegations as "natural" contact points.[144]

---

141 This latter provision was interpreted by the General Court in the *Odigitria* case. The General Court interpreted this article as a form of diplomatic protection by the EU with respect to vessels that fly the flag of a Member State.

142 The most recent example was during the political upheaval in Syria when the EEAS was ready to help with the evacuation of around 25 000 EU nationals in Syria and with hosting the diplomatic officials of four Member States in the EU delegation in Damascus (A. Miozzo's statement of May 2012, available at: <http://www.europeanvoice.com/article/imported/eu-embassy-stays-open-as-expulsions-escalate/74455.aspx> accessed May 2013). Similar operations have been carried out in Libya, Egypt and Tunisia during the spring 2011 political upheaval that affected those countries.

143 On the general role of the EEAS in the field of consular protection of EU citizens, see the December 2011 EEAS evaluation report which stated that "[...] over the past year we have also seen that the EU Delegations can play an important role in the coordination of evacuations of citizens [...]", European External Action Service (2011a) "Report by the High Representative to the European Parliament, the Council and the Commission" (22 December 2011). For an academic position on the role of the EEAS in the field of consular protection of EU citizens, see B. van Vooren and R. Wessel, *op. cit.*, n. 105, and European Parliament, AFET Committee Report on *The Role of the European External Action Service in Consular Protection and Services for EU citizens*, 2013, available at: <http://www.europarl.europa.eu/committees/de/studiesdownload.html?languageDocument=EN&file=85428> (accessed May 2013).

144 See Commission Staff Working Paper, Impact Assessment, accompanying the document, *Proposal for a Directive of the Council on co-ordination and co-operation measures regarding consular protection for unrepresented EU citizens*, SEC (2011) 1556 final, Brussels, 14.12.2011, at p. 28. A similar situation also existed before the entry into force of the Lisbon Treaty. According to the declaration of F. Frattini, Director of the DG Justice in 2007, 17% of Union citizens interviewed believed that they could seek protection from the EU's Commission delegations. See Public hearing: Diplomatic and consular protection (Centre Borschette) Brussels of 29 May 2007.

In addition, the EU delegation in Damascus has recently fulfilled diplomatic asylum tasks, by offering shelter to the consular and diplomatic officials of the Member States which did not close their representations during the armed conflict of 2012.

Therefore, it is evident that the Union is gradually expanding its powers even in the most politically sensitive foreign affairs matters. Scholarly reviews argue that the role of national embassies might gradually be transformed in the future under the impact of the change of institutional settings under the Treaty of Lisbon, and the climate of financial austerity, and represent "fall-back instruments for Member States when European diplomacy cannot deliver".[145] We can observe that, to a certain extent, this is already happening.

In short, the added value of the Treaty of Lisbon in terms of the protection of unrepresented EU citizens abroad primarily consists of enhancing the EU's role, by giving more powers and instruments to the EEAS in the field of consular protection of EU citizens, and ensuring more efficient horizontal co-operation and co-ordination among the external representations of the Member States. The EU's involvement in Georgia, Egypt, and Libya and recently in Syria has demonstrated to the citizens of the EU and to the Member States the added value brought by the EU Institutions in this domain. In these emergency situations the EU has made use of all its disaster response tools,[146] making sure that help is given to the populations of the affected third countries[147] but also to its EU populations caught in the midst of disasters.

However, in spite of the recent attainment of consular and diplomatic functions by the EU, the general norm, in both theory and practice, is that the Member State of nationality still maintains the primary responsibility for ensuring protection of EU citizens abroad. In the event of the absence of the external representation of the Member State, responsibility falls to the other Member States that are represented in the specific third countries, and,

145 See E. Hayes, "EU delegations: Europe's link to the world", in: K. E. Jorgensen and K. V. Laatikainen (eds.), *Routledge Handbook on the European Union and International Institutions, Performance, policy, power*, USA: Routledge, 2013, pp. 34–5.

146 For a detailed overview of the EU's panoply of disaster response tools, see F. Casolari, "The External Dimension of the EU Disaster Response", in: A. de Guttry, M. Gestri and G. Venturini (eds.), *International Disaster Response Law*, Hague: Springer T.M.C. Asser Press, 2012, pp. 129–155; and M. Cremona, "The EU and Global Emergencies—Competence and Instruments", in: A. Antoniadis, R. Schütze and E. Spaventa (eds.), *The European Union and Global Emergencies: A Law and Policy Analysis*, Hart Publishing, 2011, pp. 11–31.

147 Usually via the humanitarian assistance instrument. See for example, N. Keoning, "The EU and the Libyan Crisis: In Quest of Coherence?", *IAI Working Paper* of July 2011.

lastly, responsibility falls on the EU delegations, if requested by one of the Member States.

The final part of this chapter will assess the benefits of increasing the EEAS involvement for both EU citizens in need of assistance and for the Member States' budgetary expenditures.

6 Conclusion

Recent surveys of consulates and embassies of the Member States worldwide have indicated that the number of consular and diplomatic missions of the Member States has been reducing lately,[148] leaving certain geographical areas with limited external representations and an increasing number of third countries where none of the Member States are represented. At the same time, the expectations of the Member States' citizens for a prompt and effective assistance from their national governments in cases of natural or man-made disaster affecting third countries where more and more EU citizens live or travel has increased.[149] Consequently, the pressure on the Member States' executives to find ways of better responding to the needs of EU citizens for urgent protection has also increased. In this context, both the EU and the Member States have made the urgent protection of EU citizens abroad their working motto.

In spite of good intentions, the Union did not, during the pre-Lisbon Treaty period, have the necessary competence to empower its institutions to directly act for the benefit of EU citizens. When the Maastricht Treaty introduced, for the first time, a Union citizen's right to protection outside the Union's borders, the only role envisaged for the Union in this regard was limited to one sentence in the EU Treaty, whereby the consular and diplomatic representations of the Member States and the Community delegations were obliged to cooperate so

148 See R. Balfour & K. Raik, "The European External Action Service and National Diplomacies", *EPC Issue Paper* No. 73, March 2013; M. M. Schilbach, *op. cit.*, n. 22 p. 123; for Hungary, see <http://euobserver.com/economic/28315> (accessed April 2013). For Netherlands, see the Ministry of Foreign Affairs' 'Nota modernisering Nederlandse diplomatie', 8 April 2011, at p. 10 and p. 18; See Annex on *Member States' External Representations and EU Delegations in third countries* in the European Parliament Report on *Access to Electoral Rights: Citizenship, Residence and the Franchise in Local, Regional, National and European election*, Annex drafted by the M. Moraru.

149 M. Okano-Heijmans, "Changes In Consular Assistance And The Emergence Of Consular Diplomacy", in: J. Melissen and A. M. Fernández (eds.), *Consular Affairs and Diplomacy*, Martinus Nijhoff Publishers, 2011, pp. 21–43; J. Melissen, "Introduction: The Consular Dimension Of Diplomacy", in: Melissen and Fernández (eds.), *op. cit.*, n. 66 pp. 1–21.

as 'to contribute to the implementation' of the EU citizen's right to protection in third countries (former Article 20(2) TEU). In contrast with other EU citizens' rights, the drafters of the Treaty did not provide the Council with legislative powers to ensure that the Union citizen's right would be effectively applied and developed. The limitation of the Union's competence is understandable since the right to equal protection abroad of EU citizens involves highly sensitive national political issues: citizenship, foreign policy prerogative of the state, and migration. In the area of foreign policy in general, Member States have usually been resistant to changes that would have as a consequence a restriction of their national decision-making power and traditionally widely accepted freedom of international action. Consequently, the EU model of equal protection of EU citizens abroad was kept out of the reach of the Union's legislative procedures and left to the complete control of the Member States. The only instruments that the Union could have adopted to implement the EU citizen's right were political acts, such as: CFSP measures adopted by unanimous consent,[150] though, in practice, they have never been adopted, or non-binding Council Guidelines[151] adopted in the Council's specific Working Group (COCON)[152] which have been popular with the Member States due to their non-constraining effects.

The Treaty of Lisbon has completely changed this inter-governmental framework and endowed the Union with both internal and external legislative competence that it can use for the purposes of increasing the effectiveness of the protection of its citizens in the world. Finally the EU has the necessary normative and institutional setting for making its grand rhetoric and ambition to fulfil the role of an international actor operational.[153]

It is probably not just the fear of the Member States of transferring state like competences to the Union that has made the evolution of the right towards a Union-Member States shared responsibility difficult, but maybe also the origins of the EU citizenship right to equal protection abroad. The EU citizenship right was born out of the historical regional and bilateral consular and

150 From all the possible types of CFSP measures, a Joint Action would probably have been the most suited measure due to its specific operational character. In addition, CFSP Decisions could have also served the purpose of facilitating the protection abroad of EU citizens.

151 See *inter alia*, Consular Guidelines on the protection of EU citizens in third countries adopted by the COCON and endorsed by the PSC 15613/10, of 5 November 2010.

152 The COCON is made up of representatives of the Member States' Ministries of Foreign Affairs, usually working in the consular and diplomatic affairs unit.

153 See J. Larik, "Shaping the International Order as a Union Objective and the Dynamic Internationalisation of Constitutional Law", CLEER Working Papers 2011/5, 2011, p. 7.

diplomatic cooperation agreements between the European countries which are still in force. Compared to these long existing burden-sharing agreements,[154] the EU citizenship right to equal protection abroad is relatively new, and has departed from this international type of regional cooperation only in recent years under the pressure of the Commission and lately also under the pressure of the European Parliament.[155]

For some Member States, the conferral of consular assistance responsibilities upon the Union for the benefit of its citizens together with the Lisbon Treaty amendments concerning the recognition of the Union's legal personality and entrusting it with an external representation network is seen as highly problematic for their statehood.[156] With these Lisbon Treaty changes, it can be argued that the Union has ticked the last requirements needed under the Montevideo Convention on Rights and Duties of States for the existence of a State,[157] thus arguably possessing all features required by public international norms for being considered a State.[158] In the light of the impact of these Lisbon Treaty changes on the legal nature of the EU and the relation between the EU and the Member States, it is no wonder that, in spite of the climate of financial austerity, certain Member States continue to have a defensive attitude towards their foreign policy independence. Seeing the EEAS as a competitor of national Ministries of Foreign Affairs and more importantly a challenge to their statehood,[159] several Member States try to prevent the development of

154 See more on this in the Section *Horizontal implementation of the unrepresented EU citizen's right to equal protection abroad.*

155 See the amendments proposed by the European Parliament to the Commission proposal for a Directive on consular protection of unrepresented Union citizens which push for an increased role for EU delegations in the field of consular services. See Report on the proposal for a Council directive on consular protection for citizens of the Union abroad, *op. cit.*, n. 120.

156 For the UK, notably.

157 Article 1 of the Montevideo Convention on Rights and Duties of States provides: "the state as a person of international law should possess the following qualifications: a) a permanent population; b) a defined territory; c) government; d) capacity to enter into relations with the other States."

158 The question of the legal nature of the EU is a difficult subject which cannot be answered in this paper due to the limited space. Furthermore the present chapter purports to answer a more practical question, namely that of how the EU can have an impact on increasing the protection of Union citizens abroad.

159 See R. Balfour and K. Raik, *op. cit.*, n. 22 p. 17, available at: <http://www.fiia.fi/assets/news/The%20EEAS%20and%20National%20Diplomacies.pdf> (accessed March 2013).

consular functions by the EU, and of the Union delegations in the field of consular assistance of Union citizens.

In recent years there seems to have been a progressive recognition of the EU's role in directly ensuring the protection of EU citizens in third countries, in forms resembling both consular and diplomatic protection.[160] Both the practices of the EU and Member States affirm the EU power, and in certain circumstances, the obligation to ensure some sort of protection to the EU citizens in need of help in the world. However, Member States have had mixed feelings towards the endowment of the EEAS with specific consular-like functions related to protection of Union citizens:[161] relief that the Union is assuming both political and financial responsibility for Union citizens[162] versus fear of diminished external power and prestige.[163]

However in times of crisis, Member States are more prepared to make radical changes to the way in which they have historically carried out the European integration process in certain fields. The common national solutions adopted, so far, by the Member States for cutting down budgetary expenditure[164] might not be sufficient in the situation of the current financial crisis.

The need for EU intervention in securing protection abroad of EU citizens might become necessary due mainly to two reasons. Firstly, the financial austerity which has forced all Member States to rationalise their external

160 See R. Wessel and B. van Vooren, "The EEAS' Diplomatic Dreams", in: P. Quinn (ed.), *Making European Diplomacy Work: Can the EEAS Deliver?*, EU Diplomacy Papers 8/2011; J. Wouters and S. Duquet, "The EU and International Diplomatic Law: New Horizons?", *The Hague Journal of Diplomacy* 7, 2012, pp. 31–49.

161 See Report by the High Representative to the European Parliament, the Council and the Commission 22 December 2011, available at: <http://www.eeas.europa.eu/images/top_stories/2011_eeas_report_cor.pdf> (accessed February 2013).

162 See CARE Final Report, Report on Latvia at p. 297 and Chapter three Comparative Analysis at p. 663 and pp. 673–4.

163 L. Rayner, "The EU Foreign Ministry and Union Embassies", *The Foreign Policy Centre*, June 2005.

164 Such as a reduction in the numbers of personnel of the Ministry of Foreign Affairs, and especially of the number of posted diplomats. See D. Rijks, "EU Diplomatic Representation in Third Countries", *GARNET paper*, available at: <http://www.ies.be/files/repo/conference2008/EUinIA_VIII_1_Rijks.pdf> (accessed May 2013). K. Raik has also highlighted the mixed views of the Member States regarding the consular role of the EEAS, with several Member States preferring to find solutions within their own diplomatic services which would thus allow them to retain their state sovereignty over a traditional state like field of competence, such as: reductions in the numbers of personnel, allocated funds instead of sharing, not to mention transferring diplomatic or consular competence to the Union delegations. See R. Balfour & K. Raik (eds.) *op. cit.*, n. 22.

representation network, which coupled with the increasing number of EU citizens travelling and taking up residence abroad require a radical change in the future implementation of the fundamental right to consular and diplomatic protection of Union citizens in the world. Secondly, even in situations where the EU citizen in need of help has an external representation of her State of nationality or of another EU State, the intervention of the EU might prove necessary since it benefits from the stronger force of negotiation of the collective twenty-seven EU States. For example, this happens when EU citizens are arrested in third countries and, in spite of the intervention of their EU State of nationality and other EU States, there is no change in the conduct of the third country's authorities vis-à-vis the situation of the EU citizen. Several similar instances have occurred in Cuba, when two politicians were arrested;[165] during the crisis following the elections in Iran, when a French citizen was arrested and put on trial.[166] Once the EU intervened by way of clear public statements[167] and negotiations, which resembled an exercise of diplomatic protection on behalf of the EU citizens concerned, the conduct of proceedings to which the EU citizens were subject to was made more transparent and followed fair trial international standards, or the EU citizens were released from arbitrary detention. This sort of intervention of the EU Institutions directly on behalf of EU

165 In 2001, the Czech finance Minister, a member of the Czech Parliament, and a former student leader and Czech pro-democracy foundation member were arrested by the Cuban authorities on account of "conspiring against the revolution" and "had no right to impunity, whatever their position and rank". See more details at <http://edition.cnn.com/2001/WORLD/americas/01/17/cuba.czechs/>. The diplomatic intervention of the Czech Republic proved insufficient and it requested the help of the EU. A delegation of the European Parliament was also sent and after the cumulative efforts of the EU Institutions, the Czech citizens were released. See more details in J. Malenovsky, "La Pratique de la Protection Tcheque en particulier", in: J. F. Flauss (ed.), *La Protection Diplomatique: Mutations contemporaines et pratiques nationales*, Brussels: Nemesis-Bruylant, 2003, pp. 101–103.

166 See the situation of the French and British embassy employees and a French scholar who were among 100 defendants who appeared in Tehran's Revolutionary Court at a mass trial of Iranians after the crisis following the Iranian elections in 2009 (available at: <http://edition.cnn.com/2009/WORLD/meast/08/08/iran.detainee.trials/> accessed February 2013).

167 Swedish Presidency of the Council expressing its concern over the ongoing trial of an EU citizen in Tehran: "[...] actions against one EU country—citizen or embassy staff—is considered an action against all of EU, and will be treated accordingly. The EU will closely follow the trial and demand that the persons will be released promptly". See P. Vigni, *op. cit.*, n. 40 p. 25.

citizens has encouraged EU citizens in distress to request similar kinds of help directly from the EU, instead of from other EU States.[168]

The EU's commitment to ensuring protection of the human rights of its citizens abroad would go as far as making conditional the economic benefits a third country enjoys under an international treaty with the EU. In the case of an Italian priest arrested in Djibouti in October 2007, a member of the European Parliament asked the EU Council what kind of measure the EU would adopt against the behaviour of Djibouti in this specific case.[169] The Council's response to this occurrence, although not resembling an exercise of diplomatic protection on behalf of the EU citizen, does indicate the extent to which the Council would be willing to go to ensure that its citizens are protected abroad: the EU would have requested Djibouti to comply with the Cotonou Agreement, which expressly subjected economic benefits to the respect of human rights within its territory.[170]

The fact that the EU States dealing with budgetary constraints can gain from sharing capabilities and pooling their resources under the EU umbrella has already been proved by the current practice as highlighted in the previous sections.[171] One of the areas that best shows the above mentioned gains is the disappearance of the representation and coordination functions of the Rotating Presidency, which has relieved the Member States' embassies of the pressure of channelling all their resources during the 6 months period of holding the Rotating Presidency position.

The EU foreign service coordination skills have proved beneficial for ensuring protection of EU citizens in distress abroad during the Arab revolutions which started in the spring of 2011. In light of the increased number of EU

---

168 See Petition of an EU citizen asking several EU Institutions, including the HR and the EEAS, to exercise diplomatic protection on her behalf before the Egyptian authorities. See the Reply of the Head of Division, Directorate North Africa, Middle East, Arabian Peninsula, Iran and Iraq, Brussels/EEAS, 20.08.2012, Ref. Ares(2012)984358-20/08/2012.

169 Parliamentary question, E-0829/08 of 21 February 2008, available at: <http://www.europarl.europa.eu/sides/getDoc.do?pubRef=-//EP//TEXT+WQ+E-2008-0829+0+DOC+XML+V0//EN&language=EN> (accessed February 2013).

170 Council reply, E-0829/08 of 16 of April 2008, available at: <http://www.europarl.europa.eu/sides/getAllAnswers.do?reference=E-2008-0829&language=EN> (accessed February 2013).

171 See also E. Hayes, "EU delegations: Europe's link to the world", in: K. E. Jorgensen and K. V. Laatikainen (eds.), *Routledge Handbook on the European Union and International Institutions, Performance, policy, power*, New York: Routledge 2013, pp. 27–41; Paul Quinn (ed.), "Making European Diplomacy Work: Can the EEAS Deliver?", College of Europe, *EU Diplomacy Paper*, 8/2011.

tools that the EEAS can use (9 more Situation Rooms, a Crisis Platform, and express Union civil protection mechanism),[172] and the proved added value of EU delegations to the coordination of the Member States' capabilities for securing protection of EU citizens in distress abroad, the recognition of the aforementioned consular coordination and supporting tasks of the EU delegations could be of considerable help to both the Member States and for the protection of EU citizens' abroad.

The extent to which the Union delegations can actually take on more diplomatic and consular tasks ultimately depends upon agreements that are to be concluded not only between the Member States[173] but agreements which might also require the consent of third countries, since the exercise of consular protection by Union delegations directly for the Union citizens is exercised extra-territorially to the Union and does not fall within the scope of the Vienna Conventions on Consular or Diplomatic Relations,[174] nor within the customary rules of functional protection as developed by the ICJ.[175] The practice so far has, however, proved that third countries tacitly approve of the EU's exercise

172 According to A. Miozzo, Managing Director for Crisis Response at the European External Action Service, in a speech given on March 2012 at the Institute of International and European Affairs, the EEAS now has 9 Situation Rooms with which to ensure accurate and updated information regarding political situations worldwide. Another co-ordination instrument entrusted to the EU is the Crisis Platform, which is a new instrument created within the framework of the EEAS which, to date, has efficiently ensured the pooling of the Member States and the EU's resources and capabilities for the purpose of assisting EU citizens in third countries affected by disasters. The Crisis Platform has now efficiently ensured the co-ordination tasks of the Member State taking the Rotating Presidency. There are also several new expressly provided EU competences after the entry into force of the Union which can be put in practice by also involving the EU delegations in third countries, such as: humanitarian aid (Article 214 TFEU) and civil protection (Article 222 TFEU).

173 Especially within the framework of the current negotiations being carried out in the Council on the adoption of a Directive on consular protection of unrepresented Union citizens in the world.

174 The EU is not party to the Vienna Conventions on Consular and Diplomatic Relations which are open only to States.

175 Public international law recognises a right to exercise diplomatic protection to an international organisation only with regard to its agents, generally described as 'functional protection', a mechanism which the International Law Commission has described as a different mechanism than the diplomatic and consular protection of nationals which only States can exercise. See Draft Articles on Diplomatic Protection with commentaries, text adopted by the ILC at its fifty-eighth session, Official Records of the General Assembly, Sixty-first Session, Supplement No. 10, 2006 (A/61/10).

of specific mechanisms for ensuring protection of its citizens abroad by way of horizontal cooperation among the Member States and vertical cooperation among the Member States and the EU Institutions and bodies. Therefore, it is up to the Member States under their obligation of sincere cooperation with the EEAS, to turn the creation of the EU diplomatic service into an opportunity to ensure an effective fulfillment of the EU interest of effective protection of Union citizens in the world.

CHAPTER 9

Emergencies, Crises and Threats in the EU: What Role for the Court of Justice of the European Union?

Sara Poli

1 Introduction

The CJEU has rarely dealt with the legality of measures taken by the EU or its Member States to respond to a an emergency situation, whether it be caused by a natural phenomenon or a human activity. There are a number of fundamental reasons for the paucity of case law in this area.

First of all, the primary responsibility for addressing the consequences of an emergency situation lies, as a general rule, with the State of origin. This is the single EU Member State where the event causing such a situation takes place. Therefore, any challenge to responding measures, for example on human rights grounds, must be directed against such an entity. As a last resort, the individual affected by such a violation could bring an action before the European Court of Human Rights (ECHR).[1] Since the victims of a breach of

1 See, for example, the ECHR judgments *Öneryildiz* v. *Turkey* of 30 November 2004 and *Budayeva et al.* v. *Russia* of 20 March 2008. In these cases the Strasburg Court held that the emergency relief measures taken by national authorities as a result of an accident at a rubbish tip and a mudslide breached the provisions of the Convention. It should be noted that the Parties to the ECHR enjoy a certain discretion in countering a "public emergency threatening the life of the nation" (see the so-called "derogation clause in times of emergency" under Article 15 paragraph 1). Yet, under Article 15 paragraph 2, State parties are required to always comply with Article 2 ("Right to life"), except in respect of deaths resulting from lawful acts of war and Articles 3 ("Prohibition of torture"), 4 (paragraph 1) ("Prohibition of slavery") and 7 ("No punishment without law"). On the interpretation of the notion of "public emergency threatening the life of the nation" see case *Lawless* v. *Ireland* (application 332/57) of 1 July 1961; on measures not compatible with Article 15(2) see *A v. The United Kingdom*, Judgment of 19 February 2009, 3455 E.C.H.R. 5 (2009). On the law and practise of derogation clauses in international law, see E. Sommario, "Derogation from Human Rights Treaties in Situations of Natural or Man-Made Disasters", in: A. de Guttry, M. Gestri and G. Venturini (eds.), *International Disaster Response Law*, The Hague, 2012, p. 323. For the time being, the EU is not subject to the obligations of the ECHR. However, the EU institutions will also become bound by the Convention provisions, after the ongoing EU accession procedure to the ECHR is completed.

© KONINKLIJKE BRILL NV, LEIDEN, 2014 | DOI 10.1163/9789004268333_011

the human rights protected under the Convention, may take the national authorities taking emergency action before the Strasbourg Court, the CJEU is only rarely asked to scrutinize any such measure.[2]

Further reasons as to why the judges in Luxembourg have little opportunity to assess the legality of emergency measures relate to the EU constitutional framework. Prior to the Lisbon Treaty there were not many legal bases justifying EU emergency action (within or outside the EU).[3] Beforehand, the EU enacted measures related to emergency situations in order to safeguard the functioning of the internal market.[4]

Additionally, before 2009, EU action under the CFSP escaped judicial control of the CJEU, except for Article 47 of the EC Treaty. Therefore, any measure to counter emergencies within the framework of this policy could not be assessed by the CJEU, unless the CFSP Decision had a link with an EC act, as in the case of asset freezing measures against individuals supporting terrorism.[5]

Strictly speaking, there are only three events that resulted in the adoption of emergency acts which were subject to the scrutiny of the European Courts.

---

2 See, for example, case C-28/05, *G. J. Dokter, Maatschap Van den Top and W. Boekhout* v. *Minister van Landbouw, Natuur en Voedselkwaliteit* [2006] ECR I-05431. In this case, the Luxembourg Court had to consider a national measure taken to act promptly against foot and mouth disease in the light of the right to defense. The action was not upheld. The Court underlines that in a situation of emergency, it is imperative to act promptly against foot-and-mouth disease. This means that the (national) authority may take emergency measures designed to protect public health even without previously obtaining the views of the interested parties. See paras. 76–77. In other cases, the Court was asked to examine EU measures designed to prevent rather than to remedy an emergency situation. See, for example, joined cases *Booker Aquacultur Ltd* (C-20/00) and *Hydro Seafood GSP Ltd* (C-64/00) v. *The Scottish Ministers* [2003] ECR I-07411. In these cases the legality of an EU act designed to control fish diseases was unsuccessfully challenged on human rights grounds (the right to property).

3 Articles 196 (civil protection), 214 (humanitarian aid) and 222 (solidarity clause) of the TFEU were only introduced with the Lisbon Treaty. Article 222 TFEU is the real novelty of the 2009 Treaty. On this article see Blockmans' contribution to this book. The EU has acted in the area of civil protection and humanitarian aid on the basis of pre-Lisbon Treaty provisions such as Article 103 of the Euratom Treaty, in conjunction with the current Article 352 TFEU (civil protection) and the development cooperation provisions (humanitarian aid).

4 For example, the EU adopted a number of measures that had the effect of preventing national responses to an emergency in order to safeguard the functioning of the internal market in relation to bovine spongiform encephalopathy (BSE) and other crises related to food safety and/or animal health protection. See *infra*.

5 See *infra* section n. 3 on the "Kadi line of cases" starting with Case T-315/01, *Yassin Abdullah Kadi* v. *Council and Commission* [2005] ECR II-649.

The first disaster affecting the territory of the EU was the Chernobyl nuclear accident. The emergency measures taken by the EU to protect public health were subject to judicial review in a direct action.[6] However, the latter did not concern the substantive aspects of the challenged Regulation laying down maximum permitted levels of radioactive contamination of foodstuffs and of feeding-stuffs following a nuclear accident or any other case of radiological emergency.[7]

A later—and the most notorious—emergency situation was that linked to bovine spongiform encephalopathy (BSE). The restrictions applied to the import of meat from the UK and other countries prompted litigation in Luxembourg. The CJEU had to strike a balance between the right to human health (as well as the need to protect animal health) and the free movement of goods.[8] The substantive aspects of interim protective measures of the Commission or those adopted by the Member States were contested;[9] in other cases the Commission decision to resume the imports was impugned.[10]

Finally, foot and mouth disease prompted the challenge of a national measure implementing an EU act.[11] In addition, national measures aimed at preventing food safety emergencies as a result of the release of authorizations to place genetically modified organisms on the market, have also given rise to litigation between the EU and its Member States since the 1990s.[12]

In most of the cases referred to the CJEU assessed the legality of EU or national "emergency measures", designed to respond to an exceptional situation, endangering human life or health and often the environment. By their very nature,

6 Case 70/88, *Parliament* v. *Council* [1991] ECR I-4561.

7 Council Regulation (Euratom) No 3954/87, *OJ*, 1991, L 371/1. See Case 70/88, *cit.*, para. 4.

8 See Case C-157/96, *The Queen* v. *Ministry of Agriculture, Fisheries and Food, Commissioners of Customs & Excise, ex parte National Farmers' Union et al.* [1998] ECR I-02211, the order in Case C-180/96, R *United Kingdom* v. *Commission* [1996] ECR I-3903, and the judgments in Case C-180/96, *United Kingdom* v. *Commission* [1998] ECR I-2265 and Case C-365/99, *Portugal* v. *Commission* [2001] ECR I-5645.

9 Case C-428/99, *Van den Bor* v. *Voedselvoorzieningsin- en verkoopbureau* [2002] ECR I-127; Case C-477/98, *Eurostock Meat Marketing Ltd* v. *Department of Agriculture for Northern Ireland* [2000] ECR I-10695; Case C-562/08, *Müller Fleisch GmbH* v. *Land Baden-Württemberg* [2010] ECR I-01391.

10 Case C-393/01, *France* v. *Commission* [2003] ECR I-05405; C-241/01, *National Farmers' Union* v. *Secrétariat général du gouvernement* [2002] ECR I-09079.

11 See, for example, C-28/05, *cit.* n. 2.

12 See, most recently, Joined cases C-58/10 to C-68/10, *Monsanto SAS and al* v. *Ministre de l'Agriculture et de la Pêche* [2011] ECR I-07763; Case C-36/11, *Pioneer Hi Bred Italia Srl* v. *Ministero delle Politiche agricole alimentari e forestali*, judgement of 2 September 2012, nyr; Case C-165/08, *Commission* v. *Poland* [2009] ECR I-06843.

such responding measures were deemed to be adopted for a limited period of time (until the emergency situation ceased). In the light of this, we can say that they were "emergency measures" within a narrow meaning. The most recent example of such measures concern those taken to respond to the volcanic ash crisis. In the *McDonagh*[13] ruling of January 2013, the Court examined the way in which the emergency caused by the eruption of the Icelandic volcano was managed by a private party in the light of obligations stemming from EU secondary law and from an international convention to which the EU was party. As is known, the suspension of air traffic, on precautionary grounds, severely disrupted air transport services. The preliminary ruling referred to, concerns the failure of an air carrier to take the measures required by EU law to assist passengers in the exceptional occurrence of the volcanic ash crisis.

If we widen our field of enquiry to recent case-law centered around *durable* and in some cases permanent EU measures, preventing or addressing a crisis situation, or which are designed to tackle a threat, then, it is possible to identify two relevant cases.

The first is the ruling of November 2012 in the *Pringle* case[14] which focuses on one of the legal instruments designed to address the sovereign debt *crisis*. There is no doubt that the economic situation of a few Member States creates a state of durable emergency capable of threatening the stability of the euro countries as a whole and is potentially an EU-life threatening situation. The case essentially concerns the scope of the EU monetary and economic policies, including the interpretation of Article 122 TFEU, which is the emergency clause enabling the EU to provide financial assistance "where a Member State is in difficulties or is seriously threatened with severe difficulties caused by natural disasters or exceptional occurrences beyond its control".

The second relevant judgment is that of July 2013 in the *Kadi II* case that concerns the legality of EU restrictive measures to tackle the *threat* of terrorism.[15] The case raises the issue of the protection of individual rights of the addressees of the EU anti-terrorist measures.

It is clear that *McDonagh*, *Pringle* and *Kadi* are very different from each other for many reasons. For example, the first case concerns private parties' rights and obligations in the context of an emergency situation; the second one revolves around the legality of an international agreement concluded by the Member States; the third case centres on the lawfulness of EU measures.

---

13 Case C-12/11, *Denise McDonagh* v. *Ryanair Ltd*, judgment of 13 January 2013, nyr.

14 C-370/12, *Thomas Pringle* v. *Government of Ireland, Ireland and The Attorney General*, judgment of 27 November 2012, nyr.

15 See the contributions to this book of Wouters and Duquet.

The only genuine connecting factor is that in each case the CJEU examines whether the standard of behaviour that the EU or the Member States or private parties have shown to address a state of emergency (McDonagh), a crisis (Pringle) or a threat (Kadi) is compatible with EU law. The aim of this contribution is to assess the influence that the Court has exercised on the EU, its Member States and private parties in the management of the emergency, the crisis and the threat mentioned above.

There are different ways for the Court to influence how an emergency, a crisis or a threat is managed. The first is based upon the substantive standard of judicial review. The Court could decide to exercise 'minimal influence' by leaving broad discretion to the institutional actors in addressing a situation of emergency or a threat. This would be in line with the narrow standard of judicial review in a situation of normalcy[16] when the EU institutions have to assess highly complex scientific and technical facts.[17] "*In such a context, the European Union judicature cannot substitute its assessment of scientific and technical facts for that of the institutions on which alone the EC Treaty has placed that task*".[18] The alternative approach is that of the so-to-speak 'highest influence': the CJEU could strictly define the parameters that institutional actors (or private parties) must comply with in preventing or addressing an emergency or threat, regardless of the exceptionality of the event giving rise to an emergency or of the potentially devastating effect of the threat in question.

The Court has another option to affect how a crisis is managed: this is to recognise that the EU rather than the Member States has competence to deal with it. In principle, the impact of the Court on national authorities' powers would be greatest in cases where the judicature recognised that there is a legal basis in the Treaty for the EU to tackle the crisis *in lieu* of its constituent units.

16 This word is borrowed from A. Greene, "Separating Normalcy from Emergency: the Jurisprudence of Article 15 of the European Convention on Human Rights", *German Law Journal*, 2011, p. 1764.

17 According to settled case-law, the legality of EU measures requiring a complex assessment and the exercise of a wide discretion, is checked on the basis of a narrow standard of judicial review. More precisely, "where the European Union authorities have a broad discretion, in particular as to the assessment of highly complex scientific and technical facts in order to determine the nature and scope of the measures which they adopt, review by the European Union judicature is limited to verifying whether there has been a manifest error of assessment or a misuse of powers, or whether those authorities have manifestly exceeded the limits of their discretion [...]". T-291/04, *Enviro Tech Europe Ltd and Enviro Tech International, Inc.* v. *Commission* [2011] ECR II, p. 8281, para. 47.

18 *Ibid.*

Vice versa, the opposite conclusion would be an indication of "minimal influence".

This contribution will assess what is the role that the CJEU sets for itself in *McDonagh, Kadi* and *Pringle* in examining the legality of measures taken to address a situation of emergency following a natural phenomenon such as the eruption of a volcano, the threat of terrorism and the euro crisis.

2 The CJEU Interpretation of Private Parties' Obligations under EU Law in the Emergency Situation of the Volcanic Ash of 2012

The dispute in the main proceedings of the McDonagh case is directly related to one of the measures taken in response to the eruption of the Icelandic Eyjafjallajökull volcano,[19] namely the closure of Irish airspace. Hundreds of flights, including that of the applicant, were cancelled. As a consequence, the latter was held up at the point of departure for several days. During this period she incurred accommodation and other expenses due to her enforced stay. Ms McDonagh sought a refund of these expenses from the air carrier on the basis of the obligation to provide care enshrined in Regulation no. 261/2004.[20] She complained that she had not received the care from Ryanair that the airline was required to provide in case of cancellation of a flight, under the terms of the EU rules.

The CJEU has been called upon to interpret the scope of the obligations of air carriers as enshrined in the mentioned EU Regulation (and conversely the right of passengers) and to assess the validity of this act in the light of the Montreal Convention[21] to which the EU is party.[22] The agreement referred to seeks to protect air carriers *inter alia* by excluding compensation or limiting actions for damages against them.[23] By contrast, the EU Regulation aims to provide a high level of protection for passengers and is, on balance, more

19 See Alberto Alemanno's contribution to this book.

20 Regulation of the European Parliament and of the Council of 11 February 2004 establishing common rules on compensation and assistance to passengers in the event of denied boarding and of cancellation or long delay of flights, and repealing Regulation (EEC) No 295/91, *OJ*, 2004, L 46/1.

21 For the text see *OJ*, 2001, L 194/39.

22 Council Decision of 5 April 2001 on the conclusion by the European Community of the Convention for the Unification of Certain Rules for International Carriage by Air (the Montreal Convention), *OJ*, 2001, L 194/38.

23 See *infra*.

favourable to the latter than to air carriers.[24] A number of rights are conferred upon them in the event of flight cancellation, including the right to receive care from the air carrier when such a sudden event disrupts their travel plans. This right encompasses, under Article 9, the entitlement to be provided with meals and accommodation free of charge. In addition, a right to compensation is provided for.[25] However, in a situation of extraordinary circumstances, the obligation to compensate passengers for the cancellation of their flight does not apply.[26]

The referring court raises a number of questions aimed at defining the scope of the obligation for the air carrier to provide care in an exceptional situation such as the volcano eruption in this case, in the light of the Montreal Convention and EU secondary legislation.

First of all, the question is asked as to whether the cancellation of Ms McDonagh's flight in the circumstances of the volcanic ash crisis falls within the definition of "extraordinary circumstances"—thus triggering the obligation to provide care—or, in the alterative, the circumstances are of a special nature. In the latter case, Ryanair would be free from obligations. Both the AG and the CJEU interpret the material scope of the EU regulation broadly. They recognise that the exceptional circumstances of the volcanic emergency are not different from those envisaged by the Regulation, regardless of the origin and scale of such an event. In addition, the obligation to provide care does not have specific financial or temporal limits in the EU regulation. By ruling in such a way, the Court takes the side of the victim of the emergency rather than that of business operators.

The referring Court also asks whether the wide scope of the rights under the Regulation is valid in the light of the principles of the Montreal convention and the EU Charter of fundamental rights. In particular, the principles of proportionality, of an 'equitable balance of interests' referred to in the Montreal Convention and of non-discrimination. Finally, Articles 16 and 17 of the EU Charter are invoked as possible grounds for the EU Regulation's unlawfulness.

Unsurprisingly, the CJEU considers the EU regulation to be valid. The fact that the obligation to provide care entails financial consequences for air carriers does not breach the proportionality principle since the aim of the EU Regulation is to ensure a high level of protection for passengers. More broadly, the importance of the objective of consumer protection may even justify

24 This is shown, for example, by the fact that the Regulation takes into account consumer protection.

25 Article 5(1)(c) and Article 7.

26 Article 5(3).

substantial negative economic consequences for certain economic operators. In addition, air carriers may pass on the costs incurred as a result of the obligation to provide care to passengers via airline ticket prices.[27]

The principle of "equitable balance of interest", mentioned in the Montreal Convention does not affect the validity of the EU Regulation since it does not apply to the compensatory measures in question in the ruling.

The air carrier invokes the violation of the non discriminatory principle since other modes of transport are not subject to similar obligations to those at stake in the main proceedings. Invoking previous case-law, the Court dismisses this argument. It stresses that:

> the situation of undertakings operating in the different transport sectors is not comparable since the different modes of transport, having regard to the manner in which they operate, the conditions governing their accessibility and the distribution of their networks, are not interchangeable as regards the conditions of their use.[28]

The final ground invoked by Ryanair to question the validity of the EU Regulation is the breach of the right to property under Articles 16 and 17 of the EU Charter on the basis that the Regulation deprives Ryanair of the fruits of its labour and of its investments. The CJEU finds that the measure in question strikes a fair balance between the fundamental rights of air carriers and passengers. The limitations to that right are necessary and meet the general interest recognised by Union law and comply with the proportionality principle.

The final part of the judgment is dedicated to the passenger's right to compensation for failure of the air carrier to comply with its obligation to provide care. It is interesting to note that the Court confers such a right upon passengers, although it is not clearly provided for by the text of the Regulation. It is true that this right is limited to the "reimbursement of the amounts which, in the light of the specific circumstances of each case, proved necessary, appropriate and reasonable to make up for the shortcomings of the air carrier in the provision of care to that passenger"[29] and such a determination is left to the national court. However, it is noteworthy that the Court explicitly[30] creates a

27 Paras. 46–48.

28 Para. 56.

29 Para. 66, second paragraph.

30 Although AG Bot comes to the conclusion that Regulation no. 261/2004 does not limit the obligation to provide care for passengers whose flights have been cancelled owing to extraordinary circumstances, he does not go as far as the Court. He does not explicitly

remedy to the benefit of individuals affected by a situation of emergency, regardless of the financial consequences that this might have for business operators. Although the Montreal Convention does not explicitly rule out compensation for passengers in the case of a flight being cancelled due to exceptional circumstances,[31] the Court could have framed this remedy in more narrow terms. By so doing, it would have curtailed the discretion of national courts in line with the spirit of the Montreal convention that limits in various ways the right to compensation for passengers.[32]

The lesson that may be learnt from this judgment is that when EU secondary law confers upon individuals the right to receive care in the context of an extraordinary situation, the CJEU is prepared to interpret such a right very broadly, even if that interpretation is not fully supported by the terms of an international agreement to which the EU is party. For this reason, we can say that the ruling under examination is somehow inspired by the principle of autonomy of the EU legal order with respect to rules of international law, which has pervaded the "Kadi line" of cases.

3 The CJEU Assessment of the EU Measures to Counter the Threat of Terrorism in the *Kadi II* Case

On 18 July 2013 the CJEU rejected the appeal brought by the Commission, the Council and the UK against the General Court ruling of September 2010.[33] This judgment is the last act of the 'Kadi saga'. The *Kadi II* ruling is an emblematic example of judicial activism: the Court requires the EU authorities to comply with a number of conditions when implementing UNSC resolutions that target individuals in order to counter the threat of terrorism. As a result, the EU authorities' discretion in implementing the orders of the UN sanction

state that the failure to comply with this obligation entitles the victim to a right to compensation.

31 See Case C-549/07, *Friederike Wallentin-Hermann* v. *Alitalia—Linee Aeree Italiane SpA* [2008] ECR I-11061, para. 34.

32 The Convention lays down an obligation to compensate for damage occasioned by the delay, "which does not apply if it proves that it and its servants and agents took all measures that could reasonably be required to avoid the damage or that it was impossible for it or them to take such measures" (Article 19). In addition, it sets out limits of liability (Article 22) and makes any action for damage against the air carrier subject to the conditions and limits of the Convention (Article 29).

33 Judgment of 18 July 2013 in joined Cases C-584/10 P, C-593/10 P and C-595/10, P *Commission et al.* v. *Yassin Abdullah Kadi*, nyr.

committee to freeze the funds of suspected terrorists associated with the Al-Qaeda network is limited.

Let us look at the CJEU ruling in *Kadi II* in detail to appreciate the extent to which the CJEU influences the management of EU counter terrorism action.

The outcome of the case is that the CJEU upholds the GC's ruling annulling Commission Regulation (EC) No 1190/2008 of 28 November 2008 imposing certain specific restrictive measures directed against certain persons and entities associated with Usama bin Laden, the Al-Qaeda network and the Taliban[34] ("the challenged regulation"), in so far as that measure concerns Mr Kadi.

It may be recalled that the impugned act was enacted at the end of 2008. A couple of months earlier the Commission had complied with the Court's ruling in *Kadi I*[35] by disclosing to the person concerned a summary of the reasons underlying his inclusion on the list of suspected terrorists at UN level. This document was provided by the French permanent representative to the EU. Yet, the evidence and the information at the basis of the statement of reasons were not revealed on grounds of confidentiality. Mr Kadi decided to send his comments on the summary of reasons to the Commission within the time limit set by this Institution. He argued that the impugned act breached his right to a defence and to effective judicial protection since the evidence justifying his listing by the UNSC was not fully disclosed to him. In addition, his listing affected his right to property in a disproportionate manner. Having examined the information received, the Commission enacted the challenged Regulation which had the effect of confirming the inclusion of Mr Kadi within the list of natural persons targeted by restrictive measures.

As a result, a new action for annulment of this act was lodged before the GC in 2009. The latter upheld the action in 2010 on the ground that the Commission had breached fundamental rights by not disclosing the evidence and the information that were at the basis of the vague reasons adduced to justify the inclusion of Mr Kadi on the list of suspected terrorists.[36] The defendant introduced the appeal that is examined here.

---

34 *OJ*, 2008, L 322, p. 25.

35 Joined Cases C-402/05 P and C-415/05, P, *Yassin Abdullah Kadi* and *Al Barakaat International Foundation* v. *Council and Commission* [2008] ECR I-6351. In this ruling the CJEU had annulled a Regulation of 2002 (insofar as it concerned Mr Kadi) that had included the name of Mr Kadi for the first time on the list of suspected terrorists whose funds were to be frozen in the EU. This Regulation was annulled on the grounds that it breached the right to the defence and to effective judicial protection. See the judgment at first instance, Case T-315/01, *cit.*

36 Case T-85/09, *Yassin Abdullah Kadi* v. *European Commission* [2010] ECR II-5177.

It should be noted that in October 2012 the Sanctions Committee decided to de-list Mr Kadi after considering his de-listing request and the report produced by the Ombudsperson. Yet, this development does not deprive the action in question of interest, considering that Mr Kadi is only one of the persons whose funds were frozen.

In the last act of the *Kadi* saga the Court concluded that the GC had erred in law in its findings.[37] Yet, this did not affect the validity of its ruling since the impugned regulation was illegal on other grounds.

The CJEU ruling confirms its findings in *Kadi I* that all EU measures, including those which implement an act of the international body which has primary responsibility for maintaining peace and security, are subject to judicial review,[38] in the light of the fundamental rights guaranteed by the EU. Indeed, in a Union based on the rule of law, individuals may rely on judicial review against all measures.[39]

The novel aspect of the *Kadi II* ruling is that the Court makes clear that the measures designed to address the threat of terrorism are subject to the *highest level of intensity of judicial review*,[40] even if they merely implement UNSC resolutions and leave no discretion to the EU legislative authorities. Although the Court is silent on this issue, there seems to be no difference between the envisaged standard of review and that of the EU autonomous regime of restrictive measures.[41] The Court reserves for itself the role of supreme judicial authority on the lawfulness of all restrictive measures, which have their founding authority in the Sanctions committee, contrary to AG Bot's opinion.[42] In order to be

---

37 The Court considers that the GC erred in finding that the Commission had breached the rights to effective judicial protection and to the defence in refusing to disclose the information and the evidence underlying the statement of reasons. Indeed, the Commission complied with EU procedural safeguards when it disclosed the latter document. In addition, it could not have breached the aforementioned rights since the information and evidence supporting the statement of reasons was not in the hands of the Commission (paras. 138–139).

38 Para. 326 of the ruling in *Kadi I*.

39 Para. 66.

40 Contrary to the point made by the Commission, the Council and the United Kingdom, supported the view that the standard of judicial review should be a narrow one. See para. 74 of Joined Cases C-584/10 P, *cit.*

41 On the scope of judicial review for these kinds of measures see the *ONPI* case (T-228/02, [2006] ECR II-4665). AG Bot in his conclusions on the *Kadi II* case considers that the standard of review of restrictive measures of the UN and the EU listing regimes should differ. The standard of the *ONPI* case should not apply to the UN listing regime. See paras. 64–67.

42 He favoured a limited scope of judicial review. Para. 72 and following.

valid, these measures must have an adequate legal basis; in addition, the procedure followed by the EU authorities in listing the names of individuals should comply with the EU standards as set by the Court in this ruling.[43] The right of scrutiny extends to the evidence supporting the statement of the reasons to list an individual.

The Court emphasises that such an in-depth analysis is made necessary by the lack of procedural safeguards that continues to taint the UN Sanction system generally and stresses that the unsatisfactory way in which that system works is also recognised by the ECHR.[44] The CJEU further justifies its active stance on counter terrorist measures with the need to ensure a fair balance between the maintenance of international peace and security and the protection of the fundamental rights and freedoms of the person concerned.[45] Finally, the nature of the restrictive measures, in particular their substantial negative effects on fundamental rights, make a thorough assessment of their legality all the more important. In the event that procedural guarantees are not complied with, the Court will annul the contested measure and erase it retroactively from the legal order.[46] In so ruling, the CJEU discards the option suggested by AG Bot who advocates moderation in the performance of the judicial review by the EU judicature of the sanction committee decisions, given the political dimension of the listing process.[47]

The judgment presents many points of interest. The first concerns the scope of judicial review *vis-à-vis* EU measures merely transposing a UNSC resolution in the area of terrorism. This is very wide. The Court does not hide behind the fig leaf of the confidentiality of information and decides to undertake a review which is not purely formal. The fact that the information and evidence justifying the listing is confidential is not held to be in itself sufficient to screen the measure, implementing the UN freezing decision, from judicial appraisal. The second reason of interest is that the CJEU broadly interprets its power of review of CFSP decisions addressed to natural and legal persons, under Article 275 TFEU.

A further remarkable aspect of the ruling is that in the judgment the Court lays down a sort of code of procedural conduct that the EU institutions must

43 Paras. 117–118.
44 Para. 133.
45 Para. 131.
46 Para. 134.
47 Para. 80.

respect in *managing*[48] the system of restrictive measures according to the principle of good administration. This code dictates rules that concern the conduct of the EU institutions both before the listed person challenges the listing decision and after judicial action is introduced.

Firstly, as a result of the *Kadi I* ruling, the individual concerned must be informed of the evidence relied upon as the basis of the decision to list. This is, at the very least, the summary of reasons provided by the Sanctions Committee. Secondly, the EU institutions are asked by the Court to side with the individual. They have to check the information provided and be convinced that such information allows the individual to effectively make known his views on the grounds advanced against him. Should the affected person provide comments, the institutions have an obligation to examine, carefully and impartially, whether the alleged reasons are well founded, in the light of such comments and any exculpatory evidence provided with those comments.[49] Yet, the Court leaves discretion to the EU authorities in managing its relations with the sanction committee on one sensitive issue. This is the request for additional information other than the statement of reasons. Indeed, the EU authorities may decide:

> whether it is necessary to seek the assistance of the Sanctions Committee and, through that committee, the Member of the UN which proposed the listing of the individual concerned on that committee's Consolidated List, in order to obtain [...] the disclosure of information or evidence, confidential or not, to enable it to discharge its duty of careful and impartial examination.[50]

The Court is careful not to excessively curtail the discretion that these authorities enjoy in managing their relations with the Sanction committee.

Thirdly, should the decision be made to ask for additional information and evidence, then, the institutions are required to check that the supplied material supports the reasons relied on against the person concerned.[51] The

---

48 The assumption of the Court is that the EU institutions enjoy a certain degree of autonomy in managing the system of restrictive measures. The limited margin of manoeuvre of the Commission and the Council vis-à-vis the Sanction committee is underplayed by the CJEU.

49 Paras. 111–114.

50 Para. 115.

51 The Court intends that the EU institutions and the UN bodies cooperate in the spirit of Article 220(1) TFEU. It is taken for granted that the Sanction committee will give the EU authorities the requested information. Yet, this is not a given. On the contrary, the

obligation to state reasons requires that EU acts identify the individual and provide specific and concrete reasons why the competent authorities believe that the individual concerned must be subject to restrictive measures.[52]

Then, the CJEU considers the situation in which a person listed in an EU regulation decides to challenge the validity of the decision to list his name. In this case the EU authorities have the burden of proving "that the reasons relied on against the person concerned are well founded." By contrast, "it is not the task of that person to adduce evidence of the negative, that those reasons are not well founded".[53]

Then, the Court describes the role that it will perform when examining a restrictive measure. The European Courts will fully review the restrictive measure and check whether it is taken on a sufficiently solid factual basis. In order to carry out that examination, the judges may, where necessary, request the competent European Union authority to produce information or evidence, confidential or otherwise, relevant to such an examination.[54] The Commission or the Council are not compelled to make the confidential information available to the judicature. The CJEU defines two possible scenarios. The first is that they decide to keep the information confidential.[55] In this case, the Court will examine the legality of the statement of reasons on the basis of the *available* information and the observations of the person concerned and in case of insufficient evidence to support one of the reasons stated for listing, it will disregard that reason.[56] This implies that if there is not enough information for the CJEU to make a full assessment of all matters of fact and law, it will consider the listing decision as illegal.[57] The second scenario is that the competent European Union authority provides relevant information or evidence to the Court. In this case, the judicature will examine the facts alleged, the information and

---

Sanction committee could refuse to provide the information in an effort to avoid the possibility that the CJEU indirectly subjects its activity to judicial review.

52 Para. 116.

53 Para. 121.

54 Para. 120.

55 "If the competent European Union authority finds itself unable to comply with the request by the Courts of the European Union" (para. 123).

56 "If that material is insufficient to allow a finding that a reason is well founded, the Courts of the European Union shall disregard that reason as a possible basis for the contested decision to list or maintain a listing [. . .]" (para. 123).

57 Para. 137.

evidence as well as the observations submitted by the person concerned and will assess if the listing was appropriate or not.[58]

A delicate issue is the question of whether the information provided by the sanction committee through the Commission can be disclosed to the affected person. On this point, the CJEU seems to (momentarily) side with the EU authorities by acknowledging that security reasons or the conduct of the EU/ Member States international relations "may preclude the disclosure of some information or some evidence to the person concerned". There could be a request by the EU authorities to keep a batch of information confidential. In this case, the Court reserves for itself the final decision on whether (and to what extent) sensitive information may be disclosed to the individual. The balance between legitimate security considerations and individual rights is struck by the CJEU.[59] Should the CJEU consider reasons for confidentiality well founded, alternative measures to the full disclosure of information (such as a summary outlining the information's content or that of the evidence in question) may be proposed. It will be up to the Court to decide if this partial disclosure may affect the probative value of the confidential evidence.[60]

Finally, the CJEU makes clear that if one of the reasons stated by the UN Sanction committee for listing an individual is sufficiently detailed and specific, the decision to list will not be annulled. The fact that all other reasons do not meet this standard does not affect the validity of the measure in question.

In sum, the Court asserts its right to have the last word on the legality of the decision to include (or confirm the inclusion) of the name of a person on the list of suspected terrorist persons, despite the political obstacles that the conduct of international relations (based on the principle of confidentiality of information) imposes upon the EU authorities.

Having outlined the method and the steps that the CJEU will take in examining the reasons justifying the listing of an individual, it turns to examining the statement of reasons. It overrules the GC's finding that all those reasons were not sufficiently detailed and specific to justify the competent authorities' decision to subject the concerned person to restrictive measures.

---

58 "The Courts of the European Union must then determine whether the facts alleged are made out in the light of that information or evidence and assess the probative value of that information or evidence in the circumstances of the particular case and in the light of any observations submitted in relation to them by, among others, the person concerned" (para. 124).

59 Paras. 125–126.

60 Paras. 128–129.

Subsequently, the Court takes into consideration the statement of reasons provided by the Sanctions Committee as well as the comments of the person concerned. It holds that none of the "allegations presented against Mr Kadi justifies the adoption, at European level, of the restrictive measures either because the statement of reasons is insufficient, or because information or evidence which might substantiate the reason concerned, in the face of detailed rebuttals submitted by the party concerned, is lacking."[61]

4 The Influence of the CJEU on the Management of EU Restrictive Measures to Counter the Threat of Terrorism

One of the lessons to be drawn from the *Kadi II* ruling is that when restrictive measures affect human rights, the primary concern of the EU institutions should be respect for such rights. In countering a threat like terrorism, procedural rights of individuals cannot be suspended. There is a parallel between the treatment of procedural rights in the EU and that of fundamental rights such as the prohibition of torture in times of emergency under the law of the ECHR:[62] neither of them can be frozen.

The EU authorities are compelled by the Court not be neutral when procedural rights are breached at UN level; more precisely, they are required to act as a facilitator of the individual's position in asserting his rights. The ruling is likely to have a significant impact on the way the EU institutions manage the threat of terrorism through restrictive measures. Certainly, the conditions laid down by the CJEU for the management of freezing orders, which have their origin in the UN Sanction committee, place the EU authorities in an uncomfortable position with respect to the UN Sanction Committee. The situation of the EU Member States is also difficult *vis-à-vis* the UNSC. At the same time, the CJEU's criticism of the activity of the UN Sanction committee is not likely to be welcomed by this body or by the UNSC.

Kadi II offers the chance to the CJEU to affirm the importance of the rule of law in countering the threat of terrorism. As AG Bot puts it, the fight against terrorism cannot lead democracies [and the EU] to abandon or deny their

61 Para. 163.

62 Article 15 paragraph 2 of the ECHR states that certain rights protected under the Convention, including Article 3 (Prohibition of torture), cannot be derogated by State Parties even in times of emergencies.

founding principles, which include the rule of law.[63] As a result of the Court's stance, the EU becomes the champion of individual rights in global counter-terrorism action. The *Kadi* line of cases may be contrasted with other strands of the case-law in which the CJEU's review of internal legislation, designed to prevent terrorism and/or organised crime, is lenient and according to Bobek, has the effect of making "an inroad into individual freedom".[64]

One might wonder whether this ruling will put pressure on the UNSC to change the sanctioning system. It is doubtful that the UN members will decide to change that system so as to be more human right-friendly *vis-à-vis* individuals. Thus, the wide scope of judicial review defined in this ruling is likely to make the Union "a forum for appeals against or reviews of decisions taken by the Sanctions Committee,"[65] as envisaged by AG Bot.

5 The CJEU Interpretation of the Member States' Agreement Setting up the European Stability Mechanism (ESM) in the *Pringle* Case

One of the emergency clauses contained in the EU Treaties since 1993[66] is Article 122(2) of the TFEU.[67] This provision enables the EU to provide financial assistance to a Member State which is in difficulties caused by natural disasters or exceptional occurrences beyond its control. Article 122 is the "counter weight" provision[68] of the "no bail out clause," namely Article 125. The former legal basis was used to adopt Regulation no. 407/10[69] in the early phases of the Greek economic crisis. Shortly after, reliance on this provision as a basis for

63 Para. 6 of AG Bot conclusions in Joined Cases C 584/10 P, C 593/10 P and C 595/10 P, *European Commission, Council of the European Union, United Kingdom of Great Britain and Northern Ireland* v *Yassin Abdullah Kadi* of 19 March 2013.

64 For a comment on the case-law see Michal Bobek's contribution to this book.

65 See para. 71 of the AG Bot conclusions.

66 Former Article 100 TEC.

67 "Where a Member State is in difficulties or is seriously threatened with severe difficulties caused by natural disasters or exceptional occurrences beyond its control, the Council, on a proposal from the Commission, may grant, under certain conditions, Union financial assistance to the Member State concerned. The President of the Council shall inform the European Parliament of the decision taken."

68 J.-V. Louis, "Guest editorial: The no-bailout clause and rescue packages", *CML Rev.* 2010, p. 983.

69 *OJ*, 2010, L 118/1.

providing financial assistance was criticised for its doubtful compatibility with the "no bail out clause".[70]

The *Pringle* case was raised a couple of years after the outbreak of the euro crisis. At this juncture, it was clear that the Member States had given a strong preference to preventive and responding economic instruments of an intergovernmental nature to address the sovereign debt crisis rather than to EU measures.

This preliminary ruling concerns the interpretation of several articles of part III of the TFEU and other provisions of the EU Treaties.[71] It was referred by the Irish Supreme Court in order to ascertain whether the ESM, set up by the group of Member States whose currency is the euro, complied with EU law. As is known, this is a mechanism designed to address a situation of economic emergency that occurs in one or more of its founders. It was created through an international agreement concluded by seventeen Member States after Article 136 TFEU was revised by Decision 2011/199[72] of the European Council on the basis of Article 48(6) TEU. The amendment, which consisted of adding a third paragraph to Article 136, was designed, in principle, to enable Member States whose currency is the euro to create such a mechanism in order to provide financial assistance to Member States under strict conditionality. In reality, the CJEU confirmed that such a Treaty change was superfluous.[73]

Mr Pringle contested both the legality of the decision modifying Article 136 TFEU and that of the international agreement establishing the ESM, as an intergovernmental creature. In a nutshell, the referring court asked the Court to clarify whether the Member States had circumvented the EU Treaties in setting up the ESM and whether in so doing they encroached upon the powers of the EU institutions. The Court gave a negative answer and considered that the course of action taken by the Member States to create the ESM was fully compatible with the Treaties.

In this case the Court was given the chance to halt the trend of adopting measures to respond to the euro crisis outside the EU Treaty framework. Yet, it refrained from doing so. For the purpose of this contribution, the Pringle case is examined from the point of view of assessing whether the CJEU could have interpreted the EU Treaties as requiring the creation of the ESM as an EU mea-

70 For more details see M. Ruffert, "The European debt crisis and European Union Law", *CML Rev.* 2011, p. 1777.

71 Articles 2, 3 TEU, 4(3), 13 TEU; Articles 2(3), 3(1)(c) and (2), 119 to 121, 123 and 126–127 TFEU.

72 *OJ*, 2011, L 91/11.

73 See Case C-370/12, *cit.*, para. 72.

sure on the basis of the EU Treaties. In other words, it might be speculated whether the judicature could have found Treaty bases to argue in favour of the EU competence to deal with the setting of an instrument designed to address the most important crisis that the EU has ever faced.

The first question raised by the referring Court concerns the legality of Decision 2011/199 with respect to the conditions defined in Article 48(6) TEU. The *Pringle* ruling is remarkable since the CJEU for the first time assesses the legality of an act amending the Treaty and that of an act of the European Council. The conclusion is drawn that the challenged Decision was enacted in compliance with Article 48(6) TEU and does not encroach upon the powers of the EU institutions in terms of monetary policy. The ESM is an instrument of economic policy[74] but does not affect the EU powers in this area. The EU is entitled to adopt merely coordinating measures and the provisions of the EU and FEU Treaties do not confer any specific power upon the Union to establish a stability mechanism of the kind envisaged by Decision 2011/199.[75] Turning to Article 122, the Court states:

> Admittedly, Article 122(2) TFEU confers on the Union the power to grant ad hoc financial assistance to a Member State which is in difficulties or is seriously threatened with severe difficulties caused by natural disasters or exceptional occurrences beyond its control. However, *as emphasised by the European Council in recital 4 of the preamble to Decision 2011/199, Article 122(2) TFEU does not constitute an appropriate legal basis for the establishment of a stability mechanism of the kind envisaged by that decision*. The fact that the mechanism envisaged is to be *permanent* and that its *objectives are to safeguard the financial stability of the euro area as a whole* means that such action cannot be taken by the Union on the basis of that provision of the FEU Treaty (emphasis added).[76]

The Court supports the position taken by the European Council that Article 122 TFEU was not sufficient to empower the EU to create a mechanism such as the ESM. It may be argued that the CJEU could have interpreted the provisions of the EU Treaties as allowing the EU to establish a rescue fund such as the ESM, despite the fact that the EU powers in the area of economic policy are weak.

---

74 Para. 60.

75 Para. 64.

76 Para. 65.

The legal justifications found by the CJEU to exclude this solution are not thoroughly convincing. Indeed, the fact that the objective of the fund was to ensure the financial stability of the euro area as a whole is not a valid reason to exclude reliance upon Article 122. For the purpose of choosing a legal basis what matters are the purpose and the object of the envisaged EU measure. It is true that the objective of the ESM is to secure the financial stability of the euro area as a whole. The object of the mechanism, however, is to provide financial assistance to single Member States that are in difficulty, in a spirit of solidarity. The Court could have placed emphasis on the object of the measure, thus easily placing this mechanism within the material scope of 122(2). As to the second justification, the Court is right in pointing out the unsuitability of Article 122(2) as the foundation of measures designed to provide financial support in a stable manner. Indeed, being an emergency clause, it is designed to address the difficulties of Member States on an *ad hoc* and temporary basis. However, an EU mechanism could have been set up relying upon the double legal basis of Articles 122(2) and 352 TFEU. The latter provision could have been used to fill the gaps within Article 122(2). The substantive conditions of this provision were met since there is no doubt that the setting up of a permanent mechanism fell within one of the policies defined in the Treaties and was necessary to attain the objectives set out by the Treaties, namely a stable currency. In addition, a long lasting mechanism anchored to this double legal basis would not have meant an extension of the EU competence,[77] rather it was necessary for the appropriate exercise of the EU attributed competence.

The CJEU did not take the option of the double legal basis mentioned above into consideration, it merely excluded the obvious: that is that Article 352 could not be the sole legal basis of an EU act setting up the ESM on the grounds of the ERTA case law.[78] The Court narrowly interpreted the potential of the EU Treaties to support the creation of a mechanism such as the ESM. More broadly, the *Pringle* ruling shows a reluctance of the CJEU to assess the lawfulness of

77 Admittedly, in practise the use of Article 352 could be problematic since it required unanimous approval by all EU Member States, including the non euro-States. But reliance upon Article 48(6) TEU to amend Article 136 also made the approval of all EU members necessary. Moreover, the German Constitutional court's negative attitude towards the use of Article 352 in the Decision of 30 June 2009 (2BvE 2/08 *et al.*, para. 328) might have increased the Court's disquiet towards this provision.

78 Para. 67 states: "As to whether the Union could establish a stability mechanism comparable to that envisaged by Decision 2011/199 on the basis of Article 352 TFEU, suffice it to say that the Union has not used its powers under that article and that, in any event, that provision does not impose on the Union any obligation to act (see Case 22/70, Commission v Council ('ERTA') [1971] ECR 263, paragraph 95)."

the Member States' course of action in setting up the ESM. For this reason the Court may be criticised. Indeed, it sanctions the use of non EU instruments to deal with a situation of crisis which the EU was equipped to tackle.

As a result of the *Pringle* ruling the scope of Article 122 TFEU is severely reduced. It is somehow paradoxical that the EU political and judicial authorities considered that the Treaty framework did not allow the EU institutions to create an emergency mechanism to address an EU-life threatening crisis.[79] In a similar vein, although in a different context, AG Kokott emphasises that a broad interpretation of Article 125 would:

> prohibit the Member States, in a case of emergency, for example, to prevent the serious economic and social effects associated with a State bankruptcy, from voluntarily providing mutual assistance. Emergency assistance to any third State would be permitted, while emergency assistance within the Union would be banned. Such a prohibition, it appears to me, would call into question the very purpose and objective of a Union.[80]

It is submitted that when the Member States may choose between EU measures and national measures, they should prefer the former ones when there are sufficient Treaty bases, regardless of the fact that the EU action is not mandatory. Otherwise the relevant provisions of primary law are deprived of *effet utile*.

Enhanced cooperation was a further alternative to an *inter se* international agreement setting up the ESM. The Court briefly explored this issue in *Pringle*. Yet, it concluded that the lack of a specific Union competence to set up a permanent ESM, prevented the possibility to use Article 20(1) TEU.[81]

Having examined the legal arguments that the Court could have used to support the EU competence to act and declare the European Council decision illegal, did the Court really have any other choice than to ratify the Member States' decision to act outside the Treaty framework? Had the Court considered the European Council decision unlawful because it prevented an EU action, the Member States would have considered this position as an attack upon their constituent powers. In addition, "it might have caused a serious

---

79 However, it should be noted that an ESM with "an EU hat" would have presented two disadvantages: it would have been approved without parliamentary control and would have had to be financed through the EU budget.

80 Para. 143 of the view of AG Kokott of 26 October 2012 in case C-370/2012, *cit.*

81 Paras. 167–169.

relapse in the sovereign debt crisis that has plagued the eurozone, and the European Union, since 2010".[82] Even a refusal to answer the questions referred by the national court would have been inappropriate, although for different reasons.[83] In other words, alternative solutions to that envisaged by the Court were not politically appropriate. In a situation of emergency for the entire edifice of the Union, judicial activism could have jeopardised the process of European integration. Therefore, in the plenary session of the Court pragmatism prevailed over the rule of law.

6 Conclusions

This contribution has shown that the Court is seeking to establish itself as the final arbiter and guarantor of the rights of individuals within the Union when the latter counters the threat of terrorism in cooperation with the UN.[84] The standard of judicial review is unusually intense when such a threat affects fundamental human rights. In the *Kadi II* ruling the CJEU may be considered to perform a role that it is broadly similar to that of the ECHR.

The Court is also prepared to apply a wide interpretation to EU-derived rights available to victims of an emergency such as the passengers of air flights in the volcanic ash crisis. This is the case regardless of whether such an interpretation may affect the rights of other private parties such as business operators or conflict with the spirit of a Convention to which the EU is a party.

The *Kadi* and *McDonagh* cases are exemplary of an assertive role of the CJEU in defending the rights of individuals. In these two cases the Court takes an inward-looking approach in the name of the principle of autonomy of the EU legal order.

---

82 B. de Witte, "The Court of Justice approves the creation of the European Stability Mechanism outside the EU legal order: Pringle," *CML Rev* 2013, p. 806.

83 In principle, the CJEU could have declared itself as lacking competence to rule on the validity of the European Council decision emphasising the lack of jurisdiction to rule on the validity of primary law, as suggested by a number of Member States. Yet, this option was against the rule of law—since after the Lisbon Treaty the CJEU was given jurisdiction over decisions of the European Council—not to mention that it would have not been taken well by the Constitutional Courts of Member States. Such a position of the CJEU would have encouraged national courts to become "very active assessors" of EU measures addressing the euro crisis.

84 This is suggested by AG Sharpston in his opinion in Joined cases C-584/10 P, C-593/10 P and C-595/10 P, *cit.*, para. 256.

It may be concluded that the CJEU highly influences the conduct that the EU institutions and private parties (such as the air carriers) have to take in the management of a threat or in an event giving rise to an emergency. By contrast, in the *Pringle* case, by deciding to sanction the Member States' choice to use an international agreement rather than the Treaty provisions, the CJEU has pragmatically opted for judicial containment and "minimal influence". The Court gave its blessing to the course of action taken by the Member States to set up the EU rescue fund. It ruled that EU law did not prevent the creation of the ESM by way of an international agreement even though the EU Treaties contained sufficient legal bases for the EU to set up that fund. It is argued that this assessment was somehow affected by the situation of emergency in which the EU found itself as a result of the sovereign debt crises and by the spectre of possible negative reactions by national constitutional courts to different outcomes of the case.

CHAPTER 10

The Euro Crisis and the Democratic Principle

Giacomo Biagioni

1 Introduction

According to an often quoted definition, while a *rule* supplies an answer "in an all-or-nothing fashion", a *principle* is "one which officials must take into account, if it is relevant, as consideration inclining in one direction or another".[1] Such a definition, correct as it may be for all legal principles, certainly seems suitable for the principle of democracy since it does not imply the application of some given rules but rather the commitment to a general method of government. A democratic government can thus take different forms, as long as it finds its legitimacy in direct elections by the people and its institutions are accountable to the electorate. The democratic principle will not, however, in itself provide a solution for individual legal problems and can be perceived as a general source of inspiration for the legal order.

Consequently, one should not be surprised that, on the one hand, European Union law places strong emphasis upon the democratic principle, now expressly referred to in Articles 9–12 TEU, and, on the other hand, the concrete existence of a 'democratic deficit' in the EU institutional framework is often alleged.[2]

The present chapter aims to address the operation of the democratic principle in the Euro crisis and to assess the concerns expressed as to the legitimacy of the intervention of the European Union for the coordination of national fiscal, budgetary and economic policies. Unlike other contributions about the legal dimension of the Euro crisis, the chapter will not engage in an in-depth examination of all the measures adopted in order to deal with the financial and

1 R. Dworkin, *Taking Rights Seriously*, London: HUP, 1978, pp. 24 and 26. On the relevance of principles of EU law as grounds for judicial review, compared to rules, see K. Lenaerts, J. A. Gutièrrez Fons, "The Constitutional Allocation of Powers and General Principles of EU Law", *Common Market Law Review* 47, 2010, pp. 1629–1669.

2 Recently it has been argued that the real reason for the democratic deficit lies in the excessive dependence of the EU on national politics: see M. Poiares Maduro, "A New Governance for the European Union and the Euro: Democracy and Justice", RSCAS Policy Paper 2012/11, p. 18.

© KONINKLIJKE BRILL NV, LEIDEN, 2014 | DOI 10.1163/9789004268333_012

economic difficulties faced by Member States. After a general overview of the challenges to the democratic principle arising from the Euro crisis (para. 2) it has been deemed preferable to pick out three crucial subject-matters relating to the implementation of the democratic principle—the actors in the Euro crisis (para. 3), the acts of the European Union and/or its Member States in those matters (para. 4) and the existence of a power of judicial review (para. 5)—that will be analysed in turn.

2 The Democratic Principle in the European Union and the Challenges Arising from the Euro Crisis

As a matter of fact, the recognition of the democratic principle as a cornerstone of European integration dates back to even before it was clearly expressed in Articles 6 and 7 of the Maastricht Treaty.[3] However, it is often underlined that several shortcomings in the implementation of the principle can be observed.

The traditional arguments concerning the democratic deficit of the European Union can be summarized as follows. Among the EU institutions, only the European Parliament is directly elected by the citizens. Nonetheless, before the entry into force of the Lisbon Treaty, in some matters, even of core relevance, the European Parliament was confined to a merely consultative role and could only make a negligible contribution to the definition of the policies and to the adoption of the decisions of the European Union.

By contrast, in most matters, the Council and the European Commission were called upon to carry out crucial political functions, even though they do not match the traditional model of representative democracy.[4] The former, being composed of members of the Governments of the Member States, is not, in itself and as a body, accountable to the people. Rather, every single member is supposed to express the political will of his/her State, as developed through the applicable national constitutional procedures.[5]

---

3 A general assessment of the question can be found in B. Kohler-Koch and B. Rittberger (eds.), *Debating the Democratic Legitimacy of the European Union*, Lanham, MD: Rowman & Littlefield, 2007.

4 See also S. Manservisi, "La Commission européenne et la crise de la politique: d'une fonction d'intégration à une fonction de gouvernement?", *Revue du Droit de l'Union Européenne*, 2012, p. 7.

5 The accountability of the Heads of State or Government has been called into question by some scholars, as it would be relevant only at national level and would not take the specific institutional balance of the Union and its allegedly democratic character into account: J. V. Louis, "Les réponses à la crise", Cahiers de droit européen 47, 2011, pp. 359–360.

As for the Commission, the appointment procedure, involving in different ways both the Governments of Member States and the European Parliament, and the theoretical possibility of a motion of censure resemble traditional mechanisms of parliamentary democracy. However, for many reasons, such as the leniency of the control of the European Parliament, the independence of the Commissioners magnified by the high specialisation of its bureaucratic structure, the exclusive commitment to the general interest of the Union and the monopoly of the legislative initiative, the Commission is often perceived as being remote from actual political control. Of course, the same line of reasoning may apply to other institutions, such as the European Central Bank, and to the European agencies, the members of which are appointed mainly on a qualification basis (even though, as is now evident, they do not discharge purely technical functions).[6]

Accordingly, since its members are directly accountable to the people, for a long time a more effective role for the European Parliament in the decision-making process had been advocated as a necessary implication of the democratic principle.

After the entry into force of the Lisbon Treaty the commitment of the European Union to the democratic principle is now clearly expressed by Article 2 and by Title II of the TEU[7] and solemnly declared in the Charter of Fundamental Rights. Moreover, the drafters of the Lisbon Treaty did take the concerns about the actual implementation of the principle into account and devoted much effort to both clarifying its scope of application under European Union law and to improving the democratic guarantees of the decision-making processes.[8]

On one hand, the role of the European Parliament was widely strengthened, insofar as the co-decision procedure was established as the ordinary legislative procedure and extended to cover a large number of EU policy areas and the budgetary powers were equally divided between the Council and the European Parliament. On the other hand, the TEU expressly asserts the idea

---

6 For an assessment of the accountability of the European Central Bank and of the practice known as 'monetary dialogue', see F. Amtenbrink, K. van Duin, "The European Central Bank before the European Parliament: theory and practice after 10 years of monetary dialogue", in *European Law Review* 34, 2009, pp. 561–583.

7 A. von Bogdandy, "A Disputed Idea Becomes Law: Remarks on European Democracy as a Legal Principle", in: Kohler-Koch, Rittberger (eds.), *op. cit.*, n. 3 pp. 31–44; V. Cuesta Lopez, "The Lisbon Treaty's Provisions on Democratic Principles: A Legal Framework for Participatory Democracy", *European Public Law* 16, 2010, pp. 123–138.

8 See also "Editorial Comments. Direct Democracy and the European Union? Is that a threat or a promise?", *Common Market Law Review* 45, 2008, pp. 929–940.

that the European Union is based on a multi-level democracy.[9] Accordingly, the accountability of the EU's actions to the citizens is not granted solely by the involvement of the European Parliament, because the enforcement of the democratic principle also relies upon the participation of national institutions in the EU decisional procedures.[10] Such a general concept is made clear both by Article 10(2) TEU[11] and by Article 12 TEU. The latter provision calls upon national Parliaments to "contribute actively to the good functioning of the European Union", providing a list of the coordination mechanisms between European institutions and national Parliaments, as enshrined in the Treaties. The Protocol on the role of national Parliaments in the European Union and the Protocol on the application of the principles of subsidiarity and proportionality further emphasize the involvement of national institutions in the adoption of EU legislative acts and in the definition of EU policies.[12] The coordination procedures thus envisaged are, of course, additional to the usual scrutiny of the action of every single Government by its national Parliament. It is also worth noting that under Article 10(3) TEU also the principles of subsidiarity and proportionality are regarded as being connected to the democratic principle, since decisions are supposed to be taken as openly and as closely as possible to the citizen.

This summary describes the position in theory. Unfortunately, the building of EU multi-level democracy is now being shaken to its foundations by the global economic and financial crisis that has affected Member States and their sovereign debts, undermining the general stability of the European Union and threatening, in particular, the so-called Euro Area (or Eurozone). Consequently,

---

9 The difference between this model of democracy and models prevailing in Member States is discussed in A. von Bogdandy, "The European Lesson for International Democracy: The Significance of Article 9–13 EU Treaty for International Organizations", *European Journal of International Law* 23, 2012, pp. 315–334.

10 It has been argued that such a pluralistic democracy is, at least currently, the only possible model for the implementation of the democratic principle in the European Union: M. Poiares Maduro, "How Constitutional Can the European Union Be? The Tensions between Intergovernmentalism and Constitutionalism in the European Union", *Jean Monnet Working Papers* 5/04, p. 38.

11 "Citizens are directly represented at Union level in the European Parliament. Member States are represented in the European Council by their Heads of State or Government and in the Council by their governments, themselves democratically accountable either to their national Parliaments, or to their citizens".

12 On the role of national Parliaments, see K. Auel and A. Benz, "Expanding National Parliamentary Control: Does it Further European Democracy?", in: Kohler-Koch, Rittberger (eds.), *op. cit.*, n. 3 pp. 57–74.

the European institutions have devoted significant efforts in reacting to the crisis because of its strong impact on the economies of some Member States and on the European Union in general. The increasing risk of a forced exit of those States from the Euro Area and the fears for its subsequent dissolution have impelled the European Union to adopt a large number of measures, very different as to their content and form.[13]

At first, these measures focused primarily on support by the Member States to rescue the banking system.[14] Subsequently, however, the European institutions were forced to make a direct intervention in order to deal with the serious difficulties affecting several Member States in the wake of the crisis. Accordingly, the European Union, often acting concurrently with the International Monetary Fund, granted large packages of financial aid to some States, preventing—or at least controlling—their state of default.[15] Other States received support from the European Union in different forms when they experienced serious financial speculation against their sovereign debts. Financial assistance was initially granted to Greece through a series of bilateral agreements with other Member States. Subsequently, Regulation (EU) 407/2010, instituting a European Financial Stabilisation Mechanism, was enacted and the European Financial Stability Facility was established pursuant to an agreement concluded on 9 May 2010 by the 27 Member States within the framework of the ECOFIN Council and to a decision of the 16 Member States of the Euro Area, adopted on 7 June 2010.[16]

In addition, it cannot be overlooked that the Euro crisis also brought about important institutional adjustments. A revision of the TFEU was needed in order to grant an unchallenged legal basis for the establishment of a financial

---

13 The effects of the financial crisis on consumer protection and market regulation are described in N. Moloney, "The legacy effects of the financial crisis on the regulatory design in the EU", in: E. Ferran, N. Moloney, J. G. Hill and J. C. Coffee Jr., *The Regulatory Aftermath of the Global Financial Crisis*, Cambridge: CUP, 2012, pp. 111–122.

14 On the measures immediately following the financial crisis and on their efficacy, see the "Editorial Comments", *Common Market Law Review* 46, 2009, pp. 3–12.

15 For a thorough description and analysis of the financial assistance mechanisms see A. De Gregorio Merino, "Legal Development in the Economic and Monetary Union during the Debt Crisis: the Mechanisms of Financial Assistance", *Common Market Law Review* 49, 2012, pp. 1613–1646.

16 EFSF Framework Agreement, published in C-N° 1189 *Journal Officiel Grand-Duché de Luxembourg* (7 June 2010), available at: <http://www.efsf.europa.eu> (accessed 10 March 2013).

stability mechanism,[17] supposedly prohibited by the so-called 'no bail-out rule' enshrined in Article 125 TFEU.[18] Even before the entry into force of the amendment, the European Stability Mechanism was actually established, but to that end the conclusion of a traditional intergovernmental agreement between the 17 Euro Area members and the creation of an international organisation distinct from the European Union were necessary. However, it was immediately clear that the above mentioned measures of direct or indirect financial aid were to be accompanied by specific commitments of the beneficiary Member States in question to an increase in taxation revenues, to budget cuts and to economic reforms. The terms of financial aid packages were either expressly negotiated with the European Union and set forth in specific agreements, or took the form of recommendations from EU institutions to the Member State concerned. In both cases, however, these were actually perceived as being preconditions for the granting of the necessary economic support.[19]

It was also evident that the implementation of such measures had the side effect of imposing a significant social burden upon Member States that were called upon to cut their costs. Salaries of civil servants, social security benefits, and the provision of public services were especially affected and important repercussions on the labour market were observed.[20] True to form, the material impact of these measures on the population, alongside the expectations of a negative outcome, generated wide opposition from the civil society. One of the most popular arguments against the role of the European Union in the Euro crisis regards precisely the alleged eviction of the democratic

17 The reasons for the Treaty Amendment are widely discussed in B. De Witte, "The European Treaty Amendment for the Creation of a Financial Stability Mechanism", *European Policy Analysis* 6, 2011, pp. 5–6.

18 According to Article 125 TFEU neither the European Union nor Member States can assume the debts of another Member State; it is often argued that this provision also makes it illegal to grant financial aid to Member States experiencing severe difficulties. The existence of a breach of this clause is widely discussed in M. Ruffert, "The European Debt Crisis and European Union Law", *Common Market Law Review* 48, 2011, pp. 1781–1787. On the no bail-out clause and its weaknesses, see also J. V. Louis, "The No Bail-Out Clause and Rescue Packages", *Common Market Law Review* 47, 2010, pp. 976–981. The CJEU in case C-372/12, *Pringle*, nyr., held that Article 125 TFEU does not actually prevent either the EU or its Members from granting financial assistance to other Members (paras. 129–147).

19 For an assessment of the European conditionality policy in matters of financial assistance, see A. Viterbo and R. Cisotta, "La crisi del debito sovrano e gli interventi dell'UE: dai primi strumenti finanziari al Fiscal Compact", *Il diritto dell'Unione europea* 16, 2012, pp. 343–346.

20 Cf. C. Barnard, "The Financial Crisis and the Euro Plus Pact: A Labour's Lawyer Perspective," *Indiana Law Journal* 41, 2012, pp. 98–114.

principle, resulting from the Union's widespread and cumbersome intervention into national economies.

Such interventions are now likely to place very tight constraints on Member States in terms of their economic policies, after another international agreement outside the field of EU law was signed in 2012 by 25 EU Member States, namely the Treaty on Stability, Coordination and Governance in the Economic and Monetary Union (TSCG),[21] in order to provide rules concerning common budgetary discipline, coordination of economic policies and European economic governance.[22] The Treaty aims at extending the new balance of power between the Council and the Commission as envisaged by the so-called Six-pack,[23] more recently enhanced by the Two-pack in matters of fiscal and macroeconomic surveillance over Member States of the Euro Area.[24]

However, the legitimacy of an extensive intervention of the European Union into economic matters is strongly challenged, on an assumption that

---

21 The composite process of negotiation of the Treaty is described in K. Tuori, "The European Financial Crisis—Constitutional Aspects and Implications", *EUI Working Papers Law 2012/28*, pp. 19–20.

22 A thorough description and analysis of the new legal framework is contained in F. Allemand and F. Martucci, "La nouvelle gouvernance économique européenne", *Cahiers de droit européen* 48, 2012, pp. 17–99 and pp. 410–457.

23 The 'Six-Pack' is composed of five Regulations and one Directive, four of which were enacted under the ordinary legislative procedure (thus, by the European Parliament and the Council), namely Regulation (EU) 1173/2011 of the European Parliament and of the Council of 16 November 2011 on the effective enforcement of budgetary surveillance in the Euro Area; Regulation (EU) 1174/2011 of the European Parliament and of the Council of 16 November 2011 on enforcement measures to correct excessive macroeconomic imbalances in the euro area; Regulation (EU) 1175/2011 of the European Parliament and of the Council of 16 November 2011 amending Council Regulation (EC) No 1466/97 on the strengthening of the surveillance of budgetary positions and the surveillance and coordination of economic policies; Regulation (EU) 1176/2011 of the European Parliament and of the Council of 16 November 2011 on the prevention and correction of macroeconomic imbalances; Council Regulation (EU) 1177/2011 of 8 November 2011 amending Regulation (EC) No 1467/97 on speeding up and clarifying the implementation of the excessive deficit procedures; Council Directive 85/2011/EU of 8 November 2011 on requirements for budgetary frameworks of the Member States, *OJ*, 2011, L 306/1.

24 Regulation (EU) 472/2013 of the European Parliament and of the Council of 21 May 2013 on the strengthening of economic and budgetary surveillance of Member States in the euro area experiencing or threatened with serious difficulties with respect to their financial stability; Regulation (EU) No 473/2013 of the European Parliament and of the Council of 21 May 2013 on common provisions for monitoring and assessing draft budgetary plans and ensuring the correction of excessive deficit of the Member States in the euro area, *OJ*, 2013, L 140/1.

"far-reaching decisions are taken by small political elites in late night conferences without sufficient involvement of existing Union bodies and European citizens".[25] On the contrary, as such decisions regard highly sensitive questions with important social repercussions for citizens, the democratic principle would require that it is precisely these decisions that are taken bearing in mind the political preferences of the public at large. We shall now examine whether the current EU institutional framework can adequately achieve that goal.

3 The Actors

A full implementation of the mechanism of multi-level democracy enshrined in Articles 10 and 12 TEU can, of course, be achieved when the EU's action is based on the Community method and decisions are adopted under the ordinary procedure. Since the Council and the European Parliament share equal powers and national Parliaments, too, are granted some form of involvement, all the levels of representative democracy extant at Union level are put into effective operation.

In economic and monetary matters unfortunately no recourse to the Community method is made. On the contrary, special procedures involving a different distribution of powers are provided for in the TFEU. Title VIII of the TFEU underlines the role of the Commission and of the European Central Bank and grants them significant powers of action under the control of the Council and of the European Council, while a role for the European Parliament is hardly envisaged.

These procedures thus largely depart from the ordinary decision-making techniques, but the differences are even more striking in the enhanced cooperation among the Member States whose currency is the euro. The actual practice of the Member States has often disregarded these procedures, instead turning back to schemes of intergovernmental cooperation, as the establishment of the European Stability Mechanism or the conclusion of the TSCG show.

In the following sections the role of every actor in the Euro crisis will be examined in turn.

---

25 M. Poiares Maduro, "A New Governance for the European Union and the Euro: Democracy and Justice", *op. cit.*, n. 2 p. 1.

3.1 *The Prevailing Role of the European Commission and the European Central Bank*

As previously noted, one of the most remarkable features of the Economic and Monetary Union is the prominent role of the European Commission and the European Central Bank, also through their participation with other bodies, such as the Economic and Financial Committee mentioned in Article 134 TFEU and the Eurogroup.

Even though the TFEU does not grant it an autonomous decision-making power, the Commission is involved in all the most important procedures regarding Economic and Monetary Union. It is thus engaged in multilateral surveillance of the economic policies of Member States (Article 121 TFEU); it may forward proposals to the Council in matters of financial assistance to Member States (Article 122 TFEU); it enjoys monitoring and reporting powers and a right of initiative in excessive deficit procedures (Article 126 TFEU); it may exercise monitoring powers over the so-called Member States with a derogation; and it may forward proposals regarding the abrogation of derogations to the Council (Article 140 TFEU).

In turn, the European Central Bank is conferred with a central role in monetary matters within the framework of the objectives of price stability and contribution to general economic policies, as laid down in Article 127 TFEU.[26] In order to carry out its general tasks of management and implementation, it is entrusted with wide powers ranging from a general consultative and recommendatory role to the authority to take decisions or, in some cases, to make regulations.

It must be added that the European Central Bank has thus far interpreted its mandate very broadly, undertaking several initiatives not expressly provided for by the Treaties, such as the purchase of sovereign bonds issued by States in the Euro Area[27] or the recommendations aimed at ensuring that some troubled States comply with their macroeconomic policy objectives.

---

26 On the position of the ECB and the European System of Central Banks in the general Union framework, see B. Krauskopf and C. Steven, "The Institutional Framework of the European System of Central Banks: Legal Issues in the Practice of the First Ten Years of Existence", *Common Market Law Review* 46, 2009, pp. 1143–1175; C. Zilioli and M. Selmayr, "The Constitutional Status of the European Central Bank", *Common Market Law Review* 44, 2007, pp. 355–399.

27 The legal basis is the Decision of the European Central Bank of 14 May 2010 establishing a securities markets programme, *OJ*, 2010, L 124/8. According to the official position of the European Central Bank, the so-called Outright Monetary Transactions (OMTs) do comply, from the ECB's point of view, with the no-monetary financing clause laid down in Article 123 TFEU, since the purchase of Government bonds takes place on the secondary

Building upon the provisions of the TFEU, the subsequent acts adopted in order to deal with the Euro crisis expanded even further the powers of these two institutions.[28]

In matters of assistance to Member States experiencing severe economic or financial difficulties, the role of the Commission and of the European Central Bank was subsequently strengthened by Regulation (EU) 407/2010 establishing the European Financial Stabilisation Mechanism (EFSM)[29] and by the Treaty Establishing the European Stability Mechanism (ESM Treaty). The Commission and the European Central Bank are called upon, *inter alia*, to discuss with the Member State concerned, its financial situation and needs and to define the economic policy conditions subject to which financial assistance can be granted. Those conditions are to be incorporated into a Memorandum of Understanding. The Commission (alone under Regulation (EU) 407/2010 or in liaison with the ECB under the ESM Treaty) will also monitor the compliance with the economic policy conditions after the disbursement of the loan or the release of the funds to the Member State in question.

Even though the decision to grant assistance is in itself reserved to the Council under Regulation (EU) 407/2010 or to the Board of Governors under

---

market, is a monetary policy aimed at achieving price stability and does not undermine the independence of the ECB itself: see, for instance, *ECB Monthly Bulletin*, October 2012, pp. 7–9. On the non-credibility of the no-monetary financing clause and on its alleged transgression by the ECB, see D. Adamski, "National Power Games and Structural Failures in the European Macroeconomic Governance", *Common Market Law Review* 49, 2012, p. 1327 and pp. 1335–1336. A case concerning subsequent decisions regarding the purchase of Member States' bonds on the secondary market is now pending in General Court (Case T-492/12, *von Storch v. ECB, OJ*, 2012, C 32/18).

28 The problem of conferral of new tasks upon EU institutions, especially as regards the Commission and the ECB, is discussed in K. Tuori, *op. cit.*, n. 21 pp. 35–37.

29 The Regulation was enacted on the basis of Article 122 TFEU, even though that provision does not seem to apply to the Member States affected by the economic and financial crisis, as it is not an 'exceptional occurrence' beyond the control of those States. It has been argued that Article 122 TFEU could constitute a proper basis as long as the financial assistance so provided is subject to strict conditionality (A. Viterbo and R. Cisotta, "La crisi della Grecia, l'attacco speculativo all'euro e le risposte dell'Unione europea", *Il diritto dell'Unione europea* 14, 2009, p. 982), but the solution does not seem completely consistent with Article 122 TFEU, as conditionality is required in any case for Article 122 TFEU to be applicable. The question is also thoroughly discussed in B. Ryvkin, "Saving the Euro: Tensions with European Treaty Law in the European Union's Efforts to Protect the Common Currency", *Cornell International Law Journal* 227, 2012, pp. 235–240.

the ESM Treaty,[30] the practice shows, that in such urgent matters, no significant changes are usually made to the Commission's proposal.

It is also worth noting that the ESM Treaty made official the practice of the so-called 'troika' (designating the joint operation of the Commission, of the European Central Bank and of the International Monetary Fund) as a general method for dealing with the requests of financial assistance on the part of Member States.

Also in matters of coordination of economic policies and multilateral surveillance, the imposition of tighter constraints on budgetary and fiscal policies of the Member States, following the entry into force of the 'Six-Pack' and of the TSCG, implies a far more significant role for the European Commission. That institution is now empowered to monitor annual budget planning by Member States, to define principles concerning convergence towards medium-term objectives and to make recommendations with regard to draft budgetary plans of Member States in the Euro Area. Moreover, the revision of the excessive deficit procedure underlined the role of the European Commission, the recommendations of which are deemed, under certain conditions, to be adopted if the Council does not reject them with an express decision, provided that such decision meets the requirement of the so-called 'reversed qualified majority'.[31] It is also worth mentioning that under the procedure for macroeconomic imbalances the Commission is allowed to conduct an in-depth review of the economic situation of single Member States.[32]

The Commission does, however, enjoy even greater powers after the entry into force of the 'Two-Pack',[33] concerning only the Member States in the Euro Area: an enhanced mechanism of budgetary surveillance can be imposed by the Commission upon States experiencing severe financial difficulties[34] and

---

30 See also CJEU, Case C-370/12, *Pringle*, nyr., para. 161. Regulation (EU) 407/2010 and the ESM Treaty are criticized by D. Adamski, *op. cit.*, n. 27 pp. 1333–1334, who finds the main reason for the weakness of the two instruments in the fact that the decision-making power is conferred on intergovernmental bodies.

31 Such an amendment was clearly passed in an effort to prevent excessive leniency, as shown by the Council in the past: in this regard: see R. Baratta, "Legal Issues of the 'Fiscal Compact'—Searching for a mature democratic governance of the euro", *Il diritto dell'Unione europea* 17, 2012, pp. 18–21.

32 For a review of the practice of the Commission in 2012 and of the self-restraint shown with regard to several Member States, see D. Adamski, "Europe's (Misguided) Constitution of Economic Prosperity", *Common Market Law Review* 50, 2013, pp. 53–55.

33 The regulations entered into force on 30 May 2013.

34 C. Degryse, "The new European economic governance", *ETUI Working Papers 2012 14*, pp. 75–76.

an in-depth assessment of draft budgetary plans is provided for, as well as a duty of reporting *ex ante* about debt issuance by the Member States.

Mention must also be made of the Economic and Financial Committee, whose members are appointed mainly by the Commission and the European Central Bank (only one third are appointed by Member States). Its role is merely preparatory to the work of the Council and consultative within the framework of the European Semester, but the complete absence of democratic accountability is clearly striking.[35]

These measures mark a very clear development in the institutional balance regarding economic and monetary policy, adding to the central importance of those EU institutions the actions of which are mainly based on technical, rather than political, evaluations. It is often underlined that such institutions (especially, the Commission) possess a neutral expertise,[36] so that their enhanced role in economic governance should be welcomed.[37] However, it can be objected that the technical expertise is not an adequate replacement for the loss of democratic legitimacy resulting from the process.[38]

Following the above mentioned developments, the Commission and the European Central Bank will discharge significant functions in European economic governance. As a matter of fact, the Commission and the European Central Bank are going to share (by themselves or, as part of the 'troika', with the IMF, whose involvement does not actually contribute to the implementation of the democratic principle)[39] a general and discretionary power of enhancing the coordination of national economic policies. Accordingly, very tight constraints will be placed upon Member States,[40] which will no longer

---

35 The tasks of the Economic and Financial Committee are described in Article 134 TFEU: see also N. de Sadeleer, "The New Architecture of the European Economic Governance: A Leviathan or a Flat-Footed Colossus?", *Maastricht Journal of European and Comparative Law* 19, 2012, pp. 376–377.

36 Some scholars call for an evolution of the Commission towards a political government of Europe: see M. Poiares Maduro, "A New Governance for the European Union and the Euro: Democracy and Justice", *op. cit.*, n. 2 pp. 19–21.

37 The argument is often relied upon in order to show the inadequacy of the current institutional balance between the Commission and the Council, as the latter is still empowered to take decisions: see, for instance, M. Ruffert, *op. cit.*, n. 18 p. 1801.

38 A similar concern is expressed by R. Baratta, *op. cit.*, n. 18 p. 673.

39 Democratic accountability of the 'troika' is also denied by D. Adamski, "Europe's (Misguided) Constitution of Economic Prosperity", *op. cit.*, n. 32 p. 58.

40 It has been argued that the implementation of the democratic principle also places constraints upon the action of the European Union and of the Commission in particular, since it prevents structural reforms in the Member States, unless they are backed by

be able to choose from different economic priorities but will have to cope with harmonized guidelines on economic policy.

The consequences seem to be at odds with a correct implementation of the democratic principle. In the first place, the control of economic policy will be diverted from national Parliaments, usually involved in the budgetary procedures, to institutions not directly accountable to the citizens. This is a source of concern, not only because the decisions in such matters will be taken very remotely from the citizens, notwithstanding the provisions of Article 11(3) TEU, but also because the institutions involved tend to overlook, by their very nature, the wider political and social goals of economic policy focusing mainly on objectives of financial stability as enshrined in Article 127 TFEU. Such an approach is also recognised in the new criteria for multilateral surveillance as set forth in Articles 3 and 4 TSCG.

In addition, an even greater lack of democratic legitimacy can be perceived in the provisions concerning States experiencing severe financial and economic difficulties and imposing a strict conditionality upon such states. The takeover of the economic policy of those States is supposed to be a consequence of the failure of the national institutions. As such, it seems to find its root in an attitude of technocratic paternalism and distrust in genuine democratic processes. In other words, the intervention of the Commission and the European Central Bank would ultimately be aimed at 'neutralizing' democratically elected Governments and/or Parliaments insofar as they prove unable to grant economic and financial stability to their countries, causing adverse effects for the European Union as a whole or for the Eurozone.[41] Obviously, the situation can become even more alarming if functions not expressly provided for by the Treaties are exercised, as the European Central Bank allegedly did when it purchased significant quantities of sovereign bonds of some Member States in order to keep their interest rates at low levels, even though such initiatives can contribute to stabilisation in the Eurozone.[42]

---

democratic support: D. Adamski, "Europe's (Misguided) Constitution of Economic Prosperity", *op. cit.*, n. 32 pp. 58 and 83–85, who also remarks upon the inadequacy of the democratic mandate for the EMU.

41 C. Degryse, *op. cit.*, n. 34 p. 76, refers to these phenomena as 'democracy under surveillance'.

42 Some scholars deny that the purchases of government bonds by the ECB amount to a violation of the existing Treaty rules. P. de Grauwe, "The European Central Bank: Lender of last resort in the government bond markets?", *CESifo Working Paper: Monetary Policy and International Finance No. 3659*, argues that these operations fall within the scope of Article 18 of the Protocol on the Statute of the European System of Central Banks and the European Central Bank allowing the ECB to operate in financial markets also by buying and selling marketable instruments. However, even though the purchases of government

Even though one can recognize the necessity of preserving the consistency of the economic policies of single Member States with the general needs of the European Union, this cannot be allowed to outweigh the respect due to the democratic principle as a very cornerstone of European integration. Accordingly, the unavoidable primacy of institutions acting on a technical basis should be counterbalanced by a significant involvement of other actors more directly accountable to the citizens. The question is whether this is actually the case in European economic and monetary governance.

3.2 *The Governments of Member States*

As previously noted, under the TFEU the decision-making power concerning the European and Monetary Union is concentrated in the Council and, insofar as the definition of economic policy guidelines is concerned, in the European Council. That institutional balance was not altered by the 'Six-Pack', nor will it be by the 'Two-Pack'. Even though those measures place a greater emphasis on the role of the Commission,[43] the Council seems to keep a firm grip on the decision-making power concerning multilateral surveillance, excessive deficit procedures and macroeconomic imbalances.[44]

However, given the high degree of technicality of the subject matter, the Council is not expected to actually assess the content of the measures recommended or proposed by the Commission, but rather to endorse certain political inputs, it being up to the Member States to reach the final decision as to the adoption of those measures. That way, national Governments retain a wide discretion on the implementation of economic and financial governance[45] even though, as the CJEU recalled in *Commission v. Council*, it must be exercised

---

bonds on secondary markets do not directly provide liquidity to the governments, they are aimed at lowering the rates of interest paid by Member States and so they have the actual effect of indirectly granting them more liquidity.

43 According to E. Ferran, "Crisis-driven regulatory reform: where in the world is the EU going?", in: E. Ferran, N. Moloney, J. G. Hill and J. C. Coffee Jr., *op. cit.*, n. 13 pp. 29–35, the Member States retain the decision-making power, but they need the technical expertise of the Commission for the economic governance.

44 Under these procedures the Council is empowered to impose financial sanctions on Member States, but the adequacy of a measure penalizing a troubled economy is often criticized: J. V. Louis, "Les réponses à la crise", *op. cit.*, n. 5 pp. 361–362.

45 For a strong criticism see D. Adamski, "National Power Games and Structural Failures in the European Macroeconomic Governance", *op. cit.*, n. 27 p. 1341: it is argued that conferring the decision-making power on the Council is inappropriate because that institution "... cannot come up with any better economic analysis than the Commission does in its recommendation. If it deviates, the Council does so essentially due to political trading between national governments".

within the limits stemming from the Treaty provisions and following the procedures laid down in secondary EU law.[46] Since the 'Six-Pack' and the TSCG set out much tighter rules than those initially contained in Regulations (EC) 1466/97 and 1467/97 and the 'Two-Pack' is going to enhance the proceduralization of the actions of the institutions, one can foresee that the Council will have to face many constraints, especially if it is to enact decisions different from those recommended by the Commission.

For the States whose currency is the Euro, the involvement of national Governments in the procedures at European Union level also takes place through different bodies, such as the Eurogroup and the Euro Summit, initially developed as consultation meetings between Member States and subsequently formalised (the former under the Lisbon Treaty, the latter under the TSCG).

As for the Eurogroup, it has no clearly defined function under Protocol No 14 attached to the Lisbon Treaty, being committed only to discussing questions related to the 'specific responsibilities' of Member States that share the Euro. However, the activism of the body in itself and of its Presidents paved the way for a stronger role in European economic governance.[47] Accordingly, it is now called upon to take part in the multilateral surveillance envisaged under Regulation (EU) 1176/2011, acts as a Board of Governors of the European Stability Mechanism and in the future will be involved in the process of monitoring and assessing national draft budgetary plans under the 'Two-Pack'. It is also worth noting that in its periodical statements the Eurogroup pays wide attention to the programmes of financial assistance granted to Member States in difficulty and to the conditionality attached to such programmes. For the first time, in the case of Greece and more recently in the case of Cyprus, it got directly involved in the negotiation of the conditions for a financial assistance programme.[48]

The Euro Summit, in turn, gathering the Governments of Member States at the highest level and being obviously linked to the Eurogroup, is mainly empowered to discuss general issues regarding the governance of the Euro Area and the coordination of economic policies.[49] However, in a somewhat confusing development, the Euro Summit has sometimes been replaced by the

46 Case C-27/04, *Commission v. Council* [2004] ECR I-6649.

47 The role of the Eurogroup as regards euro exchange policy is assessed by M. Lòpez Escudero, "La politique de change de l'euro", *Cahiers de droit européen* 47, 2011, pp. 411–429.

48 See the Eurogroup statement on Cyprus of 25 March 2013, available at: <http://www.eurozone.europa.eu> (accessed 19 March 2013).

49 On the Euro Summit see M. Lòpez Escudero, *op. cit.*, n. 47 pp. 405–406; L. S. Rossi, "Fiscal Compact e Trattato sul Meccanismo di Stabilità: aspetti istituzionali e conseguenze dell'integrazione differenziata nell'UE", *Il diritto dell'Unione europea* 16, 2012, pp. 299–300.

gatherings of Euro Area Heads of State or Government within the framework of the European Council or of the Council in order to deal with the Euro crisis.[50] On these occasions, decisions concerning the reinforcement of the economic governance[51] of, or provision of financial assistance to, Member States in difficulty[52] have often been taken, even though a subsequent implementation by other EU institutions or by Member States has still been necessary. In this connection, it is also remarkable that the President of the European Council was greatly involved in negotiations for the granting of financial assistance, even though he does not discharge any specific role with regard to the Euro Area. The active role played by President Van Rompuy in the recent Cyprus crisis can be recalled as a clear illustration of this: not only did he take part in the negotiations between the national Government and the 'troika', but he was also reported as having been decisive in leading the crisis to a resolution.[53]

Some commentators have underlined that the increasing role of these bodies amounts to a switch towards the intergovernmental method; such an institutional change gives rise to major concerns, especially insofar as it takes place beyond the TFEU-based procedures and through new bodies, whose actions appear to be very erratic in method.[54]

A strong encroachment of that approach on to the democratic principle can be clearly envisaged for two reasons. In the first place, the practices of the Eurogroup and of the Euro Summit demonstrate a particular level of opacity, since discussions conducted and decisions reached at the relevant meetings

---

50 Sometimes, even these bodies seem to be unable to perceive themselves as distinct from one another: for instance, in the Euro Summit statement of 26 October 2011, available at: <http://www.consilium.europa.eu/uedocs/cms_data/docs/pressdata/en/ec/125644.pdf> (accessed 19 March 2013) reference is made to a decision of Euro Area Heads of State or Government and EU institutions as having been taken by the Euro Summit itself.

51 See, for instance, the statement of Euro Area Heads of State or Government of 9 December 2011, available at: <http://www.consilium.europa.eu/uedocs/cms_data/docs/pressdata/en/ec/123978.pdf> (accessed 20 March 2013), that envisages the conclusion of the TSCG.

52 See, for instance, the statement of Euro Area Heads of State or Government and EU institutions of 21 July 2011, as regards the lengthening of maturity of future EFSF loans, available at: <http://www.consilium.europa.eu/uedocs/cms_data/docs/pressdata/en/ec/123978.pdf> (accessed 29 March 2013).

53 For a clear illustration of the role of President Van Rompuy in the resolution of the Cypriot crisis see <http://www.guardian.co.uk/world/2013/mar/25/cyprus-eu-draft-agreement-bailout> (accessed 28 June 2013).

54 Concerns about the institutional balance in economic and financial matters are expressed, among others, by F. Allemand and F. Martucci, *op. cit.*, n. 22 pp. 452–455; N. de Sadeleer, *op. cit.*, n. 35 pp. 374–378.

are usually not disclosed to the general public. Even though such a course of action is often explained by the need to avoid adverse reactions by the financial markets, it can generate the risk that fundamental issues of economic governance are treated beyond any institutional form of political control, especially considering the fact that no distinct procedures and no clear voting system are laid down for these bodies. Additionally, the fragmentation of, and the confusion between, the decision making bodies does not contribute to enhancing democratic control of the decisions taken.

Secondly, it must be borne in mind that the recourse to an intergovernmental method can be deemed to comply with the democratic principle only so long as the action of the Government is subject to parliamentary control at the national level. This would rest on the assumption that the general principle of sovereign equality of Member States and their inherent freedom to act independently in intergovernmental meetings or bodies applies. However, the Euro crisis tells quite a different story. In most cases, the States of the Euro Area experiencing severe economic and financial difficulties did not have the chance to make real choices or to craft the most suitable outcomes. On the contrary, in order to receive the required financial assistance, they were bound to accept the conditions defined by other national Governments in the course of negotiations. Such a practice is being widely criticized as not being in accordance with the requirements of the democratic principle.[55] Actually, it shows clearly that in the field of economic and financial governance the balance of power between the wealthiest countries and weakest countries is of great significance, since the two groups are expected to pursue conflicting interests. Whilst in the institutional framework of the Council these contentions can be channelled into common assessments, the loose procedures of the Eurogroup or the Euro Summit do not ensure sufficient protection against the rise of national interests.

3.3 *The Role of National Parliaments and of the European Parliament in Economic Governance*

A very important side effect of the new institutional framework also concerns the role of national Parliaments in economic governance. To date, budgetary policy, involving determination of future income and expenditure of the State and affecting both fiscal policy and social policy, has been conducted by national Governments under strict parliamentary control. In a single-country

55 See C. Degryse and P. Pochet, "Monetary Union, economic coordination and democratic legitimacy", *ETUI Policy Brief*, 2011, p. 3.

perspective this is, of course, an imperative attribute of economic governance measures in order to ensure their democratic legitimacy.[56]

However, the role of national Parliaments will be devalued to a large extent by the measures implementing a reinforced economic Union. The measures concerning EFSM and ESM give a clear hint of this. On the one hand, it is very unlikely that national Parliaments will themselves be involved in negotiations with the Commission and the European Central Bank or with the 'troika' about the conditionality measures justifying financial assistance.[57] On the other hand, practice shows that it is very unusual for a national Parliament, acting under the political pressure of short-term concerns about a possible default by its country, to refuse to give its assent to the agreements reached by the Government. The sole exception was the Cypriot Parliament, which refused to endorse the conditionality measures suggested by the Eurogroup. However, ultimately, the Government managed to agree with the 'troika' on conditionality measures which did not require parliamentary approval.

The importance of parliamentary control, even within the Member States that grant financial assistance to other Members, was strongly reasserted by the German Bundesverfassungsgericht in its two judgments of 7 September 2011[58] and 12 September 2012.[59] In this regard, however, the declaration on the ESM Treaty, granting national Parliaments comprehensive information

---

56 For an explicit statement that parliamentary control as to budgetary policy is necessary for its democratic legitimacy, see BundesVerfassungsGerichtshof, BvR 987/10. For a commentary, see C. Joerges, "Europe's Economic Constitution in Crisis", *Zentra Working Papers in Transnational Studies No. 06/2012*, pp. 16–18.

57 For example, the Greek Parliament was not involved in the earlier stage of the negotiations with the "troika" and it was merely called upon to ratify the Memorandum of Understanding concluded by the Government: see E. Desli and T. Pelagidis, "Greece's Sudden Faltering Economy: From Boom to Bust with Special Reference to the Debt Problem", in: P. Arestis and M. Sawyer (eds.), *The Euro Crisis*, London: Palgrave Macmillan, 2012, pp. 139–141.

58 See F. Torres, "EMU's legitimacy and the ECB as a strategic political player in the crisis context", paper presented at the EUDO Dissemination Conference of 22 November 2012 "The Euro Crisis and the State of National Democracy", pp. 2–3: "(The Bundesverafussungsgericht) established the decision-making rights of the German parliament in any rescue package, and by analogy in any further centralization of competencies that could exceed the capacity of the federal budget and the contingency on reforms by the receiving country".

59 The importance of the judgment is underlined by M. Ruffert, *op. cit.*, n. 18 p. 1802, and A. De Gregorio Merino, *op. cit.*, n. 15 pp. 1640–1644.

about the operations effected by the Mechanism,[60] does look like the proverbial fig leaf.[61]

The actual capacity of national Parliaments to influence economic governance will be restricted from a general point of view,[62] provided that the national budgetary policy will have to comply with the common macroeconomic guidelines and the country-specific medium-term objectives, while the risk of facing excessive deficit or macroeconomic imbalances procedures will certainly place a significant burden on national economic policies.[63]

Notwithstanding this, it is not reported that any of the national Parliaments opposed the enactment of these measures and, even though the ratification process was slow-paced, especially for the Fiscal Compact, the governmental initiatives towards a reinforced economic Union were embraced completely. So, up to date national Parliaments have largely assumed a notarial function with regard to the resolutions of the respective Governments, even though it is not clear to what extent such resolutions were in accordance with the will of the people.

However, the evident loss of political weight in economic matters by national Parliaments was not compensated by a comparable enhancement of the role of the European Parliament.[64] Following the entry into force of the Lisbon Treaty, the main innovation as to the position of the European legislature in economic and monetary policy concerned the introduction of the ordinary procedure in several matters, including the multilateral surveillance (Article 121(6) TFEU), the amendment of the Statute of the European System of Central Banks (Article 129(3) TFEU) and the adoption of measures in order to use the Euro as a single currency (Article 133 TFEU). Accordingly, when it was deemed necessary to enact new legislation in order to deal with the Euro crisis and ensure a closer coordination of economic policies, the EP had to act in many cases as a co-legislator. So it was, for most of the acts composing the 'Six-Pack' and now again for the 'Two-Pack'. In addition, some representatives

---

60 Declaration on the European Stability Mechanism, 27 September 2012, available at: <http://consilium.europa.eu> (accessed 10 March 2013).

61 See also M. Ruffert, *op. cit.*, n. 18 pp. 1789–1790.

62 It has been argued that the role of the national Parliaments will be weakened while a reinforcement of the powers of the prime minister and the finance minister is to be expected: N. de Sadeleer, *op. cit.*, n. 35 p. 378.

63 See also R. Baratta, *op. cit.*, n. 31 p. 672.

64 The necessity of a cumulative involvement of national Parliaments and of the European Parliament is asserted by F. Allemand and F. Martucci, *op. cit.*, n. 22 pp. 454–457.

of the EP took part in the negotiation process leading to the drafting of the TSCG.

Even though the influence of the Parliament in the shaping of the 'Six-Pack' and the TSCG has been emphasised,[65] quite paradoxically these acts do not allow for major involvement of the European Parliament and amounted rather to a "so much promise, so little delivery" scenario.[66] However, through its participation in the legislative process, the EP was able to achieve some things, such as a general right of information and the so-called Economic Dialogue, that will allow the competent parliamentary committee to invite the Council, the Commission, the European Council or the Eurogroup to discuss both general issues of economic governance and specific issues of management of the reinforced economic Union (for example, the outcomes of an excessive deficit procedure or of a macroeconomic imbalances procedure). In addition, the Economic Dialogue will also be embedded into the European Semester, being the institutional framework in which from now on the budgetary planning of the Member States will take place.[67]

Although one can consider these achievements to be better than nothing (that is, better than being completely excluded from European economic governance) they do not seem to lead to a convincing improvement as to the implementation of the democratic principle for a number of reasons. The European Parliament will only receive information and be entitled to discuss the economic and financial issues with other institutions, but it will not be involved in the concrete management of economic governance.[68] The absence of any effective instrument to influence the recommendations of the Commission or the decisions of the Council will probably prevent the Parliament from engaging convincingly in the Economic Dialogue.[69] As a result, the EP is not likely to be able to exercise any significant role in multilateral surveillance, nor on financial assistance to Member States in difficulty, since its contribution is envisaged as absolutely negligible both under Regulation (EU) 407/2010 and the ESM Treaty.[70]

---

65 C. Fasone, "The Struggle of the European Parliament to Participate in the New Economic Governance", *EUI Working Papers RSCAS 2012/45*, pp. 7–8.

66 On the absence of a significant involvement of the EP, see L. S. Rossi, *op. cit.*, n. 49 pp. 301–302.

67 N. de Sadeleer, *op. cit.*, n. 35 pp. 364–366.

68 On the ineffectiveness of the role of the EP in the Economic Dialogue, see also D. Adamski, "National Power Games and Structural Failures in the European Macroeconomic Governance", *op. cit.*, n. 27 p. 1343.

69 The same happened with the monetary dialogue: see F. Amtenbrink and K. van Duin, *op. cit.*, n. 6 pp. 582–583.

70 For a similar remark, M. Ruffert, *op. cit.*, n. 18 p. 1790.

As the EP only gained a tiny fraction of power in economic and monetary matters, it is far from clear how it can actually contribute to enhancing the democratic legitimacy of decisions by the European institutions. One can praise the fact that discussion of such issues in the Parliament is likely to increase transparency and awareness of the procedures carried out at Union level. However this does still not imply any commitment to take the political preferences of citizens into account in the process.[71] Moreover, participation in the Economic Dialogue and in the multilateral surveillance is not granted to the plenary institution but mainly to the Economic and Monetary Affairs Committee, therefore escaping general control and giving rise to the fragmentation of the functions among the subsidiary bodies of the institution.[72]

Obviously, much will depend on the possible activism of the European Parliament (and of its Committees), insofar as it will be able to advance its influence on European economic governance in the light of its political authority. In the meantime, it is regrettable that, while recent measures have marked the effectiveness of decision-making powers of the Council and of the Commission, the EP's role remains firmly in the realm of soft law and of political suasion and does not extend to an effective role in the relevant procedures.

In conclusion, if compared with the role played in the past by national Parliaments in the definition of the economic and budgetary policies of the Member States, the empowerment of the European Parliament under the 'Six-Pack' and the 'Two-Pack' appears to be much weaker so that, at least for the time being, it does not guarantee itself an actual democratic control upon the reinforced economic Union.

4 The Acts

The non-conformity of European institutions' and Member States' actions in economic and monetary matters to traditional Community methods is clearly confirmed when one considers the acts adopted in this field. While some

71 The inability of the European institutions to take the political preferences of citizens into account is remarked upon also in R. Smits, "L'Euro(pe) à l'èpreuve?", *Cahiers de droit europèen* 46, 2010, p. 10.

72 C. Fasone, *op. cit.*, n. 65 p. 10, underlines another cause of fragmentation within the EP, recalling that "many MEPs are elected in Member States which are not affected or are only partially affected by the new measures. When the EP has to examine and decide on a case of enhanced co-operation, all MEPs, regardless of their Member States, participate in the parliamentary activity on equal footing". See also K. Tuori, *op. cit.*, n. 21 p. 47.

scholars have stressed that several different types of acts have been enacted in order to deal with the Euro crisis,[73] these acts are often not even reconcilable with the ordinary Community method and call for a mere intergovernmental cooperation between Member States.[74] Of course, the widespread fragmentation of legal instruments can in itself affect democratic control,[75] especially in the light of the fact that the decisions are taken outside the institutional processes provided for in the Treaties, endangering also their judicial review. However, the actual characteristics of the instruments employed in order to deal with the Euro crisis generate additional concerns.

As far as interference with the democratic principle is concerned, three categories of acts can be envisaged: 1) agreements negotiated as between Member States under private law; 2) agreements negotiated as between Member States under international law; 3) acts adopted in the framework of the European Union.

As surprising as it may seem, the intervention of the European institutions to deal with the Euro crisis also took place through acts enacted under private law, as was evident in the case of the European Financial Stability Facility. The so-called special purpose vehicle was instituted following two decisions of the 27 Member States within the framework of the ECOFIN Council and of the then 16 Member States of the Euro Area within the framework of the Eurogroup[76] but it was formed as a Luxembourg public limited liability company governed by the laws of the Grand Duchy of Luxembourg.[77] The rules concerning the functioning of the EFSF were subsequently established by a Framework Agreement between the Member States of the Euro Area and EFSF itself, a contract actually governed by English law.[78]

Even though the Agreement and its subsequent modifications were also approved by many national Parliaments, the application of private law is no

---

73 Also N. de Sadeleer, *op. cit.*, n. 35 p. 379, underlines the different nature of the acts adopted in economic and financial matters.

74 The necessity of the recourse to the intergovernmental method, at least as far as financial assistance is concerned, is clearly stated by A. De Gregorio Merino, *op. cit.*, n. 15 p. 1645.

75 K. Tuori, *op. cit.*, n. 21 p. 47.

76 The nature of the decisions taken by the 27 Member States within the framework of the ECOFIN Council and by the 16 Member States within the Eurogroup is discussed in A. Viterbo and R. Cisotta, "La crisi della Grecia, l'attacco speculativo all'euro e le risposte dell'Unione europea", *op. cit.*, n. 29 pp. 984–987.

77 See Article 1 of the EFSF Articles of Incorporation, available at: <http://www.efsf.europa.eu> (accessed 29 March 2013).

78 Article 16(1) of the EFSF Framework Agreement, available at: <http://www.efsf.europa.eu> (accessed 29 March 2013).

guarantee in terms of democratic principle. The management of the EFSF is in practice in the hands of the Governments, whose duty of reporting to national Parliaments is obviously far less intense than it would be if an international agreement had been at stake.

As a result of the Euro crisis, Member States also entered into several international agreements *inter se* in economic and monetary matters (not to mention non-binding agreements, like the Euro Plus Pact). Such a choice is clearly striking, especially because the mechanism of enhanced cooperation is available in the European legal order, but Member States decided not to resort to it in this case.[79] However, as far as the democratic principle is concerned, the conclusion of international agreements between Member States does not entail significant consequences: even though under the procedure for the establishment of an enhanced cooperation the consent of the European Parliament must be obtained, once it is established, the ordinary legislative procedure is not applicable and no real involvement of the European Parliament or of national Parliaments is envisaged. To begin with, frequent use was made of international agreements in the field of financial assistance. At the outset, the supposed lack of a legal basis in the TFEU induced Member States to grant financial assistance to Greece through a series of bilateral loans by other Member States. Subsequently, the conclusion of a Memorandum of Understanding became the normal way of defining the terms and the conditions of the financial assistance. However, such agreements, even if they find their legal basis in a Council decision, are negotiated by the Commission and the ECB and are performed under the supervision of those institutions (and of the IMF); consequently, they are not adopted according to a merely intergovernmental method, even though parliamentary guarantees are ultimately lacking.

Subsequently, much more significant instruments were adopted in the form of international treaties between Member States, such as the ESM Treaty and the Treaty on Stability, Coordination and Governance, the enactment of which as international agreements, was due to the fact that some decisions were expected to be binding only on some Member States. Even though the European institutions are called upon to discharge some functions and for the TSCG a future incorporation into EU law is expressly envisaged, according to its Article 15, it is clear that a different legal framework is thus established.[80]

---

79 The reasons for the choice are widely discussed in B. De Witte, "International Treaties on the Euro and the EU Legal Order", paper presented at the EUDO Dissemination Conference of 22 November 2012 "The Euro Crisis and the State of National Democracy".

80 A. Viterbo and R. Cisotta, "La crisi del debito sovrano e gli interventi dell'UE: dai primi strumenti finanziari al Fiscal Compact", *op. cit.*, n. 19 p. 365, emphasize that Article 16

While many legal issues surrounding the compatibility of these agreements with EU law may arise from that choice,[81] such issues should not give rise to serious concerns in terms of democratic guarantees since ratification is always subject to parliamentary control. However, the practice shows that the effectiveness of that control is very questionable, since national Parliaments are often motivated by the necessity of obtaining financial assistance for their State or are reacting to market stress[82] and public debate at national level often proves to be lacking. In addition, the parliamentary control, intervening *a posteriori*, is an inadequate tool insofar as the Parliament is confronted with a political commitment already assumed by the Government. Accordingly, if the Parliament does not endorse such a commitment, the Government will be forced to re-open negotiations and will often face political tensions with other Member States and greater market stress, jeopardizing the stability of the EMU or of the Euro Area as a whole. It is not by chance that, when the ratification process was slowed down, it was not the consequence of an intervention of national Parliaments but was caused by other key factors (for example, in the case of the Fiscal Compact the constitutional referendum in Ireland and the challenge before the Bundesverfassungsgericht in Germany).

However, democratic control is even more lacking when an agreement is concluded in simplified form between the Governments of the Member States on the occasion of meetings of the European Council or of the Eurogroup. Even though they are circulated in the form of statements of the Heads of State or of the Government of the Member States, they can amount to international agreements[83] when Member States enter into specific commitments with

---

TSCG envisages the incorporation of that Treaty into the legal framework of the European Union; such a provision allegedly shows that the current framework of European economic governance is only temporary and due to the extraordinary needs imposed by the economic crisis; according to R. Baratta, *op. cit.*, n. 31 p. 653, it was "a choice pursued in a situation of urgency".

81 Many of those issues were addressed, with regard to the ESM Treaty, by the CJEU in case C-372/12, *Pringle*, nyr. The Court held that the conclusion of the ESM Treaty does not in itself concern monetary policy and is not in breach either of the TFEU provisions in matters of economic policy or of the principle of sincere cooperation.

82 In some cases the urgency prevents the members of national Parliaments from even being completely aware of the commitments assumed through the agreements concluded in the framework of the Euro Area, as is reported to have happened in the Finnish Parliament when the law regarding the enlargement of the guarantees for EFSF loans was passed (see the article at: <http://www.hs.fi/english/article/Uproar+in+Parliament+over+contradictions+in+loan+guarantee+liability/1135269716134> (accessed 10 March 2013).

83 See A. Viterbo, R. Cisotta, "La crisi della Grecia, l'attacco speculativo all'euro e le risposte dell'Unione europea", *op. cit.*, n. 29 p. 987.

each other.[84] While in this way the competences of these bodies are stretched beyond the limits imposed by the Treaties, usually such agreements are not even submitted to the national Parliaments for approval. Of course, such a lack of democratic legitimacy is remedied only to some extent by the general control of the Parliament over the Executive.

Notwithstanding the prevailing role of Member States and of intergovernmental bodies, in the field of coordination of economic policies and of multilateral surveillance, the relevant provisions of the 'Six-Pack' require the adoption of EU acts. However, such acts should, for the most part, be classed as 'soft law', since the Council and the Commission will mostly make *recommendations*, deliver *opinions* and address *guidance* to Member States, while the taking of *decisions* is the last resort in the case of non-compliance. The 'Two-Pack' will also not alter the general scheme, since both the budgetary monitoring and the enhanced surveillance are supposedly carried out mostly through non-binding acts (again, opinions and recommendations).

Although soft law is not in itself incompatible with the democratic principle,[85] the superabundant use of these sorts of acts in economic governance can arouse uncertainty. Democracy requires a clearly established and discernible allocation of powers, in order to make the deciding institution accountable to the citizens.

In matters of coordination of economic policies the acts of the EU institutions will, as previously noted, interfere with the deliberative powers of the national Parliaments. However, if those acts are mainly non-binding and supposedly influence national budgetary policies by way of putting political pressure on Member States, the decision-making process is inevitably affected again by opacity, since the different responsibilities of the involved national and EU institutions become undistinguishable.

---

84 Member States sometimes show awareness of this consequence, as demonstrated by the declaration of the Slovakian Prime Minister mentioned in the statement of the Euro Area Heads of State or of Government of 2 March 2012, available at: <http://www.consilium.europa.eu/uedocs/cms_data/docs/pressdata/en/ec/128521.pdf> (accessed 20 March 2013).

85 See H. Frykman and U. Mörth, "Soft Law and Three Notions of Democracy: The Case of the EU", in: U. Mörth (ed.), *Soft Law in Governance and Regulation: An Interdisciplinary Analysis*, Cheltenham: Edward Elgar Publishing, 2004, pp. 155–170.

5 European Economic Governance and Judicial Review

It was already noted above that several shortcomings in the implementation of the democratic principle in economic and monetary matters can be observed. While this is not unfamiliar, a stronger commitment to the democratic principle will be crucial inasmuch as the new European economic governance, especially after the entry into force of the so-called 'Two-Pack', will produce stricter constraints on the Member States. In this connection, a further question requires to be asked, namely to what extent the failures of the European and national legislature in respecting democratic guarantees can be remedied by challenging acts in matters of economic governance before the courts.

As a matter of principle, it flows from Article 6 TEU and from the European Charter that the right to an effective remedy, as a key pillar of the protection of fundamental rights, is an essential element of the rule of law and of the democratic principle. Accordingly, the actual implementation of this principle must be established also taking into account the chances offered by access to the courts, insofar as they can lead to a review of those measures in order to ensure individuals' rights to democratic guarantees.

A case for assessing the importance of judicial review in this connection can also be made in the light of the fact that the recent measures concerning a reinforced economic Union were the subject of an unprecedented series of jurisdictional challenges brought by private persons or national institutions, alleging possible violations of national constitutional law, but also questioning the compliance of such measures with the provisions of the European Treaties. Consequently, these cases can help in assessing the feasibility and the limits of judicial review as a form of implementation of the democratic principle in the field of economic and financial governance.

Firstly, it is necessary to define the respective scope of jurisdiction of national courts and of the European Court of Justice in economic and monetary matters, focusing on the remedies available for individuals in those matters.[86] Thus far, after the outbreak of the Euro crisis, several cases have been brought before the General Court seeking annulment of measures adopted by the European Union. It is also worth noting that in some of these actions the

86 Other competences of the CJEU, such as those conferred by the ESM Treaty for disputes between ESM Members or between the ESM and a Member, or by the TSCG for disputes between Contracting Parties, will not be taken into account, since they do not seem to be significantly connected to the implementation of the democratic principle.

question of lack of democratic legitimacy of the measures adopted by the EU was expressly raised.[87]

However, all of these actions were declared inadmissible on procedural grounds.[88] In particular, in two cases the General Court dismissed the actions holding that the applicants were not directly concerned by the EU measures in question, either in the light of the general content of the act requiring subsequent implementation[89] or because the act only established general goals to be achieved by the State concerned with internal acts.[90]

Recently, the CJEU seemed to uphold this view in *Pringle v. Ireland*: in this case it dismissed the argument that the request for a preliminary ruling concerning the invalidity of Council Decision 2011/199 was inadmissible because the applicant in the main proceedings should have brought a direct action under Article 263 TFEU.[91] On the basis of *a contrario* reasoning one can infer

87 See in particular case T-259/10 *Ax v. Council*, nyr.

88 In case T-311/10, *Piatis v. Council and Greece*, nyr., the action was held inadmissible on different grounds: insofar as it sought the annulment of some EC Regulations concerning the introduction of the euro currency, as the complaint had been lodged after the time-limit of two months; insofar as it sought the annulment of some Greek laws and a general declaration on the illegality of some features of the Euro and insofar as it requested the General Court to issue an injunction against the Council, as the General Court was not entitled to adopt similar rulings. In case T-532/11, *Städter v. ECB*, nr., the action for annulment of some ECB decisions on temporary measures relating to the eligibility of marketable debt instruments issued or guaranteed by some Governments was held inadmissible, as the complaint had been lodged after the time-limit of two months; in case T-437/12, *Activa Referentes v. Council*, nyr., the action for annulment of Council Decision 2012/443/EU addressed to Spain on specific measures to reinforce financial stability was held inadmissible because it was brought by a company using the services of its President as a lawyer (so, not of a third person, as required by Article 19 of the Statute of the Court of Justice).

89 See case T-259/10 *Ax v. Council*, concerning an action for annulment of Regulation (EU) 407/2010.

90 See cases T-541/10 and T-215/11, *ADEDY v. Council*, nyr, concerning two actions for annulment of some Council decisions addressed to Greece with a view to reinforcing and deepening fiscal surveillance and giving notice to Greece to take measures for the deficit reduction judged necessary to remedy the situation of excessive deficit.

91 Case C-370/12, nyr. The respondent in the main proceedings relied upon the judgment in *TWD* (case C-188/92 [1994] ECR I 883) and asserted that the applicant should have brought a direct action against Council Decision 2011/199. The CJEU held that "it is not evident that the applicant in the main proceedings had beyond doubt standing to bring an action for the annulment of Decision 2011/199 under Article 263 TFEU" (para. 42). For a commentary see V. Boger, "The ESM and the European Court's Predicament in Pringle", *German Law Journal* 14, 2013, pp. 113–139.

that in the CJEU's view the applicant would not have had standing for a direct claim for annulment of the Decision.

Even though the formula used by the CJEU is not conclusive and the case referred to the Court concerning the validity of a decision introducing a Treaty amendment was very peculiar, the extant case law justifies the conclusion that individuals will be granted standing in actions for annulment of EU acts in economic and financial matters only to a very limited extent. In that connection individuals will often find an insurmountable barrier in Article 263 TFEU insofar as it requires that the act to be annulled directly and individually concerns the applicant: actually, most EU measures regarding economic and financial matters are addressed to Member States and must be enacted through national legislation, so that they do not affect the position of individuals.

Of course, the possibility of bringing challenges before national courts is still left open as happened already for Regulation (EU) 407/2010 and for the ESM Treaty.[92] In both cases the challenges before national courts were commenced precisely due to a concern for a possible deterioration of democratic legitimacy. As *Pringle* illustrates, this may ultimately lead to a request for a preliminary ruling to the CJEU, so that it can be indirectly called upon to assess the validity of those measures. However, this does not necessarily mean that, as a matter of principle, the individuals' right to an effective remedy can always be exercised, because its practical fulfilment will depend on the availability of remedies to private persons at national level.[93]

In addition, even when a remedy is actually available, its effectiveness can be jeopardized by several factors. While the deference towards political institutions and the necessity not to put the EU's and Member States' financial stability at risk may play a role, the key factor is to be found elsewhere.

The judicial review of the CJEU is more and more evolving towards a process-oriented approach, especially in politically sensitive matters, encroaching upon significant national interests. As Lenaerts puts it, in some cases "the CJEU decided not to second-guess the appropriateness of the policy

92 The Regulation and the ESM Treaty were both challenged before the German Constitutional Court, that upheld the measures with the judgments already mentioned; the ESM Treaty was also challenged before constitutional courts in Austria, Estonia and Poland and before the Supreme Court in Ireland.

93 The case law concerning the ESM Treaty shows that this does not always hold true: the Austrian Constitutional Court ruled that the application for review was inadmissible (the judgment is available at: <http://www.vfgh.gv.at> (accessed 22 March 2013); in the proceedings before the Estonian Constitutional Court the applicant was the Chancellor of Justice (an English summary of the judgment is available at: <http://www.nc.ee> (accessed 22 March 2013).

choices made by the EU legislator. Instead, it preferred to examine whether, in reaching an outcome, the EU political institutions had followed the procedural steps mandated by the authors of the Treaties. Stated simply, I argue that judicial deference in relation to 'substantive outcomes' has been counterbalanced by a strict 'process review' ".[94] Such a statement clearly has its foundations in the idea of judicial discretion as a ground for limiting the scope of judicial review.[95]

It is not necessary to assess whether such an approach is in general plausible for European courts. Doubts can, however, certainly be cast on its use in economic and monetary matters. In fact, a process-oriented approach in judicial review is acceptable when the democratic legitimacy of political institutions is beyond question, so that the substantive outcomes must be deemed to be correct as long as procedural requirements are complied with. When the democratic legitimacy of the involved institutions in itself shows significant shortcomings, however, a substantive approach seems more satisfactory, insofar as it allows the courts to also review the consistency and the reasonableness of the decisions of political institutions. Unfortunately, this does not seem to be the case in the matter in hand, so that the contribution of judicial review to the implementation of the democratic principle is lessened.

6 Concluding Remarks

The existence of several shortcomings in the implementation of the democratic principle in economic and monetary matters, following the Euro crisis, has been outlined at length. A legal framework providing for a comprehensive remedy in terms of accountability of the decision-making institutions and bodies still seems quite far away. Certainly, the Euro crisis is not the optimal

94 K. Lenaerts, "The European Court of Justice and Process-Oriented Review", *College of Europe Research Papers in Law 1/2012*, pp. 2–3. See also D. Adamski, "National Power Games and Structural Failures in the European Macroeconomic Governance", *op. cit.*, n. 27 p. 1341. The proceduralization as a key factor in the judicial review under the so-called economic constitution of the European Union (especially for the evaluation of economic and social rights) is emphasized also by C. Semmelmann, "The European Union's Economic Constitution under the Lisbon Treaty: Soul-Searching Shifts the Focus to Procedure", *European Law Review* 35, 2010, pp. 516–541.

95 A. Fritzsche, "Discretion, Scope of Judicial Review and Institutional Balance in European Law", *Common Market Law Review* 47, 2010, pp. 361–403; M. de Visser, "Judicial Accountability and New Governance", *Legal issues of economic integration* 37, 2010, pp. 41–60.

background for achieving the democratisation of decision-making processes. Special emphasis is now placed upon the efficacy of the EU's action and on its adequacy for the present challenges,[96] while the risks for the financial stability and even the survival of the Eurozone command all attention. Though justifiable to some extent, such an approach is seriously endangering the confidence of the citizens in the European Union as a whole and must increasingly be replaced, also in economic and monetary matters, with the effective enactment of the several levels of democracy referred to in the Treaties.

96 The efficacy of the action of Member States is often criticized, even though their democratic foundations are recognised: see S. Manservisi, *op. cit.*, n. 4 p. 11.

CHAPTER 11

The European Regulatory Response to the Volcanic Ash Crisis between Fragmentation and Integration

Alberto Alemanno

1 Introduction

More than twenty years after the EU removed its internal land borders, the Union still lacks an integrated airspace. This seems to be the most obvious regulatory lesson learned from the recent volcanic ash crisis that affected EU airspace on 14–25 April 2010. In this chapter, I provide an analysis of the regulatory response developed across Europe in the aftermath of the eruption of the Icelandic volcano Eyjafjallajökull and treat it as an interesting case study illustrating the effects of crises on the EU integration process[1]. While reconstructing the unfolding of events and the procedures followed by the regulators, I attempt to address some of the following questions: What did the assessment of the danger of volcanic ash mean for jetliners? Who had competence to take risk management decisions, such as the controversial flight bans? Is it true that the safe level of volcanic ash was zero? How does one explain the shift to a new safety threshold (of 2,000 mg/m^3) only five days after the event? Did regulators overact? To what extent did they manage the perceived risk rather than the actual one? How did the crisis contribute to the establishment of a more integrated EU-wide airspace?

2 The Emergency Regulatory Response

Following the eruption of Icelandic volcano Eyjafjalläjokull on 14 April 2010, a cloud of ash quickly spread across Europe, helped by favourable winds. As a result, most European civil aviation authorities closed their respective

1 For a broader analysis, see A. Alemanno, Governing Disasters—The Challenges of Emergency Risk Regulation, Cheltenam, Edward Elgar, 2011.

© KONINKLIJKE BRILL NV, LEIDEN, 2014 | DOI 10.1163/9789004268333_013

airspaces.[2] The flying bans came amid fears that the volcanic ash—a mixture of glass, sand and rock particles—could seriously damage aircraft engines. The national measures were based on the scientific advice provided by the Volcanic Ash Advisory Centre, London (VAAC)[3] and were implemented by the European Organisation for the Safety of Air Navigation (Eurocontrol).[4] From an average of 28,000 flights a day in Europe, by 17 April, when less than half of Europe's airspace was open, there were only 5,335 actual flights. Yet, even before the bans were lifted, recriminations began. The national authorities came under pressure from European airlines, several of whom had conducted allegedly successful test flights in the supposed danger zone. After three days of flying bans, all major airlines vocally claimed that authorities had been overly cautious by overestimating, in the name of the controversial precautionary principle, the extent of the ash cloud and the danger it represented for jet engines. In particular, critics disputed the model used by the VAAC London, which was originally developed to track radioactive fallout from the Chernobyl nuclear disaster in 1986,[5] and dismissed it as "theoretical."[6] National authorities defended their 'zero risk' regulatory response by claiming that their position

2 At its height on 17–18 April 2010, 17 EU Member States had a full airspace closure and two had a partial closure. At the same time, six non-EU States had a full closure.

3 Nine Volcanic Ash Advisory Centres around the world are responsible for advising international aviation of the location and movement of clouds of volcanic ash. They are part of an international system set up by the International Civil Aviation Organization (ICAO) called the International Airways Volcano Watch (IAVW). In particular, the London VAAC is responsible for monitoring and forecasting the movement of volcanic ash over the United Kingdom, Iceland and the north-eastern part of the North Atlantic Ocean.

4 Contrary to what was reported by most media, Eurocontrol is an international, not an EU, organisation. It was established in 1960 by Germany, Belgium, France, the United Kingdom, Luxembourg and the Netherlands through the Eurocontrol International Convention relating to Co-operation for the Safety of Air Navigation signed in Brussels with its main purpose being "to strengthen their cooperation in matters of air navigation and in particular to provide for the common organisation of the air traffic services in the upper air space". This convention entered into force in 1963 and has 38 Member countries, including the European Union.

5 The Numerical Atmospheric-dispersion Modelling Environment (NAME) has evolved into an all-purpose dispersion model capable of predicting the transport, transformation and deposition of a wide class of airborne materials, e.g. nuclear material, volcanic emissions, biomass smoke, chemical spills, foot-and-mouth disease. See ICAO's *Manual on Volcanic Ash*, Radioactive Material and Toxic Chemical Clouds—Doc 9691.

6 Statement by Giovanni Bisignani, Director general and chief executive of the International Air Transport Association (IATA) on 19 April 2010.

was consistent with the guidelines developed by the International Civil Aviation Organisation (ICAO).[7] In turn, scientists strenuously defended the predictions made using the NAME atmospheric dispersion model underpinning the ICAO guidelines.[8]

Meanwhile, the cloud was not moving. As Europe was facing another week of disruption, the European Commission took the initiative over the weekend of 17–18 April, with the Spanish Presidency and Eurocontrol, proposing a co-ordinated European approach. As the situation evolved, the model and the national risk management procedures were tested. It became clear to the EU Member States, national air safety authorities, national air traffic controllers and Eurocontrol that a more differentiated assessment of risk from the ash cloud was needed. Under a *prisoner's dilemma-like scenario*, however, no Member State could act independently by departing from the ICAO guidelines and taking the first step to introduce change. These guidelines are crystal clear: "The recommended procedure in the case of volcanic ash is exactly the same as with low-level wind shear, regardless of ash concentration—AVOID AVOID AVOID."[9] Five days after the commencement of the enforcement of national flying bans, the European Member States unanimously agreed, following an extraordinary meeting co-chaired by Eurocontrol and the European Commission on 19 April to move to "a co-ordinated European approach in response to the crisis."[10]

As a result, new procedures were set out which led to a partial reopening of European air space and hence reduced the human and economic impact on passengers, airlines and cargo.[11] The new measures came into force at 08.00 hours CET on 20 April and established three categories of zone, depending on the degree of contamination. The first zone was located in the central nucleus of the emissions, where a full restriction of operations was maintained; the

7 ICAO was created in 1944 under the Convention on International Civil Aviation and is headquartered in Montreal, Canada. The guidelines are contained in the *Manual on Volcanic Ash*, Radioactive Material and Toxic Chemical Clouds—Doc 9691.

8 See section 3.4, "Forecasting the Movement of Volcanic Ash Clouds", in ICAO's *Manual on Volcanic Ash*, Radioactive Material and Toxic Chemical Clouds—Doc 9691.

9 *Ibid.*, point 3.4.8.

10 See Europa, Press Release Rapid, "Volcanic Ash Crisis: Frequently Asked Questions", MEMO/10/143, Brussels, 20 April 2010 available at <http://europa.eu/rapid/press-release_MEMO-10-143_en.htm> (accessed August 12, 2013).

11 These procedures were presented by EU Commission Vice president Kallas to an extraordinary meeting of Transport Ministers, chaired by Spanish Minister José Blanco, and finally endorsed at the same meeting.

second consisted of an intermediate zone where Member States could allow flights "in a coordinated manner [with other members]" but with additional restrictions and safety controls; and the third zone, not affected by the ash, had no restrictions. These procedures, based upon a more differentiated risk assessment and paving the way for more coordinated decisions across the states, allowed for "a progressive and coordinated opening of European Air Space."[12] By 22 April, eight days after the eruption began, flights were back to normal, with 27,284 flights compared to 28,578 expected on the same day two weeks earlier.[13] Interestingly enough, Transport Ministers agreed to ask the Commission, "as long as the air traffic in Europe is not totally open", to contribute to "a smooth coordination that allows the mobility of European citizens through other modes of transport".[14]

The calm after the storm—one might have thought. Yet, the situation created by the protracted closure of European airspace had been so extraordinary that the regulatory action responsible for the disruption remained the subject of growing controversy. Beyond the personal dramatic impact upon the millions of passengers who were stranded, and the difficult implementation of the passenger's rights regulation,[15] the air industry incurred significant costs and suffered reduced revenues.[16] Incidentally, it should be noted that these costs included compensating passengers. Indeed, in the litigation that followed the disaster in question, the CJEU recognised that Articles 5(1)(b) and 9 of Regulation No 261/2004 must be interpreted as meaning that, in the event of cancellation of a flight due to 'extraordinary circumstances' of a duration such

12 Extraordinary meeting of Ministers of Transport, 19 April 2010, available at: <http://www.consilium.europa.eu/uedocs/cms_data/docs/pressdata/en/trans/113899.pdf> (accessed August 12, 2013).

13 See Eurocontrol Volcanic Ash Could Timeline, available at: <http://www.eurocontrol.int/category/keywords/volcanic-ash-cloud-timeline> (accessed 14 July 2013).

14 Extraordinary meeting of Ministers of Transport, 19 April 2010, available at: <http://www.consilium.europa.eu/uedocs/cms_data/docs/pressdata/en/trans/113899.pdf> (accessed August 12, 2013).

15 Despite the exceptional circumstances, the EU Commission considers that the Regulation on Air Passengers' Rights (EC Regulation 261/2004) remains fully applicable. Yet, it admits that, in the ongoing review of the regulation, it will "take into account the experience of the volcano ash crisis to decide whether improvements are necessary". See Note d'information de M. Kallas "Conséquences du nuages de cendres générée par l'éruption volcanique survenue en Islande sur le trafic aérien", SEC(2010) 533, at para. 26.

16 Although at the end of April it was too early to measure the impact, since some traffic that did not occur during the closure of the airspace might have taken place later on, the first figures provided by the sector calculate losses of several hundred million Euros.

as that in the main proceedings, the obligation to provide care to air passengers laid down in those provisions must be complied with, and the validity of those provisions is not affected.[17] Additionally, airports were severely hit, as well as ground handling services and tour operators.[18]

3 The Science Behind Regulations for Volcanic Ash

It seems beyond doubt that volcanic ash can cause jet engines to fail in flight.[19] An engine's heat melts the finely-ground rock, which in turn proceeds to encrust the cooler parts of the mechanism, stopping it from working. This phenomenon is called sand-blasting and it came to wide public attention in 1982 when two jumbo passenger jets lost engine power as a result of flying through clouds of ash from the eruptions of the Galunggun volcano in Indonesia.[20] Since then, volcanic ash has been internationally recognised as a potential hazard for aviation and has triggered a wide range of initiatives by the ICAO aimed at mitigating that hazard.

These incidents undoubtedly served to increase interest among the aviation community in volcanic hazards. Yet, although they revealed that mitigation of the danger posed by volcanic ash to aviation safety would require the cooperation and efforts of volcanologists, meteorologists, air traffic controllers, engine manufacturers and pilots, they were not enough to capture the interest of the airline industry. It seems that the same airline companies that today blame the authorities and the scientists for being overly cautious have always been rather reluctant to commission studies on the impact of ash on their aircraft. As a result, given the lack of technological tools capable of detecting volcanic ash, the only strategy left that guarantees flight safety seems to be the complete

17 Case C-12/11, *McDonagh* v *Ryanair Ltd*, *OJ*, 2013, C 86/2, para. 66.

18 Under EU law, tour operators are required to provide repatriation for stranded passengers and to refund or offer alternative arrangements to customers who have not started their journey as a result of the closure of European airspace.

19 To find out more on volcanic ash and its effects on aviation, see V. M. Branningan, "Alice's Adventures in Volcano land: The Use and Abuse of Expert Knowledge in Safety Regulation", *European Journal of Risk Regulation* 2, 2010, pp. 107–114. On volcanism and its consequences, see M. R. Rampino, "Super-volcanism and other geophysical processes of catastrophic import", in: N. Bostrom and M. M. Cirkovic (eds.), *Global Catastrophic Risks*, Oxford: Oxford University Press, 2008, p. 203.

20 T. Casadevall (ed.), *Volcanic Ash and Aviation Safety: Proceedings of the First International Symposium on Volcanic Ash and Aviation Safety*, Seattle: 1991; US Geological Survey Bulletin 2047, pp. iii–iv.

avoidance of these ash clouds. As mentioned above, this is the risk management strategy enshrined in the ICAO's Manual which explains why national authorities have consistently held that the presence of virtually any volcanic ash is a threat to aviation.

The major obstacle to resuming flights has been understanding aircraft tolerance levels of ash. It seems that manufacturers have agreed upon increased tolerance levels in low ash density areas, but have refused to disclose their data. It therefore remains to be seen how exactly authorities moved from the ICAO's recommended zero safety level to a level of 2,000 micrograms of ash per cubic metre within the space of five days.

By implicitly acknowledging the inherent limitations of the predominant risk analysis model, the EU Commission has decided to take two initiatives addressing the wider international dimension:

- the creation of a working group of experts, encompassing representatives from Eurocontrol, the European Air Safety Agency, Member States, ICAO and the air industry. The idea is to entrust this group with the task of establishing an inventory of the relevant technological and methodological tools at European level and in the Member States, and a research roadmap to make the most up-to-date and validated tools available to facilitate making appropriate decisions.
- the elaboration of a new methodology and coherent approach to safety risk assessment and risk management in relation to the closure of airspace to be proposed to ICAO.

The results of both initiatives were, as originally planned,[21] submitted by the EU to the ICAO general assembly in September 2010. After that, the ICAO International Volcanic Ash Task Force (IVATF) elaborated a new international standard within the ICAO for flying in volcanic ash clouds.[22] This is a globally applicable procedure to facilitate the management of flight operations through, or near, areas of known or forecast volcanic cloud through the provision of appropriate information to assist in minimising safety risk in such operations. The emerging new standard, developed by the IVATF represents, firstly, a shift from a zero risk policy to a threshold level, which has been

21 See Note d'information de M. Kallas "Conséquences du nuages de cendres générée par l'éruption volcanique survenue en Islande sur le trafic aérien", SEC(2010) 533, para. 44.

22 International Civil Aviation Organization International Volcanic Ash Task Force, "Guidance Material: Management Of Flight Operations With Known Or Forecast Volcanic Cloud Contamination", Preliminary Issue—Draft Version 3.1—19 December 2010.

rendered possible by the data obtained by engine manufacturers in the aftermath of the crisis. Secondly, it signals a change in the responsibility for the decision to fly in those circumstances by shifting it from the public authorities to the airline operators. Indeed, under the ICAO Draft December 2010 Guidance:

> For States whose airspace is potentially contaminated by volcanic ash, it is intended that the control measures specified in this document should be sufficient to satisfy their need to be confident in the ability of operators from other States to undertake operations safely into airspace that is known or forecast to be contaminated by volcanic ash; no further action on the part of States whose airspace is potentially contaminated by volcanic ash is intended.[23]

In essence, the approach is based on formalising a risk assessment procedure for use by an operator wishing to conduct such an operation and an evaluation procedure for use by that operator's State in assessing whether or not the risk of the operation in question is minimised to an acceptable level by the operator's use of this procedure. It is intended that the State of the Operator or State of Registry, as appropriate, would make this determination on behalf of all other Provider States through whose airspace the resultant flight operations are planned to be conducted.

4 The Not-Yet European Sky

As is well known by now, EU integration does not yet extend to air traffic management.[24] Only the Member States can decide whether or not to close their own airspace. As a result, the EU boasts 28 different air traffic zones, each able to impose a flying ban. Fragmentation in the European Union is the result of a historical situation in which air traffic control has been (and still is) closely associated with sovereignty, and hence confined within national borders. Indeed, air traffic control is still perceived as being governed by both national defence and sovereign interests. This also reflects one of the tenets of the

23 *Ibid.*

24 Air Traffic Management (ATM) encompasses the functions required to ensure safe and efficient movement of aircraft during all phases of operations (Air Traffic Services (ATS)), airspace management (ASM) and air traffic flow management (ATFM).

Chicago Convention according to which each State is responsible for safety supervision in civil aviation within its own jurisdiction.[25]

It would, however, be a mistake to think that efforts have not been made towards integration of EU airspace, both before and in the aftermath of the Volcanic Ash Crisis.[26] Following the adoption of the Single Europe Sky (SES I) legislation in 2004, air traffic management was brought under the EU common transport policy.[27] The idea was to redesign the European sky according to traffic flows rather than national borders. Yet, as unambiguously exemplified by the patchwork regulatory response to the current crisis, a truly 'single' sky has not been achieved.

To remedy this situation, another reform, the 'Single Sky Package' (SES II) was adopted by the European Parliament and the Council in November 2009.[28] To accelerate the full implementation of the SES, the Commission has been using the volcanic ash crisis to create political momentum. In the aftermath of the crisis, it came out with a set of encouraging proposals, most of which have now been implemented.[29]

Firstly, the creation of a crisis coordination cell, gathering together Eurocontrol, EASA,[30] Member States and air transport stakeholders. This is

---

25 Convention on International Civil Aviation, signed in Chicago in 1944.

26 Efforts to formulate an EU airspace date back to 1996 when the European Commission published a White Paper on Air Traffic Management ("Freeing Europe's Airspace") and were followed by the 1997 initiative of Eurocontrol members to open up Eurocontrol membership to the European Community.

27 The SES I consists of a Framework Regulation plus three technical regulations on the provision of air navigation services, organisation and use of the airspace and the interoperability of the European air traffic management network. See Regulation (EC) No 549/2004 of the European Parliament and of the Council of 10 March 2004 laying down the framework for the creation of the Single European Sky, *OJ* L 96, p. 1.

28 Regulation (EC) No 1070/2009 of the European Parliament and of the Council of 21 October 2009 amending Regulations (EC) No 549/2004, (EC) No 550/2004, (EC) No 551/2004 and (EC) No 552/2004 in order to improve the performance and sustainability of the European aviation system, *OJ* L 300, pp. 34–50.

29 Council of the European Union (2011) EU Volcanic Ash Crisis: Follow-Up and the Wider Scope of Crisis Management, Information from the Commission, 25 March 2011, available <http://register.consilium.europa.eu/pdf/en/11/st08/st08192.en11.pdf> (accessed August 12, 2013).

30 The European Air Safety Agency is based in Cologne and employs some 500 professionals from across Europe. It provides expert advice to the EU for drafting new legislation and is in charge of the implementation and monitoring of safety rules, including inspections in the Member States as well as of the approval of organisations involved in the design, manufacture and maintenance of aeronautical products.

exactly what the EU did not have available during the crisis. This cell institutionalises some of the *ad hoc* mechanisms established during the crisis and is empowered with the possibility of launching unmanned aircraft vehicles (UAV) to collect data.

Secondly, nomination of coordinators to facilitate the quick creation of the Functional Airspace Blocks (FAB). FABs are airspace blocks, nine in number, based upon operational requirements. These have been established regardless of State boundaries, where the provision of air navigation services and related ancillary functions are optimised and/or integrated. They were foreseen in SES II and their implementation was adopted on 3 December 2010, which together with the nomination of the FAB Coordinator provided support in facilitating the respect of the FAB implementation deadline of 4 December 2012.[31]

Thirdly, appointment of the central European Network Management. It could reasonably be argued that if the network management function had been designated prior to the crisis, the EU would have benefited from a more harmonised and coordinated approach to the risk and flow/capacity assessment; this would have given it the ability to formulate proposals for solutions quickly to be tabled within the context of SES governance structures, also taking into account the need for coordination with other neighbouring countries and regions. The Implementing Rule for Network Functions was adopted by the Single Sky Committee, along with the decision on the designation of the Network Manager, on 15 February 2011.

Fourthly, acceleration of the implementation of EASA's competences in Air Traffic Management (ATM) safety. Following the opinions issued by EASA on 28 May 2010, the agency was to assume these new competences before 2012 to ensure the safety of the European network, thus ensuring a "full system, gate-to-gate" approach to safety.

The second package of Single European Sky entered into force in 2009 and has shown great promise, especially as regards the application of a more hands-off performance oriented model of economic regulation. With the implementation of that approach, important lessons have been learned and should be included in the regulations to refine the approach. Additionally, the SES II initiative left some overlaps in legislation, so that same provisions were found in several pieces of legislation. To perform these updates, the European Commission is launching an interim update of the SES rules, called *Single European Sky 2+ (SES2+)*.

---

31 In accordance with Article 8 of the Framework Regulation, the European Commission has issued a mandate to the Eurocontrol Agency for support in the establishment of Functional Airspace Blocks (FABs).

Despite the momentum created by the volcanic ash crisis and the great promise shown by the second package of Single European Sky which entered into force in 2009, the brave proposal put forward by the Commission,[32] Member States have not yet achieved the establishment of a European Single Sky. The failure of European states to make progress towards the SES led airspace users (represented by IATA) to publish 'A Blueprint for a Single European Sky' in February 2013 which set out key SES objectives. These included the establishment of an independent economic regulator; a reduction in Air Traffic Control Centres from 63 to not more than 40; and the modernization of the ATM system.

It is largely by relying on this document that on 10 June 2013, the European Commission presented its plan "B" to speed up the implementation process of SES. The so-called SES 2+ is a package of measures aimed at challenging the current situation with state owned monopolies being responsible for providing air navigation services. In particular, the Commission proposals include several elements which are well aligned with the Blueprint: a) the designation of an independent Performance Review Body, b) the unbundling of support services, c) greater independence and competence for Civil Aviation Authorities, and d) the need for more consultation by Air Navigation Service Providers on capital expenditure.

5 Lessons Learned and Open Questions

The protracted closure of European airspace following the volcanic eruption in Iceland, together with the initially fragmented regulatory response, has shown that while precautionary measures may be life-saving, they may also be not only logistically disruptive but also economically very costly. Whether and how these costs should be taken into account at the risk management stage represents one of the most difficult questions surrounding the precautionary principle. According to many, this is also one of its greatest weaknesses.[33] Should the expected benefits of the precautions have been compared against their expected costs?[34] The EU version of the principle, reflecting the Judaeo-

32 Accelerating the implementation of the Single European Sky, COM(2013) 408 final.

33 See for example C. Sunstein, *Worst-Case Scenarios*, Cambridge, MA: Harvard University Press, 2007.

34 Even in the US, where value has been conceived for a long time solely in monetary terms, there is an emerging consensus that both expected value and expected costs should be measured in terms of well-being. Yet, to say the least, people disagree on how to define

Christian belief that one cannot put a price on life, does not seem to allow any room for this kind of regulatory exercise.[35] However, a comparative analysis of expected costs and expected benefits of precautionary measures could serve as a useful check against overreaction to recent incidents.

This seems especially true if one considers the incentives that regulators have in the aftermath of a crisis to pay undue attention to worst-case scenarios. Moreover, it is often argued that the inclusion of precautionary costs could also induce regulators, when examining risk versus risk tradeoffs, to spot 'substitute risks', i.e. hazards that materialise or are increased by risk regulation policies.[36] Thus, for instance, after the attacks of "9/11", many Americans switched from flying to driving and because driving is more dangerous than flying, thousands of people have died as a result of the switch. It is probably too early to detect the impact that flying bans have had on other public transport accidents but it might be interesting to look at the data on this.

On the other hand, one may wonder how costs can be realistically computed in a situation in which, by definition, it is not possible to assign probabilities to the various scenarios because of the alleged level of uncertainty involved. Incidentally, the latter, in turn, affects the insurability of risks.[37] Is it true, however, that authorities did not know how much ash a jet could safely tolerate? Or perhaps they knew this but had no means of measuring the average density of ash in the atmosphere. Should it emerge that authorities at the time of the eruption did not know either of the two, their regulatory response would seem to be justified and could escape criticism. On the other hand, if they did know, or could have known, this information by carrying out some more diligence and/or cooperating with the airline industry and engine manufacturers,

---

well-being (or welfare). See, e.g., R. Revesz & M. Livermore, *Retaking Rationality,* Oxford: Oxford University Press, 2008; M. Adler & E. Posner, *New Foundations of Cost-Benefit Analysis*, Cambridge: Harvard University Press, 2006.

35 A. Alemanno, Is There a Role for Cost-Benefit Analysis Beyond the Nation-State?: Lessons from International Regulatory Co-Operation, in Michael A. Livermore & Richard L. Revesz (eds.), The Globalization of Cost-Benefit Analysis in Environmental Policy, Oxford: Oxford University Press, 2013.

36 See J. D. Graham & *J. B. Wiener, Risk vs. Risk: Tradeoffs in Protecting Health and the Environment*, Cambridge, MA: Harvard University Press, 1995.

37 On the issue of insurability of risks for natural or man-made disasters, see the policy options outlined by the Commission in the Green Paper on the insurance of natural and man-made disasters, COM (2013) 213 final. See also G. Castellano, Rising from the Ashes: A Governance Perspective on Emerging Systemic Risks, in A. Alemanno, Governing Disasters—The Challenges of Emergency Risk Regulation, Cheltenam, Edward Elgar, 2011, p. 246.

then some claims of precautionary abuse might be justified. A question worth asking is whether in these circumstances some forms of regulators' liability should emerge[38]. However, if it is true that airlines and engine manufacturers have been reluctant to commission studies on the impact of ash on their aircraft, the accusation of overreaction would lose some of its evocative power.

Coming to the reaction of the European regulator, the Commission has been more prone to looking into the future than into the past and has adopted a wide range of measures aimed at better integration of EU airspace through the Single European Sky (SES).[39]

By leveraging the disruption caused by the volcanic ash crisis, the Commission successfully accelerated the implementation of SES II, thus institutionalising some of the *ad hoc* mechanisms and procedures developed during the outbreak. With the implementation of that approach, important lessons have been learned and should be included in the regulations to refine the approach. However, since the SES II initiative left some overlaps in legislation, the European Commission is currently in the process of launching an interim update of the SES rules, called Single European Sky 2+ (SES2+). Undoubtedly, the volcanic ash crisis has added new impetus to the long-running struggle to unite Europe's airspace, by demonstrating to EU citizens the limits of EU integrations in one of the most sensitive areas of public policy. The costs of a non-European sky have turned out to be higher than expected. As if any proof were needed, it is time for the EU to conquer its own sky.

38 For an insightful perspective on this issue, K. C. Lauta, Exceptions and Norms: The Law on Natural Disasters, PhD thesis, Copenaghen School of Law, 2012 (on file with the author).

39 Commission Regulation (EU) No 1191/2010 of 16 December 2010 amending Regulation (EC) No 1794/2006 laying down a common charging scheme for air navigation services, *OJ* L 333, p. 6; Commission Regulation (EU) No 691/2010 of 29 July 2010 laying down a performance scheme for air navigation services and network functions and amending Regulation (EC) No 2096/2005 laying down common requirements for the provision of air navigation services *OJ* L 201, p. 1. See Note d'information de M. Kallas "Conséquences du nuages de cendres générée par l'éruption volcanique survenue en Islande sur le trafic aérien", SEC(2010) 533.

CHAPTER 12

The Fight against Terror and the Space of Individual Freedom: A (Classic) Word of Caution

Michal Bobek

1 Introduction: The Changed Face of Terror

For more than a decade now, Europe has been learning to live with terrorism. Naturally, terrorism was not born out of the events of September 11 in New York. Before 2001, however, for most of the European population, terrorism was something to be watched on the news but something that happened either somewhere else or was largely dormant after the turbulent 1970s and 1980s. Moreover, perverse as it was in moral terms, 'European-born' terrorism, in particular its past extreme left-wing or nationalistic/separatist varieties, remained residually rational, as they aimed primarily at law-enforcement, political, business or other representatives of the believed and hated 'system'.

The situation changed dramatically after 2001. The general population ceased to be an accidental and suffering bystander or collateral damage of terrorist attacks. It became the target. The omnipresent fight against terror rhetoric and measures adopted on its basis also brought the issue into people's minds in all European countries without exception. All individuals started feeling the consequences of measures adopted at various levels with the stated aim of combating terrorism, ranging from enhanced surveillance measures and strong police presence to, at first glance, banal issues like lack of rubbish bins in public spaces, airports, railway stations etc. Some fifteen or twenty years ago, the idea that there would be, as a matter of routine, police officers armed with machine guns patrolling airports or railway stations would seem odd to most Europeans, as would the idea that all the private communications of all Europeans would be monitored.

In recent years, the European Union has been both reacting to these changes and, on the legislative level, it has also been the generator of such changes. In the name of the fight against terror(ism) and prevention or adequate reaction to emergencies caused by it, new pieces of legislation have been adopted and new instruments and tools inserted into the Treaties, in particular the Lisbon Treaty. In analysing these new instruments and legislation, first and foremost attention is being paid to the fight against terror measures in the context of

© KONINKLIJKE BRILL NV, LEIDEN, 2014 | DOI 10.1163/9789004268333_014

the Common Foreign and Security Policy and the external dimensions of the EU fight against terrorism.[1] Such a focus is understandable and natural, as new powers, competences and areas need to be analysed and filled with content.

The aim of this contribution is, however, different. It focuses on the internal dimension of EU law and the impact which the declared aim of the 'fight against terror' and legislative measures adopted on its basis have had on the state and the 'quality' of the EU legal order internally. The interest of this contribution lies in the classical or traditional EU legal instruments (regulations, directives) which have been adopted as measures in the fight against terror since 2001 and their internal life within the EU and its Member States.

A comprehensive study of all such measures is naturally outside the scope of this short contribution. It therefore takes just two significant examples of legislative measures, which have been adopted in recent years with the explicit 'fight against terror' rhetoric and justification: regulation(s) on airport and aviation security and the Data Retention Directive. Critically examining the operation of both of these instruments, it is suggested that the considerable inroads into individual freedom which both of these measures have required can hardly be justified by their appropriateness or their necessity. Furthermore, taking into account the historical sensibilities with regard to such measures in a number of post-dictatorial states and societies in Europe, it is suggested that such measures should not only be carefully and duly weighed up in the legislative process. Such measures and above all their actual application after their adoption must be made subject to critical scrutiny by the Court of Justice of the EU.

2 Example One: Airport Security and Secret Legislation

Regulation No 2320/2002 of the European Parliament and of the Council of 16 December 2002 establishing common rules in the field of civil aviation security[2] was adopted in the aftermath of the September 11 attacks in New York and Washington. The very first recital of the Regulation referred to the September 11 attacks. It stated that "*terrorism is one of the greatest threats to the ideals of democracy and freedom and the values of peace*". The prevention of (terrorist) acts of interference with civil aviation was thus the primary aim of the Regulation, as is also apparent from Article 1(1) of the Regulation.

1 See further on this topic the respective contributions of C. Hillion, J. Czuczai, J. Wouters, and S. Duquet to this volume.

2 *OJ*, 2002, L 355/1.

Further implementation of the Parliament and Council Regulation No. 2320/2002 was carried out by way of Commission Regulation (EC) No 622/2003 of 4 April 2003 laying down measures for the implementation of the common basic standards on aviation security.[3] In particular, the implementing Commission Regulation drew up a list of prohibited items, which passengers were not allowed to carry with them into the cabin of an aircraft. The list, together with other implementing provisions of the Regulation, was contained in its annex which was in accordance with Article 3 of the Regulation, "secret and not published". The Regulation foresaw that the content of the annex would be made available only to persons duly authorised by a Member State or the Commission.

As a consequence, passengers could be denied boarding at European airports if they were carrying one or more of the 'prohibited items', despite not being clearly told what such prohibited items were. This practice was challenged by Dr. Gottfried Heinrich, who was denied boarding because he was carrying tennis rackets in his hand luggage. In response to a preliminary ruling from an Austrian court deciding the case of Dr. Heinrich, the Grand Chamber of the Court of Justice held that regulations that were not published in the Official Journal have no binding force in so far as they seek to impose obligations on individuals.[4]

Prior to this decision of the Court, however, it was in fact the critical stance of the Advocate General Sharpston that made the Commission reconsider its practice. As the learned Advocate General suggested in her Opinion of 10 April 2008, regulations that, contrary to the compulsory publication requirements laid down in (then) Article 254(2) TEC, have not been published in the Official Journal of the European Union, must be deemed legally non-existent (void). The Advocate General argued that the legal order of the EU, if it wishes to maintain that it is indeed based on the rule of law, cannot tolerate the existence of secret legislation, irrespective of the declared aims such as the fight against terror. In her Opinion:

> [I]t may perhaps be suggested that the public interest in preserving rules enhancing airport security requires that the Court should either turn a Nelsonian blind eye to the clear breach of a mandatory publication requirement [...]. In my view that argument is a specious one. [...]. Similar arguments are raised not infrequently in difficult times to justify

---

3 *OJ*, 2003, L 89/9, as amended by Commission Regulation No 68/2004, *OJ*, 2004, L 10/14.

4 Case C-365/06, *Gottfried Heinrich* [2009] ECR I-1659, para. 63.

> departure from the ordinary rule of law—whether that be by suspending guarantees of fundamental rights, restricting judicial scrutiny or softening the consequences of such scrutiny. They have no place in a European Union that is governed by the rule of law and whose Court is under the Treaty obligation to ensure that 'the law is observed'.[5]

It is to the Commission's credit that after being scorned by the Advocate General, the Commission swiftly changed its policy. The Commission did not even wait for the (in the end much more 'lenient' and conceptually somewhat questionable)[6] decision of the Court of Justice, which held that secret legislation is in fact valid EU law, which just cannot impose obligations on individuals. Commission Regulation No 820/2008 of 8 August 2008 laying down measures for the implementation of the common basic standards on aviation security[7] repealed the questionable "secret" Regulation No 622/2003. The new Commission Regulation contains a full list of prohibited items, which are not to be taken by air passengers into the cabin. Now all passengers can read, should they wish to, that they are not allowed to take on board firearms, crossbows, catapults or harpoons, in other words objects one might reasonably expect to be banned. However, the passengers are also not allowed to carry such items as skateboards, kayaks, lacrosse sticks, fishing rods, and other potential assault weapons of a modern terrorist.[8]

The important point emerging from this example is that contrary to the Commission's assertions, adopting "secret legislation" in violation of EU primary law requirements was not in any way necessary for guaranteeing airport security in Europe and preventing potential terrorist attacks on civil aviation. Since 2008, the list of prohibited items has been publicly accessible, without there being any visible drop in the level of airport security.

---

5 Opinion of AG Sharpston of 10 April 2008 in Case C-365/06, *Gottfried Heinrich* [2008] ECR I-1659, para. 100. The allusion made to the '*Nelsonian blind eye*' refers to an incident ascribed to Horatio Nelson, the British naval commander in the wars with Napoleonic France. It is said that in the course of the naval battle of Copenhagen in early 1801, Nelson was ordered to disengage. Unwilling to accept the flag signals sent to his ship and refusing to retreat, he intentionally put the telescope to his blind eye. When asked why he not followed the admiralty orders, he claimed he did not see them.

6 Critically see Bobek in the case note on the *Heinrich* judgment in *Common Market Law Review* 46, 2009, p. 2077.

7 *OJ*, 2008, L 221/8.

8 Cf. Article 4.1.1. of Regulation No 820/2008.

3 Example Two: Data Retention and Surveillance

Directive 2006/24 of the European Parliament and of the Council of 15 March 2006 on the retention of data generated or processed in connection with the provision of publicly available electronic communications services or of public communications networks[9] requires all data relating to traffic and location of users of electronic communications to be stored for at least six months after the communication takes place. The data to be stored is information concerning the traffic, not the actual content of the electronic communication. In other words, information about all individual phone calls, text messages, emails, and so on is being stored by the respective service providers. The providers ought to be storing only data identifying who communicated with whom, the time, and the location of the respective parties. They ought not to, at least in theory, store the content of the communication. The stored data concerning past communications will be released by the service provider to designated national authorities for the purposes of the investigation, detection and prosecution of serious crimes.

The stated aims of the Data Retention Directive are twofold. Firstly, it is to unify the varying national laws relating to the retention of data by service providers. The disparity among such laws is said to present obstacles to the internal market for electronic communications.[10] Secondly, the even more frequently stressed aim of the same Directive is combating terrorism and organized crime.[11] Thus, even if the Directive is declared to be an internal market harmonization measure, perhaps also with a view to being able to invoke the then Article 95 TEC (currently Article 114 TFEU) as its legal basis, it could be suggested that its main purpose is in fact the declared fight against serious crime and terrorism in particular.

There are not many pieces of recent EU legislation which would have hit such massive and widespread opposition in the Member States, on both legal as well as political (civil society) grounds. In terms of law and legal

9 *OJ*, 2006, L 105/54.

10 Cf. recital 6 of the Directive No 2006/24.

11 Cf. recitals 7, 8, 10, 11. Recital No 10 expressly refers to the terrorist bombings in London on 7 July 2005 and the following declaration by the Council to "*adopt common measures on the retention of telecommunications data as soon as possible*".

proceedings, six Member States (Sweden,[12] Austria,[13] Ireland,[14] Greece,[15] the Netherlands,[16] and Germany)[17] delayed or refused to implement certain aspects of the Directive. The constitutional or supreme courts of five further Member States (Germany,[18] the Czech Republic,[19] Romania,[20] Bulgaria,[21] and Cyprus)[22] annulled parts of or the entire national laws implementing the Data Retention Directive as unconstitutional, thus making the Directive wholly or partly inoperative within those Member States.[23] On the political front, the

---

12 Case C-185/09, *Commission v Kingdom of Sweden*, [2010] *OJ*, C 80/6.

13 Case C-189/09, *Commission v Republic of Austria*, [2010] *OJ*, C 246/8.

14 Case C-202/09, *Commission v Ireland*, [2010] *OJ*, C 24/16.

15 Case C-211/09, *Commission v Hellenic Republic*, [2010] *OJ*, C 24/16.

16 Case C-192/09, *Commission v Kingdom of the Netherlands*, [2009] *OJ*, C 180/34.

17 Case C-329/12, *Commission v Federal Republic of Germany*, [2012] *OJ*, C 287/23.

18 BVerfG, 1 BvR 256/08 of 2 March 2010, available at: <http://www.bverfg.de> (accessed 25 July 2013). Further see C. DeSimone, "Pitting Karlsruhe Against Luxembourg? German Data Protection and the Contested Implementation of the EU Data Retention Directive", *German Law Journal* 11, 2010, pp. 291–318.

19 Judgment (plenary) of 22 March 2011, Pl. ÚS 24/10, available in English at: <http:// www.usoud.cz> (accessed 25 July 2013).

20 Decision No. 12581 of 8 October 2009, available in English at: <http://www.legi-internet.ro> (accessed 25 July 2013).

21 Decision of the Bulgarian Supreme Administrative Court of 11 December 2008, available at: <http://www.aip-bg.org/documents/data_retention_campaign_11122008eng.htm> (accessed 25 July 2013).

22 Decision of the Supreme Court of Cyprus of 1 February 2011, joined cases 65/2009, 78/2009, 82/2009 and 15/2010–22/2010, available at: <http://www.edri.org/edrigram/number9.3/data-retention-un-lawful-cyprus> (accessed 25 July 2013).

23 It should be noted that for similar pieces of legislation such as the Data Retention Directive, failure to implement or the later annulment of national implementing measures mean that the Directive becomes wholly inoperative at the national level. Alternatives to the non-implementation, created by the case law of the Court of Justice, are virtually excluded. Direct effect is prohibited as it would amount to vertical direct effect used by the state against the individual. Indirect effect (consistent interpretation) is also hardly possible, as there would typically be no national legislation that could be interpreted in conformity (the Directive itself was supposed to create such national legislation). Finally, it is difficult to imagine that individuals would try to bring a claim for state liability against a Member State which failed to monitor all their electronic communications. On the other hand, victims of a terrorist attack or their surviving families could hypothetically bring a damages claim against a Member State which did not monitor electronic communications and failed to prevent a terrorist attack. This appears to be just a hypothetical scenario, however, as proving a causal link between

Directive met with considerable opposition in a number of Member States, in particular in Germany.[24]

The Data Retention Directive is arguably quite a problematic measure. There is no doubt that to be effective, the fight against terrorism and against serious, in particular organized crime, necessitates access to some types of private data regarding communications of persons *reasonably suspected* of involvement in such activities. However, to automatically store data relating to *every single* communication carried out by everybody for at least six months and for up to two years? Treating everybody as a potential suspect, unless proven innocent?[25] Or better still: guilt does not matter any more. Even if innocent, the communication will continue to be monitored.

The recent challenge as to the validity of the Directive was unsuccessful.[26] The action brought by Ireland in this respect was limited, however, to just the question of the proper legal basis chosen for the adoption of the Directive, not its rule of law and human rights implications. These angles ought to be addressed in the near future, with further challenges as to the validity of the Data Retention Directive currently pending before the Court of Justice and submitted by the Irish High Court[27] and by the Austrian *Verfassungsgerichtshof* (Constitutional Court) respectively.[28]

Finally, not only may it be suggested that the Directive itself is in its scope and impact disproportionate. The national implementation in a number of Member States has proved to be even more questionable than the Directive itself. The problem lies in the strange construction of the Data Retention Directive. On the one hand, it categorically requests a massive collection and

---

the failure to monitor electronic communications and the damage caused to individuals would be in practical terms very difficult if not impossible.

24 For an illustration of this, see the web-sites of some of the civil law initiatives formed in opposition to the Directive, which were able to generate petitions or summon demonstrations involving tens of thousands of people—e.g.: <http://www.vorratsdatenspeicherung.de> or <http://blog.freiheitstattangst.de> (both sites accessed 25 July 2013).

25 Critically (with detailed technical discussion) see also L. Feiler, "The Legality of the Data Retention Directive in the Light of the Fundamental Rights to Privacy and Data Protection", *European Journal of Law and Technology* 1, 2010, available at: <http://ejlt.org> (accessed 25 July 2013).

26 Case C-301/06, *Ireland v Parliament and Council* [2009] ECR I-593. Further see case note by S. Poli, *European Constitutional Law Review* 6, 2010, pp. 137–157.

27 Case C-293/12, *Digital Rights Ireland Ltd v Minister for Communications and others*, case pending, notice published in *OJ*, 2012, C 258/11.

28 Case C-594/12, *Kärntner Landesregierung and Others*, case pending, notice published in *OJ*, 2013, C 79/7.

storage of data. At the same time, it leaves immense discretion to the Member States for choosing, when transposing the directive, which types of (serious) crime data assembled under the Directive are to be disclosed, under which procedure and to which types of national authority.[29]

This has resulted in considerable overshooting or gold-plating in the national transposition of the Directive in a number of Member States. Requests for data information archived under the Directive have been made to just about any police authority investigating any type of criminal activity, including minor crimes or offences, i.e. sometimes very distant from the original idea of the fight against terror and organized crime. The example of the Czech Republic is worrisome in this respect.[30] Law enforcement authorities started requesting lists of past mobile communications from telecommunications providers almost as a matter of routine for any type of investigation, with mobile communication surveillance becoming *the evidence* for building up a case for the police and the prosecution in the pursuit of whatever crime.

The lesson from this second example is also not difficult to draw. Disproportionate and highly intrusive EU legislation is made even worse by its national implementation. Measures introduced with the putative aim of combating terror and organized crime soon degenerate into the police authorities making their lives easier to the detriment of society at large. Naturally, all this is happening at the expense of the public image of the European Union and the EU institutions. Often, not even lawyers themselves are able to tell the difference between what is really required by the Directive and what has already been added for the convenience of national law enforcement authorities. It is difficult to argue against such accusations, primarily because the Directive does indeed require the storage of all data. It just appears that the EU legislator nonchalantly forgot to include any substantive and institutional limits. It is precisely this issue that is arguably the greatest weakness of the Directive. It legitimizes data retention measures at the national level (or certainly takes the blame for them) without being able to effectively regulate them. Metaphori-

29 Cf. Article 1(1) of the Directive (the definition of a "serious crime" for the purposes of the Directive is left to the national law of each Member State) and Article 4 of the Directive (Member States shall define the national authorities entitled to receive the information and also designate procedures).

30 Further see e.g. P. Molek, "Czech Constitutional Court Unconstitutionality of the Czech Implementation of the Data Retention Directive; Decision of 22 March 2011, Pl. ÚS 24/10", *European Constitutional Law Review* 8, 2012, p. 338–353 or M. Švarc *et al.*, "The Czech Republic", in: J. Laffranque (ed.), *The Area of Freedom, Security and Justice, Including Information Society Issues. Reports of the XXV FIDE Congress Tallinn 2014*, Tartu: Tartu University Press, 2012, pp. 261 & 278–280.

cally speaking, the situation resembles somebody organising a party that is nominally by invitation only, putting out free food and drinks, before disappearing, leaving all the doors open.

4 East, West, and the Space of Individual Freedom: Three Tentative Conclusions

In sum, the picture emerging from the previous two examples is rather discomforting for anybody who believes in individual freedom as a (if not *the*) defining value of a liberal state based upon the rule of law. In the first case, it is apparent that there was no need at all for secret legislation in order to achieve the stated aim: a high level of airport and civil aviation security. In the language of proportionality analysis, the means chosen were not even appropriate for achieving the aims stated.[31] In the second case, the means chosen appear to be disproportionate, i.e. not necessary, with respect to the stated aim. Moreover, they are bound to be misused, not to mention the simply flawed ideological foundations on which they are based. In a liberal state based upon the rule of law, one might be supervised and checked if reasonably suspected. The Data Retention Directive reverses the exception and the rule: everybody is supervised all the time by default.

Therein lies the *first* conclusion of this short reflective piece: any measure being advanced by EU or national authorities claiming to be essential and necessary in the name of the fight against terror or any other emergency must be kept at arm's length. It must be critically examined and re-assessed. Otherwise, secret legislation, total surveillance, arrests or expulsions without trials will no longer be limited to the prose of Kafka or Orwell. The role of legal scholarship in this respect is certainly not negligible. The privilege of academic freedom also brings responsibilities. The EU legal scholarship, traditionally somewhat one-sided in its outlook,[32] could certainly use a dose of healthy institutional

31 Provided that while adopting the measure, the Commission gave specific thought to what precisely was the aim of keeping the regulation secret. See in this respect paragraphs 64–66 of the already quoted Opinion of AG Sharpston in *Heinrich* (*op. cit.*, n. 5), in which she pointed out the self-contradictory nature of Commission's position. If the stated aim of (any) legislation is to regulate individual behaviour, then the appropriate means for achieving such aim can never be keeping it secret from its addressees.

32 See e.g. already H. Schepel and R. Wesseling, "The Legal Community: Judges, Lawyers, Officials and Clerks in the Writing of Europe", *European Law Journal* 3, 1997, pp. 165–188; but see more recently e.g. B. de Witte, "European Union Law: A Unified Academic

scepticism. The aim of an academic study is objective and critical cognition, not ex post explanation of institutional wisdom and orthodoxy.

It is perhaps true that such an institutional distrust might be stronger in the Central European new Member States than it is in the old Member States. Equally, there may be different sensibilities to issues like surveillance or secret legislation around Europe. The reasons lie in the past. For the post-Communist new Member States, but also for a number of other post-totalitarian States in Europe, including Germany, secret legislation or total surveillance are not just themes from social anti-utopias. They are sad memories. There indeed used to be secret collections of laws in Nazi Germany and in some countries in the Soviet legal space,[33] which were accessible only to the officials or members of the ruling party, but not to the individual members of the public. The reality of total surveillance by the secret police in the East before 1989 can perhaps be best explained visually, by watching, for instance, the revealing film "The Lives of the Others".[34]

Similar historical memories tend to be naturally translated into different value choices within the national legal and constitutional space. The space of individual freedom is a precious value that is carefully guarded, not only with respect to surveillance measures or secret legislation, but with respect to general freedom to act, including economic or commercial freedom. It is by no means suggested that individual freedom would not matter in some of the older Member States which have not had a more recent undemocratic experience. It is only suggested that the more recent such historical experience, the stronger it may become reflected in constitutional and institutional choices and acts of balancing in decision-making and adjudication. In the former "East", the guiding principle which emerged after 1989 could be said to be a general constitution of individual freedom: *in dubio pro libertate*.[35]

Discipline?", EUI RSCAS Working Paper 2008/34, also in: A. Vauchez and B. de Witte (eds.), *Lawyering Europe European Law as a Transnational Social Field*, Oxford: Hart, 2013.

33 In detail see D. A. Loeber, "Legal Rules 'For Internal Use Only'—A Comparative Analysis of the Practice of Withholding Government Decrees from Publication in Eastern Europe and in Western Countries", *International and Comparative Law Quarterly* 19, 1970, pp. 70–98 or W. E. Butler, "Unpublished Normative Acts in Post-Soviet Legal Space", *Journal of Comparative Law* 3, 2008, pp. 295–310.

34 Original title "Das Leben der Anderen", director Florian Henckel von Donnersmarck, release date 13 April 2007. The film depicts the surveillance measures, phone tapping, and flat bugging by the East German secret State Police (Stasi) in East Berlin in the 1980s.

35 Amounting to a meta-principle for solving the conflicts between other constitutional principles, defining the political ontology of a number of post-Communist systems. It is perhaps no accident that the same term has been chosen as the title of a recently

Conversely, the guiding principle of the Union and some of its older Member States` legislation and its interpretation would be much more communitarian in nature. In the case of the EU, it might amount rather to *in dubio pro integratione,* with full effectiveness and further integration being allowed to prevail over the space of individual freedom.

Therein lies the *second* conclusion: Union institutions participating in the legislative process would be well advised to take these different sensibilities into account, in particular when designing legislation considerably infringing upon individual freedom. This might perhaps have been less important in the first few years following the 2004 enlargement, where the newcomers would largely sit around silently and learn, also due to the still lasting institutional enchantment: "we finally did it, we finally belong back to Europe". However, with almost ten years having past since accession, more critical voices and views are appearing. These may be in no way hostile to the European project, rather soberly evaluating what precisely have been the trade-offs and the price paid for belonging to the Euro-club. Within this equation, the real drop in the level of protection of the individual freedom to act[36] may be a weighty factor against the benefit of belonging to the European Union. Before their accession to the EU, a number of post-Communist States in Central Europe, in particular their national constitutional courts, promoted robust visions of individual freedom as the key value within the new constitutional system. Such a move was to a great degree understandable. It represented a clear value and ideological departure from the over-regulated society and omnipresent state in Communist times. However, after 2004, a number of these freshly acquired rights and the overall space of individual freedom had to make way for different values and the more communitarian visions of the EU legal order. Individual economic or professional freedom had to make way for market regulation through production quotas.[37] A number of procedural safeguards,

published Liber Amicorum for the out-going influential vice-president of the Czech Constitutional Court, Mrs Eliška Wagnerová (M. Kokeš and I. Pospíšil (eds.), *In dubio pro libertate: Úvahy nad ústavními hodnotami a právem. Pocta Elišce Wagnerové u příležitosti životního jubilea*, Brno: Masarykova Univerzita, 2009).

36 See notably A. Albi, "An essay on how the discourse on sovereignty and the co-operativeness of national courts has diverted attention from the erosion of classic constitutional rights in the EU", in: M. Claes and others (eds.), *Constitutional Conversations in Europe: Actors, Topics and Procedures*, Cambridge: Intersentia, 2012, pp. 41–70 or A. Albi, "Ironies in human rights protection in the EU: pre-accession conditionality and post-accession conundrums", *European Law Journal* 15, 2009, pp. 46–69.

37 For example, in 2001, the Czech Constitutional Court struck down Czech national milk quotas based on the EU example (but at that time the Czech Republic being just

including a strict reading of *nulla poena sine lege*,[38] or strict prohibition of retroactivity,[39] had to make way for the *effet utile* of EU law. Finally, now it would appear that physical individual freedom from surveillance might have to make way for questionably conceived "fight against terror" measures of data retention and the like.

Therein lies the *third* and final conclusion and, for the immediate future, the greatest challenge for the Court of Justice. The Court must be seen and perceived as a genuine and sharp guardian of the Union political institutions, especially when it adopts measures similar to those discussed in this contribution, measures infringing upon the space of individual freedom. The Court of Justice's record so far is not impressive,[40] taking into account for instance the

---

an associated and candidate country) as an unconstitutional limitation of professional freedom of enterprise and action (see judgment of 14 February 2001, Pl. ÚS 45/2000, No. 96/2001 Coll.). In 2006, after accession, when the same question relating to milk quotas came up, the Constitutional Court was obliged to refrain from any substantive review and was bound to give way to primacy and uniform application of EU law (judgment of 8 March 2006, Pl. ÚS 50/04, No. 154/2006 Coll.). However, taking into account the difficulty if not impossibility of attacking regulatory measures in terms of their validity at EU level, this means in practical terms the absence of any review for the economic operators.

38 Cf. e.g. the method of reasoning of the Tribunal in Case T-324/05, *Estonia v Commission* [2009] ECR II-3681 or of the Court of Justice in Case C-255/02, *Halifax plc* [2006] ECR I-1609. In both of these cases, sanctions are created by *de facto* analogy without solid textual basis, just in the name of effective application of EU law.

39 In EU law, true retroactivity is an exception, but it is a possible exception, warranted by the existence of compelling economic interests of the Union (see e.g. Cases C-142/88 and C-92/89, *Zuckerfabrik Süderdithmarschen* [1991] ECR I-415 or C-459/02, *Gerekens* [2004] ECR I-7315). In most of the Central European constitutional legal orders, true retroactivity is constitutionally unthinkable (with the sole exception of very limited system change-related exceptions of the sort for punishing Nazi or Communist crimes).

40 The *Kadi* saga and the Court of Justice's readiness to review anti-terrorist measures as to their compatibility with fundamental rights sends a somewhat mixed message. It is true, that the Court of Justice assumed jurisdiction in such cases. On the other hand, it has repeatedly been questioned how far the displayed willingness to review was indeed ideological and how far it was just instrumental, induced by the wish to safeguard the unity of the EU legal order and extend the Court's review externally. It may be suggested that a genuine ideological commitment to individual rights may only be tested if and when upholding such rights comes at a cost to the Court of Justice and the EU legal order itself, not when somebody else (the United Nations and the Security Council, or the international legal order at large) pays the bill, so to speak. From the avalanches of academic literature on the topic, amongst the more recent contributions, see, for example, the contributions by G. de Búrca and D. Halberstam, in: G. de Búrca and J. H. H. Weiler

already quoted *Heinrich* decision of the Grand Chamber, where the Court of Justice nonchalantly held that secret legislation adopted in violation of clear primary as well as secondary law requirements remains valid law.[41] On the other hand, more recent cases,[42] in particular those decided after the entry into force of the EU Charter of Fundamental Rights, might be seen as an indication that the Court of Justice may be willing to take on a more robust role as a guardian of EU political institutions. An active and critical role of the Court of Justice will be essential in the near future,[43] in particular seeing the increased sensibilities courts and societies in post-dictatorial and post-Communist Europe show vis-à-vis such questionable measures as discussed in this short contribution, infringing upon the space of basic fundamental freedom from surveillance and supervision. Failing to assume such a crucial critical role, the Court of Justice and the EU legal order as such might find itself in situations in comparison to which cases like *Landtová*[44] could be remembered as a friendly ragging in the course of a peaceful children's matinee.

(eds.), *The Worlds of European Constitutionalism*, Cambridge: Cambridge University Press, 2012.

41 In *Heinrich* therefore, one might suggest that it was AG Sharpston who acted as *de facto* substitute judge—further see M. Bobek, "A Fourth in the Court: Why Are There Advocates General in the Court of Justice?", *Cambridge Yearbook of European Legal Studies* 14, 2011–2012, pp. 529–561.

42 Cf. e.g., with respect to data protection, in particular Joined Cases C-92/09 and C-93/09, *Schecke and Eifert* [2010] ECR I-11063. Generally see e.g. G. Arestis, "Fundamental rights in the EU: three years after Lisbon, the Luxembourg perspective", College of Europe Research Paper in Law 2/2013 or S. Iglesias Sánchez, "The Court and the Charter. The Impact of the Entry into Force of the Lisbon Treaty on the ECJ's Approach to Fundamental Rights", *Common Market Law Review* 49, 2012, pp. 1565–1611.

43 As already mentioned, two challenges relating to the validity of the Data Retention Directive are already pending before the Court of Justice, submitted by the Irish High Court and the Austrian Constitutional Court respectively (*op. cit.*, n. 27 and 28).

44 In reaction to the decision of the Court of Justice Case C-399/09, *Landtová,* judgment of 22 June 2011, n. y. r., the plenary Czech Constitutional Court held in its decision of 31 January 2012, Pl. ÚS 5/12, that the said decision of the Court of Justice is *ultra vires* and thus not applicable on the territory of the Czech Republic. This is, to our knowledge, the first case in the history of European integration in which a national (constitutional) court openly and clearly refused to follow the Court of Justice, declaring an act of the Union (a judgement of the Court of Justice), *ultra vires*. Grave and serious as such an incidence appears to be for the functioning of the EU legal order, the ensuing practice of the Czech courts, the Czech legislator as well as the Czech Constitutional Court itself would suggest that the decision will become an isolated incident. For a detailed discussion see M. Bobek,

In sum, the main massage of this contribution is indeed as its title indicates a classic word of caution with respect to exceptional or emergency measures seeking to justify their establishment or on-going existence by the need of combat terrorism. The two examples discussed suggest that such measures might be questionable in terms of their appropriateness and necessity. However, once introduced, they are only rarely critically and fully reassessed. At the same time, they quickly redefine the public space, irretrievably cutting back on the free space of the individual. Therein lies the *final* word of caution: as history from the Roman Republic to Weimar and beyond teaches us, there are perhaps less states or systems which were destroyed by genuine external or internal enemies or emergencies than there are those which fell as a consequence of inflation, overuse and inevitable abuse of exceptional or emergency powers.

"Landtová, Holubec, and the Problem of an Uncooperative Court: Implications for the Preliminary Rulings Procedure", European Constitutional Law Review 10, 2014, pp. 54–89.

PART 2

The EU as an International Actor in Managing Global Emergencies, Threats and Crises

CHAPTER 13

European Union Participation in International Financial Organizations

Christine Kaddous

1 Introduction

The European Union is today the largest exporter of goods and the world leader in trade in services. The Euro, adopted by 18 Member States, has become the second currency of the world. However, the EU, and in particular the Economic and Monetary Union (EMU), is not able to impose itself politically on the international scene. One of the reasons for this lies in its inability to translate its economic weight into political influence. The present efforts to strengthen the economic governance of the Eurozone need to be accompanied by a more unified and coherent external representation within the international financial organizations. The terms and modalities of cooperation in economic and monetary matters, in particular with the UN institutions established under the Bretton Woods system in 1944, notably with the International Monetary Fund (IMF) and the World Bank, have to be adapted to the changes which have occurred within the EU. As for the World Trade Organization (WTO), which was foreseen as the third pillar of the institutional triptyque in 1944, great progress has been made in that area since 1968. The entity first took the form of the GATT, before becoming the WTO on 1 January 1995. The representation of the then European Economic Community (EEC) was made possible following the judgment rendered by the European Court of Justice (CJEU) in the *International Fruit* case,[1] through the acknowledgment of the completion of the customs union and the establishment of the common customs tariffs which enabled the development and acceptance of the EEC's succession of its Member States in matters relating to GATT. Today, the EU is a full member of the WTO, alongside the Member States, having voting rights as provided for in Article IX of the Agreement establishing the World Trade Organization.[2]

1 CJEU, joined cases C-21-24/72, *International Fruit Company* [1972] ECR I-1219.

2 Article IX states in particular that: "… Where the European Communities exercise their right to vote, they shall have a number of votes equal to the number of their member States which are Members of the WTO… .".

© KONINKLIJKE BRILL NV, LEIDEN, 2014 | DOI 10.1163/9789004268333_015

The evolution in the EU participation in the international trade sector at the global level should be viewed as a very positive indication of what could be achieved within other international organizations, where EU competence is exclusive. However, attention must be paid to the differences which may derive from the internal rules provided for in the constituent charters of the respective organizations in which the EU aims to participate.

The financial crisis has propelled the Group of Twenty (G20) into the first position in terms of coordinating the response to the global crisis. The G20 represents more than 90% of global GDP, 80% of world trade, and two-thirds of the world's population.[3] It brings together nine advanced economies and the ten most important emerging countries from all regions in the world. Four Member States of the EU (Germany, France, Italy and the United Kingdom) are members as well as the European Union as such, which constitutes the 20th full member and the only non-State Member.

The G20 has taken on a leading role in the process of financial reform presently taking place at European and international levels. It gets support notably from the IMF for macroeconomic surveillance and from the World Bank for the governance of the global economy.[4] The present contribution aims at assessing the EU's role in these three *fora* and determining whether and how the EU's performance may be strengthened. These questions raise a certain number of concerns both within and outside the EU. There are tensions among the Member States of the EU, between the ones participating in the Euro and the ones which are outside the single currency. There is also a reluctance among specific EU Member States of the Eurozone to give up sovereignty and transfer more power to the EU. Furthermore, third countries which are members of the international financial institutions, do not all perceive the participation of the EU in these institutions positively. They consider that there is already an overrepresentation of the EU at the international level taking into account the relative loss of economic weight of the EU and the growing economic weight of new players. Apart from these obstacles, one must be aware of the internal difficulties linked to the fact that most international organizations only allow membership to States, therefore excluding any sort of EU participation.

3 See <http://www.g20.org/docs/about/about_G20.html> (accessed 9 June, 2013).

4 The two other leading institutions in the governance of the global economy are the Financial Stability Board (FSB) which gives support to the G20 for more micro-related prudential regulatory and supervisory issues, on the one side, and the Bank for International Settlements (BIS), which coordinates regulations in the field of financial services to promote international financial stability on the other side.

One of the main causes of the Eurozone crisis has been the asymmetry between centralised monetary policy and decentralised fiscal and supply side policies. The EU has responded by introducing a series of crisis management measures, which requires a reassessment of the principle of institutional balance and powers of the Member States within the EU. These new governance rules, introduced to respond to the crisis, have to be accompanied by a coherent external representation within the international financial organizations.

After an analysis of the main principles applicable to EU participation in international organizations (2), this contribution will examine the distribution of powers between the EU and its Member States in the field of EMU (3) and its projection in the field of EU external action (4) before assessing the best ways to strengthen the EU's position and role within the IMF and the World Bank as well as within the G20 (5).

2 Principles Applicable to EU Participation in International Organizations

The possibility for the EU to participate as such to an international organization depends on two factors: firstly, the conferral and division of competences between the EU and its Member States; and secondly the statute of the international organization in question.

There are no general provisions in the treaties regulating EU participation in international organizations.[5] The Lisbon treaty introduced a title VI into the Treaty on the Functioning of the European Union (TFEU) which refers to the EU's relations with international organizations and third countries and Union delegations. By virtue of Article 220 TFEU, the EU is to establish all appropriate forms of cooperation with the organs of the UN and its specialised agencies,

---

5 J. Sack, "The European Community's Membership of International Organisations", *CML Rev* 32, 1995, p. 1227; C. Kaddous, "Le droit des relations extérieures dans la jurisprudence de la Cour de justice", *Collection des Dossiers de droit européen, n°6*, Helbing: Bruylant, 1998, at p. 135; C. Flaesch-Mougin, "Les relations avec les organisations internationales et la participation à celles-ci", in : « Commentaire J. Mégret (ed.), *Etudes européennes*, Bruxelles, 2005, Chapter 6; I. Govaere, J. Capiau and A. Vermeersch, "In-Between Seats: The Participation of the European Union in International Organisations", *EFA Rev*, 2006, pp. 155–187; F. Hoffmeister, "Outsider or Frontrunner? Recent Developments under International and European Law on the Status of the European Union in International Organisations and Treaty Bodies", *CML Rev* 44, 2007, pp. 41–68.

the Council of Europe, the OSCE and the OECD.[6] It shall also maintain such relations as are appropriate with other international organizations. The High Representative for Foreign Affairs and Security Policy shall be instructed to implement this provision. On the other hand, Article 221 provides that Union delegations in third countries and within international organizations shall represent the Union.[7] However, these provisions do not expressly provide for EU membership of an international organization.[8] It is through the case law of the CJEU that the EU's capacity to participate as such in international organizations has been recognised. In *Opinion 1/76*, the CJEU considered that the Community was not only entitled to enter into contractual relations with a third country but that it also had the power, while observing the provisions of the Treaty, to cooperate with that country in setting up an appropriate entity such as the public international institution which was proposed to be established.[9] This principle was later implicitly confirmed in *Opinion 1/94*[10] where the CJEU recognised the competence of the EC to create the WTO along with the other Member States of the organization.

That being said, EU participation in international organizations may take different forms. It may vary from the status of observer to the status of full membership. Moreover, there is also not only one status of observer, but different ones depending on the constituent charters of the organizations, which may allow for more active participation of the EU and consequently largely reduce the differences between members and non-members.[11]

The rights and obligations of the observer are determined in each case by reference to the constituent charter of the organization. Such a status does not give the EU the right to vote, but it can nevertheless take part in discussions. The EU is not member of the United Nations or of any of the major UN organizations, except the FAO. It is not, for example, a member of the ILO, whereas the EU does have competences in the field of social policy; this is because the constitution of the ILO does not allow for EU membership.

---

6 Those provisions are not different in substance from the former articles of the EC Treaty, see Articles 229 to 231 TEC.

7 According to Article 221(2), Union delegations shall be placed under the authority of the High Representative and shall act in close cooperation with Member States' diplomatic and consular missions.

8 See already, C. Kaddous, *op. cit.*, n. 5.

9 Opinion 1/76 re draft Agreement establishing a European laying-up fund for inland waterway vessels [1977] ECR I-741, para. 5.

10 Opinion 1/94 re WTO Agreement [1994] ECR I-5267.

11 See F. Hoffmeister, *op. cit.*, n. 5.

The claiming by the EU of a status of full member of international organizations has faced many obstacles, the most important of which are institutional and political. At the institutional level, the fact that constituent charters of international organizations generally reserve membership to States alone, implies that the participation of the EU cannot be achieved without a modification of these acts. The political obstacle, still present today, lies in the fact that Member States of the EU are not necessarily favourable to abandoning their role in international *fora*, allowing the EU to succeed to their rights and powers. The Member States are often prepared to accept that the EU joins the "club" but not that it replaces them.

When the constituent charter of the organization allows membership for the EU and when the participation is joint with the Member States, the situation becomes complicated within the EU and within the international organization itself, in particular with regard to the question of which out of the EU and the Member States, may exercise the rights attached to membership.[12]

It is not only the Member States which are opposed to the granting of membership of international organizations to the EU. Third States have in the past invoked the legally imprecise nature of the EU and the issues related to its international responsibility. In particular, they have questioned the EU's ability to compel its Member States to respect the commitments made by it at the international level.[13] They have also highlighted the danger of setting precedents, the risk of encouraging the formation of blocks within the organization by the accession of the EU (making the decision more difficult), and the problems related to the simultaneous membership of the EU and its Member States of the same international organization. This resistance of third States still exists.

Despite these objections, internally and externally, the EU has been granted the status of full membership in many organizations.[14] It is currently a member

---

12 See, for example, an illustration of this difficulty in CJEU, Case C-25/94, *Commission v Council* [1996] ECR I-1469.

13 The existence of the infringement procedure contained within Articles 258–260 TFEU proves that this is not true. Furthermore, the case-law has demonstrated that the Commission does not hesitate to bring the matter before the CJEU when it considers that a Member State has failed to comply with commitments made by the EU on the international scene. CJEU, Case C-61/94, *Commission v Germany* [1996] ECR I-3989, para. 41.

14 To be precise one may indeed distinguish two kinds of participation as a member. The first gives the possibility to the EU to accede to an international organization, as such, an organization that has an independent existence with a developed structure. The second type occurs in the case of an international agreement on a specific subject, creating a kind of organizational structure between the parties, in order to implement its provisions.

of the FAO,[15] the *Codex Alimentarius Commission,*[16] the WTO,[17] the EBRD,[18] and the Hague Conference on Private International Law.[19] The status of full membership puts the EU on an equal footing with the Member States of the organization. The EU thus mainly acquires the right to vote, the right to make proposals and the right to speak. The difficulties raised by EU participation lie in the fact that, in most cases, the EU is not involved in the organization in question alone, but rather alongside its Member States. This joint participation is explained by the division of competences between the EU and its Member States.[20] Very often, there is a 'mixity' situation, based on the fact that many competences are shared between the EU and its Member States. Joint membership raises a number of important issues, particularly in relation to the decision-making process and voting rights. For example, how many votes should be assigned to the EU in the internal rules of the organization? How would and could these rights be exercised? Two possible models could be envisaged. The voting rights may be exercised alternatively by the EU or by its Member States, or these rights may be cumulated, allowing the EU to add its vote to those of the Member States. Such a cumulative vote is generally opposed by the other members of such organizations, who consider this modality to be an expression of a new kind of overrepresentation of the EU and its Member States within the organization. The alternative way of exercising voting rights requires a definition of the cases in which the EU votes and the ones in which the Member States vote,[21] based presumably on a clear delineation of powers between the EU and its Member States in the fields of the organization's activities.

The 'mixity' nature and the joint participation require the respect of a fundamental principle of EU law, enshrined in Article 4(3) TEU. According to the principle of sincere cooperation, the EU and the Member States shall, in full mutual respect, assist each other in carrying out tasks which flow from

---

This second category is not going to be analysed further in the present contribution. On these questions, see J. Sack, *op. cit.*, n. 5 pp. 1238–1239; and C. Kaddous, *op. cit.*, n. 5 p. 141.

15 Since 1991.

16 Since 2003. The Codex is a subsidiary common body of the FAO and the WHO, setting international standards on food safety with direct relevance for WTO agreements on the application of sanitary and phytosanitary measures.

17 The Community was one of the founders of the WTO in 1995.

18 Since 1991.

19 Since 2007.

20 C. Kaddous, *op. cit.*, n. 5 p. 141.

21 See for example the FAO.

the Treaties.[22] This principle shall also prevent the Member States from taking any measure which could jeopardise the attainment of EU objectives.

In the context of international relations, the CJEU pointed out that when it appears that the subject-matter of an agreement or a contract falls under the category of shared competences, it is important to ensure that a close association between the EU institutions and the Member States takes place both in the process of negotiation and conclusion and in the fulfilment of the obligations entered into. This duty of cooperation results from the requirement of unity in the international representation of the EU.[23] However, the first case in which the CJEU had to deal with the joint participation of the EU and its Member States in an international organization relates to the FAO. In *Commission v Council*, the main issue related to the internal Arrangement between the Council and the European Commission on the right to vote in the said organization.[24] Within the EU, the Council and the Commission had concluded an internal Arrangement for the preparation of FAO meetings, interventions and voting rights. Despite these precautions, a dispute arose and the case was brought before the CJEU. On the one hand, the Commission proposed to the Member States the adoption of a draft agreement prepared within the FAO. On the other hand, the Council confirmed an earlier decision of the COREPER, under which it was not the Commission but the Member States who should vote in the FAO Conference concerning the adoption of the envisaged agreement. After a detailed examination of the internal Arrangement, the CJEU considered that the Council had violated one of the aspects of the internal Arrangement and therefore its decision had to be annulled.[25]

The subsequent case-law gives another interesting illustration of the kind of issues which may arise from participation within an international organization. The International Maritime Organization (IMO) provides membership only for States. In *Commission v Greece*, the CJEU had to determine whether Greece, a member of the organization, was entitled to submit a proposal to the IMO, on its own behalf, in an area covered by EU law.[26] The European

22 Article 4(3) also provides that: "The Member States shall take any appropriate measure, general or particular, to ensure fulfilment of the obligations arising out of the treaties or resulting from the acts of the institutions of the Union. The Member States shall facilitate the achievement of the Union's tasks and refrain from any measure which could jeopardise the attainment of the Union's objectives".

23 CJEU, *Ruling 1/78* [1978] ECR I-2151, paras. 34–36; *Opinion 2/91* [1993] ECR I-1061, paras. 36–38; *Opinion 1/94* [1994] I-ECR I-5267, para. 108.

24 CJEU, *Commission v Council* [1996] ECR I-1469.

25 *Ibid.*, paras. 49–51.

26 CJEU, *Commission v Greece* [2009] ECR I-701.

Commission alleged that Greece had violated Article 4(3) as well as the provisions of the treaty on common transport policy. The Commission's argument was that in formulating such a proposal within the IMO forum the provisions of the EU Regulation may be affected within the meaning of the ERTA case.[27] The CJEU followed the Commission's position and considered that Greece took an initiative which was likely to affect the provision of the Regulation, and which constituted an infringement of the obligations under Article 4(3) as well as the provisions of the treaty on common transport policy.[28] It follows from this case that the duty of cooperation entails many commitments and governs situations where the EU and its Member States are members of an international organization but also situations where only the Member States are members, provided that the organization in question is active in areas which fall within EU competence. Therefore, coordination between the EU and the Member States as well as respect for sincere cooperation become fundamental for ensuring an effective representation of the EU in international organizations, whether or not the EU as such is member of the organization.[29]

---

27 *Ibid.*, paras. 16–20.

28 *Ibid.*, para. 23.

29 A new very interesting issue related to EU participation in international organizations is raised in a case pending before the CJEU (Case C-399/12, *Germany v. Council* (OIV), *OJ*, 2012, C 343/9). Germany brought an action against the Council challenging a decision by the Council adopted pursuant to Article 218(9) TFEU establishing the position to be adopted on behalf of the European Union with regard to certain resolutions to be voted upon within the framework of the international organisation for Vine and Wine (OIV) (Council Document N° 11436 adopted on 18 June 2012 at the 2176 Council meeting Agriculture and Fisheries, see Press Release 11179/12, p. 16). Germany argues that Article 218(9) TFEU was not the correct legal basis for the adoption of the decision. According to the German Government, the Treaty provision only applies to the adoption of the positions of the EU in bodies, set up by international agreements, of which the EU is a member. Therefore, it cannot be applied in relation to the representation of the Member States in bodies of international organizations in which only the Member States participate by virtue of separate international treaties. Furthermore, the German Government considers that Article 218(9) TFEU only covers "acts having legal effects", meaning acts which are binding under international law (which is not the case, according to it, with OIV resolutions). The provision at stake reads as follows: "The Council, on a proposal from the Commission or the High Representative of the Union for Foreign Affairs and Security Policy, shall adopt a decision suspending application of an agreement and establishing the positions to be adopted on the Union's behalf in a body set up by an agreement, when that body is called upon to adopt acts having legal effects, with the exception of acts supplementing or amending the institutional framework of the agreement". For a discussion of this pending case, see I. Govaere, "Novel Issues Pertaining To EU Member States Membership of Other

Article 21(3) TFEU also contributes to the achievement of the objective of an effective representation of the EU on the international scene. It requires the EU to ensure consistency between the different areas of its external action and between these and its other policies. This provision also designates that the Council and the Commission, assisted by the High Representative shall ensure that consistency and shall cooperate to that effect. In this way, the two institutions are politically responsible for achieving the goal of consistency in all areas of Union activities, and in particular in economic and monetary matters and their projection to the international arena.

Taking into account the above analysis of the main principles applicable in the sphere of external relations, one might now examine the distribution of powers between the EU and its Member States in the field of economic and monetary union in order to determine the rules applicable to the exercise of the external dimension in this field.

3 Division of Powers between the EU and Its Member States in the Field of Economic and Monetary Union

The provisions of primary law are naturally the starting point for this analysis. According to Article 3(4) TEU, the EU shall establish an economic and monetary union whose currency is the euro. This EMU relies on two main components: the economic and the monetary policies described respectively in Article 119(1) and (2) TFEU. While the economic policy is conducted by action on the part of the Member States and the EU, the monetary policy entails a definitive transfer of power from the national level to the EU. Therefore, monetary policy appears in the treaty as falling within EU exclusive competences for the countries whose currency is the euro, alongside customs union, competition rules necessary for the functioning of the internal market, conservation of marine biological resources under the common fisheries policy and common commercial policy.[30] One observation must be made at the outset. The EMU brings together competences of different nature. On the one hand, the economic policy is considered as a shared competence, and on the other hand, the monetary policy is an exclusive competence in respect of the Member States whose currency is the euro. As explained in the previous section, the

International Organizations: The OIV Case", in: I. Govaere, E. Lannon, P. Van Elsuwege and S. Adam (eds.), *The European Union in the World, Essays in Honour of Professor Marc Maresceau*, Boston-Leiden: Martinus Nijhoff, 2014, pp. 225–243.

30 See Article 3(1) TFEU.

internal distribution of powers has implications for the representation of these policies within international *fora*. Therefore, the external dimension of the EMU is complex because of the existence of competences of different nature within its two components, and because of the specificities of the constituent charters of the international financial institutions in which the EU aims to participate.

According to settled case-law of the CJEU, where the EU has an exclusive competence internally, the EU alone is responsible for the exercise of the external dimension of the same competence.[31] This basic principle applies to monetary policy and exchange rate policy. Consequently, the relevant EU institutions should act in the process of negotiation and conclusion of international agreements in these fields as well as representing the EU within the financial institutions dealing with these matters. However where both the EU and the Member States have competence, such as in economic matters, the external dimension should be exercised jointly by the EU and its Member States.

The negotiation and conclusion of agreements on monetary matters or the exchange-rate system for the euro in relation to currencies of third States is governed by a provision of primary law. Article 219 TFEU specifies the procedure to be followed in this field, which is different from the general procedure for the negotiation and conclusion of international agreements by the EU. Article 219 devotes a specific role to the European Central Bank (ECB), which sits alongside the classic role of the European Commission. While this is fully justified due the expertise and function of the ECB in monetary matters,[32] the treaty brings a new actor into the procedure of negotiation and conclusion of international agreements which modifies the existing institutional balance established in the exercise of the external dimension in the other fields of EU law. This provision has been used recently and several monetary agreements have been concluded by the EU with various third countries (Vatican City State, Principality of Andorra, Principality of Monaco and the Republic of San Marino) which use the euro as their official currency.[33]

---

31 CJEU, Case 22/79, *Commission v Council (ERTA)* [1971] ECR I-263.

32 According to Article 219(1), the Council acting on a recommendation from the Commission and after consulting the ECB or on a recommendation from the ECB, may conclude formal agreements on an exchange-rate system for the Euro in relation to currencies of third States. The Council shall act unanimously after consulting the European Parliament. See also the other paragraphs of this provision in relation to the role of the ECB.

33 See, for example, the Monetary Agreement between the EU and the Vatican City State, *OJ*, 2010, C 28/13; the Monetary Agreement between the EU and the Principality of Andorra, *OJ*, 2011, C 369/1; the Monetary Agreement between the EU and the Principality

According to Article 17(1) TEU, the European Commission shall ensure the EU's external representation, except in terms of the common foreign and security policy (CFSP)[34] and in other cases provided for in the Treaties. Specific provisions are enshrined in the Treaty on the EU's external representation in matters concerning the euro. Article 138(1) TFEU, which relates to the monetary dimension of the EMU, attributes a competence to the Council[35] to adopt a decision establishing common positions on matters of particular interest for economic and monetary union within the competent international financial institutions and conferences.[36] The second paragraph of this provision goes further and aims to ensure a "unified representation" of the Member States whose currency is the euro at the international level.[37] Whereas this Article gives details on the procedures to be respected in order to adopt different acts and measures, it does not give any indication as to the institution(s) which should represent the Eurozone. It is therefore for the Council to decide whether it will carry out this representation itself or give that power to the European Commission, the ECB or to any other entity. The situation is unclear under the Lisbon Treaty but it was also unclear under the Nice Treaty.

Different positions were defended by the EU institutions during the transition period towards the third stage of the single currency, resulting in a small "war" which was in certain respects settled by the European Council. In December 1997, the Luxembourg European Council decided that the Council and the ECB would fulfil their tasks in representing the "Community" at international level and that the European Commission would simply be associated with external representation insofar as necessary to enable it to fulfil the role assigned to it by the treaty.[38] Reacting to this decision, the Commission tried, in November 1998, on the basis of the former Article 111(4),[39] to propose

of Monaco, *OJ*, 2012, C 310/1; the Monetary Agreement between the EU and the Republic of San Marino, *OJ*, 2012, C 121/5.

34 The Treaty confers the task of representing the EU in CFSP matters on the High Representative of the Union for Foreign Affairs and Security Policy.

35 Council composed of members representing Member States whose currency is the euro.

36 This adoption of the decision must be on a proposal from the Commission and after the consultation of the ECB.

37 Paragraph 2 reads as follows: "The Council, on a proposal from the Commission, may adopt appropriate measures to ensure unified representation within the international financial institutions and conferences. The Council shall act after consulting the European Central Bank".

38 Conclusions of the Luxembourg European Council of 12 and 13 December 1997, paragraph 46.

39 Presently Article 138 TFEU.

a representation of the "Community" at the international level exercised by the Council, the Commission and the ECB[40] on an equal footing in the "Community delegation". The Commission did not succeed with its proposal and the European Council confirmed one year later, in December 1998,[41] the political approach which was decided in Luxembourg in 1997 and which still applies today, the Commission playing a complementary role to the other two institutions.

However, searching for coherence and effectiveness, the European Council emphasised the importance of the "Community" speaking with one voice on issues of particular relevance to economic and monetary union and of ensuring a timely and effective preparation of common positions and common understandings which can be presented to third parties in international *fora*.[42] Interestingly, the formula of Article 138(2) now goes even further than the European Council conclusions, referring to a "unified representation" within the international financial institutions and conferences and hence paves the route for future developments towards "unification".

Taking these legal and political elements into consideration, attention should be given to the present representation of the EU within the inter-

40 Proposal for a Council Decision on the representation and position taking of the Community at international level in the context of economic and monetary union, 9 November 1998 (COM(98)0637 final).

41 Conclusions of the European Council of 10 and 11 December 1998, paragraphs 14 and Annex II: "14. The introduction of the euro will be a major event for the international monetary system. It is imperative that the Community should play its full role in international monetary and economic policy cooperation within *fora* like the G7 and the International Monetary Fund. The European Council endorses the report of the Council on the external representation of the Community, which foresees that the President of the ECOFIN Council, or if the President is from a non-euro area Member State, the President of the Euro 11, assisted by the Commission, shall participate in meetings of the G7 (Finance).... The ECB, as the Community body competent for monetary policy, should be granted observer status at the IMF board. The views of the European Community/EMU on other issues of particular relevance to the EMU would be presented at the IMF board by the relevant member of the Executive Director's office of the Member State holding the euro Presidency, assisted by a representative of the Commission. The European Council invites the Council to act on the basis of a Commission proposal incorporating this agreement".

42 Conclusions of the European Council of 10 and 11 December 1998, paragraph 15: "The coherence and effectiveness of the Community require that it shall be able to speak with one voice on issues of particular relevance to economic and monetary union. The European Council encourages the Commission, the Council and the Member States to take the necessary action to ensure a timely and effective preparation of common positions and common understandings which can be presented to third parties in international *fora*".

national financial institutions and conferences. The next section will focus on three different *fora*: two of them are institutions created at Bretton Woods in 1944: the IMF and the World Bank, and the third one, which is not considered to be a "real" international organization, but rather a forum, is the G20.

4 Present Participation of the EU in International Financial Institutions

For the purposes of the following analysis, the EU participation within the IMF and the World Bank (4.1) will be examined separately from participation within the G20 (4.2) for reasons linked to the structure and the internal organization of the said international *fora*.

4.1 *The IMF and the World Bank*

Since its creation in 1944, the IMF has been in charge of overseeing the international monetary system to avoid exchange rate instability and huge imbalances in the international balance of payments among major economies.[43] Today its membership comprises 188 countries,[44] among which the 28 Member States of the EU. Membership is currently limited to countries.[45] Therefore, the EU is represented by its Member States, which are supposed and encouraged to coordinate their positions. The governance of the IMF is shared between

43 L. Bini Smaghi, "A Single EU Seat in the International Monetary Fund?", in K. E. Joergensen (ed.), *The European Union and International Organizations*, London: Routledge, 2009, at p. 64. See also the detailed study of the European Parliament on "External Representation of the Euro Area", study of the Directorate-General for internal policies, 2012; R. Smits, "International representation of Europe in the area of Economic and Monetary Union: legal issues and practice in the first ten years of the Euro", paper presented before the Conference: *10 years of European Monetary Union: a legal perspective*, organised by the Legal committee of the ESBC and held in Frankfurt am Main on 29–30 January 2009; A. Hervé, "The Participation of the European Union in Global Economic Governance Fora", *ELJ* (18), 2012, pp. 143–161; J. Wouters, S. Sterkx and T. Corthaut, "The International Financial Crisis, Global financial Governance and the European Union", Working paper n° 52, Leuven Centre for Global Governance Studies, 2010, pp. 1–27; J.-V. Louis, "L'Union européenne et la regulation de la finance international", in: M. Le Barbier-Le Bris (ed.), *L'Union européenne et la gouvernance mondiale*, Brussels: Bruylant, 2012, 376 p.

44 In April 2012, the Republic of South Sudan joined the IMF, becoming the institution's 188th member, see <http://www.imf.org/external/about/members.htm#number> (accessed 9 June 2013).

45 Article II of the Articles of Agreement of 1944. In order to change this provision, there is a need for the agreement of 3/5 of the IMF members representing at least 85% of voting powers as required by Article XXVIII of the Articles of the Agreement.

two decision-making entities: the Board of Governors and the Executive Board. The Board of Governors is the most important organ, which is composed of one governor, usually the Finance Minister or the President of the national Central Bank and one alternate governor per country. It meets once a year and can delegate powers to the Executive Board, which runs the operations of the IMF, supported by the work of the Managing Director.

The Executive Board is composed of 24 Executive Directors appointed or elected by member countries or by groups of countries. Different rules are applicable for the appointment or the election of this body. Specific Member States of the EU have a representative on the Executive Board, while others form part of chairs composed of groups of countries. The ECB has an observer status on the Executive Board and the International Monetary and Financial Committee (IMFC) within which the ECOFIN Presidency expresses its opinion on behalf of the EU. The European Commission has an observer status in the IMFC.

The decision-making process in the IMF is based on a quota system, which represents a key element of the definition of powers within the IMF. Unlike the General Assembly of the United Nations, where each country has one vote, decision making in the IMF was designed to reflect the position of each member country in the global economy. Each IMF member is assigned a quota that determines its financial commitment to the IMF, its voting power, its level of access to IMF financing as well as its share of SDR allocations.[46] IMF members cannot unilaterally modify their quota; these are to be reviewed by the Board of Governors and quota reform requires an extraordinary majority of 85% of the votes.[47]

As the European Commission puts it, "As the crisis has shown, it is of utmost importance for the euro area to speak with a single voice in particular on programmes, financing arrangements and the crisis resolution policy of the IMF".[48] The Commission envisages enhancing the Euro area representation within the IMF through a two-stage process. In a first stage, the country constituencies should be rearranged so as to re-group countries into euro area constituencies which could also include future euro area Member States. In parallel, observer status in the IMF Executive Board should be sought for the euro area, more

46 Under its Articles of Agreement, the IMF may allocate SDRs to members in proportion to their IMF quotas.

47 Article XXVIII of the IMF Articles of Agreement.

48 Communication from the Commission, "A blueprint for a deep and genuine economic and monetary union Launching a European Debate", COM (2012) 777, final/2, of 30/11/2012, p. 25.

precisely for the EU representing the euro area Member States in accordance with the treaties. These measures should prepare the ground for the euro area seeking, at a second stage, a single seat in the IMF bodies (the Executive Board and the IMFC).[49] The Commission has announced that it will in due course make formal proposals under Article 138(2) TFEU to establish a unified position to achieve an observer status for the euro area on the IMF Executive Board, and subsequently for a single seat.

In the Communication of November 2012, it is considered that the appropriate institution to represent the euro area in the IMF, in accordance with Article 138 TFEU, would be the Commission, with the ECB being associated with the area of monetary policy.[50] The Commission emphasizes that: "[I]n euro area matters, the European Commission has become a natural interlocutor of the IMF. In addition, more recently, the Commission and the ECB have worked closely together with the IMF in negotiating the financial assistance packages for euro area and EU Members and by collaborating in general with the Fund on surveillance. Against this background, conferring observer status on the euro area, represented by the European Commission with the ECB being associated in the area of monetary policy, is essential to increase the synergies of the cooperation between the IMF and the institutions that are at the core of the daily management of the euro area.[51]

These are the views of the European Commission which may not be shared by the Member States. As mentioned before, there are reluctances from specific EU Member States of the Eurozone to give up sovereignty and transfer more power to the EU at the international level. The debate is ongoing on these important economic and political issues. The decisions, which have to be taken by the Council on the basis of a qualified majority vote according to Article 138(3),[52] require making an overall assessment of EU participation in the IMF (pros and cons) as well as the influence which the EU may exercise on the work of the organization through the changes proposed in comparison with the present situation. The World Bank plays a crucial role in the financial and technical assistance provided to developing countries. It has expanded since its creation in 1944 to an associated group of five developing institutions, forming the World Bank Group. The group is composed

49 *Ibid.*

50 *Ibid.*

51 *Ibid.*, p. 47.

52 For these measures, only members of the Council representing Member States whose currency is the euro shall take part in the vote. The qualified majority shall be defined in accordance with Article 238(3)(a).

of the International Bank for Reconstruction and Development (IBRD); the International Development Association (IDA); the International Finance Corporation (IFC); the Multilateral Investment Guarantee Agency (MIGA) and the International Centre for Settlement of Investment disputes (ICSID). Member countries govern the World Bank Group through the Boards of Governors and the Boards of Executive Directors. These bodies make all major decisions for the organizations which are composed of 188 members. The voting system differs from agency to agency within the World Bank. For example, the IBRD, like the IMF, uses a weighted system of voting. Each member had 250 votes plus one additional vote for each share of stock held before the reform which became effective on 27 June 2012.[53] The 28 EU Member States are part of the World Bank and the representation model is based on that of the IMF. The European Commission participates as an observer in the World Bank's Development Committee. The EU policy in the field of development cooperation complements and reinforces that of the Member States. So, being a shared competence, the participation of the EU should be exercised, alongside that of the Member States. Article 4(4) TFEU states further that the EU shall have competence to carry out activities and conduct a common policy; however the exercise of that competence shall not result in Member States being prevented from participating. EU participation within the World Bank could in the long term therefore be envisaged as a joint participation.

4.2 *The G20*

This Group is the most important forum for international cooperation on economic and financial global issues. Its objectives refer to (1) policy coordination between its members in order to achieve global economic stability and sustainable growth; (2) promoting financial regulations to reduce risks and prevent future financial crises; and (3) modernizing international financial architecture.

53 Section 3(a) of the IBRD Articles of Agreement presently provides that: "a) The voting power of each member shall be equal to the sum of its basic votes and share votes. (i) The basic votes of each member shall be the number of votes that results from the equal distribution among all members of 5.55 percent of the aggregate sum of the voting power of all the members, provided that there shall be no fractional basic votes. (ii) The share votes of each member shall be the number of votes that results from the allocation of one vote for each share of stock held".

In June 2013, the United States was the largest single shareholder with 14.63% of the votes, followed by Japan (8.80%), Germany (4.62%), the United Kingdom (4.16%) and France (4.16%), see <http://siteresources.worldbank.org/BODINT/Resources/278027-1215524804501/IBRDCountryVotingTable.pdf> (accessed 9 June 2013).

The G20 is composed of 19 major economic countries,[54] including 4 EU Member States (Germany, the United Kingdom, France and Italy) as well as the EU as such. The presidency of the G20 rotates annually among its members.[55] However, the EU is not included in the rotation. The presidency leads a three-member management group of previous, current and future chairs, referred to as the "Troika", the purpose of which is to ensure transparency, fairness, and continuity from one presidency to another. The G20 does not have a secretariat of its own. A temporary secretariat is set up by the country that holds the presidency for the term of chairmanship. The creation of a G20 secretariat is under discussion, but nothing has been decided as yet.

The EU is represented within the G20 at the level of Heads of Government and States by the President of the European Council and by the President of the European Commission. EU participation at meetings of Finance Ministers and Central Bank Governors is exercised by the European Commission and the ECB. The voting system is based on consensus as there has been no treaty signed and ratified by the G20 members.

Here again, EU membership of the G20 is perceived by others as an "over-representation" of the EU in global governance. This critique is formulated by the emerging and developing countries, but also by the US, which considers that the weight given to the EU and its Member States is no longer proportionate to the regrettably diminishing economic power of the EU in the world. However, contrary to its situation with regard to the IMF and the World Bank, the EU has managed to participate as such in the G20, imposing its presence and affirming its role as a key global player in economic and financial issues of worldwide importance. This was also facilitated due to the flexibility of the system governing the functioning of G20, which offers room for ad hoc solutions.

5 Conclusions and Perspectives

The participation of the EU within international financial institutions is complex and difficult for the reasons examined in this contribution as well as due to a more general issue of external representation of the EU linked to the plurality of potential internal actors, capable of representing the EU in international *fora*. The President of the European Council, the President of the

54 These countries are: Argentina, Australia, Brazil, Canada, China, France, Germany, India, Indonesia, Italy, Japan, the Republic of Korea, Mexico, Russia, Saudi Arabia, South Africa, Turkey, the United Kingdom and the United States.

55 Russia has the Presidency in 2013.

European Commission, the ECB, the Member States (as agents for the EU) and the High Representative play a role in that context, but their competences are not always clearly defined.[56]

The distribution of powers between the EU and its Member States, which varies from one field to another in the matters covered by the IMF, World Bank and G20, and the present political situation both within and outside the EU, only allow for the formulation of a much greater, enhanced and effective coordination of the EU and its Member States at international level. The *status quo* in the representation of the EU in the said *fora* is unsatisfactory but the political will for a "unified representation" where it is possible according to Article 138 TFEU, has not yet been acquired within the EU, even after the financial crisis of 2008.

At global level, third countries can hardly be convinced of EU participation as such in the IMF and the World Bank, unless an agreement can be reached on a decrease in the number of quotas in favour of the emerging economies. These kinds of changes in the membership of these international financial institutions require formal amendments of the constituent charters, which are subject to qualified majority votes which are not easy to obtain.

Therefore the most feasible solution, until a political agreement is reached for a "unified representation", would be to promote a greater, enhanced and effective coordination, which may notably involve creating new bodies which would meet as frequently as for example the Executive body of the IMF meets in order to define common positions. This proposal has the advantage of not requiring any legislative changes but needs the political will of the Member States. It may seem trivial, but put together with the application of the general principles of EU law (duty of sincere cooperation; effective representation of the EU on the international scene) and their interpretation by the CJEU, it may provide the right framework to allow important steps to be accomplished.

The principle of sincere cooperation requires that the Member States do not act to the detriment of the EU or to the detriment of other Member States that are not participating in an international forum in the sense of the case-law developed by the Court in *Opinion 2/91* (ILO) or in *Commission v Greece* (IMO). The EU treaties provide for a system of checks and balances in order to ensure the respect of the distribution of powers between the EU and its Member States. On the one hand, a surveillance and sanctions mechanism

56 On these issues, see notably, C. Kaddous, "Role and Position of the High Representative of the Union for Foreign Affairs and Security Policy under the Lisbon Treaty", in: S. Grillerand J. Ziller (ed.), *The Lisbon Treaty. EU Constitutionalism without a Constitution Treaty?*, Springer: Verlag, 2008, at p. 205.

allows the EU to compel its Member States to respect their commitments under EU law (infringement procedures). On the other hand, the Treaty, as seen in *Commission v Council* (FAO), allows the EU institutions to exercise reciprocal control over measures taken respectively by one and the other, relating to the activities developed within international organizations (annulment procedures).

Furthermore, closer coordination should also be promoted through respect of the principle of consistency as enshrined in Article 21(3) TEU. This principle should be considered by the two politically responsible institutions, the European Commission and the Council, as a guideline of primary importance for promoting the coordination of the EU and its Member States in their actions and efforts to strengthen economic and monetary governance internally and externally.

The financial crisis has led, as in other fields of EU integration faced with global emergencies, to a consolidation of the coordination of economic and monetary issues at EU level and has encouraged the consideration of ways to strengthen the external dimension, which have to be envisaged gradually due to the political situation inside and outside the EU. In the short and medium term, one must envisage a greater, enhanced and effective coordination of the external dimension of economic and monetary policies. In the long term, the participation of the EU as such, alongside the Member States, should be made possible in the various international financial organizations.

CHAPTER 14

International Marine Environmental Law and the EU: An Adequate Framework to Address Environmental Emergencies?

Lorenzo Schiano di Pepe

1 Introduction

The present contribution focuses on the participation of the EU to international legal instruments designed to counter environmental emergencies or accidents due to marine pollution. In recent and less recent years, European coasts have been repeatedly affected by disasters caused by oil spills from tankers. A number of international conventions are actually in place to fight such threats and, after a brief outlook of the concept of "emergencies" in the environmental law sphere, the present contribution will first of all describe, on the one hand, the problems that are raised by the fact that the EU itself, unlike its Member States, is not a party to these conventions.[1] The second part of this study, on the other hand, will assess the EU's positive contribution to combat environmental emergencies or accidents caused by marine pollution taking as a test case the area of offshore oil and gas activities and the risks posed thereby. In the wake of the spill originating from the *Deepwater Horizon* oil platform, the EU has been active in acceding to relevant regional international instruments as well as in upgrading its own internal legislation in order to fill the gaps of "framework" treaties such as United Nations Convention on the Law of the Sea (UNCLOS),[2] thus proving its added value with respect to global international instruments dealing with marine pollution.

2 A Premise: Environmental Degradation Processes versus Environmental Emergencies

Most environmental degradation processes are characterized by gradual developments, progressiveness and, to a certain extent, foreseeability, as is the

1 See below, section 3.

2 See below section 4.

© KONINKLIJKE BRILL NV, LEIDEN, 2014 | DOI 10.1163/9789004268333_016

case, for example, with climate change or the loss of fauna and flora species. The reaction of the international community to such long- or medium-term environmental challenges has traditionally consisted of the adoption of framework treaties establishing a set of basic principles to be complemented, in due course, by more specific obligations, with a view to progressively modifying the behavioural patterns of States parties.[3]

Unforeseen occurrences such as maritime accidents or industrial disasters, that is "environmental emergencies," represent only a fraction (albeit of increasing relevance) of environmental concerns. Yet, as was pointed out by the Council some time ago:

> [r]ecent years have witnessed a significant increase in the occurrence and severity of natural and man-made disasters, resulting in the loss of human lives and property, including cultural heritage, the destruction of economic and social infrastructure and damage to the environment.[4]

In the past, the need has arisen for an international body of rules covering the immediate aftermaths of these occurrences. Well-established cases in point include the 1969 International Convention Relating to Intervention on the High Seas in Cases of Oil Pollution Casualties,[5] the 1990 International Convention on Oil Pollution Preparedness, Response and Co-operation[6] and the 1986 Convention on Assistance in the Case of a Nuclear Accident or Radiological Emergency.[7]

Without entering into a detailed examination of the common features of these international conventions, what is particularly note-worthy in the present context is their existence in itself, testimony to the fact that the international community has, for some time now, taken on the burden of dealing with a number of emergency situations by developing tailor-made legal regimes that are meant to take into account the peculiar features of the scenarios to which they respectively refer.

---

3 P. Birnie, A. Boyle and C. Redgwell, *International Law & the Environment*, 3rd ed., Oxford: OUP, 2009, p. 12 *et seq.*

4 Decision 2007/779/EC of the Council of 8 November 2007 establishing a Community Civil Protection Mechanism (recast), *OJ*, 2007, L 314/9, recital no. 2.

5 International Convention Relating to Intervention on the High Seas in Cases of Oil Pollution Casualties, 29 November 1969, entered into force on 6 May 1975, *ILM* 9, 1970, p. 25.

6 International Convention on Oil Pollution, Preparedness, Response and Cooperation, 30 November 1990, entered into force on 13 May, 1995, *ILM* 30, 1991, p. 733.

7 Convention on Assistance in the Case of a Nuclear Accident or Radiological Emergency, 26 September 1986, entered into force on 26 February 1987, *ILM* 25, 1986, p. 1377.

In addition, it is becoming increasingly important (even if it is not always easy)[8] to distinguish between emergency and non-emergency situations since response to environmental emergencies has recently developed as a topical subject in its own right in international and European legal discourse,[9] also in the wake of events such as the oil spill originating from the *Deepwater Horizon* oil platform in the Gulf of Mexico on 20 April 2010 and the emission of radioactive material from the *Fukushima Daiichi* nuclear power plant following the earthquake and the tsunami in Japan of 11 March 2011. These accidents have in fact demonstrated in a very dramatic fashion that, notwithstanding a certain normative proliferation, the quality of the environment is not necessarily improving and the well-being and the safety of humankind are still at the mercy of natural and man-made disasters.

3 International Regulation of Marine Pollution Caused by Ships and the Quest for an Effective External Representation of the EU

The EU takes part, together with its Member States, in a number of international environmental agreements. There is, however, a specific and yet crucial area of international environmental law where the EU is arguably still lacking a sufficient degree of external representation, namely the international governance of marine pollution caused by maritime traffic.

As is well known, the general principles relating to this sector are set at the global level by the United Nations Convention on the Law of the Sea (UNCLOS),[10] which provides, *inter alia*, for rights and duties of flag States, coastal States and port States concerning the adoption and the enforcement of rules aimed at minimising the environmental impact of maritime traffic also by preventing maritime accidents from occurring through the establishment of appropriate safety navigation standards.

---

8 The boundaries between real "emergencies" and "ordinary" environmental issues may be difficult to establish, especially with regard to occurrences which, notwithstanding their foreseeability, assume an unexpected magnitude due to a lack of, or an ineffective, response (a good example being the various "waste crises" which have recently affected the Naples area and the Campania Region in southern Italy).

9 See, e.g., A. De Guttry, M. Gestri and G. Venturini (eds.), *International Disaster Response Law*, The Hague: Springer, 2012; see also, L. Schiano di Pepe, "Inquinamento ambientale e disastri naturali: il ruolo della comunità internazionale e delle organizzazioni regionali nella gestione delle emergenze ambientali globali", in: N. Napoletano, A. Saccucci (eds.), Gestione internazionale delle emergenze globali, Naples: Editoriale Scientifica, 2013, p. 97.

10 United Nations Convention on the Law of the Sea, 10 December 1982, entered into force on 16 November 1994, *ILM* 21, 1982, p. 1261.

In such a context, a much more detailed system of norms has gradually been put in place which includes, as a most prominent example, the International Convention for the Prevention of Pollution from Ships of 1973, as supplemented by a Protocol of 1978.[11] MARPOL, as this Convention is commonly known, like any other international legal instrument having the shipping industry as its primary subject matter, has been adopted under the auspices of the International Maritime Organization (IMO), the United Nations' specialised agency responsible for safety and security at sea and the protection of the marine environment. The IMO is therefore the *forum* where proposed pieces of international legislation in this particular area are discussed by governments before going through the usual procedure of negotiation, adoption and entry into force.

Whilst the EU is a party to UNCLOS,[12] it has neither the status of member nor that of formal observer with IMO and, notwithstanding the wealth of activities carried out and currently in progress in the field of maritime safety and marine environmental protection from shipping activities,[13] it is not a party to MARPOL or other conventions of a similar technical nature.

The issue of a possible EU accession to the IMO has been repeatedly raised since 2002[14] and a "Study on the Assessment of the EU's Role in International Maritime Organizations" was prepared in 2009 upon the request of the

11 Adopted on 2 November 1978, amended by the said Protocol on 18 February 1978 and entered in force on 2 October 1983. A consolidated version of the Convention, which has since then been repeatedly amended, is published in International Maritime Organization, *MARPOL Consolidated Edition*, London, 2011.

12 Pursuant to Decision of the Council 98/392/EC of 23 March 1998 concerning the conclusion by the European Community of the United Nations Convention of 10 December 1982 on the Law of the Sea and the Agreement of 28 July 1994 relating to the implementation of Part XI thereof, *OJ*, 1998, L 179/1. See, for a series of authoritative comments, T. Treves and L. Pineschi (eds.), *The Law of the Sea. The European Union and its Member States*, The Hague: Martinus Nijhoff Publishers, 1997; reference can also be made, specifically with regard to marine environmental protection, to V. Frank, *The European Community and Marine Environmental Protection in the International Law of the Sea*, Leiden: Martinus Nijhoff Publishers, 2007.

13 See, for example, L. Schiano di Pepe, "Environmental Emergencies at Sea in the European Union's Third Maritime Safety Package", in: G. Andreone, A. Caligiuri and G. Cataldi (eds.), *Emergences environnementales et droit de la mer*, Naples: Editoriale Scientifica, 2012, pp. 363–385.

14 Recommendation from the Commission to the Council in order to authorise the Commission to open and conduct negotiations with the International Maritime Organization (IMO) on the conditions and arrangements for accession by the European Community, doc. SEC (2002) 381 final of 9 April 2002, p. 49.

European Commission.[15] In the aftermath of this publication, the Commission has expressed its intention to work towards enhancing the role of the EU within the IMO "by formalising the EU coordination mechanism and obtaining the grant of formal observer status, if not full membership".[16]

Crucially, unlike UNCLOS, the IMO Convention does not contain a clause allowing for membership of a regional organisation of economic integration, but only for co-operation mechanisms for the benefit of international organisations in general. Hence, the European Commission (rather than the Union and, previously, the Community) has been granted observer status with the IMO thanks to an exchange of letters executed on 28 June 1974 and a coordination mechanism has subsequently been established whereby, in brief, EU Member States convene before each relevant IMO meeting or event in order to discuss the position of the EU with regard to the various agenda items.[17] When it comes to actual participation in IMO committees or other bodies, however, and even when an exclusive competence of the EU is at stake, the EU cannot, because of its peculiar status, speak for itself. It is therefore usually up to a Member State, typically the one temporarily holding the rotating presidency of the Council, to express the position of the EU after which other Member States and the Commission may voice their approval and support.[18]

The problematic relationship that has just been described is not without negative consequences and calls, in the opinion of the present author, for a

15 Leuven Centre for Global Governance Studies, *Study for the Assessment of the EU's Role in International Maritime Organisations*, April 2009, available at: <http://ec.europa.eu/maritimeaffairs/documentation/studies/documents/eu_role_international_organisations_en.pdf> (accessed 30 July 2013).

16 Communication from the Commission to the European Parliament, the Council, the European Economic and Social Committee and the Committee of the Regions: "Developing the international dimension of the Integrated Maritime Policy of the European Union", doc. COM (2009) 536 final of 15 October 2009, pp. 7–8. For a different view see L. Nengye and F. Maes, "The European Union and the International Maritime Organization: EU's External Influence on the Prevention of Vessel-Source Pollution", *JMLC* 41, 2010, pp. 581–594 and by the same authors, "Legal Constraints to the European Union's Accession to the International Maritime Organization", *JMLC* 43, 2012, pp. 279–291.

17 *Study for the Assessment of the EU's Role in International Maritime Organisations*, *op. cit.*, n. 15 above, p. 47.

18 *Ibid.*, pp. 48–52 for a more detailed account of the relevant procedural arrangements and the practice relating thereto with particular reference to the difference between the adoption of *Community* (now Union) *positions* and *common positions* depending on the exclusive as opposed to shared nature of the competence of the EU (see also *ibid.*, p. 20 *et seq.*).

serious reconsideration, as is perhaps best demonstrated by the CJEU case law itself.

In *Commune de Mesquer*,[19] the Court was confronted with a series of issues of civil liability, and in particular with the question of whether or not, in the event of the sinking of an oil tanker, the producer of the heavy fuel oil spilled and the seller of the fuel and charterer of the ship may be required to bear the costs of disposing of the waste generated by the spill, even though the oil, at the relevant time, was being transported by sea by a third party. More precisely, at stake was the determination of the persons liable for the purposes of applying Directive 75/442/EEC on waste,[20] which establishes that certain categories of persons (including the "previous holders" and the "producer of the product from which the waste came") may, in accordance with the "polluter pays" principle, be held responsible for bearing the cost of disposing of waste because of their contribution to the creation of the waste and, in certain cases, to the consequent risk of pollution.

The matter is, however, also dealt with by uniform international rules, namely, the Conventions on Civil Liability for Oil Pollution Damage (CLC)[21] and on the Establishment of an International Fund for Compensation for Oil Pollution Damage (FUND),[22] both adopted on 27 November 1992. Under such regimes liability for pollution damage caused is channelled towards the ship-owner up to a certain financial limit depending on the tonnage of the ship involved and with an obligation to take out adequate insurance cover. Beyond that limit, or when the ship-owner is not able to pay or is entitled to benefit from one of the few exemption causes (the principle being one of strict liability), pollution victims are entitled to claim compensation from the International Oil Pollution Compensation Fund, which is in turn itself liable up to a certain monetary limit.

The CJEU found that whilst Directive 75/442/EEC did not preclude Member States from establishing that the ship-owner and the charterer can be liable only up to a maximum amount as well as from establishing compensation funds with resources limited to a maximum amount, if the cost of disposal

---

19 CJEU, Case C-188/07, *Commune de Mesquer v Total France* [2008] ECR I-6985.

20 Directive 75/442/EEC of the Council of 15 July 1975 on waste, *OJ*, 1975, L 194/39, as amended by Decision 96/350/EC of the Commission of 24 May 1996, in *OJ*, 1996, L 135/32.

21 The Convention is published in its consolidated version in International Oil Pollution Compensation Funds, *Liability and Compensation for Oil Pollution. Texts of the 1992 Conventions and the Supplementary Fund Protocol*, London, 2011, p. 5, available at: <http://www.iopcfund.org> (accessed 30 July 2013).

22 The Convention is published *ibid.*, p. 21.

exceeded those amounts, Member States had to "make provision for that cost to be borne by the producer of the product from which the waste thus spread came" provided however, in accordance with the "polluter pays principle", that "such a producer cannot be liable to bear that cost unless he has contributed by his conduct to the risk that the pollution caused by the shipwreck will occur".[23]

The Court rightly concluded that neither the CLC nor the FUND were binding upon the EC (now the EU), since such instruments have never been acceded to by the EC, Member States have not conferred upon the EC the relevant competences and no legally binding value can be attributed to them by way of the EC's participation in UNCLOS, which only provides, under its Article 235, for a "general obligation of cooperation" with regard to liability and compensation for damage to the marine environment.[24] This finding, however, reveals an underlying contradiction as far as co-ordination between uniform rules such as those contained in the CLC and the FUND and Directive 75/442/EEC are concerned, the latter which, unlike other more recent measures,[25] does not contain a conflict provision, thus clearly impinging on the channelling and limitation of liability principles upon which the international legal regime—to which individual Member States are parties—is based.

MOX plant,[26] decided a couple of years before *Commune de Mesquer*, had already given the CJEU the opportunity to examine the question of whether a series of provisions contained in UNCLOS and dealing with marine environmental protection fell within the competence of the (then) EC for the purposes of establishing, in turn, whether any dispute relating to marine environmental protection was to be considered, according to Article 292 ECT (now Article 344 TFEU), attributed to the exclusive competence of the CJEU, as opposed to other mechanisms for the settlement of international disputes. The Court analysed "whether and to what extent the Community, by becoming a party

23 Para. 82 of the judgment.

24 Para. 85 of the judgment.

25 Such as Directive 2004/35/EC of the European Parliament and of the Council of 21 April 2004 on environmental liability with regard to prevention and remedying of environmental damage, *OJ*, 2004, L 143/56. On these aspects of the environmental liability directive, and particularly on its Article 4, reference may be made to S. M. Carbone, F. Munari and L. Schiano di Pepe, *The Environmental Liability Directive and liability for damage to the marine environment*, *JIML* 13, 2007, pp. 341–355, esp. p. 344 *et seq.*

26 CJEU, Case C-459/03, *Commission v Ireland* [2006] ECR I-4635. For a comment on the judgment see S. Mardsen, "MOX Plant and the Espoo Convention: Can Member State Disputes Concerning Mixed Environmental Agreements be Resolved Outside EC Law?" *RECIEL* 18, 2009, p. 312.

to [UNCLOS] elected to exercise its external competence in matters of environmental protection"[27] and found that:

> within the specific context of [UNCLOS], a finding that there has been a transfer to the [EC] of areas of shared competence [was] contingent on the existence of [EC] rules within the areas covered by the Convention provisions in issue, irrespective of what may otherwise be the scope and nature of those rules.[28]

First of all, the Court affirmed that, pursuant to Article 176 ECT (now 193 TFEU), external competence of the EC (now EU) with regard to the protection of the marine environment was not exclusive but, rather, shared with Member States,[29] and that the existence of the EU's external competence regarding the protection of the marine environment was not, in principle:

> contingent on the adoption of measures of secondary law covering the area in question and liable to be affected if Member States were to take part in the procedure for concluding the agreement in question, within the terms of the principle formulated by the Court in paragraph 17 of the *AETR* judgment.[30]

As a consequence of such premise, the Court subsequently based its finding on the content of the declaration of competence rendered by the EC under Article 310 UNCLOS and in particular on the conclusion "that the matters covered by the provisions of [UNCLOS] ... [were] very largely regulated by [EC] measures"[31] and that the CJEU therefore had exclusive jurisdiction, according to current Article 344 TFEU, to deal with disputes relating to the interpretation and application of those provisions and to assess a Member State's compliance with them.[32]

The above reasoning is, however, apparently contradicted by another important judgment rendered shortly afterwards by the CJEU in *Intertanko*,[33] where

---

27 *Ibid.*, para. 96.

28 *Ibid.*, para.108.

29 *Ibid.*, para. 92.

30 *Ibid.*, para. 94.

31 *Ibid.*, para. 110.

32 *Ibid.*, para. 121.

33 CJEU, Case C-308/06, *The Queen, on the application of International Association of Independent Tanker Owners (Intertanko) and Others v Secretary of State for Transport* [2008] ECR I-4057. On the judgment see, for a general comment, P. Eeckhout, "*Case C-308/06, The Queen on the application of Intertanko and Others v Secretary of State for*

the relationship between the EC and MARPOL came under scrutiny with regard to the compatibility with MARPOL of Directive 2005/35/EC.[34] After having clarified that the EC was not a party to that particular Convention, the Court affirmed that it did not appear that the EC had assumed, under the ECT, the powers previously exercised by the Member States in the field to which MARPOL applied, so that it could therefore:

> be distinguished from [the General Agreement on Tariffs and Trade] within the framework of which the Community progressively assumed powers previously exercised by the Member States, with the consequence that it became bound by the obligations flowing from that agreement.[35]

Whilst it is true that, as a matter of principle, the EU "cannot, simply because all [Member] States are parties to MARPOL, be bound by the rules set out therein, which it has not itself approved",[36] the CJEU would appear to have overlooked the fact that most aspects dealt with by MARPOL are nowadays comprehensively dealt with by EU, formerly EC, rules, and that the unqualified reference made to the precedent represented by the *Peralta*[37] case, decided by the Court in 1994, is perhaps not totally convincing or decisive. In this respect, it may in fact well be argued that by since adopting various maritime safety packages and, in particular, the very act being examined in the *Intertanko* case, *viz.* Directive 2005/35/EC, the EU had specifically elected to exercise its powers in the field of marine environmental protection.

4 The EU's Role in Promoting Higher Standards to Prevent, Manage and React to Environmental Accidents Caused by Offshore Oil and Gas Operations

On 12 October 2010, in the wake of the *Deepwater Horizon* accident, the European Commission published a communication entitled "Facing the

---

Transport, judgment of the Court of Justice (Grand Chamber) of 3 June 2008", CMLR 45, 2009, pp. 2041–2057.

34 Directive 2005/35/EC of the European Parliament and of the Council of 7 September 2005 on ship-source pollution and on the introduction of penalties for infringements, *OJ*, 2005, L 255/11, most recently amended by Directive 2009/123/EC of the European Parliament and of the Council of 21 October 2009, *OJ*, 2009,L 2850/52.

35 Para. 48 of the judgment.

36 *Ibid.*, para. 49.

37 CJEU, Case C-379/92, *Peralta* [1994] ECR I-3453 (see para. 48 of the *Intertanko* judgment).

challenge of the safety of offshore oil and gas activities".[38] The document noted that the waters surrounding the European continent were in parts intensively exploited for the production of oil and gas, with more exploration activities taking place.

According to the communication, the number of offshore installations in the North East Atlantic alone exceeded 1,000, with over 100 in the Mediterranean and at least some units in the Black and Baltic Seas, without mentioning exploration and production activities taking place in a number of neighbouring countries.[39] A specific concern was raised with regard to the changing nature of the business and the increasing risks that this might pose, with the transformation of the European oil and gas industry in response to the progressive depletion of "easy" reservoirs.[40]

In the explanatory memorandum accompanying a subsequent "proposal for a regulation of the European Parliament and of the Council on safety of offshore oil and gas prospection, exploration and production activities", published in 2011, the European Commission noted that there were "considerable disparities and fragmentation amongst Member States' laws and practices applying to offshore activities" and that such a circumstance reflected *inter alia* "the virtual absence of international law instruments".[41]

Whilst this particular statement is probably exaggerated, it cannot be disputed that the international legal framework relating to the environmental risks posed by offshore oil and gas activities is far from satisfactory. UNCLOS, of which, as already mentioned, the EU is a party,[42] does provide—at least in principle—for a number of legal tools to prevent the possible harmful consequences of offshore activities. Due to the framework nature of the Convention, however, in order for such tools to become effective, an additional layer of international (and national) regulation of a more "technical" character is required, an objective in itself which the international community has so far failed to successfully pursue, albeit with some exceptions. International legislation covering offshore activities at the global level has in fact been developed only in part, and certainly in a far less comprehensive and effective fashion than has occurred, for example, with respect to vessel-source pollution.

---

38 COM (2010) 560 final of 12 October 2010.

39 *Ibid.*, p. 2.

40 *Ibid.*, p. 3.

41 European Commission, *Proposal for a regulation of the European Parliament and of the Council on safety of offshore oil and gas prospection, exploration and production activities*, COM (2011) 688 final of 27 October 2011, p. 3.

42 See *op. cit.*, n. 12 above.

The situation may appear somewhat less discouraging at the regional level, in particular with regard to the North Atlantic[43] and the Mediterranean Sea. As far as the latter is concerned, as is widely known, in several respects the so-called "Barcelona system"—made up of the Convention for the Protection of the Marine Environment and the Coastal Region of the Mediterranean[44] and its seven thematic Protocols[45]—provides for additional or higher environmental standards than those established by legal instruments with a global reach. This is particularly the case with regard to offshore activities, considering that an *ad hoc* Protocol was adopted as early as 1994 for the purpose of ensuring the protection of the Mediterranean Sea against pollution resulting from exploration and exploitation of the continental shelf and the seabed and its subsoil.

At the time of its adoption, the Offshore Protocol, as it is commonly referred to, was considered a very advanced instrument.[46] In general terms, it aimed

---

43 Convention for the Protection of the Marine Environment of the North-East Atlantic, 22 September 1992, entered into force on 25 March 1998, available at: <http://www.ospar.org> (accessed 30 July 2013).

44 Convention for the Protection of the Marine Environment and the Coastal Region of the Mediterranean of 10 June 1995, entered into force on 9 July 2004, on which see generally U. Leanza, "Le régime juridique de la Mer Méditerranée", *RC* 236, 1992, pp. 127–459, but also T. Treves, "L'approche régionale en matière de protection de l'environnement marin", in: *La mer et son droit. Mélanges offerts à Laurent Lucchini et Jean-Pierre Quéneudec*, Paris: A. Pédone, 2003, pp. 591–610.

45 Protocol for the Prevention of Pollution in the Mediterranean Sea by Dumping from Ships and Aircraft of 16 February 1976, entered into force on 12 February 1978 and amended by the Protocol for the Prevention and Elimination of Pollution in the Mediterranean Sea by Dumping from Ships and Aircraft or Incineration at Sea of 10 June 1995, not yet in force; Protocol Concerning Cooperation in Preventing Pollution from Ships and, in Cases of Emergency, Combating Pollution of the Mediterranean Sea of 25 January 2002, entered into force on 17 March 2004; Protocol for the Protection of the Mediterranean Sea against Pollution from Land-Based Sources and Activities of 7 March 1996, entered into force on 11 May 2008; Protocol Concerning Specially Protected Areas and Biological Diversity in the Mediterranean of 10 June 1995, entered into force on 12 December 1999; Protocol on the Prevention of Pollution of the Mediterranean Sea by Transboundary Movements of Hazardous Wastes and their Disposal of 1 October 1996, entered into force on 19 January 2008; Protocol on Integrated Coastal Zone Management in the Mediterranean of 21 January 2008, entered into force on 24 March 2011 (all texts are available on the website of the United Nations Environment Programme's Mediterranean Action Plan, available at: <http://www.unepmap.org> (accessed 30 July 2013).

46 See, in particular, T. Scovazzi, "UNEP: The Fifth Protocol to the Barcelona Convention on the Protection of the Mediterranean", *IJMCL* 10, 1995, pp. 543–546, as well as, more recently, E. Raftopoulos, "Sustainable Governance of Offshore Oil and Gas Development in the Mediterranean: Revitalizing the Dormant Mediterranean Offshore Protocol",

at preventing, abating, combating and controlling pollution resulting from a number of activities by making use of "environmentally effective and economically appropriate" best available techniques. The activities covered included, *inter alia*, scientific research concerning the resources of the seabed and its subsoil, exploration drilling, establishment of installations for the purposes of recovering resources, development drilling and various related or ancillary operations. Provisions were also made for liability and compensation in case of damage as well as for compulsory insurance.

Notwithstanding its undisputed merits (or, perhaps, as a direct consequence of such merits), the Offshore Protocol did not achieve much success until 2012, bearing in mind that the only ratifications until then had been those of Tunisia (1998), Morocco (1999), Albania (2001), Libya (2005), Cyprus (2006) and, more recently, Syria (2011), a step which had finally caused the Offshore Protocol to enter into force pursuant to its Article 32(4).

It is particularly striking that, up to 2010, the only connection between the EU, a party to the 1995 Barcelona Convention,[47] and the Offshore Protocol had been the ratification of the Protocol by one of its newest Member States, Cyprus. The situation has since then very rapidly evolved culminating in the adoption of Directive 2013/30/EU on safety of offshore oil and gas operations (short form: the Offshore Directive).[48] At some point during the legislative process, also as a consequence of the pressure exercised by some Member States and representatives of the industry,[49] the format of the proposed instrument

---

available at: <http://www.mepielan-ebulletin.gr/default.aspx?pid=18&CategoryId=4&ArticleId=29&Article=Sustainable-Governance-of-Offshore-Oil-and-Gas-Development-in-the-Mediterranean:-Revitalizing-the-Dormant-Mediterranean-Offshore-Protocol> (accessed 30 July 2013) and L. Chabason, "Offshore oil exploitation: a new frontier for international environmental law (IDDRI Working Paper no. 11/11)", available at: <http://www.iddri.org/Publications/Collections/Idees-pour-le-debat/WP%201111_chabason_offshore.pdf> (accessed 30 July 2013). Reference can also be made to L. Schiano di Pepe, "Offshore oil and gas operations in the Mediterranean Sea: regulatory gaps, recent developments and future perspectives", in: J. Juste Ruiz, V. Bou Franch (eds.), Derecho del mar y sostenibilidad ambiental en el Mediterraneo, Valencia: Tirant Lo Blanch, 2014, p. 363.

47 Decision 1999/802/EC of the Council of 22 October 1999 on the acceptance of amendments to the Convention for the Protection of the Mediterranean Sea against Pollution and to the Protocol for the Prevention of Pollution by Dumping from Ships and Aircraft, *OJ*, 1999, L 322/32.

48 Directive 2013/30/EU of the European Parliament and of the Council of 12 June 2013 on safety of offshore oil and gas operations and amending Directive 2004/35/EC on safety of offshore oil and gas operations, *OJ*, 2013, L 178/66.

49 See, for example, Oil and Gas UK, *Proposed EU Regulation on Offshore Safety*, available at: <http://www.oilandgasuk.co.uk/ProposedEURegulation.cfm> (accessed 30 July 2013).

was in fact changed from a regulation to a directive, a solution which was maintained until its final adoption.

Since the Offshore Directive is aimed at reducing the likelihood of major accidents relating to offshore oil and gas operations as well as, at the same time, limiting the consequences of such accidents, it is basically built upon two different but strictly complementary pillars. First of all, the newly adopted regime relies heavily upon the principle of prior licensing, so that offshore oil and gas operations pursuant to the Directive may only be conducted by operators who have applied for, and obtained, the appropriate licence from the competent licensing authority, thereby demonstrating their observance of minimum safety standards. Secondly, it is also meant to improve the response mechanisms in case of major accidents and for this reason specific provisions are contained in the Directive dealing with cooperation between Member States, internal and external emergency response plans to be prepared by the operator or the owner and the Member State concerned, respectively, and transboundary emergency preparedness and response, including coordinated measures with third countries.

At the end of 2012, when the legislative process aimed at the approval of the Offshore Directive was still under way, a Decision was adopted by the Council on the accession of the EU to the Offshore Protocol.[50] After recalling the ongoing efforts towards the adoption of what was then still planned as a regulation and the background to the Offshore Protocol, the Decision approves the accession to the Offshore Protocol and authorises the President of the Council to proceed to the deposit of the relevant instrument of approval.

5 Assessment, Lessons Learnt and Concluding Remarks

The developments which occurred between 2010 and 2012 with regard to the fate of the Offshore Protocol, although admittedly relating to a very specific piece of international legislation with a regional scope of application, tell us a lot about the added value that the EU may have in promoting the adoption of legal standards that prevent the likelihood of accidents, provoking marine pollution, and/or limit their consequences. The individual Member States' participation in the instrument in question had in fact proved non existent or, to

50 Decision of the Council of 17 December 2012 on the accession of the European Union to the Protocol for the Protection of the Mediterranean Sea against pollution resulting from exploration and exploitation of the continental shelf and the seabed and its subsoil, *OJ*, 2013, L 4/13.

say the least, totally ineffective for almost twenty years, a situation which will now change in the aftermath of the recent move by the EU.

The reasons for which it is possible to speak of a much welcome progress are many and of general interest for the purpose of the present discussion.

Firstly, the EU has demonstrated a high level of consistency between its internal and external actions, thus reinforcing its image as a leading actor in international environmental policymaking in particular with regard to the protection of oceans and seas. Secondly, it has provided a particularly strong incentive for Mediterranean Member States to ratify the Offshore Protocol themselves, in a spirit of cooperation between individual Member States and the institutions of the EU. Thirdly, the participation of the EU in the Offshore Protocol, combined with the recent adoption of the Offshore Directive will give institutions such as the European Commission and the CJEU even greater legitimacy to closely monitor the behaviour of Member States in fulfilling their obligations by the use of—when needed—infringement proceedings, a procedural mechanism unknown to the Barcelona Convention system which will provide an additional and highly effective compliance tool at least on one side of the Mediterranean Sea. Fourthly, and finally, the EU has clearly elected to refrain from a "race to the bottom" approach in the competition with third countries to attract potentially lucrative offshore activities, an attitude which will hopefully provide the necessary stimulus for non-EU States to ratify the Offshore Protocol so as to ensure its widespread application throughout the entire Mediterranean basin.

CHAPTER 15

The Role of the EU in Promoting International Standards in the Area of Climate Change

Elisa Morgera and Kati Kulovesi

1 Introduction

It is no secret that climate change is considered to be the greatest contemporary environmental challenge, and that it has transcended the realm of global environmental policy and law by being gradually conceived as a key threat to global security.[1] The EU has been actively promoting the multilateral recognition of climate change as a global environmental and security emergency.[2] It has also attempted to play a global leadership role in the battle against climate change since the early days of international cooperation around the issue.[3] The objective of combatting climate change has recently also been given a legal formulation in the Treaty of Lisbon where it is listed as one of the objectives of EU environmental policy.[4]

The aim of this piece is to assess whether and to what extent the European Union (EU) can be considered a world leader in stimulating the development of international climate change standards through a variety of international organizations and processes as a way of spurring necessary international cooperation. It will argue that given the slow progress towards an effective global response to the climate change challenge through multilateral cooperation, the EU has been trying to develop climate change standards internally or in

1 Notably at the 2005 UN World Summit. See discussion in E. Morgera "The 2005 UN World Summit and the Environment: The Proverbial Half-Full Glass", *Italian Yearbook of International Law* 15, 2006, p. 53. Climate change has also become an issue of discussion within the UN Security Council: F. Sindico, "Climate Change: A Security (Council) Issue?", *Carbon and Climate Law Review* 1, 2007, p. 26.

2 E. Morgera and G. Marín Durán, "The UN 2005 World Summit, the Environment and the EU: Priorities, Promises and Prospects" *RECIEL* 15, 2006, p. 1.

3 K. Kulovesi, "Climate Change in EU External Relations: Please Follow my Example (or I Might Force You To)", in: E. Morgera (ed.), *The External Environmental Action of the European Union: EU and International Law Perspectives*, Cambridge: CUP, 2012, pp. 115–148.

4 Consolidated Version of the Treaty on the Functioning of the European Union (TFEU) *OJ*, 2012, C326/47, Article 191(1).

© KONINKLIJKE BRILL NV, LEIDEN, 2014 | DOI 10.1163/9789004268333_017

cooperation with third countries. The key motivation has arguably been to promote the acceptance of such standards by the competent international organizations, or at least create a critical mass of countries engaging in climate action (mini-lateralism).[5] The paper will conclude by considering the legitimacy issues arising from this multi-faceted strategy of the EU in promoting international climate change standards.

2 The Trajectory of the EU's Strategy in Promoting International Climate Change Standards

In keeping with its leadership aspirations, the EU has attempted to use its influence to strengthen the multilateral framework for climate change mitigation under the United Nations Framework Convention on Climate Change (UNFCCC) and its Kyoto Protocol.[6] At the same time, it has sought to lead the global battle against climate change 'by example' through innovative internal climate policies and legislation.[7] Since the late 1990s, the EU has developed a rather comprehensive body of climate change law and policy. The key elements include the EU Emissions Trading Scheme (ETS) and the 20-20-20 by 2020 goal, in other words, 20%-targets for emission reductions, and for increasing energy efficiency and renewable energy by 2020.[8]

Despite efforts by the EU and several others, including developing countries that are particularly vulnerable to the negative impacts of climate change, progress made under the UNFCCC and other multilateral fora is far from adequate to prevent dangerous climate change. The 2°C target (the objective of limiting the global average temperature increase to 2°C from pre-industrial times) has formed the cornerstone of the EU climate policy since 1996, and in 2010, this objective was also formally adopted by the 195 Parties to the UNFCCC. The 2°C target is, however, in grave danger of slipping out of reach. The UN Environment Programme has estimated that there is a gap of six to

5 The term is used by S. Barrett, *Why Cooperate? The Incentives to Supply Global Public Goods*, OUP, 2012. It has also been discussed in K. Kulovesi, "Addressing Sectoral Emissions outside the UNFCCC: What Roles for Multilateralism, Minilateralism and Unilateralism?", *RECIEL* 21, 2012, p. 193.

6 Kulovesi, *op. cit.*, n. 3 above.

7 *Ibid.*

8 The history of these targets has been explained in detail in K. Kulovesi, E. Morgera and M. Muñoz: "Environmental Integration and Multifaceted International Dimensions of EU Law: Unpacking the 2009 Climate and Energy Package", *Common Market Law Review* 48, 2011, p. 829.

eleven gigatons of carbon dioxide equivalent between the emission reductions required by 2020 to meet the 2°C target, and the emission reductions pledged by countries at the inglorious 2009 UN Climate Change Conference in Copenhagen.[9] Continuing with the current climate policies is likely to result in a global average temperature increase of more than 3°C by the end of the century,[10] estimated to bring about severe environmental, economic, social and security consequences.

Given inadequate progress through multilateral cooperation over the past two decades, the EU is increasingly attempting to influence external developments and global climate policy through its internal legislation.[11] In other words, the EU has begun crafting its legislation in a way that aims to promote the development of international climate change standards at the multilateral level. In certain cases, the EU has also made access to its large and influential market contingent upon compliance with its climate standards. In this sense, the EU is using a novel mixture of multilateral negotiating positions and internal regulatory approaches that seek to export the EU's approach,[12] as well as bilateral and inter-regional cooperation with partner countries.[13]

One of the first examples—and a highly controversial one—of the EU's reliance on its internal climate legislation to influence external developments was its decision in 2008 to include emissions from both domestic and foreign airlines in the EU ETS.[14] This was followed by a variety of measures included

9 UNEP, Bridging the Emissions Gap. A UNEP Synthesis Report (UNEP, 2011), p. 8.

10 See 'The Climate Action Tracker', an independent science-based assessment, which tracks emissions commitments and actions by countries, available at: <http://www.climateactiontracker.org/> (accessed 07 May 2013).

11 Scott and Rajamani have characterized the EU's approach as 'contingent unilateralism' in J. Scott and L. Rajamani, "EU Climate Change Unilateralism", European Journal of International Law 23, 2012, p. 469. They explain that 'contingent unilateralism' includes two elements: "the application of EU climate change law to greenhouse gas emissions that are generated abroad" and that the "geographical extension contingent in the sense that the EU may agree to waive the external application of its climate change law if adequate international or third country climate change regulation has been put in place." *Ibid.*, at pp. 469–470.

12 H. Vedder, "Diplomacy by Directive: an Analysis of the International Context of the Emissions Trading Directive", in: M. Evans and P. Koutrakos (eds.), *Beyond the Established Legal Orders—Policy Interconnections Between the EU and the Rest of the World*, Oxford: Hart, 2011, pp. 105–124.

13 Kulovesi, Morgera and Muñoz, *op. cit.*, n. 8 above.

14 For comprehensive discussion, see K. Kulovesi, "Make Your Own Special Song even if Nobody Else Sings Along: International Aviation Emissions and the EU Emissions Trading Scheme", *Climate Law* 2, 2011, p. 535.

in the 2009 Climate and Energy Package, a comprehensive set of legal acts designed to implement the 20-20-20 by 2020 targets. Key elements of the Package include a revised ETS Directive, a new Directive on all forms of renewable energy (including biofuels), an effort-sharing Decision on the Member States' emissions reductions outside the emissions trading sector,[15] a Directive setting up the legislative framework for carbon capture and storage (CCS) and a Regulation seeking to reduce CO_2 emissions from passenger cars. In early October 2012 the EU also adopted a Directive on energy efficiency to complement the package.

As we have argued elsewhere, the 2009 Climate and Energy Package includes many innovative elements, some of which also aim to influence developments outside the EU.[16] For example, the revised ETS Directive increased opportunities for the EU to try to expand the carbon market by linking the ETS with trading schemes established by third countries.[17] These changes are in line with the EU's desire to create a global carbon market through interlinked emissions trading schemes. The creation of a global carbon market would be important for an effective carbon price signal and for reducing the risk of carbon leakage. Revisions to the ETS Directive also contributed to the ongoing international debate on climate finance, structured around the commitment by developed countries under the UNFCCC to jointly mobilize US$ 100 million of climate finance annually by 2020 from multiple sources. The Package contributed to this debate by changing the rules for allocating emission allowances to installations participating in the ETS so that auctioning will gradually become the main method of allocation. The Directive indicates that the Member States should use at least 50% of the auctioning revenues, or an equivalent amount, for activities related to climate change mitigation and adaptation within the EU and internationally.[18] The Commission's original proposal would have introduced a binding obligation to earmark auctioning revenues for climate finance, but this was unacceptable to the Member States.[19] While drafted in non-binding language, the climate finance provisions in the ETS Directive represent the first innovative example of how market-based mechanisms

15 Commission, "Proposal for a Decision of the European Parliament and of the Council on the Effort of Member States to Reduce Their Greenhouse Gas Emissions to Meet the Community's Greenhouse Gas Emission Reduction Commitments up to 2020" COM (2008) 17.

16 For comprehensive analysis, Kulovesi, Morgera and Muñoz, *op. cit.*, n. 8 above.

17 Directive 2009/29/EC of the European Parliament and of the Council of 23 April 2009 amending Directive 2003/87/EC so as to improve and extend the greenhouse gas emission allowance trading system of the Community, (2009) *OJ* L L140/63, Article 25(1)(a).

18 *Ibid.*, Article 10(3).

19 See Kulovesi, *op. cit.*, n. 14 above, p. 555.

can be used to generate climate funding for both domestic and international purposes.

Furthermore, the Package also introduced sustainability criteria for both European and imported biofuels to protect high-value biodiversity land and high-value carbon-stock land as well as seeking to ensure substantial reductions in greenhouse gas emissions from biofuels. The criteria have thus been set unilaterally by the EU, but were expressly based upon international reference documents.[20] Notably, the Directive indicates that the EU will endeavour to conclude bilateral or multilateral agreements with third countries containing provisions on the sustainability criteria.[21]

The EU has also prominently mainstreamed climate change into the unilateral and bilateral tools of its external relations. Specific climate change cooperation clauses have been inserted into recent bilateral/inter-regional agreements between the EU and its partner countries, containing a commitment to cooperate on trade-related aspects of the *future* international climate change regime.[22] Financial and technical assistance offered by the EU to partner countries also specifically targets various issues related to ongoing multilateral negotiations, such as the reform of the Kyoto Protocol's Clean Development Mechanism (CDM), adaptation, low-emissions development strategies and new market mechanisms.[23] Progress in the long-term climate change negotiations has also been addressed through various policy dialogues between the EU and its partner countries[24] and been institutionalised in climate-specific cooperation and dialogue initiatives, such as the Global Climate Change Alliance.[25] Successful

20 Directive (EC) 2009/28 of the European Parliament and of the Council on the promotion of the use of energy from renewable sources [2009] *OJ* L140/16 (Renewables Directive), preambular paras. 69, 73 and 77.

21 *Ibid.*, Article 18(4).

22 E.g. Free Trade Agreement between the EU and its Member States, of the first part, and Colombia and Peru, of the other [2012] *OJ* L354/3, (COPE FTA), Article 63; Free Trade Agreement between the European Union and its Member States, of the first part, and the Republic of Korea, of the other part, 6 October 2010, [2011] *OJ* L127/4 (South Korea FTA), Article 13.5(3).

23 Commission, "Environment and Natural Resources Thematic Programme—2011–2013 Strategy Paper and Multiannual Indicative Programme" (ENRTP Strategy 2011–13), 29 October 2010, 9 and 13.

24 E.g., Joint Africa-EU Action Plan 2011–2013, Partnership on Climate Change and Environment: Third EU-Africa Summit, Joint Africa-EU Strategy Action Plan (2011–2013), Tripoli 30 November 2010.

25 See: <http://www.gcca.eu>. For a discussion, G. Marín Durán and E. Morgera, *Environmental Integration in the EU's External Relations: Beyond Multilateral Dimensions*, Oxford: Hart, 2012, p. 229.

instances of these dialogues have resulted in agreement on specific common priorities between the EU and partner countries in anticipation of multilateral environmental negotiations sessions.[26]

As the above overview shows, the area of climate change has indeed become the most prominent example of the EU's deployment of a vast array of unilateral and bilateral, legal and quasi-legal instruments in its external relations to influence multilateral environmental standard-setting.[27] Some of the measures it has adopted seek to provide leadership by example and to disseminate information from regulatory innovations, hoping that this will inspire other countries to adopt similar measures in their national legal systems. Some climate measures implemented by the EU, however, are mandatory and regulate market-access to the EU, most notably the aviation scheme.[28] Others can be characterized as something in between, as in the case of the EU biofuels sustainability criteria. In this respect, the EU is allowing all biofuels to enter its market, but has created disincentives for those that do not respect the EU sustainability standards: only biofuels that fulfill the sustainability criteria will be counted against the 10% target.[29]

This overview goes to show that the EU has been experimenting with different strategies to support the development of global climate change standards. The effectiveness of these efforts in terms of promoting global climate change standards, however, remains questionable. It is therefore not yet possible to determine which approaches may have been more successful than others. That being the case, it seems useful to draw an initial typology of EU approaches in this regard:

---

26 E.g., EU-Africa Summit, "First Action Plan (2008–2010) for the Implementation of the Africa-EU Strategic Partnership" (undated), para. 8(iii), available at: <http://www.ec.europa.eu/development/icenter/repository/EAS2007_action_plan_2008_2010_en.pdf> (accessed 07 May 2013); and 12th Africa-EU Ministerial Troika Meeting, "Communiqué" Luxembourg 28 April 2009, with section Ib, titled "Climate change agenda: preparing the Copenhagen conference"; 19th EU-Japan Summit, "Joint Press Statement" Tokyo 28 April 2010, para. 12 and Annex, section 2. See discussion in Marín Durán and Morgera, *op. cit.*, n. 25 above, pp. 231–232.

27 This practice is analysed in detail in Marín Durán and Morgera, *op. cit.*, n. 25 above.

28 On this, see Scott and Rajamani, *op. cit.*, n. 11 above, pp. 475–476.

29 There has been some discussion as to whether the biofuels sustainability criteria—targeting principally the way in which biofuels enter the EU market rather than the product itself—are compatible with the market-access requirements under World Trade Organization (WTO) law. This is discussed in Kulovesi, Morgera and Munoz, *op. cit.*, n. 8 above, pp. 882–884.

Examples of EU measures	Key characteristics	International climate change standard concerned
ETS	• Market mechanism • Sanctions • Unilateral standard-setting	• Climate funding • Global carbon market • Sustainability standards for carbon credits • Aviation emissions at ICAO
Biofuels sustainability criteria	• Unilateral standard-setting (based on global references) • Incentive-based (market) approach • Certification (verification?) • Dialogue about monitoring	• CBD and biofuels
CCS Directive	• Unilateral standard setting (based on global references) • Opportunities for bilateral cooperation	• Inclusion of the CCS in the CDM
FLEGT	• Bilateral negotiations • Standard-setting based on third country national standards and global references • Incentive-based (market) approach • Involvement of international organizations	• REDD+ • REDD+ safeguards under the CBD

3 The EU and Support for Climate Change through Multilateralism and Bi/Minilateralism

Our argument here is that it is necessary to assess these efforts against the EU's Treaty-based objective to promote measures at the international level to combat climate change,[30] to promote an international system based on strong multilateral environmental cooperation and good global environmental

30 Article 191(1) TFEU.

governance,[31] and generally to "promote multilateral solutions to common problems, in particular in the framework of the United Nations."[32] The key question is whether the various mini-lateral and unilateral strategies deployed by the EU succeed in promoting multilateral environmental cooperation and governance, and whether such independent action can be deemed as legitimate from the point of view of the international community. In this regard, it is necessary in our view to assess the EU's complex strategy for influencing the development of international climate change standards from the standpoint of its compatibility with general international law and international environmental law. As to the latter point, it is necessary to expand the scope of the enquiry to the EU's impacts on various international processes (be they multilateral, bilateral or mini-lateral) that are directly or indirectly linked to global climate change standard-setting.

Firstly, the EU has actively supported the development of international climate change law multilaterally under the UNFCCC. Originally the strongest supporter of the Kyoto Protocol among developed countries, it has also consistently advocated a 'Kyoto-style' strong international legal framework, structured around legally-binding mitigation commitments and a robust compliance mechanism, in the negotiations concerning the long-term future of the UNFCCC regime. With regard to the various detailed aspects of climate policy discussed under the UNFCCC, the EU has sought to actively provide intellectual input to the process, sharing its experiences and analysis on mitigation, adaptation, finance, technology and so on.

Secondly, the EU is promoting climate-related proposals in various multilateral fora outside the UNFCCC. For example, it advocates the adoption of market-based measures under both the International Civil Aviation Organization (ICAO) and International Maritime Organization (IMO) in order to curtail the rapidly growing greenhouse gas emissions from international aviation and maritime transport. The EU is also promoting safeguards for REDD+ (Reducing Emissions from Deforestation and forest Degradation in developing countries; and the role of conservation, sustainable management of forests and enhancement of forest carbon stock in developing countries) and for biofuels in negotiations under the Convention on Biological Diversity (CBD), with

31 Consolidated Version of the Treaty on the European Union (TEU) [2010] *OJ* C83/13, 30 March 2010, Article 21(2)(h) TEU, read in conjunction with the above-mentioned provisions and Article 11 TFEU on environmental integration ("Environmental protection requirements must be integrated into the definition and implementation of the Union policies and activities, in particular with a view to promoting sustainable development.")

32 Article 21(1), second sentence TEU.

a view to injecting exogenous standards into the international climate change negotiations.[33]

Thirdly, the EU is seeking to promote the expansion and strengthening of climate change law through various minilateral and bilateral settings. It is, for example, engaged in plans to link its ETS with other emissions trading schemes, including the Australian one. The EU has also given financial support, for example, to China to develop its domestic emissions trading schemes.[34] In addition, the EU is providing bilateral assistance to developing countries to support their implementation of the international climate change regime. Although the overall amount of resources allocated to environmental cooperation by the EU remains modest,[35] climate change receives top priority for cooperation under the 2011–2013 EU environmental thematic funding (indicatively allocated €237.5 million, amounting to nearly 47% of the total budget),[36] with emphasis being placed on climate change adaptation[37] (including through the Global Climate Change Alliance), climate change mitigation[38] (in particular

33 The Council of the EU urged, in preparation for the CBD COP 11, "the CBD and its Parties to contribute actively to the development and implementation of biodiversity safeguards under REDD+ as a crucial opportunity for cooperation between the CBD and the United Nations Framework Convention on Climate Change (UNFCCC); and ENCOURAGES the use of indicators and other mechanisms to assess the impacts of REDD+ measures on biodiversity." Council, Conclusions on Biological Diversity and Biosafety, 11 June 2012, para. 7, available at: <http://www.consilium.europa.eu/uedocs/cms_data/docs/pressdata/.../130787.pdf> (accessed 07 May 2013). The REDD+ case is discussed in detail *infra*. As to biofuels, see E. Morgera, "Ambition, Complexity and Legitimacy of Pursuing Mutual Supportiveness through the EU's External Environmental Action", in: B. Van Vooren, S. Blockmans and J. Wouters (eds.), *The EU's Role in Global Governance: The Legal Dimension*, Oxford: OUP, 2013, pp. 201–203.

34 EU-China Summit Press Release, 20 September 2012, available at: <http://www.consilium.europa.eu/uedocs/cms_data/docs/pressdata/en/ec/132478.pdf> (accessed 07 May 2013).

35 As recognized by the Commission itself: the yearly average financial commitments by the EU for the environment over the period 2007–2010 was around €295 million, representing roughly 4.3% of all EU external assistance. European Commission Working Paper, "Improving Environmental Integration in Development Cooperation", SEC (2009) 555 final, p. 4. See further, G. Marín Durán, "Environmental Integration in EU Development Cooperation: Responding to International Commitments or Its Own Policy Priorities" in Morgera, *op. cit.*, n. 3 above, pp. 204–234.

36 ENRTP Strategy 2011–2013, pp. 20–23 and 28.

37 The indicative allocation for climate change adaptation is €75 million, ENRTP Strategy 2011–2013, p. 28.

38 The indicative allocation for climate change mitigation is €115 million, ENRTP Strategy 2011–2013, p. 28.

through reducing emissions from deforestation and forest degradation, low-emission development strategies, and technology transfer), and promoting investments in sustainable energy options.[39] Another priority area for external funding is to strengthen international climate change governance (indicatively allocated €39 million),[40] in order for it to be "*shaped* by the external dimensions of the EU's climate change policies (emphasis added)".[41] This is specifically geared towards supporting the work of the UNFCCC Secretariat, developing countries' participation in multilateral negotiations; and implementation of and compliance with multilateral environmental agreements (MEAs). More recently, the European Commission has proposed establishing close interlinkages between climate change, biodiversity and development funding, in a pragmatic effort to make the most of high-profile climate finance[42] internally and externally,[43]and support 'climate-proof' development.[44]

This paper will focus on two key examples on how the EU tries to promote international standards to tackle the global climate change challenge through a variety of instruments and in a variety of international fora. The two examples relate respectively to REDD+ and carbon trading.

3.1 *First Case Study: REDD+*

Forests currently contribute about one-sixth of global greenhouse gas emissions when cleared, overused or degraded, and have the potential to absorb about one-tenth of global carbon emissions projected for the first half of this century into their biomass, soils and products and store them—in principle in perpetuity.[45] Forests, however, also perform several other important environmental and socio-cultural functions that have dominated the international debate on sustainable forest management since the 1992 Rio Summit on the

39 The indicative allocation for sustainable energy is €47.5 million, ENRTP Strategy 2011–2013, p. 28.

40 *Ibid.*, pp. 26 and 28.

41 *Ibid.*, p. 25.

42 *Ibid.*, p. 17. This paragraph summarizes relevant findings on EU external funding of Marín Durán and Morgera, *op. cit.*, n. 25 above, Ch. 4.

43 See generally, Kulovesi, Morgera and Muñoz, *op. cit.*, n. 8 above.

44 Commission, "Green Paper on EU development policy in support of inclusive growth and sustainable development—increasing the impact of EU development policy" COM (2010) 629 final, 17.

45 FAO, "Role of Forests in Climate Change" (undated) available at: <http://www.fao.org/forestry/climatechange/53459/en/> (accessed 07 May 2013).

Environment and Development.[46] Sustainable forest management has been a long-standing international concern for the EU and, as such, the EU has supported addressing the issue at the multilateral level through the development of a legally binding agreement on forests[47] both at the global[48] and regional levels.[49] At the unilateral and bilateral levels, the EU has provided early and consistent external funding for the protection of tropical forests.[50]

More recently, the EU has sought to promote a global approach to deforestation through a combination of EU internal legislation with extraterritorial implications and external relations tools. Notably, the EU has been very explicit in linking these efforts to its multilateral agenda. At the internal level, the EU has first developed an action plan and then enacted a series of regulations to tackle this global problem in the short term, in the face of limited progress at the global level.[51] The EU approach is based on global soft-law commitments,[52] and is clearly designed to be compatible with ongoing, albeit partial, multilateral

46 Non-Legally Binding Authoritative Statement of Principles for a Global Consensus on the Management, Conservation and Sustainable Development of all Types of Forests (Forest Principles), 31 ILM 881 (1992).

47 G. Reischel, "The EU and the UN Forest Negotiations: A Case of Failed International Environmental Governance?" (Marie Curie European Summer School on Earth System Governance, Vrije Universiteit, Amsterdam, 24 May–6 June 2007), available at: <http://www.2007amsterdamconference.org/Downloads/07SummerSchool%20-%20Reischl.pdf> (accessed 07 May 2013).

48 The EU advocated the development of a global, legally binding instrument on forests at the United Nations Forum on Forests, e.g. Earth Negotiations Bulletin, Summary of the Fifth Session of the United Nations Forum on Forests, (2005) Volume 13, No. 133, 4, available at <http://www.iisd.ca/forestry/unff/unff5/> (accessed 07 May 2013).

49 During the Forest Europe Ministerial Conference, held in Oslo, Norway, from 14–16 June 2011, ministers of European countries and representatives of the EU adopted a mandate for negotiating a legally binding agreement on forests in Europe by 2013: see Oslo Ministerial Mandate for Negotiating a Legally Binding Agreement on Forests in Europe, 16 June 2011, available at: <http://www.foresteurope2011.org/pop.cfm?FuseAction=Doc&pAction=View&pDocumentId=29800> (accessed 07 May 2013).

50 Regulation 2494/2000 of the European Parliament and of the Council on Measures to Promote the Conservation and Sustainable Management of Tropical Forests and Other Forests in Developing Countries [2000] *OJ* L288/6; DCI Regulation, Articles 6(e) and 7(e).

51 Commission, "Forest Law Enforcement, Governance and Trade (FLEGT): Proposal for an Action Plan" COM (2003) 251 final, 3 (FLEGT Action Plan). The FLEGT Action Plan was endorsed by the Council, "Conclusions—Forest Law Enforcement, Governance and Trade (FLEGT)" [2003] [2000] *OJ* C268/1.

52 World Summit on Sustainable Development, "Johannesburg Plan of Implementation" (4 July 2002) UN Doc A/CONF.199/20, Resolution 2, 5.

efforts.[53] This approach clearly emphasises the ultimate aim of developing multilateral consensual measures to address deforestation by exporter and importer countries, step by step through a multilateral instrument or the linking of regional agreements.[54]

Deforestation issues, however, are increasingly addressed under the UNFCCC under the so-called REDD+ item.[55] This international development has led the EU to use its external relations to influence those ongoing negotiations. Thus, the EU has included references to REDD+ in its recent bilateral agreements[56] and its 2011–2013 strategy for environment thematic

53 Namely, timber species listed under the Convention on International Trade in Endangered Species (Convention on International Trade in Endangered Species of Wild Fauna and Flora, 3 March 1973, 993 UNTS 243); see FLEGT Action Plan, p. 20. The Plan also points to the need to advance work in the framework of the UN Security Council to define "conflict timber" as timber traded by armed groups the proceeds of which are used to fund armed conflict, with a view to exploring the possible set-up of an international process similar to the Kimberly Process for diamonds. *Ibid.*, p. 21.

54 FLEGT Action Plan, pp. 9 and 11.

55 REDD+ means "reducing emissions from deforestation and forest degradation, conservation of forest-carbon stocks, sustainable management of forests, and enhancement of forest-carbon stocks." This item was first officially incorporated into the agenda of the multilateral climate change negotiations in 2007 (UNFCCC COP, Decision 1/CP.13 "Bali Action Plan" (2008) UN Doc FCCC/CP/2007/6/Add.1, para. 1(b)(iii); and UNFCCC COP Decision 2/CP.13, "Reducing Emissions from Deforestation in Developing Countries: Approaches to Stimulate Action" (2008) UN Doc FCCC/CP/2007/6/Add.1, para. 3, and more recently UNFCCC COP Decision 1/CP.16, "Outcome of the Work of the Ad Hoc Working Group on Long-term Cooperative Action under the Convention" (2011) UN Doc FCCC/CP/2010/7/Add.1, at III.C: Policy approaches and positive incentives on issues relating to reducing emissions from deforestation and forest degradation in developing countries; and the role of conservation, sustainable management of forests and enhancement of forest carbon stocks in developing countries; and Annexes I–II. For a discussion of legal issues related to REDD+, see H. van Asselt, "Managing the Fragmentation of International Environmental Law: Forests at the Intersection of the Climate and Biodiversity Regime", *NYU Journal of International Law and Politics*, 44, 2012, p. 1205; and A. Savaresi, "Reducing Emissions from Deforestation in Developing Countries under the UNFCCC. Caveats and Opportunities for Biodiversity" *Yearbook of International Environmental Law* 81, 2012, p. 21.

56 Agreement Establishing an Association between the EU and its Member States, on the one hand, and Central America on the other, 22 March 2011, Article 20, available at: <http://trade.ec.europa.eu/doclib/docs/2011/march/tradoc_147660.pdf> (accessed 07 May 2013); COPE FTA, Article 286; Partnership Agreement between the Members of the African, Caribbean and Pacific Group of States of the first part and the European Community and its Member States of the other, signed in Cotonou on 23 June 2000,

funding.[57] Given that sustainable forest management and REDD+ face similar challenges related to participatory approaches to forestry and the role of forest-dependent communities, the EU is also considering using lessons learnt in the context of its Forest Law Enforcement, Governance and Trade (FLEGT) initiative[58] to provide inputs into multilateral negotiations on REDD+.[59] This would include both key concepts related to forest governance emerging from FLEGT policies and activities,[60] as well as the practical insights emerging from the FLEGT multi-stakeholder processes leading to the conclusion of forest-specific bilateral agreements (called Voluntary Partnership Agreements or VPAs).[61] This is particularly significant as it has proven particularly complex to ensure mutual supportiveness between climate change mitigation objectives, on the one hand, and biodiversity conservation and respect for the human rights of forest-dwelling communities on the other hand[62] in the multilateral negotiations on REDD+.

(Cotonou Agreement), Article 32bis, available at: <http://ec.europa.eu/europeaid/where/acp/overview/documents/devco-cotonou-consol-europe-aid-2012_en.pdf> (accessed 07 May 2013).

57 ENRTP Thematic Strategy 2011–2013, pp. 21–22.

58 FLEGT Action Plan, p. 3.

59 For a more detailed discussion, see A. Savaresi, "EU External Action on Forests: FLEGT and the Development of International Law" in Morgera, *op. cit.*, n. 3 above, pp. 149–173.

60 FLEGT Action Plan, pp. 3 and 5.

61 The EU 2005 FLEGT Regulation Setting up a Licensing Scheme for Imports of Timber Based on Bilateral Agreements (Regulation 2173/2005, [2005] *OJ* L347/1) called for VPAs to be concluded between the EU and timber-exporting third countries. The verification of the legality of harvests of timber imported into the EU is to be checked against compliance with the national law of the third State 'as set out in the VPA'—the latter reference points to a joint evaluation by the third country and the EU of the alignment of third-country national forest law with relevant multilateral standards. The VPA negotiations notably touch upon all elements of sustainability: they thus create the links between disparate pieces of national law that are needed to achieve sustainable forest management on the ground.

62 This relates to the international debate on the so-called 'safeguards' for REDD+ concerning biodiversity and forest-dependent communities. Council, "Conclusions on the Convention on Biological Diversity: Outcome of and Follow-up to the Nagoya Conference (11–29 October 2010)", 20 December 2010, para. 21, where Member States and the Commission are invited to "actively contribute to the preparation of advice on the application of relevant safeguards for biodiversity in relation to REDD+, in line with the (CBD) COP 10 decision, and facilitate the development and implementation of such safeguards under REDD+." This is already the case for the EU-Africa partnership: e.g. Third EU-Africa Summit, "Joint Africa-EU Strategy Action Plan" (2011–2013) Tripoli 30 November 2010, pp. 51–53.

What is also noteworthy in the FLEGT initiative is the cooperative approach pursued, relying on the forest-related legislation of the exporting country, in the absence of an international treaty of reference. This arguably aims to ensure the third country's ownership of the initiative, as well as to demonstrate respect for its national sovereignty over its forest resources.[63] This is then coupled with a commitment from the third country to review its national legal framework when it does not support *sustainable* forest management,[64] thus opening the door for a bilateral dialogue on the definition of this concept using national legislation of the third country as a starting point.[65] As an incentive for countries to conclude VPAs, a recent EU Regulation establishes a presumption of compliance with the due diligence requirement for timber originating from a VPA country.[66] It can therefore be argued that the EU has put in place an incentive-based approach to joint standard-setting with partner countries.[67]

Significantly, the EU has also involved an independent, specialized international organization, namely the UN Food and Agriculture Organization (FAO) in its FLEGT initiative. FAO is managing a global project funded by the EU to support African, Caribbean and Pacific countries in the review of their legislation and upgrading of their forest governance and law enforcement capacities.[68] This element is particularly significant for the legitimacy and credibility of the EU initiative, due to the fact that FAO has a long-standing and well-respected tradition of providing expert and independent advice on

63 See Forest Principles, para. 1a.

64 FLEGT Action Plan, p. 5.

65 See for instance, the case of the VPA between the EU and the Republic of Ghana (20 November 2009), available at: <http://www.illegal-logging.info/uploads/SignedAgreementECGhanaFLEGTEN.pdf> (accessed 07 May 2013).

66 Regulation (EU) 995/2010 of the European Parliament and of the Council Laying Down the Obligations of Operators Who Place Timber and Timber Products on the Market [2010] *OJ* L295/23, Articles 3–4. The legitimacy of the FLEGT approach was discussed in Morgera, *op. cit.*, n. 33 above, pp. 203–207.

67 Morgera, *op. cit.*, n. 33 above, pp. 207–208.

68 See <http://www.fao.org/forestry/acp-flegt/en> (accessed 07 May 2013). Note that while there is no formal link between the FAO FLEGT Programme and the VPAs, FAO assistance specifically targets countries based upon "their level of interest in the FLEGT Action Plan and in negotiating a VPA" through support for national and regional FLEGT/VPA workshops to share information, knowledge and lessons learnt, feasibility studies on VPA-related issues; and support for national multi-stakeholder committees in charge of VPA negotiations and for the participation of local stakeholders: FAO, Improving Forest Governance in Africa, the Caribbean and the Pacific (undated) pp. 6 and 9, available at: <foris.fao.org/static/data/acpflegt/4087ForestGovernance_EN.pdf> (accessed 07 May 2013).

the reform of national forest laws.[69] Notably, the FAO has recently announced that it is exploring synergies between FLEGT and REDD+.[70] This is particularly interesting because the EU appears to be involving an intergovernmental organization in its bid to influence multilateral standard-setting by linking experience on the ground and global negotiations in different fora (notably, the CBD).

At the operational level, it has been underlined that FLEGT and REDD+ face similar challenges during their design and implementation phases, such as unclear legal frameworks, poor information systems, weak governance, corruption and limited capacities.[71] It has also been reported that interactions between the two processes have gradually emerged, although in forms which vary from country to country. These interactions reportedly concern the stakeholder dialogue at national and local level, capacity building, and forest monitoring.[72] Notably for present purposes, interactions also include the review of the legal framework done in the context of the FLEGT VPA, which may inform national debates on securing REDD+ incentives through legal reform and establishing REDD+ safeguards.[73]

Whether FLEGT can effectively provide useful inputs into multilateral negotiations on REDD+ remains to be seen, and some commentators have cautioned against overestimating FLEGT's potential to support REDD+ negotiations, particularly because of the different focus of the two processes and the risk of a duplication of efforts.[74] While both FLEGT and REDD+ support governance reforms and include some forms of compliance verification, REDD+ has a broader scope of action in terms of comprehensively tackling forest loss in the tropics by addressing not only deforestation caused by illegal timber trading, but also forest loss caused by agricultural expansion, mining or domestic demand for fuel-wood.[75] Nonetheless, REDD+ processes could

69 See FAO Legal Office, "Legal Advisory Services: Forestry and Wildlife", available at: <http://www.fao.org/legal/development-law/forestry-wildlife-and-national-parks/en/> (accessed 07 May 2013).

70 Earth Negotiations Bulletin, CBD COP 11 Highlights, Volume 9, No. 587, 10 October 2012, available at: <http://www.iisd.ca/vol09/enb09587e.html> (accessed 07 May 2013).

71 V. Merckx, C. Van Orshoven and A. Trevisan, "FLEGT and REDD+: Interactions and Challenges" presentation at the Second EU REDD+ Projects Coordination Meeting, 3–4 July 2012, Brussels, Belgium, available at: <http://www.efi.int/files/attachments/euredd/120703_redd_and_flegt_-_interaction_and_challenges.pdf> (accessed 07 May 2013).

72 *Ibid.*

73 *Ibid.*

74 Savaresi, "EU External Action on Forests", n. 59 above.

75 *Ibid.*

also benefit from experience accrued through FLEGT-related mechanisms for monitoring, reporting and verification, as well as the definition of social safeguards (notably related to the human rights of indigenous and local forest-dwellers) that have hindered international standard-setting for REDD+ in this area.[76]

Against this backdrop, the EU has actively pursued the development of REDD+ safeguards in the context of the CBD, highlighting the need for mutual supportiveness between the international climate change and biodiversity regimes with regard to forests. Notably, the EU not only advocated the development under the CBD of advice on REDD+ safeguards, but also called for the CBD Conference of the Parties (COP) to consider means of monitoring and assessing the impacts of REDD+ on biodiversity.[77] In 2012, CBD parties eventually agreed upon advice on the application of relevant safeguards for biodiversity and the protection of the rights of indigenous and local communities to REDD+ activities. Such advice includes spelling out how CBD obligations specifically translate in the context of REDD+ activities: for instance, prioritizing the use of native communities of species; avoiding invasive alien species or developing ecosystem and species vulnerability assessments; and applying the ecosystem approach to identify sites of high biodiversity value so as to prioritize their conservation.[78] CBD Parties also recommend that national experience in implementing certain previous CBD guidelines should be taken into account, such as on forest biodiversity and protected areas,[79] biodiversity-inclusive impact assessment,[80] the ecosystem approach,[81] the Addis

76 *Ibid.*

77 Earth Negotiations Bulletin, Summary of the Eleventh Meeting of the Conference of the Parties (COP 11) to the Convention on Biological Diversity, Volume 9, No. 595, 22 October 2012, 15, available at <http://www.iisd.ca/download/pdf/enb09595e.pdf> (accessed 07 May 2013).

78 CBD Decision XI/19, "Biodiversity and Climate Change Related Issues: Advice on the Application of Relevant Safeguards for Biodiversity with Regard to Policy Approaches and Positive Incentives on Issues Relating to Reducing Emissions from Deforestation and Forest Degradation in Developing Countries; and the Role of Conservation, Sustainable Management of Forests and Enhancement of Forest Carbon Stocks in Developing Countries" (5 December 2012), Annex I.

79 CBD Decision VI/22, "Expanded Programme of Work on Forest Biological Diversity" (22 May 2002), Annex; and CBD Decision VII/28, "Programme of Work on Protected Areas" (13 April 2004), Annex.

80 CBD Decision VIII/28, "Voluntary Guidelines on Biodiversity-inclusive Impact Assessment" (15 June 2006).

81 Principles of the Ecosystem Approach, in CBD Decision V/6, "Ecosystem Approach" (22 June 2000), Annex B; and Refinement and Elaboration of the Ecosystem Approach,

Ababa Principles and Guidelines for the Sustainable Use of Biodiversity,[82] the Akwé: Kon Guidelines on cultural, environmental and social impact assessments[83] and the Tkarihwaié:ri Code of Ethical Conduct to Ensure Respect for the Cultural and Intellectual Heritage of Indigenous and Local Communities.[84] Furthermore, CBD advice also includes safeguards for the full and effective participation of indigenous and local communities in relevant policy-making and implementation processes at national and subnational levels, considering traditional knowledge, clarifying tenure issues, ensuring an equitable distribution of benefits with communities, and sharing responsibility at subnational and local levels, including with communities.

Notwithstanding progress under the CBD, the politically sensitive nature of the EU proposal should finally be emphasized: negotiations on REDD+ under the CBD encountered fierce opposition from certain developing countries. Emerging economies, in particular, appeared to see in the EU agenda of ensuring "mutual supportiveness" between the international biodiversity and climate change regime, an attempt to place multilaterally-sanctioned conditionalities to the EU and its Member States' support for REDD+ at the bilateral level.[85] It is likely that these concerns will resurface in multilateral and bilateral contexts where REDD+ safeguards are discussed or put in practice.

3.2 *Second Case Study: The EU Efforts to Promote, and to Set Standards for, the Carbon Market*

It is argued that creating a price for greenhouse gas emissions would be one of the key ways to tackle climate change. According to the Stern Review, for example, "the key aim of climate-change policy should be to ensure that those generating greenhouse gases … face a marginal cost of emissions that reflects

Based on Assessment of Experience of Parties in Implementation, in CBD Decision VII/11 "Ecosystem Approach" (13 April 2004), Annex I.

82 Addis Ababa Principles and Guidelines for the Sustainable use of Biodiversity, adopted by CBD COP Decision VII/12 (13 April 2004), Annex II.

83 Akwé: Kon Voluntary Guidelines for the Conduct of Cultural, Environmental and Social Impact Assessment regarding Developments Proposed to Take Place on, or which are Likely to Impact on, Sacred Sites and on Lands and Waters Traditionally Occupied or Used by Indigenous and Local Communities, in Article 8(j) and related provisions, CBD COP Decision VII/16F (13 April 2004).

84 CBD Decision X/42 "The Tkarihwaié:ri Code of Ethical Conduct to Ensure Respect for the Cultural and Intellectual Heritage of Indigenous and Local Communities" (29 October 2010).

85 This point was made by Brazil in a contact group on REDD+ at the eleventh meeting of the Conference of the Parties to the CBD (October 2012, Hyderabad, India): personal notes on file with author Morgera.

the damage they cause."[86] As the first supranational emissions trading scheme for greenhouse gas emissions, the EU ETS constitutes a significant milestone in the evolution of European and global climate law. In addition to launching the ETS, the EU has also been actively promoting carbon trading internationally, seeking to expand the carbon market both through the UNFCCC and through interlinked domestic and regional schemes.

While the EU ETS remains the most prominent example of greenhouse gas emissions trading, it is worth bearing in mind that it has experienced a number of serious challenges since it became operational in 2005. Most notably, setting the emissions cap at the right level to create an adequate price signal that effectively promotes low-carbon investment and innovation is proving to be a considerable challenge for the ETS. During the first trading period (2005–2007), the emissions cap was not based on monitored data and there was considerable over-allocation. For the second trading period (2008–12), the cap was tightened—but at the end of 2011, there was a surplus of 950 million allowances due to the unexpectedly dire macroeconomic situation and increasing import of international credits.[87] Given that the banking of allowances between trading periods is possible, the use of international credits is allowed and emissions have dropped in the ETS sector, a continuous oversupply of allowances during most of the third trading period (2013–2020) looks highly likely. This means that the ETS is yet again failing to create an effective carbon price signal. The European Commission has therefore been exploring possible ways of intervening in the carbon market by reviewing the timeline for planned allowance auctions and 'backloading' allowances in order to limit their supply.[88] It has also investigated other options, such as permanently withholding the necessary amount of allowances[89] to create scarcity within the market. The Commission's backloading proposal was, however, greeted with criticism by the industries covered by the ETS and by some key Member States. The European Parliament also rejected the 'backloading' proposal in April 2013. Discussion about structural changes to the ETS therefore continues.

Lessons learned from the ETS, especially the reasons why the carbon price has remained too low, appear to be valuable experiences for the EU to

86 N. Stern, *The Economics of Climate Change: The Stern Review*, Cambridge: Cambridge University Press, 2006, p. 353.

87 J. Delbeke, "Is the EU ETS Working? European Commission Perspective", 26 September 2012, available at: <http://ec.europa.eu/clima/news/docs/2012092801_ets_jd_en.pdf> (accessed 07 May 2013).

88 *Ibid.*

89 *Ibid.*

disseminate to the growing number of countries currently either planning or implementing national or sub-national emissions trading schemes, including Australia, Brazil, Chile, China, Costa Rica, India, Japan, Mexico, New Zealand, Republic of Korea and the US.[90]

At the same time as it is trying to improve the effectiveness of the ETS internally, the EU continues to promote emissions trading through multilateral, minilateral and bilateral cooperation. It has made detailed proposals for a sectoral crediting and trading mechanism in the ongoing negotiations under the UNFCCC on the New Market Mechanisms established by the UNFCCC Parties at the 2011 UN Climate Change Conference in Durban.[91] As mentioned above, the EU is also negotiating with third countries, including Australia, California and Switzerland, for the latter to link their national schemes to the ETS. The European Economic Area (EEA) and European Free Trade Association (EFTA) countries (Norway, Liechtenstein and Iceland) already participate in the ETS. In its bilateral relations, the EU is giving financial support to countries like China that are in the process of developing their own trading schemes.

Interestingly, the EU has also taken action in such areas of climate policy where multilateral cooperation has been particularly difficult. In other words, the EU has tried to influence standard-setting for the international carbon market through its internal legislation. Failing to reach a satisfactory solution through multilateral negotiations, the EU has adopted internal sustainability standards for carbon credits that are stricter than those agreed under the UNFCCC. In concrete terms, the EU has banned credits from afforestation and reforestation activities under the Kyoto Protocol's CDM form the EU ETS. It has also decided to ban credits from controversial industrial gas projects under the CDM. From May 2013 onwards, credits from projects that involve the destruction of trifluoromethane (HFC-23) and nitrous oxide (N2O) are no longer eligible to comply with obligations under the ETS.[92]

Most influential, however, has been the highly controversial decision that the EU took in 2008 to include emissions form foreign airlines alongside its

90 UNFCCC Executive Secretary Christiana Figueres, "Statement at the Carbon Forum North America", 1 October 2012, available at: <http://unfccc.int/files/press/statements/application/pdf/20121001_carbon_forum_north_america.pdf> (accessed 07 May 2013).

91 UNFCCC, "Views on the New Market-Based Mechanism. Submissions from Parties" UN Doc FCCC/AWGLCA/2012/Misc.6, 11 April 2012, pp. 7–16.

92 EU Press Release, "Commission Welcomes Vote to Ban Certain Industrial Gas Credits" IP/11/56, 21 January 2011, available at: <europa.eu/rapid/press-release_IP-11-56_en.htm> (accessed 07 May 2013).

internal aviation emissions in the ETS starting from 2012.[93] The question of emissions from international aviation and maritime bunker fuels has been debated multilaterally since the 1990s under the UNFCCC as well as within the relevant sectoral organizations, the ICAO and IMO. For global climate policy, the problem is that emissions from aviation and maritime transport are projected to increase manyfold by 2050. Their growth is eating into the already severely constrained global carbon budget to limit the global average temperature increase to 2°C. As discussed above, a gap of 8–11 gigatons of carbon dioxide equivalent exists between emissions levels in 2020 to meet this target and the current climate policies.

After years of unfruitful debates at the UNFCCC, IMO and ICAO, in 2008 the EU took a decision to include aviation emissions in the ETS from 2012 onwards.[94] It also decided to draw the boundaries of the scheme in such a way that it applies to all flights landing in, and taking off from EU airports. This has been controversial internationally given that the scheme also applies to foreign airlines. In fact, the independent action by the EU on international aviation emissions has subsequently given rise to a heated international dispute whereby the EU has been accused of, *inter alia*, using unilateral trade measures and exercising extraterritorial jurisdiction in violation of international law,[95] and failing to adequately reflect the principle of common but differentiated responsibilities and respective capabilities in the design of its aviation scheme.[96]

The EU's emissions trading scheme sets a cap for aviation emissions, calculated on the basis of the average of annual emissions during the period 2004–2006.[97] Airlines included in the scheme must also have in place a system for the annual monitoring and reporting of their greenhouse gas emissions.[98] Emissions are calculated based on the entire flight departing from or arriving at an EU airport, including for those parts of the flight that take place outside EU airspace. By the end of April each year, airlines included in the scheme are supposed to surrender allowances corresponding to their verified

93 The following overview of aviation emissions is based on Kulovesi, *op. cit.*, n. 5 above.

94 Directive 2008/101 of the European Parliament and of the European Council amending Directive 2003/87 so as to include aviation activities in the scheme for greenhouse gas emission allowance trading within the Community, [2009] *OJ* L8/3.

95 For an overview of legal arguments in this regard, see Kulovesi, *op. cit.*, n. 14 above.

96 Scott and Rajamani, *op. cit.*, n. 11 above.

97 Directive 2008/101/EC, Articles 3c(1) and (2), Article 3s.

98 *Ibid.*, Article 3g.

emissions in the previous year.[99] Directive 2008/101/EC also contains fairly strict sanctions for non-compliance with the obligation to surrender emission allowances. Accordingly, airlines failing to surrender the required number of emission allowances will incur an excess-emissions penalty of €100 for each tonne of carbon dioxide (CO_2) equivalent emitted for which the airline has not surrendered allowances.[100] Such a payment will not release the airline from the obligation to surrender the missing allowances. Ultimately, a failure to comply with the Directive may lead to a decision by the European Commission that the airline in question is banned from operating within the EU.[101]

Whilst the vast majority of foreign airlines complied with their first round of reporting obligations, the Commission drew attention to "systematic non-reporting" of their 2011 emissions by ten commercial airlines based in China (eight) and India (two).[102] Such early non-compliance with their ETS obligations by Chinese and Indian airlines relates to broader international legal and political opposition to the EU's decision to include foreign airlines within its trading scheme. As a first legal step in the battle against the inclusion of aviation emissions in the EU ETS in 2009, American Airlines, Continental Airlines, United Airlines and the Air Transport Association of America (ATAA) challenged the legality of the scheme's extraterritorial reach through UK courts. This led to a request for a preliminary ruling from the Court of Justice of the European Union (CJEU) concerning the validity of Directive 2008/101/EC in light of its alleged incompatibility with certain rules and principles of international law, namely:

(a) The principle of customary international law that each state has complete and exclusive sovereignty over its air space;
(b) The principle of customary international law that no state may validly purport to subject any part of the high seas to its sovereignty;
(c) The principle of customary international law of freedom to fly over the high seas;
(d) The principle of customary international law that aircraft overflying the high seas are subject to the exclusive jurisdiction of the country

99 *Ibid.*, Articles 6.2 and 16.3.

100 *Ibid.*, Article 16.3.

101 *Ibid.*, Articles 16.5–16.12.

102 European Commission Press Release, "Emissions Trading: Annual Compliance Round-up Shows Declining Emissions in 2011", (IP/12/477) 15 May 2012, available at: <http://europa.eu/rapid/pressReleasesAction.do?reference=IP/12/477> (accessed 07 May 2013).

in which they are registered, save as expressly provided for by international treaty;

(e) The Chicago Convention on International Civil Aviation (in particular Articles 1, 11, 12, 15, and 24);

(f) The Open Skies Agreement (in particular Articles 7, 11.2(c), and 15.3), which is an agreement between the United States and the EU and its member states aiming to open up air-transport markets; and

(g) The Kyoto Protocol (in particular, Article 2.2).[103]

In December 2011, the CJEU affirmed the validity of Directive 2008/101/EC, finding the Directive's provisions to be compatible with international law.[104] However, the outcome failed to satisfy key foreign countries whose airlines are covered by the scheme.

A coalition of some 27 countries, including Brazil, China, India, Russia, South Africa and the US, then emerged, to oppose the inclusion of international aviation emissions within the EU ETS.[105] Some of them went as far as to adopt internal measures to prevent their airlines from complying with the EU scheme. In the US, the 'European Union Emissions Trading Prohibition Act of 2011' was designed to prohibit US-based airlines from participating in the ETS. The bill passed the House of Representatives in October 2011[106] and in September 2012, the counterpart bill passed the Senate. As a result, the diplomatic conflict between the EU and the US on climate policy reached new highs in the autumn of 2012. China also prohibited its airlines from participating in the ETS and increasing fares or imposing other charges as a result of the scheme, and India instructed its airlines not to participate in the scheme.[107]

---

103 CJEU, Case C-366/10, The Air Transport Association of America, American Airlines, Inc., Continental Airlines, Inc., United Airlines, Inc. v The Secretary of State for Energy and Climate Change [2011] *OJ* C260/9 ('Case C-366/10'), Reference for a Preliminary Ruling from High Court of Justice Queen's Bench Division (Administrative Court) (United Kingdom) made on 22 July 2010.

104 *Ibid.*

105 International Centre for Trade and Sustainable Development, "Opponents of EU Aviation Carbon Law Agree on Possible Countermeasures" *Bridges Weekly Trade News Digest* (22 February 2012), available at: <http://ictsd.org/i/news/bridgesweekly/126278/> (accessed 07 May 2013).

106 H.R. 2594 European Union Emissions Trading Prohibition Act of 2011.

107 "China 'Bans' Airlines from Joining EU Carbon Scheme", *BBC News* (6 February 2012), available at: <http://www.bbc.co.uk/news/business-16901106> (accessed 07 May 2013); International Centre for Trade and Sustainable Development, "India Confirms Boycott of

The escalating international row around the ETS resulted in a surprise announcement by Connie Hedegaard, European Commissioner for Climate Action in November 2012. Hedegaard indicated that the EU had decided to "stop the clock" for one year on the implementation of the international aspects of aviation under the EU ETS.[108] In practice, this means that the EU will not require allowances to be surrendered in April 2013 concerning emissions from flights to and from the EU during 2012.[109] In 2012, the aviation scheme will therefore only apply to internal flights within the EU. While the Commission's announcement attempted to justify the move by alluding to positive developments at the ICAO and a desire to create a positive atmosphere for international negotiations, there has been plenty of speculation concerning the 'real reasons' behind the EU's decision. For one, key countries do not seem prepared to let go of their opposition to a compulsory international market mechanism for aviation emissions.[110] Rumours are also rife that the Commission's decision to stop the clock was influenced more by concerns voiced by powerful EU Member States over the economic implications of the scheme than by positive developments at the ICAO.[111] It will therefore be interesting to see what strategy the EU will employ after the one-year deadline runs out in the autumn of 2013.

At this stage, the legal and political drama surrounding the EU trading scheme for aviation emission goes to show that international standard-setting can be highly controversial politically—and very difficult even for powerful players like the EU. Regardless, there are strong legal and environmental justifications for the EU's approach towards aviation emissions. Our argument here is that this type of minilateralism could, in theory, be useful in advancing multilaterally agreed objectives, including the global goal of limiting temperature increase to 2°C—provided that it complies with the relevant norms of international law and seeks justification through multilateral fora.

EU Aviation Emissions Rule", *Bridges Weekly* (29 March 2012), available at: <http://ictsd.org/i/trade-and-sustainable-development-agenda/129985/> (accessed 07 May 2013).

108 Stopping the clock of ETS and aviation emissions following last week's International Civil Aviation Organisation (ICAO) Council, MEMO/12/854, 12 November 2012.

109 *Ibid.*

110 John Parnell, "BASIC countries threaten to block aviation emissions deal" 20 February 2013, Responding to Climate Change (RTCC), available at: <http://www.rtcc.org/basic-countries-threaten-to-block-aviation-emissions-deal/> (accessed 07 May 2013).

111 Barbara Lewis and Valerie Volcovici, "US, China turned EU powers against airline pollution law", 10 December 2012, Reuters, available at: <http://www.reuters.com/article/2012/12/10/us-eu-airlines-climate-idUSBRE8B801H20121210> (accessed 07 May 2013).

4 Conclusions: Challenges Ahead

The EU is a unique actor in the international setting—and it has also devised a uniquely complex strategy to support its international climate change standard-setting. The reliance by the EU upon minilateral and bilateral approaches in climate standard-setting is understandable given that multilateral climate cooperation continues to struggle even when urgent measures would be needed to tackle climate change. Scientific estimates show that global greenhouse gas emissions must already be reduced by 2020 in order to have a reasonable chance of meeting the 2°C target and avoiding dangerous anthropogenic climate change,[112] which are both goals agreed multilaterally by the 195 Parties to the UNFCCC. However, as explained above, the current measures to mitigate greenhouse gas emissions pledged by countries under the UNFCCC are estimated to result in more than 3°C of warming by 2100. The EU's chosen strategy of minilateralism and bilateralism seems justifiable given its objective of advancing goals agreed multilaterally under the UNFCCC.

At the same time, however, the EU must be able to respond to criticism that through its standard-setting, it unilaterally imposes its own view of international law upon third countries,[113] sparks unhealthy regulatory competition,[114] fails to respect international legal principles, such as the principle of common but differentiated responsibilities and respective capabilities,[115] pursues its own competitiveness agenda[116] or raises human rights concerns beyond its borders.[117]

In our view, when assessing the legitimacy and success of the EU as a global leader that promotes the development of international climate change standards, the Union's peculiarities as a global environmental actor should be taken into account. First of all, the Union's tendency to establish and institutionalise long-term external governance systems, often based on regulatory frameworks detailing common goals and participatory guarantees, creates conditions for easily exposing the pursuance of self-interest as opposed to the EU's "purported

112 UNEP, *Bridging the Emissions Gap*, *op. cit.*, n. 9 above.

113 Scott and Rajamani, *op. cit.*, n. 11 above; Marín Durán, *op. cit.*, n. 35 above.

114 Kulovesi, *op. cit.*, n. 14 above.

115 Scott and Rajamani, *op. cit.*, n. 11 above, p. 469.

116 G. Marín Durán, "The Role of the EU in Shaping the Trade and Environment Regulatory Nexus: Multilateral and Regional Approaches", in: Van Vooren *et al.*, *op. cit.*, n. 33 above, pp. 224–240.

117 D. Augenstein, "The Human Rights Dimension of Environmental Protection in EU External Relations Post-Lisbon", in: Morgera, *op. cit.*, n. 3 above, pp. 263–286.

commitment" to partnership and collective decision-making.[118] Secondly, the EU's constitutional requirement for coherence in its external policy translates into a legal obligation for the Union to "actively pursue" a multiplicity of objectives, including environmental protection at different levels, human rights and trade liberalisation—all under the overall ambit of contributing to multilateralism.[119] This makes the EU's role in the global fight against climate change at the same time more ambitious, potentially more balanced but also an easy target for criticism that the EU does not respect its own basic rules. Furthermore, the special nature of the EU as an international actor whose negotiating position is inherently inflexible due to the fact that it is the result of lengthy intra-EU negotiations between its 28 Member States,[120] is further compounded by the increasing interaction between internal environmental regulation and external relations.[121]

Ultimately, the legitimacy question of the EU's reliance on mini-lateralism and bilateralism (as opposed to unilateralism) as a constructive and complementary path towards international standard-setting on climate change rests upon demonstrations of good faith. With all its legal peculiarities and unique constraints, the EU still needs to show to third countries individually and to the international community as a whole that it respects the international legal order and takes into account the reasonable expectations of the other members of the international community.[122] This means protecting the reasonable interests of other States that arise from the appearances created by the bilateral or minilateral behavior of the EU.[123] In other words, it implies the need for the EU to show trustworthiness and predictability[124] in how it develops and uses its bilateral and minilateral approaches to support multilateralism.

---

118 G. De Burca, "EU External Relations: The Governance Mode of Foreign Policy", in: Van Vooren *et al.*, *op. cit.*, n. 33 above, pp. 56–58.

119 Article 21 TEU; see, further, J. Larik, "Entrenching Global Governance: The EU's Constitutional Objectives Caught Between a Sanguine Worldview and a Daunting Reality", in: van Vooren *et al.*, *op. cit.*, n. 33 above.

120 P. Leino, "The Journey Towards All That is Good and Beautiful: Human Rights and 'Common Values' as Guiding Principles of EU Foreign Relations Law", in M. Cremona and B. de Witte (eds.), *EU Foreign Relations Law*, Oxford: Hart Publishing, 2008, p. 279.

121 M. Cremona, "Expanding the Internal Market: An External Regulatory Policy for the EU?", in: van Vooren *et al.*, *op. cit.*, n. 33 above.

122 M. Kotzur, "Good Faith" Max Planck Encyclopedia of International Law, Oxford: OUP, 2012, para. 4.

123 M. Virally, "Review Essay: Good Faith in Public International Law", *American Journal of International Law* 77, 1983, p. 130.

124 S. Litvinoff, "Good Faith", *Tulane Law Review* 71, 1997, pp. 1645, 1664.

It calls for the EU to show a "genuine intention to achieve a positive result"[125] in supporting global climate change standard-setting. Demonstrating good faith, thus, necessitates systematic respect for multilateral norms as well as reliance on multilateral institutions that are essential to the effective, objective and evenhanded promotion and protection of the international community's interests.[126] To this end, the legitimacy of EU efforts to influence and support international climate change standard-setting rests upon continued responsiveness to developments within the multilateral framework, including the determinations by multilateral environmental agreements' governing and compliance bodies relating to the link between financial solidarity, capacity building, and compliance,[127] particularly in balancing the use of trade incentives and avoiding 'upsetting' multilateral determinations of common but differentiated responsibilities through bilateral routes.[128]

125 ICJ, Gulf of Maine case, [1984] ICJ Rep 246, para. 87.

126 B. Simma, "From Bilateralism to Community Interests in International Law", *Recueil des Cours* IV (250), 1994, pp. 217, 319.

127 Morgera, *op. cit.*, n. 33 above, pp. 195–208.

128 E. Morgera, "Bilateralism at the Service of Community Interests? Non-judicial Enforcement of Global Public Goods in the Context of Global Environmental Law", *European Journal of International Law* 23(3), 2012, p. 743; and Kulovesi, *op. cit.*, n. 6 above.

CHAPTER 16

EU Governance of the Threat of Piracy Off the Coast of Somalia

Bibi van Ginkel

1 Introduction

Global emergencies differ, and can entail humanitarian disasters, natural or ecological disasters, terrorism, or—as discussed in this case—piracy. The focus of this contribution will be on how the latter type of emergency is governed by the EU.[1] The term 'governance' describes the framework of powers and capabilities available to deal with a certain problem. The key question is how the problem of piracy is managed in general and whether the EU action passes a certain quality threshold and could provide any relief.

In the first section, the problem of piracy off the coast of Somalia is analysed with special attention given to the root causes. Next, an overview will be provided of the kaleidoscope of international responses to the problem, the number of actors involved, and the many attempts undertaken to coordinate all these initiatives. Subsequently, the role of the EU, its powers and capacities to deal with the issue, and the initiatives it has taken to contribute to combating piracy will be explored. Finally, the question is asked whether one can talk of a comprehensive approach to combating piracy and whether the EU action shows a genuine added value for dealing with the problem.

1 This contribution is based on a presentation given during the conference *EU Governance of Global Emergencies*, which took place on 22–23 October 2012 in Brussels. It also takes inspiration from an article written for the symposium issue on piracy of the Journal of International Criminal Justice with co-author Lennart Landman, entitled: "In search of a Sustainable and Coherent Strategy: Assessing the Kaleidoscope of Counter-piracy Activities in Somalia", 10 (4), 2012, pp. 727–748; a presentation given in Mumbai on 24 November 2012 on the occasion of the port visit of the HNLMS Rotterdam; and a paper providing food-for-thought on the future of the Contact Group on Piracy Off the Coast of Somalia commissioned by the Dutch Ministry of Foreign Affairs, written with Frans-Paul van der Putten.

© KONINKLIJKE BRILL NV, LEIDEN, 2014 | DOI 10.1163/9789004268333_018

2 The Problem of Piracy Off the Coast of Somalia

Somalia is the classic example of modern state collapse. Since the fall of the Siad Barre regime in 1991 and the bloody civil war that followed, there has been a state of chaos and lack of state authority, which has allowed piracy to grow into the structured form in which it is now presented to us.[2] One of the main challenges in terms of Somali society stems from the lack of agreement on the structure of the political system and how the system should accommodate the claims to power of rebel groups of warlords and others, that also find their basis in the clan system and the egalitarian structure of the primarily pastoral and agro-pastoral Somali communities.[3] Moreover, the growing power of pirate groups destabilises the authority of local governments by forcing the latter to choose either to support such pirate groups or lose the financial resources which they can bring to the community. Young pirates, who have recently become wealthy, might moreover call into question the power of clan leaders.[4] Speaking of one Somalia, in terms of one sovereign state with effective control over its territory, is not possible. In particular the regions in the north, Somaliland and Puntland, function quite autonomously. Somaliland, which declared independence in 1991, has always been opposed by the Transitional Federal Government (TFG) and most of the international community. Puntland was established in 1998 as a non-secessionist federal state.

Furthermore, the 'official' government in Mogadishu is struggling with the militant Islamic group Al Shabaab, which controls large parts of South-Central Somalia, and was moreover struck by a major drought and famine in recent years. Puntland in particular is considered the epicentre of piracy, harbouring most of the pirates, and home to the ports where ships dock during ransom negotiations.[5] As most members of the international community do not

---

2 See for more elaborate discussion of this topic for instance: J. Peter Pham, "The Failed State and Regional Dimensions of Somali Piracy", in: B. van Ginkel and F. van der Putten (eds.), *The International Response to Somali Piracy; Challenges and Opportunities*, Leiden/Boston: Martinus Nijhoff Publishers, 2010, pp. 31–64, or J. Dua and K. Menkhaus, "The Context of Contemporary Piracy: The Case of Somalia", *Journal of International Criminal Justice* 10 (4), 2012, pp. 749–766.

3 H. Ehrhart and K. Petretto, "The EU and Somalia: Counter-Piracy and the Question of a Comprehensive Approach", *Study for the Greens/European Free Alliance*, Hamburg, February 2012, p. 6.

4 J. Lang, 'Report of the Special Adviser to the Secretary-General on Legal Issues Related to Piracy off the Coast of Somalia', UN Doc S/2011/30, 24 January 2011, paras. 22–23.

5 Lang, *op. cit.*, n. 4 paras. 19–20.

recognise the autonomy of Puntland, official 'aid' relations have been difficult,[6] as this has been considered a *de facto* recognition of the autonomous state of Puntland. Yet, a broad consensus has emerged among experts that a bottom-up approach is more effective than a top-down strategy[7] where every official contact requires to be arranged through Mogadishu. Currently, there seems to be more room for this regional approach. At the end of 2012, the TFG was replaced by a regularly elected government and parliament, which was one of the milestones of the September 2011 Roadmap on the ending of the transition period.[8] Yet this government is only sustained with the support of troops of the African Union Mission in Somalia (AMISOM)[9] capable of controlling the capital city Mogadishu and regions along most of the borderline of South Central Somalia, leaving a large part of the country as ungoverned territory. Clearly, the new government faces major challenges, yet in general, one is hopeful, also because better prospects for ownership and leadership including at regional and district level have been created. A key element in this respect has been the important role attributed to traditional elders in this process. Another essential element though, is the need to bring the problem of Somalia 'home' and let Somalia deal with the problem of Somalia. This understanding is fully in line with the Busan principle of the 'New Deal' approach for aid effectiveness.[10]

Since Somalia is a failed State, both a functioning law enforcement system and coast guard to deal with the specific problem of piracy are lacking. Other root causes of the piracy problem can be found in the lack of options for subsistence on land and the problems caused by illegal fishing by big foreign fishing trawlers in the unguarded seas of Somalia as well as the dumping of toxic waste. These issues have damaged the growing dependence[11] of the Somali population on the country's marine resources.[12]

The illegal fishing and toxic waste dumping activities have fed into the local narrative that the piracy activities were a justified response to protect the waters, by demanding fees for 'licences' to fish in the waters they protected. However, what might have started out as genuine grievances, soon turned

---

6 Interview with policy adviser of the Dutch Ministry of Foreign Affairs, September 2009.

7 Pham, *op. cit.*, n. 2 p. 53.

8 See the signed Transition Roadmap on Somalia available at: <http://unpos.unmissions.org/Portals/UNPOS/Repository%20UNPOS/110906%20-%20Initialled%20Roadmap.pdf>

9 <http://amisom-au.org/>.

10 During a High Level Forum on Aid Effectiveness in November 2011 in Busan, the g7+ of fragile and conflict affected states agreed on a New Deal for Engagement in Fragile States.

11 Dua and Menkhaus, *op. cit.*, n. 2 p. 753.

12 Lang, *op. cit.*, n. 4 para. 12.

into a well-organised business model based on the simple driver of greed.[13] Guesstimates show that an average pirate gets a cut of earnings of between $30,000 and $40,000 annually, with high estimates of up to $78,000. Clearly, this is in stark contrast to the $500 per capita GDP in Somalia, resulting in an economy that more and more depends on the support of pirates for entire villages with the approval of clan chiefs and members of the diaspora.[14]

In addition to the circumstances caused by the internal situation in Somalia, the geographical setting has also played a significant role in the steep increase in piracy in the region. Piracy is mainly a crime of opportunity and such opportunities have been plentiful with the sea lines of communications (SLOCs) passing through the area, with the Gulf of Aden as one of its chocking points through which 33,000 ships pass each year transporting 7% of world's trade, and the vastness of the area (2,000,000 sq nmi), making it hard to secure the whole region. Furthermore, certainly in the early stages of the increase in the piracy problem, many ships lacked proper protection, and slow speed and low freeboards made it rather easy to step on board.

Although the problem of piracy has always existed, the statistics of the International Maritime Organisation (IMO) show a stark increase between 2008 and 2010. In the period from 1998 to 2007 there were approximately 25 to 50 piracy incidents per year off the East African coast, in 2008 there were 73, in 2009 there were 222 and in 2010 there were 172.[15] 2011 still showed an increase in the number of piracy incidents, but the success rate dropped from 28% in 2010 to 12% in 2011.[16] This decrease in successful piracy attacks has

---

13 Pham, *op. cit.*, n. 2 p. 43; Dua and Menkhaus, *op. cit.*, n. 2 pp. 749–766; Lang, *op. cit.*, n. 4 para. 16.

14 B. van Ginkel and L. Landman, "In search of a Sustainable and Coherent Strategy: Assessing the Kaleidoscope of Counter-piracy Activities in Somalia", *Journal of International Criminal Justice* 10(4), September 2012, p. 730; Lang, *op. cit.*, n. 4 para. 16.

15 International Maritime Organization, *Annual Piracy Statistics Report* (2008; 2009; 2010), available at: <http://www.imo.org/OurWork/Security/SecDocs/Pages/Maritime-Security.aspx> (accessed 20 January 2013).

16 Commercial Crime Services International Maritime Bureau, "As World Piracy Hits High More Ships are Escaping Somali Pirates Says", *IMB News*, available at <http://www.icc-ccs.org/news/710-as-world-piracy-hits-a-new-high-more-ships-are-escaping-somali-pirates-says-imb-report> (accessed 15 July 2013). Reports may disagree on exact figures due to unreported incidents and false alarms muddling the estimates, but the upward trend since 2008 is clear. The 2010 annual report of the International Maritime Bureau reports 'Somali piracy' incidents as numbering 22 in 2006, 51 in 2007, 111 in 2008, 218 in 2009 and 219 in 2010. The 2011 annual report of the International Maritime Bureau (IMB) notes 237 incidents of Somali piracy. These resulted in 28 successful hijackings, 470 seafarers being

been attributed to effective sea-based counter-piracy initiatives such as self-protection measures of commercial ships in accordance with the Best Management Practices 4 (BMP4)[17] and the presence of naval ships.

The *modus operandi* of the pirates in the region is different from that of pirates elsewhere, because they are not so much interested in the theft of the ships' cargo and the crew's belongings, but rather hijack in order to negotiate ransom payments for release. These ransom demands have also increased tremendously over recent years, going from an average of a few hundred thousand dollars in 2006 to $5.5 million in 2010.[18] As a result, insurance rates have skyrocketed over recent years, also contributing to an estimated total economic cost of piracy off the coast of Somalia of between 4.9 and 8.3 billion dollars for 2010.[19]

The area of operation of the pirates has also changed over recent years. In the early stages the main area of operation was near the coast line and in the Gulf of Aden, but due to the intensified surveillance of naval ships the pirates have moved as far as 1,750 nautical miles off the coast, and there have been reports of incidents as far away as the Red Sea, off the coast of India, as well as near Madagascar and the Seychelles.

Notwithstanding the large presence of naval ships, the deterrence factor in terms of fear of prosecution after arrest has not proved capable of playing a key role. On the contrary, in 2011 over 90% of the pirates apprehended by states patrolling the area were released without being prosecuted, because of lack of interest or lack of ability by states to prosecute. Although there is universal jurisdiction to prosecute, there is no universal obligation to do so, which means that it falls within the state prosecutor's discretion to decide whether they want to prosecute, if the state has implemented the relevant international

---

taken hostage, and 8 seafarers being killed. Commercial Crime Services International Maritime Bureau, *Piracy and armed robbery against ships Annual report January 1–31 December 2011* (2012), at p. 20.

17 This is a manual of "Suggested Planning and Operational Practices for Ship Operators and Masters of Ships Transiting the High Risk Area".

18 R. Middleton, "Trends in Piracy: A Global Problem with Somalia at the Core (2011)", available at <http://counterpiracy.ae/background_papers.html> (accessed 15 January 2013), at p. 2. Elsewhere, international law firm Ince & Co estimated that the average ransom payment had doubled from $2 million in January 2010 to $4 million by March 2011, see MARSH, *Piracy—the insurance implications* (2011).

19 Geopolicity, *The Economic Costs of Piracy: Pirate Ransoms & Livelihoods off the Coast of Somalia* (2011). Another study estimates the costs of piracy worldwide at 7 to 12 billion dollars annually: One Earth Future, *The Economic Costs of Maritime Piracy*, One Earth Future Working Paper, December 2010.

law into national legislation.[20] States might also decide not to prosecute due to the fear that pirates may apply for asylum.[21] Furthermore, legal shortcomings such as the absence of a clause in the criminal code prohibiting the *intent* to commit piracy might pose a problem for successful prosecution.[22] This problem of impunity is being referred to as the 'catch and release' practice.[23]

3 The International Response to Piracy Off the Coast of Somalia

In 2008, the rise in piracy attacks off the Coast of Somalia as well as the amounts of the ransoms, attracted worldwide media attention. However, piracy is certainly not a new phenomenon. After all, pirates have for a long time been considered '*hostis humani generis*'. The international response to the problem off the coast of Somalia, so far, has taken the form of a sea-based approach, a land-based approach, and a variety of initiatives coming from the private sector.

In a way it is surprising that it took until 2008 before the international community really started to pay attention, since in 2004 and 2005 many of the humanitarian transportations of the World Food Program (WFP) were already under attack. Whereas no additional actions were undertaken at first, in 2007, the IMO and WFP issued a joined communiqué in which they called for a more concerted effort to combat piracy. They argued for the need to allow ships, according to the powers attributed to war ships in Article 107 of the United Nations Convention on the Law of the Seas (UNCLOS), to enter Somali territorial waters to protect transportations of food.[24] France was the first nation to start escorting WFP ships in 2007, followed by Denmark, the Netherlands and Canada.[25]

In 2008, the United Nations Security Council (UNSC) adopted Resolution 1816 (followed by numerous other resolutions) determining that piracy committed in Somali territorial waters was considered a threat to international

---

20 D. Guilfoyle, "The legal challenges in fighting piracy", in: B. van Ginkel and F. van der Putten (eds.), *The International Response to Somali piracy; Challenges and Opportunities*, Leiden/Boston: Martinus Nijhoff Publishers, 2010, pp. 127–152.

21 Ehrhart and Petretto, *op. cit.*, n. 3 p. 38.

22 *Ibid.*

23 Lang, *op. cit.*, n. 4 para. 14. See also Preambles to UNSC Resolutions 1976 (2011), 1950(2010), 1918 (2010), 1897 (2009), and 1851 (2008).

24 International Maritime Organisation and World Food Programme, *Joint Communiqué*, 7 July 2007.

25 World Food Programme, WFP *press releases*, 2 October 2007, 2 February 2008, 8 August 2008, 26 September 2008, 23 October 2008 and 19 November 2008.

peace and security and authorizing international naval forces with the consent of the Somali authorities to conduct counter-piracy operations in Somali waters.[26] This created an exceptional situation, as was stressed by many states, since according to public international law, naval interventions by foreign states cannot take place within territorial waters.[27] They emphasized that this ability to act against what is legally termed 'armed robbery at sea' (piracy within the territorial waters) has exclusively been made possible for Somalia, and is in no way applicable to counter-piracy *per se* or anywhere else. Resolution 1846 of the same year, even extended the mandate to include activities on land to counter piracy.[28]

The protection of the WFP ships became part of the mandate of the NATO Operation Allied Provider,[29] which had a predominant mandate in counter-terrorism operation Enduring Freedom and was already present in the region. Later on, this mandate was transformed into NATO Operation Ocean Shield especially dedicated to counter-piracy.[30] After NATO, the EU followed with the setup of EU Operation Atalanta.[31] This marked the beginning of a much wider interest among different international organisations and states, such as for instance the deployment of the Combined Maritime Forces 150 (CMF 150) and later CMF 151, a voluntary multi-national naval partnership which includes up to 27 nations under the lead of the USA.[32] Individual states, such as China, India, Japan, Malaysia, Russia, Saudi Arabia, South Korea and Yemen also deployed naval ships to contribute to the patrolling activities in the region. In total, approximately 30 to 40 warships are deployed in an area 1.5 times the size of Europe. To understand these proportions, one could imagine a ship

---

26 United Nations Security Council Resolution 1816, June 2008, followed i.a. by Resolutions 1831, 1838, 1844, 1846, 1851, and 1853 (all 2008).

27 See UN Doc S/PV.5902, 2 June 2008.

28 United Nations Security Council Resolution 1846, 2 December 2008.

29 NATO Maritime Command website, available at: <http://www.mc.nato.int/Pages/home.aspx>

30 *Ibid.*

31 Council of the European Union, *Council Joint Action on the European Union Military Coordination Action in Support of UN Security Council Resolution 1816*, 2008/749/CFSP, 19 September 2008.

32 The Combined Maritime Forces (CMF) is a multinational naval partnership, which exists to promote security, stability and prosperity. Participation is voluntary. It comprises 27 nations: Australia, Bahrain, Belgium, Canada, Denmark, France, Germany, Greece, Italy, Japan, Jordan, Republic of Korea, Kuwait, Malaysia, the Netherlands, New Zealand, Pakistan, Portugal, Saudi Arabia, Seychelles, Singapore, Spain, Thailand, Turkey, the UAE, the UK and the US.

calling for help in the south of Spain, and a warship responding from the vicinity of Norway. Some of the mandates of these operations have, in addition, been expanded to include activities such as escorting, group transit escorts, patrolling, arresting, disrupting in the wider area of the Gulf of Aden and the Indian Ocean.

For the purpose of this chapter, it is interesting to zoom in on the mandate of EU NAVFOR Atalanta. Operation Atalanta was launched in December 2008 within the framework of the EU Common Security and Defence Policy (CSDP), under the Nice Treaty.[33] The Atalanta operation[34] is significant since it is the first naval operation of the EU but represents only one aspect of the EU's wider regional strategy in Somalia.[35] Based on the mandate provided by the SC Resolutions and its own Rules of Engagements,[36] the Operation conducts protection of vessels of the WFP delivering food aid to displaced persons in Somalia; the protection of the African Union Mission in Somalia (AMISOM) shipping; the deterrence, prevention and repression of acts of piracy and armed robbery off the Somali coast; and the protection of vulnerable shipping off the Somali coast on a case by case basis.[37] In addition, the Atalanta forces can arrest, detain and transfer persons who have committed or are suspected of having committed acts of piracy, as well as seize pirate vessels. Since 2012, the mandate has also included the possibility to act against some land-based targets.[38] In addition, Atalanta shall also contribute to the monitoring of fishing activities off the coast of Somalia,[39] and through MoUs with regional states (for instance Tanzania and the Seychelles).[40] Atalanta also has the ability to

33 See the website of EU NAVFOR Atalanta, available at: <http://eunavfor.eu/>.

34 The mandate has been renewed several times. The Council has recently decided to extend the operation until December 2014.

35 Council Decision 2012/174/CFSP of 23 March 2012.

36 SC Resolutions 1816 (2008), 1838 (2008), 1864 (2008), 1851 (2008), 1897 (2009), 1918 (2010), 1950 (2010), 1976 (2011), 2015 (2011), 2020 (2011), and 2077 (2012).

37 Council of the European Union: Council Joint Action 2008/851/CFSP, Brussels, 10 November 2008.

38 *Ibid.*, Article 1, para. 2.

39 Council of the European Union: Council Joint Action 2009/907/CFSP, Brussels, 8 December 2009.

40 A similar agreement between the EU and the Republic of Mauritius, based on Council Decision 2011/640/CFSP of 12 July 2011 has been challenged by the European Parliament before the Court, pending case C-658/11, European Parliament v. Council, action brought on 21 December 2011. The EP considers that the Agreement also relates to issues of judicial cooperation in criminal matters, police cooperation and development cooperation, covering fields for which the consent of the European Parliament is necessary.

transfer suspected pirates captured by the EU NAVFOR operation to competent authorities in the region with a view to their prosecution, a competence that NATO's Ocean Shield operation does not have.[41] NATO's lack of explicit competence in this field initially led to the false understanding of contributing states to the Ocean Shield operations that after capture they had no other option than to release, thereby contributing to the 'catch and release' practice discussed above. However, flag states have an autonomous competence to decide whether to prosecute,[42] which could thus imply that suspects of piracy captured by either NATO ships[43] or Atalanta ships (as long as not transferred to regional authorities) could be transferred to European jurisdictions to stand trial there.[44] In a Report of the Secretary-General of 20 January 2012, it is stated that of a total of 1,063 pirates prosecuted since 2006, 57 were prosecuted and 18 convicted by European states.[45]

As with other CSDP operations, third states also contribute to the Atalanta mission. Norway was the first non-EU state to contribute to Atalanta with a

41 It can be debated whether EU competence in this respect is evidence of the potential added value of the EU actions with respect to international action. After all, it normally depends on the discretion of the prosecutor of the flag state whether to prosecute or extradite for prosecution elsewhere (something that was not yet clear to some contributing states to the NATO operation). However, in general it is evidence of the attempts made by the international community to facilitate capacity building within the region for prosecution.

42 Under customary international law all states have universal jurisdiction to arrest and prosecute pirates. Although all states have the legal authority to capture and prosecute, there is no universal obligation to do so according to international law. According to Article 105 of the United Nations Convention of the Law of the Sea (UNCLOS) there is only a discretion to prosecute. Whether a state will prosecute is now dependent upon two things: 1) the universal jurisdiction to prosecute piracy should also be implemented in the national criminal code, and 2) the national prosecutor's office should, in accordance with its discretionary powers, decide to prosecute. For more detailed discussion on this see Guilfoyle, *op. cit.*, n. 20 pp. 127–152. For a more in-depth analysis of the difference in piracy prosecutions in national courts, see M. Gardner, "Piracy Prosecutions in National Courts", *Journal of International Criminal Justice*, 10, 2012, pp. 797–821.

43 The arrest of eleven Somali men who attacked an Italian oil tanker in January 2012 by Italian marines participating in NATO's Ocean Shield operation is evidence of the competence of flag states to decide to prosecute.

44 See for a critical assessment of the 'Catch & Release Practice', i.a. Lang, *op. cit.*, n. 4; and Ehrhart and Petretto, *op. cit.*, n. 3 p. 6 and pp. 38–40.

45 Report of the Secretary-General on specialized anti-piracy courts in Somalia and other States in the region, UN Doc. S/2012/50, 20 January 2012, para. 10. The European states that prosecuted and convicted pirates are: Belgium, France, Germany, the Netherlands and Spain.

warship.[46] Furthermore, staff officers for the Operational Headquarters have been contributed by Croatia and Ukraine. Additionally, offers by Montenegro and Serbia have been accepted and a Participation Agreement has been concluded to this effect, allowing for the contribution of naval officers.[47]

In order to coordinate the different deployments in the region by the EU, NATO and other actors, SHADE meetings (Shared Awareness and Deconfliction) have been set up.[48] In SHADE meetings, the representatives of the different navies of nations deploying to the region, enforcement agencies, the shipping industry and nations discuss tactical and operational matters. They can make agreements on communication and geographical reference standards, the sharing of operational information and assets and the synchronisation of operations. The Internationally Recommended Transit Corridor (IRTC) was developed during SHADE meetings. The IRTC functions as a designated corridor in the Gulf of Aden that directs merchant traffic away from the Somali coast and organizes it so that international navies can provide better protection. The SHADE meetings help to establish principles of coordination and cooperation, while the operational implementation consists of a mixture of *ad hoc* coordination and cooperation through several centres. Notwithstanding all of these efforts to organise better coordination and cooperation, it is important to note that although every stakeholder calls for better coordination, no one wants to be coordinated, or to operate under the command of another nation or organisation. Although the SHADE meetings do fulfil a function, it will always be suboptimal.

In addition to all of these sea-based counter-piracy measures, a number of legal as well as land-based counter-piracy measures have been developed. In particular, the Djibouti Code of Conduct Concerning the Repression of Piracy and Armed Robbery Against Ships in the Western Indian Ocean and the Gulf of Aden (more often referred to as the Djibouti Code),[49] established by the International Maritime Organisation, has played an important role. The Djibouti Code includes agreements on the conduct of shared operations, the rescue of hijacked ships and crew, interdiction and seizure of pirate vessels, and the prosecution of suspected pirates. It also provides for the exchange of

46 See <http://eunavfor.eu/mission>.

47 *Ibid.*

48 The first SHADE meeting took place in December 2008. On SHADE, see <http://oceansbeyondpiracy.org/matrix/activity/shared-awareness-and-deconfliction-shade>.

49 Signed by: Djibouti, Ethiopia, Kenya, Madagascar, the Maldives, the Seychelles, Somalia, the United Republic of Tanzania, Yemen, the Comoros, Egypt, Mauritius, Saudi Arabia, Sudan and the United Arab Emirates.

information through regional Information Sharing Centres in Mombasa (Kenya), Dar es Salaam (Tanzania), and Sana'a (Yemen). Since November 2011 these centres have also begun sharing information with the Information Sharing Centre of the Regional Cooperation Agreement on Combating Piracy and Armed Robbery against Ships in Asia (ReCAAP). The United Nations Office on Drugs and Crime (UNODC) also works on enhancing the judicial infrastructure in the region, which includes developing Somali capacity for the humane and secure imprisonment of pirates. The United Nations Development Programme (UNDP) works together with UNODC in Somalia, and with its UNDP Rule of Law and Security programme aims to develop policies and contribute to prison and custodial capacity building, invests in improving legal representation and due process for suspected pirates, and improves the security of the community at local level.

To address the underlying problems of Somali society and to monitor and advise the political process of reform, the United Nations Political Office for Somalia (UNPOS) and the International Contact Group for Somalia also play an important role.

In response to a UNSC call for more coordination among the different sea- and land-based efforts to combat piracy in the region, the Contact Group on Piracy off the Coast of Somalia (CGPCS) was established in January 2009. The informal and non-binding setup of the Contact Group creates low barriers for participation and can be considered very effective in bringing together a wide range of actors that would otherwise not have participated in a formal framework. It is also potentially the most comprehensive coordination initiative with regard to piracy off the coast of Somalia. The Contact Group has five working groups in which nations and international organisations can exchange ideas and information. Other stakeholders can also participate in the deliberations. Working Group (WG) 1 focuses on effective naval coordination and cooperation and capacity building on judicial, penal and maritime capacity of regional states. Working Group 2 deals with legal issues. Working Group 3 has contributed to the further development of the BMPs. Working Group 4's focus is on strategic communication. Finally, Working Group 5 focuses on identifying and disrupting financial networks. The purpose of the CGPCS as formulated on its website is to "facilitate the discussion and coordination of actions among states and organizations to suppress piracy off the coast of Somalia".[50]

Although a very flexible and informal platform which had a lot of support certainly at the beginning of its existence, the main question will be whether

---

50 See the website of the Contact Group on Piracy Off the Coast of Somalia, available at: <http://www.thecgpcs.org>.

the CGPCS is an adequate mechanism for achieving the aim of facilitating discussion and coordination with regard to suppressing piracy off the coast of Somalia. Related to this is the question of whether it is actually the purpose of the CGPCS, and hence its reason for existence, to completely eradicate piracy off the coast of Somalia or merely to bring it back to manageable proportions. These questions are important, because the flexible and informal platform where a lot of information exchange can take place is, at the same time, dependent upon the continued support of states and international organisations which need to stay committed to the rather undefined goal. When the work of the CGPCS proves to be effective this will be less of a problem. However, notwithstanding the number of instruments, fora, mechanisms and actors involved in counter-piracy related programmes (which are impressive) it is also clear that there is a lot of overlap in activities. Many of the topics covered by the working groups of the CGPCS are thus also on the agenda of other mechanisms. The themes of WG 1 are, in part, also on the agenda of SHADE, MSCHOA, and the Djibouti Code of Conduct. The issues discussed in WG 2 have already contributed to different capacity-building initiatives, and i.a. are going to be part of the mandate of the newly established Regional Anti-Piracy Prosecution and Intelligence Coordination Centre (Rappicc), which could possibly also look into the topics on the agenda of WG5. Furthermore, the Djibouti Code of Conduct deals with legal issues, as well as the IMO, which gives guidance on legal questions related to the use of private security companies. The focus of WG 3, the development of the BMP and the work of the IMB show some overlap. Only the work of WG 4 does not find a match in other existing mechanisms, except to a certain extent in the mandate of the UN Contact Group on Somalia or in the EU Comprehensive Strategy on the Horn of Africa. It could also be transferred to the agenda of the African Union or IGAD. With the success rate of pirate attacks going down, the question is whether states will stay as committed as they were to profit from the strength of the CGPCS in comparison to other instruments.

Even though, as mentioned, statistics show that the success rate of pirate attacks has declined in the last year, the number of attacks has not gone down by the same percentage. Strategies that really target the root causes of piracy, as far as they are implemented at all, have not been successful yet. As mentioned before, the implementation of the Roadmap and the establishment of the new government is a step in the right direction, but not one with which the underlying causes of piracy have been solved. These topics are, in any case, not really covered by the working groups of the CGPCS. Furthermore, the narratives of the pirate communities as well as the Somali community at large, are still based on the protection narrative. According to that narrative,

Somali fishermen needed to protect their sources of income from the intrusions of Western fishing trawlers that were fishing illegally in Somali waters. We can therefore conclude that in particular WG 4 on public diplomacy and strategic communication, has not been very successful in its messaging campaign. In that sense, more commitment to a flexible allocation of resources with multiple stakeholders is needed to contribute to sustainable solutions to the problem.

As mentioned, the private sector has also contributed to bringing the risk of piracy down. There is close cooperation between, on the one hand, navies and governments with, on the other hand, stakeholders in the merchant community, such as shipping companies, regulatory agencies, insurance companies, and maritime international organisations. Again, one finds an overwhelming number of active entities in this field, making coordination very difficult. Prominent actors in the Gulf of Aden region are the International Maritime Organisation (IMO), the International Maritime Bureau (IMB),[51] and the Baltic and International Maritime Council (BIMCO). The IMO is the UN agency concerned with regulating international shipping. It has long been active in the field of counter-piracy, for example through its recommendations and guidance for governments and the shipping community on the prevention and suppression of acts of piracy and armed robbery against ships. The IMO also provides statistics and reports on developments in piracy. Globally, the Piracy Reporting Centre of the IMB serves as a global contact point in the case of pirate attack. However, for the Gulf of Aden, the United Kingdom Maritime Trade Operations (UKMTO) and the Maritime Security Centre Horn of Africa (MSCHOA) play a more important role. IMB is only secondary, and reports to the IMB are more for documentation purposes than direct response.

4 EU Policies in Targeting the Problem of Piracy Off the Coast of Somalia

Since 1999, the EU has been clear on its ambition to play a role as a civil-military crisis and conflict manager.[52] The Common Security and Defence Policy (CSDP), as an integral part of the Common Foreign and Security Policy (CFSP),

51 The IMB is a division of the International Chamber of Commerce that deals with maritime crime and security.

52 European Council: Conclusions of the Presidency, Annex III: Declaration of the European Council on Strengthening the Common European Policy on Security and Defence, Cologne, 3–4 June 1999; and the Helsinki Summit 10–11 December 1999.

shall, according to Article 24 of the Treaty of the European Union (TEU) as modified by the Lisbon Treaty, "cover all areas of foreign policy and all questions relating to the Union's security, including the progressive framing of a common defence policy that might lead to a common defence". With the setup of the institutional architecture, the EU has been trying to push for some policy orientation, which—traditionally-is hard to decide upon with all Member States beforehand through the formulation of clear policy objectives. Instead, by setting up institutions and instruments, such as the Political Security Committee (PSC), the Military Committee (EUMC) and the European Union Military Staff (EUMS), as well as the introduction of concepts such as the Civil-Military Coordination (CMCO) and the creation of the Civilian Planning and Conduct Capability (CPCC), and an *ad-hoc* military Operations Centre (OpsCenter), to name just a few, the hope is to give policy direction through the activities which these organs undertake. In rather broad terms, an attempt to formulate some policy orientation has been made in terms of the European Security Strategy (ESS) adopted in 2003.[53] One challenge highlighted in the ESS, is bringing together the different instruments and capabilities, both military and civilian, and the way in which they can play a role in fragile states, especially where policies at the nexus of security and development are concerned. With this approach, the EU would certainly be able to provide an added value in situations concerning fragile states, as these elements lay down the groundwork for a comprehensive approach. Whether this has so far resulted in a comprehensive and effective approach to the problem of piracy off the coast of Somalia, can be debated.

In 2005, the EU Commission adopted the Africa Strategy: Towards a Euro-African pact to accelerate Africa's development, which takes a broad approach, including issues such as peace and security, human rights and governance, development and sustainable growth, and future partnership with Africa.[54] The Joint Africa-EU Strategy, subsequently adopted by the Council of the EU in 2007, aims to further strengthen the partnership between the EU and African states based on shared visions of some key principles.[55]

---

53 "A Secure Europe in a Better World", European Security Strategy, Brussels, 12 December 2003.

54 European Commission: EU Strategy for Africa; Towards a Euro-African pact to accelerate Africa's development, COM (2005) 489 final, Brussels, 12 October 2005.

55 Council of the European Union: The Africa-EU-Strategic Partnership. A Joint Africa-EU Strategy, Lisbon, 9 December 2007. The key principles are: the unity of Africa, the interdependence between Africa and Europe, ownership and joint responsibility, and

It was against the background of these ambitions, that the EU began its engagement with Somalia. This engagement initially took the form of humanitarian assistance, which goes back to 1994.[56] The main actor in terms of humanitarian assistance is the European Commission Directorate-General for Humanitarian Aid and Civil Protection (ECHO). Because of the necessity to adhere to the humanitarian principles of humanity, neutrality, impartiality and independence, the activities of the ECHO do not directly form a part of the EU crisis management framework and are not integrated into the structures of the European External Action Service (EEAS). Since the beginning of the 21st Century, the EU has been the largest provider of development aid in Somalia. In particular, the development instruments[57] have become more and more adept at addressing the changing situation in Somalia, including the security risks posed by piracy, and have recently begun to target the improvement of the regional response towards piracy, for instance through supporting the law enforcement agencies in the region and the implementation of the Djibouti Code. In addition, more attention has been paid to the identification and encouragement of 'home grown' governance initiatives in different parts of the country which have been supported by the local population and which do not exclude a possible future federal structure in, for instance, Somaliland or Puntland.[58] The EU has also played a role in crisis management by supporting the peace process and the implementation of the Roadmap.[59]

---

respect for human rights, democratic principles and the rule of law, as well as the right to development.

56 European Commission: Humanitarian Aid and Civil Protection: Somalia Factsheet, February 2013, available at: <http://ec.europa.eu/echo/files/aid/countries/factsheets/somalia_en.pdf>

57 European Commission: Strategy for the Implementation of Special Aid to Somalia 2002–2007, Brussels, 2002; European Commission: Somalia: Joint Strategy Paper for the period 2008–2013, Brussels 2007.

58 European Commission: Somalia: Joint Strategy Paper for the period 2008–2013, Brussels 2007: Para. 20.

59 The EU is a member of a Technical Committee established to monitor the progress of the implementation of the Roadmap. See also the support given by the EU to the Kampala Process: Council of the European Union: Council Conclusions on Somalia, 3076th Foreign Affairs council Meeting, 2011, Brussels, 21 March 2011:3.

Key instruments of the Commission have been the African Peace Facility (APF)[60] and the Instrument for Stability (IfS).[61]

In 2008, the EU began its first military engagement in the region by setting up the EU NAVFOR Atalanta operation[62] that had as its main task, protecting AMISOM. In 2010, the EU launched a military mission to contribute to the training of Somali security forces, EU Trainings Mission (EUTM) Somalia,[63] in response to the request for technical assistance of regional organizations made by Security Council Resolution 1872 of 2009. The mission, which is still on-going, focuses on command and control, specialist training, and 'train the trainer' programmes, which aim to develop Somali control of future training. Trainees additionally receive familiarisation courses in international humanitarian law, human rights law and in the protection of civilians. In 2012 the EU Council launched a new Common Security and Defence Policy mission to support regional maritime capacity building in the Horn of Africa and Western Indian Ocean states: EUCAP Nestor.[64] The latter is a regional training mission planned to become operational in the second quarter of 2013, and which will aim at strengthening the maritime capacities of eight countries in the Horn of Africa and the Western Indian Ocean. It will be a civilian mission carried out under the Common Security and Defence Policy (CSDP), augmented with military expertise, and is intended to be fully complementary to the EU Atalanta operation and the EUTM.

In an attempt to bring more coherence to the different policies, and because of the EU's ambition to develop a comprehensive approach, the Council adopted yet another 'EU policy on the Horn of Africa—towards a comprehensive EU strategy' in December 2009.[65] This policy was supposed to provide strategic guidance and formulated four principles to guide the response towards the region: 1) recognizing the need for a comprehensive approach, 2) understanding the root causes and drivers of conflict, 3) recognizing the imperative of a regional approach, and 4) building upon local ownership. In

60 Joint Council Decision 3/2003, 11 December 2003.

61 Regulation (EC) No. 1717/2006 of the European Parliament and of the Council of 15 November 2006 establishing an Instrument for Stability Launched in 2007.

62 Council of the European Union: Council Joint Action 2008/851/CFSP, Brussels, 10 November 2008.

63 Council Decision 2010/96/CFSP of 15 February 2010 on a European Union military mission to contribute to the training of Somali security forces.

64 Council Decision 2012/389/CFSP of 16 July 2012 on the European Union Mission on Regional Maritime Capacity Building in the Horn of Africa (EUCAP NESTOR).

65 Council of the European Union: An EU Policy on the Horn of Africa—towards a comprehensive EU strategy, 17383/09, Brussels, 10 December 2009.

November 2011, the Council finally adopted a 'Strategic Framework for the Horn of Africa'.[66]

The Strategic Framework for the Horn of Africa aims to guide EU action for greater peace, stability and prosperity in the region. The strategic framework sets out five areas for EU action: building robust and accountable political structures; contributing to conflict resolution and prevention; mitigating security threats emanating from the region; promoting economic growth; and supporting regional economic cooperation. The specific objectives of the comprehensive approach are to prevent and deter pirates from interrupting global maritime trade but also to contribute to a sustainable and long-term solution to piracy through building-up the capacity of the states in the region, including Somalia, to take charge of the fight against piracy. The EU also appointed a Special Representative for the Horn of Africa, Alexander Rondos.[67] He is tasked with coordinating the initiatives. Financial assistance and guidance on policies, however, comes from different organs such as the Africa desk of the EU External Action Service (EEAS) on most of the development aid programmes and the EEAS' Crisis Management Planning Department (CMPD) on the civil/military operations. The Commission's Development and Cooperation—EuropeAid Directorate-General is also involved, however. So, although the overarching ambition is to "streamline and strengthen the coordination of all actors and international donors to Somalia", the drafting and implementing of the specific policies will remain with the Commission, the Council or the Member States.

5 Is EU Governance on Piracy an Added Value? Challenges for the Future

The analysis of the problem of piracy shows the complexity of the issue. Although many resources have been allocated to the maritime response to piracy, all stakeholders agree that the solutions to the piracy problem are to be found on land. This implies dealing with the root causes of piracy, which are manifold. Both the description of the international response to piracy and the overview of EU policies on the topic show that many policies have indeed been developed to deal with the different aspects of the problem. The introductions of the different policies were not always based on a grand master

66 Council of the European Union: Horn of Africa-Council Conclusions, 16858/11 COAFR 315, Brussels, 14 November 2011.

67 *Ibid.*

plan to deal with the problem of piracy, but in many cases necessitated that existing policies were also targeted at addressing aspects of the root causes of piracy, whereas others were specifically developed for that purpose. The need for more coherence and comprehensiveness in the policy approaches was felt though, and was consequently put on the agenda of the different international platforms, such as the Contact Group on Piracy Off the Coast of Somalia. The development of the 2011 Strategic Framework for the Horn of Africa, and the development of the Djibouti Code of Conduct by the EU are also proof of that. However, the fact that existing policies now need to be fitted into an overall comprehensive approach is not obvious from the outset and thus sometimes a complicating factor. After all, one starts off with a patchwork quilt of existing policies, with possible overlaps,[68] contradicting priorities[69] and lacunae[70] of sea- and land-based counter-piracy strategies. These strategies target different policy goals, namely protection and deterrence; prosecution; capacity-building and training programmes; regional security and stabilisation; and unravelling the criminal networks in terms of financing. The challenge is thus to make these policy goals truly complementary to each other. Issues of coordination and cooperation, that became imminent, were subsequently dealt with in newly established coordination and consultation mechanisms. These mechanisms, such as the CGPCS, potentially could function as a truly comprehensive framework within which the problem of piracy including its root causes is addressed. However, what is missing is an in-depth, thorough and shared analysis of the problem which identifies the areas and the communities in society that need to be addressed. Going forward, the instruments that

68 See for instance the overview provided with regard to the activities of the different working groups of the CGPCS, and the overlap with activities of other organisations.

69 Examples of contradicting priorities can be found in the ambition to deal with corruption in a society in which the economy is largely based on an old and enduring practice in Somalia of clans and communities exercising the right to collect fees or protection money. The result of the implementation of that policy might create new economic problems for the communities. Clearly, a context-specific approach is needed in order to provide sustainable solutions. Another example can be found in the mandate of Atalanta to act against land-based targets, while the analysis of the narratives of the Somali community shows that the naval activities of the various international actors are perceived as operations to steal camels and other livestock, indicating the disconnect in communication strategies. See for the latter example also Dua and Menkhaus, *op. cit.*, n. 2 p. 765.

70 Effective strategic communication and public diplomacy to better engage with the population by setting up a successful messaging campaign to explain the different policy goals of the international community and create local ownership is still lacking.

are necessary to meet those needs require to be developed, and one needs to ensure that overlaps or contradictory or counterproductive effects are prevented from taking place. One also needs to acknowledge that other geopolitical interests are at play in the region, such as counter-terrorism, corruption, human trafficking and illegal migration, improving the humanitarian circumstances, and regional power dynamics.[71]

Some argue that we need to approach the problem through a post-conflict lens, implementing lessons learned from peace-building such as context sensitivity, pragmatic incrementalism (an approach that does not use technocratic idealized objectives), showing more sensitivity to the complexity of the situation and not assuming that there are best solutions or any wishful thinking or ambitious nation-building projects.[72] The progress made with regard to the implementation of the Roadmap, the election of the new parliament and the new government are major developments within the region, which should be reflected in the way the international community is dealing with the problem. The ambition to bring the 'Somali problem', including the problem of piracy, 'home to Somalia' in line with the New Deal approach, agreed upon in the Busan meeting on Aid effectiveness,[73] requires that the patchwork approach—but also the attempts for better international cooperation—should be brought into line with the ambitions of governments. It will also still be important to take into account that each policy creates winners and losers, and the latter can act as spoilers. At least all stakeholders should be part of the process, including local communities.

The question is whether the EU is currently dealing with the problem in an adequate fashion. The EU's Strategic Framework for the Horn of Africa,[74] shows the EU's ambition to deal with the problems in a comprehensive way. However, on closer examination it again rather comprises of a set of strategies dealing with different aspects of the problem, but which, in the author's

71 Such as the interference of regional states in Somalis' internal affairs for instance for reasons of fighting proxy wars and the fact that the different anti-piracy naval operations also serve a different purpose: namely having a naval presence in the Indian Ocean, one of the areas where the geopolitical battle regarding who has naval supremacy in the world is fought.

72 C. Bueger, J. Stockbruegger and S. Werthes, "Pirates, Fishermen, and Peacebuilding: Options for Counter-Piracy strategy in Somalia", *Contemporary Security Policy* 32, 2011, pp. 356–381.

73 During a High Level Forum on Aid Effectiveness in November 2011 in Busan, the g7+ of fragile and conflict affected states agreed on a New Deal for Engagement in Fragile States.

74 Council of the European Union: Horn of Africa-Council Conclusions, 16858/11 COAFR 315, Brussels, 14 November 2011.

opinion, together, do not qualify as a coherent strategy. This conclusion was also drawn in a Study commissioned by the Greens and the European Free Alliance on the question of a comprehensive approach of the EU Somalia strategy, in February 2012.[75] The authors of the study point out that the EU institutions are path-dependent and evolve incrementally. So the new crisis management structures such as the Political Security Committee (PSC), the Military Committee (EUMC) and the European Union Military Staff (EUMS) became part of the intergovernmental second pillar while the Commission adopted its own crisis response instruments and mechanisms and preserved its competencies in the realm of development cooperation and humanitarian aid.[76] As a result, the risk of the Council and the Commission each following a different path remains real. They even speak of different tribes of EU external action.[77] They point for instance to the 'Africa Strategy: Towards a Euro-African pact to accelerate Africa's development'[78] adopted by the EU Commission and the Joint Africa-EU Strategy adopted by the Council of the EU. In their assessment, this shows that there is much talk about comprehensiveness and coherence in the documents, but practice shows that the efforts of the EUMS and the CPCC staff to draft concepts aimed at enhancing the comprehensive approach are still unsuccessful. This might be due to the fact that there are still disagreements about the meaning, the direction and the institutional prerequisites of a comprehensive approach.[79]

The study concludes that any coherence is lacking in the comprehensive strategy. A set of more than 30 recommendations are added to the report,[80] such as the advice that EUNAVFOR Atalanta should dedicate more capabilities to monitoring the international rules and regulations on fishing activities.[81] The authors also advocate that better and more intensive joint planning and strategy building within the Union is needed.[82] For this, they argue, the EU should establish a thorough assessment of all ongoing activities of its agencies and Member States; clarify the purpose of the engagement as a whole; identify the concrete objectives; prioritize these objectives; and break them down

75 Ehrhart and Petretto, *op. cit.*, n. 3.

76 *Ibid.*, p. 9.

77 *Ibid.*, p. 11.

78 European Commission: EU Strategy for Africa; Towards a Euro-African pact to accelerate Africa's development, COM (2005) 489 final, Brussels, 12 October 2005.

79 Ehrhart and Pettreto, *op. cit.*, n. 3 p. 11. They base their conclusions on interviews with EEAS on 1 April 2011 and 13 September 2011.

80 *Ibid.*, pp. 46–48.

81 *Ibid.*, p. 35.

82 *Ibid.*, p. 44.

in terms of means and instruments available and needed.[83] Another example of how a more strategic approach can benefit the effectiveness of different initiatives, can be found in the implementation of the EUTM, for which a totally new set up of security provision structures needs to be set in place before the actual training of soldiers can take place. However, as long as there is no agreement on the overall governance model of Somalia, including the advised model of local governance systems, the EUTM will not be able to achieve real results. They furthermore, advise that the EU takes a leading coordinating role within the international community. The Strategic framework and the appointment of the Special Representative could be first steps in this respect. However, what is still missing is a "concept on how to actually align the drivers' lines of engagement of all branches that make up the different policies".[84]

6 Conclusion

When assessing the actions of the EU to counter piracy in Somalia one can state that the EU is concerned with the problem of piracy and that it has a framework of powers and financial and operational capabilities in place to deal with it. The effectiveness of the EU's action is, however, altogether questionable.

The added value of the EU lies, in particular, in its ability to address multiple aspects of the piracy problem, if it can exercise that power coherently and take a leadership role in the other international fora by monitoring the comprehensiveness and coherence of the different initiatives. To a certain extent, the EU has already provided proof of its capacity to improve cooperation with NATO, even though so far these efforts concern the engine-room level and have not overcome the political difficulties concerning EU-NATO cooperation. A further area in which the EU, in particular through its EUNAVFOR Atalanta operation, has shown a leadership role concerns its relations with China, Russia and South-Korea. Several initiatives have been deployed with regard to information sharing, closer cooperation with regard to patrolling within the IRTC, and informal cultural exchange visits on board ships, which have all contributed to building trust and overcoming cultural and linguistic barriers. Should the EU be able to improve the way in which it deals with the problem of piracy off the coast of Somalia and prove that it is able to take a leading role in the international community, this will show that the EU is an international actor capable of playing a leading role in the governance of global emergencies.

83 *Ibid.*, p. 46.

84 *Ibid.*

CHAPTER 17

The United Nations, the European Union and Multilateral Action against Terrorism

*Jan Wouters and Sanderijn Duquet**

1 Introduction

Terrorism is a major concern for the international community.[1] Terrorist attacks are sudden and unpredictable events often with far-reaching consequences for economic, social and political life. As a result, public authorities have struggled to find appropriate regulatory responses to protect citizens and society. Both the United Nations (UN) and the European Union (EU or Union) are supportive of a multilateral approach in fighting terrorism. At the same time, the continuing central role of nation States in this area, ranging from the work of intelligence services to criminal prosecution and implementation efforts, has been stressed at both global and regional levels.

The present chapter revisits counter-terrorism cooperation between the EU and UN. It will be argued that, despite the different actors and issues involved, multilateral approaches have been successfully applied. The UN and EU have developed a partnership in fighting terrorism, albeit one with particular features. Cooperation has by and large been instigated by the EU. The Union has selected the UN, with its universal mandate, to serve as a central forum for developing global counter-terrorism solutions. Over the years, it has given impetus by participating in debates, by sharing experiences and by pushing for

* The authors wish to thank Xavier Leblanc and Frederik Naert for valuable comments and suggestions made.

1 Terrorism has been identified as a key threat (European Council, "A secure Europe in a better world: European Security Strategy", Brussels, 12 December 2003) and a threat to peace and security (Report of the Secretary-General, "In larger freedom: Towards development, security and human rights for all", 21 March 2005, A/59/2005). For further reading on the perceived threat of terrorism, see S. K. Gadarian, "The Politics of Threat. How Terrorism News Shapes Foreign Policy Attitudes", *The Journal of Politics* 72, 2010, pp. 469–483; But see also F. A. Gerges, *The Rise and Fall of Al-Qaeda*, Oxford: Oxford University Press, 2011, p. 208, in which it is argued that Al-Qaeda is no longer a threat to Western societies.

© KONINKLIJKE BRILL NV, LEIDEN, 2014 | DOI 10.1163/9789004268333_019

the development of legal frameworks. UN bodies and Member States, for their part, have been responsive to interacting with EU partners.

The chapter firstly compares the institutional frameworks and related counter-terrorism strategies of the two international organisations (IOs). In a brief overview, the development by each organisation of counter-terrorism initiatives according to their own views and necessities is explained. Secondly, different modes of multilateral counter-terrorism governance are examined. The focus in this regard is on the manner in which the EU interacts with UN partners, both in formal and informal settings. In a third section, the chapter turns to a discussion on substantive interactions between key policies and norms. Three critical issues have been selected to examine how the EU influences topical debates at the global level: the streamlining of counter-terrorism action, the definition of terrorism and the sanctioning of terrorists and terrorist groups. The chapter ends with some concluding reflections.

2 Fighting Terrorism: An Institutional Comparison

Terrorism and manifestations of it have been tackled in national and international security strategies. States have been using international forums to coordinate and harmonise their counter-terrorism laws and policies. In their own right, these forums have adopted agendas for combating terrorism. Accordingly, the UN and the EU are creating legal and political shields against a threat to which even their most advanced Member States in terms of security intelligence have proved not to be immune. This section examines how and why the global and regional lines of defence differ.

2.1 *Two Paths . . .*

Neither the UN nor the EU is new to counter-terrorism. Thus far, however, they have taken different paths to achieve their goals. As early as 1937, a Convention for the Prevention and Punishment of Terrorism was concluded within the context of the League of Nations, requiring States to criminalise terrorist offences.[2] The Convention never entered into force but did represent the start of a long tradition of countering terrorism. Ever since, global instruments have

2 Convention for the Prevention and Punishment of Terrorism, done at Geneva on 16 November 1937, League of Nations Doc. C.546M.383 (1937).

been devised to address particular terrorist acts.[3] Since 1963, sixteen universal legal instruments have been developed. These have tackled, amongst other things, terrorism on board ships,[4] in aircrafts,[5] in airports,[6] terrorism using explosives,[7] terrorism using nuclear weapons,[8] and more generally the financing of terrorism.[9] The criminalisation of these 'specific terrorist acts' enabled the international community to concentrate on topics considered universal in nature and in line with the general mission and activities of the UN.[10] Yet, the adoption of an 'instrumental' approach also left potential global counter-terrorism tools untouched.[11] Consecutive attempts to conclude an all-encompassing international framework convention failed, and the International Criminal

3 B. van Ginkel, *The Practice of the United Nations in Combating Terrorism from 1946 to 2008: Questions of Legality and Legitimacy*, Antwerp/Oxford/Portland: Intersentia, 2010, p. 9.

4 Convention for the Suppression of Unlawful Acts Against the Safety of Maritime Navigation and its Protocol, signed in Rome on 10 March 1988, entered into force on 1 March 1992, *UNTS*, vol. 1678, p. 221, no. 29004.

5 Convention on Offences and Certain Other Acts Committed On Board Aircraft, signed in Tokyo on 14 September 1963, entered into force on 4 December 1969, *UNTS*, vol. 1969, p. 219, no. 10106 and Convention for the Suppression of Unlawful Seizure of Aircraft, signed in The Hague on 16 December 1970, entered into force on 14 October 1971, *UNTS*, vol. 1973, p. 105, no. 12325.

6 Convention for the Suppression of Unlawful Acts against the Safety of Civil Aviation and its Protocol, signed in Montreal on 23 September 1971, entered into force on 26 January 1973, *UNTS*, vol. 1975, p. 177, no. 14118.

7 Convention for the Suppression of Terrorist Bombings, signed in New York on 15 December 1997, entered into force on 23 May 2001, *UNTS*, vol. 2149, p. 256, no. 37517.

8 Convention for the Suppression of Acts of Nuclear Terrorism, signed in New York on 13 April 2005, entered into force on 7 July 2007, *UNTS*, vol. 2445, p. 89, no. 44004.

9 Convention for the Suppression of the Financing of Terrorism, signed in New York on 9 December 1999, entered into force on 10 April 2002, *UNTS*, vol. 2178, p. 197, no. 38349. For a complete list of all legal instruments, see <http://www.un.org/terrorism/instruments.shtml> (accessed 2 July 2013).

10 The UN has a broad mandate to work on a wide variety of issues, but its goals and coordination efforts for a more secure world are of central importance; see in particular Article 1(1) UN Charter. The EU, in its external action, also commits to the preservation of peace, the prevention of conflicts and the strengthening of international security, in accordance with the purposes and principles of the UN Charter (Articles 21 and 3(5) Treaty on European Union, *OJ*, 2010, C 83/13 (Hereinafter "TEU")).

11 See *infra* and J. Wouters, "Terrorism, Multilateralism and Regionalism: Some *Amuse-Gueule* Reflections in a Transatlantic Perspective", in W. J. M. van Genugten, M. P. Scharf and S. E. Radin (eds.), *Criminal Jurisdiction 100 Years after the 1907 Hague Peace Conference*, The Hague: T.M.C. Asser Press, 2009, pp. 68–75.

Court (ICC) does not include the crime of terrorism within its jurisdiction.[12] An attempt to fill this lacuna has been made by the judiciary.[13]

The particular enforcement efforts undertaken by the UN Security Council (UNSC or Council) are a key feature of the global fight against terrorism. The Council has extensively used its unique 'Chapter VII' powers to force national jurisdictions into compliance.[14] Operational counter-terrorism tasks have been supported by three committees established by the UNSC with a different, yet complementary mandate.[15] By contrast, the harmonisation of criminal laws has seen fairly limited global practice beyond mere information exchanges and the creation of model laws.[16]

The EU embodies a different type of counter-terrorism governance. The Union's Member States have ample experience in fighting terrorism within

---

12 The inclusion of the international crime of terrorism was a topic of discussion at the Preparatory Commissions that drafted the Rome Statute. The possible extension of the Court's jurisdiction in this regard was postponed to be considered later. However, it must be noted that certain terrorist offences may also constitute war crimes or crimes against humanity and could fall within the ICC's jurisdiction on that account: J. Wouters and F. Naert, "Shockwaves through International Law after 11 September: Finding the Right Responses to the Challenges of International Terrorism", in: C. Fijnaut, J. Wouters and F. Naert (eds.), *Legal instruments in the fight against terrorism. A transatlantic dialogue*, Leiden/Boston: Martinus Nijhoff Publishers, 2004, p. 744.

13 See UN Special Tribunal for Lebanon (Appeals Chamber), Interlocutory Decision on the Applicable Law: Terrorism, Conspiracy, Homicide, Perpetration, Cumulative Charging, STL-11-01/I, 16 February 2011, § 85. The Tribunal's contribution to the definition of terrorism is further explained later in this chapter.

14 Article 2(e) UNSC Resolution 1373, 28 September 2001, S/RES/1373 (2001).

15 These committees are: (1) The Al-Qaida Sanctions Committee (the 1267 Committee), which, on the basis of information from UN Member States, establishes and amends a list of persons solely related to Al-Qaeda. With the adoption of Resolutions 1988 and 1989 in 2011, the 1267 regime (Al-Qaeda and Taliban) was split. Committee 1267 became Committee 1267/1989 related to Al-Qaeda and a separate 1988 Committee on the Taliban was created; (2) The Counter-Terrorism Committee (UNCTC, established pursuant to UNSC Resolution 1373 and supported by the Counter-Terrorism Committee Executive Directorate (CTED)). Sanctions in this regime target individuals, groups and entities considered to be involved in terrorism over and above those covered by the 1267/1989 regime. Unlike the latter, the UNSC has left it to the Member States themselves to determine who the sanctions are targeted at; and (3) The Committee established pursuant to UNSC Resolution 1540 (2004) (The 1540 Committee) on the proliferation of nuclear, chemical and biological weapons.

16 See in this regard UNODC, Terrorism Prevention Branch, "Model Legislative Provisions Against Terrorism", available at: <http://www.unodc.org/unodc/en/legal-tools/model-treaties-and-laws.html> (accessed 2 July 2013).

their borders,[17] which has made them receptive to investing in regional collaboration.[18] Intergovernmental cooperation in the area of security and police affairs in countering terrorism has been evident right from the early days of European integration.[19] The informal Trevi Group dealt with cross-border crime and terrorism from its creation at the end of 1975.[20] Developed outside the EC Treaty framework, cooperation on this subject was later incorporated

17 Over the past thirty years, in particular the UK, Spain and France and to a lesser extent Greece, Italy and Belgium have been the target of terrorist attacks. As in previous years, in 2012, the majority of the attacks were claimed or attributed to separatist terrorism and took place in France and Spain. See Europol, "EU terrorism situation and trend report", 25 April 2013, available at: <https://www.europol.europa.eu/sites/default/files/publications/europol_te-sat2013_lr.pdf> (accessed 2 July 2013).

18 See for experiences in the UK, Spain, the Netherlands, Sweden, and Germany: M. R. Haberfeld, J. F. King and C. A. Lieberman (eds.), *Terrorism Within Comparative International Context*, New York: Springer, 2009, p. 178.

19 Early initiatives to cooperate in the fight against terrorism were also conducted within the intergovernmental settings of NATO, the Western European Union and the Council of Europe. The latter in particular acquired significant expertise prior to and following its adoption of the 1977 Convention on the Suppression of Terrorism, designed to facilitate the extradition of terrorists by listing offences (*CETS* No. 090, Strasbourg, 27 January 1977 and its 2003 amending Protocol). In the years that followed, the more general work undertaken by the Council on the related topics of extradition, mutual legal assistance and other matters of criminal law was supplemented by the conclusion of legal instruments specifically targeted at fighting terrorism: the Convention on the Prevention of Terrorism (*CETS* No. 196, Warsaw, 16 May 2005) and the Convention on Laundering, Search, Seizure and Confiscation of the Proceeds from Crime and on the Financing of Terrorism (*CETS* No. 198, Warsaw, 16 May 2005). Additionally, the Council's organs agreed upon guidelines, recommendations and declarations covering a wide spectrum of terrorism-related issues. Recently, the Committee of Ministers has focused its counter-terrorism activities on human rights (2002), the protection of victims (2005), freedom of expression (2005), identity and travel documents (2005), special investigation techniques (2005) and co-operation with Interpol (2007). The Parliamentary Assembly's actions have concerned the relationship between the fight against terrorism and human rights (2002), democracy (2001, 2004), air transport (2002), terrorist funding (2004), bioterrorism (2004), cultural activities (2004), the media (2005) and the UN and UNSC sanctioning regimes (2008). The Council of Europe has also set up a Committee of Experts on Terrorism (CODEXTER). For the latest developments, consult: <http://www.coe.int/t/dlapil/codexter/> (accessed 2 July 2013).

20 This group consisted of ministers of internal affairs and justice: see W. Devroe and J. Wouters, *De Europese Unie. Het Verdrag van Maastricht en zijn uitvoering: analyse en perspectieven*, Leuven: Peeters, 1996, p. 668; P. De Cesari, "The European Union", in: G. Nesi (ed.), *International Cooperation in Counter-terrorism*, Hampshire: Ashgate Publishing, 2006, p. 208.

into the former third pillar on Justice and Home Affairs (JHA) by the 1992 Maastricht Treaty,[21] as further reformed by the 1997 Amsterdam Treaty.[22] The bottom-up approach taken at that time left sufficient policy space for Member States to address terrorism threats within their national borders and to gradually develop joint policy responses.[23] These concerns still arise regularly, as competences in counter-terrorism issues may be shared between the Union and its Member States. The number of common Union tools to fight terrorism increased significantly post-9/11 and in the aftermath of the subsequent attacks in London and Madrid. The public shock created unprecedented political momentum, leading to an accelerated adoption and implementation of action plans and programmes.[24] Although these were criticised for being 'event-driven',[25] the EU has focused, at a more concrete level than the UN family, on the judicial dimension of fighting terrorism: criminal laws have been approximated, mutual assistance and recognition frameworks have been developed, and extradition and arrest warrant procedures have been

21 For further reading, see J. Monar, "Justice and Home Affairs: The Treaty of Maastricht as a Decisive Intergovernmental Gate Opener", *Journal of European Integration* 34, 2012, pp. 717–734.

22 A. Reinisch, "The Action of the European Union to Combat International Terrorism", in: A. Bianchi and Y. Naqvi (eds.), *Enforcing International Law Norms Against Terrorism*, Oxford: Hart, 2004, p. 121; J. Wouters and F. Naert, "Police and Judicial Cooperation in the European Union and Counterterrorism: an Overview", in: Fijnaut, Wouters and Naert (eds.), *Legal instruments in the fight against terrorism, op. cit.*, n. 12 above.

23 De Cesari, *op. cit.*, n. 20 above.

24 See the EU Action Plan to Fight Terrorism, adopted within two weeks of the 9/11 attacks (Conclusions of the Extraordinary European Council, 21 September 2001, Brussels, available at: <http://www.consilium.europa.eu/uedocs/cms_data/docs/pressdata/en/ec/140.en.pdf> (accessed 2 July 2013) which brought about the implementation of crucial parts of the 1999 Tampere Programme (Tampere European Council 15 and 16 October 1999, Presidency Conclusions, available at: <http://www.europarl.europa.eu/summits/tam_en.htm> (accessed 2 July 2013)) and the 2004 Declaration on Combating Terrorism. For further reading, see J. Wouters and F. Naert, "The European Union and 'September 11'", *Ind. Int'l & Comp. L. Rev.* 13, 2003, p. 721.

25 R. Coolsaet, "EU counterterrorism strategy: value added or chimera?", *International Affairs* 86, 2010, p. 858. However, the pendulum may have swung the other way again. In his November 2009 Discussion Paper, the EU Counterterrorism Coordinator, Gilles de Kerchove, noted the existence of a certain "counterterrorism fatigue" in the EU. See EU Counter-Terrorism Coordinator, "EU Counter-Terrorism Strategy—discussion paper", 26 November 2009, available at: <http://register.consilium.europa.eu/pdf/en/09/st15/st15359-re01.en09.pdf> (accessed 2 July 2013) at p. 2.

simplified.[26] Not all of the measures have been specific to terrorism. However, efforts of a more general nature, such as the European Arrest Warrant, have also been used in the fight against terrorism.

Building upon the latest developments of event-driven policy-making, the Lisbon Treaty introduced the most recent set of counter-terrorism mechanisms. A solidarity clause was inserted into the Treaty,[27] which obliges the Union and its Member States to assist one another *inter alia* in the event of terrorist attacks and if requested to do so (Article 222 TFEU).[28] A European public prosecutor's office (Article 86 TFEU) may also be established to deal with serious crimes with a cross-border dimension.[29] However, more than 3 years after its entry into force (1 December 2009), the novelties of the Lisbon Treaty have yet to be coherently implemented so as to become real tools in the fight against terrorism.

The development of a single treaty basis for counter-terrorist action and of a full-fledged counter-terrorism strategy with cross-cutting features was never the subject of the EU's constitutional reform processes.[30] Although this left legal qualification and competence questions unanswered, it seems to have been an unavoidable choice of policy-makers in the face of a multitude of

26 J. Wouters and F. Naert, "Of arrest warrants, terrorist offences and extradition deals: an appraisal of the EU's main criminal law measures against terrorism after '11 September'", *Common Market Law Review* 41, 2004, pp. 909–935.

27 Originally, this concept had been introduced in the EU in the 2004 Declaration on combating terrorism, see *supra*.

28 Treaty on the Functioning of the European Union, *OJ*, 2010, C 83 (Hereinafter "TFEU"). See S. Blockmans in this volume and the Joint Proposal by the Commission and the High Representative of the Union for Foreign Affairs and Security Policy for a Council Decision on the arrangements for the implementation by the Union of the Solidarity clause, Brussels, 21 December 2012, JOIN/2012/039 final.

29 Article 86(4) TFEU. The main focus of this Eurojust-linked Office would be crimes affecting the Union's financial interests. Despite the efforts of Spain and Belgium, who successively held the rotating presidency of the Council in 2010, to date, political agreement on implementation is still lacking. See Council of the European Union, Spanish presidency, "The European Public Prosecutor's Office in the European judicial area", Brussels, 15 April 2010, available at: <http://register.consilium.europa.eu/pdf/en/10/st08/st08614.en10.pdf> (accessed 2 July 2013); V. Pop, "Belgian presidency in push for EU prosecutor's office", *EU Observer*, 22 September 2010, available at: <http://euobserver.com/9/30855> (accessed 2 July 2013).

30 J. S. Vara, "The External Dimension of the Area of Freedom, Security and Justice in the Lisbon Treaty", *Eur. J.L. Reform* 10, 2008, pp. 585–586.

rather specific legal bases and different associated procedures.[31] The desire to keep distinct legal bases with different procedures while at the same time maintaining the Union's institutional balance led to the acceptance that in the Treaties the *status quo* had to be maintained.

2.2 ... *One Goal?*

The overview presented above suggests that finding appropriate regulatory responses to counter international terrorism is a complex undertaking. The reasons for this are threefold. Firstly, Member States in the UN and EU have set different counter-terrorism priorities. Secondly, and resulting from this, the governance model used in the organisations under review differs to a great extent. Thirdly, within the UN and the EU a large number of actors have taken an interest to prevent or punish terrorist acts.

Nevertheless, the UN and the EU consider the fight against terrorism to be a common one.[32] The UN frequently reiterates its strong condemnation of "terrorism in all its forms and manifestations". Member States, UN agencies and other international, regional and sub-regional organisations are expected to cooperate in its eradication.[33] Correspondingly, the EU has time and again stressed that terrorism is a threat to internal and international security, the response to which should be found globally as well as regionally.[34] Hence, both the UN and the EU consider counter-terrorism a prime example of multilevel governance. The pertinent question, to be tackled below, then becomes: how can multilateral counter-terrorism aspirations be realised?

---

31 In this regard, a parallel can be drawn between counter-terrorism and the now horizontal external relations objectives contained in Title V, Chapter 1 TEU. The latter have also not been accompanied by a single legal basis and still require implementation through different policies.

32 See e.g. Article 3(c) UNGA Resolution 60/288 on the United Nations Global Counter-Terrorism Strategy and para. 30 of the European Union Counter-Terrorism Strategy.

33 See e.g. recently UNGA Resolution 66/282 on the United Nations Global Counter-Terrorism Strategy Review, 12 July 2012.

34 See e.g. "The European Union has displayed its sincere interest in co-operating more actively and closely with all major actors towards the common goal of combating terrorism" and "the European Union believes that the fight against terrorism should be taken forward in various international organizations and bodies in accordance with the strengths and mandate of each individual body". Council of the European Union, "The Guidelines for a Common Approach to the Fight Against Terrorism", 19 March 2004, partial declassification 22 May 2008.

3 Multilateral Responses to the Threat of International Terrorism

The EU is legally bound by its own constitutional framework to "promote multilateral solutions to common problems, in particular in the framework of the United Nations" and to "establish all appropriate forms of cooperation with the organs of the United Nations and its specialised agencies".[35] This section firstly examines how the Union initiates and contributes to counter-terrorism actions via its representation in the UN's political bodies. Secondly, cooperation between the EU and the UN also materialises in the broader UN context, via interactions between specialised programmes. The final part focuses on EU-UN cooperation taking place within the Global Counter-Terrorism Forum, the Financial Action Task Force and the G7/8.

3.1 *Political Cooperation*

Interactions between the EU and the UN systems have been observed at all levels: at the highest political echelons and in the margins of Working Group meetings of UN agencies and bodies. In informal meetings in particular, the EU has been able to put across ideas and visions on UN policies and the UN Global Strategy.[36]

Participating in formal settings has been more complicated as to do so requires the EU to intervene in the State-centred UN system.[37] This has been particularly problematic in the case of UNSC meetings, which are of central importance in the fight against terrorism. The EU's actions depend upon the success of coordination between EU Member States for two reasons: the Union does not have a seat at the Council nor does it have a single foreign and defence policy. The EU can intervene at most during public UNSC sessions, under the post-Lisbon arrangements set out in Article 34(2) TEU. This provision requires Member States sitting on the UNSC to keep the High Representative and fellow

35 Article 21(1), para. 2, TEU and Article 220(1) TFEU.

36 The latest consultations made clear that the EU is not in favour of revising or renegotiating the UN Global Strategy as it stands. It rather prefers to invest in making the UN strategy more effective and its implementation more balanced. See EU Counter-Terrorism Coordinator, "EU Counter-Terrorism Strategy—discussion paper", May 2012, available at: <http://register.consilium.europa.eu/pdf/en/12/st09/st09990.en12.pdf> (accessed 2 July 2013) p. 7.

37 See regarding the tormented experience of the EU's May 2011 upgrade in the UNGA: J. Wouters, J. Odermatt and T. Ramopoulos, "The Status of the European Union at the United Nations General Assembly", in: I. Govaere, P. Van Elsuweghe, E. Lannon and S. Adam (eds.), *The European Union in the World, Essays in Honour of Marc Maresceau*, Leiden: Brill Publishers, 2013, pp. 211–223.

EU Member States informed and to defend the interests and positions of the EU. Crucially, where the EU has defined a common position on a subject which is on the UNSC agenda, EU Member States sitting in the Council are obliged to request the Council to invite the High Representative to present that position. That is, under the proviso that the format allows for non-UNSC member participation and that a common position exists for the purposes of Article 34(2) TEU. Typically, a declaration is made by the Head of the EU Delegation to the UN in New York.

Despite the possibilities for EU actors to interact with the UNSC, the centre of gravity in counter-terrorism lies with the UNSC's members. The Union, for one thing, is not involved as such in the work of the Sanctions Committees, including the Resolution 1267/1989 Sanctions Committee, which directly creates a list of terrorist suspects. It only comes into play in the implementation phase, when it gives effect to the produced terrorist lists on behalf of its Member States.[38] It is thus generally accepted that the UN "has exercised a high degree of influence over the EU in this policy area".[39] However, when acting externally, EU Member States must exercise their powers in a manner consistent with EU law.[40] Furthermore, in the implementation phase, the EU and its Member States are obliged to respect the protection of fundamental rights, principles that form part of the very foundations of the EU legal order.[41]

---

38 See Articles 75 and 215(2) TFEU and Case C-130/10 *European Parliament v. Council of the European Union, OJ*, 2012, C 130/10, in which the CJEU elaborates on the choice between these legal bases. In para. 61 it is stated "while admittedly the combating of terrorism and its financing may well be among the objectives of the area of freedom, security and justice, as they appear in Article 3(2) TEU, the objective of combating international terrorism and its financing in order to preserve international peace and security corresponds, nevertheless, to the objectives of the Treaty provisions on external action by the Union". As explained in n. 15 above, under the Resolution 1373 regime, UN Member States (or the EU on behalf of its Member States) are required to draw up their own lists of terrorist suspects. See Ch. Eckes, "The Case of Counter-Terrorist Sanctions", in: K. E. Joergensen and K. V. Latikainen (eds.), *Routledge Handbook on Europe and Institutional Institutions. Performance, Policy, Power*, London: Routledge, 2013, p. 172.

39 S. Léonard and C. Kaunert, "Combating the Financing of Terrorism Together? The Influence of the United Nations on the European Union's Financial Sanctions Regime", in: O. Costa and K. E. Jorgensen (eds.), *The Influence of International Institutions on the European Union: A Framework for Analysis*, Hampshire: Palgrave Macmillan, 2012, p. 133.

40 This is the case even in matters in the field of foreign and security policy for which the Member States have retained their competences. See CJEU, Case C-124/95, *Centro-Com v. HM Treasury and Bank of England* [1997] ECR I-81, paras. 25–30.

41 Joined Cases C-402/05 P and C-415/05 P, *Yassin Abdullah Kadi and Al Barakaat International Foundation v. Council of the European Union and Commission of the European*

One could therefore argue that on substance, to some extent, terrorist sanctions are still subject to the EU and its Member States permitting the influence of the UNSC within their common legal orders. However, this is not a view unanimously shared in EU circles. Advocate General Bot recently observed that the UNSC holds the primary responsibility for maintaining peace and security and must not be undermined by the Union as "a forum for appeals against or reviews of decisions made by the Sanctions Committee".[42] Rather, one should "develop cooperation between the Union and the United Nations" grounded in mutual confidence.[43] In this sense, confidence connotes that the EU (Courts) should not mistrust global decisions.[44] The CJEU, however, took a different stance. Omitting references to loaded notions such as "confidence" and "trust", it recently reaffirmed that appeals may be brought before EU Courts.[45] More specifically, the CJEU held that the EU Courts' role is to determine whether the competent Union authority has complied, firstly, with the procedural safeguards and, secondly, with the obligation to state reasons laid down in Article 296 TFEU.[46] In addition, reasons given by the Sanctions Committee and relied upon by EU actors have to be sufficiently detailed and specific to pass the Union's judicial review.[47]

Other invitation-only consultations have been easier for the EU to become involved in. Firstly, at high-level summits and world conferences, EU representatives have been included on a regular basis.[48] By contrast, full representation at negotiations of international agreements has been less consistent. Constitutive instruments of international organisations and/or rules of procedure of multilateral negotiation processes may or may not allow the EU to participate as a 'regional economic integration organisation' (REIO),

---

Communities ([2008] ECR I-6351, para. 304 ("*Kadi I*"), which also specifies that *all* Union measures must be compatible with fundamental rights: paras. 281 *et seq.*

42 Opinion of Advocate-General Bot, delivered on 19 March 2013, in Joined cases C-584/10 P, C-593/10 P and C-595/10 P, *Commission, Council, United Kingdom v. Yassin Abdullah Kadi* [2013] ECR-0000, paras. 71 ("*Kadi II*").

43 *Ibid.*, para. 76.

44 *Ibid.*, para. 66. See also paras. 86 and 113. In para. 85, the AG states "I consider that an effective global fight against terrorism requires confidence and collaboration between the participating international, regional and national institutions, rather than mistrust".

45 *Kadi II, op. cit.*, n. 42 above, Judgment of the Court (Grand Chamber) of 18 July 2013, para. 118.

46 *Ibid.*, paras. 111–114 and 116 of the Judgment.

47 *Ibid.*, para. 118.

48 S. Gstöhl, "EU Diplomacy After Lisbon: More Effective Multilateralism?", *Brown J. World Aff.* 17, 2011, p. 183.

enjoying similar rights and obligations as State parties.[49] When it is accorded REIO status, the EU has made good use of it, for example, by acceding to the UN Convention Against Transnational Organized Crime.[50] Importantly, the REIO status also extends to subsequent meetings and conferences, providing the EU with the opportunity to follow up on the implementation and possible modifications of the convention.[51] As a final possibility, the EU may be accorded observer status. This was the case at the 2005 International Conference on the Revision of the Suppression of Unlawful Acts against the Safety of Maritime Navigation.[52] The European Commission participated in the Conference that adopted the 2005 Protocol to the Convention.[53] The latter aims to prevent and suppress terrorism against ships and to improve security both aboard and ashore.[54]

Secondly, at the UN General Assembly (UNGA), its committees and working groups, the EU enjoys a more enhanced observer status. The Union is registered on the list of speakers entitled to present common positions and to participate in the Assembly's debates.[55] When the UNGA organises negotiations on

---

49 Provisions may also include specific rules on voting procedures. The REIO will typically only be allowed to vote if it has the necessary competence to do so and only with the number of votes of its Member States, provided that those States do not exercise their own votes. See D. B. Hollis, "Why State Consent Still Matters: Non-State Actors, Treaties, and the Changing Sources of International Law", *Berkeley J. Int'l L.* 23, 2005, p. 159.

50 See the REIO clause of Article 36(2) UN Convention Against Transnational Organized Crime and the Council Decision of 29 April 2004 on the conclusion, on behalf of the European Community, of the United Nations Convention Against Transnational Organised Crime, *OJ*, 2004, L 261/69.

51 The EU and its Members States were active participants in the 2012 Vienna Conference of the Parties; See the Report of the Conference of the Parties to the United Nations Convention against Transnational Organized Crime on its sixth session, held in Vienna from 15 to 19 October 2012, CTOC/COP/2012/15. The representative of the EU presented the opening statement on behalf of the Member States and 12 countries in its geographic surroundings (§ 4) and co-sponsored draft resolutions (§§ 40 and 72).

52 IMO, Report on the 2005 International Conference on the Revision of the SUA Treaties, 26 October 2005, A 24/15(b).

53 Diplomatic Conference on Aviation Security held under the auspices of the International Civil Aviation Organization in Beijing from 30 August to 10 September 2010.

54 Article 4 of the Protocol criminalizes the use of a ship as a device to further an act of terrorism and as a means of transport for various terrorism-related materials or for persons who have committed an act of terrorism.

55 UNGA Resolution 65/276, adopted on 3 May 2011, A/RES/65/276 (2011). Note that the enhanced observer status does not apply to other principal UN organs: see Note of the Secretary-General, Participation of the European Union in the work of the United Nations, 1 June 2011, A/65/856, para. 3.

multilateral conventions, it is common practice for the EU to be invited.[56] The EU has used these invitations, among others, to present statements that pushed for the adoption of a legal instrument on nuclear terrorism in the UNGA Ad Hoc Committee on International Terrorism.[57] This goal was achieved, subsequently, in 2005, when the UNGA adopted the Convention for the Suppression of Acts of Nuclear Terrorism.[58]

As a third possibility, the EU can acquire a specific *ad hoc* status. An example is the Counter-Terrorism Centre (UNCCT), endorsed by the UNGA following an initiative taken by the Government of Saudi Arabia.[59] The UNCTT's Advisory Board is composed of its Chair, Saudi Arabia, 20 States, the CTITF Chairman (functioning as secretary and *ex officio* member of the Advisory Board) and the Union as the sole and permanent 'guest member'. This status, not provided for by the 2011 launch agreement, allows it to fully participate in the Centre's activities among selected Member States.[60]

3.2 *Judicial and Police Cooperation*

When operational counter-terrorism cooperation is established, increasing transnational collaborations between police forces and justice services is of paramount importance. The UN bodies have been developing harmonisation and mutual assistance programmes.[61] The Office on Drugs and Crime (UNODC) has taken on the mission of implementing the universal legal regime against terrorism. This is the largest UN programme mandated to deliver counter-terrorism related technical assistance. Its Terrorism Prevention Branch specifically focuses on the improvement of mutual legal assistance and extradition procedures, by developing model laws and legislative guides. The UNODC houses a number of projects on the prevention of (organised) crime and terrorism. In these, working relations with EU agencies are maintained.

---

56 F. Hoffmeister and P. J. Kuijper, "The status of the European Union at the United Nations", in: J. Wouters, F. Hoffmeister and T. Ruys (eds.), *The United Nations and the European Union: An Ever Stronger Partnership*, The Hague: T.M.C. Asser Press, 2006, p. 28.

57 G. de Vries, "Cooperation between the European Union and the United Nations in counterterrorism", in: Wouters, Hoffmeister and Ruys (eds.), *op. cit.*, n. 56 above, p. 307.

58 The Convention, however, does not contain a REIO clause. Accordingly, the EU was unable to become a party to it. See Article 24(3) which states "this Convention shall be open to accession by any State".

59 UNGA Resolution 66/10 on the United Nations Counter-Terrorism Centre, 7 December 2011, A/RES/66/10.

60 See Chapter II, para. II, Government of the Kingdom of Saudi Arabia Contribution Agreement to launch the United Nations Center for Counter-Terrorism (UNCCT), New York, 19 September 2011, *United Nations Juridical Yearbook*, 2011, pp. 65–69.

61 De Vries, *op. cit.*, n. 57 above, p. 309.

An example is the EU sponsorship of UNODC programmes,[62] and the cooperation of a number of its agencies, e.g. Frontex and Eurojust, with the UNODC's Terrorism Prevention Branch. Instruments are of a political nature: working arrangements[63] and memoranda of understanding enable these collaborations.[64] More concretely, cooperation primarily consists of the organisation of joint training sessions and seminars, participation in meetings and the exchange of information.[65] The EU-UN exchanges in UNODC settings are of a practical nature which allows for concrete interactions. The EU is rich in history and practice when it comes to enhancing counter-terrorism collaboration between Member States. Good practices and experiences can be shared and mutual learning enhanced. This allows for collaborations in which the UN and EU partners are to a greater extent on an equal footing.

3.3 *The EU at the UN: A Coordinated Discourse?*

Terrorism has steadily gained attention across the UN spectrum. Throughout, the EU has been able to influence global counter-terrorism processes. Still, one may wonder whether the Union has been contributing to the fullest extent possible in terms of its abilities. The answer is far from one-dimensional. Judging by its failed attempts to push for the conclusion of a comprehensive UN convention on terrorism, the EU has not been able to achieve its goals. However, reaching agreement on this document has proved to be a complicated exercise. The Union has faced considerable external opposition. On top of that,

---

62 In 2010, the EU contributed US $15.6 million. Part of the EU funds is also used by the UNODC Counter Piracy programme and its efforts to fight illicit drug trafficking in West Africa. See Press release, "UNODC Executive Director meets European Union officials and attends NATO briefing on mission to Brussels", 15 March 2011, available at: <http://www.unodc.org/unodc/en/eds-corner/March2011/unodc-executive-director-meets-european-union-officials-and-attends-nato-briefing-on-mission-to-brussels.html> (accessed 2 July 2013).

63 In April 2012, Frontex and UNODC signed such a working arrangement aimed at strengthening cooperation between the two agencies in the field of crime prevention and human security. See <http://www.unodc.org/unodc/en/frontpage/2012/April/unodc-and-eu-border-management-agency-sign-cooperation-agreement.html> (accessed 2 July 2013).

64 Eurojust and UNODC signed a memorandum of understanding, available at: <http://eurojust.europa.eu/doclibrary/Eurojustframework/agreements/MoU%20between%20Eurojust%20and%20the%20United%20Nations%20Office%20on%20Drugs%20and%20Crime%20(2010)/Eurojust-UNODC-2010-02-26-EN.pdf> (accessed 2 July 2013), entry into force: 26 February 2010.

65 See Articles 7 and 8 of the Eurojust-UNODC memorandum of understanding, 26 February 2010.

divergent views between EU Member States on particular issues, including some of the core questions such as a common definition of terrorism and the scope of the acts to be covered by it, have yet to be resolved.[66] Yet, the on-going attempts do demonstrate determination to reach a solution.[67]

It is thus all the more interesting to study how the EU is contributing to the fight against terrorism in a broader context. Which instruments are being used to achieve results in countering terrorism at the UN? Showing consistency, the EU has strongly relied upon tools of diplomacy. Especially since the entry into force of the Lisbon Treaty, the EU's toolbox has expanded to allow for increased common action.[68] This concerns, firstly, diplomacy in the strict sense. The multilateral Union Delegations in New York and Addis Ababa house specialists tasked with facilitating the fight against terrorism.[69] Secondly, and even more important, is the Union's deployment of tools of public diplomacy.

---

66 De Vries, *op. cit.*, n. 57 above, p. 307.

67 See the many statements made by the EU on this subject: e.g. Statement by Minister Michael Postl, Austrian Federal Ministry for Foreign Affairs, on behalf of the EU, Ad Hoc Committee on Terrorism, New York, 1 March 2006; and recently: "The EU remains engaged in the negotiation process of a Comprehensive Convention on International Terrorism and committed to its successful conclusion. In this regard, we would like to recall the readiness to consider the 2007 proposal without further modifications. This, however, presupposes that other delegations are willing to accept the 2007 proposal as is"; Statement on behalf of the EU and its Member States by Roland Tricot at the UN Sixth Committee, 8 October 2012, New York: "As we stated on many occasions in the past, most recently during the Sixth Committee last fall, the development of an international legal instrument such as the draft Comprehensive Convention on International Terrorism is an important endeavour of the international community to strengthen the international legal framework aimed at combating terrorist acts. Such a convention would coherently supplement the existing body of international law on terrorism"; Statement on behalf of the EU and its Member States by G. Marhic, Minister Counsellor, EU Delegation to the UN, Ad Hoc Committee established by General Assembly resolution 51/210 of 17 December 1996, 8 April 2013, New York.

68 See, among others, S. Duke, "Providing for European-Level Diplomacy after Lisbon: The Case of the European External Action Service", *The Hague Journal of Diplomacy* 4, 2009, pp. 211–233; M. Emerson *et al., Upgrading the EU's Role as Global Actor*, Brussels: CEPS, 2011, p. 144; J. Wouters, D. Coppens and B. De Meester, "The European Union's External Relations after the Lisbon Treaty", in: S. Griller and J. Ziller (eds.), *The Lisbon Treaty: EU Constitutionalism Without a Constitutional Treaty?*, Vienna: Springer, 2008, pp. 143–203.

69 The Moscow and Washington DC Union delegations deploy JHA counsellors and Europol liaison officers. Th. Renard, "EU Counterterrorism Policies and Institutions after the Lisbon Treaty", Policy Brief, *Center on Global Counterterrorism Cooperation*, September 2012.

The following paragraphs focus on how the EU is promoting these instruments within the context of the UNGA and the UNSC.

The EU Member States have a long tradition of coordinating positions in the UNGA and, if conceivable, at the UNSC.[70] Before a common position can be expressed at the international level, negotiations take place within the relevant EU bodies. Coordinating capacity lies with the relevant Council working parties: the Working Party on Terrorism (COTER; CFSP aspects of terrorism) and the Terrorist Working Group (TGW; AFSJ aspects of terrorism). Subsequently, the common position is taken to the UN and presented on behalf of the EU or on behalf of the EU and its Member States.

The merits of this practice are clear. It enables the EU to politically express its own will as well as, where appropriate, the collective will of its 28 Member States.[71] It can be argued that the consensus-building in itself is already a major success for European foreign policy.[72] In a multilateral context, coordination exercises furthermore contribute to the visibility of the EU.[73] In other words, it

---

70 F. Hoffmeister, "Outsider or Frontrunner? Recent developments under international and European law on the status of the European Union in international organizations and treaty bodies", *Common Market Law Review* 44, 2007, pp. 41–68, at pp. 65–66. See for example, recently, at the UNSC: Statement on behalf of the EU and its Member States by H. E. Th. Mayr-Harting, Head of the EU Delegation to the UN, at the Security Council Open Debate on "Threats to international peace and security caused by terrorist acts: Comprehensive approach to counter-terrorism", 15 January 2013, New York; Statement on behalf of the EU and its Member States by I. Vrailas, Deputy Head of the EU Delegation to the UN, at the Security Council Debate on Committees established pursuant to 1267 (1999)/1989 (2011), 1373 (2001) and 1540 (2004) resolutions, 14 November 2012, New York; at the UNGA and its Sixth Committee: Statement on behalf of the EU and its Member States by R. Tricot, First Counsellor, Legal Adviser, EU Delegation to the UN, at the Sixth Committee Working Group on Measures to eliminate international terrorism; remarks on the fight against nuclear terrorism in the Statement on behalf of the EU by H. E. Th. Mayr-Harting at the UN 67th General Assembly Resolution on the Report of the IAEA, 5 November 2012, New York.

71 Furthermore, often, candidate Member States as well as States in Europe's geographical surrounding align themselves with the Union's coordinated positions. As an example, see the alignment of the then acceding Member State Croatia, the Candidate Countries of the former Yugoslav Republic of Macedonia, Montenegro, Iceland, and Serbia, the Countries of the Stabilisation and Association Process and potential candidates, Albania and Bosnia and Herzegovina, as well as Ukraine, Armenia and Georgia, with the Statement made by Mayr-Harting, 15 January 2013, *op. cit.*, n. 70 above.

72 R. Dover, "From CFSP to ESDP: The EU's Foreign, Security, and Defence Policies", in M. Cini, and N. Pérez-Solórzano (eds.), *European Union Politics*, Oxford: Oxford University Press, 2010, p. 256.

73 Hoffmeister and Kuijper, *op. cit.*, n. 56 above, p. 15.

allows the EU and its Member States to be perceived as a 'bloc' by other actors in global discussions on terrorism.[74] This is where the EU can steer debates in the UNGA and its Sixth Committee. The latter bodies are strongly influenced by preferences and priorities set by Member States. Consequently, priorities that have been pre-agreed upon by a well-organized collective of States, are likely to result in leadership in multilateral settings.[75] Admittedly, measuring the direct influence of common EU positions in the UNGA is tricky.[76] No exact parameters exist to assess the EU's performance. For that reason, it is interesting to consider what happens when Member States do *not* manage to present a coordinated position.[77] Relations between the EU and its Member States at the UNGA have indeed been tested in terrorism debates. A notorious and ill-fated episode occurred in the autumn of 2011, when the UK insisted upon the delivery of statements on behalf of the 'EU and its Member States' rather than solely on behalf of the EU as a single entity. The British action brought about negative consequences for the EU's functioning in counter-terrorism debates. Due to persistent objections, the EU was not able to deliver a great number of carefully prepared declarations within the UNGA, including on counter-terrorism.[78] As a result, the EU and its Member States did not speak up on counter-terrorist initiatives for which their political support had always seemed obvious.

In the UNSC, the negotiation context is completely different due to the Council's composition and its deliberations taking place behind closed doors.[79] It has been reported that if the US, China and Russia are sitting around the UNSC table with Europeans presenting a coordinated position, bargaining

74 J. Wouters, J. Odermatt and T. Ramopoulos, "The Lisbon Treaty and the Status of the European Union in the International Arena", in: *Mediterranean Yearbook 2011*, Barcelona: IEMed 2011, p. 170.

75 P. J. Tallberg, *Leadership and Negotiation in the European Union*, Cambridge: Cambridge University Press, 2006, pp. 4–5.

76 The analysis of the performance of the EU in multilateral settings is currently understudied. Useful research tools are nevertheless provided by K. E. Jørgensen, "Analysing the performance of the European Union", in: *Jørgensen* and Laatikainen, *op. cit.*, n. 38 above, pp. 86–101; and N. Van Willigen and Y. Kleistra, "Evaluating diplomacy", *ibid.*, pp. 102–112.

77 See on split votes, E. Paasivirta and D. Porter, "EU coordination at the UN General Assembly and ECOSOC", in: Wouters, Hoffmeister and Ruys (eds.), *op. cit.*, n. 56 above, p. 45.

78 See also J. Borger, "EU anger over British stance on UN statements", *The Guardian*, 20 October 2011, available at: <http://www.guardian.co.uk/world/2011/oct/20/uk-eu-un-statements-wording> (accessed 2 July 2013).

79 France and the UK, being permanent members, hold a power of veto. Of the ten non-permanent members, up to three (and theoretically even four) EU Member States could be elected as well.

resembles "bilateral cooperation between the EU and these countries in a multilateral context".[80] In line with this finding, Verbeke argues that the critical mass of the EU in the UNSC should enable it to achieve its ambition to be a credible actor in security issues given that it is represented by, on average, four members within the UNSC.[81] Considerable practice indeed shows that EU actors increasingly co-sponsor draft resolutions and present common statements, including on terrorism and related topics.[82] Nevertheless, this may also fail to reflect the reality of the steering of debates by Member States rather than the Union. The Mali crisis serves as a recent example in which France pushed for action simultaneously in the UNSC and in the Council of the EU. French President Hollande, in his speech at the UN High-level meeting on the Sahel in September 2012, called for the UNSC to urgently meet Mali's call for an African-led force to address the terrorist threat in the northern part of the country.[83] France presented a draft resolution in the UNSC, supported by the UK, Germany and the three African members (South Africa, Morocco, and Togo), which was adopted unanimously on 12 October 2012.[84] France thus succeeded in convincing its fellow European States in the UNSC and the remaining

80 S. Biscop and E. Drieskens, "Effective Multilateralism and Collective Security: Empowering the UN", in K. V. Laatikainen and K. E. Smith (eds.), *The European Union and the United Nations: Intersecting multilateralisms*, Hampshire: Palgrave Macmillan, 2006, p. 120.

81 J. Verbeke, "EU coordination on UN Security Council matters", in: Wouters, Hoffmeister and Ruys (eds.), *op. cit.*, n. 56 above, pp. 49–60.

82 Hoffmeister and Kuijper, *op. cit.*, n. 56 above, p. 17. See also Statement on behalf of the EU and its Member States by H. E. Th. Mayr-Harting, Head of the EU Delegation to the UN, at the Security Council Open Debate on "Threats to international peace and security caused by terrorist acts: Comprehensive approach to counter-terrorism", 15 January 2013, New York; Statement on behalf of the EU by H. E. Mr. M. Palouš, Permanent Representative of the Czech Republic to the UN, Open Debate in the Security Council, Briefings by Chairmen of Subsidiary Bodies of the Security Council (Counter-Terrorism Committee, 1267/1989 Committee, and 1540 Committee), 26 May 2009, New York; Statement on behalf of the EU, H. E. Ms. K. Lintonen, Permanent Representative of Finland to the UN, UNSC, Public Meeting, Joint briefing of the Chairpersons of the Al-Qaeda/Taliban Sanctions Committee, the Counter-Terrorism Committee and the Committee established pursuant to Security Council Resolution 1540 (2004), 28 September 2006, New York.

83 Speech by F. Hollande, President of the French Republic, High-level meeting on the Sahel, New York, 26 September 2012, available at: <http://ambafrance-us.org/spip.php?article3911> (accessed 2 July 2013).

84 UNSC Resolution 2071 (2012), 12 October 2012, S/RES/2071 (2012). A follow-up resolution that was adopted unanimously in December 2012, authorised the deployment of the African-led International Support Mission to Mali (AFISMA): UNSC Resolution 2085, 20 December 2012, S/RES/2085 (2012).

Member States in the Council of the EU.[85] As such, it served as a bridge builder between the EU, its Member States and the UNSC.

In sum, to perform well at the UNGA and the UNSC, the EU and its Member States should invest in early coordination. Precisely because the EU promotes its tools of public diplomacy, it should be mindful of how it is perceived in multilateral settings.

3.4 *Informal Cooperation*

Counter-terrorism cooperation between the UN, EU and other multilateral partners also takes place outside the institutional frameworks discussed above. The reasons for this are threefold. Partaking in club-like multilateral forums has proved to be a good alternative for overcoming some of the bureaucratic hurdles associated with the UN and other international organisations. Secondly, similar to informal cooperation within institutionalised settings, meetings organised outside the UN system apply less strict participation rules, which is beneficial to non-State actors such as the EU. Finally, these informal forums often have a selected 'like-minded' membership.[86] Success can be achieved through a flexible consensus among motivated participants.

The EU and UN actors collaborate in the Global Counter-Terrorism Forum (GCTF), launched in 2011. The GCTF serves as an informal contact group that deliberately moved away from the UN to, oddly enough, discuss the carrying out of counter-terrorism regulations promulgated by the organisation.[87] The mechanism furthers the implementation of the universally agreed counter-

85 Council of the European Union, "Council conclusions on the situation in Mali 3191st Foreign Affairs Council meeting", Luxembourg, 15 October 2012, para. 2.

86 Addressing international concerns in smaller groups of like-minded States has been clearly put forward in disarmament and proliferation initiatives. The Proliferation Security Initiative (PSI) is one such multilateral response by a group of like-minded countries that tackles the proliferation of weapons of mass destruction by both States and terrorist groups. See for further reading on the PSI: J. Yoo and G. Sulmasy, "The Proliferation Security Initiative: a Model for International Cooperation", *Hofstra L. Rev.* 35, 2006, p. 405.

87 The EU is the sole international organisation to be represented. The 30 founding members of the GCTF are: Algeria, Australia, Canada, China, Colombia, Denmark, Egypt, the EU, France, Germany, India, Indonesia, Italy, Japan, Jordan, Morocco, the Netherlands, New Zealand, Nigeria, Pakistan, Qatar, Russia, Saudi Arabia, South Africa, Spain, Switzerland, Turkey, the United Arab Emirates, the United Kingdom, and the United States. See <http://www.thegctf.org> (accessed 2 July 2013).

terrorism instruments and, more broadly, complements and reinforces existing multilateral counter-terrorist efforts.[88]

Informal multilateral collaboration on the identification of the movement of terrorist finances, the review of terrorist financing techniques, and the implementation of counter-measures, occurs in the Financial Action Task Force (FATF).[89] The European Commission is a member of this network since its establishment by the 1989 G-7 Summit, and relevant UN bodies, the UNODC and the UNSC's 1373 and 1267/1989 Committees have acquired observer status.[90] FATF Recommendations strive for the criminalisation of terrorist financing offences in domestic jurisdictions—relying upon the 1999 UN Convention on the Suppression of the Financing of Terrorism—and national cooperation with the UNSC sanctions' system.[91] In its actions, the Task Force seeks the support of high level organisational partners. The taking on board of the Commission as well as other regional players provides it with an invaluable regional outreach platform.[92] Interestingly, interaction with the UN is also brought about. The FATF has been referred to in a number of UNSC Resolutions, most importantly, in Resolution 1617 which strongly urged Member States to implement the FATF recommendations on terrorist financing.[93]

---

88 See US Department of State, Global Counterterrorism Forum Fact Sheet, available at: <http://www.state.gov/r/pa/prs/ps/2011/09/172010.htm> (accessed 2 July 2013).

89 See FATF, International Standards on Combating Money Laundering and the Financing of Terrorism and Proliferation, 2012, available at: <http://www.fatfgafi.org/media/fatf/documents/recommendations/pdfs/FATF%20Recommendations%20(approved%20February%202012)%20reprint%20May%202012%20web%20version.pdf> (accessed 2 July 2013).

90 Other observing UN bodies and agencies are the International Monetary Fund (IMF) and World Bank. On the EU side, the European Bank for Reconstruction and Development (EBRD), the European Central Bank (ECB), Eurojust, and Europol have also acquired observer status.

91 Recommendations 5–7, Financial Action Task Force, "International standards on combating money laundering and the financing of terrorism & proliferation" (2012), available at: <http://www.fatf-gafi.org/media/fatf/documents/recommendations/pdfs/FATF_Recommendations.pdf> (accessed 2 July 2013).

92 N. Beekarry, "The international anti-money laundering and combating the financing of terrorism regulatory strategy: a critical analysis of compliance determinants in international law", *Nw. J. Int'l L. & Bus.* 31, 2011, p. 172.

93 Para. 7, UNSC Resolution 1617, 29 July 2005, S/RES/1617 (2005), as reiterated in para. 41 Resolution 1989 (2011). See also the references to the FATF in UNSC Resolution 1810, 25 April 2008, S/RES/1810 (2008) (taking into consideration the guidance of the FATF framework); Resolution 1929, 9 June 2010, S/RES/1929 (2010) (welcoming the guidance issued by the FATF to assist States in implementing their financial obligations); Resolution

Following the establishment of the FATF, the G-7/8 has remained active in combating international terrorism. Since 1977, the EU/EC has been officially represented at every G-7/G8 summit. Yearly summits bring together Heads of State and Government as well as the presidents of the European Commission and European Council, respectively. Ministerial meetings are also organised gathering ministers in their respective fields of competence and EU civil servants.[94] In 1995, world leaders adopted a set of principles to combat terrorism at the Halifax Summit. The standards were further developed at the Ottawa Ministerial on Terrorism (December 1995) and at the Lyon Summit (June 1996), and endorsed at the Paris Summit (July 1996).[95] *Ad hoc* counter-terrorism experts meetings and conferences have been organised regularly since then. The Group of Twenty, for its part, has mainly remained preoccupied with the fight against terrorist financing. In 2001, a G-20 Action Plan on Terrorist Financing was adopted, in which implementation of the relevant UNSC Resolutions and international standards set by the FATF was aimed for.[96]

1977, 20 April 2011, S/RES/1977 (2011) (taking into consideration the guidance of the FATF framework); Resolution 2094, 7 March 2013, S/RES/2094 (2013) (welcoming the FATF's new Recommendation on targeted financial sanctions related to proliferation). See also Commission on Narcotic Drugs Resolution 39/5 (1996), E/CN.7/1996/RES/5 on the encouragement of each Member State to require the establishment by banks and other financial institutions of customer identification policies and to broaden anti-money-laundering measures, and of the United Nations International Drug Control Programme to strengthen cooperation with the Financial Action Task Force.

94 See J. Huigens and A. Niemann, "The G8 1/2: the EU's contested and ambiguous actorness in the G8", *Cambridge Review of International Affairs* 24, 2011, pp. 629–657; A. Hervé, "The Participation of the European Union in Global Economic Governance Fora", *European Law Journal* 18, 2012, pp. 143–161.

95 G-8, Ministerial Declaration on Countering Terrorism, 12 December 1995, Ottawa, available at: <http://www.g8.utoronto.ca/terrorism/terror96.htm>; G-8, Declaration on Terrorism, 27 June 1996, Lyon, available at: <http://www.g8.utoronto.ca/summit/1996lyon/terrorism.html> and G-7/P-8 Ministerial Conference on Terrorism, Agreement on 25 Measures, 30 July 1996, Paris, available at: <http://www.g8.utoronto.ca/terrorism/terror25.htm>. (all accessed 2 July 2013). See for further reading S. Gstöhl, "Informal governance and the G8", in: T. Christiansen and Ch. Neuhold (eds.), *International Handbook on Informal Governance*, Cheltenham: Edward Elgar Publishing, 2012, pp. 255–275 and A. Niemann and J. Huigens, "The European Union's role in the G8: a principal-agent perspective", *Journal of European Public Policy* 18, 2011, pp. 420–442.

96 Communiqué, "G20 Action Plan on Terrorist Financing", Ottawa, 17 November 2001, available at: <http://www.g20.utoronto.ca/2001/2001communique.html#action> (accessed 2 July 2013).

This overview shows a positive relationship between the EU's aspirations and counter-terrorism activities carried out by informal networks. Participating in the networks complements the EU's external counter-terrorism action. In the informal groups described above, a general tendency exists to focus on sensitive issues. As well as implementation concerns that are taken on board, the topic of combatting the financing of terrorism stands out. Exchanging information on money flows necessarily takes place in a sphere of confidence. In this respect, the EU's participation proves useful to monitor some of the most high-level international interactions in the field.

4 The Contribution of the EU to the Global Fight against Terrorism

This section examines concrete synergies resulting from diverse exchanges between the UN and the EU. The analysis will focus upon three critical counter-terrorism issues: the streamlining of counter-terrorism action, the definition of terrorism and the sanctioning of terrorists and terrorist groups. The singling out of these topical issues will allow us to further observe different modes of interaction between the EU and the UN.

4.1 *Coordinating Terrorism Action*

A relatively simple, yet effective, way for the EU to cooperate with the UN is by sharing good practices. As indicated, mutual learning has been included in the EU-UNODC cooperation. However, it can also be applied to confront problems encountered by UN bodies that have been dealt with by the EU as well. The overview presented in section 2 discerned parallelisms in the layered counter-terrorist activities of both organisations, especially with regard to the difficulties experienced in governing the whole.[97] As explained, the fight against terrorism has involved multiple legal instruments. Likewise, powers have been assigned to various actors. Both the UN and the EU have been struggling to synergise action across policy fields into a political-strategic framework. This holds true in particular since multiple legal bases are maintained in the EU and the UN systems to fight terrorism in all its different guises.

97 E. Herlin-Karnell, "The EU as a promoter of values and the European Global Project", *German L.J.* 13, 2012, p. 1240.

Nevertheless, in both organisations, the desire was felt—at least in strategic terms—to reconnect counter-terrorism initiatives.[98] The topic was addressed by the UN and the EU, almost simultaneously and in a rather similar way. In 2005, for the first time,[99] the EU developed a 'European Union Counter-Terrorism Strategy', based upon four pillars ('Prevent', 'Protect', 'Pursue' and 'Respond').[100] Shortly thereafter, in 2006, the UNGA decided to adopt a Global Counter-Terrorism Strategy, which set out the framework for the collective effort of the UN system on countering terrorism.[101] At the global level, furthermore, the EU suggested that the UNSC appoint a UN system-wide coordinator on counter-terrorism, based on positive experiences at the regional level. The position would mirror that of its own counter-terrorism coordinator, to give a central focus and higher visibility to counter-terrorism efforts within the UN. Such efforts otherwise tend to be undermined by the diverging objectives of the large number of agencies and bodies involved.[102]

4.2 *Defining Terrorism*

Global legal definitions of terrorism are rare if not non-existent.[103] In fact, only moderate attempts have been undertaken to remedy this. The UN Special Tribunal for Lebanon has defined 'transnational terrorism' as a customary international crime.[104] UNSC Resolution 1566 (2004) included a description of

---

98 See e.g. Council of the European Union, The European Union Strategy for Combating Radicalisation and Recruitment to Terrorism, Brussels, 24 November 2005, available at: <register.consilium.eu.int/pdf/en/05/st14/st14781-re01.en05.pdf> (accessed 2 July 2013).

99 See J. Argomaniza, "Post-9/11 institutionalisation of European Union counter-terrorism: Emergence, acceleration and inertia", *European Security* 18, 2009, pp. 155–156.

100 Council of the European Union, The European Union Counter-Terrorism Strategy, Brussels, 30 November 2005, available at: <register.consilium.eu.int/pdf/en/05/st14/st14469-re04.en05.pdf> (accessed 2 July 2013) (hereinafter: "EU Counter-Terrorism Strategy").

101 UNGA Resolution 60/288, adopted on 8 September 2006, and its review Resolutions 62/272 and 64/297. For an overview of the most recent counterterrorism activities, see UNGA, United Nations Global Counter-Terrorism Strategy: activities of the United Nations system in implementing the Strategy, Report of the Secretary-General, 4 April 2012, A/66/762.

102 EU Counter-Terrorism Coordinator, *op. cit.*, n. 36 above, p. 7.

103 B. Saul, "Legislating from a Radical Hague: the United Nations Special Tribunal for Lebanon Invents an International Crime of Transnational Terrorism", *Leiden Journal of International Law* 24, 2011, p. 685.

104 The Appeals Chamber identified a peace-time customary international law crime of terrorism consisting of three elements: (i) the perpetration of a criminal act (such as

acts of terrorism that has been used for international cooperation purposes.[105] Prior to this, the 1999 Financing Convention already contained a fairly generic definition, which later on served as a model for the operational part of Resolution 1373.[106] The Convention criminalises the providing and collecting of funds for acts specified in the many UN conventions and protocols countering terrorism, as well as:

> Any other act intended to cause death or serious bodily injury to a civilian, or to any other person not taking an active part in the hostilities in a situation of armed conflict, when the purpose of such act, by its nature

---

murder, kidnapping, hostage-taking, arson, and so on), or threatening such an act; (ii) the intent to spread fear among the population (which would generally entail the creation of public danger) or directly or indirectly coerce a national or international authority to take some action, or to refrain from taking it; (iii) a transnational element: see UN Special Tribunal for Lebanon, *op. cit.*, n. 13 above, § 85. The Tribunal's definition was subsequently applied to interpret domestic terrorism offences under Lebanese law. It must be noted that legal academics have questioned the reasoning of the Tribunal, and even considered it to be a case of disguised legislative activism; Saul, *op. cit.*, n. 103 above, p. 678.

105 UNSC Resolution 1566, 8 October 2004, S/RES/1566 (2004), § 3. While not expressly framed as a definition of terrorism, the Resolution recalls "that criminal acts, including against civilians, committed with the intent to cause death or serious bodily injury, or taking of hostages, with the purpose to provoke a state of terror in the general public or in a group of persons or particular persons, intimidate a population or compel a government or an international organization to do or to abstain from doing any act, which constitute offences within the scope of and as defined in the international conventions and protocols relating to terrorism, are under no circumstances justifiable by considerations of a political, philosophical, ideological, racial, ethnic, religious or other similar nature, and calls upon all States to prevent such acts and, if not prevented, to ensure that such acts are punished by penalties consistent with their grave nature". Subsequently, this description of terrorism, together with its three cumulative characteristics, was endorsed by UN Special Rapporteur on counter terrorism and human rights Scheinin in his report on the promotion and protection of human rights and fundamental freedoms while countering terrorism, E/CN.4/2006/98 (2005), §37. See also the references to, as well as the proposed modifications of, the definition in the report on the UN High-level Panel on Threats, Challenges and Change, "A More Secure World: Our Shared Responsibility", A/59/565 (2004), paragraph 164(d); UN Secretary-General, In larger freedom: towards development, security and human rights for all, UNGA (59th Session), 21 Mar 2005, § 91.

106 E. J. Husabø, "The Interaction between Global, Regional and National Regulation in the Definition of Terrorism", in: A. Follesdal, R. A. Wessel and J. Wouters (eds.), *Multilevel Regulation and the EU: The Interplay between Global, European and National Normative Processes*, Leiden/Boston: Martinus Nijhoff Publishers, 2008, p. 171.

> or context, is to intimidate a population, or to compel a government or an international organization to do or to abstain from doing any act.[107]

The Financing Convention and even more explicitly, UNSC Resolution 1373 (2001), have prompted States to alter national definitions, as well as corresponding judicial procedures. Because of the rather vague description of acts of terrorism, there have been inconsistencies in the domestic implementation of the Resolution.[108] More generally, the non-existence of a generic definition of terrorism has encouraged the cherry picking of definitions: legislators and judges have transferred definitions agreed upon in a rather specific context from the regional or national level to the global one and visa versa.[109] In doing so, they engage in a delicate exercise. Classifying criminals and offences as terrorist may have far-reaching legal repercussions for individuals.[110] The former Special Rapporteur on the promotion and protection of human rights and fundamental freedoms while countering terrorism, Martin Scheinin, has warned that

> In the absence of a universally agreed definition of terrorist acts, some States have included in their national counter-terrorism legislation a broad range of acts which do not, in terms of severity, purpose or aim, reach the threshold of objectively being considered terrorist acts, or the threshold required for exclusion from refugee status.[111]

The current legal disarray can be resolved by increasing efforts at the UNGA to produce a global definition of terrorism. The EU has clearly taken on the mission of advancing negotiations. Continuously, the Union and its Member States have made use of their speaking rights to advocate the development of such a definition.[112] In this matter the EU can rely on its own experiences

---

107 Article 2(1) Financing Convention.

108 S. Setty, "What's in a Name? How Nations Define Terrorism Ten Years after 9/11", *University of Pennsylvania Journal of International Law* 33, 2011, pp. 1–64, discusses the implementation of the resolution in the US, UK and India.

109 See Husabø, *op. cit.*, n. 106 above.

110 See R. Young, "Defining Terrorism: The Evolution of Terrorism as a Legal Concept in International Law and Its Influence on Definitions in Domestic Legislation", *B.C. Int'l & Comp. L. Rev.* 29, 2006, pp. 23–103.

111 UNGA, Report of the Special Rapporteur on the promotion and protection of human rights and fundamental freedoms while countering terrorism, A/62/263, para. 66.

112 Statement at the formal plenary session of the UNGA by H. E. Mr. J. M. Hoscheit, Permanent Representative of Luxembourg to the UN, on behalf of the EU, who stated that "the EU

in defining terrorism and harmonising national laws. The Council Framework Decision of 13 June 2002 on combating terrorism, which was last amended in 2008, established a definition of 'terrorist offences'.[113] Earlier, in December 2001, the Council had already released Common Position 931 on the application of specific measures to combat terrorism including a definition of terrorist acts and persons, groups and entities involved in those acts.[114] Representatives of the EU and its Member States have taken this know-how to the UNGA to argue in favour of establishing "an operational definition of the perpetration of a terrorist act rather than attempting to define the phenomenon of terrorism in all its complexity".[115] This approach clearly resembles the way in which agreement was sought between EU Member States when they considered the same topic.

The EU's efforts peaked in 2005, when it made the elaboration of a universal definition of terrorism a priority for the 60th General Assembly.[116] The 2005 campaign was supported by EU statements in a variety of UN meetings that referred to this aim.[117] Regrettably, rather quickly, the drive to push for a defini-

considers that agreeing on a definition of terrorism and concluding a comprehensive international convention on terrorism are key elements", 6 April 2005. The statement on behalf of the EU, by H. E. Sir E. Jones Parry, Permanent Representative of the UK to the UN, at the Informal meeting of the plenary to discuss the revised text of the Draft Outcome Document of the High-level Plenary Meeting of the General Assembly, 28 July 2005, UNGA, New York, put it this way: "we must agree to conclude a comprehensive convention on international terrorism, at the latest during the sixtieth session of the General Assembly, including a legal definition of terrorist acts".

113 Council Framework Decision of 13 June 2002 on combating terrorism (2002/475/JHA), 13 June 2002, *OJ*, 2002, L 164/3. In 2008, three more offences linked to terrorism were added to this list: public provocation, recruitment, and training for terrorism. See Council Framework Decision 2008/919/JHA of 28 November 2008 amending Framework Decision 2002/475/JHA on combating terrorism, *OJ*, 2008, L 330/21. See for a further analysis *inter alia* E. Dumitriu, "The E.U.'s Definition of Terrorism: The Council Framework Decision on Combating Terrorism", *German Law Journal* 5, 2004, pp. 585–601; Wouters and Naert, "The European Union and 'September 11'", *op. cit.*, n. 24 above.

114 Council Common Position of 27 December 2001 on the application of specific measures to combat terrorism (2001/931/CFSP), *OJ*, 2001, L 344/93.

115 Statement by Mr. P. Rietjens on behalf of the EU in the Working group created by Resolution 51/210 of the General Assembly of 17 December 1996, "Measures to eliminate international terrorism", 15 October 2001, New York.

116 EU Priorities for the 60th Session of the UNGA, Brussels, 22 July 2005.

117 See the Statement at the informal plenary session of the UNGA to continue an exchange of views on the recommendations contained in the report of the High Level Panel on Threats, Challenges and Change (HLP) by H. E. Mr. J. M. Hoscheit, Permanent Representative of

tion ebbed away again. Although still prioritised by the EU at the 2006 session of the UNGA,[118] few statements referred to it in the following period. The finding of a universal agreement seemed 'distant'.[119] A strategic prioritisation by the EU nevertheless remains in order. If not as a matter of principle or legal obligation,[120] the EU should pursue legal clarity out of self-interest. Protection gaps affect the EU internally and externally, as will be explained in the following paragraphs.

For over a decade now, terrorism has been recognized as a special offence in all EU Member States. The 2002 common definition was used in subsequent Common Positions and Decisions on the operational part of counter-terrorism action and for the adoption of mutual recognition laws.[121] Even if the European system generally functions well, there is room for improvement. EU Member States still struggle to domestically consistently implement definitions of terrorist offences.[122] The building of a global consensus may further

---

Luxembourg to the UN, on behalf of the EU, 27 January 2005, who explained that "the EU shares the belief of the HLP that achieving consensus in the framework of the GA on an overall definition of terrorism would be highly valuable"; Statement by H. E. J. Freeman, Head of the UK Delegation to the Biennial Meeting of States to consider the implementation of the UN programme of action on small arms and light weapons, on behalf of the EU, 14 July 2005, New York, thanking the UNSC for including a proposal on the agreement of a common definition in his report. This discussion was also addressed by the EU in the UNSC: see Statement to the UNSC on the Counter-Terrorism Committee (CTC) by Mr. M. Bichler, Deputy Permanent Representative of Luxembourg to the UN, on behalf of the EU, 18 January 2005, New York, who welcomed "the particular value of achieving, as soon as possible, consensus on a legal definition of terrorism". In the same sense, see EU Presidency Statement at the UN 2005 World Summit, 14 September 2005, New York.

118 See EU Priorities for the 61st UN General Assembly, 18 July 2006, Brussels.

119 B. Ferrero-Waldner, European Commissioner for External Relations and European Neighbourhood Policy, "The External Dimension of the Fight Against International Terrorism", Statement to the European Parliament plenary session, Strasbourg, 14 February 2007: "While the UN has not yet agreed on a definition and while such an agreement seems distant, I would like to recall that relevant universal conventions and protocols provide a common legal understanding of what constitutes an act of terrorism".

120 See Articles 3(5) and 21(1) TEU.

121 O. Bures, "EU Counterterrorism Policy: A Paper Tiger?", *Terrorism and Political Violence* 18, 2006, p. 67.

122 See, for example, NGO criticism related to France's definition of terrorist organisations: "The broad definition and expansive interpretation of *association de malfaiteurs* translate into a low standard of proof for decisions to arrest suspects or to place them under investigation by a judge. Indeed, casting a wide net to ensnare large numbers of people who might have some connection with an alleged terrorist network has been one of

benefit European harmonisation efforts. It may result in the revision of the internal legal framework or at least broaden the possibilities of cooperation with third countries.

Important questions arise regarding the current stance of the EU and its Member States on the design of a global definition. In earlier statements, the Union and its Member States argued in favour of an operational definition. This could be translated into a set of minimum rules on terrorism that UN Member States would be obliged to adopt and respect. Offences would be listed as terrorist acts to be criminalised domestically. In theory, this would benefit the further development of global mutual assistance programmes, and as such, extend the EU systems in place to third countries. However, problems of recognition would presumably arise. It seems unlikely that UN Member States would recognize each other's broad national definitions. In the context of increased mutual recognition programmes, a tighter global definition would seem beneficial. Such a definition would also include a restriction upon what individual States may define as terrorism. It is highly uncertain, though, whether at this point in time sufficient political will can be found within the EU to defend such a position, let alone, whether fellow UN Member States would be ready to accept it. Once again, EU Member States have to coordinate in order to steer debates within the UNGA in a direction that benefits the EU as a whole.

Secondly, the 2013 Mali intervention illustrates how the EU and its Member States are affected by the lack of a universal definition in their external policies. Definitional difficulties concerned the categorisation of terrorist organisations, their command and control structures, and criteria for membership.[123] UNSC Resolution 2085 authorised the deployment of the African-led International Support Mission to Mali (AFISMA) in light of the "urgent need to counter the increasing terrorist threat" in the country.[124] Subsequently, and at the request of the local government, France intervened in Mali to fight

---

the characteristics of investigations into *association de malfaiteurs*". See Human Rights Watch, "Preempting Justice: Counterterrorism Laws and Procedures in France", 2008, available at: <http://www.hrw.org/reports/2008/france0708/france0708web.pdf> p. 2 (accessed at 2 July 2013); and UNGA, Report of the Special Rapporteur on the promotion and protection of human rights and fundamental freedoms while countering terrorism, A/63/223, that discusses the definition of terrorist crimes in Spanish statutory law and judicial practice.

123 UNGA, Special Rapporteur on the promotion and protection of human rights and fundamental freedoms while countering terrorism, 26 September 2012, A/67/396, p. 11.

124 UNSC Res. 2085, recital 3; Security Council Press Statement on Mali, SC/10878, available at: <http://www.un.org/News/Press/docs/2013/sc10878.doc.htm> (accessed 2 July 2013).

'terrorism' and 'terrorist groups'. This terminology was copied by the EU's High Representative.[125] However, France encountered legal obstacles in defining terrorist groups in Mali.[126] In the absence of a globally accepted definition, French officials referred to UNSC Resolution 2085's general mandate.[127] The latter Resolution stated that jihadist rebels were to be considered 'terrorist organisations' because of their listing under the UNSC's sanctions regime.[128] Two of the groups involved in the Mali conflict had indeed been subjected to sanctioning by the international community prior to the 2013 intervention.[129] However, other groupings operating in the conflict had not.[130] Referring to

---

125 In its official statement, president Hollande repeated that "France—at the request of the President of Mali and in compliance with the Charter of the United Nations—has committed herself to supporting the Malian army in the face of the terrorist aggression threatening the whole of West Africa" and that "France has no special interest in this operation other than to protect a friendly country, and no goal other than to fight terrorism". See Statement by M. François Hollande, President of the Republic, following the select defence council, Paris, 12 January 2013. See also Statement by EU High Representative Ashton on the situation in Mali, Brussels, 11 January 2013, A 8/13, in which she states that "I am very concerned about the military movements initiated by terrorist groups in the north of Mali and condemn in the strongest terms their attacks against Malian forces and the occupation of the city of Konna". See also Council conclusions on Mali, 3217th Foreign Affairs Council meeting, Brussels, 17 January 2013.

126 Legal problems arose in terms of interpreting the UNSC Resolution 2085 rather than in terms of criminal prosecution purposes.

127 See statement by President Hollande, *op. cit.*, n. 125 above, and Press conference given by Laurent Fabius, Minister of Foreign Affairs, Paris, 11 January 2013.

128 See UNSC Res. 2085, para. 2: "Demands that Malian rebel groups cut off all ties to terrorist organizations, notably Al-Qaeda in Islamic Maghreb (AQIM) and associated groups, and take concrete and visible steps to this effect, takes note of the listing of Movement of Unity and Jihad in Western Africa (MUJWA) on the Al-Qaeda sanctions list established and maintained by the Committee pursuant to resolutions 1267 (1999) and 1989 (2011) and further reiterates its readiness to continue to adopt further targeted sanctions, under the above-mentioned regime, against those rebel groups and individuals who do not cut off all ties to Al-Qaeda and associated groups, including AQIM and MUJWA".

129 Available at: <http://www.un.org/sc/committees/1267/AQList.htm> (accessed 2 July 2013).

130 The National Movement for the Liberation of Azawad (MNLA) and the Harakat Ansar al-Dine are such groups. See BBC, "Mali crisis: Key players", 24 January 2013; The Economist, "Jihad in Africa: The danger in the desert", 26 January 2013. For further reading, see also Th. Christakis and K. Bannelier, "French Military Intervention in Mali: It's Legal but . . . Why?", *Blog of the European Journal of International Law*, 25 January 2013, available at: <http://www.ejiltalk.org/french-military-intervention-in-mali-its-legal-but-why-part-i/#more-7483> (accessed 2 July 2013).

these groups as terrorist on this ground is therefore at odds with the current state of international law. The European definitions equally were not successfully applied. Firstly, France was unable to rely on the common European definition of terrorist acts and actors as these have a limited territorial scope.[131] Secondly, for unknown reasons, neither France nor EU actors had explicitly sought recourse to the definition introduced by 2001 Common Position 931. Given the external dimension of the classification problem, this would have made sense: the scope of the Common Position is less restricted than that of the Framework Decision.

The much desired legal certainty in this area justifies EU efforts working towards a global definition. In this regard, it should be borne in mind that, even in the case of an agreed definition, disagreements may exist about how to apply and interpret it. Nevertheless, terrorism laws can only be advanced when attempts are undertaken to adopt a legal framework. The best way for the EU to influence this process is to breathe new life into the discussions by applying its public diplomacy tools. Therefore, EU Member States must first decide on their position on the matter. Subsequently, reviving the 2005 campaign of repeated statements and the explicit prioritising of the matter in the UNGA seems a preferable way forward.

4.3 *Sanctioning Terrorists and Terrorist Groups*

Often portrayed as being two distinct and irreconcilable regimes, the EU's constitutional framework faces complications when implementing sanctions imposed upon individuals and entities by the 1267/1989 Committee.[132] The frictions between the global and regional level have become a prime example

---

131 Article 9 of the 2002 Framework Decision on combating terrorism covers terrorist acts committed against the EU and its Member States. An additional condition is added for the application of the Framework Decision to the case of terrorist acts targeting a third country or an international organisation: it must be perpetrated on the EU's territory, by a European national/resident or for the benefit of a legal person established in the EU.

132 To implement the relevant decisions of the UNSC that seek to list and sanction individuals and organisations, the Council enacted Regulation No 881/2002 of 27 May 2002 imposing certain specific restrictive measures directed against certain persons and entities associated with Usama bin Laden, the Al-Qaeda network and the Taliban, *OJ*, 2002, L 139/9, most recently amended by Commission Implementing Regulation (EU) No 439/2013 of 13 May 2013 amending for the 192nd time Council Regulation (EC) No 881/2002 imposing certain specific restrictive measures directed against certain persons and entities associated with the Al Qaida network, *OJ*, 2013, L 129/34. For further reading, see M. den Boer, "Soft, Smart and Strategic. The International Dimension of EU Action in the Fight Against Terrorism", in: M. Cremona, J. Monar and S. Poli (eds.), *The External*

of a conflict of (interpretations of) human rights obligations and the rule of law under different legal orders.[133] Nevertheless, a certain degree of cross-fertilisation of the interpretation of underlying concepts—e.g. due process guarantees—between the UN and EU can also be observed. Counter-terrorism measures taken by the EU in the aftermath of 9/11 were moderated in favour of human rights guarantees in the years that followed.[134] Especially particular cases where measures generally had gone too far, most notably the counter-terrorism sanctions regime, have evolved in response to the case-law. This subsection examines how the EU has, to some extent, simultaneously succeeded in subjecting the UNSC sanctions regime to mechanisms that lessen the potential for abuse.

Initially, the UNCTC's policy on human rights was that it considered this regime to be outside the scope of its mandate.[135] The UN listing of terrorists was not based on general, published, criteria nor did it provide for the right to appeal such decisions. Different aspects of this practice were found to be clearly incompatible with European (and international) human rights standards. Over the years, counter-terrorism restrictive measures imposed by the UNSC have been the object of extensive case law before the EU courts.[136] More

---

Dimension of the European Union's Area of Freedom, Security and Justice, P.I.E. Peter Lang, 2011, Cahiers du Collège d'Europe 13, 2011, pp. 341–363.

133 But see Opinion of AG Bot, *op. cit.*, n. 42 above, para. 85: "The mutual confidence which must exist between the European Union and the United Nations is justified by the fact that the values concerning respect for fundamental rights are shared by those two organisations". Likewise, in its 2013 *Kadi* Judgement, the CJEU refers to fundamental rights and freedoms as being shared values of the UN and the EU. According to the Court, judicial review is indispensable to ensure a fair balance between the maintenance of international peace and security and the protection of those shared values. See Para. 131 CJEU *Kadi II, op. cit*, n. 45 above.

134 See, for example, on data protection, the meeting of certain privacy protection concerns raised by the European Parliament in the latest versions of the PNR and the SWIFT agreements with the USA. See for experiences in the UN: Setty, *op. cit.*, n. 108 above, p. 18.

135 As the first Chairman in a briefing to the UNSC on 18 January 2002 stated: "The Counter-Terrorism Committee is mandated to monitor the implementation of resolution 1373 (2001). Monitoring performance against other international conventions, including human rights law, is outside the scope of the Counter-Terrorism Committee's mandate. But we will remain aware of the interaction with human rights concerns, and we will keep ourselves briefed as appropriate. It is, of course, open to other organisations to study States' reports and take up their content in other forums".

136 The European Court of Justice (CJEU) has been fully involved, especially when it considered Committee 1373 sanctions, initiated and carried out by Member States in the driving seat, as compared to 1267/1989 Committee sanctions.

concretely, targeted individuals have invoked the flaws in the protection of human rights and judicial standards commonly accepted under EU law.[137] The *Kadi* saga exemplifies these tensions. In its 2008 *Kadi I* judgment, the Court of Justice of the European Union (CJEU) found EC regulations based on listings under UNSC Resolution 1267 to be in breach of the right to be informed of the reasons on the basis of which the sanction was imposed and the right to be heard.[138] Under the UNSC Resolution 1373 regime, one may recall the *Sison*[139] and the *OMPI, PMOI I* and *II* cases.[140] In Resolution 1373 cases, the CTC does not identify the persons or groups subject to fund-freezing measures. Instead, it is for the UN Member States (or in these cases, the Council) to do so. Sanctions against Mr. Sison were annulled for a lack of reason-giving and, subsequently, on the basis that Sison had never been investigated, prosecuted or convicted for any specific act of terrorism. Similarly, in the *OMPI* and *PMOI* cases, the Court reiterated the EU's threshold for human rights guarantees when imposing autonomous sanctions.

This strong stand by the EU courts, as well as repeated calls by EU Member States and NGOs to adopt due process standards as well as a criminal justice approach, have influenced the UNSC's position. A more proactive approach was adopted to meet the most fundamental critical claims raised in these court cases.[141] The UNSC broke new ground in terms of respect for the rights of the defence with the adoption of Resolutions 1822 (2008), 1904 (2009) and

137 For further reading on this, see Ch. Eckes, "EU counter-terrorist sanctions against individuals: problems and perils", *European Foreign Affairs Review* 17, 2012, pp. 133–156.

138 CJEU *Kadi I, op. cit.*, n. 41 above. For further reading, see G. de Búrca, "The EU, the European Court of Justice and the International Legal Order after Kadi", *Harvard International Law Journal* 51, 2009, pp. 1–50.

139 Case T-47/03, *Jose Maria Sison v. Council of the European Union* [2007] ECR II-73; Case T-341/07, *Sison v. Council* [2011] ECR II-7915. The Council had adopted a decision to include the name of Mr Sison, a Philippine national whose refugee status was rejected on the grounds that he was included in the list of persons whose assets are frozen under UNSC Res. 1373. Sison appealed the Dutch decision to add him to their 'assets freezing list' on 13 August 2002, which had been followed by a similar decision by the Council on 28 October 2002 and the re-adoption of sanctions in 2007. The General Court, however, reasoned in 2011 that the Dutch asylum appeal decisions were concerned with the legality of the rejection of the asylum procedure, not the terrorism allegations.

140 Case T-228/02, *Organisation des Modjahedines du peuple d'Iran v Council* [2006] ECR II-5665 ["*OMPI*"]; Case T-256/07, *People's Mojahedin Organization of Iran v Council* [2008] ECR II-3019 ["*PMOI I*"]; Case T-284/08, *People's Mojahedin Organization of Iran v Council* [2008] ECR II-3487 ["*PMOI II*"].

141 C. H. Powell, "The United Nations Security Council, Terrorism and the Rule of Law", in: V. V. Ramraj (ed.), *Global Anti-terrorism Law and Policy*, Cambridge: Cambridge University Press, 2012, p. 21; Opinion of AG Bot, *op. cit.*, n. 42 above, para. 81.

1989 (2011).[142] Listing decisions now contain references to the importance of upholding human rights. These formal notifications are supplemented with substantial ones: an—admittedly basic[143]—statement of the reasons why someone has been listed is also provided.[144] In addition, general criteria for listing someone have been published to improve transparency in the listing process.[145] The most recent positive development was the creation, in 2009, of the function of an Ombudsperson in the 1267/1989 Committee as a direct consequence of the CJEU's 2008 *Kadi* judgment and lobbying by the Union and its Member States.[146] The Office of the Ombudsperson contributes to the provision of fairness and transparency, thus improving the Committee's

---

142 See also UN Security Council, Al-Qaeda Sanctions Committee, Guidelines of the Committee for the Conduct of Its Work, 30 November 2011.

143 Eckes, "The Case of Counter-Terrorist Sanctions", *op. cit.*, n. 38, p. 175.

144 UNSC Resolution 1735 (2006), S/RES/1735, para. 5: "Decides that, when proposing names to the Committee for inclusion on the Consolidated List, States shall [...] provide a statement of case; the statement of case should provide as much detail as possible on the basis(es) for the listing, including: (i) specific information supporting a determination that the individual or entity meets the criteria above; (ii) the nature of the information and (iii) supporting information or documents that can be provided; States should include details of any connection between the proposed designee and any currently listed individual or entity". See also UNSC Resolution 1822 (2008), S/RES/1822, para. 13, which directs the Res. 1267/1989 Sanctions Committee, after a name is added to its list, to make accessible on the Committee's website a narrative summary of reasons for listing for the corresponding entry or entries on the list.

145 See UNSC Resolution 1988 (2011), para. 3, for entities and other groups and undertakings associated with the Taliban; UNSC Resolution 1989 (2011), S/RES/1989, paras. 4–5, for entities and other groups and undertakings associated with Al-Qaeda. In its 2005 Resolution 1617, the UNSC had already provided clearer criteria as to what the term 'associated with' means. See, however, Szewczyk, who questions whether the wider purpose that the Council should serve can be implemented procedurally, for example, by providing criteria. He argues that "those problems would not be alleviated simply through clearer communication": B. M. J. Szewczyk, "Variable Multipolarity and U.N. Security Council Reform", *Harvard International Law Journal* 53, 2012, p. 488.

146 The Office of the Ombudsperson was established pursuant to UNSC Resolution 1904 (2009) and its mandate enhanced pursuant to UNSC Resolution 1989 (2011). As the Ombudsperson has acknowledged: "The decision of the ECJ, coming at the culmination of ongoing criticism—academically, politically and otherwise—as to the lack of a fair and transparent process, led directly to the adoption of resolution 1904 (2009) and the establishment of the Office of the Ombudsperson". See K. Prost, "Lecture at the Institute of Legal Research on the invitation of the Ministry of Foreign Affairs and the national autonomous University of Mexico", 24 June 2011, p. 4, available at: <http://www.un.org/en/sc/ombudsperson/pdfs/Mexico%20Presentation%20-%2024%20June%202011%20(English).pdf.> (accessed 2 July 2013).

overall effectiveness and legitimacy. It was Austria's Permanent Representative to the UN and then Chair of the Sanctions Committee, Thomas Mayr-Harting, who stated that this body "improved the procedures of the sanctions regime in terms of due process".[147] An informal group of like-minded States, including six EU Member States,[148] strongly pushed for the establishment of the office and the procedures that came with it. The group's spokesman referred to these as being "fair and clear procedures for placing individuals and entities on sanctions lists and for removing them, as well as for granting humanitarian exemptions". The like-minded group furthermore indirectly referred to the EU's contribution when acknowledging that the improvements contained in the Resolution "corresponded to concerns of Group's members and regional organizations".[149] In this area, the Union and its Member States have been able to export rule of law mechanisms to the global level. In individual cases, the Office of the Ombudsperson has indeed been rather successful in better linking the global and regional legal systems. It even brought about a delisting decision in the—for the EU—symbolic *Kadi* case on 5 October 2012, following its extensive report and the delisting request submitted.[150]

While the new dynamics should be welcomed, a number of remarks are in order. Firstly, the UNSC still does not provide petitioners with an independent review mechanism nor an effective remedy.[151] The function of an Ombudsperson, although most likely beneficial in individual cases, cannot be confused with that of a judicial body.[152] The review procedures do not

147 Press release on Security Council Resolution 1904 (Press Release), 17 December 2009, available at: <http://www.un.org/News/Press/docs/2009/sc9825.doc.htm> (accessed 2 July 2013).

148 The group consisted of Belgium, Costa Rica, Denmark, Germany, Finland, Lichtenstein, the Netherlands, Norway, Sweden and Switzerland.

149 See Press release, UNSC, 6247th Meeting, "Security Council amends United Nations Al-Qaida/Taliban sanctions regime, authorizes appointment of ombudsperson to handle delisting issues", SC/9825.

150 UNSC Press Release, SC/10785, "Security Council Al-Qaida Sanctions Committee deletes entry of Yasin Abdullah Ezzedine Qadi from its list", 5 October 2012. The EU decision to delist Kadi followed a week later: see Commission Implementing Regulation (EU) No 933/2012 of 11 October 2012 amending for the 180th time Council Regulation (EC) No 881/2002 imposing certain specific restrictive measures directed against certain persons and entities associated with the Al Qaida network, *OJ*, 2012, L 278/11.

151 G. L. Willis, "Security Council targeted sanctions, due process and the 1267 Ombudsperson", *Georgetown Journal of International Law* 42, 2011, p. 688.

152 The Ombudsperson sees it this way: "In my opinion, the dialogue process and the preparation of the report, as they are operating in practice, bring a form of 'independent review' to the 1267 regime. It is, of course, not a review of any Security Council or

establish which standard of review applies nor state with whom the burden of proof rests.[153] The Ombudsperson furthermore operates within the political context of the UNSC under an essentially limited mandate. Solely Committee 1267/1989 decisions in the Al Qaida regime can be examined, not those taken in the Taliban regime, nor those taken by any other Sanctions Committee.[154] However, the like-minded States are pushing for an extension of the Ombudsperson mechanism to other Sanctions Committees.

The question remains how these dynamics at the UNSC have been received in EU circles. On the one hand, a full review of regulations implementing UN Resolutions still seems appropriate. For the reasons outlined above, the sanctions regime may still be at odds with the EU legal order.[155] In particular, as long as no effective remedy is available at the international level EU courts have a central role in judicially reviewing the cases of individuals.[156] On the other hand, it has also been argued that the new developments in the global

---

Committee decision as such action would conflict directly with the UN Charter. Rather it is a review of underlying information for the purpose of a decision yet to be made by the Committee. It may not be the concept of traditional judicial review as it is known, but it is a form of review. An independent third party is looking at the underlying information and providing views on it to the decision maker"; Prost, *op. cit.*, n. 143 above, p. 7.

153 D. Hoerauf, "The United Nations Al-Qaida sanctions regime after U.N. Resolution 1989: Due process still overdue?", *Temp. Int'l & Comp. L.J.* 23, 2012, p. 214.

154 UNSC Resolution 1989 (2011), S/RES/1989, para. 21. The Ombudsman equally does not review cases of individuals being listed following restrictive measures taken against their country. It would be interesting to examine the due process differences between counter-terrorism and 'geographical' sanctions. See in this regard the CJEU case law on the subject and the extent to which the latter accepts (or not) distinctions, in for example the cases of *Fulmen* and *Mahmoudian* (joined cases T-439/10 and T-440/10 [2012]; Iran), *Tay Za* (Case C-376/10 P [2012]; Burma/Myanmar) and *Bamba* (Case T-86/11 [2012]; Ivory Coast).

155 Powell, *op. cit.*, n. 141 above. But see Opinion of Advocate General Bot, 19 March 2013, *op. cit.*, n. 42 above.

156 See Para. 126 in Case T-85/09, *Yassin Abdullah Kadi v Commission* [2010] ECR II-5177, in which the General Court concluded that, "in circumstances such as those of this case, its task is to ensure—as the Court of Justice held at paragraphs 326 and 327 of Kadi—'in principle the full review' of the lawfulness of the contested regulation in the light of fundamental rights, without affording the regulation any immunity from jurisdiction on the ground that it gives effect to resolutions adopted by the Security Council under Chapter VII of the Charter of the United Nations." As upheld in paras. 68 and 97 of the CJEU *Kadi II* Judgment of 18 July *op. cit.*, n. 45 above. See for further reading P. Eeckhout, "Fundamental rights and the interface between second and third pillar", in: A. Dashwood and M. Maresceau (eds.), *Law and Practice of EU External Relations*, Cambridge: Cambridge University Press, 2008, pp. 104–128.

sanctions regime may have altered the standard of review to be applied by the EU Courts. The argument has been made that extra due process guarantees provided for by the Ombudsperson should result in a less intense standard of review.[157] As Advocate General Bot sees it, the Office of the Ombudsperson "has made it possible to raise the quality of the list considerably. It would be paradoxical if the Court failed to take account of the improvements to which it has directly contributed, even though the Office of the Ombudsperson is not a judicial body".[158] The CJEU indeed explicitly took into account the improvements added to the listing procedures in its latest *Kadi* judgment. Unlike its Advocate-General, though, it considered the efforts made at the UN level to be insufficient.[159] In other words, while the CJEU took note of the procedural changes, it remains of the view that these "do not provide to the person whose name is listed [...] the guarantee of effective judicial protection".[160]

5 Concluding Remarks

The EU has been a driving force in a broad range of UN counter-terrorism activities. Despite its limited competences in the field, the Union has gradually acquired the necessary know-how to fight terrorism. Practices have been translated into multilateral action, leading to interesting dynamics. Global partners have been considering solutions proposed by the EU, sometimes resulting in successes (the streamlining of the architecture of the UN's counter-terrorism system), moderate successes (e.g. the greater willingness of the UNSC 1267/1989 sanctions regime to consider review mechanisms) or

157 Advocate General Bot puts it this way: "The improvements to the procedure within the United Nations allow, in particular, the presumption to be made that the reasons cited in support of listing are based on sufficient evidence and information. The EU judicature should not therefore perform an intensive review of the justification for listing on the basis of the evidence and information on which the assessments made by the Sanctions Committee are based". In his view, the "presumption of justification" can be rebutted "during the implementation procedure within the Union, in the course of which the listed person may adduce new evidence or information"; Opinion of AG Bot, *op. cit.*, n. 42 above, paras. 87–88.

158 *Ibid.*, para. 83.

159 Interestingly, to determine the applicable standard for what constitutes a breach of effective judicial protection in the EU, the CJEU referred to the standard as endorsed by the European Court of Human Rights in its *Nada v. Switzerland* judgment, 12 September 2012 (No 10593/08, not yet published in the Reports of Judgments and Decisions), para. 211.

160 CJEU *Kadi II*, *op. cit*, n. 45 above, para. 133.

working points to be followed up (e.g. the definition of terrorism). Interestingly, in all cases, even in those where the EU has not (fully) attained its goals, an interaction has been established between the relevant actors of the UN and the EU. Discussions have involved the UNSC, EU Courts, Union representatives and Delegations, the UN Secretary-General and Member States. This chapter has shown that the EU's commitment to contributing to the fight against terrorism has clearly benefited the global debates and practices. The results of these dynamics have, in turn, influenced EU policies and the rethinking of common positions.

Moreover, the EU has managed to lead by example and by dialogue. Firstly, the setting of examples and the sharing of experiences has taken place on strategic aspects of counter-terrorism policy-making. In addition, the EU's input has also been welcomed in legal debates. The EU has been a front-runner in the sense that it has internally been dealing with issues that have only later surfaced at the global level. Secondly, in all aspects of the global fight against terrorism the EU has deployed its diplomatic tools. The EU has acquired visible presence in virtually all major counter-terrorism activities of the UN while respecting participation rules. For a number of EU policies a way forward has also been found through participation in informal initiatives organised outside the UN framework. Both approaches require constant internal coordination efforts by the EU and its Member States. To further increase the EU's leadership position in countering terrorism, the streamlining of actions and visions of Member States will be a key element.

CHAPTER 18

China-EU Experience and Budding Cooperation in Emergency Management

Veronika Orbetsova and Jing Men

1 Introduction

Emergencies can be defined as sudden and unforeseeable events that call for immediate measures which would minimise negative impact.[1] When an emergency provokes a "serious disruption of the functioning of a community or a society causing widespread human, material, economic or environmental losses" that cannot be coped with by the affected community, the emergency becomes a disaster.[2] The International Federation of the Red Cross and the Red Crescent Societies (IFRC) divide disasters into two broad categories: natural hazards and technological or man-made disasters. Natural hazards[3] include geophysical (tsunamis, earthquakes, volcanic eruptions and landslides), climatological (droughts, extreme temperatures and wildfires), hydrological (floods and avalanches) and biological hazards (disease epidemics and insect or animal plagues).[4] Technological and man-made hazards comprise famines, displaced populations, industrial accidents, transport accidents, environmental degradation and pollution accidents. This typological description present in Chinese law defines emergencies as "natural disasters, calamitous accidents, public health accidents and public security incidents, which occur abruptly and cause or may potentially cause serious social harm".[5]

Indeed, disasters can result in a wide array of losses including human, economic, material and environmental ones. To a large extent, the consequences of a disaster depend on the capacity of communities and societies to deal

1 *Glossary of Humanitarian Terms*, Reliefweb, Draft Version, August 2008, p. 24, available at: <http://www.who.int/hac/about/reliefweb-aug2008.pdf> (accessed 11 June 2013).

2 *Ibid.*, p. 22.

3 The term 'natural hazards' is preferred to the term 'natural disasters' because the latter may erroneously convey the assumption that the latter are the result of 'natural' phenomena.

4 International Federation of Red Cross and Red Crescent Societies (IFRC), "Types of disasters, definition of hazard", available at: <http://www.ifrc.org/en/what-we-do/disaster-management/about-disasters/definition-of-hazard/> (accessed 11 June 2013).

5 "Emergency Response Law of the People's Republic of China", 30 August 2007, Article 1 and Article 5.

© KONINKLIJKE BRILL NV, LEIDEN, 2014 | DOI 10.1163/9789004268333_020

with the disaster. The IFRC holds that the impact of a disaster depends upon the scope of the hazard, the vulnerability of the affected community, and the capacity of the community to respond to it.[6] This is why disaster or emergency management is of crucial importance.[7] Emergency management encompasses the organisation and management of emergency relief operations, the immediate response to global emergencies and long-term disaster relief actions which aim to lessen the impact of disasters. Indeed, investing in disaster risk prevention and preparedness is crucial not only for the saving of human lives, but also for achieving long-term goals of sustainable development and poverty eradication. According to the European Directorate General Humanitarian Aid and Civil Protection (DG ECHO) every €1 spent on disaster prevention saves €4–7 being spent on disaster response.[8] Using similar logic, Chinese law specifies that when it comes to the management of emergencies, priority is to be given "to prevention and combining prevention with emergency response".[9]

The management of emergencies occurring on the territory of a country is primarily the responsibility of the affected state. However, the management of large scale hazards and trans-boundary hazards, or global emergencies, is sometimes beyond the power of individual states. In such cases, according to international law, in respect of sovereignty, territorial integrity and national unity, assistance to a disaster stricken country is provided "with the consent of the affected country and, in principle, on the basis of an appeal by the affected country".[10] It is, furthermore, emphasised that international assistance to affected countries and regions should be closely coordinated with the receiving state. Such assistance includes supplies (food, water, shelter, blankets, medical equipment, etc.), relief personnel and specialised teams (search and rescue teams, medical staff, etc.), relief equipment and medical and technical assistance. Assistance also comprises long-term measures of prevention and planning which increase the capacities of communities to respond to emergency situations in a timely and effective manner and reduce the risk of disaster.

---

6 IFRC, "What is a disaster", available at: <http://www.ifrc.org/en/what-we-do/disaster-management/about-disasters/what-is-a-disaster/> (accessed 11 June 2013).

7 According to the *Glossary of Humanitarian Terms, op. cit.*, n. 1 p. 24, the terms 'emergency management' and 'disaster management' are interchangeable.

8 European Commission, DG ECHO, "Factsheet, Disaster Risk Management", May 2013, p. 1, available at: <http://ec.europa.eu/echo/files/aid/countries/factsheets/thematic/disaster_risk_management_en.p> (accessed 9 June 2013).

9 "Emergency Response Law", *op. cit.*, n. 5 Article 1 and Article 5.

10 United Nations, General Assembly Resolution 57/150, "Strengthening the effectiveness and cooperation of international urban search and rescue assistance", 16 December 2002, p. 1, available at: <http://www.ifrc.org/Docs/idrl/I238EN.pdf> (accessed 10 June 2013).

According to Oxfam international, on average almost 250 million people per year are affected by disasters.[11] As global warming and climate change become more and more visible, the number of global emergencies has dramatically increased in the last century: in 1992 the Centre for Epidemiology of Disasters reported 221 disasters which affected 78 million people, whereas in 2011 the number of disasters worldwide grew to 336, the number of victims soared to 209 million and the economic cost was evaluated at US$366 billion.[12] Even though no country is spared from large-scale hazards, the geographical location and the huge territory of countries like China make them prone to such global emergency situations. This chapter is concerned with China-EU experience and cooperation in emergency management. It will first study China's enhanced efforts in emergency management and its growing global experience in disaster relief, then review the EU's experience in this field and in the third part, examine the recently developed EU-China cooperation in managing emergencies. Facing a growing number of natural disasters in recent years, the Chinese state has been making efforts to strengthen its emergency management capacity. Moreover, China increasingly involves itself in the management of global emergencies both at the regional level—in the Asia-Pacific region—and at the global level. However, as China is still developing its capacities, cooperation with well-established and worldwide-recognised actors in the field of humanitarian aid and disaster management such as the European Union (EU) is of paramount importance.

2 China as a Player in Emergency Management

2.1 *Emergency Cases in China*

According to the OFDA/CRED International Disaster Database, China is the country that has experienced the highest number of disasters per year since 2000.[13] China is among the countries with the highest mortality risk index concerning natural hazards. Between 1980 and 2010 more than 2.8 billion

---

11 Oxfam international, "Summary", *The Right to Survive: The humanitarian challenge for the twenty-first century*, Oxfam Publishing, 2009, p. 2, available at: <http://www.oxfam.org/sites/www.oxfam.org/files/right-to-survive-report.pdf> (accessed 11 June 2013).

12 Data from the Centre for Epidemiology of Disasters quoted in "What silent disasters are saying", Devex, 19 February 2013, available at: <https://www.devex.com/en/news/what-silent-disasters-are-saying/80342> (accessed 11 June 2013).

13 "Disasters according to EM-DAT and Charter activations between 2000 and 2010", International Charter Space and Major Disasters, available at: <http://www.disasterscharter.org/web/charter/emdat> (accessed 11 June 2013).

people were affected by natural hazards, with an average of 90 million per year.[14] Floods, storms and earthquakes are among the most common natural hazards China has to face, with floods being undoubtedly the most devastating disasters. The floods of 2002, 2003 and 2007 are classified in the top 10 most costly natural hazards in terms of the number of people affected.[15] Moreover, seven of the ten natural hazards that affected the highest number of people in Asia between 1980 and 2008 occurred in China and all of them were floods. Several hundred thousand people per year are affected by technological hazards of different types.[16]

Perhaps one of the deadliest and most damaging disasters that China had to deal with was the strong earthquake which hit Wenchuan in May 2008 killing 875,000 people.[17] More than half of the casualties were children—most of whom were buried under the 3,000 schools that collapsed.[18] The economic damage was estimated at US$85 billion, making the 2008 earthquake by far the costliest disaster that occurred in China since the beginning of the 20th century.[19] The scope of the earthquake coupled with the difficulties accessing the affected region, made it impossible for the Chinese government to rely only on its own resources. On 14 May 2008, two days after the earthquake, the Chinese government formally requested assistance from the international community so as to respond to the needs of the disaster-hit population.[20] This earthquake is a milestone in the development of China's emergency management: it not only showed the solidarity and the high mobilisation of both the

14 Data from EM-DAT: The OFDA/CRED International Disaster Database, Catholic University of Louvain, version from August 2011, quoted in "China Disaster Statistics", Preventionweb, available at: <http://www.preventionweb.net/english/countries/statistics/?cid=36> (accessed 11 June 2013).

15 Centre for Research on the Epidemiology of Disasters (CRED), "People's Republic of China Country Profile, Natural Disasters", EM-DAT, The International Disaster Database, data version from July 2012, available at: <http://www.emdat.be/result-country-profile> (accessed 11 June 2013).

16 Data from EM-DAT: The OFDA/CRED International Disaster Database, Catholic University of Louvain, data version from August 2011, quoted in "Asia Disaster Statistics", Preventionweb, available at: <http://www.preventionweb.net/english/countries/statistics/index_region.php?rid=4> (accessed 11 June 2013).

17 Data from EM-DAT, quoted in "China Disaster Statistics", *op. cit.*, n. 14.

18 UNISDR, *The Asia-Pacific Disaster Report* 2012, p. 37.

19 CRED, *op. cit.*, n. 35.

20 UNICEF, "China requests emergency supplies to aid in quake recovery", 15 May 2008, Sichuan, China, available at: <http://www.unicef.org/infobycountry/china_43935.html> (accessed 15 June 2013).

government and the society, thus reinforcing national unity, but also shed light on the flaws and difficulties in dealing with large-scale natural hazards. It was also a lesson-learning experience for China as it uncovered the gaps in coordination between different governmental and non-governmental actors at local and national levels. The Wenchuan earthquake triggered a number of institutional reforms and led to the launch of numerous initiatives in China at local, national and international levels.

2.2 *Recent Developments in China*

As a matter of fact, China's efforts in disaster management were noticeably strengthened after the outbreak of the severe acute respiratory syndrome (SARS) epidemic in 2003. When fighting against SARS, the Chinese leadership developed awareness of the high risks of the mismanagement of emergency situations and set up a disaster management system. Many officials who have proved incapable of coping with hazards have been dismissed. To quote but two examples, former health Minister ZHANG Wenkang was discharged for the SARS cover-up in 2003, and former environment Minister XIE Zhenhua resigned in 2005 for mismanaging the Songhua River pollution accident.[21]

In the following years, a number of legislative measures have been adopted and specialised institutions have been created. The most significant legislative innovation was the adoption of the "Emergency Response Law of the People's Republic of China" in 2007. The law regulates the distribution of competences between central and local governments, as well as prevention, monitoring and early warning, emergency handling and relief and post-emergency rehabilitation. According to the "Emergency Response Law", the responsibility for the overall precautionary plans in response to national emergencies lies with the State Council Emergency Management Office (EMO). Local governments then develop specific precautionary plans in accordance with the laws, regulations and rules adopted by the EMO.[22] The law stipulates that the governments at national, province and city levels should monitor the sources of danger which may provoke emergencies and take preventive measures. Such measures include establishing a sound training system for control of emergencies and specialised training for staff members in charge of emergency management, organising professional and voluntary emergency rescue teams and ensuring good coordination in their combined efforts, implementing emergency response education, taking fiscal measures in order to guarantee the funds

21 Y. Xie, "Institute to teach officials crisis management", *China Daily*, 8 June 2010, available at: <http://www.chinadaily.com.cn/china/2010-06/08/content_9946684.htm> (accessed 14 June 2013).

22 "Emergency Response Law", *op. cit.*, n. 5 Chapter II, Article 17.

required for emergency response and developing a risk insurance system financed by the government for big disasters.[23] Lists of concrete measures to be taken in cases of natural disasters, calamitous accidents and public health incidents, and social safety incidents are provided as well.[24]

In terms of monitoring and early warning, the law foresees the creation of a "unified national information system for emergencies."[25] The lower level governments are responsible for regularly collecting data, analysing it and informing the higher level immediately in the event that a serious emergency is likely to occur. Local governments are bound by law to issue warnings to the general public and inform the public regularly and in a timely manner.[26] In addition, the central government has to publish timely information about the management of the emergency. Moreover, the law envisages public-private partnerships so as to "ensure the production and supply of the materials for emergency rescue, of daily necessities and of the gears for emergency handling."[27] Additionally, the importance of the involvement of local communities in organising the public to rescue each-other is recognised.[28]

In November 2008, as part of its efforts to develop emergency management capabilities after the 2008 earthquake and as a follow-up to the regulation issued by the State Council, the Chinese government established the National Institute for Emergency Management (NIEM) within the Chinese Academy of Governance, directly under the State Council. The NIEM reports directly to the State Council EMO. The Institute is designed to train officials from ministerial to grassroots levels in coping with natural and technological hazards. According to QIAO Renyi, Executive Deputy Director of the NIEM, more than 2,000 officials will be trained every year.[29] The curriculum of the NIEM comprises lectures by experienced officials and combines a theoretical approach with case studies of typical emergencies. Particular emphasis is being put on disaster preparedness and in particular on the improvement of the policy framework, the development of action plans and specially tailored exercises.[30] The core activities of the NIEM are distributed between the Departments of Training

23 *Ibid.*, Articles 20–26.

24 *Ibid.*, Article 49 and Article 50.

25 *Ibid.*, Chapter III, Article 37.

26 For a detailed description of the step-by-step measures to be taken by local governments in the case of a strong probability of an emergency occurring, i.e. early warning, please see "Emergency Response Law of the People's Republic of China", *op. cit.*, n. 5 Article 42–45.

27 *Ibid.*, Article 32.

28 *Ibid.*, Article 55.

29 Xie, *op. cit.*, n. 21.

30 J. Stromseth, Country Representative for China of the Asia Foundation, "Questionnaire accompanying the nomination of the NIEM for the Sasakawa Award", 2013.

and Education, International Affairs, Policy and Research. The NIEM focuses on the development of practical capacity building programmes for local and national level government officials. Up to now, more than 4,000 senior government officials and professionals from the private sector and from non-governmental institutions have taken part in the training offered by the NIEM.[31] Moreover, more than 600 directors and emergency management trainers have taken part in the Training of Trainers programmes.[32] The NIEM has published a number of books and articles with a research focus on risk assessment, early warning systems, technological safety, roles of NGOs in disaster management, leadership during emergency operations, etc. The *National Annual Report of Emergency Management* is considered a guideline for emergency management in China.[33] The NIEM stimulates exchanges of knowledge and experience of relevant actors involved in disaster management operations by organising annual forums and conferences on disaster management.

Another legislative development worth mentioning is the inclusion of disaster management in China's 11th and 12th Five-Year Plans. In the Comprehensive Disaster Reduction Plan issued in 2007 within the framework of the 11th Five-Year Plan, special emphasis is put on the need for local governments to "mainstream disaster reduction into their economic [sic] and social development plans."[34] Disaster prevention and reduction is an integral part of the 12th Five-Year Plan. A separate chapter in this Plan is dedicated to the strengthening of water conservancy, disaster prevention and reduction system building.

2.3 *China's International Experience of Emergency Management*

The *Asia-Disaster Report* of 2012 states that the "Asia-Pacific region is the most disaster-prone area in the world" and "the most seriously affected one" with over 2 million people killed from 1970 to 2011, "accounting for 75 per cent of all disaster fatalities globally".[35] Hydrological disasters are reported as the most frequent and most devastating ones. China, as the biggest and most affected

---

31 NIEM, "Application of the NIEM for the Sasakawa Award", 27 February 2013, p. 7, available at: <http://www.preventionweb.net/files/workspace/30411_0cagniemsletterinitiativechallengea.pdf> (accessed 14 June 2013).

32 *Ibid.*

33 *Ibid.*

34 HFA, *China: National Progress Report on the Implementation of the Hyogo Framework for Action 2011–2013—Interim*, 31 October 2012, PreventionWeb, available at: <http://www.preventionweb.net/files/28446_chn_NationalHFAprogress_2011-13.pdf> (accessed 15 June 2013).

35 United Nations Economic and Social Commission for Asia and the Pacific (ESCAP) and the United Nations Office for Disaster Risk Reduction (UNISDR), *Reducing Vulnerability and Exposure to Disasters, the Asia-Pacific Disaster Report 2012*, p. xxi, available at:

country, has a crucial role to play in relation to disaster management in the Asia-Pacific region.

Chinese rescuers are, indeed, participating more and more actively in international disaster management operations in the Asia-Pacific region. China sent a 42-member team to Southeast Iran after the earthquake that hit the region on 26 December 2003. This Chinese International Search and Rescue Team (CISAR) was the first Asian rescue mission to arrive.[36] Shortly after the 8.7-magnitude earthquake and the tsunamis it triggered devastated the island of Sumatra in Indonesia, the CISAR dispatched a team of 70 rescuers that worked for nearly 30 days in the worst-hit Aceh Province, treating more than 10,000 victims.[37] The Chinese team, composed of professional rescuers, medical workers and seismologists, was one of the most active after the May 2006 earthquake in Indonesia.[38] The CISAR rescue team sent to Pakistan after the deadly earthquake that shook the country on 8 October 2005, assumed the role of UN Rescue Mission Coordinator in the area.[39] This was a significant recognition of the efforts of the two Chinese rescue teams sent to the most devastated areas of Pakistan. Five years later, when Pakistan faced the most severe floods to affect the country in 80 years, the Chinese government sent a 116-member team accompanied by four helicopters to join the rescue and epidemic prevention mission.[40] By the end of the rescue operation, the CISAR team had provided assistance to 25,700 victims.[41]

China played a major role in the initiation and deepening of the collaboration in disaster reduction between Asian states. Indeed, the first Asian Ministerial Conference on Disaster Risk Reduction was held in September

---

<http://www.unescap.org/idd/pubs/Asia-Pacific-Disaster-Report-2012.pdf> (accessed 11 June 2013).

36 The Chinese International Search and Rescue Team (CISAR) was established in April 2001. In May 2003, the CISAR sent a team of 30 experienced rescuers and three sniffer dogs to earthquake-stricken Algeria. This mission to Northern Algeria is emblematic since it was the first Chinese rescue team deployed in a disaster-hit foreign country. For the 12 years of its existence the CISAR has participated in a number of rescue operations both at home and abroad. Y. Wang (ed.), "Backgrounder: Major International rescue operations carried out by CISAR", *Xinhua News Agency*, 13 March 2011, available at: <http://news.xinhuanet.com/english2010/world/2011-03/13/c_13776466.htm> (accessed 11 June 2013).

37 *Ibid.*

38 *Ibid.*

39 *Ibid.*

40 *Ibid.*

41 *Ibid.*

2005 in Beijing.[42] China took an active role in the drafting of the Beijing Action Plan for Reducing Disaster Risks in Asia, and the Delhi and Kuala Lumpur Declarations on Disaster Risk Reduction in Asia, adopted in 2007 and 2008 respectively.[43] Moreover, cooperation in disaster relief with other regional powers has been fostered through a number of documents and actions of the Shanghai Cooperation Organisation (SCO), of which China is a founding member. Indeed, the SCO Charter clearly states "mutual assistance in preventing natural and man-made disasters and elimination of their implications" as one of the areas of cooperation.[44] The Inter-Governmental Mutual Aid Agreement signed in 2005 between the SCO member states and the 2007–2008 Action Plan for Mutual Aid in Disaster Relief established the legislative framework for high level meetings of the institutions in charge of emergency management, joint drills and exhibitions of special equipment.[45] Recently, a joint disaster drill was held on 11–16 June 2013 in Shaoxing, Zhejiang province. Around 1,000 participants from China, Kazakhstan, Kyrgyzstan, Russia and Tajikistan took part in a simulation of disaster relief measures based on the scenario of a deadly 8-magnitude earthquake hitting a large city in Zhejiang province. This included "rescue operations in crashed planes, collapsed buildings, exploded oil tanks, subway buses and carriages".[46]

These interventions demonstrate not only the growing recognition by the Chinese government of the importance of increasing the country's capacity to cope with disasters, but also the will of China to become and to be considered as a major actor in disaster management in the Asia-Pacific region. On the one hand, the way a country deals with natural and man-made disasters within its boundaries as well as in other countries and regions affects the image of the country not only domestically, but also internationally. Disasters have

42 ASEM, 'ASEM Workshop on Cooperation on Capacity Building of Disaster Relief', 27–30 May 2009, Chengdu, China, available at: <http://asemworkshop.mca.gov.cn/article/Background/> (accessed 27 June 2013).

43 *Ibid.*

44 SCO, Charter of the Shanghai Cooperation Organisation, 7 June 2002, Article 3, available at: <http://www.sectsco.org/EN123/show.asp?id=69> (accessed 28 June 2013).

45 D. Medvedev, former President and current Prime-Minister of the Russian Federation, "Opening Address at Expanded Session of Shanghai Cooperation Organisation Council of Heads of State", 16 June 2009, Yekaterinburg, available at: <http://archive.kremlin.ru/eng/speeches/2009/06/16/2200_type82914_217959.shtml> (accessed 28 June 2013).

46 Y. Arintoc, "SCO members conducted a disaster drill which aims to enhance cooperation", *the China Voice*, 17 June 2013, available at: <http://www.thechinavoice.com/sco-members-conducted-a-disaster-drill-which-aims-to-enhance-cooperation/> (accessed 28 June 2013).

both short-term consequences—loss of human lives and damage of property and infrastructure—and long-term negative effects on the economy, sustainable development, the state of public health, water and food safety, the provision of natural resources, etc. If a disaster is not managed in an effective and timely manner, negative spill-over effects can be aggravated which in turn will contribute to the creation of a negative country-image. On the other hand, a quick and adequate response to an emergency situation can increase both the credibility of state institutions and contribute to the construction of a positive country-image.

China's commitment to increase its own disaster management capacity and actively engage in international disaster relief operations is visible on many levels. China clearly states its support for joint efforts of disaster relief at the United Nations at the General Assembly and Security Council Meetings of the UN. For instance, at the 67th Session of the General Assembly, under the agenda item on "Strengthening of the coordination of humanitarian and disaster relief assistance of the United Nations, including special economic assistance", the Chinese Ambassador LI Baodong stated:

> As a developing country prone to natural disasters, China knows all too well the sufferings disasters inflict on the people affected. Therefore, the Chinese Government attaches great importance to international cooperation in the humanitarian field, actively participates in multilateral and bilateral humanitarian assistance, and shares with other developing countries experience and technologies of coping with natural disasters.[47]

China is an active member of a number of UN structures involved in emergency management. For instance, the China National Space Administration is a member of the *Charter on Cooperation to Achieve the Coordinated Use of Space Facilities in the Event of Natural or Technological Disasters*.[48] The Charter aims to strengthen cooperation between space agencies and space system

47 B. Li, Ambassador, Permanent Representative of China to the UN, statement at the 67th Session of the GA under agenda item 70: Permanent Mission of the People's Republic of China to the UN, "Strengthening of the coordination of humanitarian and disaster relief assistance of the United Nations, including special economic assistance", 13 December 2012, available at: <http://www.china-un.org/eng/chinaandun/economicdevelopment/humanitarian/t998099.htm> (accessed 15 June 2013).

48 *Charter on Cooperation to achieve the Coordinated Use of Space Facilities in the Event of a Natural or technological Disasters*, 25 April 2000, available at: <http://www.disasterscharter.org/web/charter/charter> (accessed 10 June 2013).

operators and by doing so to increase the effectiveness of the response to disasters. China actively participates in the work of the United Nations Platform for Space-based Information for Disaster Management and Emergency Response (UN-SPIDER) and was involved in the establishment of the International Centre for Drought Risk Reduction.[49]

In its endeavour to set the image of a responsible player in disaster management, China seeks recognition from the United Nations. In 2013 the NIEM was nominated by the Asia Foundation for the UN Sasakawa Award for Disaster Risk Reduction.[50] The application of the NIEM for the Sasakawa award is a symbolic gesture of commitment of the Chinese government to disaster management not only of emergencies within China, but also of global emergencies. Moreover, the partnerships established between the NIEM and foreign institutions under the framework of the Sino-EU, Sino-German, Sino-British and Sino-USA partnerships confirm NIEM's ambitions to mobilise not only national, but also international resources.[51]

In 2009, the CISAR successfully passed the evaluation of the International Search and Rescue Advisory Group (INSARAG) External Classification.[52] The latter is a peer review process of international urban search and rescue (USAR) groups which was developed and endorsed by the INSARAG, a "network of disaster-prone and disaster-responding countries and organisations dedicated to urban search and rescue (USAR) and operational field coordination."[53] The INSARAG was established in 1991 and its Secretariat is located within the Emergency Services Branch of the United Nations Office for the Coordination of Humanitarian Affairs (OCHA) in Geneva. INSARAG is committed to increasing the effectiveness of emergency preparedness and response activities,

---

49 Chinese government, "China's Actions for Disaster Prevention and reduction", "VI. International cooperation in Disaster Prevention and Reduction", p. 7, available at: <http://english.gov.cn/official/2009-05/11/content_1310629_7.htm> (accessed 27 June 2013).

50 United Nations, "Chinese Academy of Governance—National Institute of Emergency Management", The Sasakawa Award 2013, available at: <http://www.unisdr.org/2013/sasakawa/documents/nominees/ChineseAcademyGovernance.pdf> (accessed 14 June 2013).

51 NIEM, "Application for the Sasakawa Award", *op. cit.*, n. 31 p. 8.

52 Z. Lin (ed.), "China's international search and rescue team attains IEC certificate", *China View, Xinhua News Agency*, 15 November 2009, available at: <http://news.xinhuanet.com/english/2009-11/15/content_12458149.htm> (accessed 10 June 2013).

53 United Nations Office for Coordination of Humanitarian Affairs (OCHA), "International Search and Rescue Advisory Group (INSARAG): Overview", available at: <http://www.unocha.org/what-we-do/coordination-tools/insarag/overview> (accessed 10 June 2013).

improving the interaction and cooperation between USAR teams working in the disaster areas. Moreover, INSARAG is mandated to develop international procedures, guidelines and best practices. INSARAG guidelines were recognised as the main reference for coordinating international USAR response by the UN General Assembly Resolution 57/150—"Strengthening the Effectiveness and Coordination of International USAR Assistance".[54] This is why the recognition of the CISAR as a heavy USAR qualified for participation in international deployments involving "difficult and complex technical search-and-rescue operations" is of crucial importance for China both in terms of disaster relief capacity building and in terms of positive country image building.[55]

China was the first country to send assistance to earthquake stricken Haiti in 2010. China sent a CISAR emergency rescue team of 60 people and a 43-member Chinese medical care and epidemic prevention team to Haiti.[56] Moreover, China shipped around 90 tons of in-kind assistance, including food, water and water-purification equipment, portable power generators emergency lights, clothing, medicines, and tents.[57] In addition to the US$1 million of emergency humanitarian aid to Haiti announced by the RCSC, the Chinese government pledged US$4.4 million of assistance relief supplies.[58] With the memory of the devastating earthquake in Wenchuan still alive, not only the Chinese government, but also the Chinese society showed empathy to Haitians. The Financial Tracking Service (FTS) of OCHA estimates at more than US$14 million the humanitarian funding provided to Haiti by China in

54 United Nations General Assembly, *Resolution adopted by the General Assembly 57/150*, "Strengthening the Effectiveness and Coordination of International USAR Assistance", 16 December 2002, p. 3, available at: <http://www.ifrc.org/Docs/idrl/I238EN.pdf> (accessed 10 June 2013).

55 For more information on INSARAG, please see OCHA, "INSARAG Preparedness—Response", INSARAG: timeline of events, 16 July 2012, available at: <https://docs.unocha.org/sites/dms/Documents/insarag_poster_timeline.pdf> (accessed 11 June 2013).

56 UNOCHA, "Haiti Emergencies for 2010: List of all humanitarian pledges, commitments and contributions in 2010", Financial Tracking Service, 12 June 2013, available at: <http://fts.unocha.org/reports/daily/ocha_R10c_C91_Y2010_asof___1306120204.pdf> (accessed 12 June 2013).

57 K. Georgieva, EU Commissioner for International Cooperation, Humanitarian Aid and Civil Response, "EU-China—A Partnership for a More Resilient World", speech delivered at the Launch ceremony of EU-China Disaster Risk Management Project and the inauguration of the China-EU Institute of Emergency Management, Beijing, 15 June 2012, available at: <http://europa.eu/rapid/press-release_SPEECH-12-449_en.htm?locale=FR> (accessed 7 June 2013).

58 UNOCHA, "Haiti Emergencies for 2010", *op. cit.*, n. 56.

the first six months following the earthquake.[59] This disaster relief operation is even more significant given the absence of diplomatic relations between China and Haiti.[60]

3 EU's Experience in Emergency Management

During the last decade, disasters killed more than 80,000 Europeans and caused economic losses of more than €100 billion.[61] In this regard, the *Treaty on the Functioning of the European Union* emphasises the importance of "cooperation between Member States in order to improve the effectiveness of systems for preventing and protecting against natural or man-made disasters."[62] Over the years, the EU has developed valuable institutional experience in coordinated disaster response to emergencies both inside and outside the Union. The EU delivers assistance to disaster stricken areas both within its boundaries[63] and in third countries through two main channels—civil protection (emergency relief efforts both inside the EU and in third countries)[64] and humanitarian aid (only for disaster relief efforts outside the EU).[65] The European Civil Protection Mechanism (CPM), established in 2001, is the main instrument for European civil protection.[66] The CPM is activated automatically if the country requesting assistance is a Member State. When a country which is not an EU Member State makes an appeal for assistance to the EU, the European Commission needs to consult the Presidency of the Council. In the first ten years of its existence, the CPM was used for more than 150 disasters worldwide.[67] The Monitoring and Information Centre (MIC) is the

59 UNOCHA, "Haiti Emergencies for 2010: Total Humanitarian Funding per Donor in 2010", FTS OCHA, 12 June 2013, available at: <http://fts.unocha.org/reports/daily/ocha_R24c_C91_Y2010_asof___1306120204.pdf> (accessed 13 June 2013).

60 The Republic of Haiti is one of the few countries which recognises and has diplomatic relations with Taiwan and not with the People's Republic of China.

61 European Commission, "Factsheet, Disaster Risk Management", *op. cit.*, n. 8 p. 1.

62 European Union, *Consolidated Version of the Treaty on the Functioning of the European Union (TFEU)*, C326/47, *OJ*, 2012, Part III, Title XXIII Civil Protection, Article 196(1).

63 Article 222(b) of the TFEU.

64 Article 196 of the TFEU.

65 Article 214(1) of the TFEU.

66 Besides the 28 EU Member States, Former Yugoslav Republic of Macedonia, Iceland, Liechtenstein and Norway also participate in the CPM.

67 European Commission, *Special Eurobarometer 383, Civil Protection, Report,* conducted by TNS Opinion & Social at the request of Directorate-General Humanitarian Aid and Civil

'operational heart' of the CPM. The MIC plays three main roles: it is the contact point for requests and offers of assistance; it acts as a coordinator of European assistance through the CPM; and it disseminates information on civil protection response and preparedness.[68] The civil protection response of the EU used to be based on voluntary participation in the CPM of EU Member States both in the form of trained expert teams and in-kind assets.

This scheme, although an achievement in itself, made it difficult to plan disaster relief operations in advance.[69] In order to tackle this issue and to ensure better coordinated, better adapted to the circumstances, more timely and efficient responses to natural and man-made disasters, the EU went a step further by creating the European Emergency Response Centre (ERC). The ERC, which opened its doors on 15 May 2013, manages "civil protection intervention modules", made up of "pre-identified Member States' response assets [...] that can immediately be deployed to any large scale emergency".[70] This means that a voluntary pool will be made up of the resources that the countries participating in the CPM commit themselves to providing. These resources, placed on standby, will be ready for instant deployment "as part of a coherent European response".[71] The ERC is expected to ensure "cooperation and coherence of EU action at an inter-institutional level, focusing on coordination mechanisms with the European External Action Service, the Council and Member States" as well as to enhance "cooperation between civil protection and humanitarian aid authorities in Member States".[72] The ERC merges the functions of the MIC for civil protection and the Crisis Room for humanitarian crises, thus optimising resources and enhancing effectiveness. The daily work of the centre consists in the monitoring of global emergencies, the collection and analysis of real-time information on disasters and the preparation and deployment of equipment, rescue teams and experts. The centre envisages a process of

---

Protection, June 2012, p. 2, available at: <http://ec.europa.eu/public_opinion/archives/ebs/ebs_383_en.pdf> (accessed 8 June 2013).

68 For further information on the MIC, please see European Commission, DG ECHO, "Monitoring and Information Centre", available at: <http://ec.europa.eu/echo/policies/disaster_response/mic_en.htm> (accessed 9 June 2013).

69 European Commission, Directorate General Humanitarian Aid and Civil Protection, Emergency Response Centre, "ECHO Factsheet", April 2013, available at: <http://ec.europa.eu/echo/files/aid/countries/factsheets/thematic/ERC_en.pdf> (accessed 8 June 2013).

70 *Ibid.*, p. 2.

71 *Ibid.*

72 *Ibid.*

identification and continuous evaluation of the shortcomings of the management of emergency situations.

Led by the desire to involve European citizens in the management of the constantly increasing number of global emergencies, on 19 September 2012, the European Commission submitted a proposal to the European Council and the European Parliament for the establishment of a European Voluntary Humanitarian Aid Corpse—EU Aid Volunteers.[73] This global initiative will allow the training and deployment of around 10,000 European citizens (or long-term residents of an EU Member State) eager to support communities struck by disasters for the period 2014–2020. The trained volunteers will provide valuable support to humanitarian organisations working in disaster-struck societies. Local organisations will benefit from capacity-building measures as 7,000 local staff and volunteers of local organisations will actively take part in the initiative as well.[74] Furthermore, 10,000 online volunteers will support the EU Aid Volunteers remotely. In the long run, the actions of the EU Aid Volunteers will create a positive spill-over effect both in the communities where the volunteers are deployed and in the EU. The resilience of European communities will indeed indirectly be enhanced as more EU citizens will receive specific training to cope with disasters.

According to the Special Eurobarometer survey on Civil Protection launched in March 2012, coordination of disaster response efforts at EU level is seen as necessary. 92 percent of the respondents to the survey agreed "that not all countries have sufficient national means to deal with a major disaster on their own", 82 percent agreed "that a co-ordinated EU action in dealing with disasters is more effective than actions by individual countries" and 89 percent agreed "that the EU should help any non-EU country worldwide hit by disasters by co-ordinating the sending of experts and equipment to affected areas".[75]

Indeed, over the years both the EU institutions and EU Member States have developed expertise in disaster risk reduction, early warning systems, disaster prevention measures, and disaster-response systems. European experience

73 European Commission, "Proposal for a Regulation of the European Parliament and of the Council Establishing the European Voluntary Humanitarian Aid Corpse, EU Aid Volunteers", COM(2012) 514 final, 19 September 2012, Brussels, available at: <http://ec.europa.eu/echo/files/aid/euaidvolunteers/com2012-514_proposal regulation_cn.pdf> (accessed 12 June 2013).

74 European Commission, DG ECHO, "EU Aid Volunteers: Commission proposes new global humanitarian initiative", available at: <http://ec.europa.eu/echo/euaidvolunteers/index_en.htm> (accessed 12 June 2013).

75 European Commission, *Eurobarometer 383*, p. 4.

and lessons learnt in developing and implementing different disaster relief measures such as developing earthquake-resilient building codes and flood management measures are of particular relevance for China which is often affected by earthquakes and floods.[76] In this regard, the experience of countries like the Netherlands which have been exposed to flood-related emergencies throughout their history, can be very valuable to China. Moreover, given that the EU Member States have been confronted for many decades with hazards linked to urbanisation and industrialisation, the EU's knowledge of the management of big agglomerations and the prevention of man-made hazards can be very valuable for China.

The EU is thus a valued partner not merely because it is one of the major donors when it comes to disaster relief but also because of its experience and good practice in coordinated, timely and efficient response to emergencies both inside and outside the Union. From this perspective, EU-China cooperation is particularly relevant for both partners. Regardless of the difference of nature of the two partners (China being a nation-state and the EU—a complex entity uniting nation-states) China nonetheless comprises entities with different degrees of autonomy in governance. At a regional level, analogously to the EU the coordinated actions of which are critical for the management of emergency situations in the European region, China plays a critical role in the Asian region. In this context it is worth mentioning the Asia-Europe Meeting (ASEM) Workshop on Capacity Building of Disaster Relief organised by China in May 2009 in Chengdu. This Workshop aimed to enhance cooperation between Asian and European states and establish channels of exchange in "disaster early warning, risk assessment, emergency relief, technology cooperation and personnel training among ASEM partners."[77]

4 EU-China Cooperation in Managing Emergencies

Both the EU and China are parties to the *10-year Hyogo Framework for Action* (HFA) which was adopted in 2005 after the World Conference for Disaster Reduction was held in Kobe, Japan. The main goal of the HFA is to "substantially reduce disaster losses by 2015 by building the resilience of nations and communities to disasters".[78] The document recognises the crucial role of cooperation with third countries and organisations in the management of

76 Georgieva, "EU-China—A Partnership for a More Resilient World", *op. cit.*, n. 57.

77 ASEM, "ASEM Workshop . . .", *op. cit.*, n. 42.

78 UNISDR, *Hyogo Framework for Action.*

global emergencies. In her speech on 15 June 2012, Kristalina Georgieva, the EU Commissioner for International Cooperation, Humanitarian Aid and Civil Response, stressed the importance of solidarity "in the face of more frequent and more devastating disasters" both "at home and elsewhere on our planet".[79] Experience has proved that exchange of good practices and cooperation between different international actors in disaster preparedness, prevention and response is crucial for the delivery of effective and timely response, markedly lowers transportation and other costs, helps ensure adequacy and complementarity and avoids duplications of assistance materials. The Wenchuan earthquake showed the absolute necessity of coordinating disaster response efforts so as not to overburden the remaining infrastructure and guarantee the most efficient way to deliver assistance to the most vulnerable. The resilience of communities in the face of natural or technological hazards can be considerably increased by cooperation through joint training programmes. Moreover, *China's Comprehensive Disaster Prevention and Reduction Plan* (*2011–2015*) recognises the heavy financial and economic consequences of disasters and envisages increased investment in comprehensive emergency management measures across government sectors.[80]

Between 1995 and 2010, the European Commission provided €25.8 million to China in support of efforts to deal with earthquakes, floods, snowstorms and droughts that hit the country. In 2008, immediately after China requested international assistance in support of national disaster management efforts, the EU CPM was activated. EU Member States provided in-kind assistance (over 20,000 tents, more than 40,000 blankets, medical and food supplies, clothing, water purification and other relief materials)[81] and more than €2 million of humanitarian aid used to provide water, food, shelter, sanitation, health and other necessary items.[82] Moreover, two teams of European experts were present on the ground to facilitate the handling of the above-mentioned assistance.[83]

---

79 Georgieva, "EU-China—A Partnership for a More Resilient World", *op. cit.*, n. 57.

80 UNISDR, *The Asia-Pacific Disaster Report 2012*, p. xxiv.

81 For a full list of the assistance provided by EU Member States to China, please see UN OCHA, "China emergencies for 2008: List of all humanitarian pledges, commitments and contributions in 2008", FTS UN OCHA, 12 June 2013, available at: <http://fts.unocha.org/reports/daily/ocha_R10c_C44_Y2008_asof___1306120204.pdf> (accessed 13 June 2013).

82 European Commission, "The EU and China launch a joint project for managing disaster risks", Press release, 15 June 2012, Brussels, available at: <http://eeas.europa.eu/delegations/china/press_corner/all_news/news/2012/20120615_en.htm> (accessed 14 June 2013).

83 *Ibid.*

4.1 *EU-China Disaster Risk Management Project*

At the 12th EU-China Summit in Nanjing on 30 November 2009, then-Premier WEN Jiabao and President Jose Manuel Barroso placed an emphasis on emergency management cooperation. On 29 November 2010, Commissioner Georgieva and then State Councillor MA Kai signed an agreement for enhanced cooperation in the field of disaster management. The two sides agreed upon the first bilateral project in this field—the EU-China Disaster Risk Management (DRM) Project. The DRM Project establishes a "long-term and effective platform facilitating cooperation" both at a strategic level to design "holistic and cross-cutting policies" and at an operational level to cope with the challenges of disaster preparedness, relief and post-disaster management.[84] The Project aims to enhance China's capacities to respond to disasters as well as to harmonise the European and the Chinese disaster risk management systems. It will allow the exchange of knowledge and expertise and will contribute to a "more efficient and cost-effective response and preparedness for disasters".[85] Indeed, the agreement foresees that the EU will share with China information and expertise "of both, specialised Commission services and specialised agencies and authorities of the EU Member States".[86] The DRM Project will be implemented by a consortium of specialised bodies of the EU Member States led by the French Ministry of Interior. The Chinese counterparts are the NIEM of the China Academy of Governance and the EMO.[87] The total budget for the EU-China DRM Project is €9 million, of which €6 million will be provided by the Development and Cooperation Instrument of the EU.[88] China committed itself to contribute €3 million in-kind.

EU-China cooperation in managing emergencies entered a new stage on 15 June 2012 when the EU-China DRM Project was formally launched in Beijing, in the presence of the EU Commissioner for International Cooperation, Humanitarian Aid and Civil Response, Kristalina Georgieva. As Commissioner

---

84 Georgieva, "EU-China—A Partnership for a More Resilient World", *op. cit.*, n. 57.

85 K. Georgieva, EU Commissioner for International Cooperation, Humanitarian Aid and Civil Response, quoted in "EU, China sign agreement on disaster risk management", 30 November 2010, *English.news.cn*, available at: <http://news.xinhuanet.com/english2010/china/2010-11/30/c_13627623.htm> (accessed 9 June 2013).

86 Delegation of the European Union to China and Mongolia, "EU and China launch the 'Disaster Risk Management' project", 29 November 2010, Beijing, p. 1, available at: <http://eeas.europa.eu/delegations/china/documents/news/20101129_01_en.pdf> (accessed 14 June 2013).

87 European Commission, "EU-China Disaster Risk Management Project (Financing Agreement)", Delegation of the European Commission to China.

88 *Ibid.*

Georgieva explained, this Project will build upon the successful experience of the EU-China River Basin Management and create synergies with two recently-established bilateral dialogues—the China Europe Water Platform and the EU-China Partnership on Sustainable Urbanisation, both launched in the spring of 2012.[89] Moreover, on 15 June 2013, the EU-China Institute for Emergency Management was inaugurated.

4.2 *The EU-China Institute for Emergency Management and Prospect for Future Cooperation*

The EU-China Institute for Emergency Management was established under the first core component of the EU-China DRM Project—capacity development. This joint European-Chinese institute is based in the NIEM and acts as a resource centre assisting the NIEM in strengthening its capacity building and advisory role in support of the State Council Emergency Management Office.[90]

The first Short Term Training Programme on Emergency Management was organised in Tianjin in collaboration with the NIEM of the Chinese Academy of Governance.[91] Held from 12 May until 7 June 2013, the training featured presentations and case studies on disaster management from the EU and China and gathered 70 representatives from the Chinese State Council Emergency Management Offices and national and local state owned enterprises working in the field of security and disaster management. This training, the first of its kind, is said to be the precursor of a number of long-term initiatives that will be implemented through the EU-China Institute for Emergency Management. The latter includes an official Short Term Training Programme Certificate which is expected to be implemented in October 2013, and Masters and PhD Programmes in Public Administration and Emergency Management, which are being designed jointly by European and Chinese experts.[92]

This new dialogue on emergency management puts emphasis on the opportunities for both partners to learn from each other. It opens the door to closer cooperation between the EU and Member State institutions, Chinese

89 Delegation of the European Union to China and Mongolia, "EU and China launch the 'Disaster Risk Management' project", *op. cit.*, n. 86.

90 European Commission, "EU-China Disaster Risk Management Project (Financing Agreement)", *op. cit.*, n. 87.

91 Delegation of the European Union to China, "EU-China Disaster Risk Management Project—Highlights 2013", 7 June 2013, available at: <http://eeas.europa.eu/delegations/china/press_corner/all_news/news/2013/20130607_en.htm> (accessed 13 June 2013).

92 *Ibid.*

institutions and key international organisations with expertise on disaster management.

Bilateral cooperation in disaster management is only in its initial phase. However, the strong commitment of both the EU and China to improving the effectiveness and quality of their respective disaster response mechanisms and the management of global emergencies, gives an impetus for the development of the partnership in this field. In this regard, the successful cooperation between the European Red Cross Societies and the Red Cross Society of China (RCSC)[93] during the relief phase of the Sichuan earthquake in 2008 can serve as an example. The Emergency Response Units deployed in Sichuan province were subsequently donated to the RCSC and now form an integral part of the Emergency Response Teams of the RCSC which have been deployed on different occasions, including to the Qinghai earthquake in 2010.[94]

5 Concluding Remarks

China and the EU are two important players in the world. China, as the rapidly emerging power and currently the second largest economy; and the EU, as an influential regional organisation of developed countries, have a lot to share in the field of emergency management. China is one of the countries most affected by natural disasters. The lessons learnt concerning disaster relief and emergency management have been reflected in the legislation brought in and projects undertaken by the Chinese leadership in the past ten years. The SARS outbreak in 2003 triggered serious efforts in this field, but the policy of the new government in Beijing during that year, marked by the principle of 'people first', played a decisive role in all the changes. The over thirty-year-reform remarkably stimulated Chinese economic growth, but the one-sided emphasis on growth and the pursuit of GDP somehow led to the neglect of some natural and social problems which gave rise to an increase in social unrest. Stability and inclusive growth became key to China's sustainable development.

---

93 The Red Cross Society of China is well-equipped with ambulances, motorcycle and bicycle ambulances and deploys disaster relief teams not only inside Beijing and in its surroundings, but also throughout the country. See N. LaFleur, "EU's top humanitarian official stresses cooperation and learning from China Red Cross", Red Cross EU Office, available at: <http://www.redcross.eu/en/Red-Cross-EU-Office/NEWS-ROOM/PREVIOUS-NEWS/Commissioner-Georgieva-visits-China-Red-Cross/> (accessed 11 June 2013).

94 N. LaFleur, *op. cit.*, n. 93.

In this sense, government capacities are particularly challenged in the face of disasters and emergencies. Therefore, to increase such capacities and develop effective and efficient mechanisms in this field would not only help improve the quality of disaster relief actions, but also earn credit and maintain legitimacy for the government in Beijing. Against such a background, we see an increasing commitment both domestically and internationally by the Chinese government to emergency management and involvement in rescue operations. Furthermore, China-EU cooperation in this field has also been noticeably enhanced in recent years. The rapid development of cooperative projects between China and the EU is not only mutually beneficial, but also supportive to international emergency management.

Index